THE EURO IN THE NATIONAL CONTEXT

THE EURO IN THE NATIONAL CONTEXT

EDITED BY
JEAN-VICTOR LOUIS

BIICL
BRITISH INSTITUTE OF
INTERNATIONAL AND
COMPARATIVE LAW
www.biicl.org

Published and Distributed by
The British Institute of International and Comparative Law
Charles Clore House, 17 Russell Square, London WC1B 5JP

British Library Cataloguing in Publication Data
A Catalogue record of this book is available from the British Library

ISBN 0–903067–67–6

Typeset by Cambrian Typesetters
Frimley, Surrey
Printed in Great Britain by Biddles Ltd.,
Guildford and King's Lynn

ACKNOWLEDGEMENTS

We would like to express our gratitude to the European University Institute, the European Central Bank, the Banque Nationale de Belgique and the Deutsche Forschungsgemeinschaft. The support of all these institutions in the whole research project has been substantial and constant.

The assistance of the Trans European Policy Studies Association (TEPSA) is also gratefully acknowledged, especially at the rapporteur selection stage.

Julio Baquero Cruz, Stefania Baroncelli, Alessandra Chirico and Assimakis Komninos have been the research associates throughout this project. Alexandra George collaborated in the editing process.

Last but not least, we would like to thank the British Institute of International and Comparative Law for providing the venue for this publication.

CONTENTS

INTRODUCTION xvii
Jean-Victor Louis

AUSTRIA 1
Herta Baumann and Helmut Lang

1. Political and economic aspects 1
   Helmut Lang
   1.1 Introduction 1
   1.2 Public opinion 1
      1.2.1 Framework 1
      1.2.2 Overview of the surveys 3
      1.2.3 Public opinion and the EU 3
      1.2.4 Trust in European institutions and bodies 4
      1.2.5 Support for the single currency 5
      1.2.6 Arguments for and against the euro 7
      1.2.7 The external value of the euro 8
      1.2.8 Information about the single currency 9
      1.2.9 Change-over to the euro notes and coins 10
      1.2.10 Other topics 10
   1.3 Financial institutions 11
      1.3.1 Reactions to monetary policy decisions 11
      1.3.2 The weakness of the euro or the strength of the dollar 13
      1.3.3 Reactions to the referendum in Denmark 15
   1.4 Institutional and procedural matters 16
      1.4.1 Introduction 16
      1.4.2 The government 16
      1.4.3 The Freedom Party (FPÖ) 20
      1.4.4 The Austrian parliament 21
   1.5 Trends towards spill-over 21
      1.5.1 Co-ordination of macroeconomic policy 21
      1.5.2 Tax harmonisation 23
      1.5.3 Social policy 23
      1.5.4 External projection of the euro 23

2. Legal framework 24
   Herta Baumann
   2.1 Changes in the legal framework 24
      2.1.1 Introduction 24
      2.1.2 Dual display of prices 24

2.1.3 Conversion and exchange of bank notes and coins 25
2.1.4 Company law 25
2.2 The Austrian stability pact 26
2.3 Experiences with the consultation mechanism 26
2.4 National law from the EC-perspective 27
2.5 The application of the law 28
2.6 Institutional aspects 30
2.6.1 The foreign reserve assets 30
2.6.2 Allocation of the monetary income 30

Bibliography 31

BELGIUM 33
Paul Magnette and Soukaïna Farès

1. The political framework 33
Paul Magnette
1.1 A timid politicisation of euro-discussions 33
1.2 Political discussions about the euro: Belgium supports the institutionalisation of an economic authority 33
1.3 Debating the ECB policies: the role of social partners 36
1.4 Public opinion: permissive consensus 38
1.5 Conclusions: a debate limited to Belgian élites 40

2. Les attitudes des institutions financières belges à l'égard de la politique monétaire de la BCE 41
Soukaïna Farès
2.1 Introduction 41
2.2 Le 'BILAN' de l'euro 43
2.3 La dépréciation de l'euro 43
2.4 Les conclusions de la presse financière concernant l'euro 45
2.5 Les marchés obligataires / actions 46
2.6 La politique monétaire de la BCE 47
2.7 Indépendance et transparence de la BCE 49
2.8 L'UEM et l'élargissement 50
2.9 Résumé de la situation 51

ON THE OUTSIDE: DENMARK AND THE EURO 53
Karsten Skjalm

1. Introduction 53

2. The Maastricht legacy 54
2.1 Maastricht 54

2.2 The lessons from the Maastricht ratification process 59
2.3 1995–98: Growing divide between the Danish EU-debate and the European integration process 62
2.3.1 Euro-X episode 62
2.3.2 The Amsterdam referendum campaign 65
2.3.3 Autumn 1998: the turning point in the Danish EMU-debate 67

3. Denmark's derogation status: rights and obligations 70

4. Economic policy 75

5. The Euro referendum 77
5.1 Arguments and voters' concerns 77
5.2 EMU and political integration 80

6. Legal framework 81
6.1 The law as it stands 81
6.2 Legislation allowing further use of the euro 82
6.3 Consequential amendments 83
6.4 Central bank legislation 83
6.5 National law from the EC perspective 83
6.6 The application of the law 84

Bibliography 84

FRANCE 87
Jacques Le Cacheux and Régis Chemain

1. Quels risques d'inflation? 87
Jacques Le Cacheux
1.1 Introduction 87
1.2 La double faute de la BCE 88
1.3 Une politique monétaire plus active? 89
1.4 La banque centrale et les marchés financiers 91
1.5 La fin des largesses budgétaires? 92
1.6 La fiscalité 93
1.7 En guise de conclusion 94

2. Legal framework 96
Régis Chemain
2.1 Changes in the legal framework 96
2.1.1 Legal framework relative to the modification of some legal amounts expressed in francs 96
2.1.2 National guidelines for the introduction of banknotes and coins in euros 98
2.1.3 Instruments and procedures for the monetary policy of the Banque de France 99

2.1.4 Introduction of the euro to Monaco 99
2.2 National law from the EC perspective 100
2.3 The application of the law 102
2.4 Institutional aspects 102

Bibliography 102

GERMANY 105
Susanne Hägele and Ingo Linsenmann
With a contribution by Peter Christian Müller-Graff

1. Summary 105

2. Political and economic aspects 106
2.1 Public opinion 106
2.2 Assessment of ECB monetary policy decisions and the development of the exchange rate 110
2.2.1 Monetary policy decisions of the ECB 110
2.2.1.a Interest rates decisions 110
2.2.1.b Inflation projection 119
2.2.1.c Money growth 120
2.2.1.d Interventions 121
2.2.2 The development of the exchange rate 125
2.3 Institutional and procedural matters 131
2.3.1 General perception of institutional issues of EMU related policies 131
2.3.2 Strengthening of the Euro-group and external representation 133
2.3.3 The joining of Greece 134
2.3.4 The Danish referendum 136
2.3.5 Debate on enlargement and the reform of the ECB governing council 138
2.4 Trends towards spill-over 139
2.4.1 Tax harmonisation and social policy 140
2.4.2 Co-ordination of macroeconomic policy and monetary policy (policy-mix) 142

3. Legal framework 143
3.1 Changes in the legal framework 143
3.1.1 Results of the EMU working party (*AS WWU*) 143
3.1.2 Practical implementation of the exchange of notes and coins 146
3.2 National law from the EC perspective 146
3.3 The application of the law 147
3.4 Institutional aspects 148

3.4.1 The reform of the Bundesbank 148
3.4.2 The reform of prudential supervision in Germany 151
3.4.3 Constitutional aspects of the reform of prudential supervision in Germany 153
3.4.4 Other issues 156

Bibliography 157

GREECE 171
Anthony Papayannides

1. Greece joins the Euro-zone: political parties, economic actors and public opinion 171
2. The end-run of the drachma to join the Euro-zone 174
3. Technical adaptations of the frame of monetary policies to the euro 176
4. Legal/institutional adaptations—The final alignment 177
5. The remaining inflationary pressures of the Greek economy 178

IRELAND
Alan Stuart

1. Political and economic aspects 181
   1.1 Public opinion and awareness of the euro 181
   1.2 Irish financial institutions' attitudes towards EMU 184
   1.3 Political aspects of the euro 189
   1.4 Political parties 190
   1.5 Anti-Europe interest groups 193
   1.6 Trade unions 194
   1.7 Employers' organisations 194
2. Trends towards spill-over 195
   2.1 Tax harmonisation 196
   2.2 Social policy 196
   2.3 Macroeconomic policy co-ordination 197
   2.4 The neutrality debate 198
3. Legal framework 198
   3.1 Domestic provisions in the Economic and Monetary Union Act 1998 199
   3.2 The Central Bank Act 1998 and its implications 200
   3.3 National law from the EU perspective 202
   3.4 The application of the law 202

Bibliography 202

ITALY 205
Marina Mancini and Silvia Nenci

1. Political and economic aspects 205
Silvia Nenci
1.1 Public opinion and the euro 205
1.1.1 Surveys 205
1.1.2 Articles in the press 207
1.2 Financial institutions 208
1.2.1 The weakness of the euro 208
1.2.2 ECB policy measures 210
1.3 Institutional and procedural matters 210
1.4 Trends towards spill-over 214
1.4.1 The debate on EU reforms 214
1.4.2 Fiscal policy and tax harmonisation 217
1.4.3 Competitiveness 218
1.4.4 Pension reform 219
1.4.5 The labour market 220

2. Legal framework 221
Marina Mancini
2.1 Changes in the legal framework 221
2.1.1 Law of treaties 221
2.1.2 National law 223
2.2 National law from the EC perspective 224
2.3 The application of the law 224
2.4 Institutional aspects 225
2.4.1 Relationship between the Bank of Italy and the Italian government 225
2.4.2 Relationship between the Bank of Italy and the European Central Bank 225

Bibliography 226

THE NETHERLANDS 227
Jeannette Mak and Frank Elderson

1. Political and economic aspects 227
Jeannette Mak
1.1 Introduction 227
1.2 Public opinion 229
1.3 Financial press and financial institutions 232
1.3.1 Monetary decisions of the ECB and the euro-dollar exchange rate 233
1.3.2 Referendum on the euro in Denmark on 28 September 2000 238

1.3.3 Accession of Greece and further enlargement of EMU 239
1.4 Institutional and procedural matters 239
1.5 Trends towards spillover 242

2. Legal framework 243
Frank Elderson
2.1 Changes in the legal framework 243
2.1.1 Introduction 243
2.1.1 Brief overview of the main features of the law as it stood at the end of 1999 243
2.1.1.a Bank Act 1998 243
2.1.1.b Further legislation which required adaptation in view of Article 109 EC 246
2.1.2 Developments during the year 2000 248
2.1.2.a Protection of the euro: Act of 11 November 1999 and Euro-counterfeiting Bill 248
2.1.2.b Adaptation of legislation in relation to the introduction of the euro 250
2.1.2.c Euro Temporary Act on regulation procedures 251
2.1.2.d Amendment of certain provisions of Book 2 of the Civil Code 252
2.1.2.e Cash changeover 253
2.1.2.f Act on the financing of decentralised public authorities 254
2.2 National law from the EC perspective 255
2.3 The application of the law 257
2.4 Institutional aspects 257

SPAIN 259
Juan Carlos Monedero Fernández-Gala and Manuel López Escudero

1. Political aspects and trends towards spillover
Juan Carlos Monedero Fernándex-Gala 259
1.1 La continuidad del *relativo* optimismo europeísta 259
1.2 La opinión pública española respecto del euro 261
1.3 El punto de vista empresarial 266
1.4 El Banco de España 268
1.5 Los sindicatos: la apuesta por el *spill over* 270
1.6 Los partidos políticos 272
1.7 El euro en los medios de comunicación 276

2. Legal framework 279
Manuel López Escudero
2.1 El proyecto de ley general de estabilidad presupuestaria 280

2.2 El canje de pesetas por euros 284
2.3 Disposiciones Referentes al Banco de España 287
Bibliography 289

SWEDEN 291
Eric Clapham

1. Political and economic aspects 291
1.1 Public opinion 291
1.2 Financial markets 300
1.2.1 Opinion about EMU membership 300
1.2.2 Openness and transparency of the ECB 301
1.2.3 ECB and monetary policy 302
1.2.4 Convergence programme 303
1.3 Institutions 303
1.3.1 Political parties 303
1.3.2 Social Democratic Party 304
1.3.3 Other parties 306
1.3.4 Politics and the EMU referendum 307
1.3.5 Ecofin Council and Euro-group 308
1.3.6 Trade unions: LO 308
1.4 Trends towards spillover 310
1.4.1 Stabilisation policy 310
1.4.2 Prices level and EMU membership 311
1.4.3 Practical preparations 312
1.4.4 Taxes 313

2. Legal framework 313
2.1 Background 313
2.2 Swedish legal convergence 314
2.3 Accounting in euro 314

Bibliography 317

UNITED KINGDOM 319
Alexis Krachai, Hosein Jahanshahi, Lazaros Panourgias and Mads Andenas

1. Political and economic aspects
Alexis Krachai and Hosein Jahansashi 319
1.1 Public opinion 319
1.1.1 Summary 319
1.1.2 General attitude towards the euro 319
1.1.3 Analysis 322
1.2 Financial institutions 324

1.2.1 Aim of ECB monetary policy 324
1.2.2 ECB monetary policy decisions in 2000 324
1.2.2.a M3 growth 324
1.2.2.b Interest rates 324
1.2.2.c Straight from the president's mouth 325
1.2.3 Reactions in the United Kingdom 325
1.2.3.a The Bank of England 326
1.2.3.b Systemic issues arising from ECB monetary policy decisions 326
1.2.3.c The Treasury 327
1.2.3.d The London Investment Banking Association (LIBA) 327
1.2.3.e The National Association of Pension Funds (NAPF) 327
1.2.3.f The Association of British Insurers (ABI) 327
1.2.3.g Mortgage associations 328
1.2.4 Reactions from the financial press 328
1.2.5 Reactions regarding the weakness of the euro *vis-à-vis* other currencies 328
1.3 Institutional and procedural matters 329
1.4 Trends towards spillover 332
1.4.1 Tax harmonisation 332
1.4.2 Social policy 333
1.4.3 Co-ordination of macroeconomic and monetary policy 333
1.4.4 External projection of the euro 333

2. The euro, EMU and UK law 334
Lazaros E. Panourgias and Mads Andenas
2.1 Overview 334
2.2 Private law issues 337
2.2.1 Continuity of contracts 337
2.2.2 Conversion and rounding 338
2.2.3 Substitution of euro for the currencies of the participating Member States 339
2.2.4 Accounting 340
2.2.5 Invoices 341
2.2.6 Tax issues 341
2.2.6.a 'Euroconversion' 341
2.2.6.b Tax payments in euro 342
2.2.7 Listing securities in euro 343
2.3 Institutional issues 343
2.3.1 Monetary policy 343
2.3.2 Government debt management 344

2.3.3 Supervision 344
2.3.3.a Capital adequacy 347
2.3.3.b *Three Rivers* 347
2.3.3.c Payments system 349

THE EURO-GROUP AND ECONOMIC POLICY CO-ORDINATION 351
Jean-Victor Louis

1. Introduction 351
2. The co-ordination, its nature and its limits 352
3. The co-ordination procedures 355
4. The Economic and Financial Committee (EFC) and the Economic Policy Committee (EPC) 362
5. Possible orientations 365
5. Concluding remarks 368

Bibliography 370

INTRODUCTION

The present volume brings together a series of national reports that examine the introduction of the euro and the relevant economic, political, and legal developments throughout the year 2000 in most of the Member States of the European Union: Austria, Belgium, Denmark, France, Germany, Greece, Ireland, Italy, the Netherlands, Spain, Sweden, and the United Kingdom. These reports are produced in the framework of the '*Eurospectator*' research project of the European University Institute of Florence. The latter's ambition is to cover the period from the beginning of the third stage of the European Economic and Monetary Union, that is from 1 January 1999, until the introduction of euro coins and notes, that is until the end of year 2001, to be more precise, until 28 February 2002, when the transitory period of double circulation of old national currencies and euros will have ended.

The first set of reports that were produced in the framework of the *Eurospectator* research project and that covered the year 1999, were published as Working Papers of the Law Department of the European University Institute (EUI Working Papers Law No 4 to 9). The countries that were treated that year were ten: Austria, Belgium, France, Germany, Greece, Italy, Portugal, Spain, Sweden, and the United Kingdom.

There are some differences between the present 2000 series and the first set of reports for 1999. A number of changes have occurred in the composition of the network of collaborators to the programme. There are for the first time, reports on Denmark, Ireland, and the Netherlands. A 'Community' report has also been prepared, dealing with institutional aspects of economic co-ordination.

Meanwhile, all three 'out' countries are now examined. It was indeed important to have an extensive report on Denmark, the year of the referendum. Dr Skjalm presents an interesting synthesis of the approach to EMU, and indeed to the EU itself, in his country. We are also happy to have been able to add to the economic and political science oriented report of the Federal Trust a report on the legal developments in the UK, due to Professor Mads Andenas and Lazaros Panourgias of the British Institute of International and Comparative Law. In addition, Eric Clapham produced, as last year, a well-documented interdisciplinary report for Sweden. The Netherlands are now well covered, both on the legal aspects, treated by Frank Elderson, of the Nederlandsche Bank, and on the political science aspects, analysed by Jeannette Mak, a researcher of the Department of Political and Social Sciences of the EUI. Alan Stuart, the new member of the team for Ireland, succeeded in presenting in a single paper, the situation in Ireland, in 1999 (when no *Eurospectator* report had been produced) and in 2000, in an interdisciplinary way. It is interesting to read his comments on the public opinion and on the attitude of political parties and trade unions, in the light of the negative result of the referendum on the Treaty of Nice.

At this stage, we do not intend to proceed to any substantial conclusions from this collection of reports. It is envisaged that after the completion of the entire programme, with the future production of reports for the period January 2001 to February 2002, a conference will take place in October 2002, which will evaluate the whole project and draw general conclusions. However, that does not prevent us from making some comments based on what has been achieved up to now.

A basic remark is that the opinion on the euro reflects the attitude of each country on the European Union in general. That is true in Sweden where, as the current report observes, only 34 per cent of the population think that the participation of their country to the Union is a good thing according to Eurobarometer no 54 (Autumn 2000), and a majority of the population is against the euro. On the contrary, although that seems to be an exception to the rule, in the Netherlands the attitude towards the euro is more favourable than towards the European integration in general. In many countries the increasingly favourable trend to the euro has been broken in the Spring 2000. It is not the case in Spain where the support for the euro has steadily increased in the year under review. It is difficult to find an easy explanation for the decrease of support for the euro. Obviously, its weakness on the exchange markets was only one of the elements that could have played a role, because, as observed in the German report, the polls did not reflect a change in the opinion when the euro exchange rate recovered somewhat. In the three 'out' countries, the fact that the economic situation was reasonably good, despite the non-participation to the EMU was surely an element that played in favour of Eurosceptic attitudes. The euro is not a priority in the opinion of the general public in or outside the Euro-area. Sometimes polls are conducted in order to scrutinise the awareness of the population of the euro and not the attitudes on the EMU, as the author of the Irish report explains and, as the year 2000 was still well away from the start of the circulation of monetary signs in euro in January 2002, not very much was done in order to inform the public, as commented in the Austrian report. General campaigns have only started in the summer of 2001. That explains why in some countries like Italy, where the support to the euro is important, the citizens appear to know very little about it. The authors of the reports have observed that, as a rule, the results of polls conducted by national private or public institutes are less optimistic on the attitude of the public towards the euro, than the ones of Eurobarometer. It is the case, for example, in Germany, in the Netherlands and in Spain. It has been pointed out by the Spanish report that this may be due, in some cases, to the way questions are put in national questionnaires. Needless to say that this observation does not imply any negative appreciation as to the polls conducted by the Commission that have at least the merit to be the only ones putting the same questions all over the Union.

Specific factors have influenced the attitudes towards the EMU and the Union in some countries. The perspective of the entry of the drachma in the monetary union, at the beginning of 2001, was an element invoked in the electoral campaign in Greece, as mentioned by the Greek rapporteur, as it also was by Premier Aznar in the Spanish elections of 2000. For the Austrian report, opinion polls in this country were obviously influenced by the 'sanctions' adopted by the other fourteen EU Member States against the participation of the party of Mr Haider in the Government. The UK remains a special case. The attitude of the opinion seems very much influenced by the lack of strong leadership of the government on the subject of Britain joining the euro and it is interesting to notice that some polls ask the question: 'if the government were to strongly urge that Britain should be part of a single currency, how would you vote?'. The negative attitude of the British public is also due to the reluctance of the government to see the decision to be taken as a political one.

The opinions of the financial sector are not easy to collect. The managers of financial institutions are not keen on expressing definitive opinions on the monetary policy. Reservations are formulated by economists of the banks or in articles of the professional press that use to refer to 'financial markets', when they make some critical points on the variations of interest rates or the interventions of the ESCB on the exchange markets (see the report of Ms Farès). The official standpoint is generally, as noted in the Federal Trust report, one of global approval in contrast with the criticisms, sometimes contradictory, expressed in the financial press. The same occurred in Italy, where the president of the Italian Banking Association is quoted as saying, for example, that the increase of the interest rate in August 2000, was 'equilibrated'. The positions of individual economists are much more diversified. The report of Jacques Le Cacheux is exemplary of the concerns raised, on the one hand, by the interest rate policy of the ECB, and, on the other hand, by the 'inflexible' application of the Stability and Growth Pact.

In the Euro-area, the euro is not at the centre of political debates. Paul Magnette observes, in the Belgian report, that the situation is perhaps in evolution, not because there would be an opposition to the euro as such, but rather considering the social issues that are raised in the development of a discourse on the kind of EMU desirable. It is not without meaning that in Belgium only the trade unions debate on the kind of EMU they would approve of. The current discussion on structural reforms in the labour markets and the revision of the 'excessive' generosity of the welfare state, in particular in the field of retirement schemes can develop into an important controversy between the authorities and the social partners. The initiatives of the French and Belgian Ministers of Finance in order to strengthen the Euro-group are inspired by the will of Treasuries in the Member States not only to affirm the authority of the Executive towards the ECB, while preserving the latter's independence, but also to keep controlling the process. 2000 was a year of impressive growth but the fruit of this 'prosperity' was not mainly used in order to reduce the remaining debt that, as it is well known, is still very considerable in some Member States, and the European co-ordination was not an exemplary one. The orientation was more on using this extra revenue in order either to decrease the fiscal pressure or to increase the expenses in sectors considered as priorities (Le Cacheux). There was also no European concerted action when oil prices increased. Reactions were purely national ones and this despite the repeated calls for a closer co-ordination of economic policies and for a growing role for the broad economic guidelines. Discussions concerning the opportunity to maintain unchanged the Stability and Growth Pact only re-appeared in 2001 with the worsening of the conjuncture.

Most legal developments concern technical measures for the introduction of the euro. A lot of provisions had to be taken in company law, accounting law, social law, taxation law, criminal law, procedural law, etc, in order to settle some questions raised by the change-over. It is particularly interesting to look at the way the UK, as an 'out' country, that happens to be the most important financial centre, has interpreted the new monetary law of the Community and taken all practical measures for the smooth working of the single currency. The Dutch legal report describes the measures that have been adopted in order to adapt the central bank legislation to the integration into the ESCB, a matter that, for most of the other countries has been dealt with in the first set of reports. The same is true for Ireland. Sweden presents the singularity to be, by its own will, a country with a derogation that is normally subject to the obligations of such a country. As the report of the ECB on convergence, published in 2000, observes, Sweden, that has amended its constitution in order to give independence to the Sveriges Riksbank, has not started with the lasting procedure of constitutional revision, that is necessary for the integration of the central bank in the ESCB, when Sweden will participate, as it has the obligation to do, in the third stage of the EMU. Our former colleague, Robert Sparve, the general counsel of the Riksbank, has insisted on the fact that such a preparation could start without delay in order to permit the participation of Sweden in the monetary union, if and when it is so decided. Such preparation would be reversible in case of a negative referendum. However, as mentioned by the Swedish rapporteur, the starting of the procedure of revision could be considered as not respectful of the democratic decision to be taken by the Swedish people on EMU participation. Such participation has to be in conformity with the convergence criteria, the one on exchange rate policy included.

The German report, prepared with the contribution of Professor Müller-Graff, raises the issue of conformity with the German Constitution of the conferral to the Bundesbank of complete power of prudential supervision. His view is that arguments in favour of the non-conformity are more convincing. It seems that this debate is no longer timely, because the reform would create an Allfinanz supervision authority that would not be the Bundesbank. The central bank would preserve the operational responsibilities it has now. The question of the reform of the Bundesbank has not been settled either in 2000. The Bundesbank was since its creation a rather centralised institution notwithstanding the existence of Länderzentralbänken and the participation of their presidents to the Zentralbankrat. This structure has been for years very useful for the President of the Bank as a kind of alibi for not accepting any decision on monetary policy forced upon him. It was not for him to decide, for example, on interest rates, but for an organ where regional elements were supposed to have more weight than orientations based on the necessities of international or European cooperation. With the participation of Germany to the monetary union, such a complex structure is redundant. Anyway, both the Direktorium and the Zentralbankrat have lost their decision-making competencies. It is a fact that some members of the Board of the Bundesbank have a tendency to forget this in their comments on monetary policy. Nevertheless, there is no simple solution to such questions that are prone to considerations of political equilibrium between the centre and the periphery, in a context of increasing protagonism of the Länder.

Quite apart from these institutional questions, one should, once again, remark that no report mentions problems related to the continuity of contracts, a subject that has been extensively treated by the literature, but has not apparently, up to now, had any relevance at all in the practice.

As far as the possible follow-up of the EMU is concerned, rapporteurs (for Germany and Italy) observe that the IGC 2000 and the Treaty of Nice were not concerned at all with the strengthening of the political institutions as a necessary counterpart to the role of the ECB and ESCB in the monetary union. Title VII on Economic and monetary policy was almost unchanged after Nice, except for the parsimonious introduction of qualified majority voting in some provisions, and the Protocol on the ESCB statute was only touched in order to allow for new principles for the composition of the Governing Council (Article 10). As noted in the French report, taxation harmonisation still has to be based on unanimity.

The German report mentions the open perspectives in the field of macro-economic policies and fiscal harmonisation, as a result of the Cardiff process and the Lisbon open method of co-ordination, as well as political efforts to solve the long-lasting problem of taxation of income savings. It remains to be seen, if we are on the way towards 'more supranational modes of governance' (Wessels/Linsenmann 2001). The Eurogroup is increasingly concerned with structural problems, for example, in the labour market and in the pensions sector. However, the pragmatism (in the form of soft law), underlined in the Dutch report, that characterises the provisions of the Maastricht Treaty in the field of economic co-ordination, remains the dominant feature in the approach of the authorities to these problems.

JEAN-VICTOR LOUIS

LIST OF CONTRIBUTORS

Mads Andenas, Director of the British Institute of International and Comparative Law, London

Herta Baumann, MMag, Scientific Consultant at the Austrian Institute for International Affairs, Vienna

Régis Chemain, Maître de conférences, Université de Paris X, Nanterre

Eric Clapham, Stockholm School of Economics

Frank Elderson, Senior Lawyer, Legal Department, De Nederlandsche Bank NV

Soukaïna Farès, Assistante de recherche au groupe d'études politiques européennes (GEPE), Brussels

Susanne Hägele, Universität Köln

Hosein Jahanshahi, Research Assistant, Federal Trust for Education and Research, London

Alexis Krachai, Research Officer, Federal Trust for Education and Research, London

Helmut Lang, Scientific Consultant at the Austrian Institute for International Affairs, Veinna

Jacques Le Cacheux, Directeur du Département des Études, Observatoire Français des Conjonctures Économiques

Ingo Linsenmann, Universität Köln, Forschungsinstitut für Politische Wissenschaft und Europäische Fragen, Cologne

Manuel López Escudero, Universidad de Granada, Facultad de Derecho, Departamento de Derecho Internacional Público

Jean-Victor Louis, Professor at the European University Institute and at the Université Libre de Bruxelles

Paul Magnette, Lecturer at the Université Libre de Bruxelles

Jeannette Mak, Researcher, Department of Social and Political Sciences, European University Institute, Rome

Marina Mancini, Istituto Affari Internazionali, Rome

Juan Carlos Monedero Fernández-Gala, Universidad Complutense de Madrid, Facultad de Ciencias Políticas

Silvia Nenci, Istituto Affari Internazionali, Rome

Lazaros Panourgias, Research Fellow at the British Institute of International and Comparative Law and Legal Advisor, European Bank for Reconstruction and Development, London

Anthony Papayannides, EKEME, Athens

Karsten Skjalm, Senior Research Fellow, Danish Institute of International Affairs (DUPI), Copenhagen

Alan Stuart, Institute for European Affairs (IEA), Dublin

AUSTRIA

Herta Baumann and Helmut Lang

1. Political and economic aspects
Helmut Lang*

1.1 Introduction

In the year 2000, public debate in Austria was dominated by two topics. First, the appointment of the new government coalition between the People's Party (Österreichische Volkspartei—ÖVP) and the Freedom Party (Freiheitliche Partei Österreichs—FPÖ), and the ensuing measures of the other 14 EU Member States.[1] Secondly, the controversial discussions about the federal budgets (in spring about the budget for the year 2000; from summer and onwards about the budgets for the years 2001 and 2002) and about the accompanying austerity measures.[2] The main reason for the reduction of the public deficit and for the achievement of a balanced budget by 2002 was that it was necessary for the monetary union and because Austria had the highest public deficit of all countries within the Euro-area. However, monetary union did not itself play a significant role in the public debate.

1.2 Public opinion

1.2.1 Framework

The results of public opinion polls during the year 2000 were clearly influenced by the sanctions imposed on the Austrian government by the fourteen EU Member States. Although the sanctions were only diplomatic bilateral measures, their symbolic impact was enormous. The government and the most influential media successfully drew the picture of small and innocent Austria (and its population) being treated terribly unfairly by the European Union and the other fourteen Member States. Newspapers were full of contemptuous letters by angry citizens against the EU. Examples of unjustified bad treatment of Austrians in other Member States were dealt with excessively.[3] Members of the government, such as the Minister of

* Scientific Consultant at the OIIP (Austrian Institute for International Affairs), Operngasse 20B, A–1040, Wien.

1 See Chs 1.2.1 and 1.4.2.

2 See below for more information about the budgets.

3 See an overview of several sanctions in areas other than diplomatic relations in *Der Standard*, 21 Apr 2000.

Finance, Karl-Heinz Grasser, suggested retaliatory measures such as the suspension of Austrian contributions to the EU budget.[4] Representatives of the opposition parties were accused of treason if they did not unambiguously join the condemnations of the 'unjustified sanctions' against Austria. In the presence of the Minister of Justice, Haider even suggested using the criminal law to prosecute politicians who do not defend Austria against the sanctions of the other 14 EU Member States.[5] The government decided to organise a popular initiative unless the sanctions were lifted by autumn. Its text included suggestions such as 'Should the sanctions against Austria be lifted immediately' or 'Should the right of every EU Member State be secured to nominate its government on the basis of free and democratic elections' (*Der Standard*, 12 July 2000).[6]

To sum up, this sometimes-bizarre public debate had the following features:

- The sanctions were perceived as unfair, unjustified and as a serious insult to the whole country and to its entire population.
- Any responsibility for the situation by the Austrian government was denied.
- The measures were seen as EU measures and this influenced views about the EU, as well as perceptions of institutions not involved in the discussion about the sanctions (such as the European Central Bank).

Two other aspects should be mentioned in the context of the interpretation of public opinion polls about the euro in the year 2000. First, any public debate about the euro was limited to the continuous decline of the euro in relation to the dollar. Although many commentators—most notably the governor of the Austrian Central Bank, Klaus Liebscher—tried to dissipate concerns, the main message was that it had lost value. Secondly, the year 2000 was a transitional year between the start of monetary union at the beginning of 1999 and the final preparations for the introduction of euro

[4] The Minister withdrew his threat after a spokes person of the Commission had indicated that a suspension of contributions to the EU budget would be a breach of the Treaties and would be followed by a fine (*Der Standard*, 18 Apr 2000).

[5] This statement of Haider and especially the reaction of the Minister of Justice, who thought that this was an interesting idea, were heavily criticised by the 'three wise men' in their report about the policies of the new government and the 'political nature' of the Freedom Party as an attack on the freedom of criticism (Ahtisaari, Frowein, Oreja, 2000, 28). On the basis of this report by the 'three wise men' the other fourteen EU Member States lifted the sanctions against Austria's government because they 'would become counterproductive' (Ahtisaari, Frowein, Oreja, 2000), 33.

[6] Constitutional experts heavily criticised the planned popular initiative and called it an abuse of the constitution (*Der Standard*, 12 July 2000). Art 49b (1) of the Federal Constitution states that a popular initiative can be held 'on a matter of fundamental and overall national importance for *whose settlement the legislature is competent*. [. . .] Elections and matters subject to a decision by a court or an administrative authority cannot be the topic of a plebiscite' (emphasis added).

coins and notes in 2001. As a consequence, the year 2000 did not see any major public information campaign about the euro.

1.2.2 Overview of the surveys

The following information is drawn from the two Eurobarometer surveys published in the year 2000 (Eurobarometer 52 and 53) and from two surveys conducted on behalf of the Austrian government (more precisely: the 'Euro-Initiative' of the Austrian government). All surveys mentioned so far are based on samples of 1,000 face-to-face interviews. It is important to bear in mind the time at which the fieldwork was done. Eurobarometer study number 52 was carried out in October and November 1999. This was after the general elections on 3 October 1999, and before the beginning of serious negotiations for the formation of a new government. The fieldwork of the first Austrian survey was done between 19 January and 18 February 2000. During this time the coalition talks between the Social Democratic Party and the People's Party failed, the coalition negotiations between the ÖVP and the Freedom Party were successfully concluded, and the government was installed in spite of heavy national and international protests. Eurobarometer survey 53 was conducted in April and May 2000, after the initial storms of protest had weakened slightly, but emotions were still aroused and the 'sanctions' dominated the public debate. The second survey's fieldwork on behalf of the government was done between 21 June and 21 July 2000. During that time, the 'three wise men' were appointed (on 12 July) to investigate the Austrian government's positions on human rights and the 'nature' of the Freedom Party.

1.2.3 Public opinion and the EU

Overall support for Austria's EU membership was highly volatile over the last two years.[7] In late 1998 38 per cent of Austrian citizens perceived EU membership to be a good thing, whereas 19 per cent saw it as a bad thing (Eurobarometer 50, 41). Support for EU membership slightly deteriorated in spring 1999, supposedly due to the institutional crisis and the war in Kosovo (Eurobarometer 51, 24–5).[8] In autumn 1999 the support level increased significantly to 42 per cent, and opposition dropped to 18 per cent (Eurobarometer 52, 26). This was the strongest increase in net support of all Member States (+11 per cent).[9] However, Austria still had the third lowest level of support for EU membership compared to the other

[7] The upwards and downwards trends coincided with the aggregated EU development but were more accentuated.

[8] 36 per cent of Austrians regarded EU membership as a good thing, 23 per cent as a bad thing.

[9] Net support levels in Spain, Portugal and Belgium each rose by 9 per cent.

Member States, and one of the highest opposition levels. The Spring 2000 Eurobarometer survey clearly showed the impact on public opinion of the *sanctions* against Austria. The proportion of Austrians that supported Austria's membership had fallen by 9 percentage points; the proportion that believed Austria's membership to be a bad thing had increased by 7 percentage points. (Eurobarometer 53, 8). Support levels decreased only slightly in the European Union as a whole. We find an even more significant drop in public opinion in the answers about whether the country had benefited from EU membership. In October and November 1999 45 per cent of Austrians believed that the country had benefited from EU membership. But 32 per cent thought that Austria had not benefited (Eurobarometer 52, 28). In Spring 2000, the number of Austrians perceiving benefits had dropped to 34 per cent (–11 per cent); the number thinking that Austria had not benefited increased to 48 per cent (+16 per cent). Therefore, the net result plunged from +13 per cent to –14 per cent. (Eurobarometer 53, 10)

1.2.4 Trust in European institutions and bodies

The level of trust in European institutions and bodies plunged and the level of distrust increased significantly. The amount of trust lost seems to roughly coincide with awareness of the respective institutions and bodies. The most significant drop in trust levels concerned the European Parliament, which lost 12 percentage points in the six months from Autumn 1999 to Spring 2000. Trust levels for the Commission fell by six percentage points, the Council of Ministers by five points, the Court of Justice and the European Central Bank by four points. The increase of the levels of distrust in the same period was even more significant. Distrust in the European institutions and bodies increased by 12 points for the European Parliament and the Council of Ministers, nine points for the ECB, and eight points for the Commission and the Court of Justice. Trust in the least known institutions and bodies n the European institutions and bodies—the European Ombudsman, the Committee of the Regions and the Social and Economic Committee—did not change significantly. However, the levels of distrust increased by seven percentage points for all three. Due to the European Parliament's heavy losses—at the end of 1999 it was the relatively most trusted European institution in Austria—the positions of the three most trusted institutions and bodies changed. In spring of the year 2000 the Austrian people most trusted the European Court of Justice (45 per cent), followed by the ECB (42 per cent), and the European Parliament and the Commission (40 per cent each). Compared with the other Member States, the level of trust in the European Parliament was significantly lower than in the majority of the Member States. In 11 Member States between 68 per cent (Ireland) and 52 per cent (Denmark) of the population trusted in the EP. The EP had the lowest support in Germany (46 per cent), Sweden, Austria (both 40 per cent) and the UK (27 per cent). The EU-15 average was 52 per cent. Trust in the ECB was also one of the lowest compared with other Member States and the lowest level of the Euro-zone.[10] However, it was still close to the EU average of 43 per cent (Eurobarometer 53, Annex 2.8.).

1.2.5 Support for the single currency

Support for key issues[11] decreased, mainly in favour of 'don't know' answers but with one notable exception: support for the proposal 'There has to be one single currency, the euro, replacing the schilling and all other national currencies of the Member States of the European Union' fell from 58 per cent (Eurobarometer 52, annex B.42) to 48 per cent (Eurobarometer 53, annex B.37), and opposition to this proposal increased from 30 per cent to 38 per cent. With 48 per cent, Austria had the lowest support level for the single currency of all countries of the Euro-zone, including Greece, but the opposition level was significantly lower than in Finland. It was remarkable that, at the same time, 61 per cent of Austrians supported the suggestion that the EU Member States should have a common defence and security policy. This result is difficult to explain without recourse to additional data.

The answers to the two proposals concerning the ECB[12] changed significantly less. The independence of the ECB is supported by 63 per cent (–4 per cent compared to Eurobarometer 52), and 68 per cent think the ECB should be accountable to the European Parliament (–6 per cent compared to Eurobarometer 52). The falling support for the accountability of the ECB could be the consequence of the significant loss of reputation by the EP.

Unlike the Eurobarometer, the surveys conducted on behalf of the Austrian government did not show any significant drop in the support levels for the euro. From summer 1997 the surveys used almost the same question[13] to ask for opinions about the euro. In October 1999 17 per cent of Austrians said they were very much in favour of the single currency and 46 per cent said they were in favour. Taken together, 63 per cent were

[10] The ECB had lower trust levels than in Austria only in Sweden (41 per cent), Greece (39 per cent) and the UK (19 per cent).

[11] Single Currency and related issues, common foreign policy, common defence policy, subsidiarity, support of the European Parliament for the Commission and whether EU matters should be taught at school.

[12] 'With the single currency, the euro, there has to be a European Central Bank which is independent of the Member States' and 'The European Central Bank has to be accountable for its decisions to the European Parliament'.

[13] The wording of the question was updated after the introduction of the euro at the beginning of 1999.

positive. In February 2000, 16 per cent were very much in favour and 46 per cent in favour of the single currency. In August 2000 the numbers were 22 per cent and 40 per cent respectively. This means that the cumulative support level ('very much in favour' and 'in favour') did not change significantly throughout the whole year and was, somewhat surprisingly and contrary to the results of the Eurobarometer, not influenced by the political developments in Austria. It is not easy to find an explanation for this phenomenon. One reason could be that the Eurobarometer survey took place at a time when emotions still were running high and the public debate about the sanctions continued to be lively. By summer, the emotions had somewhat subsided and the decision to install the 'three wise men' already suggested that the situation would normalise. Another explanation could be that the Eurobarometer survey contains exclusively EU topics that could have led, under the circumstances of Spring 2000, to a reinforcement of negative opinions about the EU. Finally, the wording of the questions is very different. The Eurobarometer question mentions the replacement of the national currency and includes the term 'European Union', both of which could evoke negative feelings compared with the wording of the question in the Austrian surveys. However, these are only speculations in the absence of data. It will be interesting to see whether the support levels in the next Eurobarometer survey return to the previous levels.

Broken down according to standard socio-demographic variables, the results of the Austrian surveys largely reflect the aggregated data of the Eurobarometer for the Union as a whole. Men are more likely to support the euro than women, and support for the euro increases with the level of education. The age group least likely to support the euro is people aged 60 and over; this group has a relatively high percentage of women and people with lower educational levels.

Asked whether they expect personal advantages or disadvantages from the introduction of the euro, 29 per cent of Austrians said in summer 2000 (25 per cent in February) that they expected personal advantages, and 30 per cent expected disadvantages (24 per cent in February). 40 per cent expected neither advantages nor disadvantages (51 per cent in February). Men, young people and people with higher education were the most likely to be optimistic about personal advantages. Almost half of the people with higher education expected personal advantages; only 18 per cent of those expected disadvantages. Only 22 per cent of people with lower educational levels expected personal advantages; 34 per cent of them feared disadvantages. The difference between men and women is significant: only 23 per cent of women expected advantages (37 per cent of men) and 37 per cent expected disadvantages (23 per cent of men).

1.2.6 Arguments for and against the euro

For the third time, the government survey in summer 2000 asked for arguments for and against the euro.[14] Respondents had to choose from given lists of arguments that contained 25 arguments for and 19 arguments against the euro. Unfortunately, since the list of arguments against the euro lacked some important considerations,[15] certain shortcomings should be kept in mind.

Comparing the results of Summer 2000 with those of March 1998 the following general observations can be made.

First, every argument in favour of the euro had less support in Summer 2000.[16] Part of the explanation could be that, in March 1998 (shortly before the final decisions to enter the third stage of Monetary Union were taken by the European Council at the beginning of May), the euro was a topic of public debate; at this stage, the government was running a comprehensive campaign in favour of the euro. Another part of the explanation for the weaker support for arguments in favour of the euro is most likely to be the impact of the sanctions.

The majority of arguments against the euro also lost support, but less significantly than the arguments in favour of the euro. Some arguments had slightly gained support and only two arguments gained significantly (more than 2 per cent). Interestingly, those were not political arguments, as would have been expected as a consequence of the sanctions. Those proposals were that the euro would be much weaker than the schilling (+4 per cent), and that people who do not know much about money matters will suffer disadvantages (+7 per cent).

Secondly, the arguments in favour of the euro have much more support than those against. The three most important arguments for the euro have the support of 70, 65, and 58 per cent respectively, the most frequently chosen arguments against the euro got the support of 50 per cent (each of the first two) and 42 per cent.

The arguments in favour of the euro were predominantly the expression of personal and economic advantages. The five most important arguments were (the numbers in brackets show the results in percentage terms in summer 2000 and in March 1998): the transfer of payments in the EU will be easier (70; 78); removal of the necessity to change money and pay money exchange fees (65; 76); better comparability of prices (58; 70);

[14] These questions were also included in the surveys in Dec 1997 and Mar 1998.

[15] Some examples of missing arguments against the Euro: the change-over to the new currency will be difficult; the value of the smallest banknote is much too high; the euro is losing its value against the dollar; holidays in Mediterranean countries will become more expensive.

[16] With the exception of two out of the three least important arguments, which gained statistically insignificant percentage points.

shopping in the EU will be easier (56; 71); and no more exchange rate losses (47; 58). Political arguments for the single currency were not considered to be very important. 27 per cent supported the proposal that the euro improves co-operation in Europe (40 per cent in March 1998), and only 14 per cent thought that the single currency contributes to peace in Europe (14 per cent in 1998). The most important arguments against the euro were predominantly political. The five most important were (results in percentage points): with the removal of the schilling Austria loses part of its identity (50; 50); Austria will be more dependent on decisions in Brussels (50; 48); economic policy in Austria will be more influenced by Brussels and the ECB (42; 49); people who do not know much about money matters will suffer disadvantages (41; 34); and, other economically weaker EU countries will be financed by those with stronger economies (35; 48).

Another interesting aspect should be mentioned. The connection between monetary union and the reduction of public deficits and public debt (which usually means austerity measures) is either not well known or not considered to be an important argument concerning the euro. The proposals mentioning public debt are among the two least important reasons for or against the euro.[17] The proposal 'In order to finance monetary union taxes have to be raised' is supported by 24 per cent of Austrians and ranks in the lower half of arguments against the euro. However, this argument does not mention public debt and is probably perceived to refer to the changeover costs.

Another interesting argument against the euro is the following: 'The euro makes it impossible for Austria to leave the EU.' This is supported by 34 per cent (32 per cent in 1998), which makes it the seventh most important argument against the euro.

1.2.7 The external value of the euro

The summer 2000 survey on behalf of the government asked Austrians whether they thought that the decline of the euro against the dollar would have affected them personally. Seven per cent answered that it would have positive effects for them, 22 per cent said it would have negative effects, 32 per cent stated it would not have affected them, and 39 per cent thought that it was too early to say.

In February 2000 the survey asked whether people thought that the common currency helped the Austrian economy in the international competition against the dollar and the yen. 50 per cent said that the

[17] The argument 'The government can reduce the public debt' was the least supported argument in favour of the euro (supported by 9 per cent). The suggestion 'Public debt will increase' was the second least supported argument against the euro (supported by 16 per cent). Of course, very much depends on the given proposals and their wording.

common currency helped, 19 per cent said it would not help, and 31 per cent did not have an opinion. In October 1999 59 per cent had supported the view that the euro helped in the international competition (18 per cent no; 23 per cent don't know).

A clear majority of Austrians (55 per cent) thought in February 2000 that monetary union helped the Austrian defence against international financial speculation. 15 per cent held the view that Austria could better defend itself alone, while 30 per cent did not know. In October 1999, 65 per cent had thought that it was better to defend the currency together, only 19 per cent did not hold any view. This remarkable increase in 'don't know' answers seems to be the result of the sanctions against Austria. People did not change their mind that it would be better to defend against speculation alone, but it was much more difficult to admit that it would be easier in co-operation with the other Member States.

A survey published at the beginning of October asked Austrians whether the depreciation of the euro disturbed them: 45 per cent answered with 'no', and 51 per cent with 'yes'.[18] Broken down by party affiliation, 48 per cent of Social Democrats, 62 per cent of Freedom Party supporters, 34 per cent of People's Party followers, and 52 per cent of Greens said that they were disturbed by the weak euro.

1.2.8 Information about the single currency

According to the Eurobarometer survey conducted in April and May 2000, 59 per cent of Austrians felt very well (11 per cent) or well informed (41 per cent) about the euro, which was an increase of 4 per cent compared to the previous survey. In this respect, Austria ranks fifth—after the Netherlands, Finland, Luxemburg and Belgium—in feeling better informed. 39 per cent felt not very well (31 per cent) or not at all informed (8 per cent).

These results roughly coincide with the results of the studies on behalf of the Austrian government. In summer 2000 51 per cent said they felt very well (9 per cent) or well informed (42 per cent) about the euro, 48 per cent felt not very (38 per cent) or not at all informed (10 per cent). Since the peak in March 1999 people have felt ever less informed. This trend can be explained by the reduction of media coverage to normal levels after the introduction of the euro at the beginning of 1999, and the absence of public campaigns for the euro in the year 2000.

Seventy-eight per cent says that they have received information about the single currency (Eurobarometer 53). According to the Summer 2000 survey on behalf of the Austrian government, 60 per cent of Austrians

[18] Survey conducted by the OGM institute; 501 interviews; published in 'Format' 40/2000, 83.

have actively informed themselves about the euro; 39 per cent said that they had not.

Without going into details, it can be said that the great majority of information about the euro is received from three sources: banks (financial institutions), newspapers and television (or the Austrian Broadcasting Corporation, which includes radio).

1.2.9 Change-over to the euro notes and coins

Forty-three per cent of Austrians think they will quickly get accustomed to the euro notes and coins. 31 per cent expect that they will need a long time until the get familiar with the euro, and 26 per cent do not know yet. The answers to this question did not change significantly over the years.[19] Analysis by standard demographic variables shows, as expected, that those groups that are more likely to support the introduction of the euro (men; younger people; well-educated people) also expect that they will adapt rapidly to the euro.

1.2.10 Other topics

A study conducted from 31 January 2000 to 9 February 2000 asked several interesting questions.[20] The main results are presented below.

A large majority of Austrians (87 per cent) has heard about the fall of the euro against the dollar, although people were not sure about the positive and negative effects of the exchange rate development. 47 per cent thought that exporters would benefit from the falling euro, 27 per cent expected advantages for importers. Correspondingly, 29 per cent held the view that exporters would suffer disadvantages, and 48 per cent saw disadvantages for importers. For the Austrian economy as a whole, 47 per cent expected negative effects, while only 18 per cent expected positive effects.[21] The study did not ask for the reasons for these expectations. People probably expected negative effects from rising crude oil prices.

The answers to the question about who should represent Austria in the ECB in Frankfurt are very interesting. The people had four given alternatives and answered as follows (the first number represents 'yes'-answers in percentage points, the second 'no'-answers; 'don't know'-answers are not shown): the association of banks (23; 38); the Minister of Finance (28; 50); the Austrian Central Bank (64; 18); the Minister for Foreign Affairs (17; 62). A two-thirds majority chose the right answer. However, the

[19] In Oct 1998 the numbers were 41 per cent (adapt quickly), 27 per cent (long term) and 32 per cent (don't know).

[20] The sample included 970 people over 18 years old. Interviews were made by telephone.

[21] The percentage of neither/nor and don't know is not shown.

results show that additional alternatives could have been interesting (for example: the finance committee of the Austrian parliament; the Federal President; the social partners).

1.3 Financial institutions

1.3.1 Reactions to monetary policy decisions

The reactions to ECB monetary policy decisions and to the weakness of the euro against the dollar and other currencies can not be completely separated because most commentators assumed a connection between these two developments. The EMU Council's decisions to increase the interest rates several times in the year 2000, and also the decision to intervene on behalf of the euro in September, were extensively criticised by commentators. The main points of critique were the inconsistency of the ECB monetary policy strategy, the supposed orientation of the exchange rate, and the endangering of economic growth in the Euro-zone.

The ECB monetary policy strategy consists of two 'pillars'. The first pillar is the money supply; the second comprises several other influences on the price level. According to many commentators, the interest rate decisions of the ECB were not consistent with this strategy and therefore sent mixed signals to the markets. The chief economist of the Creditanstalt Bankverein, one of Austria's biggest banks, pointed out that the reference value of the money supply had been continuously surpassed since the beginning of 1999 without any clear reaction from the ECB.[22] Additionally, the interpretation of the indicators of the second pillar remained unclear (*Der Standard*, 31 August 2000). This led to the question whether the ECB oriented itself along the money supply or directly along inflation (Schulmeister, 2000b). Other observers used these arguments to defend the ECB's monetary policy. They argued that the ECB showed that it was flexible and reacted on the basis of a comprehensive evaluation of the economic situation, rather than mechanistically executing its policy according to simple indicators (Gnan/Schubert, 2000, 596). That this led the strategy—at least temporarily—in the direction of inflation targeting only stressed the flexibility of the concept (Mooslechner, 2000, 79).

The ECB's handling of the development of the exchange rate was also heavily criticised. For a long time, the ECB strictly denied that the exchange rate would have any influence on its decisions. Nevertheless, the ECB increased interest rates six times in the year 2000, without any significant growth in the core inflation rate. This led ECB watchers to the

[22] Despite the growth of monetary supply about the reference value of 4.5 per cent, the ECB council decided to lower interest rates on 8 Apr 1999.

conclusion that the ECB in fact tried to influence the exchange rate.[23] However, the euro continued to fall after each interest rate increase. This supposedly had two reasons. First, the markets interpreted the ECB's measures as attempts to support the euro's exchange rate. Secondly, one of the main reasons for the exchange rate development was the economic growth differential between Europe and the United States. Since rising interest rates signalled lower economic growth in the Euro-area, a further decline of the euro followed inevitably (Schulmeister, 2000c).[24] Equally criticised were the ECB's interventions to support the euro's exchange rate. They seemed only to confirm that the ECB followed—against its monetary policy strategy—an exchange rate goal. Worse, the interventions could be interpreted as giving in to political pressure after the Ministers of Finance of the Euro-zone had issued a statement in September that a strong euro was in the interest of the Euro-zone, and after they had considered the possibility of interventions under the impression of rising oil prices and Europe-wide demonstrations of angry car owners, lorry drivers and carriers (*Der Standard*, 8–12 September 2000). The Austrian Minister of Finance was clearly in favour of ECB interventions to support the euro (*Der Standard*, 12 September 2000). Furthermore, it looked as if the ECB wanted to influence public opinion in Denmark shortly before the referendum on the euro (*Wirtschaftsblatt*, 29 September 2000).

Ernest Gnan and Aurel Schubert, two high-ranking staff members of the Austrian Central Bank, came to different conclusions in their evaluation of the first two years of the Euro-system.[25] In their opinion, the pragmatic two-pillar strategy worked well and took into account the uncertainties of the new monetary policy regime. The ECB did not, as expected by critics, react mechanistically to fluctuations of monetary supply. At the beginning the multitude of potentially important indicators in the two pillars led to uncertainties about monetary policy. Nevertheless, the decisions of the ECB were largely anticipated by the markets, which contradict the critique that the Euro-system acted opaquely and unpredictably (Gnan/Schubert, 2000, 596–7). Another interpretation of the same data is that the ECB did not lead the financial markets but rather followed them (Zotter, 2000, 37).

Another issue was the effect of rising interest rates on economic growth. Opinions were divided on this point. Representatives of official institutions tended to assure markets that economic growth would not be endangered, whereas many commentators warned of negative effects for the country's

[23] See also 'Finanznachrichten' July 2000: A comment to the interest rate decision of 3 Feb 2000 includes the same arguments: unclear strategy of the ECB, supposed exchange rate orientation, not exactly defined indicators in the second pillar.

[24] The same arguments are expressed in a commentary to the interest rate increase on 5 Oct 2000, in: 'Format', 41/2000, 85.

[25] The article reflects the personal views of the authors and is not necessarily identical with the views of the Austrian Central Bank.

economic development. After each monetary policy decision, the ECB council and its members, including the governor of the Austrian Central Bank, Klaus Liebscher, promised that it would not endanger the strong economic growth in the Euro-zone. Many observers were of a different opinion (see for example 'Wirtschaftsblatt', 17 March 2000). They argued that by following its arbitrary reference values, the ECB was slowing economic growth with higher interest rates to compensate for the inflationary pressure caused by rising oil prices ('Wirtschaftsblatt', 27 October 2000). One day before the 27 April interest rate decision, Erhard Fürst, chief economist of the Association of Austrian Industrialists (Industriellenvereinigung), appealed to the ECB not to increase interest rates. He argued that the ECB should observe the core inflation rate, which did not indicate any sign of economic overheating (*Der Standard*, 27 April 2000).

1.3.2 The weakness of the euro or the strength of the dollar

The development of the exchange rate kept alive an intensive discussion about its reasons. This faded as soon as the euro recovered at the end of the year. The whole debate showed that economic theory does not offer any convincing and broadly accepted explanation for exchange rate developments. The following is a summary of the most frequently used, and the most interesting, arguments.

The 'official' explanation for the decline of the euro offered by the ECB and its council members included the following arguments: the exchange rate development does 'not appear to be appropriate when looking at fundamentals'. The depreciation of the euro is not in line with the strong economic fundamentals of the Euro-area and also not in line with international balance of payment positions (*Duisenberg*, 12 September 2000, 6). Furthermore, the more important internal value of the currency is satisfactory. Duisenberg and Liebscher also repeatedly reminded governments and other organisations of the latter's responsibility to achieve sustained and non-inflationary growth in the Euro-area. Among other things, they demanded reforms of the tax and social security systems, and reforms of labour and product market regulations. However, they did not use the argument of over-regulation in the Euro-area to explain the depreciation of the euro.

An analysis by the Raiffeisen Zentralbank, one of the biggest banks in Austria, also mentioned the growth differential as an important reason for the exchange rate development, and added the argument of insufficient structural reforms in Europe (*Der Standard*, 4 May 2000). An economist of the Institute for Advanced Studies expressed the same opinion: the economic growth differential cannot be removed by monetary policy measures but only with structural reforms (*Der Standard*, 26 April 2000).

One important line of argument can be summarised under the heading:

'psychological explanations'. The psychological element consists of the irrational belief of many people (obviously including many journalists) that a strong euro is important and good for Europe, and that the external value of the currency is an important indicator of the stability of the currency. Populists, such as Haider, could exploit these irrational elements by arguing that the depreciation showed that the euro is not a stable currency and that it is therefore a failure[26] ('Format' September 2000). Economists tried in vain to explain that currency fluctuations are perfectly normal, that the internal value of the currency is the decisive indicator of a stable currency (especially in the Euro-zone with its relatively small amount of external trade), and that a lower euro stimulates exports (Schulmeister, 2000a). Some economists suggested avoidance of the term 'euro weakness' in favour of talk of a strong dollar (*Der Standard*, 21 April 2000). One commentator put it in the following way: 'The weakness of the euro consists of the anxious comparisons with the dollar' ('Finanznachrichten' September 2000)

It was sometimes argued that the difference between the Federal Reserve and the ECB, and perhaps even more importantly, the difference between their presidents Alan Greenspan and Wim Duisenberg, adds to the weakness of the euro. The ECB is still a very young institution and has yet to gain the trust of the markets. This is a long-term process and it is made more difficult by the ECB's current behaviour which is, as already mentioned, perceived by many observers to be inconsistent (*Die Press*', 3 May 2000). One commentator put it in the following words: 'the financial markets allow a high Greenspan-bonus on the one hand and ask for an additional ECB risk charge' (*Wirtschaftsblatt*, 27 October 2000).

Political arguments to explain the weakness of the euro were also important. In an article at the end of May, Dietmar Schweisgut[27] argued that purely economic explanations are not sufficient. In his view, the weakness of the euro is mainly an expression of the absence of a political identity for the Euro-zone. The main argument is that the representatives of the Euro-zone Member States do not show any willingness to complement the reality of the single currency with an efficient institutional framework in terms of economic policy co-ordination and external projection of the euro. The Euro-group, acting in a legal grey area, is not able to fulfil these functions and is barely visible to an external observer. In international organisations such as the IMF or the G7, Germany, France, and Italy in fact represent the Euro-zone. The result is that the Euro-zone does not have any identity. All these reasons contribute to the weakness of the euro (Schweisgut, 2000). The governor of the Austrian Central Bank,

[26] The Minister of Finance, Karl Heinz Grasser, contradicted his party leader and declared that the euro had great internal stability, *Der Standard*, 29 Feb 2000).

[27] Schweisgut is a former department head in the ministry of finance and is now Austria's ambassador in Japan.

Klaus Liebscher, seemed to argue in this direction when he stated at the end of the year that the growth differential between Europe and the US is only part of the explanation for the euro's weakness. He claimed that the main problem was that the economic policy co-ordination would be perceived as insufficient (*Der Standard*, 5 December 2000). In Summer, Liebscher explained that the long-lasting decision-making processes in the EU (for example, in difficult matters such as tax co-ordination or harmonisation) could damage the image of the EU. The markets, in turn, could react to this political weakness with a weaker assessment of the euro (*Trend*, 7 August 2000, 190).[28]

An article by two experts of the Austrian Central Bank added to interesting considerations. The financial markets see the enlargement process as a potential problem for the future policy of stability, and the financial markets in Europe are not as liquid and homogeneous as the US markets (Gnan/Schubert, 2000, 599).

Another interesting explanation for the weak euro turned up in April, after the leader of the Freedom Party, Jörg Haider, had suggested that Austria could leave the EU if the sanctions were not lifted. According to the newspaper *Der Standard*, this statement—combined with the political uncertainty in Italy after the resignation of Prime Minister D'Alema—further weakened the euro. The newspaper quoted a London-based exchange strategist and maintained that Haider's statements would be taken seriously by international financial analysts (*Der Standard*, 21 April 2000).

1.3.3 Reactions to the referendum in Denmark

Most of the Austrian reactions to the referendum on the introduction of the euro in Denmark on 28 September 2000 referred to the sanctions against Austria. Haider said that the result of the referendum demonstrated the people's profound distrust of the Brussels-based technocrats, and reflected the euro's weakness. Peter Westenthaler, the leader of the parliamentary group of the Freedom Party, called the referendum a 'wonderful signal'. It did not only show opposition to the euro but also to the EU central bureaucracy. Contrary to his party colleagues, Karl Heinz Grasser, the Minister of Finance, characterised the Danish decision as very unfortunate: it expresses the apprehension of the people of a small country about their vote in the European Union, which could have been influenced by the sanctions against Austria. However, the Minister continued, the vote was highly irrational because the Danish currency remains pegged to the euro. Therefore Denmark does not have any room for manoeuvre in

[28] Political arguments for the weakness of the euro can also be found in several issues of 'Finanznachrichten' (issues 20, 37, 38/2000).

monetary matters and cannot exert any influence in the Euro-group and the ECB. Chancellor Wolfgang Schüssel assumed that the Danish people feared losing their identity and sovereignty. The Minister for Foreign Affairs, Benita Ferrero-Waldner, regretted a political setback for Europe. She was convinced that the sanctions against Austria had played a role in the decision of the Danish people (*Der Standard*, 30 September/1 October 2000).

1.4 Institutional and procedural matters

1.4.1 Introduction

As already mentioned in the introduction—apart from the decline of the euro—EMU matters have not been topics of public debate in the year 2000. It is therefore impossible to report on many of the points raised by the questionnaire. Most institutions did not publish any significant opinion concerning euro-related topics. Generally speaking, one can assume that the positions of the public institutions and organisations have not changed in the last year. The most likely exceptions to this rule—the government and the Freedom Party—are examined closely.

1.4.2 The government

The general elections held on 3 October 1999 led to a complex political situation.[29] After four months of difficult negotiations, the new government coalition (comprising the People's Party and the Freedom Party) was sworn in on 4 February 2000 by Federal President Thomas Klestil. The Freedom Party's participation in the new government triggered worldwide criticism, because the FPÖ (and especially its leader, Jörg Haider) were perceived to be far right, populist and xenophobic. On 31 January 2000, the Portuguese Prime Minister, Antonio Guterres, issued a statement on behalf of the 14 other EU Member States, saying that they would suspend all bilateral contacts with the Austrian government, if it included the Freedom Party. These measures were implemented after the ÖVP and the FPÖ agreed to form a coalition government.

On the initiative of the Austrian Federal President, the leaders of the two coalition parties, Wolfgang Schüssel (ÖVP) and Jörg Haider (FPÖ), signed a declaration before the new government was sworn in. This declaration was intended to reassure the EU Member States, and other concerned countries, of Austria's continued commitment to common European values and principles such as the rights and freedoms enshrined in the European Convention on Human Rights and the principles laid

[29] For more details see the Austrian report 1999.

down in Article 6 of the European Union Treaty. It also contained a commitment to Austria's membership in the European Union and the monetary union:

The Federal Government is committed to the European peace project. Co-operation between the coalition parties is based on a commitment to Austria's membership in the European Union.

The Federal Government desires to strengthen Austria's position as a performance and competition oriented economic location. That is the basis for securing existing employment, creating new jobs and ensuring prosperity in our country. Austria's accession to the European Union and an assured participation in the European Monetary Union were and remain important preconditions for the future of the economy and employment in Austria.[30]

In its working programme, the government coalition refers to EMU with the following paragraph:

One decisive precondition for the development of the European integration process in the 21st century is the success of a consolidated Economic and Monetary Union and a stable euro, the strength of which is founded on close co-ordination of the macro-economic policies of the EU Member States. The Federal Government regards its efforts to obtain more budget discipline, which is in any case inevitable for national economic reasons, as a contribution to the success of the Economic and Monetary Union, to EU employment policy and to the global position of the euro (Österreichische Bundesregierung, 2000, 7).

The responsibility for the internal co-ordination and the external representation of EU-policy now lies in the hands of the People's Party.[31] The Minister of Finance, Karl-Heinz Grasser, belongs to the Freedom Party. However, the department responsible for information concerning the common European currency was moved from the Ministry of Finance to the Federal Chancellery.

The first priority of the new government was to agree on a federal budget for the year 2000, and to present the updated stability programme for the period 2000–3 to the Commission and the Council.[32] The projected overall public deficit for the year 2000 had been set at 1.7 per cent of GDP by the stability programme 1999–2002. To this figure, the federal government deficit should contribute –2.2 per cent, the 'Länder' and local authorities should provide a surplus of 0.5 per cent of GDP. The starting point for the new government was difficult for several reasons: the

[30] Excerpts from the 'Declaration: Responsibility for Austria—A Future in the Heart of Europe', signed by Wolfgang Schüssel and Jörg Haider on 3 Feb 2000, in the presence of Federal President Thomas Klestil.

[31] The former coalition had a co-responsibility in EU-matters of the Federal Chancellery (SPÖ) and the Ministry for Foreign Affairs (ÖVP).

[32] According to the Stability and Growth Pact, the updated stability programmes have to be presented at the end of each year. Due to the lack of a new government and of a budget for the year 2000, Austria got the permission to submit her stability programme later.

previous government had implemented tax reform and increased family allowances taking effect in the year 2000. This endangered the projected public deficit. These measures were estimated to burden government finances in 2000 by some 0.9 per cent of GDP (Europäische Kommission, 1999, 24). The Commission warned that the public deficit would widen to 2.6 per cent of GDP in 2000 without 'additional significant savings (or revenues)'. The Commission concluded that 'in the absence of additional means the deficit in 2000 would be clearly above the objective set in the stability programme of a deficit of 1.7 per cent of GDP' (Europäische Kommission, 1999, 24). This outlook put Austria a full percentage point behind the next worst country, France. In political terms, the situation was especially difficult for the Freedom Party, which had promised costly measures in the election campaign, such as a flat-tax and the 'children-cheque'[33] (Freiheitliche Partei Österreichs, 1999, 20 and 31).[34]

The budget for the year 2000 was presented to parliament on 21 March 2000 by the Minister of Finance and adopted by parliament on 18 May 2000. It was designed to use many one-off measures (such as the increase of indirect taxes and public charges) to reach the goal set by the stability programme. The budget was heavily criticised for lacking sustained measures and structural reforms and for being insufficiently ambitious.

It was very interesting to observe how the national and international criticism of the budgetary measures, and the updated stability programme (presented on 28 March 2000), finally led to the definition of new deficit goals. The government and stability programmes both planned to achieve a balanced budget in the long term. The projected public deficit for the years 2001, 2002 and 2003 should be 1.5 per cent, 1.4 per cent, and 1.3 per cent respectively. This consolidation course was criticised on several occasions by the governor of the Austrian Central Bank, Klaus Liebscher. In his speech at the general meeting of the Austrian Central Bank on 18 May, Liebscher said the efforts of the government to reduce the deficit and public debt were not ambitious enough and, in effect, not in conformity with the Stability and Growth Pact which demands deficits 'close to balance or in surplus'. Liebscher pleaded for primarily expenditure-based and structural reform measures, especially concerning the social system, the health system, public administration as well as deregulation, privatisation and more flexibility of the labour markets (Liebscher, 2000b).

In their April economic outlook for the years 2000 and 2001, the two

[33] Every mother should get 5.700 schillings per month for a child under the age of 7 years. For each additional child under the age of 7 she should get 2.850 schillings per month (FPÖ—Der Haider-Prinzhorn Plan (Manifesto for the general elections), Vienna, 1999, 32.)

[34] In the government programme the Freedom Party had already made significant concessions (no flat tax, 'children cheque' only for two years—with a possible third year if parental leave is split between the parents—and a postponement until 2002).

most important Austrian economic research institutes[35] expressed serious doubts about the sufficiency of the planned government measures to meet even the modest goals set out in the stability programme. They concluded that additional consolidation efforts would be necessary. In its spring economic forecast, the European Commission stated that, due to one-off measures, increased revenues and an economic growth dividend, the deficit for the year 2000 should be in accordance with the objective of the stability programme. However, for 2001 the Commission predicted a deficit of 2 per cent of GDP 'unless compensated by additional significant savings (or revenues)' (Europäische Kommission, 2000a, 39). The Commission also criticised the Austrian stability programme as being insufficiently ambitious (*Der Standard*, 27 April 2000). On 8 May 2000, the Ecofin Council examined the updated Austrian stability programme for the period 2000–3. In its opinion, the Council regretted that in the 1998–1999 period, the above-trend growth was not used to further reduce the deficit and the public debt. On the contrary, the debt ratio had increased in 1999. The Council further regretted that 'the goal of attaining the 60 per cent of GDP reference value for the gross consolidated debt has been postponed by three years to 2005'. The Council noted that 'the updated stability programme is not fully in line with the requirements of the Stability and Growth Pact as it does not give a large enough safety margin to prevent the deficit from breaching the 3 per cent of GDP reference value in the event of a cyclical downturn'. Therefore, the Council asked for a more ambitious consolidation of government finances and urged the government to reduce the deficit targets in the next programme update. It also 'invited' the Austrian government to aim to attain the 60 per cent of GDP reference value by 2002. To achieve that goal, the one-off measures of the budget 2000 would have to be replaced by permanent measures and expenditure savings (Ecofin Council, 2000). In reaction to this opinion of the Council, Austria's Minister of Finance, Karl-Heinz Grasser, announced that the consolidation efforts would be intensified, that structural reforms would replace one-off measures and that a public deficit of 1.3 per cent of GDP should be achieved by 2002 (instead of 2003 as predicted in the stability programme). Similar criticism came form the OECD (*Der Standard*, 31 May 2000) and the IMF (*Der Standard*, 25 May 2000; Österreichische Nationalbank-Pressedienst, 2000).

At the end of May, the Ministry of Finance unofficially talked about its intention of reducing the public deficit to 0.9 per cent by 2002 and 0.4 per cent by 2003 (*Der Standard*, 25 May 2000). After the meeting of the Eurogroup and the Ecofin Council on 5 June 2000, the Minister of Finance announced a deficit goal of between 0 and 0.5 per cent for the year 2003. The Ministers of Finance had decided to take advantage of better-than-expected

[35] The Institute for Advanced Studies and the Austrian Institute of Economic Research.

economic growth and to advance the consolidation targets. At the beginning of July the government started to talk about balancing the budget by 2002, and on 11 July the government officially decided to strive to achieve that goal. The government announced a 'reform dialogue' to start three days later which should include all stakeholders; in a first step, it defined the balanced budget by 2002 as the common goal. The Social Democratic Party and the Green Party did not participate, but they accepted bilateral talks with the Minister of Finance a few days later. The draft budget for the years 2001 and 2002 was presented on 1 September 2000 and triggered controversial discussions. The main points of criticism:

- The budgetary measures are primarily concentrated on the revenue-side (about two-thirds according to the estimate of the European Commission; see Europäische Kommission, 2000b, 37), which increases the already high government revenue/GDP ratio to about 47 per cent in 2001 (*Der Standard*, 30 November 2000).
- The introduction of university fees, which until recently had been explicitly ruled out by the responsible minister and the Chancellor.
- The social incompatibility of the measures.
- The adherence of the government to expensive measures agreed in the government programme (which is based on much higher deficit projections), notably significant reductions of non-wage labour costs and the increase of child allowances.

The budget for 2001 was adopted by parliament on 6 December 2000 with the votes of the government coalition parties.

On 19 December 2000, the government published the updated stability programme for the years 2000–4. This is based on the new strategic goal of a balanced budget by the year 2002.

1.4.3 Freedom Party (FPÖ)

The Freedom Party had always been the party most critical of the euro. In 1997 it had organised a popular initiative in favour of the schilling, arguing for a postponement of the third stage of EMU (see *Eurospectator* 1999). However, on entering the government the Freedom Party committed itself to EMU and the need to reduce the federal deficit.

In practice, the Freedom Party applied a double strategy. Members of the government adhere to the positions put down in the government programme and the government declaration. But the former party leader (until the end of April 2000) and governor of Carinthia, Jörg Haider—who still is by far the most influential member of the Freedom Party—continues to argue against the euro. This ambiguity was best expressed when, at the end of February, Haider said the euro is a failure ('Mißgeburt'; an ill-conceived child). He pointed out that it had been promised that the euro would be as strong as the schilling and as stable as the German mark. Referring to the external value of the euro against the dollar, Haider said that this was obviously untrue. The public had therefore been lied to. However, the Minister of Finance, Karl-Heinz Grasser, shortly afterwards praised the euro as 'wanted child', and stressed the internal stability of the new currency (*Der Standard*, 29 February 2000; *Format* September 2000).

1.4.4 The Austrian parliament

According to Article 32.5 of the Austrian Central Bank Act, the governor and the vice-governor of the Central Bank have to report to the finance committee of the Austrian parliament about monetary policy measures at least twice a year. In the year 2000, these reports took place on 12 January and on 29 June. The sessions of the committee are not public. Therefore, only short summaries of the reports of the governor and the vice-governor are available (Österreichisches Parlament, 2000). In their reports, the governor and the vice-governor of the Austrian Central Bank seemed to closely follow the published statements of the ECB, and largely coincided with the reports given by Duisenberg to the Economic and Finance Committee of the European Parliament. The heads of the Central Bank explained that the several ECB interest rate increases were made in order to address upside risks to the price stability in the Euro-area, and that both pillars of the monetary policy strategy had indicated upward pressure. Both times, Governor Liebscher used the opportunity to stress that monetary policy alone cannot provide for a prolonged period of non-inflationary growth. Efforts and reforms in many policy areas (such as labour markets or product markets) would be necessary to achieve that goal. In January, the governor called for more efforts to reduce the public deficit. In June, he welcomed the more ambitious goals of the government and again stressed the importance of sound public finances. The governor also referred to the development of the exchange rate and explained the depreciation of the euro against the dollar, mainly with reference to the stronger US economic growth. He stressed that the ECB did not have an exchange rate goal, but that the exchange rate is one of several indicators of the second pillar of the monetary policy strategy.

1.5 Trends towards spillover

1.5.1 Co-ordination of macroeconomic policy

The need for the better co-ordination or harmonisation of policies such as employment and social policy or economic and fiscal policy, is mainly argued in two ways.

The first line of argument says that there is a need for better co-ordination and harmonisation of policies at the EU-level to complement the single currency. The starting point was the legal provisions found in the EC Treaty and in the Stability and Growth Pact. A variety of co-ordination procedures in many policy areas have developed on this basis. Although these procedures are not legally binding, their elements (such as reports, benchmarks and peer reviews) in fact reduce the national room for manoeuvre. In addition, the EU discussion defines the Maastricht criteria with increasing details, and moves from the 'deficit criteria' in the direction of the quality and sustainability of public finances.

The second line of arguments appears at the level of the nation states. It is argued that, in connection with the single currency, the common market intensifies economic competition and also the competition among the Member States. The quality of a location depends on many different factors, such as tax and social systems, regulations of labour, capital, services and goods markets, infrastructure, efficiency of public administration,[36] education and training, adaptability and flexibility.[37] This argument works in two directions: it demands national deregulation, and it requires European co-operation and regulations to avoid unfair competition and distortions of the common market.

The current government supports both lines of argument, at least in principle. On the occasion of the European Council in Lisbon in March 2000, the Minister of Finance, Karl Heinz Grasser, characterised it as very reasonable that the EU develops to an economic, financial and social model (*Der Standard*, 24 March 2000).

A working group organised by the Ministry of Finance—comprising of representatives from other ministries, the social partners, the Austrian Central Bank, regional and local authorities and economists—discussed the possible need to adapt Austrian economic policy to the new framework of monetary union. Several working papers dealing with this question are published on the homepage of the Ministry of Finance (see for example Part, 2000). The areas of fiscal policy, wage and price policies, structural policy and capital markets are discussed. The main argument seems to be that the new framework makes it even more important to carry out reforms in order to maintain Austria's competitive position. Since this discussion takes place at the level of experts, political arguments or alternatives (such as the need or intention to decide some matters at the European level) are not discussed.

[36] See for example, 'Finanznachrichten', Mar 2000: The consequences of monetary union on the public sector are underestimated and not sufficiently discussed. Good governance is an essential factor for the quality of a location.

[37] See, eg, Liebscher (2000a) and Beirat für Wirtschafts- und Sozialfragen (1998), 99–101.

1.5.2 Tax harmonisation

Austria always argued for the need to establish minimum European levels of certain direct taxes, such as corporate taxes and taxes on capital to avoid a competitive race towards lower taxes (See *Eurospectator* 1999). During the Portuguese presidency in the first half of the year 2000, the discussion about the taxation of capital gains in the EU shifted from direct taxation (opposed by the UK) to the exchange of information among the Member States about the identity and the capital gains of nationals from other EU countries. Austria (and Luxembourg) opposed this compromise because of its traditional banking secrecy. Banking secrecy is constitutionally protected in Austria. After Luxembourg accepted the compromise, Austria at first threatened to uphold its veto at the European Council in Feira, but it finally gave in. Commentators suggested that Austria's tactics had to be interpreted in the context of the sanctions, and that the threat of a veto was a gesture directed at the Austrian public.

1.5.3 Social policy

Austria argues that:

> a general shift of social policy to the decision-making institutions of the European Union does not make sense. Neither would such a shift be possible in many areas, because of different traditions in national social security systems and the rather different levels of development of Member States (Beirat für Wirtschafts- und Sozialfragen, 1998, 104).

However, it is acknowledged that economic and political integration necessitates a closer co-ordination of social policies. Austria therefore supported the EU level developments in the year 2000, most notably the initiation of the 'Lisbon-process', and the 'social policy agenda' supported by the European Council in Nice. Public debate at the national level scarcely took notice of these developments. In the framework of public deficit reduction, the national debate was dominated by the new term 'social accuracy of aim'. This is supposed to mean that only those in need should receive social transfers, or that well-off people should receive fewer benefits from public transfers.

1.5.4 External projection of the euro

The lack of a political identity within the Euro-zone, and the lack of a coherent external representation, were described in Chapter 1.3.2 as reasons for the depreciation of the euro. According to many experts (including the governor of the Austrian Central Bank), it will be necessary to develop an efficient institutional framework. This is required, not only for internal co-ordination, but also for external representation.[38] However, this will be a long-term project that depends on the political will of the Euro-zone Member States' governments to give up some of their sovereignty, and to join forces.

2. Legal framework
Herta Baumann**

2.1 Changes in the legal framework

2.1.1 Introduction

The main part of the legal amendments necessary to introduce the single currency was adopted before 2000. In addition to the adjustment of laws and regulations that contain schilling amounts or schilling references, new substantive changes were made concerning the dual display of prices, the conversion and exchange of bank notes and coins, and the conversion of the capital of a co-operative society into euro. In the field of public finance, it was necessary to amend the system set up to co-ordinate the budgetary and financial activities of the territorial authorities.

2.1.2 Dual display of prices

In order to ensure legal certainty in connection with the changeover to the euro, and to avoid unjustified price increases on the occasion of the changeover, the 'Euro-Währungsangabengesetz'[39] was adopted. This law basically regulates the dual display of prices for the period from 1 October 2001 to 28 February 2002 and its period, however may be prolonged by the Federal Government. Specifically, the 'Euro-Währungsangabengesetz' specifies that all businesses that are obliged to display monetary amounts to consumers must display such amounts in both currency units. The law also affects business activities carried out by the territorial authorities of the State if such authorities act in their capacity as private business enterprises. Furthermore, the law provides special rules in order to ensure a cost-effective implementation of the law. Therefore, small businesses, petrol stations, bookstores and taxi-drivers can also comply with the obligation by displaying price lists or conversion tables. The local administration authorities are responsible for supervising compliance with the dual display of currencies and for executing administrative penal procedures. A euro price commission will be established as an advisory body to the

[38] See Ch 1.3.2.

** Scientific Consultant at the OIIP (Austrian Institute for International Affairs), Operngasse 209B, A-1040, Wien.

[39] BGBl I No 110/1999.

Federal Minister of Economics and Labour. This commission will have the particular task of receiving and dealing with complaints, and it will provide information about the legal provisions.

2.1.3 Conversion and exchange of bank notes and coins

The Euro-area Finance Ministers have agreed that the period of dual circulation of notes and coins should not last for more than two months. In Austria, the 'Eurogesetz'[40] provides that the period for dual circulation of notes and coins will be two months. During these months it will still be possible to use the schilling in cash payments. The schilling loses its legal tender status after 28 February 2002. In order to make sure that there will be sufficient circulation of notes and coins from the beginning of 2002, euro bank notes and coins will be frontloaded to commercial banks, the business sector, and the public sector from 1 September 2001. Moreover, euro coins will be issued to consumers in the form of 'starter kits', which can be acquired at commercial banks and post offices from 15 December 2001. Consumers should have the chance to familiarise themselves with the new coins some days before the euro notes and coins are introduced. However usage of the frontloaded euro bank notes and coins in cash payments will not permitted before January 2002.

The 'Euro-Währungsangabengesetz' regulates costs of cash exchange during the dual circulation phase for notes and coins. Under this law, banks are not allowed to charge for exchanging schilling for euro up to a maximum amount of 50,000 schillings (the 'average household' amount). After 28 February 2002, commercial banks are free to decide on the conditions under which they will exchange notes and coins. In any case, the Austrian National Bank and its branches in the provinces will continue to exchange euro for schilling free of charge after 28 February 2002. There is no time limit for this exchange option. Until 31 March 2002 it will also be possible to exchange, free of charge, old currencies of the Euro-area up to an equivalent amount of 3,000 euro per person per day at the Austrian National Bank and its branches.

2.1.4 Company law

With the '1. Euro-Justiz-Begleitgesetz', the foundation was laid to establish new joint stock companies in euro and to convert the joint capital of an existing company into euro (see *Eurospectator* 1999). With the adoption of the 'Euro-Genossenschaftsbegleitgesetz',[41] the same rules are now applicable to co-operative societies.

[40] BGBl I No 72/2000. [41] BGBl I No 136/2000.

2.2 The Austrian stability pact

With the adoption of the Austrian Stability Pact and the Consultation-Mechanism, a new framework was established to co-ordinate the budgetary and financial activities of the territorial authorities in order to fulfil the budget criteria of the European Stability and Growth Pact. The Austrian Stability programme for the period 1998 to 2002 stated that the budgetary policy target 'is a public budget deficit of 1.5 per cent of GDP by 2002'. The Austrian Stability Pact provides rules and procedures to fulfil this obligation (see *Eurospectator* 1999). In mid-2000 the new government set the new goal of achieving a balanced budget by 2002. The updated stability programme, published in December, states: 'By 2002 Austria will reduce the public deficit to 0 per cent of gross domestic product (GDP), with the Federal Government deficit coming down to 0.75 per cent of GDP.' This means that the budgets of the provinces and local authorities will have to contribute a budget surplus of 0.75 per cent of GDP. The federal government needed the full co-operation of the provinces and local authorities to reach this target. Therefore the provinces and the local authorities had a strong position in the financial burden-sharing negotiations, which took place during the year 2000.[42] On 16 October, the federal government, the provinces and the local authorities adopted the financial burden-sharing arrangements ('Finanzausgleich') up to 2004, and agreed on the joint achievement of the deficit target of 0 per cent of GDP in 2002. The provinces undertake to contribute an average budget surplus of not less than 0.75 per cent of GDP. This task should be reached as a result of structural reforms, including savings in the staff expenditure on provincial teachers. The current system of housing assistance will be reformed and a standing working party will be set up to examine structural changes in the health system. The local authorities undertake to achieve a balanced budget. The agreements amending the Austrian stability pact are binding, and a penalty system will be set up as a safeguard. In exchange for their concessions, the provinces and local authorities achieved a large part of the tax revenue transfers they demanded.

2.3 Experiences with the consultation mechanism

As far as it can be seen, the consultation mechanism is strengthening the position of the provinces and the local authorities.

[42] The Provinces and the local authorities receive a share of the federal income taxes. The 'Finanzausgleich', a financial burden sharing arrangement, governs the division of financial recourses and stipulates the precise figures of the transferred revenues for a period of three or four years. The new financial burden sharing agreement is applicable from 2001 to 2004.

A true partnership begins to develop between the local authorities, the Länder and the federal government. The partners cannot block new legislation but can require that the necessary financing be made available for its application. The costs of introducing new laws must thus be evaluated before new legislation passes Parliament. The true importance of the 'Consultation Mechanism' is not the question of receiving additional financial resources, but of clarifying the costs entailed by new legislation and of opening negotiation and discussion procedures to avoid the introduction of costly and useless provisions.[43]

Before the introduction of the consultation mechanism, the provinces and local authorities were involved in the normal consultation process during the introductory stage of draft laws. In this process, up to one hundred institutions were invited to give an opinion on draft laws. Thus the opinions of the provinces and local authorities formerly occurred at the same level as those of many other participants in the consultation procedure. The consultation mechanism gives the provinces and local authorities a new instrument with which to participate in the drafting process of federal laws. Although the consultation mechanism is also applicable in the case of new legislation by the provinces, the experience shows that the mechanism is used mainly by the provinces and local authorities 'against' federal legislation (see Bußjäger, 2000, 600 et seq). So far, there have been several negotiations in the Consultation Committee, although the committee has not had to decide on the covering of costs, and the Constitutional Court has not had to settle a dispute arising out of the agreement. The constant 'threat' of starting the consultation mechanism, and the danger of a disagreement on the covering of the financial costs of a draft law, has prevented the territorial authorities with legislative power from submitting potentially costly bills to the other territorial authorities, and has helped them to draw up texts that were better adapted and acceptable. The whole Mechanism, with its mandatory provisions to clarify the costs entailed by new legislation, compels the federal government and the government of the provinces to evaluate the costs of new legislation, and this is an important step to an economic use of the financial resources (see Bußjäger, 2000, 600 et seq).

2.4 National law from the EC perspective

During the year 2000, only few new laws and amendments concerning the introduction of the single currency were adopted. As already mentioned, the main part of the necessary legislation was implemented before 2000. As stated in the 1999 *Eurospectator* Report, from the EU-Perspective 'legislation in Austria is compatible with the requirements of the Treaty and the ESCB-ECB Statute.' There is no suggestion that the legislation introduced during 2000 had not fulfilled the Community law requirements.

[43] See: <http://www.staedtebund.at>.

2.5 The application of the law

In general, the legislation concerning the introduction of the euro has not led to an increase in court proceedings.[44] Only a few cases concerning the Euro-legislation were brought to court during the year 2000. The Ministry of Justice does not systematically observe the euro related proceedings, as it believes that this is not necessary. An expert of the Ministry of Justice stated that the new legislation is clear, comprehensive and leaves no room for uncertainties. Court proceedings concerning this new legislation are therefore unlikely. Since the principle of continuity of contracts in case of an alteration of the legal tender is settled national case law, no court proceedings concerned this principle (see *Eurospectator* 1999). The only area in which proceedings had been brought was in the area of company law. Some proceedings had already been pending in this realm, and some Supreme Court decisions have been published. The main problem concerns the conversion of a company's capital from schilling to euro. Because of the unavoidable rounding differences, unintended changes in the shares and the voting rights are possible. Furthermore, since the conversion of the capital leads to 'unsightly' amounts,[45] the members of a company often decide to increase or reduce capital in order to gain a smooth amount. Although the solution of these problems is mainly a question of the drawing up of contracts, an increase in court proceedings in this realm is likely. This is particularly so after 1 January 2002, when entries in the company register are only possible after the conversion of the capital into euro.

Two Supreme Court decisions are worth mentioning in this regard. For the purpose of the easier changeover of the companies, the '1.Euro-Justiz-Begleitggesetz' contains provisions that simplify the decision-making process within the company. In general, an amendment of the statutes requires a majority of three-quarters of the votes in the general meeting. The new legislative amendments concerning the conversion of the capital require only a single majority of the votes. However, in case 6 Ob 240/99h, the Austrian Supreme Court decided that these provisions are not applicable for limited liability companies where there is a reduction in capital. A limited liability company had applied to the Registration Court for an entry in the company register. The general meeting had approved the conversion of the capital into euro and the smoothing of the amounts with a reduction in capital. The application was rejected by the Registration Court and this was upheld by the Supreme Court. The appli-

44 Interview with an expert of the Ministry of Justice.

45 Before the amendments due to the single currency, the minimum joint capital of a limited lability company in Austria had to be at 500,000 schillings and the minimum amount of a share had to be at 1,000 schilling. After the conversion these amounts will be at 36,336.42 euro and at 72.67 euro. The new minimum amounts were fixed at 35,000 euro and at 70 euro.

cant argued that the amendment was effected under the scheme provided by the '1. Euro-Justiz-Begleitgesetz'. However, the Supreme Court explained that, for the creditors' security, the company law provides for a special procedure in case of a reduction in capital. These provisions were not altered by the new legislation. Companies may therefore not rely upon the provisions that simplify the decision-making process, where the protection of the creditors is in danger. The conversion of the capital does not require a smoothing of the amounts; if the members of the company wish to smooth the amounts, they should observe the relevant provisions and procedures.

The second decision concerns the law of the land register. The relevant proceeding was brought to court, before the new euro-legislation had been enacted, but it shows how court decisions influenced that legislation. Under the 'Verordnung über wertbeständige Rechte' (Decree on fixed-value rights), a registration of a mortgage securing a debt payable in a foreign currency was not allowed. That provision states that mortgages may be created only in schilling or by reference to the price of fine gold. In 1997 an application was made to the Registration Court for a registration of a mortgage denominated in German mark. The Court refused the application. The applicants lodged an appeal on a point of law before the Austrian Supreme Court. In Case 5 Ob 87/99a the Austrian Supreme Court decided to stay proceedings and to refer to the European Court of Justice for a preliminary ruling. The Supreme Court asked if the Austrian legislation providing that a registration of a security right in respect of a foreign-currency debt is valid only where it is denominated in schilling constitutes a restriction of the free movement of capital and payments compatible with Article 56 of the EC Treaty. The European Court of Justice decided that those rules were not compatible with Article 56 EC. Even if the Decree on fixed-value rights was designed to ensure the foreseeability and transparency of the mortgage system, and therefore to enable lower-ranking creditors to establish the precise amount of prior-ranking debts, the cost of such effects is a lack of security for creditors, whose debts are denominated in foreign currencies.

In the legislative process for the introduction of the euro the law in question was repealed. Entries of mortgages in the land register are now allowed if denominated in a currency of a Member State of the European Economic Area. A new question arising out of the repeal of the Decree on fixed-value rights is the possibility to enter value-guarantee-clauses in the land register. The Austrian Supreme Court refused such an entry in case 5 Ob 256/99d, and it argued that the registration of such clauses places the principle of the clarity and transparency of the land register in danger. However, this is not generally recognised in the academic literature and the decision has been severely criticised. A change in the case law is likely.

2.6 Institutional aspects

Two aspects concerning the Austrian Central bank (Nationalbank) and its position within the ESCB were discussed during 2000.

2.6.1 The foreign reserve assets

The Austrian Central bank held a larger amount of foreign reserve assets than it needed to transfer to the ECB. Hence, an amount of approximately 121 bn schilling (8.79 bn euro) remains with the central bank (see Hauner 2000, 86). As the consolidation of the public budget and the way to a balanced public budget calls for a great effort, the federal government searched for new capital sources. It seemed to find them in the foreign reserve assets. However, the Austrian Central Bank had always stressed its independence, the prohibition under Article 101 EC on the financing of public authorities, and the required approval of the ECB for any decision about the remaining foreign reserve assets. The central bank stated that, in its view, the use of the foreign reserve assets for the consolidation of the budget is not appropriate. Furthermore, it asked for a suspension of the discussion until after the introduction of the bank notes and coins.[46]

2.6.2 Allocation of the monetary income

The allocation of the monetary income of the ECB was a second topic that was discussed during 2000. Since this allocation will take place not before 2002, the discussion is still in its preliminary stages. On the one hand, under Article 32 of the ESCB-ECB Statute, each national central bank transfers its monetary income 'derived from its assets held against notes in circulation and deposit liabilities to credit institutions'. On the other hand, the allocation of the monetary income to the central banks shall be in 'proportion to their paid up shares in the capital of the ECB'. Since the Austrian schilling is a popular currency (especially in the Eastern European countries), the amount of notes in circulation is higher than the amount of the share in the subscribed capital. Therefore, the Austrian National Bank's share in the monetary income that must be transferred to the ECB will be higher than the share it will receive from the ECB. The difference could amount to approximately 100 million schilling (7.27 million euro) (*Wirtschaftsblatt*, 30 November 2000). The Austrian Central Bank stated that it is aware of this problem, but it predicts a much smaller deficit of 35 million schillings (2.54 million euro). Furthermore, the Austrian Central Bank negotiates a new allocation key, since under Article 32.2 of the

46 Österreichische Nationalbank, Pressedienst, 6 Feb 2001, see: <http://www.oenb.at/presse_p.htm>.

ESCB-ECB Statute, the Governing Council may find an alternative method to measure the monetary income 'for a period of not more than five years'. Moreover, the Austrian Central Bank stated that this period should be extended to ten years by the Council applying Article 42 of the ESCB–ECB Statute.

Bibliography

Ahtisaari, Martti; Frowein, Jochen; Oreja, Marcelino (2000), *Report*, Paris.

Beirat für Wirtschafts- und Sozialfragen (1998), *Wirtschaftspolitische Handlungsspielräume*, Wien.

Bundesministerium für Finanzen (2000a), *Österreichisches Stabilitätsprogramm, 2000–2003*, Wien.

—— (2000b), *Österreichisches Stabilitätsprogramm, 2000–2004*, Wien.

Bußjäger, Peter (2000), 'Rechtsfragen zum Konsultationsmechanismus', in *Österreichische Juristen-Zeitung*, 2000, p. 581.

Duisenberg, Willem F (2000), *Introductory statements at the hearing before the Committee on Economic and Monetary Affairs of the European Parliament*, Brussels.

Ecofin (1999), *Stability Programme of Austria (1998–2002)—Opinion of the Council*, Brussels.

—— (2000), *Updating the Stability Programme of Austria (2000–2003)*—Opinion of the Council, Brussels.

Eurobarometer 52 (2000), Brussels.

—— 53 (2000), Brussels.

Europäische Kommission (1999), *Europäische Wirtschaft—Herbstprognose für 1999–2001*, Brüssel.

—— (2000a), *Europäische Wirtschaft—Frühjahrsprognose für 2000–2001*, Brüssel.

—— (2000b), *Europäische Wirtschaft—Herbstprognose für 2000–2002*, Brüssel.

Federal Ministry of Finance (2000), *Changeover to the euro in the Public Sector*, Vienna.

Freiheitliche Partei Österreichs (1999), *Der Haider-Prinzhorn Plan*, Wien.

Gnan, Ernest; Schubert, Aurel (2000), 'Zwei Jahre Europäische Zentralbank—Bisherige Erfahrungen mit der Europäischen Wirtschafts- und Währungsunion', in *Österreichisches Bankarchiv* 7/2000, 591–604.

Hauner, David (2000), 'Die Fremdwährungsreserven der OeNB—Wie groß ist der Spielraum?', in *Zeitschrift für Wirtschaft und Gesellschaft*, 2000, 81.

Lachs, Thomas (2000), 'Ein schwacher Euro?', in *Arbeit & Wirtschaft*, 12/2000, 28–31.

Liebscher, Klaus (2000), *Die Rolle der nationalen Zentralbanken in der WWU (Rede am 23.11.2000 im Forschungsinstitut für Europafragen an der Wirtschaftsuniversität Wien)*, Wien.

—— (2000), *The euro and the Austrian Viewpoint—Perspectives for Central and Eastern Europe. (Rede am 30.11.2000 in Antwerpen vor dem Belgian Financial Forum)*, Wien.

—— (2000), 'Vom Schilling zum Euro', in *Österreichisches Bankenarchiv* 2000, 3.

—— (2000a), *Der Euro—Eine Herausforderung für den Wirtschaftsstandort Österreich (Rede vor dem Burgenländischen Wirtschaftsbund und Management Club Burgenland)*, Bad Tatzmannsdorf.

—— (2000b), *Rede des Gouverneurs bei der Generalversammlung der ONB am 18.5.2000*, Wien.

Mader, Peter (2000), 'GmbH und Währungsumstellung—Hinweis für die Praxis', in *Wirtschaftsrechtliche Blätter*, 2000, 193.

Market-Institut (2000a), *Die Einstellung der Österreicher zum Euro (zehnte Welle)*, Linz.

—— (2000b), *Die Einstellung der Österreicher zum Euro (elfte Welle)*, Linz.

Mooslechner, Peter (2000), 'Geldpolitik und geldpolitische Strategie in Zeiten der Währungsunion: veränderte Rahmenbedingungen—neue Herausforderungen', in Österreichische Nationalbank (ed.), *Berichte und Studien* 2/2000, Wien, 74–87.

Östereichische Gesellschaft für Europapolitik (2000), *Der Euro und die Mitgliedschaft in der Europäischen Union—Das Meinungsklima im Februar 2000*, Wien.

Österreichische Bundesregierung (2000), *Zukunft im Herzen Europas—Das Regierungsprogrammem*, Wien.

Österreichische Nationalbank—Pressedienst (2000), *IMF Public Information Notice über die Artikel-IV-Konsultationen mit Österreich*, Wien.

Österreichisches Parlament (2000), *Parlamentskorrespondenz (diverse Nummern)*, Wien <http//www.parlinkom.gv.at>.

Part, Peter (2000), *Österreichische Budgetpolitik in der WWU*, Bundesministerium für Finanzen, Working Paper 5/2000 <http//www.bmf.gv.at/publikationen/_ startframe.htm>.

Radl, Sabine (2000), 'Euro kostet Nationalbank 25 Milliarden', in *Wirtschaftsblatt*, 30 November 2000.

Rothschild, Kurt W (2000), 'Defizite: Realität und Hysterie', in *Der Standard*, 22 August 2000, 27.

Schauer, Martin (2000), 'Die Euro-Umstellung und ihre Auswirkungen auf das Wohnrecht', in: *Wohnrechtliche Blätter*, 2000,1.

Schulmeister, Stephan, (2000a), 'Der Euro im Zeitalter des Finanzkapitals', in *Der Standard*, 22 May 2000, 18.

—— (2000b), 'Eurokurs, Ölpreis und EZB', in *Der Standard*, 18 September2000, 18.

—— (2000c), 'Wie die EZB den Euro schwächt', in *Der Standard*, 13 November 2000, 20.

Schweisgut, Dietmar (2000), 'Euroland: Warum so abgebrannt?', in *Der Standard*, 30 2000, 31.

Walterskirchen, Ewald (2000a), Konjunkturprognose, in *WIFO Monatsberichte* 4/2000.

—— (2000b), Konjunkturprognose, in *WIFO Monatsberichte* 7/2000.

—— (2000c), Konjunkturprognose, in *WIFO Monatsberichte* 10/2000.

Weigand, Arno and Gröller, Konrad (2000), 'Rundes Grundkapital mit runden Anteilsbeträgen der Stückaktien nach Euro-Umstellung?', in *ecolex* 2000, 284.

Zotter, Thomas (2000), 'Die Europäische Zentralbank in der Euro-Falle?', in *Arbeit & Wirtschaft* 12/2000, 32–8.

BELGIUM

Paul Magnette and Soukaïna Farès

1. The political framework
Paul Magnette*

1.1 A timid politicisation of euro-discussions

As explained in last year's report, European integration has always been an object of consensus among Belgian political leaders and organised interests.[47] The conviction that Belgium is too small and too open an economic space to manage a truly independent monetary policy is so widespread that the existence of the euro is very rarely contested and discussions about monetary policies are usually very limited.

However, the year 2000 has given rise to some timid politicisation of these discussions. The European political agenda gave the Belgian Finance Minister, Didier Reynders, opportunities to state his own views—largely shared by the coalition government and most political parties—about the institutional organisation of economic policies (1.2). Meanwhile, the policies implemented by the ECB have led to criticisms from some left-wing political parties and trade unions (1.3). The two major trade unions (socialist FGTB and Christian-Democrat CSC) have set up committees to scrutinise the ECB's decisions, and they frequently publish reports on these questions. In a context characterised by the absence of broader political discussions about monetary issues, they tend to become the two major 'euro-watchers'.

1.2 Political discussions about the euro: Belgium supports the institutionalisation of an economic authority

Belgian leaders have been quite active in European debates about the euro in 2000, particularly during the second semester. The Prime Minister, Mr Guy Verhofstadt, has frequently followed a classic Belgian line, arguing that the euro should give rise to spillover, in terms of economic and social integration. Mr Verhofstadt, a fervent admirer of Mr Blair's third way, has frequently argued that the European Union should try to reconcile economic growth with social solidarity and sustainable development. He

* Lecturer, Université Libre de Bruxelles, 39 Avenue F.D. Roosevelt, B-1050, Bruxelles.

47 See D. Devos and P. Magnette, *Belgian Report, Euro Spectator: Implementing the Euro, EUI Working papers, Law Department*, 2000/5, 58 et seq.

has presented the euro as the cornerstone of these European ambitions. Without being very clear about what he means by 'economic and social integration', he has notably supported the idea of developing 'social benchmarking' in implementing the guidelines of the Lisbon Summit (*L'Echo de la Bourse*, 21 March 2000). This viewpoint is shared by the Finance Minister who, in order to answer public worries about the value of the euro *vis-à-vis* the dollar, argued that the external value of the euro is not an important matter when compared to its contribution to economic growth, budgetary stability and structural reforms (*L'Echo de la Bourse*, 2 March 2000).

Throughout the year the Belgian Finance Minister also strongly supported French suggestions that the Euro-group be strengthened in order to establish a dialogue with the ECB. This had been discussed in Belgium well before this year. The former government, led by a Flemish Christian-Democrat (Jean-Luc Dehaene), was ideologically very close to Mr Duisenberg's doctrine, however the idea of enhancing the visibility and coherence of this political organ was supported by most left-wing and French-speaking parties. In September 1998, the French-speaking Christian-Democrat Finance Minister Jean-Jacques Viseur had suggested to his European colleagues that a two-year Presidency of the then Euro-XI be established (the president would have been elected by his peers, and would have been assisted by a vice-president, if he was drawn from one of the three Member States that are G7 members). Currently a member of the parliamentary opposition, Mr Viseur has again supported this idea in the Belgian media (*L'Echo de la Bourse*, 16 June 2000); he argues that the Commission lacks legitimacy and that the ECB's role is too narrowly defined to allow it to become 'the face' of the euro.

The Finance Minister argued all year for the strengthening of the Euro-group, for a dialogue between the latter and the ECB, and for the enlargement of its tasks. In May 2000 he argued that, since the president of the ECB is invited to Ecofin meetings, the president of the Euro-group should be invited to participate in some ECB board meetings (*L'Echo de la Bourse*, 6 and 17 May 2000, 2 June 2000). Without being given the right to vote, the Euro-group president would help make European monetary decisions more coherent and would enhance their visibility. In September 2000, Mr Reynders publicly regretted the fact that Mr Duisenberg did not attend the Euro-group meeting in Versailles (at a time when he was participating in a discussion with American businessmen in Canada). Mr Reynders declared this absence to be 'totally abnormal' in a period of public doubts about the exchange rate of the euro (*L'Echo de la Bourse*, 12 September 2000). At the end of the same month, Mr Reynders agreed with his French colleague and the commissioner Pedro Solbes Mira, that the interventions of the ECB, the US Federal Reserve and the Bank of Japan to support the euro, were excellent decisions 'responding to the reactions expressed by the Finance Ministers of the Euro-zone' (*L'Echo de la Bourse*, 23 September 2000).

All these interventions have followed the same argument: the Euro-zone needs a coherent political authority to avoid cacophony and to establish a dialogue with the ECB, without affecting its independence. Mr Reynders frequently supported this argument during the second semester. Recalling that Belgium would hold the presidency of the Euro-zone for the whole of 2001 (as Sweden is not part of the Euro-zone), he used different press conferences and interviews to present a programme for this presidency. In order to further Mr Fabius's initiatives, Mr Reynders intended to institutionalise the Euro-group and to transform it into a 'weighty political organ' (*L'Echo de la Bourse*, 21 November 2000). The president of the Euro-group, he argued, must be the only voice speaking for the Euro-zone, and unauthorised comments of his colleagues would 'not be welcome' (*L'Echo de la Bourse*, 19 December 2000). He added that the group could now deal with a large set of questions: from the 'quality of public expenses', to the preparation of the summits dedicated to the 'Lisbon follow-up', so that it would actually cover a broad range of economic and social policies. Though it remains an informal organ, Mr Reynders saw the Euro-group as a 'kind of enhanced co-operation' (*L'écho de la bourse*, 19 December 2000) and he believed its role would become increasingly crucial after enlargement because new Member States would not be able to become Euro-zone members in the short term.

Another idea developed by Mr Reynders—that will be a priority of the Belgian presidency—is that the control of financial institutions should be improved. He believes that national central banks could play this role because they are aware of the peculiarities of local markets. If co-ordination proved possible between the national central banks, it would be useless to create a new supranational organ to deal with these tasks (*L'Echo de la Bourse*, 4 December 2000). This idea was welcomed by national central banks and associations of private financial organisations, but still needs to be discussed at the political level.

Concrete questions concerning the transition to notes and coins in euro have not given rise to much discussion. The Finance Minister has continued to plead for a short transition period, and the director of the National Bank (who acts as a 'general commissioner for the euro') has supported this strategy. While worrying that only a very small proportion of Belgians use the euro for the time being in their everyday transactions, the Minister presented a set of actions designed to help consumers accept the transition easily (*L'Echo de la Bourse*, 30 November 2000).

While these discussions are focused on the general philosophy of monetary policies in the EU, and particularly its institutional organisation, discussions about the actual policies led by the ECB have been very rare and limited to social partners. A kind of implicit division of labour explains that, while the government focuses on the reform of the institutional framework, social actors try to hold the ECB accountable for its decisions.

1.3 Debating the ECB policies: the role of social partners

Our previous report mentioned the fact that trade unions were the only actors to publicly state their opinions about monetary policy. This has remained true so far and might be explained in part by the Belgian political situation. The coalition government brings together liberal (right wing), socialist and green parties, and it does not face a very strong opposition (only Christian-Democrats and some small regionalist and extreme right-wing parties). This quite fragile coalition government tries to avoid discussions that are prone to left-right dichotomies and that would undermine its own stability. Nevertheless, a classic left-right cleavage can still be observed around the spillover expected from the euro. While right-wing parties, employers' organisations and some economists hope that the euro will strengthen budgetary discipline and induce more labour market flexibility, left-wing parties and trade unions call for a 'regulatory spillover'. This would consist of the rise of an 'economic government' and the creation of a European fiscal and social basis, designed to avoid (or at least to limit) social and fiscal dumping.

Notably, the French-speaking socialist party, defining its priorities for the Belgian Presidency, has asked to:

> strengthen co-ordination of economic policies and dialogue with the ECB to take account of full employment and durable growth (Parti Socialiste, Priorités pour la présidence belge de l'Union européenne, Brussels, 11 Dec 2000).

Better co-ordination of fiscal policies, support for public services and investment in the field of scientific research are also part of this party's objectives. They are still understood as elements of its ambition to transform the EU into a 'federal Europe'.

In a more precise document that defines its general economic orientations, the Flemish *Socialistische partij* has defended similar points (Socialistische Partij, *Goedgekeurde resolutieteksten*, *Economisch contract*, Brussels, 2000). This document argues that social security, fiscal matters, wages, and labour market are currently subject to strong competition, and lead to social and fiscal dumping. More co-ordination of these matters should be organised in order to avoid the weakening of national acquisitions through spontaneous market harmonisation, and this should be decided by qualified majority voting. This party also envisaged a system of budgetary compensation through a federal budget that would help countries suffering from the consequences of policies led by other countries to draw investments via fiscal reforms. The same document pleads for a revision of the ECB's mandate, which it says should not only (or not primarily) try to reduce inflation but should also take employment and growth into account.

Trade unions have supported these claims and have made studies criticising the ECB's policy. In its fourth report on monetary policy in the EMU (Brussels, 2000), the CSC trade union (Christian-Democratic) explains that:

> a monetary policy guided by the sole concern of price stability (. . .) damages the credibility of the currency. (. . .) A single-minded and exclusive focus on preserving inflation below 2 per cent at all times and at all cost will not pay off. Increasing interest rates even further will almost certainly result in slowdown of economic growth, thus providing the basis for a new fall in the euro exchange rate and thereby locking the ECB in a vicious circle.

In the sensible context of the 'oil crisis', the trade union pleads for a less strict position:

> external shocks such as an oil price jump can lift inflation swiftly above the 2 per cent ceiling, thereby forcing the ECB to follow restrictive monetary policy even when the acceleration in inflation is temporary and has nothing to do with the malfunctioning markets inside EMU. Other central banks in the world take such situations into account by focusing on core instead of headline inflation as well as through somewhat higher inflation targets.

The other major trade union—the socialist FGTB—shares this analysis. It added that:

> continued wage moderation, together with fiscal tightening might overcompensate the potential inflationary consequences of the oil shock, thereby resulting in actual deflation. The other danger is that monetary policy might mistakenly read the temporary acceleration of inflation as a permanent one and might trigger a new but completely unnecessary stability conflict over an inflation objective of 2 per cent instead of 1 per cent (FGTB, Second report on monetary policy in the EMU, Brussels, 2000).

In common documents, the two trade unions have suggested an alternative monetary policy based on these critical findings:

> With one European currency and with one common monetary policy, the possibility exists of implementing a policy that is tailored to the economic needs of EMU itself. The choice is very clear. Either embarking on an anti-inflationary policy that keeps inflation at an all-time low. (. . .) This rigid attitude from the ECB would also trigger a new stability conflict over an inflation rate that, although accelerating, is still so limited that it does not constitute a problem. Such an option would come down to solving US-inflationary problem at the expense of the EMU recovery. The alternative is to tolerate a limited or temporary breach of the arbitrary and self-imposed ceiling of 2 per cent inflation, due to the dollar appreciation. Such a policy would also deliver the US its much-needed imported disinflation, while at the same time sheltering the EMU-recovery from an unnecessary

stability conflict (FGTB-CSC, Understanding the ECB's policy making, An increase that does not threaten the recovery in EMU yet, Brussels, 16 Feb 2000).

A more recent common document (FGTB–CSC, *Pour une politique monétaire favorable à l'emploi et la croissance*, Brussels, 13 December 2000), argued once again that the weakness of the euro *vis-à-vis* the dollar is due to the fact that European growth is limited by a narrow monetary policy and remains weaker than American growth. And it pleaded for a larger growth of the monetary amount, a break in the enhancing of interest rates and a limitation of this rate if the euro were to become stronger than the dollar.

However, the politicisation of these policies has thus far been limited to experts. The media has not reported these documents and they have not yet given rise to parliamentary discussions. By contrast, employers' associations have continued to support perfectly opposing arguments. After the UNICE thanked the ECB for its policy (*L'Echo de la Bourse*, 21 March 2000), the Belgian Federation of Employers (FEB) argued that the euro's weakness is an advantage for European exports. Agreeing with trade unions that this weakness is a consequence of the fact that the growth rate had been lower in Europe than in the US, employers pleaded for a more flexible labour market in order to reach US standards. A more flexible use of labour, combined with a strict monetary policy, should support growth (FEB, *Focus Euro*, Brussels, April 2000). Despite these divergences, trade unions and employers nevertheless managed to reach common positions within the 'Conseil central de l'économie' (CCE) in order to define their priorities for the Belgian presidency. These included institutional reform of the EU, pursuing the Lisbon objectives, macroeconomic co-ordination (including some form of fiscal co-operation), sustainable development and international trade (*L'Echo de la Bourse*, 12 December 2000). Once again, one identifies the Belgian consensus on European integration—recently revived by Belgium's position during the Nice summit—combined with the Belgian 'social model' and the use of vague objectives to avoid conflicts. This helped to produce the new Belgian line.

1.4 Public opinion: permissive consensus

The last Eurobarometer polls confirm that the Belgian population largely supports the euro. As in the former survey, 76 per cent of persons polled in March–April 2000 answered that they were 'for' the Euro. Belgium thus has the third highest score in the EU, after Italy and Luxembourg, and it is a particularly high score. The general support for the euro in the EU has been declining since the end of 1998, after a two-year period of constant growth (47 per cent 'for' in March 1997; 64 per cent in

September 1998; 61 per cent in March 1999; 58 per cent in March 2000).[48] Belgium is an exception to this evolution.

The general level of confidence in the EU declined from 1994 to 1999 in Belgium; it has been growing during the last year. In March 2000, 62 per cent of persons think that, 'generally speaking (. . .) Belgian membership of the European Union is a good thing'. This is up from 47 per cent one year earlier, with Belgium ranking seventh. The same results are reached when the other classic Eurobarometer question is asked: 'Taking everything into consideration, would you say that Belgium has on balance benefited or not from being a member of the European Union?' Sixty per cent of persons answer that Belgium has benefited from EU membership, while only 44 per cent thought this a year earlier. Support for the euro remains larger than general support for the EU.

Asked whether they think monetary matters should be dealt with at the national or European level, 80 per cent of persons in March 2000 were in favour of European decision-making. Belgium had the highest score. The former experience of a monetary association with Luxembourg might help explain this enthusiasm, even though the dimensions of this experience are not comparable with the euro. More probable is a hypothesis made by many political scientists who suggest that, in this field as in others, the EU appears to be an efficient public authority that is able to tackle problems the national government is unable to handle. Generally speaking, there is a tendency to view the EU as a remedy for internal evils in countries in which it is perceived that the political system is in crisis (Belgium, Italy, Greece) and confidence in the national government is therefore low.

Some monetary peculiarity exists in this phenomenon. As far as other competence in other fields is concerned, people are less enthusiastic about European action in Belgium. While 73 per cent see humanitarian aid as a valuable common policy, and 62 per cent view defence as such, EC unemployment and immigration policies are only supported by 55 per cent, while health and social welfare achieve only 36 per cent support.

However, 93 per cent of persons see fighting poverty and unemployment as Union priorities, 89 per cent believe peace, security and fighting organised crime is a priority while successfully implementing the euro is seen as priority by 'only' 72 per cent. These results can be explained by a classic hypothesis. According to most political scientists, the end of the century was characterised by deep worries among European citizens concerning their physical and material security. In political sciences jargon, they are 'materialistic citizens',[49] and this explains why they mention all 'security matters' as priorities.

[48] Similar trends may be observed in the Euro-zone: there were 52 per cent for in Mar 1997; 70 per cent in Sept 1998; 68 per cent in Mar 1999.

[49] See D Klingemann and D Fuchs (eds), *Citizens and the State, Beliefs in Government, Vol.I*, Oxford, Oxford University Press, 1995.

The average level of support for the ECB is rather high in Belgium (49 per cent), and slightly better than one year earlier (42 per cent). It is much weaker than in the Benelux partners (70 per cent NL, 59 per cent L), but remains much higher than the EU average (27 per cent). This is a medium score when compared with other EU institutions. The European Parliament is now trusted by 61 per cent (50 per cent one year earlier), the Court of Justice by 55 per cent (44 per cent in 1999), the Commission by 57 per cent (40 per cent in 1999), and the Council by 49 per cent (36 per cent in 1999). More instructive is the fact that 28 per cent have no opinion about this question (only 11 per cent in the case of the EP, and 12 per cent for the Commission). This high level of 'no answer' responses can be understood as an indication that the ECB has relatively low notoriety (only 27 per cent think it plays an important role).

The existence of the ECB and its independence of Member States are usually not debated in Belgium: 74 per cent of persons asked support this independence. This simply means that Belgians see the independent ECB as a normal consequence of the EMU, and it is therefore less debated in Belgium than in some other Member states. 84 per cent also think that the ECB has to be accountable to the European Parliament.

Belgians usually think that they have received information about the single currency (87 per cent), though a much smaller proportion feel 'informed' (69 per cent). These are relatively high levels compared to the EU averages (75 per cent, 52 per cent respectively) and to the Euro-zone averages (84 per cent, 52 per cent respectively). These scores are close to, and somewhat higher than, the Euro-12 average. Most people have been informed by television (63 per cent) and banks (52 per cent).

1.5 Conclusions: a debate limited to Belgian élites

The Belgian situation is rather stable. Belgians have always perceived their country to be a small and open economic space. Since the beginning of the century, Belgian élites and citizens have praised interdependence, co-operation and integration.

These long-term elements, combined with a natural Belgian disdain for political discussions, probably explain why the euro is not a much-debated issue. Nationalist extreme right-wing parties are the only segment of the Belgian citizenry who criticise Europe as a whole, and the euro in particular. But even this group does not reject them. Beyond this opposition, a classic left-right cleavage can be observed around the spillover expected from the euro. While right-wing parties, employers' organisations and some economists hope that the euro will strengthen budgetary discipline and induce more labour market flexibility, left-wing parties and trade unions call for a 'regulatory spill-over' consisting of the rise of an 'economic government' and the creation of a European fiscal and social basis designed to avoid fiscal and social dumping. This reflects discussions elsewhere in the EU, and notably in the economic and monetary committee of the EP. Official Belgian positions usually amount to a compromise between these two positions due to the coalition between these two wings in the government.

Public opinion generally ignores these discussions—with the exception of 'cognitively mobilised' citizens, who echo them—and shares the Belgian élite's general confidence in the EU and in its monetary policies.

2. Les attitudes des institutions financières belges à l'égard de la politique monétaire de la BCE

Soukaïna Farès*

2.1 Introduction

La mise sur les rails de l'Union monétaire, avec l'introduction de l'euro au 1er janvier 1999, avait été perçue par le secteur financier comme étant tout d'abord le symbole d'une unité et d'une identité européenne.

La Banque ARTESIA avait écrit[50] que l'euro était un véritable accélérateur de la croissance économique, puisque son utilisation favoriserait les échanges transfrontaliers et l'intégration du marché.

Pour les institutions bancaires, l'avènement de la monnaie unique était synonyme d'une plus grande transparence dans la fixation des prix. Son utilisation allait entraîner des avantages considérables pour la population et ce sous forme de meilleurs prix et de taux d'intérêt les plus bas possible. L'UEM était dés lors un catalyseur du progrès économique et social en Europe, catalyseur qui allait parachever les contours de l'ordre économique mondial au 21e siècle. Un article publié dans le 'Bulletin de la FEB', le mensuel économique le plus lu en Belgique, avait mis l'accent[51] sur les principaux défis et risques liés à l'introduction de l'euro vus par les présidents de trois grandes banques en Belgique.

M. Rémi Vermeiren, président de la banque KBC, avait mis l'accent sur les conséquences énormes au niveau des recettes et des coûts (suppression des recettes liées aux transactions de devises et de change entre les monnaies de l'UEM[52], coûts additionnels pour les adaptations aux TI, formation, information). Dés lors, les premiers défis pour la banque KBC étaient l'adaptation des programmes informatiques à l'euro, la communication d'informations aussi bien aux collaborateurs qu'aux clients ainsi que la formation de ses employés. Outre ces frais de conversion à court

* Assistante de recherche au Groupe d'études politiques européennes (GEPE)

50 Notes économiques, ARTESIA Banque, n°203, décembre 99.

51 Bulletin FEB, n°11, novembre 1999.

52 Recettes estimées selon l'association belge des banques en 1997 à plus de 20 milliards BEF/an.

terme, les risques et défis de l'UEM étaient essentiellement liés à l'élargissement d'échelle, soudain, du marché financier.

M. Herman Verwilst, président de la Banque Fortis, avait attiré l'attention sur l'intégration plus approfondie du projet européen qui élargissait le champ d'action des banques à l'échelle européenne et qui multipliait de ce fait la concurrence directe. Selon lui, les banques devaient dans ce contexte continuer à devancer leurs clients, qui pensent dorénavant et agissent de plus en plus au niveau européen.

Le président de la BBL, M. Michel Tilmant, avançait que l'élargissement du marché domestique à l'UEM impliquait l'acquisition d'une taille suffisante pour continuer à intervenir parmi les 'major players'. L'avènement de l'UEM avait poussé les banques belges à apporter de modifications stratégiques dans leur offre de service et de produits. A long terme, les banques belges pensent que l'euro engendrera un secteur bancaire plus fort et plus compétitif. L'environnement monétaire stable obtenu grâce à l'euro peut, lui aussi, avoir un impact favorable sur le système bancaire au sein de l'UEM. En revanche, le président de la BBL, M. Michel Tilmant avait estimait que la stabilité monétaire et les taux d'intérêt structurellement peu élevés pourraient cependant constituer une menace pour le rendement des transformations de durées, qui constituent l'un des piliers de l'activité bancaire classique, si l'écart entre les taux courts et les taux longs devait, lui aussi, se réduire de manière structurelle (écrasement de la marge d'intermédiation).

En résumé, l'UEM engendre des défis considérables pour le secteur bancaire belge qui reste convaincu que les entreprises ont aussi beaucoup à faire pour adapter leurs systèmes et surtout leurs stratégies à l'UEM.

En effet, l'Association belge des Banques avait fait le point de la situation et avait constaté suite à une enquête[53] qu'elle avait menée auprès d'un groupe cible que l'utilisation de l'euro, comme monnaie scripturale, était encore très faible surtout chez les particuliers et les entreprises (respectivement—de 0.5 pour cent et—de 5 pour cent).

Cette tendance n'avait rien de surprenant ni d'inquiétant car, selon l'ABB, les entreprises n'allaient s'occuper de leur passage à l'euro qu'après le 1er janvier 2000. Le dernier eurobaromètre de la FEB du mois d'octobre 2000 laisse transparaître une évolution à ce niveau. En effet, l'utilisation externe de l'euro (envoi de factures, etc.) par les entreprises belges a déjà atteint un niveau relativement élevé (61 pour cent des entreprises belges) mais son utilisation interne (rémunérations, comptabilité, etc.) par ces entreprises reste très modeste.

Avec l'arrivée de l'euro fiduciaire en janvier 2002, la FEB partage le même souci que le Ministre des affaires économiques, M. Charles Picqué, concernant la préparation des entreprises belges au passage définitif à l'euro.

[53] Enquête menée par l'Association Belge des Banques, mars 1999.

2.2 Le 'BILAN' de l'euro

Le débat sur le 'BILAN' de l'euro s'est souvent résumé en Belgique, comme d'ailleurs dans les autres États membres, à une analyse de la valeur de celui-ci par rapport au dollar. Les journaux ont souvent associé la baisse du cours de l'euro face au dollar à un premier 'échec' de la monnaie unique, dans la mesure où cela refléterait un manque de crédibilité de l'euro. Or, il apparaît suivant le magazine 'la Banque'[54] que le parcours baissier de l'euro a été très opportun, en soulageant les exportateurs européens.

Entre euphorie et amertume, les avis des milieux financiers belges concernant le bilan de l'euro restent partagés. Selon le Courrier économique et financier de la KBC banque,[55] la deuxième année d'existence de l'euro n'a pas été, à maints égards, des plus facile. Ainsi, sa valeur externe par rapport au dollar US n'a cessé de faiblir presque tout au long de l'année. À la différence de 1999, l'objectif de la stabilité des prix à l'intérieur de l'UEM a en outre été mis en péril, ce qui a amené la Banque centrale européenne, à l'automne 2000, à intervenir sur le marché des changes pour soutenir le cours de l'euro.

Le développement rapide de l'usage international de la monnaie unique en 1999 a subi un coup d'arrêt en 2000. L'accession de l'euro au statut international se fait de manière graduelle et demandera par conséquent du temps. De même, la perspective d'une extension rapide de l'UEM aux trois pays 'out' restants après l'adhésion de la Grèce semble s'évanouir depuis le 'non' qui a sanctionné le référendum danois.

Techniquement parlant, les quotidiens et revues financiers belges estiment que les deux premières années de l'euro se sont toutefois déroulées sans heurts sur les marchés monétaire et financiers et il semble également que le passage à la troisième phase de l'UEM, qui verra l'émission de pièces de monnaie et de billets de banque en euro, sera un succès. Ainsi, le quotidien 'L'Echo'[56] avait précisé dans un article que le premier bilan de l'euro était 'extrêmement positif'.

2.3 La dépréciation de l'euro

'L'euro n'est pas la monnaie forte qu'il était censé être au départ'.[57] Cette opinion reste partagée par plusieurs quotidiens et magazines financiers qui remarquent que l'euro s'est déprécié de quelque 30per cent par rapport au dollar au cours des 22 premiers mois de son existence. Même si la monnaie unique européenne avait amorcé une prudente remontée durant ces

[54] Banque magazine, n° 605, juillet-août 1999.
[55] Le Courrier économique et financier-KBC, n°1, janvier 2001.
[56] L'Echo, 18 février 2000.
[57] Vecteur- Fortis Banque, n° 12, février 2001.

derniers mois, son cours par rapport au dollar reste inférieur à la valeur du début 1999.

L'un des rares points qui font l'unanimité des journaux est que l'euro est sous-évalué depuis un bon moment. Les avis restent par contre divergents concernant la juste valeur ou le cours d'équilibre de l'euro par rapport au dollar. En dépit de l'appréciation qui se dessine depuis octobre 2000, l'euro reste considéré aujourd'hui par la presse comme sous-évalué à raison de 10 à 15 pour cent minimum. Cette dépréciation est due, suivant les analyses de certains observateurs, à plusieurs raisons, dont la politique monétaire de la BCE.

Ainsi, dans un article du magazine 'Vecteur',[58] on explique que les marchés financiers pointent volontiers un doigt accusateur vers la BCE lorsqu'il s'agit d'expliquer la défaillance de l'euro. Ils estiment que la BCE n'est pas à la hauteur de sa tâche et font référence au manque de transparence du processus décisionnel, aux interventions intempestives des ministres des finances à propos du cap à suivre dans la période liminaire, ou encore aux déclarations parfois contradictoires des membres du conseil des gouverneurs, avec comme corollaire une certaine confusion à propos de la stratégie monétaire, des paramètres vraiment déterminants pour la politique monétaire, etc.

Toutefois, la dépréciation de l'euro a été perçue comme un point positif étant donné qu'elle avait contribué à soutenir la croissance économique au sein de la zone euro. Chose qui n'était pas, selon la presse, superflue.

Sur ce point, la Banque nationale de Belgique avait à son tour salué dans les rapports[59] l'action de l'Eurosystème qui, selon elle, avait manifestement réussi à stabiliser les attentes relatives à l'évolution des prix, assurant de la sorte les conditions d'une croissance durable. La Banque ajoutait que le recul du prix du pétrole et l'appréciation de l'euro survenus à la fin de 2000 avaient limité les risques d'inflation bien que les résultats des négociations salariales restaient déterminants à cet égard.

D'autre part, il était précisé que certains avantages de l'euro ne se manifesteraient que progressivement: les effets de l'approfondissement du marché intérieur, par l'élimination du risque de change, la réduction des coûts de transaction et la transparence accrue des prix, seront graduels et se renforceront à partir de 2002, quand les monnaies nationales auront complètement disparu.

D'autres avantages ne pourront être concrètement appréciés qu'après un certain temps. Ainsi, ce serait seulement dans quelques années que chacun pourrait constater que l'Eurosystème avait bien rempli sa mission de maintien de la stabilité des prix.

[58] Ibid.

[59] Rapports présentés par le gouverneur au nom du conseil de régence, le 2 février 2000 et le 31 janvier 2001.

Quant aux effets d'entraînement que la monnaie unique exercera sur l'intégration européenne dans d'autres domaines et son influence sur le système monétaire international, la Banque trouvait qu'il était encore trop tôt pour les évaluer. Selon la BNB, les premiers pas de l'euro sont déjà qualifiés de prometteurs.

De plus, la stratégie de la politique monétaire a fait montre de son adéquation au nouveau contexte et elle a permis à l'Eurosystème d'hériter de la réputation des banques centrales ayant obtenu les meilleurs résultats en termes de stabilité des prix, tout en tenant compte des incertitudes nées du changement de régime monétaire. Le relèvement des taux d'intérêt amorcé en novembre 1999 et poursuivi en 2000 visait essentiellement à assurer le maintien de la stabilité des prix. Un tel resserrement de la politique de taux était généralement attendu et a été bien accueilli dans les marchés financiers. A court terme, l'action de l'Eurosystème n'a pas détérioré les perspectives de croissance, car elle est restée mesurée et a seulement servi de contrepoids à l'incidence d'autres facteurs, telle la dépréciation de l'euro.

Notons au passage que la dépréciation de l'euro par rapport au dollar n'a pas eu la même incidence sur la Belgique qui est moins sensible aux variations du cours du dollar. En effet, si l'on se réfère à la dépréciation totale du cours du change effectif des États Membres entre fin 1998 et fin 2000, on se rend compte que le recul est moindre en Belgique étant donné que ses échanges commerciaux s'effectuent en grande partie avec d'autres états membres de l'UEM.

2.4 Les conclusions de la presse financière concernant l'euro

Dans un article sur la 'Valeur de l'euro' publié dans le magazine Tendencies Review,[60] un auteur[61] conclut que la situation que traverse l'euro pour l'instant sera différente à long terme: aux États-Unis, la période de croissance exceptionnelle semble toucher à sa fin, tandis que l'économie européenne sort de sa période de rigueur dictée par le traité de Maastricht. Par conséquent, l'attente de rendements toujours plus élevés aux États-Unis va s'affaiblir et l'image de l'euro en tant que monnaie d'investissement va s'améliorer.

D'autre part, la fin du marché haussier des années 90 va également tempérer la tendance d'investissement structurelle aux États-Unis, une évolution qui ne peut qu'améliorer les perspectives de l'euro à long terme.

Cet avis est partagé par un autre magazine[62] même si celui-ci estime que

[60] Tendencies Review, n°50, *la valeur de l'euro*.

[61] Stefaan Van Langendonck, économiste au département de recherche macro-économique internationale de KBC Asset Management.

[62] Perspectives économiques, Dexia Banque, février 2001.

l'euro ne profite que peu de la vague de pessimisme qui entoure l'économie américaine. La méfiance, dont a fait l'objet l'euro, s'estompe lentement. Le magazine pense que l'euro ne pourra décoller vraiment que s'il y a une faiblesse prolongée de l'économie américaine. Comme cette hypothèse est loin d'être certaine, il envisage une légère appréciation de la devise européenne.

2.5 Les marchés obligataires/actions

L'évolution des différentiels d'intérêt sur les marchés obligataires depuis la mise en place de l'UEM est également un sujet qui a suscité plusieurs réactions de la part de la presse économique et financière.[63]

Dans un article du magazine 'Vecteur',[64] on précise que l'introduction de l'euro laissait entendre une nouvelle réduction des différentiels d'intérêt sur le marché des obligations d'état: cette introduction était supposée accroître la séduction des obligations des petits États Membres aux yeux des gestionnaires de portefeuilles extérieurs à l'Union et, partant, réduire le différentiel d'intérêt -ou spread- entre ces états et l'Allemagne.

En pratique, les choses se sont déroulées autrement: les petits États Membres, principales victimes, constatent que depuis 1999, les conditions auxquelles ils peuvent faire appel au marché obligataire se sont relativement détériorées par rapport à celles dont peut bénéficier le gouvernement allemand. En Belgique, le différentiel d'intérêt par rapport à l'Allemagne pour ce qui est des obligations d'état à 10 ans s'est creusé entre 1998—avant la 3ème phase de l'UEM—et 2000, de 19 à 33 points de base en moyenne. A cela s'ajoute qu'à l'inverse de ce que l'on observait dans ces pays avant l'UEM, le spread avec l'Allemagne est plus important dans les petits pays qui ont rallié l'UEM (comme la Belgique) que dans ceux qui n'en font pas (encore) partie, comme le Danemark et la Suède.

Vu l'évolution favorable des finances publiques, due aux efforts et aux politiques budgétaires encadrées par le pacte de stabilité et de croissance, cet élargissement du spread ne peut en tout cas pas être imputé à une augmentation du risque de crédit. En 2000, contrairement à l'Allemagne, la Belgique a affiché un excédent budgétaire. En outre, elle est parvenue à réduire considérablement son taux d'endettement. De 122 pour cent du PIB en 1998, le gouvernement belge espère le ramener à 104 pour cent fin 2001. L'article conclut que le fonctionnement du marché obligataire européen doit être amélioré et rendu plus homogène. Dans le cas de la Belgique, ce serait peut être aller un peu trop loin. Il faut en effet relativiser le coût de l'actuel différentiel d'intérêt pour le Trésor. Vu l'échéancier de la dette publique, la disparition du spread représenterait au maximum une

[63] Voir l'Echo, 15 décembre 2000—Le Soir, 30 décembre 2000.
[64] Vecteur, Fortis Banque, n° 12, février 2001.

économie supplémentaire de EUR 25 millions l'an en paiements d'intéréts, soit 0.01 pour cent du PIB.

Sur un autre plan, l'intégration européenne a également marqué de son empreinte les marchés d'actions. Avec l'avènement de l'UEM, l'augmentation de l'influence sectorielle sur le cours de l'action était prévisible étant donné que la structuration de la zone monétaire favorisait une plus grande spécialisation. L'UEM établit dés lors un cadre compétitif dans lequel seules les entreprises les plus efficaces survivront.

Selon le Directeur Général Asset Management de KBC Bank,[65] M. Stefan Duchateau, ce processus peut être préjudiciable aux plus petites entreprises—dont les belges. Il a expliqué que lors de la constitution d'un portefeuille sectoriel, on prenait d'abord les valeurs les plus importantes, de sorte que les petites entreprises pouvaient rester sur la touche. Il a ajouté que la différence entre l'évolution des plus petites bourses et celle des grandes se remarquait déjà. Ainsi, et en raison de l'attrait des valeurs les plus importantes, l'évolution de la bourse belge a pris du retard sur celle des grandes bourses. De plus, les différences qui subsistent entre les pays en matière de fiscalité, de politique sociale, etc. font que le cours des actions est toujours soumis à l'influence du 'pays'. De ce fait, M. Duchateau concluait que plusieurs obstacles subsistaient encore à la réalisation d'un marché des capitaux, vraiment unifié en Europe. Pour y arriver, il faudrait selon lui, uniformiser les directives comptables, le contrôle prudentiel, les règles relatives à l'autonomie de gestion, etc.

2.6 La politique monétaire de la BCE

Le projet de l'euro est perçu favorablement par les particuliers et les entreprises en raison de la simplification attendue pour les voyages internationaux et le commerce au sein des 12 pays.

Quant à la presse économique et financière, sa réaction face à la politique commune de l'Eurosystème varie mais tend en général à exprimer la même idée: les choix de la BCE ne sont pas toujours faciles. Les effets ne sont pas toujours bénéfiques pour l'euro.

En février 2000, les sentiments restaient mitigés pour le premier anniversaire de l'euro. La presse estimait en outre que l'objectif principal de la BCE, à savoir la stabilité des prix, a été réalisé, malgré l'accélération de l'inflation. La décision de la BCE de relever ses taux directeurs en avril avait provoqué une certaine déception dans les milieux financiers qui pensaient que la détente des prix pétroliers allait entraîner une baisse de l'inflation au second semestre : avec la faiblesse de l'euro, cet espoir était déçu et on se demandait si cette faiblesse arrivait à un bon moment.[66]

[65] Voir le Bulletin FEB, n° 11, novembre 1999.
[66] Conjonctures économiques, Dexia Banque, mai 2000.

Les interventions de la BCE qui ont précédé celle où elle avait agi seule, à savoir le 3, 6 et 9 novembre, ont trouvé des échos plutôt positifs. En effet, la première intervention de la BCE en automne 2000 (22 septembre) en coordination avec les banques centrales des EU, du Japon, du Royaume-Uni et du Canada avait provoqué une certaine euphorie dans les milieux financiers belges étant donné que le cours de l'euro s'était apprécié de 7 pour cent. Bien que cette appréciation n'était plus que de 1 à 2 pour cent (lors des interventions unilatérales de novembre) et que l'euro ne s'était pas redressé face au dollar dans les semaines qui avaient suivi, les interventions du SEBC sur le marché des changes n'étaient pas qualifiées pour autant d'inefficaces. Leur impact restait quand même perçu comme 'modeste'.

En effet, le quotidien 'Le Soir'[67] avait qualifié l'intervention de la BCE en novembre d'une 'guérilla' de longue haleine. Cette opération, selon le même quotidien, n'était pas de grand effet puisqu'elle avait requinqué la monnaie européenne, sans parvenir à la maintenir durablement au dessus du seuil de 0.87 dollar. Quelques jours plus tard, le même quotidien[68] saluait l'intervention de la BCE sur les marchés des changes et trouvait qu'elle avait choisi le meilleur instrument qui soutenait l'euro tout en n'étant pas néfaste à la croissance économique.

Les déclarations des hommes politiques nationaux et des banquiers centraux du SEBC (concernant l'évolution des marchés financiers et la nécessité d'interventions sur les changes) ont été fortement critiquées par la presse: la contradiction que laissait transparaître leur contenu[69] a créé pas mal de confusion et a maintenu un épais brouillard sur la politique monétaire et de change future de l'UEM. Bien qu'après la première intervention, l'euro se soit à nouveau déprécié rapidement, les propos tenus en octobre par le président de la BCE, M. Duisenberg avaient suscité l'impression que la propension du SEBC à intervenir de nouveau et de manière régulière était minime.

La décision de la BCE en décembre 2000 de laisser inchangés ses taux directeurs ainsi que son objectif pour la masse monétaire avait démontré, selon certains quotidiens,[70] qu'elle n'était pas encore prête à se montrer plus laxiste. Le maintien de la valeur de référence de la masse monétaire avait, quant à lui, surpris un bon nombre d'analystes qui pronostiquaient un relèvement en raison de l'amélioration de la conjoncture européenne.[71]

Le taux de change de l'euro n'est pas lié aux seules interventions de la BCE sur les marchés des changes. En effet, dans le Courrier économique et financier de la KBC,[72] on explique que la tendance baissière de l'euro en

[67] Le Soir, 7 novembre 2000.
[68] Le Soir, supplément économique, 17 novembre 2000.
[69] Voir le courrier économique et financier, KBC, n°1, janvier 2001.
[70] L'Echo, 15 décembre 2000.
[71] Voir L'Echo du 15 décembre 2000.
[72] Courrier économique et financier, KBC Banque, n°1, janvier 2001.

2000 était moins liée à la spéculation directe qu'aux abondantes sorties de capitaux en provenance des pays de l'UEM et à destination des EU. Cela fait présumer que les interventions en soi, n'ont, au bout du compte, pas tellement pu inverser l'orientation des cours de change. Selon le même article, si l'euro s'est raffermi depuis décembre 2000, cela tient surtout aux indications d'un net ralentissement de la croissance économique aux EU et à la réduction progressive de ces sorties de capitaux.

Cela dit, l'amélioration de la conjoncture européenne qui a augmenté le volume des liquidités nécessaires au bon fonctionnement de l'économie, laisse présager quand même un geste de la BCE à ce niveau. Nombre d'experts estiment que les sept hausses de taux décidées par la BCE ont déjà contribué à essouffler la croissance. En outre, la remontée de l'euro et la baisse des prix du pétrole ont contribué à faire reculer légèrement l'inflation ainsi que les risques pesant sur les prix à moyen terme.

2.7 Indépendance et transparence de la BCE

'Informer la population de la zone euro en s'exprimant avec clarté est le défi adressé à la BCE.'[73] Quelques mois après sa naissance en juin 1998, la presse[74] estimait que sur papier, la BCE avait toutes les garanties de pouvoir poursuivre ses objectifs de manière indépendante. Elle trouvait qu'elle devrait cependant faire preuve d'une ouverture suffisante dans sa communication et la justification de ses décisions pour confirmer cette indépendance politique et cette légitimité sur le terrain.

Après les premiers résultats affichés, et lors d'un débat[75] organisé en préparation au 24e Vlaams Wetenschappelijk Economisch Congres, certains intervenants avaient mis l'accent sur les dangers qui guettaient la politique monétaire. Ils estimaient que certaines interventions s'imposaient notamment en ce qui concernait l'Euro-11: selon eux, l'Euro-11 doit être officialisé et il faut continuer à le développer. On fait remarquer que ce groupe pourrait remplir un rôle en matière de coopération et d'harmonisation, en complément de la BCE qui est chargée de la politique monétaire unique.

Le secrétaire général du Ministère des Finances, M Grégoire Brouhns, avait également attiré l'attention sur ce sujet lors d'une communication faite à une journée d'étude.[76] Il faisait remarquer que l'Euro-11 restait une enceinte d'échange de vues économiques et financiers entre États

[73] Extrait de la communication de M Willem F Duisenberg, président de la Banque centrale européenne, Francfort-sur-le-Main, avril 2000.

[74] Bulletin de la Générale de Banque, décembre 1998.

[75] Débat organisé sur le thème de l'UEM, 30 novembre 1999, ARTESIA Banking Corporation.

[76] Voir Bulletin de documentation, Ministère des Finances, SED, n°2 mars-avril 1999/Communication à la journée d'étude tenue à Bruxelles le vendredi 13 novembre 1998.

partageant un même destin monétaire. Ni plus ni moins. Selon lui, l'Euro-11 a été conçu dans le voisinage du Conseil ECOFIN et ceci a été conçu comme étant quelque chose de normal dans la mesure où la plupart des questions traitées relevaient des attributions de ce conseil.

Toutefois, M. Brouhns avait souligné que dans la mesure où certaines réformes structurelles relevaient des attributions d'autres conseils, il convenait d'organiser une coordination communautaire ad hoc. Le concept Euro-11 devrait, selon lui, être élargi à d'autres conseils. Enfin, il estimait que la crédibilité de l'UEM restait à consolider. Pour ce faire, deux entreprises restaient à réussir:

- d'une part, la coordination-surveillance des politiques économiques nationales,
- et d'autre part, le dialogue entre la BCE et le conseil ECOFIN-Euro-11.

2.8 L'UEM et l'élargissement

L'adhésion de la Grèce porte le nombre d'États membres de l'UEM à 12. Cette adhésion était attendue de longue date, même si la presse économique trouvait que l'économie grecque était structurellement encore très faible et fragile. Certains magazines[77] voient dans cette adhésion une décision politique visant la réunion des Balkans à l'UE.

Quant aux résultats du référendum danois sur l'introduction de l'euro, le 'non' ne repose pas suivant la presse sur une logique économique. Lors du scrutin, la population danoise s'est essentiellement laissé guider par des facteurs émotionnels, comme la crainte d'une union politique ou la perte d'un système de sécurité sociale favorable. Dans le Courrier économique et financier de la KBC,[78] on pense qu'elle sera probablement à nouveau appelée à se prononcer sur l'euro dans quelque cinq ans au plus tôt. Économiquement parlant, les conséquences du 'non' danois ne sont pas tellement importantes pour la zone euro. Selon la FEB,[79] les conséquences négatives de cette décision affecteraient essentiellement les entreprises danoises qui seraient privées de certains avantages de la monnaie unique. Sur le plan psychologique et politique, les effets sont plus profonds. Ainsi, la Suède a vu se renforcer son euroscepticisme, suite au 'non' danois.

Selon le Courrier économique et financier de la KBC, le vote anti-euro des Danois n'a eu qu'un impact marginal au R.U. Au cours de la décennie écoulée, l'opinion publique britannique était de toute façon déjà opposée à une adhésion à l'UEM. Le scénario d'un isolement complet du Royaume Uni, en tant que seul État Membre de l'UE ne participant pas à l'UEM, est cependant devenu moins probable.

77 Notes économiques, ARTESIA Banque, juin 2000.
78 Courrier économique et financier, KBC Banque, n°1, janvier 2001.
79 Voir FEB infor (Newsletter hebdomadaire), n°33, 6 octobre 2000.

Quant à la perspective de l'élargissement de l'Union européenne, les 13 pays qui sont officiellement candidats devront, une fois membres de l'UE, répondre aux critères de Maastricht pour participer à l'UEM. La plupart des candidats remplissent déjà le critère se rapportant aux finances publiques ou en sont très proches. Pour les critères relatifs à l'inflation, aux taux d'intérêt et à la stabilité des cours de change, le Courrier économique et financier de la KBC avance qu'il leur reste un long chemin à parcourir.

2.9 Résumé de la situation

Enfin, la situation pourrait être résumée comme suit: tout d'abord, les milieux financiers ne voient pas en général dans la faiblesse de l'euro un signe d'une bonne ou d'une mauvaise politique. Même s'ils restent persuadés que ce n'est que dans quelques dizaines d'années que l'on saura si l'UEM est une bonne ou mauvaise solution, ils trouvent que, techniquement parlant, l'euro est déjà un succès.

Plusieurs observateurs trouvent leur argument dans la crise de la Dioxine qu'a connue la Belgique au printemps 1999 et qui aurait sans doute eu un impact négatif sur le BEF, si cette devise avait encore été autonome. Grâce à l'euro, cette crise n'a guère eu de répercussions financières et économiques mais bien politiques.

Dans le même ordre d'idées, le gouverneur de la Banque Nationale de Belgique, M Guy Quaden, avait mentionné dans un de ses discours[80] que l'introduction de l'euro avait indéniablement contribué à créer un cadre économique plus stable dans les États membres. Il avait ajouté que cette stabilité était d'autant plus remarquable dans le cas de la Belgique pour laquelle la crise de la Dioxine aurait engendré de lourdes conséquences (macro-économiques) si l'euro n'était pas là. Sur un autre plan, il avait avancé que le manque de confiance de la part des entreprises et des consommateurs suite à la crise du pétrole en septembre 2000 avait tendance à se dissiper grâce aux performances qu'avait réalisé l'euro vers la fin de la même année. L'augmentation des prix du pétrole n'avait pas, selon lui, sérieusement touché la croissance économique européenne et la BCE avait fait ce qu'elle devait faire en matière d'inflation en intervenant plusieurs fois tout au long de l'an 2000. Enfin, il trouvait que les marchés avaient tendance à devenir plus réalistes: ils ne conservaient plus que les bonnes informations concernant le dollar et les mauvaises concernant l'euro, comme c'était le cas avant.

L'euro, reste selon la BNB, une monnaie qui a fait ses preuves sur les marchés financiers et elle fera davantage ses preuves auprès du grand public une fois qu'elle sera une monnaie tangible.

[80] 'De Hanze' International Club of West-Flanders, Speech of Guy Quaden, Bruges, 11 Jan 2001.

Sur le plan pratique, l'utilisation de l'euro comme monnaie scripturale, reste relativement limitée en Belgique même si l'introduction des pièces et des billets en euro approche à grands pas. En revanche, la Belgique fait partie du peloton de tête dans la zone euro en matière d'organisation d'un passage harmonieux à l'euro.

Cela dit, plusieurs aspects requièrent encore l'attention, comme cela fut constaté par le Commissariat général à l'euro lors de sa 6ème réunion plénière.[81] Il s'agit essentiellement de l'adaptation de la législation et de la réglementation, du basculement définitif des administrations publiques à tous les niveaux et de la préparation des PME et des particuliers.

En ce qui concerne l'union économique et monétaire, certains observateurs pensent qu'elle n'est pas encore une réalité et ses effets ne verront le jour que si la BCE tient compte des différences régionales dans l'élaboration de sa politique monétaire.

D'autres soulignent que le taux uniforme de la BCE est trop bas pour les pays qui affichent une croissance rapide, mais peut-être trop élevé pour les pays qui sont à la traîne et concluent que les pays ayant des chiffres de croissance et d'inflation divergents pourraient rencontrer des difficultés à collaborer. Pour faire face à cela, ils estiment que la BCE devrait recourir à d'autres instruments économiques.

En outre, la phase 3 de l'UEM est caractérisée par une double asymétrie à laquelle, plusieurs analystes attirent l'attention: la première asymétrie se réfère à la centralisation du pôle monétaire autour de la BCE qui prend place comme centre d'impulsion et de pouvoir et la décentralisation du pôle économique autour des États membres qui conservent l'essentiel des instruments de la politique économique. Cette forme d'asymétrie n'est pas impossible à surmonter.[82] Mais dans la situation actuelle de l'Union, elle risque de mettre à l'épreuve, durant quelques années encore, le degré de solidarité entre les États membres. La seconde asymétrie renvoie à la distinction entre les participants à la monnaie unique et les non participants. De ce fait, l'UEM est vue comme une union à deux vitesses à laquelle il faudra s'accommoder aussi longtemps que le processus d'élargissement est devant nous.

Enfin, la prochaine présidence belge donne beaucoup d'espoir aux milieux économiques et financiers belges dans la mesure où ils souhaitent qu'elle contribue à changer, de manière significative, l'environnement économique et financier européen.

[81] Voir Communiqué de presse 29 novembre 2000.

[82] Voir lettre mensuelle socio-économique du Secrétariat du Conseil Central de l'Economie (juin 1999).

ON THE OUTSIDE: DENMARK AND THE EURO

Karsten Skjalm *

1. Introduction

The year 2000 was a decisive year for Denmark's relation to the euro. Many international observers had long anticipated that Denmark was much closer to taking a plunge into the Euro-zone than Britain and Sweden, and that it would therefore be the first country among the 'wait-and-see brigade' to hold a referendum about the euro. Denmark was, through its long tradition of a fixed exchange rate policy and its strong desire to strictly adhere to the convergence criteria, to a large extent already behaving as though it was a member of the Euro-group. In addition, since late 1998 opinion polls had revealed a strong, if not overwhelming, stable majority of voters wanting to join the 3rd stage of the EMU. The prospect of an early referendum gained ever increasing political momentum when, at that point in time (October 1998), the Social Democratic-led government started to take on the special Danish exemption from the single currency that Denmark obtained as a part of the Edinburgh decision in 1992. On 9 March 2000, Prime Minister Poul Nyrup Rasmussen finally decided to call a referendum to take place on 28 September 2000.[83]

The referendum was widely regarded as crucial for Denmark's overall status in the European Union. On the one hand, the outcome of the referendum would decide whether Denmark should participate in one of the most dynamic core areas in the EU, the Euro-area. On the other hand, a negative vote in the referendum would very likely block successive referenda in the two other areas in which Denmark maintained exemptions according to the Edinburgh agreement: the CFSP, and home and justice affairs. The Danish euro-referendum was followed with great interest in Britain and Sweden because the outcome was likely to have an important impact on the outlook for an early euro-referendum in those countries. In a sense, the Danes were also voting for the Britons and Swedes.

As it turned out, a majority of 53.1 per cent of the voters decided to vote 'No'. The outcome was hardly surprising as the pro-euro camp lost its

* PhD, Senior Research Fellow, Danish Institute of International Affairs, Nytorv 5, DK-1450, Copenhagen.

[83] *Berlingske Tidende*, 10 Mar 2000, Nyrups historiske beslutning.

lead in the polls immediately after the referendum was called in March 2000. The polls indicated a dead heat during most of the campaign, until in early September when a decisive trend towards a 'No'-vote emerged. Politically, the negative outcome has left Denmark's EU policy in a state of disarray. Economically, the immediate effects were limited. The 'No'-vote had little immediate impact on the Danish currency, the kroner, and the short-term interest rate spread *vis-à-vis* the euro rate (this had widened during the campaign and has returned to its previous level of around 30 basis points).

In the light of the extremely important referendum event, this contribution to the *Eurospectator* project goes beyond the questions and the time period we have been asked to analyse. The paper is structured as follows. The second section provides a lengthy analysis of the Danish EMU debate since the IGC 1991 and up to the point when the referendum campaign started in March 2000. The third section aims to clarify the treaty obligations and rights of Denmark's status as a Member State with derogation from the final stage of EMU. The section furthermore attempts to discuss the implications of this membership status for Danish economic policy, and it also includes a brief discussion about the economic arguments in the referendum campaign. The fourth section describes the main principles behind the Danish economic policy in recent years, as well as the economic situation in the year of the referendum. In the fifth section we return to the political debate on the euro during the referendum campaign. The section attempts to provide a tentative analysis of the reasons for the outcome of the referendum. However, it should be borne in mind that the jury is still out on this important question, and we will have to await more definitive conclusions until comprehensive analysis and data are available. The sixth and final section describes the legal framework of the euro in Denmark.

2. The Maastricht legacy

2.1 Maastricht

When EMU was put on the agenda at the Hanover summit in June 1988, Denmark was governed by a pro-European conservative-liberal coalition. Two years earlier, in February 1986, the government had won an advisory referendum on the Single European Act, even though the Social democratic opposition managed to rally 70 per cent of their voters behind a 'No'-vote. The defeat at the referendum forced the Social Democratic Party (Socialdemokratiet, SDP) to revise its European policy. This process accelerated in the late 1980s when the SDP's spokeswoman on foreign affairs, Ritt Bjerregaard, and the party chairman and parliamentary leader, Svend Auken, gradually took over the leadership of the party's European policy.

Initially, the SDP was very sceptical, if not hostile, to the idea of a European monetary union. But this opposition weakened considerably during 1989 and 1990. By contrast, the government came out in favour of EMU from the beginning, counting that its room for manoeuvre on European policy was steadily widening. In spring 1990, the conservative-liberal coalition even supported the Kohl and Mitterrand suggestion of a fast track that would launch EMU as early as 1993.

This partial party-political realignment laid the ground for a broad inter-party agreement on the Danish platform for the 1991 Intergovernmental Conference (IGC). The 'Danish Memorandum on IGC' was signed by the government parties [Conservatives (*Det Konservative Folkeparti*), Liberals (*Venstre*) and Social Liberals (*Det Radikale Venstre*)] and the Social Democrats, and supported by the two small centre-right parties, the Centre Democrats (*Centrumdemokraterne*) and the Christian People's Party (*Kristeligt Folkeparti*). The Progress Party (*Fremskridtpartiet*) and the Socialist People's Party (*Socialistisk Folkeparti*), which constituted the far right and the left wing of the parliament respectively, remained hostile to the IGC. A Social Democratic Party still struggling with internal disagreement heavily influenced the memorandum. It contained the following main points concerning EMU:[84]

- EMU was viewed as a natural extension of the creation of the internal market. In order to reap the full economic benefits of EMU, in particular exchange rate stability, growth and employment, the memorandum favoured a rapid transition to the final stage, keeping the second stage as short as possible.
- The memorandum considered it natural that the primary objective of the monetary policy of the European Central Bank (ECB) be price stability, while the Ecofin-council should take care of other objectives when setting economic policy, including growth and employment. The memorandum suggested that the objective of full employment should be 'expressly included among the higher principles of the Community'. With a view to ensuring achievement of the Community's economic policy objectives, the Ecofin Council should be strengthened. This would also facilitate the necessary co-ordination between the Council and the ECB.
- Regarding the foreign exchange policy towards third countries, the memorandum suggested that the Ecofin Council make decisions concerning formal exchange rate arrangements, including realignment of central parities and the size of fluctuation bands, whereas the ECB should be responsible for the daily conduct of exchange rate policy. Here too, it was important to assure the Council of 'the necessary influ-

[84] Danish Government Memorandum, approved by the Market Committee of the Folketing, 4 Oct 1990.

ence'. This could be done through regular meetings between the chairman of the Ecofin Council and the ECB.
- Finally, in the area of fiscal and budgetary policy, the memorandum was strictly against the Council being able to make legally binding decisions about a Member State's 'budget surplus or deficit or its revenue and expenditure, just as distribution policy must remain a national matter. Anything else would be unacceptable to the national parliaments'. Multilateral surveillance and peer group pressure were regarded as sufficient to maintain budgetary discipline. At the time, taking this stance far from isolated Denmark. Only the German government insisted on legally binding criteria for budgetary policies.

In the final analysis, the Danish delegation—and in retrospect, this may come as a surprise—entered the IGC on a platform that was not dissimilar to the French one. At the intergovernmental conference, Denmark often broke ranks from the German-Dutch alliance to which it traditionally had belonged. However, apart from an ill-fated proposal to narrow the bands of exchange rate fluctuations in the second stage, Denmark kept a low profile throughout the EMU negotiations.

Meanwhile, political constellations were changing on the domestic scene. The Social Democrats won a spectacular victory at the parliamentary election in December 1990, and they were only a few seats short of ousting the Conservative-Liberal government. The party had still not solved its internal tensions over its European policy. As soon as it became clear that the Maastricht Treaty would not include any real institutional framework for promoting growth and employment, the opposition to a pro-European policy stiffened among the backbenchers and constituencies within the party. The Social Democrats' strengthened parliamentary position meant the government could not ignore the party's concerns.

This became clear in the final lap of the IGC when the British government pressed for a general opt-out clause on EMU in the Treaty. With the exception of Denmark, all the Member States rejected this position on the grounds that it would undermine the credibility of the whole process if all Member States did not give a clear and irrevocable pledge of their intent to go all the way with EMU. The issue was solved at marathon meetings of the Ecofin Council, one week before the Maastricht Summit. One protocol—that applied only to the UK—allowed the British government to decide (independently of the European Council) whether or not the UK was going to take part in the third stage of EMU. Another protocol—that applied to Denmark—allowed for a double Danish referendum on EMU shortly before the transition to the final stage (at the time most likely in 1996). The reason for separating the issue in two protocols was that the Danish delegation did not want the same protocol as the United Kingdom because their motivations were not the same.

Although the Maastricht Treaty, in its entirety, went beyond what had been suggested in the Danish memorandum, all political parties supported the Treaty, with the exception of the Progress Party and the Socialist People's Party.[85]

The Conservative and Liberal Parties, which had formed the government since the 1990 election, gave similar reasons for supporting EMU.[86] According to the Conservatives' spokesman, Henning Grove, Denmark's monetary sovereignty now meant that the Danish National Bank could wait half an hour to change the interest rate after the Bundesbank had moved on its rates. The Liberal Party's spokeswoman, Ms Charlotte Antonsen, said that, in reality, Denmark had given up its monetary sovereignty when the capital movements had been liberalised in the 1980s. EMU was thus a natural extension of the internal market. Monetary sovereignty had become obsolete *pari passu* with the implementation of the Single European Act, and EMU would furthermore reduce the transaction costs and risk of exchange rate instability (which were costly for Danish companies). EMU would therefore contribute to growth and employment.

The Social Democrats' spokesmen, Bjoern Westh and Ivar Noergaard, also spoke in favour of the Treaty, although Ivar Noergaard would have liked the Treaty to mention the objective of full employment on an equal footing with price stability. The main reason for SDP's rather positive attitude was that the above-mentioned EMU-protocol had provided Denmark with a wait-and-see option.

The Socialist People's party argued against the Maastricht Treaty, which was seen as the foundation of a United States of Europe, implying a tremendous centralisation of power. The party also argued against EMU on economic grounds, believing that the convergence criteria and the monetary constitution would create more unemployment. The Progress Party, which could only support an EC in the form of a greater free-trade area, was squarely against the Treaty.

85 The smallest political party in the parliament, the Christian People's Party had however become openly split on the Treaty.

86 Fortryk af Folketingets Forhandlinger, 17 Mar 1992, Col. 7784–7792. On 10 Mar 1992, the government put forward a bill which would authorise the government to ratify the Maastricht Treaty, technically by changing the Danish accession law of 11 Oct 1972. The bill went through a first parliamentary reading on 17 Mar 1992. The pros and cons of EMU, and the Maastricht Treaty as a whole, were repeated at the second and third reading on 30 Apr and 12 May, and they also dominated the subsequent referendum debate. At the end of the third reading on 12 May, the parliament authorised ratification of the Maastricht Treaty with 130 votes in favour and only 25 votes against. Since a majority of 5 to 6 existed, there was no need for a referendum in legal terms. However, for political reasons, the government had already decided to hold a referendum on 2 June 1992.

During the short referendum campaign, the small anti-Union movement (organised mainly in various non-parliamentary movements) faced a massive political constellation consisting of all the parties represented in parliament (with the exception of the two smaller parties mentioned above), the business community, the trade unions and almost all the major newspapers. However, the opinion polls showed a narrow race, indicating that the political elite was seriously out of tune with the general public. In the last ten days before the referendum, the polls moved in the direction of an increasing 'Yes'-majority. The last poll, conducted one day before the referendum, had a 45.7 per cent 'yes' vote and a 40.8 per cent 'No', with 13.5 per cent undecided. Nonetheless, the referendum on 2 June gave a narrow 'No' vote victory. 49.3 per cent voted in favour of the Treaty, 50.7 per cent voted against. At 81.3 per cent, the turnout was rather high.

Despite the Danish 'No', the 11 other Member States decided to carry on with their ratification processes, leaving it to the Danish government to create a formula for Denmark's participation in the European Union. Needless to say, the negative vote left the Danish political elite in a state of disarray, not least the Social Democrats whose voters had defied the party line in large numbers.

At the Social Democratic Party congress in September 1992, the party consequently readjusted its platform arguing against Danish participation in EMU's third stage, as well as in the defence dimension, including the WEU, union citizenship, and supranational co-operation in justice and home affairs. During the summer of 1992, various exit polls and academic surveys unanimously singled out these four areas as main reasons for the 'No' vote. In the run-up to the referendum, the Socialist People's party had published its demands for renegotiations in case of a 'No' vote, mentioning that Denmark should be kept out of the four policy areas. The same demands were raised in a joint-declaration of the anti-EU movements shortly before the referendum.

In October 1992, the Social Democratic Party, the Socialist People's Party and the Social Liberal Party worked out a proposal to solve the Danish problem. The core of the paper, *Denmark in Europe*, consisted of the four points mentioned above: Denmark should be allowed to be exempt from the third stage of EMU and the defence dimension, and should be allowed to be uncommitted with respect to union citizenship and supranational co-operation in home and justice affairs. Furthermore, an agreement should be legally binding and time-unlimited. The paper was presented to the Conservative–Liberal government as a *fait accompli.* Although it disliked the paper, the government supported it, knowing that it would fall from power if it failed to do so. The European Council meeting in Edinburgh on 11–12 December 1992 generally accepted the Danish demands as presented in the 'National Compromise' (*Denmark in*

Europe). On Denmark's relation with EMU, the European Council concluded:[87]

1. The Protocol on certain provisions relating to Denmark attached to the Treaty establishing the European Community gives Denmark the right to notify the Council of the European Communities of its position concerning participation in the third stage of Economic and Monetary Union. Denmark has given notification that it will not participate in the third stage. This notification will take effect upon the coming into effect of this decision.
2. As a consequence, Denmark will not participate in the single currency, will not be bound by the rules concerning economic policy which apply only to the Member States participating in the third stage of Economic and Monetary Union, and will retain its existing powers in the field of monetary policy, according to its national laws and regulations, including powers of the National Bank of Denmark in the field of monetary policy.
3. Denmark will participate fully in the second stage of Economic and Monetary Union and will continue to participate in exchange-rate co-operation within the European Monetary System (EMS).

When the Maastricht Treaty, as supplemented by the Edinburgh decisions, was sent to a second referendum on 18 May 1993, there was a clear majority of 56.7 per cent voting 'Yes'. 43.3 per cent voted 'No'. (The turnout had increased slightly to 86.5 per cent). At no time during the campaign was the positive vote threatened.

2.2 The lessons from the Maastricht ratification process

In the debate that followed the 'No'-vote in June 1992, there was broad agreement that the European integration process was proceeding much faster than the general public was willing to accept. The political parties and movements suggested different responses to this lesson.

According to the pro-European parties (in particular the Liberal Party, and, to a certain extent, the Conservatives), the political establishment should make greater efforts to explain why European integration had to move into higher gear in response to external events (particularly the unification of Germany and the profound changes in Eastern Europe), as well as why Denmark needed to belong to the core of this process. Early on, the Liberal Party—led by Uffe Ellemann-Jensen (the Danish Foreign Minister, 1982–93—made clear that it wanted to get rid of the exemptions as soon as possible.

[87] European Council and the arrangements for Denmark, Conclusions of the Edinburgh summit, 11–12 Dec 1992.

This position created frequent frictions with the Social Democrats, which in early 1993 finally formed a coalition government under the leadership of Poul Nyrup Rasmussen. Apart from respecting the national compromise, the Social Democrats emphasised that the European Union needed to be brought closer to the concerns of the citizens. This implied a strengthening of the principles of subsidiarity, transparency and openness, as well as making employment, the environment and social welfare priority issues.

The Socialist Party (*Socialistisk Folkeparti*) emerged deeply divided from the ratification process. The pro-European wing broadly subscribed to the strategy suggested by the Social Democrats, whereas the Eurosceptics emphasised the need to halt the integration process. If this was not possible because it required support from other Member States, Denmark should ask for more opt-outs. Since the mid-1990s, the Socialist Party leadership had aimed at forging a consensus between the two camps by emphasising the need to strengthen EU co-operation in some soft-issue areas (especially environmental policies, although the Member States' right to keep higher standard should be strictly obeyed) and stressing the need for a more flexible Europe, with a view to the Eastern enlargement.

The outright sceptics camp consists of the far right (mainly the Danish People's party, *Dansk Folkeparti*, created in 1995 through a split in the Progress party and the fourth biggest party in parliament after the 1998 election) and the left (The Red-Greens, *Enhedslisten* which gained four seats in parliament at the 1994 election), as well as the two political movements outside the national parliament, the June Movement (*Junibevægelsen*, which supports Denmark's membership although it wants European integration rolled back to the situation prior to Maastricht, that is, the single European market) and the People's Movement Against EC (Folkebevægelsen mod EF, which wants Denmark to leave the EU). This multicoloured host of parties and movements continuously warned the public against the slippery slope of European integration and warned the political establishment against fiddling with the opt-outs.

Apart from the Liberal Party's frequent snipes at the exemptions, the second referendum in May 1993 was followed by broad agreement from the political parties to stick to the national compromise. Nevertheless, the Prime Minister often had to remind the public that 'the exemptions stand. They are not, and will not, be up for discussion'. The reason for this was threefold.

First, between late 1994 and the general election on 11 March 1998, the government often trailed in the polls after the Conservative-Liberal coalition. In this period, the Liberal Party decisively became the biggest opposition party; at times the polls indicated that it was even bigger than the Social Democrats. The Liberal Party's hostile attitude towards the exemptions thus formed part of a larger strategy of keeping a distinctive opposition profile, while the Social Democrats' fierce protection of the exemptions was one way of presenting itself as an honest and responsible governmental party concerned with the real needs of the citizens.

Another reason for the Prime Minister's frequent interventions was the mounting external pressure on the exemptions. As long as European integration kept moving, it was evident that at least some of the exemptions would have to be evaluated at some point in time. Otherwise Denmark would gradually move further away from the core of the European Union when some of the policy areas concerning the exemptions were deepened. By late 1995, when the European Council made it clear that the euro would be launched at the date envisaged in the Treaty (1 January 1999), the further construction of the EMU architecture started to accelerate. Three years later, the construction of the European defence policy also started to accelerate.

However, the mounting external pressure did not imply, that the government's pronouncements increasingly lacked domestic credibility. For five years after 1993 opinion polls unanimously showed a clear and almost rock-steady majority of voters favouring the preservation of the EMU opt-out.

The opinion polls also revealed that, among the pro-European parties, the Social Democratic voters (particularly unskilled labour and the unemployed, who traditionally count among the party's core voters) were the strongest opponents of abandoning the exemption. Within these voter segments, the Social Democrats have since 1994 lost voters in rather large numbers to the EU-sceptic parties, the Socialist People's Party and the Danish People's Party. Although this voter movement cannot be explained by the European question, it contributes to explaining the Social Democratic leadership's fierce protection of the exemptions, especially when one takes into account that the government has often trailed in the polls after the Conservative-Liberal coalition.

Finally, after 1993, the Prime Minister and his cabinet always looked ahead to one very likely event: another EU-referendum, this time on the Amsterdam Treaty. Constitutionally, this referendum was not necessary if a majority of five-sixths was available in the parliament. Such a majority probably existed, but it was politically inevitable after the events in 1992 and 1993.[88] The government knew that the referendum was a big political gamble, but it had no other option if it wanted to preserve the trust of the

[88] According to Art 20 of the Danish Constitution, a referendum is not necessary if the treaty in question does not imply any transfer of sovereignty. That the new treaty would imply transfer of sovereignty became clear when the Irish draft treaty was put forward in the run-up to the Dublin Summit in December 1996. From that moment the Danish voters were almost certain to vote in another referendum. See *Politiken*, 6 Dec 1996, 'EU-reform kræver afstemning' and *Jyllandsposten*, 6 Dec 1996, 'Danmark på vej mod ny EU-afstemning'.

voters. It also knew that a positive vote would be against all odds, if it started to play with the status of the exemptions. Throughout the years, the strong anti-Union movement had repeatedly warned the voters that the government would take on the exemptions one day.

For these reasons, it was evident that the EMU exemption—and any other exemptions—would not be up for discussion in the long period leading up to the referendum on the Amsterdam treaty. As soon as it became clear during the Intergovernmental Conference that the new Treaty would imply a transfer of sovereignty, and that a new Danish referendum would become necessary, even the chairman of the Liberal Party and leader of the opposition (Uffe Ellemann-Jensen) announced that the Danish voters were not prepared for a referendum on the exemptions, and that a public debate would be futile.[89] From that moment in the second half of 1996, the Danish debate on EMU was closed.

2.3 1995–98: Growing divide between the Danish EU-debate and the European integration process

2.3.1 The Euro-X episode

Thus, both public discussion on the EMU exemption and political discussion about what the EMU negotiations on the Stability Pact and the ERM-II meant for Denmark and its position in Europe, became taboo. This was despite the fact that EMU-related issues, particularly the Stability Pact, always took centre-stage during the Intergovernmental Conference.[90]

There was one notable exception, namely, the political events around the creation of the Euro Council in late 1997. Briefly described, the background for the Euro Council was as follows: in November 1995, the German finance minister Theo Waigel launched his proposal for a 'Stability Pact' to enforce budgetary discipline in the third stage of EMU.[91] In France, Waigel's proposal was viewed as another attempt to tilt the EMU construction towards the German Maastricht vision. This prompted French finance minister Jean Arthuis to revive the old French idea of an 'economic government' in order to 'counterbalance' the strengthened monetary pillar in the EMU construction.[92] For a long time this French

[89] At the Liberal Partyís annual congress in Sept 1996, Uffe Ellemann-Jensen said that the time was not ripe and it would be 'a capital offence' to make a referendum now when the polls unanimously showed a firm public opposition to abandoning the exemptions. See *Politiken*, 23 Sept 1996, 'Venstre trækker i EU-bremsen'.

[90] The only newspaper persistently trying to raise a political debate on EMU and on the Danish EMU-exemption was the business newspaper, Boersen, especially thanks to its strongly engaged editor, Mr Leif Beck Fallesen.

[91] See Waigel (1995).

[92] See e.g. the section, 'Pôle monétaire, et pôle politique' in Arthuis (1998), 219–22. See also *Financial Times*, 18 June 1996, 'France proposes EMU club to co-ordinate economic policies'. See also the interview with Arthuis in *La Tribune* on 23 Sept 1996 in which he says:

idea met with fierce resistance from the Bundesbank and the German government, which saw it as another bold French attempt to get around the independence of the European Central Bank.[93] Having ensured a satisfactory agreement on the Stability Pact at the Dublin Summit, as well as strong and very clear French guarantees that the new institution would not interfere with the independence of the ECB, Waigel and the Bundesbank finally abandoned their resistance at a Franco-German meeting in Lyons in March 1997.[94] In turn, France accepted that—in order to emphasise the German philosophy underlying the single currency project—the new body would be called 'the stability council'. Another round of negotiations followed the French socialists' surprising electoral victory in May-June 1997, ending with the new French government giving the same guarantees as the previous one.[95] The council was re-dubbed Euro-X, with the 'X' being filled in by the number of the participants in EMU (to be decided in May 1998). Having reached a second Franco-German compromise, it became clear that the French wanted to deny access to the non-members of EMU (including Denmark, Sweden, the UK, and probably Greece), and also to use this council to discuss all sorts of issues that were, not exclusively related to the Euro-zone[96] (such as labour market and employment policies, tax policies and social issues).[97]

The Franco-German deal was an immediate threat to the position of the future 'outs' of the euro. Although Germany insisted that the Euro-X council would be informal, without any decision-making power, there was a risk that real negotiations (including agenda setting) would take place in the Euro-X council. The prospect that the Euro-X council could 'pre-cook'

'There needs to be a balance between the monetary and political authority . . . With the euro and the stability council, our wish for an appreciating dollar would be heard more clearly'. It was exactly such remarks, which evoked the German fears.

[93] See, eg, remarks by State Secretary Jürgen Stark, in *Financial Times*, 20 June 1996; interview with Otmar Issing, at the time chief economist in the Bundesbank, in *Wirtschaftswoche*, 15 August 1996; interview with Hans Tietmeyer, President of the Bundesbank, in *Die Zeit*, 23 Jan 1997; interview with Johan Wilhelm Gaddum, Vice-President the Bundesbank, in *Handelsblatt*, 30 January 1997; and finally the remarks by Theo Waigel at the World Economic Forum in Davos on 2 Feb 1997, cited in *European Report*, 5 Feb 1997.

[94] *Financial Times*, 13 Mar 1997, 'Waigel reassured over EMU Stability Council'.

[95] See *International Herald Tribune*, 20–21 Sept 1997, 'Jospin Accepts Central Bank'; *Les Echos*, 22 Sept 1997, 'Sommet de Weimar: Paris et Bonn renouent avec les concessions mutuelles'; and *Wall Street Journal*, 15 Oct 1997, 'Germany and France agree at last on 1999 Economic Policy Forum'.

[96] The issues exclusively specific for the Euro-zone are admittedly hard to define. But according to a narrow reading of the Treaty, they are: 1) decisions on penalties under the Stability Pact; 2) decisions on formal exchange rate arrangements in the Euro-zone; 3) decisions on the design of euro notes and coins.

[97] See in particular speech by Pierre Moscovici, French Minister of European Affairs at the IFRI-Institute on 14 Oct 1997 (Moscovici (1997)) and Dominique Strauss-Kahn's article in *Financial Times* on 28 Nov 1997 (Strauss-Kahn (1997)), as well as interview with Strauss-Kahn in *Der Spiegel*, 8 Dec 1997.

Ecofin negotiations and decisions threatened to undermine the status of the latter, to which the 'out' countries belonged. At worst, the Ecofin council would be reduced to a place for formal endorsement of deliberations that had already taken place in the Euro-X council. This would undermine the bargaining power of the future 'outs'.

Thus the 'out' countries' ministers barked loudly when the proposal was put forward at the Ecofin council meeting in November 1997. Beside the Swedish finance minister, Erik Asbrink, the Danish minister of economy, Ms Marianne Jelved, spoke most loudly against the proposal. Jelved repeatedly claimed that the Franco-German proposal divided the EU into blocs, thereby putting the unity and solidarity of the Union at risk, and that it probably breached the EU Treaty. Speaking after the Ecofin council's first formal discussion at its meeting on 17 November 1997, Jelved said:

> This is the first time in EU's history that not all Member States can participate in a council in which real decisions can be made. [The council] therefore undermines the solidarity, which is the foundation of co-operation in the EU . . . If you get two classes of members, what would then happen when Hungary and other Eastern European countries join the Union? Would it be possible to create the traditionally positive climate, which keeps the Union together? I would like to question that (. . .) [The point is that the other Member States] want a formal endorsement from all ministers of finance and economy to establish a council in which not all can participate. And in Euro-X they will discuss all important issues. The Treaty does not specifically allow for this, and therefore I cannot accept [the council].[98]

This statement nicely encapsulated the main arguments Mrs Jelved made in the heated discussions in the weeks prior to the Luxembourg Summit in December 1997. Jelved also made an additional argument, mainly for domestic consumption. Speaking at the annual meeting of the Danish Bankers' Association in Copenhagen on 3 December 1997, she said:

> This [Euro-X] case also demonstrates that the Danish opt-outs weaken our possibilities and influence in European Union co-operation. For Europe's sake, but not least for our own sake, it is therefore important that we get a 'Yes' on 28 May 1998, to the Amsterdam Treaty.

One should not question Jelved's real motives for making such a fuss about the creation of the Euro council. Her concerns were genuine and right, and she fought a hard fight behind the closed doors of the Ecofin Council. She initially tried to make the council as unofficial as possible,[99]

[98] *Politiken*, 18 Nov 1997, 'Jelved: EU vil brÊkke over'.

[99] Specifically, she attempted to deny the Euro-countries' access to EU facilities, including buildings, interpreters, covering of travelling costs, dinner and drinks. Here, it should be noted that for regular Ecofin meetings, the EU budget pays for the flights of most ministers and their assistants, around thirty-three interpreters plus stand-by translators, two assistants to serve coffee and handle sound and other technical problems and dinner served by outside

then she questioned the legality of the council, and she later attempted to define clear restrictions for the council's agenda. Her final approach was to try to ensure that Denmark would have formal access to the council. Her attempts were all in vain, as the future would soon reveal.

That Jelved might also have had a domestic agenda is reasonably clear. The Swedish finance minister, Erik Asbrink, and Prime Minister Göran Persson never made the point that their voters should have it clear about the adverse consequences for Sweden of not being member of the Euro-X council and that it was time the voters evaluated their attitudes to the EU. In fact, Asbrink and Persson repeatedly made the opposite point, claiming that the Euro-X council might create a negative domestic backlash. Speaking at a news conference after the jobs summit on 20 November 1997, Persson said:

> it would be up to the Swedish people to decide whether to join in the future. But if [the Euro countries] act harshly, if they act without feeling for national opinion, they might close the door.[100]

Jelved never appealed to the Euro countries to take into consideration the possible negative reaction the creation of the Euro-X council might evoke among the Danish voters. This was despite the fact that Denmark was rapidly approaching a referendum on the new EU-treaty, the outcome of which could easily create the same kind of European disarray as in 1992. Instead, she appealed to the Danish voters.

Throughout the years, Jelved—who is also the chairman of the Social Liberal Party, the junior partner of the government—never tried to hide the fact that she was a staunch supporter of EMU, and that she would like Denmark to participate as soon as possible. But until late 1998 (see below), she never openly tried to launch a political debate about the EMU opt-out. Her official position was the same as the Prime Minister's: 'The opt-outs stand. They are not up for discussion before, during, and after the (Amsterdam) intergovernmental conference'. At times, she hinted at the obvious, namely, that this could change in the future. Instead of overtly attacking the opt-outs, Jelved pursued a subtler tactic: whenever she had the chance, she pointed to the fact that Denmark was losing influence by remaining on the outside.

2.3.2 The Amsterdam referendum campaign

The main objective of the Intergovernmental Conference in 1996–7 was to prepare the European Union institutionally for enlargement. However, it

caterers. The costs of laying on such council meetings have never been calculated. See *Reuters*, 14 Nov 1997, 'Who pays for dinner—threat to EMU policy deal'.

100 *Reuters*, 20 Nov 1997, 'EU leaders air EMU dispute at jobs summit'.

quickly became clear that the negotiations on the Stability Pact and other EMU-related issues absorbed the energy, leaving institutional reform with a secondary status in the conference. Only little progress had been achieved on it during the Irish presidency. The Dutch presidency, which took over in January 1997, soon realised that the negotiations could not proceed until after the election in Britain, and a new British government—hopefully a new Labour government—had been installed. A furher unexpected setback occurred when Jacques Chirac, the French president, dissolved the French parliament in late April 1997, calling for general elections on 25 May and 1 June, only two weeks prior to the Amsterdam summit. Consequently, the EU largely failed to achieve its official IGC mission, namely, the reform of its institutions. The Member States managed to streamline the decision-making procedures along the co-decision procedure. However, the transition to majority voting within fields, where unanimity still applied, was limited, as were the all-important adjustment of voting weights in the Council of Ministers and the number of commissioners a Member State could obtain. These important reforms were postponed to a future mini-conference, which was concluded in Nice in December 2000.

One could easily argue that the 1996–7 IGC revealed the true weights of objectives among the core-countries in the EU: before the Eastern enlargement, European integration had to be deepened, not only with the launch of the euro but also with further economic policy integration. Nonetheless, EMU was a taboo in the Danish debate. The Eastern enlargement was presented to the public as though it were the only major integration project in preparation. Almost all the Danish political parties and movements whole-heartedly supported the Eastern enlargement project; Eastern enlargement offered the Danish government an opportunity to have a say in European affairs at a time when it was in a weak position to influence the other major integration project (EMU). Denmark, thus, became one of the staunchest supporters of Eastern enlargement, particularly regarding enlargement to incorporate the Baltic countries (whose participation was always in doubt). For this reason, compared to the Economic and Monetary Union, Eastern enlargement received overly much publicity in the Danish media between 1995 and 1998. The EU-sceptics supported Eastern enlargement for two reasons. First, they believed that the enlargement would put an end to further integration ('more Union' as it is dubbed in the Danish debate). Due to the size and heterogeneity of the future EU, the EU would at the very least have to give up the unity principle allowing for looser associations (flexibility). Secondly, they sensed that it would be a capital political crime to question the enlargement.

EMU was conspicuously absent from the agenda of the Amsterdam referendum campaign, the more so since the campaign took place at the same time as the European Council made its all-important decision to launch the euro with 11 Member States on 1 January 1999 (only seven months away), and as the European Central Bank was about to be created. By the end of the referendum campaign, the Danish Prime Minister made the dubious promise that if the voters voted 'Yes', it would significantly slow down progress towards 'more Union', because the road to a larger and more heterogeneous EU would be cleared. He also promised that he did not envisage any new referenda for at least another four years.[101]

The arguments of the EU-sceptical parties and movements were also troubled with fault lines. They claimed that a 'Nc'-vote would also halt the integration process, as it would create a similar European shock to that in 1992, causing the other Member States to stop and think once again. Therefore, Denmark should not insist on new exemptions this time. In any event, such exemptions would be difficult to construct because of the few changes in the Treaty. Denmark should instead raise the stakes much higher by insisting on an overall renegotiation of the Treaty. The main purpose of such a renegotiation would be to allow scope for all applicant countries, and not only five as stated in the 'enlargement protocol'. This line of argument not only rested on a misreading of the protocol and the spirit of the enlargement process in general, it was also logically incoherent. On the one hand, the EU-sceptics claimed that a renegotiation on the Treaty was necessary to prepare the Union for full enlargement. On the other hand, they were strictly against any re-weighting of Council votes to favour the larger Member States, and they also resisted movements towards more majority voting in the Council as well as ceilings on the number of commissioners that might cause the smaller Member States to loose their commissioner.

In the end, the pro-European camp prevailed and the Amsterdam Treaty was approved by 55 per cent of the voters (45 per cent voted against).

2.3.3 Autumn 1998: the turning point in the Danish EMU-debate

With the Amsterdam Treaty hurdle cleared, the Danish government could finally start addressing the EMU exemption. The main problem was the many promises made by it to stick to the exemptions. The government had to wait for the right moment. As late as 15 September 1998, the Social Democratic Party congress made another resolution on preserving the exemptions.

To the surprise of almost everybody, Prime Minister Poul Nyrup Rasmussen finally moved one month later. In an interview with five regional newspapers published on 18 October 1998, Nyrup Rasmussen

[101] *Berlingske Tidende*, 26 May 1998, 'Poul Nyrup: EU slækker tempoet' and the interview in *Weekendavisen* on the referendum day 28 May 1998, 'Nyrup: Ikke flere traktater'.

said that there would be no Danish referendum on EMU before 2002. He added that he:

did not at any moment reproach the Danish population for not being able to relate to a theoretical project [such as the EMU]. The population should quietly be able to watch the EMU-countries' co-operation developing for better or for worse. The population would have to see whether the baby grows big and strong before it could relate.[102]

Despite the dubious remark on the EMU being a theoretical project—made at a time when the Euro was only few weeks away—the real point was that, for the first time, the Prime Minister contemplated the idea of a referendum on EMU.

The ball started rolling from this point. Indicating that he meant business, Nyrup Rasmussen repeated his statement in a string of interviews over the next weeks. Quoted in leading daily newspaper *Berlingske Tidende* on 24 October 1998, the Prime Minister said: 'I don't know when [to have a referendum]. But when I weigh the pros and cons, the conclusion is this: Yes, I think there will be a referendum on the EMU.'[103] In a later interview with *Berlingske Tidende*, he made it clear that only the EMU-exemption would be up for discussion.[104] After the Pörtschach summit in late October, he said: 'it will be extremely unwise for the preservation of Denmark's interests if we started saying: Not see, not hear, and not speak. We cannot every time hide behind our exemptions and say, we do not dare, we will not'.[105]

The real puzzle was the timing of Nyrup Rasmussen's campaign. Why now? In the series of interviews, he kept on returning to one theme: the global financial crisis. For instance, in the 24 October interview with *Berlingske Tidende*, he said that the Euro-zone had shown great resistance to 'the wild birds of the financial markets': 'If the EU is able to manage the financial crisis, this will be the best signal to give the Danish population in the coming debate on EMU'.[106] The all-important point was that, despite showing strong economic fundamentals and having pursued a rock-steady fixed exchange rate policy for years (unlike the Euro-countries, some of which had weaker economic fundamentals), Denmark was not immune to the August and September financial crisis. In August, the Danish National Bank had to support the krone using dkr 16bn of its reserves,[107] and in late September it had to resort to the expensive interest rate instrument, increasing the discount with no less than 1 per cent (from 4 to 5 per cent).

102 *Aalborg Stiftstidende*, 18 Oct 1998, 'Drop den krisesnak'.
103 *Berlingske Tidende*, 24 Oct 1998, 'Nyryp: Danmark skal stemme om ØMU'.
104 Ibid, 29 Oct 1998, 'Nyrup: Kun debat om ØMU'.
105 Quoted in *Berlingske Tidende*, 29 Oct 1998, 'Historien om et forudsigeligt EU-opgør'.
106 *Berlingske Tidende*, 24 Oct 1998, 'Nyrup: Danmark skal stemme om ØMU'.
107 Danmarks Nationalbank (1998), 9.

The financial crisis threatened the foundations of Denmark's economic policy.

Another likely factor determining the timing was that the leading opposition party, the Liberal Party, as well as circles in the business community, seized the financial crisis to launch another siege of the EMU-exemption. From the outbreak of the attack on the Danish kroner, Liberal Party members, including its new chairman, Anders Fogh Rasmussen, put pressure on the government to commit itself to a referendum on EMU, possibly by 2001 so that Denmark could join EMU when the single currency is put into circulation.

A final important factor determining the timing was the development of the opinion polls: on 12 October 1998, a few days before Nyrup Rasmussen was interviewed by the regional papers, the reputable *Greens Analyseinstitut* (the only poll institute that has tracked the public attitudes to the four exemptions on a monthly basis), published the first poll in history that indicated that a significant majority of the voters were ready to give up the EMU-exemption and vote in favour of joining EMU. 41 per cent said they would vote 'Yes' in a referendum on EMU; 37.5 per cent said they would vote 'No'. Just as significantly, the poll also showed for the first time that a majority of Social Democratic voters would vote in favour of joining EMU (42 per cent against 40 per cent). However, the Prime Minister rejected suggestions that he had been looking at the polls before making his intervention.

During 1999, the Danish euro-debate tended to focus more on the question of when to have a referendum than the substantial political and economic issues related to the single currency. To the extent that the political parties were discussing the substantial issues, they were mainly reiterating their Maastricht arguments for joining or not-joining the single currency. For this reason, the Liberal Party urged the Prime Minister to proceed and called for a snap referendum: 'We have already had the debate, so let's go on. . .'. However, the Prime Minister was wary about the risk of another Maastricht referendum—and, in particular, about his own social democratic constituencies' lukewarm attitude to joining the euro and to EU-integration in general—and he maintained that it was necessary to have a lengthy debate about the pros and cons of joining, before he would consider an actual date for the referendum. The political parties were scarce of funds and staff and did not seem to be eager to engage in a very long campaign, but they all attached enormous weight to the issue. For this reason, political pressure mounted on the Prime Minister to set a date for the referendum. In Summer 1999, after consulting his own party, the Prime Minister announced that unless something unexpected happened (such as a currency crisis), the euro referendum would be held somewhere between the Social Democratic Party congress in September 2000 (a congress that was expected to conclude the party's internal euro debate) and the next parliamentary election in March 2002.[108] On 9 March 2000, the Prime Minister announced that the referendum would take place very early within this time interval, namely on 28 September 2000. Nothing unexpected had happened, but the government had become increasingly aware that the mounting political momentum necessitated an early referendum. Postponing the date of the referendum would not add value to the debate; it might actually be counter-productive as it could produce the mixed signal that the government itself was unsure about whether joining the euro was the best thing for Denmark. Postponing the referendum also entailed the risk that the euro debate would be entangled with wider EU integration issues, such as the IGC on the Nice Treaty and the European defence dimension, the negotiations of which were likely to accelerate in the late autumn of 2000. The Prime Minister and his government wanted to steer the euro debate clear of these thorny issues, and therefore decided to choose one of the earliest possible dates within the timeframe that the Prime Minister had laid down.

3. Denmark's derogation status: rights and obligations

Denmark retains its national currency and competence over its monetary and exchange rate policy. This means that Denmark's central bank maintains its power to issue notes and coins in Denmark, and formal control over short-term interest rates for banks' and credit institutions' drafts and deposits in the central bank. In consultation with the central bank, the government likewise maintains control over the Danish exchange rate policy. In other words, the Danish krone will not be irreversibly locked *vis-à-vis* the Euro-countries' currencies, and it will not be replaced by the euro while Denmark maintains its opt-out.

This means that Denmark does not participate in the Euro-system's decision-making bodies.[109] As the governor of Denmark's national bank is not represented at the ECB governing council,[110] and a Dane cannot be appointed to the ECB's executive board,[111] no Dane sits at the table when monetary policy decisions are made in the EU. In addition, Denmark has no right to vote on possible exchange rate policy guidelines or formal arrangements connecting the euro to other big currencies (the dollar and the yen) in the Council of Ministers unless it participates in the euro.[112] Finally, Denmark does not participate in the Euro-countries' representation in international institutions such as the G7 and the IMF. In the European System of Central Banks (ESCB), Denmark only participates in

108 *Politiken*, 13. Aug 1999, 'Nyrup: Euroafgørelse i S næste år'.
109 Art 43 in the ESCB Protocol.
110 Art 112 EC and Art 43 in the ESCB Protocol.
111 Art 43 in the ESCB Protocol.
112 Art 111 EC and Art 43 in the ESCB Protocol.

the General Council that does not have any competence concerning the common monetary and exchange rate policy. The General Council is solely a contact body for the exchange of information between the Euro-countries' and the non-participating Member States' central banks.

Even though Denmark does not participate in the single currency, this does not mean that the country has full formal control over its monetary and exchange rate policy. As a Member State with derogation, Denmark has to respect a number of obligations that are stipulated in the Treaty and in secondary legislation.

First, Denmark's central bank must in accordance with the Treaty and the ESCB-ECB Statute be independent.[113] Secondly, Denmark is required to adjust its monetary policy with a view to maintaining price stability[114] (although this does not have to be the central bank's *primary* objective).[115] Price stability has indeed become a primary objective of the monetary policy of all EU Member States, but this seems to reflect a global trend rather than developments within the EU.

The objective of price stability can be pursued in two ways: first the non-participating Member States can pursue a *fixed exchange rate policy* by tying their monetary policy to that of the ECB within the framework of the ERM2. Secondly, the non-participating Member States may independently pursue an inflation target without support from the Euro-system. Denmark has chosen the first model. When Greece joins the single currency in 2001, Denmark will be the only non-participating Member State in the ERM2. Britain and Sweden have so far chosen an inflation target and flexible exchange rates.

According to the Treaty, the non-participating Member States shall treat their exchange rate policies as a matter of common interest.[116] The Council of Ministers therefore monitors their exchange rate policies in order to prevent major exchange rate fluctuations that could harm the internal market and the Euro-countries' competitiveness.[117] The non-participating Member States are required to regularly submit convergence programmes that contain medium-term objectives, and inflation and exchange rate forecasts.[118] If the Council of Ministers finds that the

113 Art 108 EC and Art 7 in the ESCB Protocol.

114 Arts 2, 4, 116.2 and 117.2 EC and Art 2 of the ESCB Protocol.

115 Art 109 EC.

116 Art 124 EC.

117 Art 99 EC and Council Regulation 1466/97.

118 The non-participating Member States' obligation to pursue a stability-oriented monetary and exchange rate policy is also expressed in the Council of Ministers' resolution on the establishment of the ERM2 in 1997. The resolution stresses that permanent economic convergence between the Euro-zone and the non-participating Member States is a precondition for exchange rate stability between the euro and other EU currencies. In order to achieve this, all Member States must pursue a stable monetary policy geared towards price stability. According to the resolution (para 1.2), this is deemed necessary to ensure a functioning internal market and to avoid trade distortions between the Member States. The ERM2 agreement, thus, provides an institutional framework which 'contributes to secure that Member States outside the Euro-zone . . . orientate their policies towards stability and economic convergence which helps them to join the euro later' (para 1.3).

content of the convergence programmes should be strengthened, the Council may ask the non-participating Member State to adjust its programme. If necessary, the Council can make such recommendations public. The Treaty thus produces a clear asymmetry between the Euro-zone and the non-participating Member States' mutual influence on monetary and exchange rate policies. The non-participating Member States have no influence on the Euro-zone's monetary and exchange rate policy but, through their qualified majority in the Council of Ministers, the Euro-members can forward recommendations as to the non-participating Member States' monetary and exchange rate policy.

Membership of the ERM2 is a precondition for joining the euro. But in the Danish (and British) case, membership is purely voluntary because of the permanent opt-out from the single currency that Denmark obtained as a part of the Edinburgh decision. Membership of ERM was an explicit objective of the national compromise that laid the foundation for the Edinburgh decision in 1992. This objective also reflects Denmark's tradition of a fixed exchange rate policy. In September 1998, Denmark successfully reached an agreement with the Euro-countries, which provides a narrower fluctuation band of ±2.25 per cent of the krone's central rate *vis-à-vis* the euro.

During the referendum campaign it was hotly debated whether the new ERM agreement is better or worse than the old system and, more specifically, whether the ECB would rescue the krone in case of a speculative attack. The debate especially centred on the quality of the safety net that the ERM2 is supposed to set for the Danish currency. On the surface, the ERM2 agreement provides a strong safety net by obliging the participating central banks to provide automatic and—in principle—limitless support when the currencies reach the margins of the fluctuation band.[119] In the Danish referendum debate, this was often understood to mean that there would be no risk of speculative attacks that would force the Danish central bank to raise its interest rates or devaluate the krone. The experience from the old ERM and other fixed exchange rate arrangements seemed to be forgotten by many Eurosceptics.

First, it was ignored that the ERM2 agreement—like the old ERM agreement revised in 1993—includes a clause that allows the ECB to suspend its intervention obligations if it finds that the intervention support threatens its primary objective of price stabililty. This clause was also an important part of an agreement between the Deutsche Bundesbank and the German government, which the former made use of in the September 1992 lira crises.[120] Secondly, the old ERM experience shows that, during major speculative attacks, the central banks often are disinclined to obtain large

[119] Council Resolution 97/C236/3 of 16 June 1997.
[120] See Emminger (1979) and (1986).

credits because the debt has to be repaid after a short period of time. They thus prefer to unilaterally raise the short-term interest rate instead. This leaves the non-anchor country (in this case Denmark) with almost all the burden of twenty-five adjustments in defending the currency. Maintaining a fixed exchange rate therefore has its price. Contrary to the old ERM agreement, the ERM2 agreement clearly states that the short-term interest rate is to be regarded as a primary weapon against currency attacks. Thirdly, contrary to the old ERM, the central banks (including the ECB) can call for adjustments of the parity rates between the euro and the krone. Considering that the Eurosceptics often presented the ECB as a non-accountable and non-democratic supranational body, it is quite interesting that this aspect was also often ignored in the Danish referendum debate. Finally, the debate tended to neglect that it is an implicit precondition of intervention support that Denmark pursue a stability oriented economic policy that aims to *permanently* fulfil the convergence criteria, and that takes into consideration the Council of Ministers' recommendations concerning possible adjustments of Denmark's convergence programme. For these and other reasons, it is questionable whether the new ERM2 arrangement provides the same sort of currency security that Denmark enjoyed under the old ERM. However the pro-European parties failed to get this important argument across in the referendum debate.

When disentangling the substance of the Danish EMU-opt out, it becomes clear that the opt-out is almost exclusively connected to the provisions regarding *monetary union*. As for *economic union*, there are almost no differences between the obligations of the Euro-countries and non-participating Member States. The two exceptions concern the rules on budgetary discipline, namely, the Council's option to issue a third recommendation of rectifying excessive deficits,[121] and on the application of sanctions (non-interest bearing deposits and fines) as a last resort in the case of persistent excessive deficits.[122] As these provisions are only the final steps in a chain of escalating countermeasures, Denmark does in fact participate in most of the excessive deficit procedure.

In the Danish referendum debate, the sanction provisions in the excessive deficit procedure achieved much attention. Less observance was paid to the intermediate steps in the procedure that also apply to Denmark as a non-participating Member State. In the DUPI report on the development of the European Union since Maastricht (requested by the Parliament and submitted in April 2000), we argued that it cannot be ruled out that Denmark is economically more vulnerable to the intermediate steps in the excessive deficit procedure as a non-participating Member State than it would be if it were to join the euro. The reason is that, in conjunction with its fixed exchange rate policy, Danish budgetary policy has to observe two

[121] Art 104.9 EC. [122] Art 104.11 EC.

set of financial restrictions: one stems from the bond markets, the other from the currency markets. The Euro-countries do not individually face any discipline from the currency markets as they no longer have a national currency. As the Delors report mentioned as early as 1989, the empirical evidence shows that the currency markets typically impose a much tougher fiscal discipline because they are far more volatile and react much faster than the bond markets. As long as it remains outside the euro, Denmark thus has a greater incentive to avoid excessive deficits—even in the short run—if it is to avoid hikes in interest rates that harm investments, the housing sector, and ultimately growth and employment. Thus, Denmark also faces a greater time pressure to make the necessary budgetary adjustments before the Council decides to make its recommendations public as a second step in the escalating chain of political countermeasures. It is therefore doubtful whether Denmark has more room for budgetary manoeuvre outside the euro than it would have if it joined the euro. This point was later made in another important report submitted by four leading Danish economists,[123] and the government also endorsed it.[124]

Apart from these two exceptions, Denmark's economic policy is no less tied up by the rules and provisions concerning fiscal policy, labour market policy, tax policy, social policy, and so on, than the Euro-countries. Denmark does not have special opt-outs in any of these policy areas, but this was not well understood in the Danish euro debate. The most important theme in the campaign was the euro's implications in terms of further political integration (see below). One of the most important Eurosceptic arguments was that the euro would trigger much deeper political integration within the policy areas mentioned. Membership of the euro would drag Denmark on an irreversible path towards a federal Europe, and might even threaten the very foundations of the principles of the universal Danish welfare state (that is, if tax and social policies were to be harmonised as feared by the Eurosceptics). The arguments were dubious for a number of reasons. But what is important in this context is that, even if the euro were to lead to further political integration, Denmark would be dragged along with this integration irrespective of whether or not it was a member of the euro. This was not made perfectly clear to the voters during the referendum campaign.

The argument becomes even stronger when the strengthened role of the Euro-council is taken into consideration. Much of the political debate evolved around the infamous 'seat at the table' argument, but the complex relationship between the Council of Ministers and the Euro-group was not well understood by the politicians, the press or the public during the

123 Rådet for Europæisk Politik (2000).

124 *Berlingske Tidende*, 30 Apr 2000, 'Euroen gavner velfærd'; *Berlingske Tidende*, 11 Aug 2000, 'Euro vil give selvstændighed'.

campaign. Instead, the pro-euro camp focused on Denmark's co-influence on the ECB's monetary policy, if it joined the euro. This argument was quite easy to dismiss because the Eurosceptics could refer to the ECB's status as an independent body charged with pursuing a European-wide monetary and exchange rate policy, which does not take into consideration the special needs of individual countries.

In conclusion, the economic case for joining the euro ought to be quite clear for a country like Denmark, whose economic policies already respond as though it was a member of the Euro-zone. But for a number of reasons that we will discuss in section 5, the government and the pro-European parties failed to convince the voters.

4. Economic policy

As mentioned above, Denmark's ERM membership follows a long fixed exchange rate tradition. In the Bretton Woods period from 1948 to 1973, in which the Danish krone was tied to the US Dollar, the krone was adjusted only twice (both times simultaneously with the devaluation of the British pound in 1949 and 1967). These episodes can largely be explained in terms of the weight of the Danish agricultural export and its dependence on the British market at the time.

After the sudden change in the international business cycle after the 1973/74 oil price shock, there was a period of frequent and often one-sided devaluations of the Danish krone. Between 1976 and 1982 the krone was devalued no less than eight times *vis-à-vis* the Deutsche Mark, which functioned as the anchor currency in the Snake and later in the EMS. In a historical perspective, this devaluation policy should be viewed as a brief intermezzo compared with the fixed exchange rate policy that has been pursued with considerable stringency both before and since.

In the beginning of the 1980s, it was acknowledged that the devaluation policy could not permanently improve Danish competitiveness and its prospects for growth and employment. Typically, the devaluation only created a brief sigh of relief before wages and prices began to catch-up. When the conservative-liberal parties (Conservatives, Liberal Party, Centre Democrats and the Christian People's Party) assumed power in 1982, a fixed exchange rate policy within the ERM was declared to be a corner stone in Denmark's economic policy. As was the case in many other Member States, it took some time before the unfavourable inflation rate development was reversed. The period between 1983 and 1987 witnessed a growing and significant current account deficit that necessitated a significant tightening of the fiscal policy in 1987 ('kartoffelkuren'). At that point, the social partners also made an agreement to maintain moderate wage development. These measures greatly contributed to eliminating the inflation gap *vis-à-vis* Germany in the following years, and to restoring the balance of payments, thus adding greater stringency to the fixed exchange rate policy.

When the Social Democrats and three junior parties (The Social Liberal Party, Centre Democrats and the Christian People's Party) assumed power in 1993, the fiscal policy was slightly eased in light of the mounting economic recession after the German re-unification. However, this relaxation of fiscal policy (amounting to around 0.5 per cent of GDP) paid due respect to the fixed exchange rate policy and owed much to the increased room for manoeuvre created by the moderate wage and price development and by a considerable surplus in the balance of payments.

Despite the widening of the exchange rate bands within the ERM in 1993 and the permanent derogation from the third stage of EMU (opening no less than two windows of opportunity for de-coupling the Danish krone from the Deutsche Mark), from 1994 the Danish central bank started to pursue an even tighter exchange rate policy that was similar to that of the Netherlands and Belgium. Since 1997, the Danish central bank has aimed to keep a narrow band of around 0.25 to 0.50 per cent against the Deutsche Mark (and against the euro from 1999). For this reason, the Danish government was very keen to reach an agreement with the ECB on a very narrow band (±1 per cent was suggested) in the new ERM. At the informal Ecofin Council meeting in Vienna of 25–26 September 1998, it was agreed to link the Danish kroner to the euro within an old ERM-styled band of 2.25 per cent while maintaining the existing parity from 1987. Although the agreement fell short of the Danish government's desire, the latter was generally very relieved that it had been possible to reach accord, especially in the light of the global financial turmoil in August and September 1998.

Despite the fixed exchange rate policy, the Danish economic business cycle became significantly desynchronised from that of the core EMU-countries between 1993 and 1998. Rapid economic growth, particularly in 1993 and 1994, and an impressive reduction of unemployment (from around 12 per cent in 1993 to 4.5 per cent in 1998), supported by active labour market reforms, made it possible for Denmark to fulfil the convergence criteria without painful austerity measures. Since 1996, Denmark has fulfilled all the five convergence criteria.

But the impressive economic growth also led to a deterioration of the external current account and to pressures on the labour market, followed by wage increases. In 1998, the parliament decided to significantly tighten economic policy (the 'Whitsun Package') in order to dampen domestic demand and ease the pressure on the labour market. The inflation rate has remained high during 2000 due to increasing energy prices and to the higher value of the dollar *vis-à-vis* the euro (and, thus, the Danish krone). In October 2000, the year-on-year increase in Danish (harmonised) consumer prices was 2.8 per cent. This is largely in line with the Euro-area

(2.4 per cent). However, core inflation has significantly decreased since autumn 1999 as the Whitsun package has started to take effect. Economic growth in the first half of 2000 was higher than expected (3 per cent) due to a sharp increase in private investment and exports.[125]

According to its November 1998 convergence programme that was updated in 1999, the Danish government aims to keep the budget surplus above 2 per cent of GDP, and to reduce the public debt ratio from 56 per cent to below 40 per cent by 2005.[126] These objectives comply with the spirit and the letter of the Stability and Growth Pact, and the Council's Broad Economic Policy Guidelines mainly aim to meet the challenges of the ageing of the population without large future tax increases or reductions in public services. The fiscal objectives also serve to underpin the fixed exchange rate policy. The budget surplus is estimated at 2.7 per cent in 2000 (compared with 2.8 per cent in 1999); this is well above the 2 per cent target. Gross public debt has been reduced from 55.8 per cent to 48.3 per cent of GDP since 1998.

As in the past, the Danish central bank has followed the ECB's interest rate decisions very closely throughout 2000. However, uncertainty about the result of the euro referendum forced the central bank to increase the short-term interest rates unilaterally in late August. The marginal lending rate and the rate on deposits were thus increased by 0.2 per cent on 22 August and again on 29 August. On the 29 September, the day after the referendum, the official rates were once again raised by 0.5 per cent.[127] Contrary to claims by the pro-European parties, the krone was not subject to any major weakness either before or after the referendum. In the approach to the referendum, the short-term interest rate spread in the money markets did widen from 0.21 per cent in March to a maximum level of 1.75 per cent prior to the referendum. Since then, the spread has moved back to 0.3–0.4 points. Likewise, the Danish Central Bank has reduced the official rates slightly (by 0.1 per cent on 13 and 27 October).

5. The Euro referendum

5.1 Arguments and voters' concerns

When the campaign began in March 2000, the political parties and movements immediately engaged in a tug-of-war to control the euro agenda. Was the euro referendum mainly an economic issue or was it a political

125 A main explanatory factor of the high investment activity is that the need for restoration of dwellings and buildings for business purposes in the wake of the hurricane in Dec 1999 was stronger than estimated. The total damages of the hurricane is estimated at a little more than 1 per cent of GDP; Ministry of Economic Affairs (2000).

126 Ministry of Economic Affairs (1999), 1.

127 Following the interest rate increases by the ECB, the Danish central bank also raised the official interest rates by 0.25 per cent on 31 Aug and on 5 Oct 2000.

issue?[128] In line with the long Danish tradition, the pro-European parties primarily used economic arguments while the Eurosceptic parties and movements almost exclusively used political arguments. The Eurosceptics' paramount argument against joining the euro was that the single currency had unleashed an uncontrollable path towards a European federal state that would demolish the basic features of the Danish welfare state or the Danes' national character if Denmark were to join.[129] Using economic arguments, the Social Democratic Party launched a counter-offensive arguing that euro membership would provide a shelter against currency attacks, and that such attacks were in fact the greatest threat to the Danish welfare state, employment and economic well being. The other pro-European parties' main political argument for joining the Euro was that it would enable Denmark to have a say in economic matters and in the overall European integration process. According to these parties, the creation of the Euro-group was the most visible sign so far that Denmark had lost political influence by remaining on the outside.

It very quickly became clear that the pro-European parties were losing ground among the voters. By March a number of polls already indicated that the 'Yes'-camp had lost its lead.[130] From April to late August, most polls indicated a very narrow race, but in early September a more stable trend toward a 'No'-vote finally emerged.

As mentioned in the introduction, we will have to await more analysis and data before more definitive conclusions can be drawn. As pointed out in Section 3, there is no doubt that the pro-European parties had difficulty communicating their economic arguments to the voters. The Danish Economic Council gave the worst blow to the pro-side's economic arguments when its May 2000 biannual report argued that the economic effects of joining were likely to be small and uncertain.[131] Most Danish economists heavily disputed the report's analysis and conclusions, but it achieved a lot of publicity in the media.[132] Throughout the campaign, the Eurosceptics constantly referred to the report and argued that it proved that the euro was primarily a political issue.

[128] According to a Greens poll published in *Boersen* on 4 Aug 2000, 36.2 per cent of the voters believed that the euro referendum was mainly about political issues whereas only 19.9 per cent believed it was mainly about economic issues. 38.2 per cent correctly believed that the political and economic issues could not be separated. In April the contrasting figures were: political issues 32.1 per cent, economic issues 23.4 per cent, economic as well as political issues 38.9 per cent. The figures show that the Euro-sceptics had some success in convincing the voters that the euro referendum was mainly about political issues.

[129] See e.g. *Berlingske Tidende*, 12 Apr 2000, 'Opgør om danskhed og pensioner'.

[130] *Berlingske Tidende*, 11 Mar 2000, 'Snævert flertal mod euroen'.

[131] Det Økonomiske Sekretariat (2000).

[132] *Boersen*, 25 May 2000, 'Vismænd stemplet som inkompetente', *Boersen*, 29 May 2000, 'Nationalbanken konfronterer vismændene'.

A more fundamental reason why the pro-European parties had difficulty communicating the economic case for joining the euro to the voters may be found in the literature concerning economic voting behaviour. This literature is supported by hundreds of empirical studies and generally shows that the voters attach greater weight to their pocket books and the state of the economy when they go to the ballot box. According to this literature, understanding complex economic relationships and economic policy arguments are less important than actual economic well being when voters assess the performance of the government. Moreover, the empirical studies generally show that voters are myopic or short-sighted. Voters seem to quickly forget the lessons of the past, and to take only the (more or less) present state of the economy into consideration when forming expectations for the future. If this also holds true for the Danish voters in the euro referendum, it is not surprising that the pro-European parties' economic arguments did not convince. The voters had forgotten all about the frequent currency crises of the past. They instead tended to focus on the extremely well-performing economy with a stable currency, stable and rather low interest rates, a historically low unemployment rate, and a solid budgetary surplus. The mood among many voters seemed to be: 'if the Danish currency isn't broke why fix it with a new, uncertain, and so far imaginary currency which has moreover lost much of its value against the dollar since it was introduced in 1999'. Many voters ironically failed to recognise that the Danish krone was just as 'weak' as the euro because of the close link between the two currencies.

The Eurosceptics never failed to seize an opportunity to point to the strength of the Danish economy and the weakness of the euro *vis-à-vis* the dollar. They used the image of Titanic, claiming that it did not make any economic or political sense to embark on a sinking ship. And when the euro witnessed another major downturn against the dollar in the beginning of September, the polls finally started to point in the direction of a clear 'No'-vote. According to a poll published in the financial daily *Borsen*, no less than 33 per cent of the voters in September indicated that the fall of the euro was likely to influence their vote. The fall of the euro was also a god-sent opportunity for the Eurosceptic camp to bolster their argument that the euro did not work unless it was underpinned by a much stronger political superstructure.

The hypothesis that the state of the economy mattered more than the political debate is supported by a poll published shortly after the referendum, in *Mandag Morgen* on 2 October 2000. The poll revealed that the voters neither considered the pro-European parties' nor the Eurosceptic parties' most important arguments to be credible. In fact, by a significant margin, the voters considered the campaign of each camp to be lacking credibility.

5.2 EMU and political integration

Since the Danish referendum campaign tended to centre on political issues, it is not surprising that the link between EMU and political integration became one of the hottest themes in the debate. One could identify three positions in the Danish debate: the two fringe groups, both represented by Eurosceptic political parties and movements, attached great importance to the asymmetrical construction of EMU (that is, the fact that the monetary and exchange rate policy has been centralised at the supranational level, whereas the general economic policies basically remain nationally anchored). This asymmetry became the point of departure in their arguments as to why EMU would either break down or had to be fixed by much deeper political integration.

One group—represented by nationalist or conservative Eurosceptics—maintained that EMU remains a method of co-operation between sovereign nation states with individual national iterests, political institutions and stable loyalty bonds between national institutions and citizens. For this reason, and in the light of past experiences and the different national traditions in Europe, the group seriously doubted whether it was possible to achieve the enduring and sufficient measure of political solidarity among the Member States that communitarisation of the monetary policy required. The asymmetrical construction of EMU would give rise to a persistent tension between the supranational monetary body and the national institutions, and among the Member States. The tension would be likely to reach boiling point in the foreseeable future, and this would probably result in the breakdown of EMU. For this reason it was better for Denmark to remain on the outside, or at least wait and see how the project would evolve.

The other group reached the opposite conclusion, believing that the political tensions would trigger much deeper political integration in terms of a much higher degree of supranationalism (perhaps even the formation of a federal state), 'harmonisation' and the 'centralisation' of important areas (particularly within core welfare areas such as taxes, labour market policies, pensions and social policies). This would not only exacerbate the EU's democratic deficit, but would also threaten the very foundation of the Danish welfare state. This group was represented by the June Movement, Peoples Movement Against the EC, Socialist People's Party, Red/Green Alliance and Christian People's Party.

The third group—represented by the pro-European parties—maintained that they could see no reason why the euro would not work or why the asymmeterical construction of EMU needed rectification in terms of deeper political integration. There is no doubt that this view reflected the pro-European parties' long-held hesitation to admit, or even discuss, the dynamics of European integration. But there was also substance to the view. After all, the Treaty and secondary legislation in the EMU area clearly stipulated the rights and obligations of the Member States and the EU institutions, and the experience from more than forty years of European integration generally shows that the Member States have tended to adhere to their obligations as long as these are clearly spelled out. In fact, in a historical context, the EU as an international organisation is just as unique as EMU is as a currency union. Furthermore, the EMU construction is not as asymmetrical as it initially seems. That the general economic policies basically remain national preserves does not imply that no co-operation takes place. In certain areas, where the risk of national free-riding that could damage the currency union is particularly high, the co-operation is quite binding and is enforced by sanctions, if the Member States do not abide with the rules (that is, the Stability and Growth Pact). In most areas of economic policy, the EU makes use of 'soft' co-ordination instruments such as broad economic policy guidelines, best practices, benchmarking, surveillance, information exchange, codes of conduct and peer group pressure.[133] This is sensible because the co-ordination aims to accommodate the Member States' special needs and respect their prerogatives, but it also ensures a certain co-ordination of their economic policies. The latter is also important because of the high level of economic interdependence in the EU. By the end of the campaign, the pro-European parties finally began to admit that the EMU construction might change in the direction of further political integration in the future. This change of mind was sensible, although it perhaps came too late to change the outcome of the referendum. The argument was sensible because economic co-operation—like all other forms of co-operation in the EU—is organic and is bound to change when the politico-economic circumstances change and new challenges arise.

In conclusion, the fact that the Danish pro-European political parties tend to take a defensive stance towards European integration, and that the Danish referendum campaign centred mainly on political issues, helps to explain the outcome of the referendum.

6. Legal framework[134]

6.1 The law as it stands

With the decision of the Edinburgh European Council, Denmark has notified—in accordance with Protocol no 12 on certain provisions relating to Denmark attached to the Treaty—that it will not participate in the third stage of the European Monetary Union (EMU). According to Protocol no 12, Denmark will be treated as a Member State with a derogation, and the currency in Denmark remains the Danish krone.

133 Skjalm (2000).
134 This section is written by Lis Waage, Juridisk Sekretariat, Danmarks Nationalbank.

As Denmark has not adopted the euro, the euro is legally considered a foreign currency in Denmark. It was therefore not strictly necessary to adopt new legislation, apart from that changing the reference from ECU to euro. The new legislation will be described below. Furthermore, Denmark will have to fulfil certain criteria and Treaty obligations concerning its central bank. This will also be dealt below.

The law related to the euro can be divided into two categories. First, changes to legislation that were necessary due to the fact that the euro has replaced the ECU and a number of European currencies since 1 January 1999. Secondly, changes to legislation that will make it easier for Danish enterprises after the introduction of the euro. From a legal perspective, the euro does not (with a few exceptions) enjoy a special status compared to other foreign currencies, and the Danish krone remains the legal tender currency in Denmark.

The Ministry of Economic Affairs has requested all ministries to indicate which legislation should be amended as a consequence of the introduction of the euro. This exercise has led to the adoption of the 'Euro-package',[135] which contains all the legislation adopted as a consequence of the introduction of the Euro in the then eleven participating Member States.

6.2 Legislation allowing further use of the euro

In two important areas—accounting and the share value of limited liability companies—legislation has been passed that goes further in allowing the use of the euro than what was strictly necessary from a legal point of view.

In order to facilitate the introduction of the euro for Danish enterprises and to ensure that they can compete on a level playing field in attracting foreign investors, the Accounting Act[136] has been amended to allow certain companies to prepare their annual reports, accounts, consolidated accounts, semi-annual reports and statements on the source and application of funds in euro. The Danish Commerce and Companies Agency can furthermore allow such companies to prepare these documents in other currencies that are relevant to the company in question. It should be noted that the Danish legislation provides the euro with the same status as the Danish krone in this respect, as it is not necessary to prove that the euro is a relevant currency for the company (whereas this must be demonstrated if other foreign currencies are to be used).

The Statutory Order[137] of the Accounting Act has thus been amended to allow bookkeeping in euro. According to this statutory order, a

[135] Act No 1056 of 23 Dec 1998.
[136] Act No 526 of 17 June 996.
[137] Act No 1006 of 23 Dec 1998.

company may only change its currency at the beginning of a new financial year and cannot revert to the Danish krone.

Various fiscal laws have therefore been amended in order to allow the accounts used for fiscal purposes to be in foreign currencies. However, all statements required by the Danish tax authorities must be converted into the Danish krone according to rules set by the Minister for Taxation (although such rules have not yet been set). Furthermore, the Public Limited Liability Companies Act[138] and the Private Limited Liability Companies Act[139] have both been amended to allow these companies to issue their share capital in either the Danish krone or the euro. By executive order, the Danish Commerce and Companies Agency may allow the share capital to be issued in other currencies. Such an executive order[140] was announced on 19 July 1999 and came into force on 2 August 2000. Again, the euro enjoys the same legal status as the Danish krone, unlike foreign currencies in general.

6.3 Consequential amendments

Amendments have been passed to change references from ECU to Euro in the following acts and executive orders issued in accordance with these acts:

- The Commercial Banks and Savings Banks . . . Consolidated Act[141]
- The Act on Investment Firms[142]
- The Act on Measures to Prevent Money Laundering[143]

6.4 Central bank legislation

There has been no amendment to the Danish Central Bank Act[144] due to the adoption of the euro in the participating Member States (see below).

6.5 National law from the EC perspective

According to the Treaty, the EMI and the Commission have examined the compatibility between each Member State's national legislation, including the statutes of its national central bank, and Articles 108 and 109 EC and the ESCB-ECB Statute.

A distinction was made between central bank independence and legal integration of national central banks in the ESCB. As Article 108 of the

[138] Act No 545 of 20 June 1996.
[139] Act No 378 of 22 May 1996.
[140] Executive Order No 604 of 19 July 1999.
[141] Consolidated Act No 829 of 25 Nov 1998.
[142] Consolidated Act No 741 of 9 Oct 1998.
[143] Act No 348 of 9 June 1993.
[144] The National Bank of Denmark Act (Act No 116 of 7 Apr 1936).

Treaty applies to Denmark, the Danish central bank had to fulfill the requirements of central bank independence, whereas the requirements in relation to becoming an integral part of the system are relevant only in connection to a Danish adoption of the euro.

Both the Commission and the EMI had concluded in their 1998 reports that the statute of Danmarks Nationalbank does not contain any incompatibilities in the area of central bank independence. The legal integration of Danmarks Nationalbank in the ESCB is not a question for the time being and other legislation does not need to be adapted unless Denmark adopts the single currency.

6.6 The application of the law

There have not been any judgments published in the Danish weekly law review[145] in connection with the introduction of the euro in the 11 participating Member States. Since the presumption rule concerning replacement of a reference to the ECU by a reference to the euro and the provision on continuity of contracts in Regulation 1103/97 also apply to Denmark, proceedings will presumably be very limited, if any. The Minister for Taxation has stated[146] that redenomination to euro of shares and bonds from the currencies of the eleven participating Member States will be regarded as a sale. The same applies to redenomination of the shares of Danish companies to euro. Redenomination of bonds denominated in the Danish krone to euro will, on the other hand, be regarded as redemption prior to maturity/sale and buy of a new bond. The decision also deals with the issue of taxation of differences due to redenomination.

The Danish Financial Supervisory Authority has also stated that conversion of debt from one of the currencies of the 11 EMU Member States to euro should not be considered as new debt for the purposes of the order on speculation no 868 of 25 November 1997. The euro is, however, still considered a foreign currency.

Bibliography

Arthuis, J. (1998), *Dans les coulisses*, Paris: Plon.

Det Økonomiske Sekretariat (2000), *Dansk Økonomi, Forår 2000.*

DUPI (2000), *Udviklingen i EU siden 1992 på de omrÂder der er omfattet af de danske forbehold*, Copenhagen: Dansk Udenrigspolitisk Institut.

Emminger, O (1979), 'Die Europäische Währungssystem und die deutsche Geldpolitik', Handelsblatt 26 March 1979.

—— (1986), *D-mark, Dollar, Währungskrisen: Errinnerungen eines ehemahligen Bundesbankpräsidenten*, Stuttgart: Deutsche Verlag.

[145] Ugeskrift for Retsvæsen.

[146] DEP of 19 Jan 1999, 98–620–69.

Ministry of Economic Affairs (1999), *Updated Convergence Programme*, http://www.oem.dk.

Ministry of Economic Affairs (2000), *Økonomisk oversigt 2000*, <http://www.oem.dk>.

Rådet for Europæisk Politik (2000), *Danmark og ØMU'en. 2. Økonomiske aspekter*, Aarhus: Systeme og Rådet for Europæisk Politik.

Skjalm, K. (2000), *En stadig tættere union? ØMU'en og den politiske integration*, Working Paper 2000/5, Copenhagen: Danish Institute of International Affairs.

Strauss-Kahn, D. (1997), 'We're in this together', *Financial Times* 28 November 1997.

Waigel, T. (1995), *Stabilitätspakt für Europa und Finanzpolitik in der dritten Stufe der WWU*, Bonn: Bundesministerium der Finanzen, 10 November 1995.

FRANCE

Jacques Le Cacheux and Régis Chemain

1. Quels risques d'inflation?
Jacques Le Cacheux*

1.1 Introduction

Après les quelques soubresauts qui ont suivi le lancement de la monnaie unique européenne, liés aux contrecoups des crises asiatique et russe sur la croissance et le commerce mondiaux, l'activité européenne a connu une période assez longue de dynamisme, certes bien loin des allures américaines, mais suffisamment prononcée pour que le chômage subisse, dans toute la zone euro, un recul remarquable, que l'accroissement spontané des recettes fiscales redonne aux politiques budgétaires nationales des marges de manœuvre qu'elles n'avaient plus depuis le début de la décennie précédente, et que les responsables de la politique monétaire européenne se préoccupent des tensions inflationnistes plus que d'un éventuel soutien à l'activité. La politique monétaire européenne a donc été progressivement durcie au cours de l'année 2000, pour des raisons tant internes (l'existence présumée de tensions inflationnistes) qu'externes (la faiblesse persistante de la monnaie européenne vis à vis des autres grandes devises, notamment le dollar américain): de novembre 1999 à décembre 2000, le taux d'intérêt court a été relevé à six reprises, dont cinq au cours de l'année 2000, passant de 2,5 pour cent à 4,75 pour cent (un demi-point au début novembre 1999, puis à nouveau un quart de point au début février 2000, un quart de point encore en mars, et à nouveau un quart de point fin avril, un demi-point en juin, un quart de point à la fin août et un autre quart de point début octobre). Dans le même temps, l'euro s'est presque constamment déprécié par rapport aux autres devises, et même les interventions directes de la BCE sur les marchés des changes (la première, en concertation avec les banques centrales américaine et japonaise, la seconde isolément) n'ont guère permis de redresser un taux de change demeuré aux alentours de 0,85/0,9 dollar pour un euro.

La France a assumé la présidence de l'Union européenne pendant le second semestre de l'année 2000. Dès lors, on aurait pu s'attendre à un

* Professeur à l'Université de Pau et des pays de l'Adour, Directeur du Département des Études, OFCE, Paris; Observatoire français des conjonctures économiques (OFCE), 69 Quai d'Orsay, F-75340, Paris Cedex 07.

activisme du gouvernement français sur les grands dossiers économiques européens, notamment en raison des positions défendues dans le passé sur des sujets tels que les institutions européennes, leur fonctionnement et les règles concernant les prises de décision, le gouvernement économique de la zone euro, l'harmonisation fiscale et les dangers de la concurrence fiscale en Europe, etc. En réalité, toutefois, comme chacun sait, le sommet européen de Nice, censé réformer en profondeur les institutions avant l'élargissement de l'UE aux pays d'Europe centrale et orientale (PECO), n'a pas produit de résultats à la hauteur des espérances et n'a fait que remettre les décisions sur la plupart des questions importantes; de même, à quelques exceptions près, les progrès accomplis durant la présidence française sur les dossiers économiques, fiscaux et monétaires sont, en définitive, très minces.

1.2 La double faute de la BCE

Tant les hausses de taux d'intérêt que la dépréciation de la monnaie européenne ont suscité, dans la presse et de la part des analystes financiers, des critiques acerbes. En effet, après une décennie de faible croissance économique et de montée quasi continue du chômage en France, la plupart des commentateurs craignaient qu'un durcissement trop précoce de la politique monétaire européenne ne menace la poursuite de la reprise—engagée dès 1997 et plus soutenue en France que dans les autres grands pays membres de l'union monétaire européenne, alors que la réalité des tensions inflationnistes n'apparaissait pas toujours très clairement: certes l'amélioration progressive de la situation des marchés du travail—avec la plus forte création d'emploi depuis les années soixante (près d'un million et demi) et une baisse de près d'un million du nombre de chômeurs entre l'été 1997 et la fin de l'année 2000—s'est traduite par l'apparition, prévisible, de quelques difficultés de recrutement, d'offres insuffisantes de certaines qualifications et de pressions à la hausse de certains salaires; certes les hausses de prix du pétrole et celles des prix des importations, consécutives à la dépréciation externe de la monnaie européenne, ont imprimé à l'indice des prix à la consommation quelques petites marches d'escalier; mais aucun de mécanismes de transmission de l'inflation, qui avaient caractérisé les précédents chocs pétroliers, n'était à l'œuvre pour alimenter une véritable reprise de l'inflation. En définitive, la hausse de prix en France en 2000 aura été inférieure à 2,5 pour cent, soit un peu moins que la moyenne de la zone euro, mais un peu supérieure à l'objectif que la banque centrale européenne (BCE) s'est fixé pour la zone dans son ensemble. Et s'il est vrai que certains pays membres ont pu connaître des situations de surchauffe justifiant un durcissement de leurs conditions monétaires—notamment les Pays-Bas et l'Irlande, la conjoncture française n'appelait vraisemblablement pas de tels remèdes, en tout cas pas aussi tôt dans la phase de reprise; une telle appréciation valant également, et *a fortiori*, pour des pays tels que l'Allemagne et l'Italie, dont le redémarrage avait été plus tardif encore que celui que de l'économie française. Les annonces successives de hausses de taux par les autorités de la BCE ont donc été fortement critiquées, notamment par des parlementaires—jusque et y compris des membres influents de la Commission des finances de l'Assemblée nationale, certains allant même jusqu'à réclamer la démission du président de la BCE.

Dans le même temps, les hausses successives des taux d'intérêt européens apparaissaient comme des tentatives d'influer sur le cours de change externe de l'euro, mais en vain, ce qui posait le problème de la crédibilité de la BCE et de ses dirigeants. En effet, la plupart des analyses journalistiques et des commentaires des analystes financiers portaient un jugement négatif sur la dépréciation de l'euro vis à vis du dollar et du yen, même si cette évaluation est demeurée modérée en France, la plupart des propos—y compris ceux émanant de membres du gouvernement—soulignant également les avantages que présentaient pour l'économie de la zone euro et la compétitivité de ses producteurs, une dépréciation de la monnaie européenne par rapport aux monnaies des pays concurrents. Malgré cette analyse, nombreuses ont été les critiques à l'égard de la faiblesse de la monnaie européenne, risquant, selon beaucoup, de compromettre sa crédibilité et reflétant le manque de crédibilité des autorités qui la gèrent. Il est vrai que la plupart des resserrements de la politique monétaire européenne, dont on attendait généralement une appréciation de l'euro, ont été suivis d'accès de faiblesse de la monnaie européenne sur les marchés des changes; de même, les deux tentatives d'interventions directes sur les ces marchés n'ont guère été probantes pour soutenir le cours de la devise européenne face aux autres grandes devises. Bien que les avis divergent sur les causes de cette faiblesse persistante—ou, plus précisément, de la force persistante du dollar américain, (rendement anticipé, décalage conjoncturel, effets de l'attractivité de l'économie américaine sur les capitaux du reste du monde), peu de commentateurs souhaitaient une dépréciation plus marquée de l'euro, et la plupart s'attendaient, en fin d'année 2000, à une appréciation vis à vis du dollar, qui ne s'est guère matérialisée.

1.3 Une politique monétaire plus active?

Depuis le lancement, en janvier 1999, de la monnaie unique, la BCE n'a été confrontée qu'à des situations relativement classiques de tensions inflationnistes, à l'exception de l'épisode du 'trou d'air' du premier semestre 1999, au cours duquel elle avait voulu faire la preuve de son indépendance en résistant aux pressions politiques, allemandes et françaises notamment, et en n'assouplissant que tardivement sa politique monétaire. Par la suite, la robustesse de la croissance européenne, sa vigueur même dans certains pays membres (Espagne, Irlande, Pays-Bas notamment) et la situation extérieure de la zone euro—hausse des prix du pétrole en dollar et dépréciation de l'euro aggravant ses conséquences internes et renchérissant les exportations en provenance du reste du monde—ont incité les autorités monétaires européennes à adopter des orientations plus restrictives, dans la poursuite de la stabilité monétaire que le traité de Maastricht et les statuts de la BCE posent en objectif prioritaire de cette dernière. Bien que souvent critiquée pour son excès de zèle anti-inflationniste, dans un contexte où le dépassement du seuil critique de 2 pour cent d'inflation annuelle dans la zone apparaissait certes probable—et effectivement observé pour l'année 2000, la BCE a pu augmenter fréquemment ses taux d'intérêt directeurs, la seule hésitation portant sur la date et l'ampleur des hausses.

La conjoncture européenne du début de l'année 2001, pourtant, semble bien différente. L'inflation dans la zone euro demeure certes relativement vive, notamment dans certains pays membres—ceux qui enregistrent une croissance très soutenue, le plus souvent ceux qui ont également un retard de développement—mais le pic de hausse des prix est apparemment passé et tous les experts tablent sur un reflux de l'inflation dès le second semestre 2001, l'objectif d'un rythme moyen de hausse des prix dans la zone euro inférieur à 2 pour cent l'an étant probablement respecté à partir du début de l'année 2002, au moment de la mise en circulation des pièces et billets. Tandis que le reste du monde entre en récession, sous l'effet de la brusque décélération de l'économie américaine et des crises financières qui secouent plusieurs grands pays émergents (Argentine et Turquie, notamment), le ralentissement perceptible de l'économie européenne, même s'il est moins prononcé qu'ailleurs et vraisemblablement passager, soulève la question de la réactivité de la BCE face aux évolutions conjoncturelles, dès lors que la stabilité monétaire semble assurée à moyen terme: étant donné la longueur probable des délais d'action de la politique monétaire sur l'activité et les prix, faut-il réduire rapidement le taux d'intérêt directeur que contrôle la BCE? Ou bien son niveau du début de l'année 2001 est-il approprié aux conditions macro-économiques de la zone euro? Il ne fait guère de doute que le changement brutal de l'environnement économique mondial modifie les conditions économiques et monétaires en Europe, de même que les fortes baisses des cours boursiers américains et européens risquent d'avoir un effet de richesse négatif, incitant les ménages à réfréner leurs ardeurs consommatrices. Ces inflexions de la conjoncture européenne, particulièrement sensibles dans certains pays (Allemagne et Italie, en particulier) devraient inciter à des modifications dans les orientations des politiques macro-économiques dans la zone euro. L'incertitude porte davantage sur l'ampleur et la durée prévisibles du ralentissement en Europe, et sur l'opportunité, pour la BCE, de tenter un 'réglage fin' de la conjoncture européenne.

1.4 La Banque centrale et les marchés financiers

Le comportement de la BCE est souvent opposé à celui de la Réserve Fédérale Américaine, la banque centrale des États-Unis, et la faible réactivité de la première souvent contrastée au pragmatisme de la seconde. Il est vrai que la Réserve Fédérale Américaine a joui, ces dernières années, d'une crédibilité et d'un prestige considérables auprès de l'opinion et des marchés financiers, notamment par ce qu'elle s'est montrée très réactive et que l'économie américaine a bénéficié, pendant près d'une décennie, d'une croissance spectaculaire. Les responsables de la banque centrale américaine n'ont pas, non plus, hésité à assumer une responsabilité en matière de stabilité financière, en commentant les évolutions boursières ou celles du taux de change du dollar, ou en manipulant les taux d'intérêt en réponse à de fortes variations, à la baisse, des cours boursiers. La BCE ne devrait-elle pas faire preuve du même pragmatisme et de la même réactivité?

Les difficultés ne manquent pas. En premier lieu, il convient de rappeler que les objectifs fixés à chacune des deux banques par les textes ne sont pas les mêmes: alors que la BCE se voit confier la tâche prioritaire d'assurer la stabilité monétaire, les autres buts (croissance économique, stabilité financière, notamment) n'étant que subsidiaires, la Réserve Fédérale Américaine a, depuis l'Employment Act de 1946, la mission de soutenir la croissance et l'emploi tout en maintenant la stabilité monétaire, c'est-à-dire que tous ses objectifs sont sur le même plan. En outre, les divergences au sein de la zone euro et la diversité des appréciations sur la situation globale de l'Union ne facilitent pas la prise de décision au sein du Conseil de la BCE, constitué des gouverneurs des douze banques centrales des États membres et du directoire de la BCE: tandis que certains pays connaissent un ralentissement marqué, d'autres sont encore en surchauffe. Enfin, la BCE souffre d'un problème de crédibilité que ses rares tentatives d'activisme n'ont pas résolu: lorsque à deux reprises à l'automne 2000, elle est intervenue directement sur les marchés des changes pour tenter de redresser le cours de l'euro vis à vis du dollar, les conséquences n'ont guère été à la hauteur des attentes; et de même, les relèvements de taux d'intérêt n'ont, la plupart du temps, pas sensiblement influencé le taux de change de l'euro. Une baisse des taux dans la zone euro permettrait-elle de redresser les cours boursiers européens? Rien n'est moins sûr. Mais plus fondamentalement, une banque centrale doit-elle se préoccuper de la stabilité des marchés financiers? A l'évidence, les responsables de la Réserve Fédérale Américaine le pensent, de même que bon nombre d'économistes aujourd'hui, qui insistent sur les liens étroits entre bourses et conjonctures, notamment par l'entremise des effets de richesse; mais il semble que la culture de la BCE, sous l'influence d'un passé récent marqué par la lutte contre l'inflation, et d'une économie européenne longtemps peu encline à la finance de marché, n'ait pas faite sienne cette orientation.

1.5 La fin des largesses budgétaires?

La conduite des politiques budgétaires nationales s'est révélée, depuis le passage à l'euro, beaucoup plus facile que ne l'imaginaient les concepteurs des traités de Maastricht—qui organisait le passage à la monnaie unique et en fixait les conditions de participation (les fameux critères de Maastricht)—et d'Amsterdam—qui pérennise, sous le nom de Pacte de Stabilité et de Croissance, les exigences imposées aux politiques budgétaires nationales, et notamment l'obligation de soumettre à la Commission Européenne un programme pluriannuel conforme aux Grandes orientations de politiques économiques (GOPE) définies conjointement par les Douze,[147] et de respecter la limite de déficit public fixée à 3 pour cent du PIB, sauf circonstances exceptionnelles dues à une récession 'sévère' (dont la définition est précisée dans le Pacte). La conjoncture a, en effet, été favorable et, au lieu des difficultés attendues, c'est la gestion politique des 'cagnottes fiscales' qui a suscité les tensions les plus vives.

Face à des recettes budgétaires plus abondantes que prévu, les gouvernements européens avaient le choix entre une accélération de la consolidation budgétaire—pour atteindre plus vite l'objectif d'un budget équilibré en temps de haute conjoncture et d'une réduction rapide de la dette publique—et des largesses budgétaires sous forme de baisses d'impôts ou d'accroissement de dépenses publiques. Contrairement aux souhaits de la BCE et de la Commission, favorables à un retour plus rapide à l'équilibre des finances publiques en Europe et à un recul plus prononcé des endettements publics, la plupart des autorités nationales, et notamment le gouvernement français, ont choisi de relâcher un peu la pression exercée depuis près d'une décennie sur les dépenses publiques, tant dans le domaine des grands services publics (justice, police, éducation, etc.) qu'en matière de protection sociale (dépenses de santé, minima sociaux, etc.), et de réduire les prélèvements obligatoires. Ces baisses d'impôts, le plus souvent des impôts directs—bien qu'en France le taux normal de TVA ait été abaissé d'un point (de 20,6 à 19,6 pour cent) au printemps 2000 et certains services (travaux de réparation des logements) placés dans la catégorie des dépenses taxées au taux réduit de 5,5 pour cent—n'ont pas été coordonnées. Elles se sont accompagnées, dans certains pays, de réformes fiscales ambitieuses, dans d'autres d'ajustements plus mineurs; mais elles ont aussi manifesté les tentations de concurrence fiscale qui animent les gouvernements européens dans le contexte de l'union économique et monétaire.

[147] Depuis janvier 2001, la Grèce a rejoint les onze membres fondateurs de l'union monétaire (Allemagne, Autriche, Belgique, Espagne, Finlande, France, Irlande, Italie, Luxembourg, Pays-Bas, Portugal).

De manière générale, la coordination des politiques budgétaires nationales des pays membres de la zone euro n'a pas été exemplaire, en raison des divergences de vues sur les objectifs et les moyens de les atteindre et des écarts de conjoncture qui sont demeurés importants depuis le lancement de la monnaie unique. En effet, alors que, dans certains pays, la baisse des prélèvements obligatoires est présentée comme le meilleur remède au faible dynamisme de l'activité, d'autres gouvernements considèrent qu'il est préférable d'augmenter certaines dépenses publiques ou de lutter plus activement contre les inégalités économiques en redistribuant davantage. En outre, la controverse survenue au début du printemps 2001 à propos des orientations de politique macro-économique irlandaise est venue rappeler la difficulté de se coordonner au-delà des règles édictées dans le Pacte de stabilité et de croissance: ainsi l'Irlande, dont les finances publiques respectent scrupuleusement les critères formels du traité de Maastricht et du Pacte de Stabilité, a-t-elle été réprimandée par ses pairs et la Commission pour mener une politique budgétaire 'irresponsable', parce que trop expansionniste dans le contexte national d'une économie au dynamisme étonnant (avec un taux de croissance annuel voisin de 10 pour cent), mais à l'inflation également hors norme (environ 5 pour cent par an en 2000, contre un peu plus de 2 pour cent en moyenne dans la zone euro).

1.6 La fiscalité

La question de la concurrence fiscale avait été présentée par le gouvernement français comme l'une des difficultés majeures que la présidence française se devait, sinon de résoudre, du moins d'amoindrir. Pour ce faire, les autorités françaises comptaient sur les vertus de la coordination des politiques budgétaires et sur l'aboutissement des négociations, depuis longtemps engagées mais difficiles, sur le 'code de bonne conduite' pour la fiscalité des sociétés, et sur la directive concernant la fiscalité de l'épargne, ou plus précisément des placements financiers des particuliers. Aucun de ces trois chantiers n'a abouti à des solutions vraiment satisfaisantes, même si quelques avancées ont été faites.

En dehors des discussions sur les grandes orientations de politique économique, la coordination des politiques budgétaires et fiscales nationales est demeurée toute théorique. En pratique, chaque gouvernement national a continué de préparer et d'annoncer indépendamment ses décisions, même lorsqu'il s'agissait de domaines ayant des conséquences sur les partenaires, comme la fiscalité des sociétés. Ainsi le gouvernement allemand a-t-il annoncé une ambitieuse réforme fiscale, et le gouvernement français des modifications substantielles de la fiscalité, notamment des personnes—mais aussi de la taxe professionnelle—sans la moindre concertation, ces réformes nationales allant, d'ailleurs, dans des directions sensiblement différentes, ce qui augure mal de l'émergence d'une fiscalité européenne[148].

L'adoption du 'code de conduite' marque, cependant, un certain progrès en matière de limitation de la concurrence fiscale que se livrent les États membres pour attirer les entreprises à l'intérieur de l'espace économique et monétaire européen. Une liste de pratiques 'dommageables', selon la définition de l'OCDE, a été établie et de nombreux traitements discriminatoires sont désormais hors-la-loi. Pourtant, cette liste ne permet pas de recenser les nombreuses formes occultes de concurrence fiscale qui demeurent et elle n'apporte pas de réponse aux pratiques non discriminatoires, mais néanmoins assurément concurrentielles que sont tentés de mettre en œuvre les gouvernements nationaux dans les circonstances présentes.

En outre l'accord obtenu au Conseil Ecofin du 27 novembre 2000 sur le principe d'une directive comportant obligation d'une imposition minimale effective des revenus des placements financiers des personnes au sein de l'Union européenne a été présenté comme une grande victoire de la présidence française. Il est vrai que l'opposition des gouvernements britannique et luxembourgeois a toute tentative en ce sens jusqu'alors a finalement été vaincue, du moins dans la forme. Mais quant au fond, cet accord ne prévoit guère de mesures précises très contraignantes et comporte un calendrier très lâche et des clauses de sauvegarde telles que la réalité des progrès est beaucoup plus mince que les apparences.

Enfin, contrairement aux intentions affichées avant le début de la présidence française, le sommet européen de Nice n'a pas produit de résultats tangibles sur les questions économiques et fiscales. En particulier, les questions fiscales font toujours partie du champ des décisions prises à l'unanimité, et non à la majorité qualifiée comme semblaient le souhaiter les responsables français. Les possibilités de concurrence fiscale entre États membres, dans le domaine de la fiscalité du capital (épargne financière et entreprises), bien sûr, mais aussi, si la mobilité des personnes devait s'accroître au cours des années à venir, de la fiscalité des revenus des personnes et de la parafiscalité (cotisations sociales), ce que l'accord sur la fiscalité n'envisage nullement à ce stade.

[148] Les orientations contenues dans l'étude sur la fiscalité que préparent les services de la Commission ne sont, de ce fait, pas susceptibles d'être beaucoup plus ambitieuses.

1.7 En guise de conclusion

L'année 2001 s'est close sur le sommet de Nice, que la présidence française avait voulu exemplaire, mais qui, en dépit de quelques avancées sur les questions institutionnelles—et notamment une refonte sensible des pondérations, tant au sein du Conseil qu'au Parlement européen, dont les grands pays sortent renforcés—et sur la Charte des droits fondamentaux, a engendré un sentiment d'échec que les discours triomphalistes des responsables politiques français ne sont pas parvenus à dissiper. En effet, comme on l'a rappelé plus haut, l'élargissement du domaine des décisions prises à la majorité qualifiée n'a pas été jusqu'à toucher des questions telles que la fiscalité, et les changements de pondération ont, apparemment, rendu plus faciles la constitution de minorités de blocage. En outre, la question de la parité entre l'Allemagne et la France, qui avait fait l'objet d'un consensus depuis le début de la construction européenne, a été réouverte et le poids de l'Allemagne a, en définitive, été accru, tant au Parlement que dans la formation de minorités de blocage au Conseil. Enfin, et surtout, les grandes questions institutionnelles, et celles qui touchent à l'avenir de l'Europe à 25, ont été renvoyées à une prochaine conférence intergouvernementale, en 2003–2004, avec, à la clé, un nouveau traité. Certes le débat sur le devenir de l'UE a été relancé, avec, au début de l'année 2001, les contributions du SPD allemand et du Premier ministre français; mais le sentiment d'atermoiement prévaut, et l'on peut se demander si un nouveau traité tous les trois ans est, réellement, souhaitable. D'autant que certains pays, à l'instar de l'Irlande pour le traité de Nice, pourraient rechigner à les ratifier.

En matière de politiques économiques, l'année 2001 devrait permettre de clarifier les choix faits dans les traités. En particulier, le ralentissement sensible de l'activité dans la zone euro devrait inciter les autorités monétaires et budgétaires à modifier le cours de leurs politiques. La BCE adoptera-t-elle une attitude plus pragmatique, une politique plus réactive? Et les gouvernements nationaux respecteront-ils, contre vents et marées, les engagements en matière budgétaire lors de la définition des grandes orientations à moyen terme, comme les y incitent la Commission et la BCE? Ou bien, dans le respect de lettre, sinon de l'esprit du Pacte de stabilité, choisiront-ils d'assouplir leurs politiques budgétaires et de laisser se creuser à nouveau un peu les déficits publics pour laisser jouer pleinement les stabilisateurs automatiques? Les réponses à ces questions contribueront à mieux éclairer les analystes, les marchés financiers et l'opinion publique européenne sur les conditions d'exercice des responsabilités en matière de politiques macroéconomiques, à la veille de la mise en circulation des pièces et billets en euro, et de la disparition programmée des monnaies nationales.

2. Legal framework
Régis Chemain**

2.1 Changes in the legal framework

Despite a relative disaffection of the public for this subject, France seems to be one of the most advanced countries of the Euro-group concerning the preparation of the introduction of notes and coins in euro on 1 January 2002.

Undoubtedly, the government made great progress on this point. Two important national measures have to be analysed: the Parliament adopted an act authorising the government to change by ordinance redenominate amounts expressed in francs in legal texts and the National Euro Committee specified the calendar for the introduction of banknotes and coins in euro after 1 January 2002.

2.1.1 Legal framework relative to the modification of some legal amounts expressed in francs

Regulation 974/98/EC of the Council of 3 May 1998[149] provides in its Preamble the following:

> as from the end of the transitional period references in legal instruments existing at the end of the transitional period will have to be read as references to the euro unit according to the respective conversion rates; . . . a physical redenomination of existing legal instruments is therefore not necessary to achieve this result; . . . the rounding rules defined in Regulation (EC) No 1103/97 shall also apply to the conversions to be made at the end of the transitional period or after the transitional period; . . . for reasons of clarity it may be desirable that the physical redenomination will take place as soon as appropriate (recital 20).

Taking into account this analysis, an inter-ministerial committee worked in order to track all the rules affected by the introduction of the euro. It distinguished four categories of rules. Some amounts that are revalued each year can be simply converted with a strict application of the conversion rate with due respect to Community rules on rounding. The same can be done for all the texts, which have no incidence on public expenditures and resources (salaries etc.). A third category includes indicative thresholds, which have to be adapted for the sake of clarity; these modifications will have limited financial consequences. On the opposite, the inter-ministerial committee identified 700 money amount references in legal texts, for which clarity was essential, and whose adaptation could have significant financial implications.

** Maître de Conférences, Université de Paris X (Nanterre), 30 Rue des Bernardins, F-75005, Paris.

149 OJ [1998] L 139/1, 11 May 1998.

In order to ensure the adaptation of such money references in those legal texts corresponding to the two last categories, the government requested the parliament's necessary authorisation. This is the object of the *loi n° 2000–517 du 15 juin 2000 portant habilitation du gouvernement à adapter par ordonnance la valeur en euros de certains montants exprimés en francs dans les textes législatifs.*[150] The possibility of temporary delegation of a part of the legislative power to the government is in conformity with Article 38 of the French Constitution.

This law authorises the Government to take by ordinance all necessary measures in order to adapt amounts expressed in francs in several legal texts. The ordinances will have to be submitted to parliament for ratification.

The adaptation of these amounts will have to respect two important principles. First, it should in no way lead to an increase of any pecuniary sanctions or any penalties (legal neutrality). The second principle is more demanding: the ordinance must have no significant incidence on public expenditures and resources (economic neutrality). Although these two principles are plainly justified and self-explicable, their respect by the government will strongly complicate its work and will not be easy to monitor. During the debate in parliament, the rapporteur of this act proposed that the latter should provide for a limit of 7 per cent to any variation of amount as a result of its conversion.[151] Although this limit is very important in view of the legal and economic neutrality principles, it was not included in the act itself. The government, however, politically committed itself to respect this margin and rightly argued that such a legal margin would lead people to think that the intention of the amounts' adaptation is to increase public resources.

Government *ordonnance portant adaptation de la valeur en euros de certains montants exprimés en francs dans les texts législatifs* of 19 September 2000 entered into force on 1 January 2001. It modifies some amounts, in order to achieve round sums in euro as thresholds. The modification of these amounts is operated in different ways. Some adjustments are made using limits attached to the ordinance, indicating the parity or correspondence between an amount in francs and its counter-part in euro. The act makes reference to various limits: one applicable to pecuniary sanctions or penalties, one to a series of other provisions (amounts figuring in texts of commercial, civil, administrative, social or criminal law), another to some tax law provisions. Other adjustments are expressly made by the ordinance itself without any reference to limits. Eventually, a general rule written down in the text may necessitate some further adaptations.

150 JORF n°138 du 13 June 2000, 9063

151 In the preliminary draft of ordinance submitted by the Government to Parliament during the debates, he notes that the adaptation of the amount of the hunting licence fee would lead to an increase of 31 per cent of its price!

Parliament had to ratify this ordinance before March 2001. At this occasion it could monitor the government's taking into account of the above-mentioned economic and legal principles.

2.1.2 National guidelines for the introduction of banknotes and coins in euros

France is one of the first countries that adopted a plan for the introduction of coins and banknotes in euro. This plan was prepared and adopted at administrative level, by the National Euro Committee under the direction of the Economy and Finance Ministry.[152]

This national plan takes into account the provisions of Regulation 1103/97/EC of the Council of 17 June 1997[153] concerning the circulation of euro coins and banknotes from 1 January 2002 and the withdrawal of national monetary signs at the latest 6 months after this date. Moreover, the national French plan, pursuant to the Ecofin Decision of 8 November 1999, has shortened this period of double circulation.

The National Euro Committee has provided for three different stages:

- During a preparatory phase all interested parties will be supplied with coins (September 2001) and banknotes (December 2001). This concerns all banks, shops, etc. After 15 of December 2001 the public will be able to obtain a 'euro purse', as a starter-kit, in order to familiarise themselves with the new money.
- The simultaneous circulation of euro and franc will go on for 6 to 8 weeks with effect from the 1.1.2002. Thus the circulation of francs should end at the latest during the second week of February. During this period shops should always give change in euro. This phase will certainly be the most critical for the acceptance of the euro by the public. We must underline at this occasion that Community rules provide only for a deadline for the disappearance of national currencies, as legal tender (at the latest, six months after the end of the transitional period). They do not organise or impose a co-ordination between members of the Euro-group on this subject and it is to be regretted that national monetary signs will not disappear at the same time.
- During a third phase, not yet delimited, coins and banknotes denominated in franc could be changed for euro in all banks; after the end of that phase, this operation will still be possible for one year for coins and for ten years for banknotes but only at the Bank of France.

[152] National Euro Committee, 'National guidelines for the introduction of pieces and banknotes in euros', 11 Feb 2000.

[153] OJ [1997] L 162/1, 19 June 1997.

2.1.3 Instruments and procedures for the monetary policy of the Banque de France

Following Guideline 7/2000 of the ECB Governing Council of 31 July 2000 concerning instruments and procedures for the Euro-system monetary policy, the Banque de France adopted a decision in order to adapt its own monetary instruments.[154]

This decision specifies that, in order for financial institutions to be counterparts in monetary policy operations, they must abide by the rules adopted by the ECB or by the rules approved by it after being defined by national central banks. In such a case national requirements must at least be submitted to the ECB. Measures for controlling risks will also respect ECB requirements.

The same decision prescribes in the same spirit that open market operations will have to be in conformity with Community law.

The decision confirms the full integration of the Banque de France in the Euro-system.

2.1.4 Introduction of the euro to Monaco

In 1925 the Principality of Monaco had accorded the status of legal tender to French francs in its territory. The monetary agreements between France and Monaco (Exchange Control Agreement of 14 April 1945, exchange of letters of 18 May 1963 and of 27 November 1987) allow the principality to issue coins at a quota of 1/500 with regard to coins issued by the Banque de France. To comply with the declaration included in the Maastricht treaty, Monaco expressed its readiness to introduce the euro in the principality in the same way as in France. Council Decision 1999/96/EC of 31 December 1998 empowered the French government to negotiate a new agreement in the name of the Community, in order to allow the principality to officially use the euro as legal tender. Notwithstanding the fact that these negotiations are not yet officially over, it is known that Monaco will be able to issue some euro coins with a national face. All the elements concerning the conditions of this power to issue coins should be defined before autumn 2001 (after a Community agreement concerning this issue has been reached). In fact, the current system concerning the power of Monaco to issue a quota of franc coins should be exactly reproduced: the principality will be able to issue 1/500 of the euro-coins that the French Mint will be allowed by the ECB to issue.

154 Banque de France, Decision n° 00–1 of 13.12.2000 concerning instruments and procedures for its monetary policy.

2.2 National law from the EC perspective

Although there seems to be no obvious contradiction between national and European Community law, we will point out in this section a few problems concerning the powers of parliament as to the budget.

The fiscal powers of government and parliament are largely based on the *Ordonnance 2–59 du 2 janvier 1959*. This specific legal act, considered part of the French Constitution, appears now to be inadequate and needs to be thoroughly modified and modernised in order to reinforce the role of parliament. This question was extensively debated during the past year, and the European integration took an important place in the debate. The European Commission, apart from criticising severely the French economic programmes, made also reference to this ordinance's inadequacies, especially as far as EC economic monitoring and the necessity of protecting parliament's powers are concerned.

Without making an exhaustive commentary of this legislation and of the reforms under discussion, reference should be made to a few problems of compatibility with Community law. These problems are usually resolved in a pragmatic way by the Community and French institutions, but they would certainly be reduced, if some aspects of French financial organisation were reformed. Thus, the European monetary union is an occasion to improve some important aspects of the French budgetary regime.

A first problem concerns more the French institutions themselves than the EU. This problem is one of budgetary calendar: the budget is necessarily voted for only one year while the EMU imposes to each Member State to present a stability (or convergence) programme covering several years. This means that in national law such a programme cannot definitively bind the parliament, even if the finance ministry obtains its political support on a draft programme. Thus, the government could prepare and present this programme to the Community with no debate in parliament.[155] In practice, it has the opportunity to present to parliament an act on public expenditure applicable to several years,[156] but the constraints included in such a text are not so important, since parliament can contest this text every year at the stage of adoption of the next year's national budget.

In other words, the French financial organisation provides for a very

[155] On 23 Dec 1998 the Minister of Finance presented the first French stability programme before the pertinent committee of the Assemblée Nationale (Assemblée Nationale, *Rapport du groupe de travail sur l'efficacité de la dépense publique et le contrôle parlementaire*, 27 Jan 1999, 39).

[156] In order to prepare France for the EMU a special law was adopted in 1994 concerning a five-year plan for the control of public finances (*Loi d'orientation quinquennale des finances publiques du 24.1.94*).

rigid framework for fiscal programming. Normally public expenditure needs an annual approach, which means that the execution of the French stability programme could be difficult, if it is not supported by parliament. The latter might consider that with the European economic policy co-ordination, it looses its prerogatives, while the Community institutions could have doubts on the French government's capacity to respect its commitments. The reform of the ordinance must address this problem. Several solutions are envisaged. Even if the one-year principle is not affected, a long-term vision is necessary. That could take place through the legal recognition of the practice of the debate on long-term budgetary guidelines. In order to insure that this duly takes into consideration the stability programmes, the new law would impose on the government the duty to present and attach to the 'projet de loi de finances de l'année' the national stability programme and perhaps that of other EU Member States.

Furthermore, the calendar for the elaboration of the French budget does not coincide with the Community calendar of economic co-ordination and supervision. These differences between Community and national parliamentary calendars are the cause for the government's transmission of not-to-date information to the Commission in March that is usually updated in December. At the same time, parliament is not well involved in the elaboration of the stability programme, which is prepared too soon. Meanwhile, the debate on next year's budget will have to respect such a programme, although the available data do not coincide with the latest information. The updated programme transmitted by the government in December will be itself constrained by the annual budget voted just before. So there is a risk of incoherence between the stability programme and the budget legislation, which is hard to reduce.[157]

Therefore, France is supposed to transmit its economic data to the European Union before the end of March, while the French Parliament will vote on the budget with more precise economic data in December. The parliament, therefore, is not well involved in this process and the government has to bring to date its plans and the information used by the Commission in order to evaluate French economic policy. This problem does not have an easy solution: solutions that are envisaged accept the necessity for the French Government to transmit updated programmes; in addition, it is suggested that the parliament should take duly into account the stability programme, when debating on the annual budget. It is also envisaged to present to the European Union a provisory stability programme before March and to update it before September.[158]

[157] *Rapport du groupe de travail sur l'efficacité de la dépense publique et le contrôle parlementaire*, ibid, 37.

[158] Sénat, *Rapport d'information sur le fonctionnement des services de l'État dans l'élaboration des projets de lois de finances*, N° 485, session ordinaire 1999/2000, 63.

Another issue worth mentioning is that the EMU should facilitate the modification of French public accounting rules in order to respect the European accounting system. Thus, the reform of the ordinance of 1959 should lead to the development of what is called *comptabilité* en 'droits constatés', which means that an operation is registered as soon as it appears for all products and charges it generates without taking into account the year of the realisation of this operation (for the moment, it is only registered as profit and payment realised during the year). This new method should allow a better control of the national budget.

2.3 The application of the law

We first have to mention a judgment of the Paris Court of Appeal of 1.7.99, only recently published. This judgment is one of the first rendered by the civil courts on the introduction of the euro. In this case the court had to correct a judgment, which contained a material error concerning the conversion of a debt denominated in escudos and converted in francs. The court corrected this error by an exact application of the conversion rules included in Article 4.4 of Regulation 1103/97 by converting first the debt from escudos to euro and then from euro to francs. However, strangely enough, the Court does not refer expressly to this provision. Instead, it refers very generally to Regulations 974/98 and 2866/98.[159] The reasoning of the court should have been more precise.

2.4 Institutional aspects

In the last years, especially before important elections, the role of the national central bank was severely debated. It was not the case this year. On the contrary, the Banque de France seems to have been able to assert its independence and autonomy from the government: in his annual report to parliament and during his audition by the Senate, the governor clearly presented his preoccupations with regard to the '35–hour' law (on working time) and to the insufficient pace of reduction of the French deficit.

Bibliography

Banque Centrale Européenne (BCE): Bulletin mensuel, différents numéros.

Les Cahiers français (2000a): *Monnaie et politique monétaire en Europe*, n° 292, Paris, La Documentation française.

—— (2000b): *L'Europe en perspective*, n° 293, Paris, La Documentation française.

Commissariat général du Plan (1999): *Le gouvernement économique de la zone euro, Rapport du groupe de réflexion présidé par Robert Boyer*, Paris, La Documentation française.

[159] OJ [1998] L 359/1, 31 Dec 1998.

Conseil d'analyse économique (CAE) (2000): *Questions européennes, Rapport du CAE*, n° 27, octobre, Paris, La Documentation française.

Dupont, Gaël; Le Cacheux Jacques; Sterdyniak Henri; Touzé Vincent (2000): 'La réforme fiscale française: bilan et perspectives', Revue de l'OFCE, n° 75, octobre.

Fayolle, Jacky; Le Cacheux Jacques (2001): 'Après la présidence française: l'Union européenne, entre l'euro et l'élargissement', Lettre de l'OFCE, n° 202, janvier.

Fitoussi, Jean-Paul (2000): *Rapport sur l'état de l'Union européenne 2000*, Paris, Fayard et Presses de Sciences-Po.

Le Cacheux, Jacques (1998a): 'L'union monétaire, étape vers l'Europe fédérale?', in *Entre Union et nations, l'Europe et l'Etat*, sous la direction de Anne-Maris Le Gloannec, Paris, Presses de Sciences-Po.

—— (1998b): 'Tax Competition in the European Union: Present and Prospects', préparé pour le Forum économique franco-allemand, CEPII-ZEI, Paris, juillet; paru dans la série ZEI Policy Paper, n° B16.

Le Cacheux, Jacques (2000): 'Business Taxation and Firms Location Decisions: A Survey of European Empirical Studies', Document pour la Direction Fiscalité de la Commission européenne, avril.

TAXUD (2001): The Key, bulletin de la Direction générale 'Taxation and Customs Union', n° 15, March.

GERMANY

Susanne Hägele and Ingo Linsenmann***[160]
With a contribution by Peter Christian Müller-Graff

1. Summary

This report surveys political, economic and legal developments concerning the EMU in Germany in 2000, resulting in the following picture:

- The German public in its majority was sceptical about the introduction of the euro because its low exchange rate against the dollar made it appear like a weak currency, and because Germans are still attached to the more familiar German mark. Approval rates for the new currency declined in German polls and did not recover when euro rates did. However, despite a seasonal anti-euro hype, Europe in general and the euro were not a top priority of German citizens.
- Analysts and political actors in Germany closely followed the ECB Council's decisions on interest rates, the interventions and the discussion about the inflation projection. While employers' organisations, banks and ECB-watchers generally approved the ECB's monetary policy and by and large anticipated moves correctly, trade unions were strongly against interest rate hikes. Economic think tanks criticised the 2-pillar strategy and the communication skills of the ECB. Starting the year rather positively, they later warned against an overly tight monetary policy in the wake of the oil price crisis. The publication of the inflation projection was received negatively by the markets but received encouraging comments by some academic economists.
- Opposition parties used the weakness of the euro to pour blame on the government's policies. Otherwise the EMU and the euro were not a central issue in Parliament, apart from the debate about the German stability programme. The principle of central bank independence was respected.

* Universität zu Köln.
** Universität zu Köln, Forschungsinstitut für Politische Wissenschaft und Europäische Fragen, 6 Gottfried-Keller Str., D-50931, Köln.

[160] The authors wish to thank Peter-Christian Müller-Graff and Wim Kösters for comments and Eva Hammächer for her support. The following abbreviations are used in the current study: BöZ = Börsen Zeitung; DBR = Deutsche Bank Research; FAZ = Frankfurter Allgemeine Zeitung; FR = Frankfurter Rundschau; FT = Financial Times; FTD = Financial Times Deutschland; NZZ = Neue Züricher Zeitung; SZ = Süddeutsche Zeitung; VWD = VWD—Finanz- und Wirtschaftsspiegel. 'Auszüge' refers to the extracts of press articles published by the Bundesbank (61 issues in the year 2000): Deutsche Bundesbank (ed) (2000), *Auszüge aus Presseartikeln*, Frankfurt am Main.

- Comments by French Finance Minister Fabius about strengthening the Euro-group triggered traditional German reactions against a 'gouvernement économique', but subsequent extreme plans by the Belgian Finance Minister Reynders were much less criticised.
- Concerning trends towards a 'spill-over' of EMU realities into other policy fields, there were comments about the lack of a political pillar/counterpart to strengthen the currency. Different voices mentioned harmonisation of taxation, company law or capital markets and the macro-economic policy-mix. However the attention focused more on German internal politics, and the connection was not often made between the issues of economic policy, the major tax reform undertaken by the Red/Green government coalition, and the European policy co-ordination context.
- In the legal framework, after the key adaptations had been enacted in 1998 and 1999, the federal government and the Länder proceeded towards detailed adaptations in a large number of acts containing amounts in D-Mark, especially concerning so-called 'signal amounts'.
- The practical adaptation process and preparations for the forthcoming introduction of banknotes and coins went on steadily. To facilitate the introduction of banknotes and coins in 2002, the government decided to allow 'starter-kits' to be distributed to the population starting 17 December 2001.
- The only known lawsuit before a German court concerned a private complaint that the forced introduction of the weak currency euro formed an infringement on the constitutional right of ownership, but the Constitutional Court refused to accept it.
- The adaptation of the federally structured German central bank system to the new realities of the EMU still needs to be settled. The dispute revolves around the future of the Land central banks, which the Finance Ministry and the Bundesbank directorate advise to dissolve. Linked with this debate is the discussion about the reform of banking or prudential supervision. The intention of the federal Ministry of Finance is to merge the present three supervisory institutions into one federal agency.

2. Political and economic aspects

2.1 Public opinion

The general trend in 2000 was the revival of the public debate about the 'sacrifice' of the Deutsche Mark, mostly due to a loss of confidence in the euro that was perceived as a weak currency, especially in its exchange rate to the US dollar. The conservative newspaper FAZ argued that 'Germans fear more and more that they may have exchanged their beloved D-Mark, the symbol of reconstruction after the War, against a weak currency' (FAZ 8 September 2000, p.13). Attachment to the D-Mark is another reason: Germans seem to want to 'stick to the familiar', 'afraid of the unknown' (Tagesspiegel, 25 February 2001). The president of the Bundesbank Ernst Welteke agreed that

> the strong Mark is associated with the resurfacing of Germany after World War II. Our currency has also become one of the major reserve currencies worldwide. And then the Germans lost their money twice in the last century (interview with Welt am Sonntag, 4 March 2001).

One opinion poll suggested the diffidence might stem from the fact that the euro has not yet been introduced in the everyday life of citizens in the form of coins and banknotes and therefore seems remote and somewhat unreal (BdB Demo/skopie 8/2000, 18). In the hope of dispelling those fears, the 2001 advertising campaign organised by the German government will be an 'earnest' one, and focus on words like 'security', 'freedom', 'community', democracy' and 'achievement' (Stuttgarter Nachrichten, 6 March 2001, and SZ, 14 December 2000, 32).

The opinion polls in 2000 reflected the population's scepticism: after a short period of 'euphoria' in early 1999, when the euro was introduced, approval levels descended again (Noelle-Neumann/Petersen 2000, 297).

The Euro-Barometer no 53 (spring 2000) percentages of 50 per cent pro and 39 per cent against the euro were optimistic compared with German polls: The report 'Allensbacher Daten zum Euro' (Allensbacher Berichte 2000), was entitled 'major loss of confidence in the euro—66 per cent of Germans worry about the loss of value of the common European currency'. The proportion of people feeling that the 'euro most likely brings disadvantages for me' varied between 43 per cent in March, 51 per cent in October (BdB Inter/esse 11/2000), and 63 per cent in May (Infrastest dimap May 2000).

Euro-Barometer no 54 in autumn 2000 was again more optimistic than German polls, stating support for euro in Germany 47 per cent (-3 per cent from no 53), whereas a December 2000 enquiry for Institut Louis Harris by Emnid indicated approval for the euro in Germany only 29 per cent. Even the recent recovery of the exchange rate did not seem to help (dimap for Bild, see Yahoo Deutschland, 7 January 2001). Early polls in 2001 confirm the 2000 trend, with the Allensbach Institute stating that '20 per cent have confidence in the euro, 73 per cent have little confidence or none at all' (Allensbacher Berichte 2001, also DSGV/Emnid March 2001: two out of five interviewees welcome the euro-introduction and less than two fifths have confidence in the euro).

Question: 'Are you in favour or against the single European

currency?'[161]

An additional point of interest raised by the organisation of savings

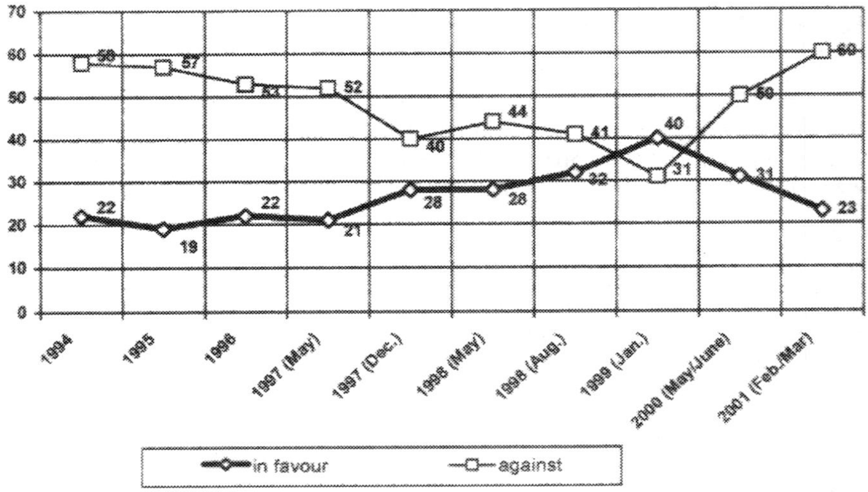

banks (Deutscher Sparkassen- und Giroverband, DSGV), was the degree of information among the public about the relevant dates for the introduction of euro banknotes: more people subjectively considered themselves well informed than was actually the case when concrete dates were asked: Half the interviewees thought they knew the right date, but, when asked to name it, only a quarter of all interviewees actually did (DSGV/Emnid March 2001).

A more detailed look at the examined polls confirms last year's observation that there are notable differences between East and West, obviously a specific German problem. Even a decade after reunification there is still no unified public opinion. Generally, support for the euro is lower in Eastern Germany. Again Eurobarometer polls are more optimistic than polls carried out by German institutions: whereas Euro-Barometer no 54 states 41 per cent are against in the West, and 55 per cent against in the East, German figures in July indicated 47 per cent against in the West versus 60 per cent against in the East (Allensbacher Berichte 2000). In

161 From: Allensbacher Berichte (2000; 2001). Note that the question changed in the year 2001: 'Do you think that the decision to introduce the Euro was good or not good?'. However, the Allensbach poll is the only poll starting as early as 1994 asking the same question until the year 2000 continuously.

March 2001 the euro introduction was considered 'not a good decision' by 58 per cent of West and 69 per cent of East Germans (Allensbacher Berichte 2001), while 38 per cent of all Germans had confidence in the euro but only 26 per cent of East Germans did so (DSGV/Emnid March 2001).

Beyond this particularity, the cleavages in public opinion registered in other Member States according to age, gender, education and political affiliation can be found in Germany as well.

- Age: 45 per cent of people under 30 years of age were optimistic about the euro in the longer run, but only 30 per cent of people over 60 years were so (Allensbacher Berichte 2001).
- Gender: men appeared more confident than women by 15 per cent (DSGV/Emnid March 2001).
- Education: 41 per cent of all Germans approved the introduction of notes and coins, but among high school degree/A-level holders and university graduates the proportion was 59 per cent (DSGV/Emnid March 2000). Meanwhile, 50 per cent of management level employees and higher-ranking civil servants were optimistic about the euro in the longer run, as opposed to 28 per cent of low-skilled workers (Allensbacher Berichte 2001).
- Political affiliation: in July 2000 the Allensbach Institute asked the question 'Are you for or against the euro?': Greens responded with 38 per cent pro, the conservative CDU/CSU 31 per cent pro, the social-democratic SPD 31 per cent pro, the liberal FDP 27 per cent pro, the socialist PDS only 15 per cent pro. Approval rates were higher when the question was asked differently, again by the Allensbach Institute, in March 2001: 'Concerning the euro, do you believe that in the long run advantages will prevail over disadvantages?' Greens were pro by 51 per cent, followed by FDP with 45 per cent, SPD with 39 per cent, CDU/CSU 36 per cent and PDS 31 per cent.

All those figures must nevertheless be seen in perspective: concern with Europe in general and the euro in particular was not the top priority in German public opinion, as analysed by the monthly observer 'Politbarometer', which asked interviewees to name problems of particular concern. In 2000, Europe and the euro appeared among the ten top problems in May, June, and then from September through December, but it never made the top five. Its highest ranking was 6 out of 10 in October. Worries about the euro were less prominent than unemployment, taxes, pensions, frauds, and xenophobic political radicalism (Politbarometer monthly polls, January 2000–January 2001).

A series of interviews conducted by the authors in Berlin with representatives of the political parties in the Bundestag confirmed that the euro is not an issue they are confronted with in their constituencies.

Parliamentarians do not find they spend a lot of time discussing the euro with their voters (this was reported by Social-Democrats, Socialists, Greens and Conservatives, we could not speak with the liberal party FDP). Even the PDS voters, mainly from Eastern Germany, while being against the euro in principle, seem to accept it since the decision is now irrevocable. But all parties do expect a media-induced populist 'panic' shortly before Christmas 2001 (interviews with representatives of the SPD, Greens, PDS, and CDU). How big the problem will be is seen to depend on the state of the economy around that time. If unemployment rates are high, the panic may be worse (Greens interview).

2.2 Assessment of ECB monetary policy decisions and the development of the exchange rate[162]

2.2.1 Monetary policy decisions of the ECB

2.2.1.a Interest rates decisions

During the year 2000, the ECB Governing Council met twenty-four times in order to take decisions on interest rates and, contrary to the year 1999, raised interest rates six times without moves in the other direction. Most notable has been the first rate hike on 3 February and the fifty points rise on 8 June. Furthermore, analysts and political actors in Germany closely followed the interventions of the ECB and of other central banks as well as the inflation projection in December and the decision on the reference value of money growth.

When looking at the comments made by political and economic actors in Germany in the year 2000 with regard to the ECB's monetary policy and especially to interest rates decisions, some regular patterns are noticeable. Right up to the end of the year, most employers' organisations and economic actors from banks and ECB-watchers were backing the general direction of the ECB's policy. At the end of the year, there were a slowly growing number of comments which indicated that a turning point was coming closer and that the ECB would start lowering the interest rates within the first half of the year 2001. However, a substantial number of ECB-watchers were still asking for even higher interest rates. Comments by the main political parties were rare with the exception of the SPD parliamentary group in the Bundestag.

Throughout the year, the trade unions were against any interest rate hikes. Both the DGB and the DAG regularly called for a lowering of the interest rates and strongly criticised the rate moves of the ECB. Mainly, they rejected the view of the ECB that inflation was on the rise due to the

162 Note that this chapter includes the assessment of financial institutions and the specialised press as well as of the political actors in Germany.

increased oil price and criticised some of the rate hikes as an inappropriate tool to combat the weakening of the euro's exchange rate *vis-à-vis* the US-dollar.

For the trade unions, higher interest rates slow down economic growth and would 'kill' the economic recovery in Euroland and Germany. This would have direct consequences for employment. In a 'sharp criticism', the DAG saw 'exaggerated fear of inflation' on behalf of the ECB that would 'ruin the considerable economic upturn including unfortunate consequences for labour markets' (DAG press release, 5 October 2000). The interest rate hike at the end of August was commented as a 'totally excessive and counter-productive reaction to the euro-weakness' (DAG press release, 31 August 2000). At the same time, trade unions claimed that they had done their macro-economic share by enabling moderate pay agreements, which have signalled a high degree of internal stability orientation (ibid.).

Trade unions did not see serious risks of inflation that would justify the ECB's 'unnecessary playing the monetary policy muscleman' (DGB press release, 8 June 2000). Core inflation was significantly below the ECB's margin of 2 per cent and any rise in the interest rates would slow down the economy with Germany falling back even further than the US economy (DGB press release, 29 August 2000). Furthermore, the restrictive monetary policy of the ECB had severe consequences on the mortgage market and on the construction market which is a key sector for economic growth in Germany (ibid.).

Higher interest rates were not seen as an appropriate tool to combat the weakening of the euro's exchange rate *vis-à-vis* the US-dollar. In addition, an alleged lack of reforms in the area of taxation, labour market and social policy in Europe cannot be taken as a sweeping reason for the weakness of the currency: 'This is purely the production of ideology, in order to safeguard some advantages in the societal distribution battle (gesellschaftlicher Verteilungskampf)' (DGB press release, 28 June 2000).

In February, already two days in advance, financial markets in Germany and ECB-watchers were quite certain that a rate hike was imminent. Norbert Walter of Deutsche Bank said that he understood the comment made by Wim Duisenberg when leaving the Ecofin meeting, that the weak euro would threaten price stability, as a sign of market preparation by the ECB (Yahoo Deutschland[163], 1 February 2000/c). Walter would have preferred strong and earlier action of the ECB as the euro is in direct competition with the US-dollar and thus was even in favour of interventions. The economic development of the Euro-zone is getting stronger and could cope with higher interest rates. 'The markets demand a signal

[163] Note that Yahoo Deutschland publishes articles provided by press agencies. For abbreviations of newspapers, see n 1.

from the ECB that it firmly stands with the euro, otherwise the euro would look like an unloved child', was one of the other ECB-watchers' comments (Yahoo Deutschland, 1 February 2000/d). Peffekoven, one of the wise men of the Sachverständigenrat, however pointed to the risks for public finances if long term interest rates would rise (Yahoo Deutschland, 1 February 2000/b). Contrary to market opinion, trade unions were against any rate hikes. 'All economic indicators would show that it would hamper economic activity in Europe, it would nip the recovering domestic demand in the bud', said Putzhammer of the German Trade Union Federation DGB (Yahoo Deutschland, 1 February 2000/a).

The German employers' associations consequently welcomed the unanimous decision of the ECB. The Association of German Banks (BdB) saw preventive measures against forthcoming inflation risks, while for the German Association of Chambers of Industry and Commerce (DIHT) the move was comprehensible. However, it should be avoided to give the impression that the move was motivated by the currency's weakness. The Association of German Public Sector Banks (Bundesverband Öffentlicher Banken Deutschlands, VÖB) criticised the timing of the decision. For the VÖB it came too late to prevent a further weakening of the euro against the US-dollar, yen and the pound sterling, while it was unnecessary—'we should not exaggerate the fear of inflation'—and too early for the Federal Association of German Industry. The German white-collar union (DAG) saw the economic recovery weakened both in Germany and in the Euro-zone (SZ, 4 May 2000, 25).

At the same time, the main political parties were either positive or neutral in their reactions. For the SPD parliamentary group's economic spokesperson, the move would not endanger the economic upturn, while the FPD was in favour of not letting the rate gap between the US and the Euro-zone to widen even further. German Central Bankers, by adding to Duisenberg's comments made in the press conference, communicated to the press that the weak exchange rate had only a limited role in the decision of the ECB (Bundesbank chief economist Hermann Remsperger and Bavarian Landeszentralbank president Zeitler) and that it was mainly due to the rising risk of inflation that the decision was deemed necessary (Bundesbank president Welteke). He added that there is no risk to slow down economic growth as there is enough liquidity available for the German economy (Reuters agency reports of 3 February 2000, Spiegel-online of 3 February 2000).

Currency analysts from banks were rather negative than positive, as the rate hike would be perceived as a sign of weakness. The ECB was forced to react on the weak euro, an analysis that was further underpinned by the explanation given by Duisenberg. Had the ECB raised interest rates only in March, the explanation provided by the raising oil prices and wage costs would have been more convincing (see also DBR, 4 February 2000, p. 2).

For the time being, the reputation of the ECB was damaged. (Die Welt, 4 February 2000). The ECB had tried to find a compromise between reversing the trend of the deteriorating exchange rate and not putting the economic recovery in Euroland at risk. However, this compromise 'is not really convincing and might not impress the markets' (NZZ online, 4 February 2000)

Finally, the decision was seen as a warning signal to the social partners, especially in Germany. If the trade union would demand significant wage increases, the ECB would have to react quickly by increasing the rates even further (SZ, 4 May 2000, p. 25)

By March, the anticipation of the ECB monetary decisions and the reactions towards it became more uniform. Already in early March, a new move was anticipated in order to stop raising inflation at the outset (SZ, 1 March 2000, p. 25). The rate hike on 16 March was welcomed by the DIHT since fears of inflation were fuelled by the weak euro and rising oil prices (Yahoo Deutschland, 16 March 2000/a). It praised the ECB for its good preparation in advance. The BDI remarked that tackling structural reforms in Europe and especially in Germany will be more important than to trail the interest rates trends of the US (Yahoo Deutschland, 16 March 2000/d). For the BdB, the rise was a measure justified by the situation with rising energy prices, economic growth in the Euro-zone, the continuous weak exchange rate and wage demands of German trade unions that have adverse effects on stability. The social partners will have to secure moderate wage agreements in order to prevent further inflation (BdB Press release, 16 March 2000).

The DAG made, again, clear that for the trade union this 'would slow down economic growth, will not hold on inflation caused by external factors and will not lead to a strengthened external value of the currency' (Yahoo Deutschland, 16 March 2000/c). The policy of short, rapid steps leaves the markets uncertain while at the same time inflation caused by the oil price will go down in forthcoming months for statistical reasons, added the DGB (Yahoo Deutschland, 16 March 2000/b).

German ECB-watchers of the banks were positive about the move and expected further hikes either in April or in May (Yahoo Deutschland, 16 March 2000/e).

The chairman of the Sachverständigenrat, Donges, who was not convinced by the way the ECB explained its decision, raised criticism. He thought the explanations given by the ECB 'a little bit volatile' as it used the money stock in 1999, the exchange rate in February and the fear of importing inflation in March.

Looking at the leading experts' reports being published in Germany, the perception of the ECB's monetary policy looks as follows. In their spring report (Frühjahrsgutachten) of April 2000, the six main economic research institutes were content with the interest rate turn of November 1999 and the consecutive hike in February. It was 'justified' on the basis of both the economic upturn and the worsening price perspectives. Even if these would lead to some kind of dampening of the economic cycle, no severe restrictive consequences were seen. The ECB had no reason to further stimulate economic activity as the production gap was seen as diminishing, inflation was turning towards the upper limit defined by the ECB itself and the money stock was expanding rapidly as did the credit volume (Frühjahrsgutachten 2000, 68). On the other hand, the Frühjahrsgutachten did not deem it necessary that interest rates be raised by more than 50 points until Autumn, taking into account that second-round effects caused by the oil price rise would hardly be worth mentioning.

The Frühjahrsgutachten was positive about the monetary strategy pursued by the ECB as it provided an 'appropriate orientation'. However, it was rather critical with regard to the basis of this strategy as adopted by the ECB as well as to the communication strategy of the ECB. It criticised that too many diverging official comments were made concerning the perceived weakness of the euro *vis-à-vis* other currencies.[164] Furthermore, 'the juxtaposition of the two pillars was sometimes problematic as they resulted in different signals' (Frühjahrsgutachten 2000, 68). Referring to the hike in November 1999, the report remarked that the M3 increase was already flattening out while this was given as the key explanation to the move itself. 'This has made monetary policy difficult to comprehend' (Frühjahrsgutachten 2000, 69). In a longer paragraph, the report was less convinced on the M3 indicator.

In a dissenting opinion, two institutes thought the interest rate hikes in November 1999 and early 2000 were not justified. The tightening of the monetary line was seen as being in opposition to the economic aim to foster economic growth (Frühjahrsgutachten 2000, 71–2) while at the same time inflation rose only temporarily due to the oil price and the exchange rate and wage policy was still stability-oriented.

In June, some commentators forecast with precision the 50 points rise already some days in advance (FAZ, 5 June 2000, 35). However, it was also recommended that the ECB should stay calm as it is not only the differences in economic growth and interest rates in the US but also the lacking acceptance of the currency by international investors and the public that lead to the current weakness of the exchange rate. Interest rate hikes were not seen as the best way to counter-balance those effects (FAZ, 22 May 2000, 33). Deutsche Bank Research agreed with the analysis of

[164] On the other hand, the Frühjahrsgutachten in April backed the ECB in its policy not to publish minutes of the Governing Council meetings. Taking into account the policy of the Bundesbank in the past, this would hardly add to the credibility of the central bank. 'The successes of the central bank to maintain price stability and to avoid big mistakes, that is not to over-stimulate or slow down the economy, is most important. Since the beginning of the currency union, these mistakes are hardly noticeable' (Frühjahrsgutachten 2000, 57–8).

Duisenberg that risks for inflation still existed, despite concerns voiced by mainly 'Anglo-Saxon observers that the ECB might already be overdoing it' (DBR, 16 June 2000, 1).

In August, the interest rate rise was expected by the markets, thanks to a good communication strategy of the ECB (see also DBR, 25 August 2000, 1). Most ECB-watchers 'praised' the ECB; for them, the strategy of the ECB was correct in keeping a check on inflation, while at the same time supporting economic growth (Yahoo Deutschland, 31 August 2000/b, FAZ, 31 August 2000, 31). Some analysts and employers' associations, for example the DIHT, were less satisfied with the twenty-five-point rise, which was too 'timid', and expected the necessity for further decisions in the near future (Yahoo Deutschland, 31 August 2000/a, DBR, 1 September 2000, 1).

Most newspapers also in October were in line with the decisions of the ECB. The FAZ saw the hike, as based on money growth, still higher than the reference value of the ECB, and rising inflation was putting internal price stability at risk. However, as the interest rate rise was 'a surprise', it moderately criticised the lacking preparation of the ECB: 'surprises should not be part of a strategy for a medium-term monetary policy' (FAZ, 6 October 2000, p. 13). The BdB, again, saw the move as 'justified' both with regard to the two pillars of the ECB's strategy and the continuously high oil price. There would still be the danger of second-round effects (BdB press release, 5 October 2000). However, and in line with the comments made in August, some analysts remarked that most indicators were actually unchanged since August, and some, including the oil price and the exchange rate, were even going in the opposite direction. The question remained why the ECB had not raised the interest rates by 50 points two months earlier (Wirtschaftsdienst 2000/X, 589).

In their autumn report (Herbstgutachten), published after the last rate hike of 5 October, the opinion of the institutes had changed considerably and moved in the direction of the two dissenting institutes in spring. Although they acknowledged that price stability was endangered by the rise in crude oil prices and the continuous euro devaluation, they advised the ECB not to tighten monetary policy even further. The main reason given was that inflation was mainly caused by the oil price, an external price shock to be taken for granted by the central bank. If the ECB was to balance out this raise in inflation by trying to slow down or even reverse internal inflation within the Euro-zone, this would result in a clear drop of economic activity (Herbstgutachten 2000, 74). As the macro-economic conditions for monetary policy are neutral, there is no reason to overreact.

In an alternative—though unlikely—scenario, the institutes would envisage the need for action on behalf of the ECB: in case oil-price related inflation becomes enduring and would result in a reversal of the moderate wage policy of the social partners, the ECB would have to prevent a wage-price spiral by tightening monetary policy. The Herbstgutachten warned that this—as history shows—would lead to a stabilisation recession. While criticising the communication strategy of the ECB, the institutes did not detect a general loss of trust in the central bank. Clear indicators for this are low long-term interests and the absence of high-risk premia for euro investments (Herbstgutachten 2000, 79).

The annual report (Jahresgutachten) of the Council of Economic Advisers (Sachverständigenrat zur Begutachtung der gesamtwirtschaftlichen Entwicklung), published on 15 November, was rather critical with both the communication and the monetary strategy of the ECB. With regard to the monetary strategy of the ECB the Jahresgutachten remarked, that, although it is positive to maintain a two-pillar strategy and thus safeguard a high discretionary power, this can lead towards some kind of 'discretionary anything-goes' (Jahresgutachten 2000, 24). The Jahresgutachten noted that in its official explanations of the monetary decisions, the ECB did not make clear which of the two pillars was effectively responsible for the decisions (Jahresgutachten 2000, 77). On the other hand, the Jahresgutachten rejected criticism put forward after the various rate hikes within the year 2000. A stability oriented monetary policy has to act preventively. Interest rates thus have to be channelled upwardly in time, instead of keeping them on a low level, and the reaction must come only at a time when the price climate has already got significantly worse (Jahresgutachten 2000, 296). Since monetary policy measures show their effect only after considerable time, a central bank has to aim at price developments in the medium-term future and should not orientate itself at current inflation rates (Jahresgutachten 2000, 297). Furthermore, the fact that the Euro-zone enjoys liquidity, proves that the monetary policy is not restrictive. In sum, the Jahresgutachten supports the ECB in its monetary policy and—at least with regard to the results—supports it in its stringent approach in combating inflation: 'It has nothing to do with excessive inflation fears, but, instead, with reliability and credibility with regard to the intention of stability' (Jahresgutachten 2000, 298).

Furthermore, as the ECB has a broad set of indicators assessing price risks for the Euro-zone, it leads to an non-transparent arrangement of the second pillar. 'It is not known to the public, how the second pillar indicators are weighted by the ECB when assessing inflation dangers' (Jahresgutachten 2000, 24) On the other hand, the Jahresgutachten was positive with regard to the definition of inflation as provided by the ECB, that is less than 2 per cent in the medium term. There would still be some room for manoeuvre but at the same time it would be transparent enough to stabilise the expectations of the market participants (Jahresgutachten 2000, 299).

The Jahresgutachten was critical towards the attempts to establish a core inflation rate for the Euro-zone as the new stability target for the central bank by taking out volatile energy prices and food prices fluctuating according to the season. 'A drop of the value of money for the public is a drop of the value of money regardless of which prices are responsible for it' (Jahresgutachten 2000, 296).

By the end of the year, comments became more sober. Market would tend to see greater danger for the economy than for inflation if the interest rates would rise even further, 'each new step would be a mistake that would have to be corrected later on by the ECB when economic indicators would deteriorate' (FTD, 30 October 2000). In November, this analysis was being confirmed by the ECB's inaction and most commentators saw another rise as less and less likely (FTD, 16 November 2000).

The ECB was seen as 'being in a jam'. On the one hand, by raising interest rate to combat inflation the ECB would be accused of stifling economic growth. On the other hand, by not raising the rates the ECB would be blamed for not doing enough against growing fears of inflation. Looking at the lower crude oil price and at the higher exchange rate, *Die Welt* concluded that after Euroland had outstripped the US in economic growth in the third quarter of 2000 it seems reasonable to expect that interest rates in Euroland have peaked and will go down in spring 2001. (Die Welt, 14 December 2000). In December, a number of analysts were actually expecting a reduction of the interest rates and accused the members of the Governing Council of being 'scared cats' (FR, 15 December 2000) and of showing their lack of self-confidence by not changing the direction of monetary policy in order to support Euroland's economy. Some ECB-watchers were in favour of further increases. The EMU-Monitor suggested in November that money growth was still above the reference value, which, in addition, should not be lowered by the ECB in order to secure its credibility (Yahoo Deutschland, 29 November 2000). A majority of analysts asked by Reuters at the end of November were expecting a medium-term increase by 25 points as both inflation pressure and the euro-weakness had not vanished (Handelsblatt, 24 November 2000).

In their end-of-the-year reflections, most newspapers were certain that 'the next interest rate move of the ECB would go downward' (BöZ, 30 December 2000) as money growth was gradually getting closer to the ECB margin of 4.5 per cent.

On another level, the interest rates decisions of the ECB were also commented with regard to the activities of the American Fed. A 'race' between the two central banks was detected in which the activities of the ECB were measured according to the moves of the Fed. Eventually, while the decisions of the Fed were taken as such, the ECB was always considered as either moving behind the Fed, which was taken as 'following suit', or trying to be the frontrunner of the two central banks. In March it was thought that,

> it is no disadvantage for Duisenberg and his team, that they were quicker with their decision than the Americans. The demonstration of a bit of independence from the world biggest financial power won't do any harm unless it degenerates in an interest rates race for investors money (SZ, 17 March 2000, 4).

By June, however, 'the last interest tango' was envisaged (FAZ, 8 June 2000, p. 31).

Assessments of the ECB's monetary strategy and its decisions from the political parties in Germany were rare. In January, the SPD parliamentary group remarked that an increase of the interest rates would be rather the opposite of an appropriate signal for economic growth (SPD parliamentary group press release, 31 January 2000). In February, it made clear that the euro would need no support by higher interest rates as the weakness would only be temporary (SPD parliamentary group press release, 3 February 2000). In April, an increase was considered not necessary as inflation was low and inflation prognosis were positive (SPD parliamentary group press release, 27 April 2000) The SPD parliamentary group only moderately commented on the June decision to raise the interest rates in saying that this decision was not 'imperative'. The decision, however, was not seen as an immediate danger for economic growth in Germany and in the EU as a whole (SPD parliamentary group press release, 08 June 2000).

The CDU/CSU parliamentary group does not make any explicit reference to the policy-making of the ECB taking account of the latter's independence (interview CDU/CSU, 6 February 2001). However, strong emphasis is put on the ECB's task to ensure price stability (CDU parliamentary group press release, 22 November 2000).

For the PDS parliamentary group, the fundamental problem is not the policies carried out by the ECB, but instead the Treaty provisions and the orientation of the Treaty as 'anti-Keynesian'. The ECB being the guardian of monetarism not only is it neglecting but also is bound to neglect any political objectives put forward by democratic institutions. However, comparing the attitude of the ECB with that of the Bundesbank when being responsible for monetary policy, 'it did not turn out to be as bad as one could imagine taking the Treaty provisions as a starting point' (PDS interview, 9 February 2001).

The liberal Free Democrats FDP supported throughout the year the restrictive monetary policy of the ECB. For them, the central bank had no choice to do otherwise as the weakness of the euro also endangered the internal stability of the currency. The ECB had to counter-balance imported inflation and to prevent a further flow of capital into the US-market (FDP parliamentary group press releases, 16 March 2000, 26 April

2000, 30 August 2000). The interest rate hike in October looked 'almost as an act of despair', as the situation could not be reversed (FDP parliamentary group press release, 5 October 2000). For the FDP, only structural reforms to be carried out by the Euro-Member States and especially Germany and France could re-establish the necessary market confidence in the euro. Among other reforms, the FDP specifically demanded reforms of the social security systems, more flexibility for the labour and goods markets as well as a systematic reduction of energy taxation. Furthermore, it accused the French government of questioning the independence of the European Central Bank with rather clumsy comments in August.

2.2.1.b Inflation projection

ECB-watchers and analysts in Germany commented extensively on the decision of the ECB to publish some kind of inflation projection at the end of the year for which the ECB staff and not the Governing Council is responsible.[165] The decision to opt for projections based on a fixed interest rate and a constant exchange rate against the US-dollar left the markets overwhelmingly disappointed. For most, this kind of projections was of limited value (FTD, 20 December 2000; FAZ, 21 December 2000, 17). Others saw merely some public-relations effort on behalf of the ECB to demonstrate more transparency without limiting the scope for independent action by the Governing Council (VWD, 19 December 2000). Finally, some of the institutional actors feared that markets and analysts would take the publication of a projection more as a prognosis, thus unnecessarily creating pressure on the ECB in case the projected inflation rate is not met. The fact that the projection is not officially approved by the Governing Council of the Board, won't help either (BöZ, 25 November 2000, 6, FAZ, 16 October 2000, 33) as the market has to 'second-guess to what extent the council believes its own staff's forecast' (DBR, 17 November 2000, 1). It would basically add to the existing confusion about the monetary strategy of the ECB and might lead to self-fulfilling prophecies in case wage demands by the trade unions would consider it appropriate to compare the actual inflation rate with the projection of the ECB. If the actual inflation rate is lower, trade unions might demand higher wage increases, which would in turn push inflation rates (position of the BdB in its economic report October 2000).

The Herbstgutachten (see above) in October made clear that it appreciated the announcement of the ECB to publish their inflation projection and reminded that the institutes had recommended such a move six

[165] It was noted that this projection was merely for the sake of Duisenberg who had unilaterally announced the publication in October 1999 at the European Parliament leaving his fellow members of the Governing Council to 'grimly' accept this decision in order not to further harm Duisenberg's reputation in the public (BöZ on 17 Nov 2000).

months ago. As the inflation projection would be a scenario with a given monetary policy, it would be a standard towards which the ECB could orientate itself. 'Monetary action or inaction will be more comprehensible to the public. It will strengthen credibility and stabilise the expectation of economic actors' (Herbstgutachten 2000, 75). However, the ECB should give a commentary to it in order to avoid misunderstandings and a sense of insecurity of the public. It has to make clear that there will be a natural uncertainty with the projection and that it will be one among numerous other indicators which will serve as the basis for its decisions.

The Jahresgutachten warned that

> the publication of the inflation projection will only help the central bank to build up credibility and carry out a forward looking monetary policy, if the latter assumes the inherent obligation to report seriously by putting the inflation projection at the centre of the second pillar and if it meets the increased demand with reference to its communication policy. This is not an easy undertaking [Jahresgutachten 2000, 24, see also 301 et seq]. 'Therefore, it is even more important that the presentation and commenting of the inflation projection *by all members of the ECB Council* will be done in the same way clearly and comprehensibly' (Jahresgutachten 2000, p. 303, emphasis added).

However, the Jahresgutachten expects a qualitative improvement of monetary policy with this projection. Since monetary policy risks to address necessary measures too late—caused by the long lags of 2–4 years until interest rate impulses show effects, with the publication of the inflation projection it will be easier for the ECB to prevent this mistake. It will be easier to pursue a preventive monetary policy and to counter-balance emerging price risks at an early stage (Jahresgutachten 2000, p. 303).

2.2.1.c Money growth

At the end of the year, analysts were awaiting the decision of the ECB on its first pillar of the monetary strategy, ie money growth. In a poll carried out by Financial Times Deutschland before the December decision of the ECB to keep the reference value at 4.5 per cent, more than two thirds of the analysts thought it appropriate to raise it to 5 per cent (although only 40 per cent thought that the ECB would do so) (FTD, 11 December 2000). For most analysts, the potential output growth was already higher than assumed by the ECB and keeping the reference value would be a sign of a restrictive monetary policy of the ECB. Raising the growth rate of the money stock from 4.5 to 5 per cent would demonstrate, that the ECB believes in a higher potential output growth and in an advancement of the new economy in Europe (Die Welt, 14 December 2000). Also the big research institutes in autumn advised the ECB to fix the M3 reference value to 5 per cent instead of 4.5 per cent, because the velocity of circulation had dropped significantly (see also similarly Jahresgutachten 2000, 304). For the trade unions, the low money target of 4.5 per cent is unreasonable as capital markets can not only accommodate more money but need it, too, during the current restructuring (interview with DGB, 7 February 2001).

Contrary to this perception, the EMU-Monitor advised the ECB not to raise M3 money growth to 5 per cent as the key indicators do not permit such a move and as 'increasing the reference value in times of rising inflation rates risks damaging the credibility of the ECB's commitment to price stability' (EMU-Monitor press statement, 29 November 2000). The EMU-Monitor consequently asked for higher interest rates in case the M3 growth is not decreasing within the next months. It could also be understood by this move that first the ECB intends to lower interest rates in the near future, and secondly, it has lost its confidence in economic growth. Thirdly, if the 'new economy' should be supported by such a move, the ECB would be ill advised to do so as the 'new economy' has yet to demonstrate its capacity to contribute to economic growth in Europe without adding to inflation (BöZ, 7 December 2000, 9). In the end, also the two umbrella organisations of savings banks (DSGV) and public banks (VÖB) welcomed the decisions to keep the reference value as a 'clear sign for the continuation of its stability oriented strategy', which will further strengthen the reputation of the ECB (Yahoo Deutschland, 14 December 2000). The ECB had finally settled on a projection that resembles the former money targeting of the Bundesbank, 'a resemblance to the DM which will only do good to the euro' (VWD, 24 November 2000).

2.2.1.d Interventions

Calls for an intervention of the ECB and other central banks in order to help stabilising the exchange rate of the euro grew louder over the Summer in Germany, even though analysts were not certain if, how, and when interventions would actually be successful. Then, the first intervention of the G7 central banks in September was widely commented not only by analysts, but also by political actors. Already a few days before the actual intervention, tension rose after the Euro-group meeting in Versailles with consecutive 'conflicting signals' of European policymakers (FT, 13 September 2000, 1). At that time, Bundesbank council members repeatedly pointed out, that interventions would be counter-productive when being used against a market trend (ibid). Market analysts however thought that interventions would instead help to counter-balance extreme irregularities between supply and demand (FAZ, 13 September 2000, 31).

The intensity with which international markets were following each single move of the central bank was once again demonstrated in mid-September when the ECB announced that it would sell inflows deriving from the interest income of foreign reserve assets against euro. This 'surprise move' of the ECB was widely regarded as a disguised intervention but at the same time most analysts underlined that the announced 2.5 bn euro were not sufficient to achieve a turning point at the foreign exchange market (e.g. SZ, 15 September 2000, 25). The 'ballon d'essai' was thus 'all but brilliant' showing that the central bankers themselves had no idea what to do (FAZ, 15 September 2000, 13). Consequently, this kind of intervention was considered as 'a joke' that went 'awfully wrong' (FAZ, 18 September 2000, 49), but 'not calling it an intervention had the nice side effect that ECB could not be blamed if it turned out to be a dud' (DBR, 15 September 2000, 1).

When the G7 central banks finally intervened, analysts were mildly surprised about the fact that they did so before the G7 finance meeting in Prague the following weekend and that the Federal Reserve participated in the intervention (FAZ, 23 September 2000, 13). The reaction was mixed. In order to achieve a long-lasting turning point of the exchange rate development, many analysts saw two options for the ECB. On the one hand, it could have raised interest rates by about 2 per cent, thus balancing out the differences in interests between the US and Euroland. However, the consequences would have been a 'brutal monetary contraction' and a 'crashing downswing of economic activity' (see for this quote and the following, Handelsblatt, 26 September 2000). On the other hand, the ECB could have waited for an unstable market situation and provoke a change of mood with a conclusive intervention strategy. Instead, the ECB did so, although 'the attempt was too early', as the current exchange rate level was not completely wrong. Still, the US was considered the better place for long-term investments and economic growth in the US is too strong to initiate a swing in market expectations. Euroland 'remains number two'.

In a more broader sense, the intervention was considered as yet another attempt to counter-balance the lack of the more fundamental reforms necessary for Euroland, especially the future political side of the European Union and an economic policy being more dynamic and less re-distributive, accelerating deregulation and trying to break-up the entrenched patterns of corporatism in continental Europe (FAZ, 23 September 2000, 13).

For the Bundesbank it was necessary to demonstrate the market that the ECB and the other G7 central banks were actually able to do a concerted action (vice-president Stark in FAZ, 26 September 2000/a). Also the BdB approved the intervention strategy because it could discourage speculation (SZ, 25 September 2000, 26). Although the ECB had no obligation to intervene as the internal stability of the currency was not under real threat, the intervention could help to overcome the psychological problem. Comments in the same direction were made by top German bankers who praised the joined intervention as a sign of a shared feeling of responsibility and the proof of the leadership strength of the ECB (FAZ, 26 September 2000, 31). These positions, however, were strongly criticised by former minister Graf Lambsdorff, who saw some kind of opportunism as ad hoc interventions had been rejected in the past by the economists (*Die Welt*, 30 September 2000, 14).

The Herbstgutachten was cautious in its assessment of the intervention on the foreign exchange market by the ECB and other central banks. Although the first intervention was only meant as a 'signal', there would always be the risk of a failure. The leading economic research institutes were sceptical as to whether the intervention would lead to a stable reversal of the exchange rate development for two reasons. First, interventions are only successful if the financial markets fundamentally change their expectations on the future development of the exchange rate. Secondly, it is difficult to define an 'equilibrium exchange rate', as it depends on expectations of the relation of purchasing power, of the interest rates differences and the future economic dynamics in the countries.

The institutes did not rule out that the there is some 'fundamental weakness of the euro against the US-dollar' (Herbstgutachten 2000, 78) and that the market, therefore, is not completely wrong. They mentioned the strong economic dynamics of the United States and high productivity gains leading to a high attractiveness of investment in the US. This, however, could change, taking also into account the ability of the US to further finance their enormous trade balance deficit. A slow-down of economic activity in the US, already envisaged by the institutes in autumn 2000, might lead to a re-assessment of the trade balance deficit by the markets, which could further weaken the exchange rate of the dollar.

As a conclusion, the Herbstgutachten was cautiously positive with regard to the future development of the exchange rate of the euro, stating that 'numerous scenarios give every reason to believe that in the medium-term the exchange rate of the euro will be noticeably above the current value' (Herbstgutachten 2000, 78). The institutes recommended a coherent approach of all actors involved in order to foster confidence in the Euro-zone. For this, the ECB should strictly stay on its stability-oriented course and at the same time should intensify efforts to communicate it clearly to the public. Furthermore, economic policy should play its part as should fiscal and wage policy remain stability oriented (Herbstgutachten 2000, 79). There were clear indicators for this in recent months, and growth prospects were much better than they have been in recent years.

The CDU was cautious about the political autonomy of the ECB with regard to demands put forward by the finance ministers. Duisenberg not attending the Ecofin in September was thus a good and 'clear sign for the ECB's independence' (CDU/CSU EU-spokesperson Hintze in the Bundestag, 12 September 2000). In a joint action by the leading central banks the SPD saw a pleasant and supportive signal for the sense of their responsibility for the world economy (SPD parliamentary group press release no 802, 29 September 2000).

The interview given by ECB President Duisenberg to The Times on 16 October 2000, in which he discussed the chances of renewed interventions to help the euro, was then badly received in Germany. Duisenberg's outspokenness was called a 'deadly sin' (SZ, 18 October 2000, 3). He was described as 'under pressure' and putting 'the credibility of the ECB at stake' (FAZ, 25 October 2000, 33). In the following days, a resignation of Duisenberg was widely discussed, but for the sake of stability there was a clear preference for Duisenberg staying president (SZ, 19 October 2000, 27; BöZ, 20 October 2000; FAZ 20 October 2000, 13). Even the German Finance Ministry felt obliged to officially state that there is no debate on the future of Duisenberg as ECB-President (SZ, 18 October 2000, 3).

Troubled by Duisenberg's Times-Interview, the mood turned quite negative at the end of November. While some still thought the September intervention was done 'with great bravura' (SZ, 17 October 2000, 25), consequently backed by an interest rate hike early October, others repeated that it had been too early and that the support of the Fed was only lukewarm (interview with Manfred Neumann in SZ, 27 October 2000, 27). Almost all analysts, however, were sure that the interview had done a great disservice to the aim to stabilise the exchange rate against the US-dollar. In a poll, 60 per cent of German top managers spoke against further interventions (Handelsblatt, 19. October 2000). The 'mistrust in the market' did not really help to change expectations of traders (FAZ, 25 October 2000, 33). The ECB should let the euro fall until the markets would themselves decide on the turning point, because otherwise the ECB would only lose out to the speculators who would be invited to do so by further actions (interview with Manfred Neumann in SZ, 27 October 2000, 27).

The November interventions were either greeted or condemned as futile by analysts in the press. On the positive side, it was noted that the ECB was intervening with the current trend as the exchange rate was gradually moving upwards. This was, thus, a timing that 'fits perfectly with chapter one of the central bankers' handbook for interventions' (DBR, 3 November 2000, 1). A 'broad approval' was noted as it became clear for the markets that, taking the enormous foreign exchange reserves of the central banks of the ESCB into account, there is a potent opponent who is willing to act (see for example Peter Bofinger in *Die Welt*, 7 November 2000). Furthermore, it was noted that the ECB demonstrated how it wants to live through the presidential election in the US, since, in the past, after each election, the exchange rate of the US-dollar against the Deutsche Mark rose considerably (BöZ, 7 November 2000, 4). On the other side, the fact that the ECB acted unilaterally (although later in the month it became obvious that the BoJ had helped the ECB) was noted with concern and, as a consequence, analysts saw the interventions as doomed to fail. Others remarked that although it would have been better if the ECB could have acted in co-operation with the Fed and other Central Banks, it is simply wrong to believe in the opposite. It was only because of the understanding of the markets that the Fed would not intervene due to the ongoing election campaign that the ECB was able to surprise the markets. The ECB should keep up with its courage. (BöZ, 15 November 2000, 9).

The main aim of the ECB was to give a signal that it considered the exchange rate in October as the bottom line. Although some thought this inappropriate immediately after the first interventions in November, most commentators later that month and in December were certain that the ECB achieved exactly this aim. It had not been the aim of the ECB to achieve a defined appropriate exchange rate (BöZ, 15 November 2000, 9). Also Bundesbank president Welteke used this broad understanding in December at the Bundesbank's annual press conference, by arguing that the ECB had shown its capacity to act and that it got rid of the doubts whether or not it would be able to use the intervention instrument effectively (NZZ online, 7 December 2000).

The Jahresgutachten, with regard to the interventions in September and November of the year 2000, reminded that strong deviations from an explicable fundamental exchange rate level were not that unusual since the collapse of the Bretton Woods system. Therefore, the European Central Bank should rely on a reversal of the trend instead of putting its credibility at stake. The central bank should avoid to raise doubts about its orientation towards internal stability of the euro. 'Only by maintaining and communicating a course which is oriented towards consistently safeguarding price stability, does monetary policy do the best possible in this situation to strengthen the external value of the euro' (Jahresgutachten 2000, 308).

2.2.2 The development of the exchange rate

The debate on the exchange rate developed according to the deterioration of the external value of the euro throughout the year. At times, the weak exchange rate was the title story and the topic of the editorials of many newspapers in Germany. It was however also noted that nowhere else in Europe the public and the media got so exited about the exchange rate (SZ, 27 April 2000, 27).

In the first half of the year, references to the weakness of the euro were less urgent than in Autumn of 2000. Thus, in February the SPD saw the weakness as 'temporary' (SPD parliamentary group press release, 3 February 2000). In April it stated that Europe should not throw itself into a state of panic as the internal value of the euro is outstandingly good (SPD parliamentary group press release 27 April 2000). The ECB's task to ensure internal price stability is still met and purchasing power is stable. The liberal FPD, however, was certain that the 'weak currency' was reflecting the lacking competitiveness of Euroland and that there is considerable danger of imported inflation. FDP EU-parliamentary-group spokesperson Haussmann noted the following in the Bundestag on the results of the Lisbon European Council meeting:

> In my view, the weakness is in reality the result of a comparison of systems. On the one hand, there is the Anglo-Saxon, flexible, open, one could say, libertarian economic and social system. On the other hand, there is the more bureaucratic, continental European and less flexible economic system. Until you do not decide on thorough reforms in taxation, labour and wage law, we will not achieve a lasting hard euro (6 April 2000 debate, Bundestagsprotokoll 14/098).

Summarising the explanations given throughout the year, there were four main reasons given in the German economic press and by ECB-watchers (for alternative enumeration, see e.g. SZ, 8 September 2000/b, 2).

First, the US was basically performing much better than Europe. Although the economies of all Euro-zone Member States were in a better shape than during most of the second half of the nineties, there were still clear differences among the Member States. While some of the small and medium-sized Member States were performing very well (albeit with some negative results such as higher inflation rates, see for example Ireland and the Netherlands), the three larger Member States Germany, France and Italy were not showing economic dynamism necessary to outperform the US. As a consequence, positive news on the American economy, which were numerous during the year 2000, were 'rewarded' by a rising US-dollar, as investments in the US were considered much more beneficial than in Euroland. Each piece of information on negative indicators in the main economies of the Euro-zone had deteriorating effects on the exchange rate of the euro. At the same time, and this came to a surprise to most analysts, 'good news' on Euroland showed virtually no positive effect on the exchange rate during the year 2000. In addition, the relationship between the ups and downs at the American stock market and the exchange rate of the US-dollar ceased to exist, thus invalidating one of the fundamentals of the international markets. It was therefore concluded that not only did the markets fail to believe in the strength and prospects of the European economies, but, at the same time, they failed to believe in the 'young central bank ECB' as being able to take care of its currency. Without any doubt, this analysis became a self-fulfilling prophecy right up to the all-time low in October.[166] It was also noted that there was a clear gap between the perception of Euroland in the US and in Euroland itself,

[166] In a rather sarcastic comment, the SZ already at the end of Jan 2000 (SZ on 29/30 Jan 2000, 25) demanded a global currency named 'Globo', but saw the biggest obstacle in the fact that at this point, there would be no other currency towards which the 'Globo' could be argued upwards or downwards.

with the US and its media rather thinking that the euro is not worth investing in it (Deutsche Bank chief economist Norbert Walter in FAZ, 30 October 2000, 35). While the 'old continent' was 'ill, decadent and divided', the US was exclusively defined by 'positive "imagines agentes" ' (SZ, 8 May 2000, 19). This would also give a partial explanation for the fact that while Euroland was performing much better than the Japanese economy, the exchange rate against the yen also deteriorated considerably.

Secondly, markets had serious 'doubts about the political will' of the politicians to back up the single currency with the necessary reforms to be carried out in and by the Member States (FAZ, 1 February 2000, 31). It is the politicians who are responsible for the weak euro as they had demonstratively declared that they would implement tax reforms, restructure deeply entrenched social security systems (both pension and health systems) and liberalise all necessary areas of the economy (FAZ, 2 May 2000, 33). As some investors had trusted these announcements in 1999, they are now retreating from the European market having lost substantial capital, thus adding to the deterioration of the exchange rate. It is, therefore, not the ECB that is to blame, as it had done what it was supposed to be doing, ie keeping inflation at bay (ibid.).

The debates within and actions of a number of Euro-zone Member States in September through tax reductions, in order to compensate for the rising oil prices, were taken as yet another indicator for the problems created by the lack of stronger discipline in economic policy. Most commentators criticised the French government for its move to give in to popular protest as well as the German reaction to soften certain rules for income and wage taxes. BuBa president Welteke went as far as criticising the government as he 'would have preferred if all European states would have uniformly done nothing' (Frankfurter Allgemeine Sonntagszeitung, 24 September 2000). Another example was given by reference to the different approaches as to the money obtained with the auctions of the UMTS/3G-licences (*Die Zeit*, 26 October 2000).

Thirdly, market analysts and the relevant media criticised throughout the year conflicting statements made by politicians and central bankers alike. During the first half of the year for some analysts politicians showed too few concerns about the deteriorating exchange rate *vis-à-vis* the US-dollar. They claimed that the euro 'would not be defended' and that 'appeasing statements by finance ministers' (e.g. after the Ecofin meeting in January) weakened ECB-statements on the inflation risk caused by the weakness (SZ, 2 February 2000, 25). Chancellor Schröder's comments in early September, that a weak euro favours (German) exports and is, therefore, good for the economy, provoked very negative reactions from the opposition parties and the press, which accused Schröder's statement of 'poisoning' confidence in the euro and of being responsible for the following further rate plunge (SZ, 8 September 2000, 1, 2 and 25).

The Jahresgutachten was also critical towards comments made by politicians that in principle a devaluation could be welcomed, as having expansive economic effects: 'this did the stability aim of the central bank a disservice' (Jahresgutachten 2000, 305). It, however, also stated that '[although] discordant statements of monetary decision-makers and the continuous devaluation of the European single currency irritated the public, [this] . . . was not reflected in raising inflation expectations' (Jahresgutachten 2000, 23).

While, for some, the conflicting statements were one of the main reasons for the plunge, the more uniform statements, at the same time, were also considered as detrimental to the exchange rate. The monotonous repetition of the perceived fact that the 'euro is undervalued' by institutions (e.g. by the Euro-group and the Commission), politicians and central bankers alike became flat, as these statements had obviously no effect (see, eg, comments made by the chairman of the Sachverständigenrat, Jürgen Donges, in Welt am Sonntag, 23 April 2000, 53; SZ, 8 September 2000/b, 2). As a consequence, commentators started questioning the empirical content of this message and argued that in the end, maybe there is no undervaluation (e.g. EMU Monitor; FAZ, 30 November 2000, 17).

In addition, the French call for a better co-operation between governments by strengthening the Euro-group, which had a democratic legitimacy, in order to establish a counterweight to the ECB, was taken as a further sign for the markets that Euroland's politicians could not be trusted (SZ, 22/23 July 2000, 25; FAZ, 24 August 2000, 1).

Fourthly, and finally, the fact that the euro is still a 'virtual' currency had further consequences for the lacking trust of the markets and the public as a whole. As prices remained stable, it seemed to be the stable Deutsche Mark that is responsible for it, while the euro lost its value every day at the foreign exchange market. Thus, if wages and pensions had been paid in euro already, people would have started to associate the internal price stability with the euro. However, until now, the euro lacks symbolism (FAZ, 2 September 2000, 13) and in the absence of any other instrument to measure the success of the currency, the public turned to the exchange rate and added to the bad reputation of the currency (BöZ, 22 November 2000).

This also was applied to the new profession of ECB-watchers. As the single currency and the ECB naturally are under stronger and more critical examination than the eleven national currencies before, there are always some analysts who blame the ECB for doing something or for not taking the expected decision (BöZ, 2 September 2000). Norbert Walter of Deutsche Bank compared the growing number of analysts with the decreasing number of central bankers to give an explanation that 'you will always find a fly in the ointment' when looking at the activities of the ECB

(*Die Welt*, 2 January 2001).

A slightly different debate addressed the economic consequences of the weakness of the euro. The Herbstgutachten, published at the time of the all-time low of the euro against the US-dollar, remarked that the devaluation consists of direct and indirect price effects. Second-round effects resulting from higher import prices are not to be expected, although stimulated exports could in return result in better price margins for domestic producers, being favoured by more expensive imports. These effects are much more relevant for the medium-term inflation development as they would spread into other areas and thus result into an increase of inflation dynamics (Herbstgutachten 2000, 77). Until now, these effects do not jeopardise the medium-term stability goals of the ECB.

It was also taken as a new kind of 'euro-sclerosis'—a term rather used in the first half of the 1980s, the fact that most Europeans do not understand the completely different situation Europe is experiencing since the start of the third stage of EMU. Most of them continue to think in national terms and thus overestimate the effects of the weak euro for their own economy. At a time where foreign (ie, non-Euroland) trade only amounts to 16 per cent of GDP compared to up to 60 per cent (for the Netherlands) before the EMU, the effects cannot be compared. Most Europeans do not take into account that, as a consequence of this, inflation does not soar and internal stability is secured (FAZ, 13 November 2000, 35). Thus, the euro-weakness 'does not matter' and Europe should learn from the US by adopting a policy of 'benign neglect' (*Die Zeit*, 11 May 2000, 32, also former Chancellor Helmut Schmidt in *Die Zeit*, 7 September 2000, 1).

Furthermore, outside the party political debate, certain remarks made by politicians noted that the weak euro has its advantages for the export-oriented German economy. At the same time, there was a warning that the industry should not become over-optimistic and postpone cost reduction efforts due to the favourable exchange rate. The BDI reminded the industry that only because of the strict policy of the Bundesbank in the past had the German economy improved its international competitiveness (Welt am Sonntag, 23 April 2000, 54).

Only at the end of the year analysts were finally relieved that fundamentals of the US as well as of Euroland's economy were more and more reflected in the improvement of the exchange rate (FAZ, 22 December 2000, 25, Welt am Sonntag 31 December 2000, 49). '2001—the year of the euro' (without a question mark in SZ, 27 December 2000, 4 and 4 January 2001, 4, with a question mark in an article of Norbert Walter in FAZ 2 January 2001, 25) was expected, fuelled by the possible recession in the US and the devastating impression of the vote count in the presidential elections. It remains to be seen, if the stronger euro is in fact a weaker US-dollar (Welt am Sonntag 31 December 2000, 49) as one must be reserved with confidence being low, with no progress visible with regard to the heterogeneity of the comments made by politicians and central bankers, and with a missing coherent economic and fiscal policy for Euroland (SZ editorial, 29 December 2000, 4).

Of course, the weak euro was also used in the party political debate in Germany, in which the opposition accused the government of being counter-productive in securing a strong currency. Already in April, the CDU/CSU claimed that the politics of the German government would make 'Germans poorer' (SZ, 25 April 2000, 1). Reacting to the claim of Chancellor Schröder, that 20-year-old analysts at the stock markets are dictating the exchange rate, the Bavarian Prime Minister Stoiber accused him of being part to blame for the weak euro (*Die Welt*, 2 November 2000). In October, the CSU parliamentary group leader in the Bundestag, Glos, accused the government of 'playing down the high-explosive risk-mix for stability, economic growth and jobs' and of 'inactivity' (Handelsblatt, 19 October 2000). The CDU saw Schröder's 'free and easy attitude to the euro-weakness as unacceptable' (CDU/CSU parliamentary group press release, 7 September 2000). For the CDU, this inactivity also led partly to the failure of the Danish referendum (CDU/CSU parliamentary group press release, 29 September 2000). Looking at macro-economic policy, the euro suffers from an inadequate policy to overcome economic, social, fiscal and labour market problems of the Euro-zone countries and especially of Germany, being the biggest Member State (CDU/CSU parliamentary group, 2000, 26–7).

This interpretation was consequently rejected by the parties in government. The Green MP Wolf replied to these accusations by referring to the exchange rate of the US-dollar to the Deutsche Mark in 1985 and to the continuous statements on behalf of the finance ministers calling for a strengthened euro (speech of Margareta Wolf in the Bundestag, 14 September 2000, Bundestagsprotokoll 14/118). References in the first half of the year 2000 by the governmental parties to the implicit positive effect for exports, especially for the German export-oriented economy, were numerous (see, eg, The Green MP Kerstin Müller in the Bundestag, 11 May 2000, Bundestagsprotokoll 14/102).

For the PDS, it is mainly the lack of a political union and the emerging enlargement that is problematic for the external value of the single currency (PDS parliamentary group press release, 29 September 2000). In the Bundestag, the PDS launched in May a written question on the effects of the undervaluation of the euro for the national budget (Bundestagsdrucksache 14/3460, 25 May 2000).[167]

The parliamentary group of the FDP took the chance of the euro weak-

[167] In its answer, the government saw only indirect consequences. It would mainly effect those areas where payments are made in US-dollar, for example in development policy. Additional expenditure would be approved by the Finance Ministry (Bundestagsdrucksache 14/3617 on 16 June 2000).

ness to accuse the German governmental coalition of being the main reason for the lack of confidence of the international financial markets in the single currency. As Germany is the biggest Member State, it needs to lead the way for other big Member States that had abandoned the ECB in its quest for a stronger euro (FDP parliamentary group press release, 6 November 2000). In more than twenty press releases on the euro-weakness throughout the year it correlated the exchange rate with demands to the government to pursue structural reform in Germany, including more flexible labour and goods markets, the abolition of the 'Eco-tax', and pension and social security reforms (eg FDP parliamentary group press release, 17 May 2000). The FDP, however, acknowledged that also the media had to change its reporting by putting more emphasis on the fact that internal stability of the currency was more or less achieved (FDP parliamentary group press release, 30 October 2000).

2.3 Institutional and procedural matters

2.3.1 General perception of institutional issues of EMU related policies

Looking at the debates in the Bundestag throughout the year, with some of the debates being officially about EMU and/or the euro, European issues were not in the centre of the discussion. The presentation by the Finance Minister and the consecutive discussion of the Convergence Report 1999 basically revealed that almost nobody in the Bundestag was prepared to discuss issues linked to either the euro or the work of the ECB (Bundestagsprotokoll 14/113). Only two written questions on the euro were posed to the government throughout the year 2000, one from the PDS on the exchange rate (see above), and one from MPs of the CDU/CSU on the change-over scenario (Bundestagsdrucksache 14/3832, 4 July 2000).[168] Furthermore, in the parliamentary debates on the annual budget for 2001 the Stability and Growth Pact was neither mentioned as an incentive nor as a disciplinary factor for the government's proposal on the budget deficit for 2001, with the exception of the Finance Minister. Otherwise, EMU was only mentioned by the opposition parties with regard to the exchange rate and the responsibility of the government for the devaluation. However, to put it differently, there was no real evaluation of the policies pursued of the ECB in Parliament or by the parliamentary groups in the Bundestag. This can be taken as a sign for the understanding of the parties that it should not be one of their tasks to assess the ECB's policy-making, which could be interpreted as political interference threatening the independence of the Central Bank.

The only real debate took place during the Bundestag questioning-time

168 The answer of the government was given in Bundestagsdrucksache 14/3908, 20 July 2000.

on the updating of the German stability programme by the government in October 2000 (Bundestagsprotokoll 14/123). Fiscal policies of other Member States and the Stability and Growth Pact were also basically the only co-ordination policy on which the media in Germany reported (e.g. on Germany FAZ, 29 February 2000, 17, on Italy FAZ 8 March 2000, 19; on France BöZ, 25 November 2000). The criticism on Austria's programme got some media coverage, too (FAZ, 27 April 2000, 22; SZ, 9 March 2000, 23; 13 June 2000, 25).

In the interviews carried out with the spokespersons for EU-affairs of three out of four parliamentary groups in the Bundestag, it turned out that EMU-awareness and related processes on the European level, including the Euro-group, is rather low. When it comes to the important institutions, such as to the Economic and Financial Committee being in charge of the preparation of both the Ecofin and the Euro-group meetings, or to the Economic Policy Committee preparing, among others, the Broad Economic Policy Guidelines and the 'Cardiff-reports', parties in the Bundestag hardly know of their existence.[169] However, the issue-specific committees of the Bundestag discuss government documents, which form part of the 'Cardiff' and 'Luxembourg' processes (BMF interview no 3).[170] Those topics seem to be reserved to parliamentarians sitting in the relevant committees and to an 'epistemic community' (Haas 1992) of ministerial officials, industry representatives and trade unionists who handle the European agenda.

With regard to the penetration of EMU-provisions into the national arena and into national policy-making, the government has now the position that the situation has to be improved (BMF interviews no 1 and 2, BMWi interview). For this, the government has restructured its annual economic policy report 2001, which has been prepared in the year 2000 (Jahreswirtschaftsbericht 2001), by emphasising its European dimension. More precisely, it tries to demonstrate, on the one hand, the European underpinning of policy choices on the national level by the government, and, on the other hand, the interconnectedness of German national policies with that of other EU Member States. For example, the annual economic policy report 2001 is written on the basis of the German chapter of the Broad Economic Policy Guidelines (BMF interview no 3). This 'new

[169] This assessment is also valid for the media and even for the specialised press. In *Die Zeit*, the former head of the EMU directorate of the Finance Ministry, Collignon, spoke of a 'jungle of methods and procedures' (*Die Zeit*, 26 Oct 2000), but it is noteworthy that this comment was indeed done by a civil servant. The 'Cologne process' and the 'Cardiff process' are completely absent from the media.

[170] Parliamentarians are more interested in aspects of EMU which are of relevance to their constituency. For example, the Economic Committee of the Bundestag is highly interested in the work of the Economy Ministry for the changeover and its consequences for small and medium-sized industry (BMWi interview).

approach' should also be introduced into other documents and into the handling of other policies, such as the national report on structural reforms ('Cardiff'). It was said that the Finance Minister himself has developed this idea in order to improve the national dialogue on EMU issues in the political debate (BMF interview no 2).

Looking at the Stability and Growth Pact, the likelihood of a national stability pact between the national, local and regional level is low. Apart from the fact that the main part of governmental debt lies with the national level, the real political issue between the national and the regional level as well as among the Länder themselves is the 'Länderfinanzausgleich' (financial adjustment among the Länder). A national stability pact is thus 'not an issue at all' (BMF interview no 1), although the government officially asks for some kind of national regulation (Jahreswirtschaftsbericht 2001, 32).[171]

2.3.2 Strengthening of the Euro-group and external representation

German newspapers and analysts carefully took note of the proposals made by the French Finance Minister Fabius and the informal developments during the French presidency of the Euro-group. His claim that it would be necessary to 'upgrade' the chairperson of the Euro-group by making him or her solely responsible for the representation of a coherent fiscal policy in Europe were considered as 'reasonable' and 'fitting into the logic of the Economic and Monetary Union' (FAZ, 26 September 00/b), especially with regard to the external representation of the euro in international financial organisations and meetings. In the long run, it will be necessary to have a single voice in international institutions, in order to be taken seriously.[172] In addition, his proposals for better co-ordination and working methods of the Euro-group were considered as improvements (SZ, 11 September 2000), as were those on the timing of the meetings and on the press conference after the Euro-group meetings (FAZ 22 August 2000).

But Fabius' implicit proposals in favour of inflation targets set by the finance ministers themselves were considered as an equivocal statement that was completely superfluous (Handelsblatt, 30 August 2000). This kind of approach was not taken as strengthening the Euro-zone with a better co-ordination of its policy mix (*Die Zeit*, 26 October 2000). Fabius' remarks, thus, triggered off the traditional German reactions against the French idea of a 'gouvernement économique' (Commissariat Général du Plan 1999; also Wessels/Linsenmann 2001), which is in principle directed

171 See on a German national stability pact also Hellermann (2000).

172 In May, the FTD pledged for a 'high representative for EMU Fiscal Policy' that should be elected by the finance ministers for longer than just the six months of one presidency (FTD, 10 May 2000).

against the independence of the Central Bank: 'Every attempt of the [French] EU-presidency to establish a second Mr Euro next to ECB-President Wim Duisenberg would only create new mistrust at the markets' (Tagesspiegel, 10 September 2000). Also BuBa president Welteke and vice-president Stark briskly rejected the French proposals (SZ 22/23 July 2000, p. 25; BöZ, 14 July 2000).[173]

The Jahresgutachten was against a strengthening of the role of the Euro-group vis-à-vis the European Central Bank, too, as this might lead to a political influencing of the ECB in its aims and monetary decisions. 'Everything should be avoided which would provoke the danger of a loss of credibility for the new currency' (Jahresgutachten 2000, 299). However, it was also noted that not every statement 'from Brussels, Paris or Berlin on the exchange rate is an attempt on the autonomy of the central bank' (FAZ, 26 September 2000/b).

The German Finance Ministry is rather positive with regard to the co-operation between the ECB and the Euro-group. It does not see any serious attempts by the French government to undermine the independence of the central bank. Quite on the contrary, the discussions with the president of the ECB at Euro-group meetings is successfully used by Duisenberg to elaborate on the monetary policy of the ECB. If the finance ministers understand the policy of the ECB, the ECB gains more independence (BMF interview no 2). It was acknowledged that the Euro-group has become more and more institutionalised in the last two years, albeit without detriment to the ECB but instead to the Ecofin.

It is interesting to note that the presentation made by the Belgian Finance Minister at the end of the year 2000 of his own strategy for the first one-year presidency of the Euro-group was mostly welcomed by the German press, despite the fact that some of the Belgian proposals went further than the French plans (BöZ, 22 December 2000). The proposals, including a separate secretariat for the Euro-group and an even closer co-ordination of the fiscal policies of the Member States, were not taken as futile, since the political actors will have to take into account the very negative experiences with the exchange rate during the year 2000 (ibid.).

2.3.3 The joining of Greece

The press coverage of Greece's accession to the Euro-zone started in May with the positive proposal of the European Commission. Earlier, the presi-

[173] Earlier the year, Karl Lamers, spokesperson on foreign policy of the CDU/CSU parliamentary group, had proposed a 'European economic government' adopting binding decisions for the Euro-zone as a precondition to solve the current problems (relating to the exchange rate) (press release CDU/CSU parliamentary group, 2 May 2000). This proposal, which is clearly a minority position in his party, was put in the framework of an up-date to his and Schäuble's concept of 'Kerneuropa' in the light of the IGC 2000.

dent of the Landeszentralbank Hesse, Reckers, officially warned the heads of state and government not to neglect the shaky fulfilment of the criteria by Greece as some analysts, for example from the IMF, suggested that the turnaround in Greece would not be long-lasting: 'In my view, it would be appropriate to postpone the accession of Greece for at least one year' (LZB Hessen press release, 27 April 2000).

Most commentators saw a 'candidate with minor defects' (SZ, 3 May 2000, 2) as it was still uncertain that the efforts of Greece would be long-lasting, because the Greek government had only temporarily reduced certain excise taxes in order to meet the criteria. It was, however, considered as a political decision not keeping Greece out of the Euro-club any longer. With this, 'the EU would step by step leave the path of a strict interpretation of the Maastricht criteria' (ibid.). It was the 'worst possible moment' for the European Commission to propose Greece's accession on the day that the euro hit another all-time low at the foreign exchange market (*Handelsblatt*, 4 May 2000). But there was no choice for the European Commission to postpone its proposal as it had to follow the 'fall from grace' precedent of the accession of Belgium and Italy in 1998 (ibid; see also NZZ, 20 June 2000). Also the Jahresgutachten pointed to the high gross government debt of 104.4 per cent in 1999 and to the favourable conditions in Greece that helped to meet the price stability criterion in 1999 (Jahresgutachten 2000, 86; for the favourable conditions, see also Handelsblatt, 1 November 2000). However, while some saw 'a new risk' (Handelsblatt, 4 May 2000), or were rather sceptical as to the lasting effects of recent efforts (DBR, 26 May 2000), for others 'the accession of the drachma will neither strengthen nor weaken the euro' (BöZ, 4 May 2000). The key role will still be with the finance ministers in the Euro-group that will have to ensure that decisions are followed with strict discipline (ibid.).

During the debate in the Bundestag on the results of the Feira European Council meeting, Finance Minister Eichel made clear that the government was happy that Greece succeeded in fulfilling the Maastricht criteria after a long and difficult but successful convergence process. He reminded Greece that it should not slacken its efforts to fulfil the stability programmes to follow (Bundestagsprotokoll 14/111, 10456). Contrary to the SPD, the CDU/CSU parliamentary group was against the accession of Greece to the Euro-zone. In the light of the weakness of the euro, it demanded a very strict and complete adherence to the Maastricht criteria. The joining of Greece should, thus, only take place, when gross government debt is considerably lower than at present and when it becomes clear that low inflation is actually a stable feature in Greece: 'The admission of Greece at this point in time would backfire' (CDU/CSU parliamentary group press release, 3 May 2000; see also CDU/CSU MP Gerd Müller in the above-mentioned debate, p. 10470). It consequently voted against a motion of the governmental parties on the position of the government at the Feira European Council that included a paragraph on the accession of Greece (Bundestagsdrucksache 14/3514, 7 June 2000). The FDP suggested a special time table for Greece—and also for potential other new members: first there should be a European Council meeting including the finance ministers that would decide on a binding time table for structural reforms. 'Only after such a preparation, the accession of Greece to the Euro-zone would be sensible' in macro-economic terms (FPD parliamentary group press release, 3 May 2000).

At the end of the year 2000 and the beginning of 2001, German commentators once again reviewed the accession of Greece to the Euro-zone with the Greek government having almost 'miraculously' succeeded (Wirtschaftsdienst, 2001/I, 6). The Euro-zone has become more heterogeneous as the Greek inflation rate was higher than the Euro-zone's average. Having lost the possibility of an independent monetary policy and having to deal with the Frankfurt policy which is not exactly suitable for its small and peripheral national economy, it will create the need for an even stricter fiscal and income policy (NZZ, 3 January 2001). However, most analysts were welcoming the accession that would not pose any danger for the stability in Euroland (Yahoo Deutschland, 2 January 2001). Also the positive remarks made by the ECB in its monthly bulletin were noted (BöZ, 12 January 2001).

2.3.4 The Danish referendum

Already before the referendum actually took place, most newspapers were not only speculating about the consequences of a 'lost referendum', taking into account that the opinion polls prior to 28 September 2000 were showing negative trends, but were also reporting extensively on the campaign. This may be taken as a sign how important the referendum was taken in Germany (eg FAZ, 28 September 2000, 7). Clearly, the consequence of the referendum for the European Union as a whole, and for Euroland in particular, was not exactly seen in the joining of the economically relatively unimportant Denmark—it was noted with particular relief that the euro exchange rate hardly reacted (SZ 30 September/1 October 2000, 1; FAZ 30 September 2000, 25; Berliner Zeitung, 30 September/1 October 2000, 4), but rather in the implications it will have on the state of the euro in Sweden and, above all, in the United Kingdom. The way the Danes voted ('to be in or not to be in') was also considered as an important element in the British debate on joining the EMU (FAZ, 15 September 2000/b, 13). In this respect, the negative result of the referendum was then also regarded as a boost for Euro-sceptics in the UK (SZ, 30 September/1 October 2000, 2; Wirtschaftsdienst 2000/X, 590).

It was also noted that most of the arguments used by the opponents of the single currency in Denmark were rather populist than actually factual. For example, the slogan that the introduction of the euro would be the single biggest transfer of sovereignty for Denmark and the fact that this slogan despite its incorrectness was successful was taken as a sign that the European project is obviously too complicated to positively 'sell' it to the citizens (FTD, 28 September 2000, 29). To put it differently, one of the positive effects of the Danish defeat was that 'the next candidates would be wise to learn from the Danish example and start a timely public discussion about the merits of becoming insiders' (DBR, 29 September 2000, 1). But the situation in Germany would not be all that different. A similar referendum in Germany—which would be unconstitutional—would have led to 'similarly catastrophic' results (SZ, 30 September/1 October 2000, 1; Berliner Zeitung, 30 September/1 October 2000, 1).

Finally, the referendum was considered as an important contribution to the on-going debate on the future of the European integration process. The various scenarios of a multi-speed Europe with differentiated integration were now confirmed, since the Danes finally destroyed the project of only one single integration stage supported and joined by all Member States. As a consequence, a 'hard core' Europe does exist already, that is the Euro-zone, with Member States using the economy as a 'launching pad for a confederation (*Staatenbund*)' (*Die Welt*, 30 September 2000, 1; FTD, 28 September 2000, 29; see also *Die Welt*, 24 October 2000).

The German parties also commented on the failure of the referendum. For the CDU, it was a setback for the integration process. Whereas the economic consequences are only minor, political and psychological effects for European integration are much more serious (CDU/CSU parliamentary group press release, 29 September 2000). Furthermore, for the CDU/CSU it was 'a slap in the face of German European policy' and a result of the government's negligence in the handling of the euro exchange rate (Berliner Zeitung, 30 September/1 October, S. 1). The PDS was rather grateful that the Danes used their constitutional right to decide on whether or not they want to join the Euro-zone. The Danes were not at all impressed by the supporting interventions of the central banks and the comments made at the G7 Finance meeting with regard to the undervaluation of the euro. It recalled that the PDS demanded such a referendum also for Germany (PDS parliamentary group press release no 1947, 29 September 2000).

The Greens took note of the result with regret because it would pose a new challenge for European policy. It needed to be made clear that the euro is not only a monetary project but rather a political project to maintain and extend the Community model (Green parliamentary group press release no 0581/2000, 29 September 2000). The SPD saw limited consequences for the economy with the exception of the cross-border trade between Denmark and its bordering countries, which is of particular importance for the Danish economy (SPD parliamentary group press release no 802, 29 September 2000). For the FDP, it was a setback for Europe, which not only resulted from the wrong policy against Austria but from lacking economic and institutional reforms in the Euro-zone. Only these would create the necessary confidence of the international financial markets (FDP parliamentary group press release, 29 September 2000).

2.3.5 Debate on enlargement and the reform of the ECB governing council

The debate on the reform of the Governing Council in the light of the enlargement towards Central and Eastern Europe was limited to a few articles and statements. The Börsen-Zeitung saw the need for an optimisation of the Treaty provisions as a precondition for the 'qualitative improvement of the product euro' because without a reform the interests of national central bankers would dominate the ECB council too much (BöZ, 20 September 2000). As the 12 candidate countries and Turkey currently only represent 7 per cent of the EU's GDP while representing 40 per cent of the population, BuBa-President Welteke posed the question 'if with the current institutional framework . . . a unified monetary policy could be pursued' (cited in BöZ, 28 November 2000). He urged the political actors to clarify this question soon and unambiguously in order to prevent false assessments on both sides. It was noted, that it would not only be national interests but indeed 'small states' national interests that would determine the monetary policy directions of the ECB (FTD, 3 May 2000).

The German Finance Ministry would have liked the ECB to come forward with a proposal during the year but the ECB governing board could not agree on a common standpoint. After the (non-)decision had been taken at the Nice European Council,[174] various solutions are now possible for the Finance Ministry. However, a 'German seat' in the governing board will be a condition. A mixing together with the nationalities of the executive board members will be one of the options, even if this would be against one of the 'holy principles' of the ECB (BMF interview no 2).

The Deutsche Bank chief economist Norbert Walter proposed a formula that would more or less maintain the current weight of the executive board within the governing council (FAZ, 25 April 2000, 33). In a similar vein, the Financial Times Deutschland argued that the number of governing council members is not important, if first the ECB council starts having a formal voting on decisions—as provided for by the Treaty and the ESCB-ECB Statute provisions, and if secondly the executive board is united when tabling proposals. So far, a united board needs roughly a third of the

174 See new Art 10.6 of the ESCB–ECB Statute and Declaration No 19 to the Treaty of Nice.

national central banks presidents. This relation won't change much in a Euro-zone with 20 members and 26 ECB council members, provided that decision-making by majority is actually used (FTD, 3 May 2000).

In the light of the Danish referendum, it was also noted that Europe should do its utmost to prevent the impression that the Euro-zone is only attractive to poor, ie to present and future 'cohesion funds' countries, while strong economies such as Denmark, Sweden and the UK stay deliberately apart. In this respect, the strict application of the Maastricht criteria should be secured by giving the ECB governing council the right to veto any new accession to the Euro-zone (BöZ, 20 September 2000). Following this argumentation, the BuBa president Welteke, who demanded stronger Maastricht criteria for the countries currently enjoying a candidate status with the EU, triggered off an additional debate in Germany. The magazine *Der Spiegel* reported on a paper of the Bundesbank sent by Welteke to both Foreign Minister Fischer and Finance Minister Eichel, in which doubts were raised that new Member States would be as much committed to the fight against inflation as the current Member States are. Economies catching up with the standard of living in the EU would inevitably produce and accept higher inflation rates. As a consequence, it would be very probable that political pressure would increase to water down the stability criteria and the stability course of the Euro-system (Der Spiegel 49/2000, 132). 'Real criteria' should therefore be added to the existing ones, which was translated as a new criterion evaluating the economic strength of the country concerned. Peter Schmidthuber (former member of the European Commission and former member of the executive board of the Bundesbank) was cited saying that 'nominal and real convergence would have to be pursued at the same time' (VWD, 6 December 2000).

2.4 Trends towards spill-over[175]

Naturally, politicians debated in German newspapers both the relation between the Intergovernmental Conference for the revision of the Amsterdam Treaty and the development of EMU. In particular, the gloomy prospects of a real leap forward at the Nice European Council meeting for the future of the integration process and the weakness of the euro were seen as connected developments. Looking from the position of a central banker, Ottmar Issing asked for a 'workable political structure for Europe' even if monetary union has managed to function without a political union (FTD, 15 September 2000).

The lacking 'political pillar' which would strengthen the currency was noted and it was expected that the EMU, further integrated by federal (following the principle of subsidiarity) political structures, would form an 'own circle' within the European Union (FAZ, 23 October 2000). This

[175] Note that the 'external projection of the euro' is covered by Ch 2.3.2.

kind of 'EMU hard core' would thus be the 'political pillar' needed for the euro (ibid.). Consequently, there was no reference to any kind of support resulting from the Nice results for the single currency.

2.4.1 Tax harmonisation and social policy

The major debates on taxation policies and harmonisation which have dominated Germany during the year 1999 and especially during Lafontaine's term in office as finance minister came to an end in 2000 as most of the political discussions centred on the 'reform projects' of the government, ie the 'big tax reform', the introduction of the Eco-tax on 1 January 2001 as well as the reform of the pension system, with the latter going to be decided in mid-2001.[176] Nevertheless, the national agenda of the Federal government until the next elections in 2002 in the area of economic, fiscal and employment policy, as well as with regard to structural reforms (liberalisation and deregulation of gas, electricity, postal and telecommunication markets) coincides with the central items on the European agenda in these policy areas, as it is well reflected in the various 'co-ordination processes' at the European level ('Luxembourg' and 'Cardiff'), and as was again reinforced in the detailed policy agenda of the Lisbon European Council. The Lisbon-strategy and the 'new open method of co-ordination' should indeed foster the relationship among policy areas and move forward the social agenda of the Union (Chancellor Schröder in the Bundestag, Bundestagsprotokoll 14/098, 6 April 2000).

Thus, in a broad sense one could argue that there are trends towards 'spill-over' from the EMU and from the internal market project (Wessels/Linsenmann 2001; Dyson 2000). Moreover, 'Member States will eventually take further steps towards more supranational modes of governance in the field of fiscal, economic, and employment policy as well, adjusted to the specific characteristics of the policy field' (Wessels/Linsenmann 2001).

Looking at spill-over trends in the stricter sense, the government does not see the need for regulating the differences between corporation taxes and peak rates of (income) tax at European level through harmonisation measures. The government is looking more at those taxation policies that are designed to attract foreign capital (Eichel, 19 October 2000; BMF interview no 2). Furthermore, harmonisation is seen as necessary in the area of VAT and capital income taxes as a result of EMU (BMF interview no 2). For other taxes, such as income tax or corporation taxes, tax competition would be given preference to harmonisation. Thus, *political*

176 For a detailed account of the controversy between the proponents of 'ordo-liberalism' and 'managed capitalism' in the current government and the legacy of Lafontaine, see Dyson (2001).

debates on 'races to the bottom' resulting from tax competition died out, somehow also related to the Feira decision on savings taxation in June and to the consequent agreement on 'substantial content' in late November by the Ecofin (Council of the EU, 26/27 November 2000).[177] Finally, the government sees the necessity of further harmonisation of energy taxation, although it doubts that the proposed directive for the restructuring of the Community framework regulations on the taxation of energy products will be adopted soon (Jahreswirtschaftsbericht 2001, p. 38).

In the interviews, the CDU/CSU claimed that they would opt for a strengthened harmonisation of taxation policy, especially with regard to indirect taxes and to a unified tax on profits, while at the same time labour market regulations should remain decentralised (CDU/CSU interview). The PDS is rather split on the whole European integration process with some being fundamentally against the 'capitalistic project', some believing in the national level rather than in the European one for the best arena for pursuing a 'social agenda', and with others being in favour of more democratic structures at the European level. With regard to a deepening of the EMU policies there seems to be a majority of the parliamentary group in favour of a 'real' economic and social union including a transfer of sovereignty (PDS interview).

For the BDI, representing German industry, advantages and disadvantages of a further integration have to be weighed against each other. If spill-over would mean further harmonisation in the area of taxation and social policy, it would rather be a negative and counter-productive development for competition conditions in German industry. Instead, competition among Member States as to advantages of an industrial location would be better served by rules that prevent unfair competition and a distortion of the common market principles (see the energy sector in France). The BDI is against a further integration of employment policy as it doubts that reforms of labour market regulations that are necessary for Germany would be implemented via the European level (BDI interview).

Furthermore, 'Europe badly needs more efficient capital markets' (Norbert Walter in DBR, 15 December 2000, 5). Although market capitalisation was seen as almost identical with that of the US on an aggregated calculation, capital markets in Europe are still fragmented with high institutional and financial barriers—such as different trading systems—preventing an integrated market (Handelsblatt, 24 October 2000). This needs to go hand in hand with a 'political standardisation' including co-ordination of economic policy and common foreign and security policy

[177] Germany is going to implement the necessary legal adaptations following the Feira decisions until the end of the year 2002. Among the steps to be made one may refer to changing the rules of the bankers' duty to maintain confidentiality and Art 30a.3 of the Tax Act (MP Poß on 29 June 2000, Bundestagsprotokoll 14/111, 10463).

(ibid.). European standardisation must also apply to taxation systems, common accounting standards, as well as to the regulation and deregulation of the banking system, which would help to harmonise European capital markets. The Lamfalussy group of wise men on the development of a European capital market was thus seen as a first but not yet sufficient step in the right direction (FTD, 17 August 2000). The same analysis also applies to the Commission's Financial Services Action Plan (Jahreswirtschaftsbericht, 2001, 61–2).[178]

In addition, company law in Europe is seen as in great need of a further harmonisation, including its implementation and enforcement, so that, for example, investors and share-holders can be sure that an unsuccessful management bears its responsibilities and securities are actually used also for companies outside the specific national arena (FTD, 17 August 2000). Thus, the need for a pan-European securities regulator is obvious but it will take years if not decades until the national authorities are willing to give up their powers. In this respect, the failure of the attempted fusion of the London SE and the Deutsche Börse into 'iX Exchange' was seen not as a sign of unwillingness among the actors, but rather as caused by different national regulations (BöZ, 13 September 2000).

2.4.2 Co-ordination of macroeconomic policy and monetary policy (policy-mix)

One of the key policy areas in which progress is demanded as a direct consequence of monetary union is indeed economic policy, as the imbalance between a monetary policy being decided at the European level and economic (and fiscal) policy being still in the hands of national institutions is seen as a major risk for EMU. Even if there are no official attempts to change the Treaty provisions, the Finance Ministry does see the need of a further deepening of the economic policy co-operation. This could be the introduction of stricter provisions for the monitoring mechanisms and the screening processes of economic policy (Article 99 EC). In the light of a non-existing dominating central state—especially when comparing the EU with the US—provisions for the Member States have to be more binding (BMF interview no 2). Thus, the German government has moved away from former Bundesbank-dominated positions to avoid any tight co-ordination of economic policy (Dyson 2001).

With regard to the various co-ordination procedures, the government is

[178] In its report on structural reforms within the 'Cardiff-Process', the government enumerates the various legislative processes introduced in the year 2000 with regard to capital markets and financial services, ie a bill on rules for corporate take-overs, the Registered Stock Act, drafts for the Fourth Financial Markets Promotion Act and the setting up of a group of experts on corporate governance (see Federal Ministry of Economics and Technology, 2000, 37).

content with the progress made in the year 2000:

The individual policy areas have so far been able to supplement each other, making a policy-mix oriented to growth and stability. A wage trend oriented to stability and employment over the medium term, successful fiscal policy consolidation and significant progress in structural reforms have supported the ECB in its stability policy task. The EU and the Euro-zone have thus become more resistant to external shocks' (Jahreswirtschaftsbericht 2001, p. 25). The procedures are considered as 'necessary instruments to realise a vital overall strategy for sustained economic growth, more and better jobs and greater social cohesion. It will remain a lasting task to tighten the existing procedures of economic policy co-ordination and to improve their interaction and thus to achieve synergy effects (ibid, 23; in the same vein, BMF-interviews nos 2 and 3; BMWi-interview).

3. Legal framework

3.1 Changes in the legal framework

3.1.1 Results of the EMU working party (AS WWU)

This co-ordination group, created in 1995 and chaired by the Federal Ministry of Finance, includes senior civil servants from all federal ministries, and—with observer status—representatives of the Bundesbank, the Chancellery, the Press and Information Office, the Länder and cities.[179] It still exists in 2001 and it co-ordinated the drafting of numerous laws and procedures to implement the euro in Germany. In July 2000, the group published a comprehensive report, its fourth, on the introduction of the euro into legislation and public administration. The working party will dissolve after January 2002, but before that it still functions as a forum for information exchange and it already published its fifth report.[180] The preparatory legal work as such is completed (BMF interview no 2; BMWi interview).

After the key legal adaptations have been enacted during the years 1998 and 1999, the change-over to the euro also results in detailed legal adaptations in a vast number of acts which contain amounts in German marks (see 4th report by the EMU working party, July 2000, 41–6). The conversion of Deutsche Mark 'signal amounts', ie round sums usually fixed as thresholds for tax exemption limits, fines, and fees, if conducted purely mathematically, would result in 'awkward' signal amounts in euro. Therefore, the amounts need to be realigned. This implies political decisions by the competent departments who have to find a balance between the interests of those supporting realignment at a lower level and those in

179 See *Eurospectator* German report for 1999 (Linsenmann/Müller 2000).

180 The fifth report has been published on 20 June, 2001: <http://www.bundesfinanzministerium.de/infos/eurogeld1/5aswwubericht.pdf>.

favour of a higher level. Amounts whose realignment affects citizens directly, ie with external price and cost relevance, are more sensitive than those that affect only the internal administrative sphere, ie the budgets of public authorities. However, the distinction is in some cases difficult to make, since even threshold values with a primarily internal administrative or organisational purpose may entail financial effects for citizens. Another consideration is the impact on the credibility and acceptance of the euro of a public perception that the conversion may be used to 'make everything more expensive' through a general smoothing to a higher level. A gradual and transparent process is asked for. Possible solutions pinpointed by the EMU working party were:

- An effort by the government to reduce the value of signal amounts—with the possible consequence of lower revenues.
- For laws, which need to be amended anyway in the transitional period, 'awkward' amounts in Deutsche Mark could be fixed in a way yielding 'rounded' euro amounts.
- An averaging approach means increases in one place would be offset by reduction in another. Of course, areas would have to be defined carefully and sufficient transparency for citizens would have to be taken into consideration.

Among the dozen of acts that were passed and partly already adopted, the one on the smoothing of euro amounts in tax law (*Steuer-Euroglättungsgesetz*, StEuglG) of 19 December 2000 (BGBl I, no 57, 23 December 2000) particularly addresses the problem of smoothing signal amounts in pivotal tax acts, including the Income Tax Act, Corporation Tax Act, Trade Tax Act, etc. It essentially chooses to realign amounts in favour of the taxable persons (4th report EMU working party, 43). The European Commission complimented the German government for the preparations for the introduction of euro banknotes and coins, and for that piece of legislation in particular (European Commission 2001, 22–3). Finance Minister Eichel announced in the Bundestag that the government's choice to round amounts down in favour of taxpayers would mean a total 350 million Deutsche Mark less tax income (Bundestagsprotokoll 14/123, 11785).

The realignment of amounts in legislation of the various ministries has been put together in comprehensive laws (*Artikelgesetze*) on the introduction of the euro, in most cases in one for each ministry. From these *Euro-Einführungs-Gesetze*[181] the fourth has already been enacted whereas the other ones are still in the legislative procedure by the time of writing.

- The Fourth Act (*Viertes EuroEG*) regulates conversion to the euro in social

[181] For the first three Acts (Euro-Einführungs-Gesetze) see *Eurospectator* German report for 1999 (Linsenmann/Müller 2000).

and labour law (BGBl I, no 60, 29 December 2000).

- The Fifth Act (*Fünftes EuroEG*) was drafted by the Ministry of Agriculture and concerns provisions in the agriculture and forestry sector (Bundestagsdrucksache 14/4555, 9 November 2000).
- The Sixth Act (*Sechstes EuroEG*) concerns regulations in the area of public administration, immigration, foreigners' and nationality law (Bundesratsdrucksache, 10/01, 5 January 2001).
- The Seventh Act (*Siebtes EuroEG*) regulates the conversion into euro of fees and fines in the environmental sector (Bundestagsdrucksache 14/5641, 23 March 2001).
- The Eighth Act (*Achtes EuroEG*) handles conversion issues in the health sector (Bundestagsdrucksache 14/5930, 26 April 2001).
- The Ninth Act (*Neuntes EuroEG*) is a joint product of the Ministry of Economics and Technology and of the Ministry of Education and Research and includes honoraria for architects and engineers (Bundestagsdrucksache 14/5937, 26 April 2001).
- The Tenth Act (*Zehntes EuroEG*) handles conversion measures in the area of transport, construction and housing, as well as family, senior citizens, women and youth.[182]
- The Eleventh Act (*Elftes EuroEG*) regulates the conversion into euro in the area of competence of the Ministry of Defence (Bundestagsdrucksache 14/5436, 6 March 2001).
- A Twelfth Act (*Zwölftes EuroEG*) concerns excise taxes and has been prepared by the Ministry of Finance (Bundestagsdrucksache 14/6143, 25 May 2001).

In addition, there are several other acts not included in the numbering of the *Euro-Einführungs-Gesetze*. An act has already been enacted on the supervision of insurance companies (BGBl I, no 58, 27 December 2000), whereas a conversion law for the *Lastenausgleichsgesetz* (Bundestagsdrucksache 14/5440, 6 March 2001)[183] is pending. In the area of competence of the Ministry of Justice, there have been several legal adaptations. Two acts are already enacted: one concerns stock-market shares (*Namensaktiengesetz*) (BGBl I, no 4, 24 January 2001) and the other converts fees and indemnification rates of a number of acts in the judicial area (*KostREuroUG*) (BGBl I, no 19, 4 May 2001). More are to follow: one on civil procedural law (*Reform des Zivilprozesses*), and six minor ones regulating different aspects of legal provisions.[184]

Finally, also at the regional level, the sixteen Länder have adopted the

[182] Unaccounted for at the time of writing.

[183] *Lastenausgleich*: compensation paid to individuals for damage and losses during and immediately after the Second World War. There are still some pensions being paid under this scheme.

[184] Statute introducing the euro in professional law, in administration of justice, in civil,

local legislation necessary for euro conversions and for rounding amounts in euro (European Commission 2001, p. 26).

3.1.2 Practical implementation of the exchange of notes and coins

On 8 November 1999 the EU Finance Ministers agreed to allow a restricted amount of euro coins to be released to the public in the second half of December 2001 (Council of the EU, 08.11.99). As in other Eurozone countries, the German government chose to take advantage of this option. The Ministry of Finance, the Bundesbank, representatives of the industry and services, as well as banks and consumer organisations, agreed upon the following measures to introduce the so-called starter-kits:

On 1 September 2001, the Bundesbank will provide credit institutions with the new currency, including up to 53 million mixed coin packages for distribution to the population until the end of the year. Credit institutions can give out those starter-kits with euro coins as of 17 December 2001. The starter-kits contain 20 coins worth 10,23 euro and will be given out in exchange for 20 DM, without charging any fees. The aim is that the population should familiarise itself with the new coins and use them for payment starting 1 January 2002. For blind people there is an additional possibility to receive euro banknotes, printed only on one side. This should contribute to a better adaptation to the new currency. The euro coins and notes will become legal tender and replace the Deutsche Mark as of 1 January 2002, when the 'legal big bang' takes place, and shall not be accepted for payment before that date. As a way of facilitating the transition, it will be possible to pay in Deutsche Mark until 28 February 2002, but change will be given only in euro (see *Eurospectator* German report for 1999; Linsenmann/Müller 2000).

Since police forces are under the authority of the Länder, measures of crime prevention with reference to the introduction of the euro are coordinated by a project group (Projektgruppe EURO) founded on 5 May 2000 and composed of representatives of all Länder police forces as well as of border police and of the federal criminal office (Bundeskriminalamt). The co-ordination at the federal level lies with the Ministry of the Interior (Bundestagsdrucksache 14/3908, 20 July 2000).

3.2 National law from the EC perspective

Conflicts or inconsistencies of the legislation and regulations adopted during 2000 *vis-à-vis* Community law are not known to the authors.

criminal and regulatory offences procedural law; second statute amending the law of compensation for damage; statute introducing the euro in financial statement law; amendment of the regulations governing administrative courts; statute amending rules of costs in the area of intellectual property; statute amending distress exemption limits.

3.3 The application of the law

There was a constitutional complaint brought in December 2000 by the *Effecten-Spiegel* before the Federal Constitutional Court against the third act on the introduction of the euro (*Drittes EuroEG*) based on Article 14.1 of the Basic Law (*Grundgesetz—GG*), ie on the protection of ownership. The plaintiff was a weekly stock-market journal based in Düsseldorf that specialises in derogatory accusations against the government and the banking system about all that concerns the euro. The accusation that the *Drittes EuroEG* was contrary to the constitutional right of ownership was based on the claim that the euro, which replaces the DM as the only valid currency in Germany following the *Drittes EuroEG*, has proven to be a currency of unstable value. Replacing the DM by the euro was therefore considered by the plaintiff to be hurting the right of ownership of anyone who owns money currently denominated in DM. The Constitutional Court by ruling on 9 February 2001 refused to accept the complaint.[185]

Apart from this case, proceedings and judgments during 2000 including private and public law issues, are not known to the authors.

There were also no legal debates, strictly speaking, on the euro in the German legal literature in 2000. There was some discussion in the last FIDE (International Federation for European Law) congress about laws that had to be adapted, consequently to the introduction of the euro, in particular in the interest of a functioning capital market.[186] The media did ask repeatedly for legal advice on the question whether Germany had the right to leave the Euro-zone (which of course it has not). This happened before the Danish referendum as well as during the exchange rate plunge of the euro against the dollar.

Finally, there have been reports in the German press concerning the employer status of the ECB. Employees' tasks description, the promotion system and the wage scales are not clearly defined, and this is in contradiction with standards of national labour laws (SZ, 28 November 2000, 21; Tagesspiegel online, 3 December 2000). The two internal unions representing the ECB personnel (USE, Union of the Staff of the ECB, and IPSO, International and European Public Services, together about 24 per cent of ECB employees) have filed a lawsuit in case T-238/00 with the European Court of first Instance in Luxembourg, arguing that the ECB cannot refuse to enter into wage negotiations and cannot restrict the right to strike. A small group of employees has followed and filed a lawsuit in case T-20/01, in their own name, asking for a an examination of a standard clause in ECB contracts which stipulates that contracts are subject to general personnel rules in their most recent version, allowing the ECB to change

185 Unpublished decision 2 BvR 2226/00.

186 Papers have not been published.

conditions of employment unilaterally at any given time (information provided by USE and IPSO). However, although the ECB is located in Frankfurt, the matter is really a European one and does not fall under German law.

3.4 Institutional aspects

Institutional adaptations at the national level resulting from Economic and Monetary Union are still under way in Germany. As reported in the *Eurospectator* report 1999, this concerns mainly the federally structured German central bank system. In the year 2000, the question of institutional reforms of the system of banking or prudential supervision has to be added to the list of disputed issues in the political arena in Germany.

Due to the fact that the reform of prudential supervision will also affect the position of the Bundesbank, which is so far also responsible for debt management and involved in the banking supervision, both issues are considered together by some of the political actors, a development that has not helped to solve any of the problems. In addition, the interests of the various actors involved in this question differ substantially, being further complicated due to the Bundesrat's involvement in the legislative procedure to amend the Bundesbank Act.[187]

3.4.1 The reform of the Bundesbank

With regard to the reform of the German central bank system the Bundesbank, the ministries of finance of the federal and regional levels, and finally the Länder central banks have continued their political battle in the year 2000 on the 'centralist'-'federal' model dichotomy. A question of particular importance is the involvement of the Länder central banks in the key institutional bodies of the Bundesbank as well as in the reform of the executive organs of the latter. While the Ministry of Finance and the finance ministries of the Länder had requested an expert commission to present a report on the structural reform of the Bundesbank (BMF Bericht zur Strukturreform der Bundesbank, presided by Karl Otto Pöhl, 4 July 2000), the Ministry of Finance was, due to political reasons, unable to proceed with the legislative procedure in the presentation of a draft act in the year 2000.

Undisputed is the fact that with the creation of the ESCB the focus of monetary decision-making has shifted from the national to the EU level (FAZ, 4 July 2000). As a consequence, it is not the German Zentralbankrat (Central Bank Council) that decides on monetary questions anymore, and, following Article 7 of the ESCB–ECB Statute, the

[187] A draft of the government can be blocked by a two-thirds majority of the Bundesrat, which requires an—unlikely—two-thirds majority in the Bundestag in order to be overruled.

Zentralbankrat is not even allowed to instruct the president of the Bundesbank on his voting behaviour in the ECB Governing Council. Thus, the role and composition of the Zentralbankrat has to be adapted as the Bundesbank is in need of an efficient management system in order to be 'competitive' with other national central banks within the ESCB (BMF Bericht, see above). Finally, and there is also a consensus on this aspect, the present structure is extremely costly, with staff numbers being disproportionately high compared to other central banks (SZ, 29 August 2000). A 30 per cent cut in staff numbers (currently slightly below 16.000) is envisaged by all political actors.

An additional argument for the reform was put forward by the Bundesbank president Welteke, who complained about the personal statements of the independent Länder central bank presidents that added too many voices to the German position and irritated Euro-system partners (Ernst Welteke quoted in BöZ, 4 July 2000). Contrary to this position, the Länder central banks argued that they are closer to the citizens and to smaller and medium-sized enterprises, and thereby contribute to feelings of confidence and trust in the stability of the euro.[188] By slightly neglecting the new decision-making structure of the ESCB, the Länder governments mainly argue that the Bundesbank president needs the advice of independent presidents of Länder central banks in the Zentralbankrat.

The Pöhl Commission proposed (by a majority of its members) to abolish first the independent status of the presidents of the Länder central banks and secondly, the current role of the Zentralbankrat. It should be replaced by a single executive organ with ten members (replacing the Directorate, the Zentralbankrat, and the executive boards of the Länder central banks). The nine Länder central banks should turn into five regional agencies of the Bundesbank presided by a regional president. These should be members of the single executive organ next to the president, the vice-president and three other members nominated on a proposal by the Federal government (while the regional presidents are nominated on a proposal by the Bundesrat).[189]

While the proposals of the Pöhl commission suited both Welteke (Bundesbank press release, 6 July 2000) and Finance Minister Eichel,[190]

188 This position was especially promoted by the president of the Central Bank of Bremen, Lower Saxony and Saxony Anhalt, Hans Helmut Kotz (LCB Bremen, Lower Saxony and Saxony-Anhalt, press statement, 15 May 2000) and by the president of the Central Bank of North-Rhine-Westphalia, Eberhard Heinke (LCB of North-Rhine Westphalia, press release, 4 Dec 2000).

189 The position of the Pöhl Commission was also supported by the Jahresgutachten (2000, 87). The new structure should be oriented to more efficiency and to an effective participation of the Bundesbank president in the ECB Governing Council. The Zentralbankrat in its present form and independent Länder central banks are not any more needed in EMU (ibid.).

190 The general idea of a centralised and streamlined institution was also supported by an opinion of the Federal Court of Auditors (FAZ, 27 Apr 2000, 21).

most Länder finance ministers and Länder central banks' presidents were strictly against the abolishment of the federal structure of the Bundesbank. Thus, the effort to have a mixed expert commission helping to find a compromise between the different levels failed (see also Welteke in FAZ, 7 September 2000, p. 18).

The Finance Ministers of Bavaria, North-Rhine-Westphalia, Lower Saxony and Saxony pleaded together and across party lines for the upholding of the present decentralised structure throughout the year (SZ, 29 May 2000, 25; SZ, 29 August 2000). In a 'cornerstone paper' at the end of the year, which was based on an earlier draft of September 2000, they again put forward the position of the Länder governments by proposing a solution with a directorate of eleven members, five nominated by the Federal government and six—rotating—from the nine LCBs (SZ, 29 May 2000, 25).

The December 'cornerstone paper' was thus not welcomed by Finance Minister Eichel who had reasons to hope that the Länder would be more willing to compromise, e.g. by presenting a 50–50 proposal on the directorate and by willing to reduce the number of Länder central banks to five (BöZ, 16 November 2000). Also the Directorate of the Bundesbank unanimously rejected the paper, criticising the enormous co-ordination costs and redundant work inherited in the proposed structure and concluding that it would prevent an efficient running of the Bundesbank (Bundesbank press release, 13 December 2000). Thus, Welteke again put forward his own point of view, pleading for a new, streamlined solution that would allow substantial savings of time, bureaucracy and money, and a more homogeneous decision-making procedure. His proposal at the end of the year included eight-member directorate, with the government nominating president and vice-president and the remaining six proposed by a mixed federal government/Länder commission. The Länder central banks should become local agencies of the Bundesbank, lose their 9 presidents and give up their supervision duties (SZ, 28 December 2000, 24).

The government, represented by Finance Minister Eichel, had generally sided with the streamlined, money-saving proposals put forward by the Bundesbank and the Pöhl Commission, albeit without being too outspoken (interview with Eichel in BöZ, 30 December 2000). Eichel was put into the unpleasant role of a mediator between the Länder finance ministers and the media-oriented Bundesbank president and it was only in January 2001 that he came forward with the first official contribution of the federal government. By that time, criticism of his indecisiveness had grown with many fearing that this would damage the reputation of the Bundesbank (VWD, 3 January 2001). On 25 January 2001, Eichel finally announced the proposed outline of the government draft that included the abolishment of the Zentralbankrat and the replacement of the Directorate by a central executive board (with a president, a vice-president and four other members all nominated by the federal level). In return, the Länder central banks and their presidents should be preserved, the latter however not any more being involved in the decision-making structures in the Bundesbank (FTD, 26 January 2001). With this structure, the 'German monetary authority would obtain an efficient and lean structure' (SZ, 26 January 2001, 23).

While the banks (BdB) welcomed the proposal and the Bundesbank was unable to comment due to disagreements in the Zentralbankrat (Bundesbank press release, 25 January 2001), the Länder were overtly critical (SZ, 26 January 2001, 23). By that time, however, the focus of the debate turned more to Eichel's institutional proposals on prudential supervision (see below). With the legislative procedure to amend the Bundesbank Act—the final draft legislation of the government was finally adopted by the Federal cabinet on 30 May 2001 (BMF press release, 30 May 2001)—certainly not to be finalised in the year 2001, the debate on the Bundesbank reform will continue for another year.

3.4.2 The reform of prudential supervision in Germany

The second major institutional reform project is the structure of the national supervision of the banking, insurance and securities markets. Here, the interests of the political actors are definitely different from those on the issue of the BuBa reform; in particular the Bundesbank itself and the Ministry of Finance have diverging opinions. At present, there are three institutions in Germany that fulfil supervisory tasks: the Federal Banking Supervisory Office (Bundesaufsichtsamt für das Kreditwesen) in co-operation with the Bundesbank, the Federal Insurance Supervisory Office (Bundesaufsichtsamt für das Versicherungswesen) and the Federal Securities Supervisory Office (Bundesaufsichtsamt für den Wertpapierhandel). Since the beginning of the debate the intention of the Ministry of Finance has been to create a single federal agency.

Conflicts revolved in particular around the issue of banking supervision. While the Bundesbank demanded the full integration of banking supervision into the Bundesbank, claiming that already it is carrying out most of the data collection and the processing of reports submitted by the institutions, the FBSO proposed to merge all functions of banking supervision under its own authority (SZ, 22 March 2000, 26). Since the actual 'on-site supervision' is actually decentralised to the Länder central banks, the latter and the Länder governments support the Bundesbank in merging the banking supervision into the Bundesbank (e.g. LZB Hesse press release, 27 April 2000).[191] The Bundesbank suggested the banking supervision should

[191] The president of the LCB of North Rhine-Westphalia, Heinke, estimates that about three quarter of staff currently involved in the prudential supervision are actually located at the Länder central banks' level (LZB NRW press release, 4 Dec 2000).

be attributed solely to the Bundesbank, because it has the most expertise and is closest to the markets. Synergy effects for a more efficient and focused supervision could be created by a combination of banking supervision, monetary policy and transactions under one roof. On the other hand, having first-hand information about banking trends and activities would support the overall role of the national central bank in keeping the financial system stable. The Bundesbank could report to the Ministry of Finance without a breach of constitutional and European independence requirements, which do not include supervision (Bundesbank monthly report, September 2000, 33–45; speech by Ernst Welteke in Stuttgart, see BöZ, 17 July 2000). The position of the Bundesbank was supported by the Pöhl Commission (see above), and, in an unprecedented way, by the European Central Bank.[192]

The possible extended role of the Bundesbank was also discussed with regard to the status of independence of the Bundesbank. Those against a merging of the FBSO into the Bundesbank argued that the lacking democratic legitimacy of the Bundesbank would be in conflict with an autonomous role in prudential supervision. The Bundesbank rejected this view extensively in its monthly report in September 2000:

> The argument sometimes heard, ie that the Bundesbank's autonomy cannot be reconciled with its simultaneously assuming responsibility for banking supervision, is invalid; the transfer of prudential competence to the Bundesbank would be quite clearly in keeping with Article 88 of the Constitution. Parliamentary and thus political responsibility for this area could be secured in the form of a right on the part of the Federal Ministry of Finance to issue instructions to the Bundesbank on questions relating to banking supervision. The Finance Ministry's banking supervisory instructions would be addressed directly to the Bundesbank's central managing body and would then be passed on to the departments and main offices (42).

This position of the Bundesbank, however, is not undisputed, especially as the topic is of central relevance for other national central banks within the ESCB, as it might eventually lead to some kind of European regulatory institution in which the ECB will be involved (see below, chapter 3.4.3).

In general, banks, bank associations and large companies have been arguing in favour of a single authority being in charge of banking supervision (and indeed of prudential supervision in general), albeit without siding with the Bundesbank, with the governmental plans or with the FBSO (SZ, 30 March 2000, 27).

During the year 2000, the Ministry of Finance went ahead with its intention to merge all three institutions into one single authority by estab-

[192] See detailed overview of banking supervision in the Euro-zone in the ECB monthly report April (2000, 53–70) as well as the position of the ECB on the role of central banks in prudential supervision, published in March 2001, which was taken as a direct response to the plans of the German government.

lishing a 'forum for financial market supervision' in November. The agreement between the FBSO, the Federal Insurance Supervisory Office, Federal Securities Supervisory Office, and the Bundesbank was signed in November, and foresees biannual meetings between the presidents and additional senior staff members and should make proposals on measures to facilitate the co-operation between the agencies and the Bundesbank, on issues of common interest, especially with regard to the participation in international committees, and on the implementation of the current supervisory legislation (BöZ, 3 November 2000, 1, agreement reprinted on p. 6).

It came as no surprise when Eichel announced the intention of the government to propose a 'Federal Agency for Financial Market Supervision' (Bundesanstalt für Finanzmarktaufsicht) in late January 2001. The minister referred to the creation of a single and integrated financial market in which the banking, insurance and securities industries sell the same products to the same customers using similar distribution channels. Thus, a single regulatory body would be able to protect investors by creating a common set of rules and at the same time would strengthen Germany's place in European and world financial markets (BMF press statement, 25 January 2001). In addition, it can be understood as a reaction to the recent series of mergers between insurance companies and banks in view of creating an 'efficient and neutral supervisor' (BMF press statement, 11 April 2001).

The reaction to the governmental proposal by the different actors reflected the positions put forward earlier. The Bundesbank, backed by strong comments by the ECB, criticised the diminished role allocated to the Bundesbank for banking supervision in the proposal, especially as it was unclear in what way the Bundesbank would still be involved (Bundesbank press release, 25 January 2001). The banking associations were overwhelmingly supportive of the BMF proposal (BdB press release, 25 January 2001), while the Länder criticised 'this package of horror against federalism' (SZ, 26 January 2001, 23).

The draft legislative act to be proposed by the Finance Ministry, which has to be adopted by the Federal cabinet is still pending.[193]

3.4.3 Constitutional aspects of the reform of prudential supervision in Germany[194]

A reform of the prudential supervision in Germany can only be realised, if the constitutional principles are respected. The conformity of the different

[193] As of May 2001, a new draft can be downloaded at <http://www.bundesfinanzministerium.de>.

[194] Chapter written by Peter-Christian Müller-Graff.

reform models with the German constitution (*Grundgesetz*—GG) is debated. Although a full consensus on the constitutional questions has not yet emerged, we will proceed to an overview of the different aspects. An exact legal analysis on this matter requires treating the different reform plans separately. However, there is a common starting point on which all the different reform plans are based on: all reform alternatives concern the scope of application of Articles 87.3 and 88 GG. Article 88 GG specifically refers to the Bundesbank and lays down its original area of responsibility. In contrast Article 87.3 GG concerns federal authorities in general and fixes the requirements for the establishment of a new federal authority. Article 87.3 GG is subdivided into two sentences differentiating according to the structure of the new federal authority and according to the degree of involvement of the already existing authorities of the Länder. The most important practical consequence of the question as to which of the mentioned Articles has to be applied is that Article 87.3 s 2 GG requires an absolute majority in the Bundestag and additionally the assent of the Bundesrat, whereas Article 87.3 s 1 and Article 88 GG only demand a simple majority in the Bundestag.

As mentioned above, one of the reform plans is to integrate the banking supervision completely into the Bundesbank. This suggestion is also controversial. Some authors and the Bundesbank itself think that a reform in this way would be in conformity with Article 88 GG (Maunz 1982: Art. 88 GG FN 41; Bundesbank monthly report, September 2000, 44), whereas others plead for the taking into consideration of Article 87.3 GG, since the scope of application of Article 88 GG would be exceeded.[195] In fact, Article 88 GG which is lex specialis with reference to Article 87.3 GG can only be applied, if the Bundesbank is affected in its function as a currency or note bank (Stern 1998, 146; Herdegen 1998: Art. 88 GG FN 41). Though there is to a certain degree a connection between supervision on the one hand and the tasks based on the function of a currency or note bank on the other hand, the arguments of the authors who take the stand that a complete supervision can not fall under Article 88 GG are more convincing (Hahn 1982, 33 et seq, 70 et seq).

Against this background one has to examine the relation between Article 88 and 87.3 GG, in order to find out, if Article 87.3 GG is applicable, which means that the requirements of Article 87.3 GG have to be fulfilled. There is almost a general consensus that Article 87.3 GG is not only applicable when new authorities are established but also when powers are transferred to an existing authority (Lerche 1992: Art. 87 GG FN 175, 213, 217; Jarass/Pieroth 2000: Art 87 FN 9, 12). The suggested integration plans differ as far as the contribution of the Länder central

[195] In the concrete case not yet decided, but with this tendency the Federal Constitutional Court in the decision BVerfGE 14, 197, 216 et seq.

banks is concerned. Keeping on an 'integrated on-site-supervision' of the Länder central banks seems, at first glance, to lead to an application of Article 87.3 s 2 GG, since the former would be a subordinated authority in the sense of that provision. As a result, the requirements of Article 87.3 s 2 GG, which demands an urgent need for a reform and additionally the assent of the Bundesrat, would have to be fulfilled. However, it has to be considered that the provision in question has to be interpreted teleologically, and hence it has to be taken into consideration that it aims to protect the power of the Länder (Lerche 1992: Art. 87 GG FN 211). Since there would be no reduction of the competence of the Länder when keeping on an 'integrated on-site-supervision', Article 87.3 s 2 GG would not be applicable. Hence, the reform plan would be in accordance with the Constitution as long as the amendment is contained in a statute, as demanded by Article 87.3 s 1 GG.

In case the integration of the Länder central banks is combined with an indirect de facto supervisory power, the legal situation would be the same. If they are completely integrated into the Bundesbank and thereby all of their supervision activities cease, Article 87.3 s 2 GG would a priori not be applicable, so that the result would be the same as for the 'integrated on-site-supervision' and the 'integrated indirect de facto supervision'.

As mentioned above, the alternative to these integration models would be the establishment of a single authority by merging the three existing authorities (FBSO, FISO and the FSSO) into one. The stripping of the supervision power from the Bundesbank does not violate Article 88 GG, since this power is not one of the original competencies of the Bundesbank mentioned in that provision.[196] Although the new authority would be the result of a merger, the creation of the new authority would require an act of parliament according to Article 87.3 s 1 GG. As far as the legal form of the new authority is concerned, the choice would be up to the legislature.[197] The possible participation of the Länder central banks in the new authority and the constitutional question of the applicability of Article 87.3 s 2 GG correspond to the integration model treated above. Depending on the degree of participation of the Länder central banks Article 87.3 s 2 GG would be either not applicable a priori or not applicable because it has to be interpreted teleologically.

As a result, one can conclude that it seems that the variety of constitutional questions and problems could be solved no matter which reform model is opted for. However there is no full consensus in the constitutional debate on this issue.

[196] See Federal Constitutional Court in the decision BVerfGE 14, 197, p. 215 et seq.
[197] Ibid, 37, 1, 25.

3.4.4 Other issues

Lastly, the redistribution of monetary income within the ESCB is a possibly contentious issue between the Bundesbank and the ECB. According to Article 32 of the ESCB–ECB Statute the allocation of the monetary income among the national central banks is to be in proportion to their paid up shares in the capital of the ECB. However, the Governing Council decided, based on Article 32.3 of the Statute, to postpone the application of this provision until the year 2002. By using the derogation clause in Article 51 ESCB-ECB Statute, the application could be further postponed until 1 January 2007 (Sinn/Feist 2000a, 21).

The issue is to be settled by the ESCB itself, but questions repeatedly arose in Germany on the possible consequences for the Bundesbank (protocols of the press conferences of the Bundesbank: Bundesbank press releases 7 December 2000, 5 April 2001). The monetary income of the Bundesbank is comparatively higher than in other EU Member States because the ratio of cash transactions to the total GDP is higher in Germany than in other countries and because the Deutsche Mark is used extensively abroad (Handelsblatt 19 April 2001). Under the current transitional calculation, the allocation of monetary income resulted in 2000 in a net liability of 4 million euro for the Bundesbank (a transfer of 14 million in the common pool and a return of 10 million euro) (Bundesbank Annual Report 2000, 177).[198]

In particular, Sinn and Feist from the IFO-institute estimate that 'the accidental redistribution of seignorage wealth in the Euro-system' (Sinn/Feist 2000b) will amount to a loss of up to 30 bn euro for Germany, an estimation that was not rejected, albeit not approved, by the members of the Bundesbank Directorate (Bundesbank press releases 7 December 2000, 11; 5 April 2001, 13). The Bundesbank does not want to officially make public its opinion in order not to weaken its bargaining position within the ESCB (ibid.).

It is also to be expected that in the context of the allocation of monetary income discussions will reappear in Germany on the assessment of the very high foreign reserve assets, bearing in mind that also former finance minister Waigel fought a 'gold war' (Duckenfield 1999) against the Bundesbank (VWD, 14 February 2001, 4 April 2001).

198 In the year 2000 the annual surplus of the Bundesbank amounted to 8.4 bn euro (against 3.9 bn euro for 1999, the higher figure being mainly due to higher interest rates), which is transferred to the Federal Government. There, 3.5 bn euro are used by the government to finance regular expenditures and the rest goes into debt relief.

Bibliography

1. Interviews

BDI interview, Bernhard Welschke, head of European politics department, and Reinhard Kudiß, member of staff of the economics department of the BDI, Berlin, 6 February 2001.

BMF interview no 1, Federal Ministry of Finance, head of division within the Directorate-General 'E' on European Affairs, Berlin, 7 February 2001.

BMF interview no 2, Federal Ministry of Finance, head of division within the Directorate-General 'E' on European Affairs, Berlin, 8 February 2001.

BMF interview no 3, Federal Ministry of Finance, head of division within the Directorate-General 'I' on fundamental aspects, Berlin, 7 February 2001.

BMWi interview, Federal Ministry of Economics and Technology, head of division within the Directorate-General 'I' on economic policy, Berlin, 7 February 2001.

CDU/CSU interview, Jürgen Hart, member of the working group, European Union' of the CDU/CSU parliamentary group in the Bundestag, Berlin, 6/7 February 2001.

DGB interview, Andreas Botsch, head of department structural and environmental policy at the Federal Executive Board of the DGB, Berlin, 7 February 2001.

'Grüne' interview, Christian Sterzing, MP, spokesperson on EU affairs of the Bündnis 90/Die Grünen parliamentary group in the Bundestag, Berlin, 8 February 2001.

PDS interview, Uwe Hiksch, MP, spokesperson on EU affairs of the PDS parliamentary group in the Bundestag, Berlin, 9 February 2001.

SPD interview, Günter Gloser, MP, spokesperson on EU affairs of the SPD parliamentary group in the Bundestag, and Carlos Jahnsen, member of working group 'European Union', Berlin, 7 February 2001.

2. Articles and books

Commissariat Général du Plan (1999). *Le gouvernement économique de la zone euro*. Rapport du groupe de réflexion présidé par Robert Boyer, Paris: La Documentation française.

Duckenfield, M (1999). 'The *Goldkrieg*: Revaluing the Bundesbank's Reserves and the Politics of EMU', 8(1) *German Politics*, 106–30.

Dyson, K (2000). 'EMU as Europeanization: Convergence, Diversity and Contingency', 38(4) *Journal of Common Market Studies*, 645–666.

—— (2001). 'Germany and the Euro: Redefining EMU, Handling Paradox, and Managing Uncertainty and Contingency', in K. Dyson (ed.), *European states and the euro: playing the semi-sovereignty game*. Oxford: Oxford University Press (forthcoming).

Frühjahrsgutachten (2000). Deutsches Institut für Wirtschaftsforschung, Berlin et al. (eds.), *Die Lage der Weltwirtschaft und der deutschen Wirtschaft im Frühjahr 2000*, concluded in Hamburg am 14 April 2000.

Haas, P (1992). 'Introduction: Epistemic Communities and International Policy Co-ordination', 46(1) *International Organization* 1–35.

Hägele, S and Wessels, W (2000). 'Euro-Gruppe und Wirtschafts- und

Finanzausschuss', in W Weidenfeld and W Wessels (eds), *Jahrbuch der Europäischen Integration 1999/2000*. Bonn: Europa-Union Verlag, 107–10.

Hahn, HJ (1982). 'Die Deutsche Bundesbank im Verfassungsrecht', 113(2) + 113(3) *Bayerische Verwaltungsblätter, Zeitschrift für öffentliches Recht und öffentliche Verwaltung* 33–7 + 70–5.

Hellermann, J (2000). 'Die Europäische Wirtschafts- und Währungsunion als Stabilitätsgemeinschaft und der nationale Stabilitätspakt in der bundesstaatlichen Solidargemeinschaft' 35(1) *Europarecht* 24–41.

Herbstsgutachten (2000). Deutsches Institut für Wirtschaftsforschung, Berlin et al (eds), *Die Lage der Weltwirtschaft und der deutschen Wirtschaft im Herbst 2000*, concluded in Halle (Saale) 20. October 2000.

Herdegen, M (1998). 'Art. 88', in T Maunz and G Dürig (eds), *Grundgesetz-Kommentar*. München: Beck.

Jahresgutachten (2000). Sachverständigenrat zur Begutachtung der gesamtwirtschaftlichen Entwicklung (eds), *Chancen auf einen höheren Wachstumspfad, Jahresgutachten 2000/01*, Wiesbaden November 2000.

Lerche, P (1992). 'Art 87', in T Maunz and G Dürig (eds), *Grundgesetz-Kommentar*. München: Beck.

Linsenmann, I, and Müller, T (2000). 'German Report', in J-V Louis (ed), *Euro Spectator: Implementing the Euro. National Reports: French Report / German Report*. EUI Working Paper LAW no 2000/6, San Domenico: European University Institute, 57–109.

Maunz, T (1982). 'Art 88', in T Maunz and G Dürig (eds), *Grundgesetz-Kommentar*. München: Beck.

Noelle-Neumann, E, and Petersen, T (2000). 'Die öffentliche Meinung', in: Weidenfeld and Wessels (eds), *Jahrbuch der Europäischen Integration 1999/2000*, Bonn: Europa-Union Verlag, 295–300.

Pieroth, B (2000). 'Art 87 GG', in HD Jarass and B Pieroth (eds), *Grundgesetz für die Bundesrepublik Deutschland (GG). Der Kommentar für Ausbildung und Praxis*. München: CH Beck.

Sinn, H-W, and Feist, H (2000a). 'Der Euro und der Geldschöpfungsgewinn: Gewinner und Verlierer durch die Währungsunion', in: *ifo Schnelldienst 31/2000*, <http://www.ifo.de/orcl/owai/SD31-00Text.pdf>.

—— (2000b). 'The accidental redistribution of seignorage wealth in the Eurosystem', in: *CESifo Forum* 3/2000, <http://www.ifo.de/orcl/owai/special3–00.pdf>.

Stern, K (1998). 'Die Notenbank im Staatsgefüge', in Deutsche Bundesbank (ed.), *50 Jahre Deutsche Mark. Notenbank und Währung in Deutschland seit 1948*. München: C H Beck, 141–98.

Wessels, W, and Linsenmann, I (2001). 'EMU's impact on national institutions', in K Dyson (ed), *European states and the euro: playing the semi-sovereignty game*. (Oxford: Oxford University Press) (forthcoming).

Wirtschaftsdienst 2000/X: 'Erneute Zinserhöhung', 589.

Wirtschaftsdienst 2000/X: 'Votum gegen den Euro', 590.

Wirtschaftsdienst 2001/I: 'Griechenland im Euro-Club', 6.

3. Documents

Allensbacher Berichte (2000), *Großer Vertrauensverlust gegenüber dem Euro*, Institut für Demoskopie Allensbach, no 11, July 2000.

—— (2001), *Das Vertrauen in den Euro sinkt*, Institut für Demoskopie Allensbach, no 7, March 2001.

BdB Demo/skopie 8/2000: Bundesverband deutscher Banken (ed) (2000), Deutschland im Wandel: Der Wirtschaftsstandort im Zeichen der Globalisierung, Demoskopie—Umfragen, Meinungen, Gesellschaftstrends no 8, May 2000, <http://www.bdb.de/html/02_politik/sub_02_demoskopie/ pol_02. asp>.

BdB (Bundesverband deutscher Banken), 'Energiepreisanstieg trübt den Konjunkturhorizont', economic report—October 2000.

BdB Inter/esse 11/2000: Bundesverband deutscher Banken (ed.) (2000), Infodienst Inter/esse no 11/2000, November 2000, <http://www.bdb.de/ html/02_politik/ sub_01_interesse/pol_01.asp>.

BdB press release, 16 March 2000: 'Stabilitätspolitische Vernunft der Tarifparteien gefordert'.

—— 5 October 2000: 'Bankenverband: Leitzinserhöhung stabilitätspolitisch gerechtfertigt'.

—— 25 January 2001: 'Allfinanzaufsicht stärkt den Finanzplatz Deutschland'.

BGBl I, no 57, 23 December 2000: Gesetz zur Umrechnung und Glättung steuerlicher Euro-Beträge (Steuer-Euroglättungsgesetz-StEuglG) vom 19 December 2000, in Bundesgesetzblatt (Federal Law Gazette) Jahrgang 2000 Teil I Nr. 57, Bonn 23 December 2000, 1790–809.

—— no 58, 27.12.00: Gesetz zur Änderung des Versicherungsaufsichtsgesetzes, insbesondere zur Durchführung der EU-Richtlinie 98/78/EG vom 27. Oktober 1998 über die zusätzliche Beaufsichtigung der einer Versicherungsgruppe angehörenden Versicherungsunternehmen sowie zur Umstellung von Vorschriften auf Euro vom 21 Dezember 2000, in: Bundesgesetzblatt Jahrgang 2000 Teil I Nr. 58, Bonn 27 December 2000, 1857–76.

—— no 60, 29 December 2000: Gesetz zur Einführung des Euro im Sozial- und Arbeitsrecht sowie zur Änderung anderer Vorschriften (4. Euro-Einführungsgesetz), 21 December 2000, in: Bundesgesetzblatt Jahrgang 2000 Teil I Nr. 60, Bonn 29 December 2000, 1983–2019.

—— no 4, 24 January 2001: Gesetz zur Namensaktie und zur Erleichterung der Stimmrechtsausübung (Namensaktiengesetz—NaStraG), 18 January 2001, in Bundesgesetzblatt Jahrgang 2000 Teil I Nr. 4, Bonn 24 January 2001, 123–6.

—— no 19, 4.05.01: Gesetz zur Umstellung des Kostenrechts und der Steuerberatergebührenverordnung auf Euro (KostREuroUG), 27 April 2001, in: Bundesgesetzblatt Jahrgang 2001 Teil I Nr. 19, Bonn 4 May 2001, pp. 751–762.

BMF, Bericht zur Strukturreform der Bundesbank, presided by Karl Otto Pöhl, 4. Juli 2000, <http://www.bundsfinanzministerium.de/bbank/bbank.pdf>.

BMF press statements (Ministry of Finance)

—— 25 January 2001: Allfinanzaufsicht und Bundesbankstrukturreform stärken Finanzplatz Deutschland (no F. 18 (D. 8)).

—— 11 April 2001: Reformen für den Finanzplatz Deutschland (no F. 76 (D. 33)).

—— 30 May 2001: Verabschiedung Bundesbankstrukturreform im Kabinett (no F. 109).

Bundesbank, Annual Report 2000, Frankfurt April 2001.

—— Monthly report, no 9, 52. Jg., September 2000.

Bundesbank press release, 6 July 2000: Strukturreform der Bundesbank.

—— 13 December 2000: Stellungnahme des Direktoriums der Deutschen Bundesbank zum Eckpunktepapier zur Bundesbankstrukturreform der Länder vom 6. Dezember 2000.

—— 25 January 2001: Pressenotiz zur Presseerklärung des Bundesministers der Finanzen zur Allfinanzaufsicht und der Bundesbankstrukturreform.

—— 4 May 2001: Protokoll der Pressekonferenz im Anschluss an die Zentralbanksitzung der Deutschen Bundesbank am 4 April 2001—nach Bandaufnahme.

Bundesratsdrucksache, 10/01, 5 January 2001: Gesetzentwurf des Bundesrates: Entwurf eines Gesetzes zur Umstellung von Vorschriften des Dienst-, allgemeinen Verwaltungs-, Sicherheits-, Ausländer- und Staatsangehörigkeitrechts auf Euro (Sechstes Euro-Einführungsgesetz).

Bundestagsdrucksache, 14/3460, 25.05.00: Kleine Anfrage der Abgeordneten Dr. Christa Luft, Dr Uwe-Jens Rössel und der Fraktion der PDS: 'Kursveränderungen des Euro'.

—— 14/3514, 7 June 2000: Resolution by MPs from the governing coalition: 'Europäischer Rat in Feira—Europa entschlossen voranbringen'.

—— 14/3617, 16 June 2000: Antwort der Bundesregierung auf die Kleine Anfrage der Abgeordneten Dr. Christa Luft, Dr. Uwe-Jens Rössel und der Fraktion der PDS—Drucksache 14/3460—'Kursveränderungen des Euro'.

—— 14/3832, 4 July 2000: Kleine Anfrage der Abgeordneten Gerda Hasselfeldt, Heinz Seiffert, Norbert Barthle, Otto Bernhardt, Leo Dautzenberg, Jochen-Konrad Fromme, Dr. Reinhard Göhner, Hansgeorg Hauser (Rednitzhembach), Dr. Michael Luther, Erich Maaß (Wilhelmshaven), Hans Michelbach, Hans-Peter Repnik, Norbert Schindler, Diethard Schütze (Berlin), Wolfang Schulhoff, Klaus-Peter Willsch, Elke Wülfing und der Fraktion der CDU/CSU: 'Reibungslose Durchführung des Euro-Bargeld-Umtausches'.

—— 14/3908, 20 July 2000: Antwort der Bundesregierung auf die Kleine Anfrage der Abgeordneten Gerda Hasselfeldt, Heinz Seiffert, Norbert Barthle, weiterer Abgeordneter und der Fraktion der CDU/CSU—Drucksache 14/3832—'Reibungslose Durchführung des Euro-Bargeld-Umtausches'.

—— 14/4555, 9 November 2000: Gesetzentwurf der Bundesregierung: Entwurf eines Gesetzes zur Umstellung von Vorschriften im land- und forstwirtschaftlichen Bereich auf Euro (Fünftes-Euro-Einführungs-Gesetz).

—— 14/5436, 6 March 2001: Gesetzentwurf der Bundesregierung: Entwurf eines Gesetzes zur Umstellung soldatenversorgungsrechtlicher und anderer Vorschriften auf Euro (Elftes Euro-Einführungs-Gesetz).

—— 14/5440, 6 March 2001: Gesetzentwurf der Bundesregierung: Entwurf eines Gesetzes zur Umstellung auf Euro-Beträge im Lastenausgleich und zur Anpassung der LAG-Vorschriften (LAG-Euro-Umstellungs- und Anpassungsgesetz—LAG-EUAnpG).

—— 14/5641, 23 March 2001: Gesetzentwurf der Bundesregierung: Entwurf eines Gesetzes zur Umstellung der umweltrechtlichen Vorschriften auf den Euro (Siebtes Euro-Einführungsgesetz).

—— 14/5930, 26 April 2001: Gesetzentwurf der Bundesregierung: Entwurf eines Gesetzes zur Umstellung von Gesetzen und anderen Vorschriften auf dem Gebiet des Gesundheitswesens auf Euro (Achtes Euro-Einführungsgesetz).

—— 14/5937, 26 April 2001: Gesetzentwurf der Bundesregierung: Entwurf eines Gesetzes zur Umstellung von Gesetzen und Verordnungen im Zuständigkeitsbereich des Bundesministeriums für Wirtschaft und Technologie sowie des Bundesministeriums für Bildung und Forschung auf Euro (Neuntes Euro-Einführungsgesetz).

—— 14/6143, 25 May 2001: Gesetz zur Änderung von Verbrauchsteuergesetzen und des Finanzverwaltungsgesetzes sowie zur Umrechnung zoll- und verbrauchsteuerrechtlicher Euro-Beträge (Zwölftes Euro-Einführungsgesetz—12.EuroEG).

Bundestagsprotokoll (Official Records of Parliament), 14/098: 98. Sitzung des Deutschen Bundestages, 14. Wahlperiode, Berlin, 06.04.00: Abgabe einer Regierungserklärung zu den Ergebnissen der Sondertagung des Europäischen Rates vom 23./24. März 2000 in Lissabon, 9080–117.

—— 14/102: 102. Sitzung des Deutschen Bundestages, 14. Wahlperiode, Berlin, 11.05.00: Abgabe einer Regierungserklärung: Deutschland im Aufbruch—Moderne Wirtschaftspolitik für neue Arbeitsplätze, 9484–528.

—— 14/111: 111. Sitzung des Deutschen Bundestages, 14. Wahlperiode, Berlin, 29 June 2000: Abgabe einer Regierungserklärung: Zu den Ergebnissen des Europäischen Rates in Feira am 19/20 Juni 2000, 10455–10473.

—— 14/113: 113. Sitzung des Deutschen Bundestages, 14. Wahlperiode, Berlin, 5 July 2000: Befragung der Bundesregierung zum Bericht über die Entwicklung der Konvergenz in der Europäischen Union im Jahre 1999.

—— 14/118: 118. Sitzung des Deutschen Bundestags, 14. Wahlperiode, Berlin, 14.09.00: Erste Beratung des von der Bundesregierung eingebrachten Entwurfs eines Gesetzes über die Feststellung des Bundeshaushaltsplans für das Haushaltsjahr 2001 (Haushaltsgesetz 2001).

—— 14/123: 123. Sitzung des Deutschen Bundestages, 14. Wahlperiode, Berlin 11 October 2000: Befragung der Bundesregierung: Aktualisierung des deutschen Stabilitätsprogramms, pp. 11783–11788.

CDU/CSU parliamentary group press releases, 2 May 2000—Lamers: 'Fünf Herausforderungen für die Europäische Union', <http://www.kas.de/publikationen/2000/berichte/mai/lamers.html>, Download: 17 April 2001.

—— 3 May 2000—Hintze: 'Aufnahme Griechenlands in die Euro-zone verschieben. Kursverfall birgt Gefahr importierter Inflation', <http://www.cducsu.bundestag.de/texte/hintze5li.htm>. Download: 17 November 2000.

—— 7 September 2000—Hintze: 'Schröder verkennt den Ernst der Situation. Zum historischen Tiefstand des Euros', <http://www.cducsu.bundestag.de/texte/hintz57i.htm>. Download: 17 November 2000.

—— 12 September 2000—Hintze: 'Deutschlands Zukunft in Europa—Unionsvorschläge zu Reform und Erweiterung der EU', <http://www.cducsu.bundestag.de/texte/hintze4r.htm>. Download: 17 November 2000.

—— 29 September 2000—Hintze: 'Europäische Regierungen sind Schuld: Euro-Einführung scheitert in Dänemark', <http://www.cducsu.bundestag.de/texte/hintz60i.htm> Download: 17 November 2000.

—— 22 November 2000—Hintze: 'Richtigkeit der Euro-Einführung bestätigt. Zur Herbst-Konjunkturprognose der EU', <http://www. cducsu.bundestag.de/texte/hintz70i.htm>. Download: 31 January 2001.

CDU/CSU parliamentary group, 'Für eine bessere Politik. Bilanz nach zwei Jahren Rot-Grün.', Berlin 2000.

Council of the EU, 8 November 1999: 2212. Council meeting—Ecofin, Press Release Brussels (8 November 1999)—Press: 328—Nr: 12514/99.

—— 26/27 November 2000: 2312. Council meeting —Ecofin, Press Release Brussels (26 November 2000)—Press: 453—Nr: 13861/00.

DAG press release, 5 October 2000: 'DAG übt scharfe Kritik an Leitzinserhöhung'.

—— 31 August 2000: 'DAG zur Leitzinsanhebung: ‹berzogene und kontraproduktive Reaktionen auf Euro-Schwäche'.

DGB press release, 16 March 2000: 'Scharfe Kritik des DGB an Zinserhöhung: Keine stichhaltige Begründung, Trippelschritte verunsichern Erwartungen'.

—— 8 June 2000: 'DGB kritisiert 'unnötige Kraftmeierei' der Europäischen Zentralbank'.

—— 29 August 2000: 'DGB warnt Europäische Zentralbank (EZB) vor weiterer Zinserhöhung'.

—— 28 June 2000: 'Putzhammer: Euro-Schwäche nicht ideologisch missbrauchen'.

DSGV/Emnid: Deutscher Sparkassen- und Giroverband (DSGV)/Emnid press release 25/2001, 23 March 2001: 'Euro-Skepsis nach wie vor stark'.

ECB press release, 14 September 2000: 'Sales of foreign exchange interest income by the European Central Bank (ECB)', <http://www.ecb.int/press/00/pr000914 .htm>.

—— 14 September 2000: 'Geldpolitische Beschlüsse', <http://www.ecb. int/press/00/pr000914de.htm>.

—— Position of the ECB on role of central banks in prudential supervision, March 2001. <http://www.ecb.int/ pub/pdf/ prudentialsupcbrole_ en.pdf>.

Eichel, Hans, 19 October 2000: 'Europäische Wirtschaftspolitik', Rede anlässlich der Eröffnung des Eurochambres Kongresses 2000 in Berlin <http//www.bundes finanzministerium.de>.

EMU Monitor press statement no 6, 29 November 2000.

Euro-Barometer 53: European Commission (ed) (2000), *Eurobarometer. Die öffentliche Meinung in der Europäischen Union*, no 53, Brussels October 2000.

—— 54: European Commission (ed) (2000), *Eurobarometer. Die öffentliche Meinung in der Europäischen Union*, no 54, Brussels April 2001.

European Central Bank (2000), *Monthly Report April 2000*, Frankfurt A.M.

European Commission (2001), *Report on the preparations for the introduction of euro notes and coins. Communication from the Commission to the Council, the EP, the ECS and the ECB*, COM (2001) 190 final, Brussels 3 April 2001.

FDP parliamentary group press releases, 16 March 2000: Brüderle: 'Zinsschritt der EZB ist konsequent'.

—— 26 April 2000: Brüderle: 'Zinserhöhung durch Europäische Zentralbank wahrscheinlich'.

—— 3 May 2000: Haussmann: 'Beitritt Griechenlands zur Währungsunion muss stabilitätspolitisch vorbereitet sein'.

—— 17 May 2000: Brüderle: 'Euro gerät weiter unter Druck'.

—— 30 August 2000: Brüderle: 'EZB-Zinserhöhung unvermeidbar'.

—— 29 September 2000: Haussmann: 'Ein schlechter Tag für Europa'.

—— 5 October 2000: Brüderle: 'Zinserhöhung grenzt fast an Verzweiflungstat'.

—— 30 October 2000: Haussmann: 'Innere Stabilität des Euro darstellen'.

—— 6 November 2000: Brüderle: 'Bundesregierung muss EZB-Kampf für stärkeren Euro endlich unterstützen'.

Federal Ministry of Economics and Technology 2000: *Structural reforms on the goods, services and capital markets in Germany in 2000. Third national report pursuant to the conclusions of the European Council at Cardiff on 15/16 June 1998*. Documentation no 483, Berlin <http://www.bmwi.de/Homepage/download/english/Doku483_E.pdf>.

4th report of the Federal Ministry of Finance EMU Working Party (2000), *The Introduction of the Euro into Legislation and Public Administration*, July 5th 2000.

Green parliamentary group press release, 29 September 2000—0581: Müller/Sterzing: 'Grüne bedauern das dänische Nein zum Euro'.

Infratest dimap (2000), *Umfrage zur politischen Stimmung im Mai 2000 im Auftrag von ARD/ 'bericht aus berlin' und 9 Tageszeitungen.*

Jahreswirtschaftsbericht (2001), Bundesministerium für Finanzen (ed.), Continuing on the Course of Reform—Strengthening the Dynamic of Growth. The German Government's Annual Report on Economic and Fiscal Policy, Annual Economic Report 2001, Bonn, <http://www.bundesfinanzministerium.de/jwb/indexe.htm>.

LZB Bremen, Lower Saxony and Saxony Anhalt press release, 15 May 2000, in: Auszüge no 25, 6–11.

LZB Hessen press release, 27 April 2000: 'Bankenaufsicht unter dem Dach der Bundesbank zusammenführen, Anpassung der Zinspolitik muss noch weitergehen, Euro-Beitritt Griechenlands zurückstellen', <http://www.bundesbank.de/lzbh/de/pressenotizen/notizen/notiz270400.htm> Download: 12 April 2001.

LZB NRW press release 4 December 2000: 'LZB-Präsident Eberhard Heinke fordert dezentrale Strukturen', <http://www.bundesbank.de/lzb-nrw/de/pressenotizen/notizen/ press800.htm>.

PDS parliamentary group press release, 29 September 2000—no 1947: Rössel: 'Euro—nein Danke!'

Politbarometer (2000–2001): Forschungsgruppe Wahlen E. V. Mannheim (ed), *Poltibarometer—Monatliche repräsentative Umfrage*, January 2000–January 2001.

SPD parliamentary group press releases, 31 January 2000—0076: Schwanhold: 'Euro durch Wachstumskurs stärken—keine EZB-Zinserhöhung'.

—— 3 February 2000—0085: Poß: 'Der Euro braucht keine Stützung'.

—— 27 April 2000—0373: Wieczorek: 'EURO: Aufmerksamkeit ja—Panik nein!'

—— 8 June 2000—0500: Wieczorek: 'Zinspolitik: Für Waschstum und Arbeitsplätze'.

—— 29 September 2000—802: Poß/Wieczorek: 'Trotz Dänen-Votum: Stabilisierung des Euro in Sicht'.

4. Newspaper articles

Berliner Zeitung, 30 September 2000/1 October 2000: 'Euro-Länder geben sich nach Nein der Dänen betont gelassen', 1.

BöZ, 4 May 2000: 'Testat mit erhobenem Zeigefinger', in: Auszüge no 22, 6.

BöZ, 4 July 2000: 'Welteke will Führung aus einem Guss', in: Auszüge no 31, 2.

BöZ, 14 July 2000: 'Bundesbank rügt Aussagen von Fabius', in: Auszüge no 33, 13.

BöZ, 17 July 2000: 'Politik und Märkte im Zeichen des Euro' (Ernst Welteke), in: Auszüge no 33/2000, 2–6.
BöZ, 2 September 2000: 'Cool bleiben, EZB!' (Bernd Wittkowski), in: Auszüge no 42, 10–11.
BöZ, 13 September 2000: 'Europäisches Kapitalmarktrecht wichtiger denn je' (Rüdiger von Rosen), in: Auszüge no 44, 18–19.
BöZ, 20 September 2000: 'Reformen statt Wählerschelte' (Friedrich Heinemann), in: Auszüge no 45, 9–10.
BöZ, 20 Octover 2000: 'Wortloses Eingeständnis', Download: 20 October 2000.
BöZ, 3 November 2000: 'Finanzaufseher gründen Forum zur sektorübergreifenden Kooperation', 1.
BöZ, 7 November 2000: 'EZB gewinnt Glaubwürdigkeit zurück' (Annette Becker), 4.
BöZ, 15 November 2000: 'Jetzt bloß den Mut nicht verlieren' (Annette Becker), in: Auszüge no 55, 9.
BöZ, 16 November 2000: 'Neuer Plan für Bundesbankreform im Gespräch'.
BöZ, 17 November 2000: 'Nur Duisenberg zuliebe' (Christian Burckhardt).
BöZ, 22 November 2000: 'Der wahre Wert des Euro' (Christian Burckhardt), <http://www.boersen-zeitung.com/online/redaktion/aktuell/BZ226006.HTM>.
BöZ, 25 November 2000: 'BVR für geldpolitische Atempause der EZB', 6.
BöZ, 25 November 2000: 'Französische Haushaltspolitik im Zwielicht' (Jörg Foshag), <http://www.boersenzeitung.com/online/redaktion/aktuell/BZ229052. HTM>.Download: 25 November 2000.
BöZ, 28 November 2000: 'Weltekes Warnung an die EU' (Christian Burckhardt), 10–11.
BöZ, 7 December 2000: 'Mit dem alten Geldmantel ins neue Jahr' (Christian Burckhardt), 9.
BöZ, 16 December 2000: 'Faltlhauser attackiert Bundesbankpräsident'.
BöZ, 22 December 2000: 'Belgien feilt am Euro-Profil' (Christof Roche), in: Auszüge no 61, 11–12.
BöZ, 30 December 2000: 'M3 wächst deutlich langsamer'.
BöZ, 12 January 2001: 'Lob für Konvergenz Griechenlands'.
BöZ, 3 February 2001: 'ëBundesbank bleibt in Aufsicht eingebunden''.
DBR, 26 May 2000, EWU-Monitor no 85: 'Griechenland—zwölftes Mitglied der EWU', 1.
DBR, 4 February 2000, Frankfurt Voice no 5: 'ECB refi hike—More to come', 2–3.
DBR, 16 June 2000, Frankfurt Voice no 24: 'ECB—still accommodative', 1.
DBR, 25 August 2000, Frankfurt Voice no 34: 'ECB: Why (not) wait?', 1.
DBR, 1 September 2000, Frankfurt Voice no 35: 'ECB: Back to Trippelschritte', 1.
DBR, 15 September 2000, Frankfurt Voice no 37: 'ECB intervention—what intervention?', 1.
DBR, 29 September 2000, Frankfurt Voice no 39: 'Denmark: 50 bp—Euroland:?', 1.
DBR, 3 November 2000, Frankfurt Voice no 44: 'ECB—interventions, elections and the euro', 1.
DBR, 17 November 2000, Frankfurt Voice no 46: 'ECB: offering a view into its crystal ball?', 1.

DBR, 15 December 2000, Frankfurt Voice no 50: 'Initial report of the Lamfalussy Group' (Norbert Walter), 5–6.

Der Spiegel, no 49, 4 December 2000: 'Aktive Beratung' (Christian Reiermann), 132.

Deutsche Bundesbank, Auszüge aus Presseartikeln no 26, 30 May 2000: Ansprache von Ernst Welteke, Präsident der Deutschen Bundesbank, zur Verabschiedung von Landeszentralbankpräsident Dr. Guntram Palm und der Amtseinführung von Helmut Schieber, in Stuttgart, 26 May 2000, 2–3.

Die Welt, 4 February 2000: 'Die Welt, Geteiltes Echo auf Zinsanhebung', <http://www.welt.de/daten/2000/02/04/0204fi150317.htx>.

—— 30 September 2000: 'Der Euro trotzt dem Nein der Dänen', 1.

—— 30 September 2000: 'Die zwei Europas' (Nikolaus Blome), 1.

—— 30 September 2000: 'Nach den Interventionen steckt die EZB in einer Zwangslage' (Otto Graf Lambsdorff), 14.

—— 24 October 2000: 'Was Europa den Dänen verdankt' (Anja Dalgaard-Nielsen), in: Auszüge no 52, 13.

—— 2 November 2000: 'Stoiber: Bundesregierung mitschuldig an schwachem Euro', <http://www.welt.de/daten/2000/11/02/1102de200043.htx>.

—— 7 November 2000: 'Die Amerikaner müssen eine Führungsrolle übernehmen' (Interview with currency expert Peter Bofinger), <http://www.welt.de/daten/2000/11/07/1107wi200946.htx>.

—— 14 December 2000: 'Nach dem Wachstumsgipfel ist nun der Zinsgipfel erreicht' (Stefan Borstel), <http://www.welt.de/daten/2000/12/14/1214wi209142.htx>.

—— 15 December 2000: 'Behutsame Geldpolitik' (Ralf Neubauer), <http://www.welt.de/daten/2000/12/15/1215wi209419.htx>. Download: 15 December 2000.

—— 15 December 2000: 'Duisenberg sieht Euro-Trendwende', <http://www.welt.de/daten/2000/12/15/1215wi209422.htx>. Download: 15 December 2000.

—— 2 January 2001: 'Zurzeit verbietet es sich, Dollar zu verkaufen' (Deutsche-Bank-Chefsvolkswirt Walther—Interview), <http://www.welt.de/daten/2001/01/02/0102wi212723.htx>.

Die Zeit, 11 May 2000: 'Mut zu neuem Denken' (Wilfried Herz), 32.

—— 7 September 2000: 'Der Euro ist stabil' (Helmut Schmidt), 1.

—— 26 October 2000: 'Euro statt Ego' (Klaus-Peter Schmid), in: Auszüge no 53, 7–9.

FAZ, 1 February 2000: 'Zweifel am politischen Willen', 31.

FAZ, 29 February 2000: 'Lob und Tadel für deutsches Stabilitätsprogramm', 17.

FAZ, 8 March 2000: 'Die Euro-Dividende hilft Italien, das Defizit zu verringern', 19.

FAZ, 25 April 2000: 'Morgenröte über dem Euroland' (Norbert Walter), 33.

FAZ, 27 April 2000: 'EU kritisiert mangelnde Etatkonsolidierung in Wien', 22.

FAZ, 27 April 2000: 'LZB-Präsidenten kritisieren Rechnungshof', 21.

FAZ, 2 May 2000: 'Der Ausverkauf des Euro erhitzt die Gemüter' (Holger Steltzner), 33.

FAZ, 22 May 2000: 'Die Gefahr übertriebener Zinserhöhung steigt' (Holger Steltzner), 33.

FAZ, 5 June 2000: 'Handle in der Zeit, dann wirkt es in der Not' (Thorsten Polleit), 35.

FAZ, 8 June 2000: 'Der letzte Zinstango' (Heinz Brestel), 31.

FAZ, 4 July 2000: 'Welteke für eine Bundesbank-Führungsstruktur aus einem Guss', 17.

FAZ, 22 August 2000: 'Die "Euro-group" soll ein Gegengewicht zur EZB werden', in Auszüge no 39, 1.

FAZ, 24 August 2000: 'Die Banken rufen nach finanzieller und logistischer Hilfe bei der Einführung des Euro', 1–2.

FAZ, 24 August 2000: 'Gradmesser Euro', 1.

FAZ, 31 August 2000: 'Die Märkte rechnen fest mit einer Zinserhöhung', 31.

FAZ, 2 September 2000: 'Eine Währung ohne Symbolkraft' (Claus Tigges), 13.

FAZ, 7 September 2000: 'Der gute Ruf der Bundesbank steht auf dem Spiel' (Claus Tigges), 18.

FAZ, 8 September 2000: 'Der Euro trudelt und beunruhigt die Bürger', 13.

FAZ, 13 September 2000: 'Rufe nach Interventionen zugunsten des Euro', 31.

FAZ, 15 September 2000/a: 'Devisenverkäufe der EZB stützen den Euro nur kurz', 13.

FAZ, 15 September 2000/b: 'Rein oder nicht rein' (Bettina Schulz), 13.

FAZ, 18 September 2000: 'Auch diese Abstimmung wird eine Zitterpartie' (Jasper von Altenbockum), 7.

FAZ, 18 September 2000: 'Der Intervention folgt das Rekordtief für den Euro' (Holger Steltzner), 49.

FAZ, 23 September 2000: 'Die Notenbanken stützen den Euro', 13.

FAZ, 26 September 2000: 'Ölpreis und Euro treiben die Aktienkurse', 31.

FAZ, 26 September 2000/a: 'Der Ölpreis ist kein Grund zur Panik' (Jürgen Stark), in: Auszüge no 46, 3/4.

FAZ, 26 September 2000/b: 'Eine Stimme für die Finanzpolitik' (Gerald Braunberger), in: Auszüge no 47, 7/8.

FAZ, 29 September 2000: 'Auch diese Abstimmung wird eine Zitterpartie', 7.

FAZ, 30 September 2000: 'Eurobörsen reagieren kaum auf Votum der Dänen', 25.

FAZ, 6 October 2000: 'Für den Euro', 13.

FAZ, 16 October 2000: 'Vorsicht, Inflationsprognose!' (Michael Hüther), 33.

FAZ, 20 October 2000: 'Der Zentralbankrat stützt Duisenberg', 13.

FAZ, 23 October 2000: 'Der Euro braucht eine politische Stütze' (Thomas Mayer), in: Auszüge no 52, 9.

FAZ, 25 October 2000: 'Interventionen zeugen vom Misstrauen gegenüber dem Markt', 33.

FAZ, 30 October 2000: 'Der Euro ist kein sterbender Schwan (Norbert Walter), 35.

FAZ, 13 November 2000: 'Ein Euro ist ein Euro' (Klaus Friedrich), 35.

FAZ, 30 November 2000: 'Der Euro ist aus guten Gründen schwach', 17.

FAZ, 21 December 2000: 'Die 'Projektion' der EZB bleibt vage', 17.

FAZ, 22 December 2000: 'Der Euro gewinnt an Stärke', 25.

FAZ, 2 January 2001: '2001: Jahr des Euro?' (Norbert Walter), 25.

FR, 15 December 2000: 'Angsthasen'.

Frankfurter Allgemeine Sonntagszeitung, 24 September 2000: 'Mir wäre am liebsten gewesen, alle hätten nichts getan', Interview mit Bundesbankpräsident Welteke', in Auszüge no 46, 2–3.

FT, 13 September 2000: 'Policymakers give conflicting signals over euro intervention', 1.

FTD, 3 May 2000: 'Euroland dehnt sich aus—doch die EZB will bleiben, wie sie ist' (Norbert Häring), 4–5.

FTD, 10 May 2000: 'Die politische Schwäche der europäischen Währung', in: Auszüge no 23, 11–12.

FTD, 17 August 2000: 'Integrationskraft der Finanzmärkte ist trotz Euro gering (Stephen Cecchetti), 7–8.

FTD, 15 September 2000: 'Europa braucht eine tragfähige politische Struktur' (Otmar Issing), in: Auszüge no 44, 13.

FTD, 28 September 2000: 'Ein Tritt für den Euro und Europa' (Wolfgang Proissl), 29.

FTD, 30 October 2000: 'FTD-Zinsprognose: Ab 2002 mehr Wachstum bei weniger Inflation' (Cosima Jäckel/ Norbert Häring), Download: 25 November 2000.

FTD, 16 November 2000: 'EZB lässt die Leitzinsen unverändert', <http://www.ftd.de/pw/ed/FTDHUWDZLFC.html>. Download: 17 November 2000.

FTD, 11 December 2000: 'FTD-Zinsprognose: Volkswirte fürchten zu knappen Geldmantel' (Cosima Jäckel und Norbert Häring).

FTD, 15 December 2000: 'EZB enttäuscht die Zinshoffnungen in Europa' (Norbert Häring, Doris Grass), <http://www.ftd.de/pw/eu/FTD976811088217.html>. Download: 15 December 2000.

FTD, 20 December 2000: 'EZB-Schätzungen deuten stabile Zinsen an', <http://www.ftd.de/ub/fi/FTDEBT04ZGC.html>. Download: 21 December 2000.

FTD, 26 January 2001: 'Eichel plant grundlegenden Umbau von Bundesbank und Finanzaufsicht' (Claus Hulverscheidt), <http://www.ftd.de/pw/de/FTDRLF6EIC.html>. Download: 29 January 2001.

Handelsblatt, 4 May 2000: 'Neues Risiko' (Eberhard Wisdorff), in: Auszüge no 22, 5.

—— 30 August 2000: 'Zweideutige Reden über Inflationsziele schaden der europäischen Währung' (Eberhard Wisdorff), in: Auszüge no 42, 11–12.

—— 26 September 2000: 'Die Europäische Zentralbank hat die Geduld verloren' (Manfred J. M. Neumann), in: Auszüge no 46, 10–11.

—— 19 October 2000: ' "Verharmlosung und Nichtstun"—CSU wirft Schröder Sorglosigkeit in Finanzsachen vor', Download: 20 October 2000.

—— 20 October 2000: 'Deutschlands Top-Manager sind gegen Euro-Intervention der EZB', Download: 20 October 2000.

—— 24 October 2000: 'Ein starker Euro bedarf einer weiteren politischen Integration Europas' (Horst Löchel), in: Auszüge no 52, pp. 9–10.

—— 1 November 2000: 'Athen wappnet sich für den Euro-Beitritt', in: Auszüge no: 53, pp. 13–14.

—— 24 November 2000: 'Experten rechnen mittelfristig mit weiterer EZB-Zinserhöhung', Download: 28 November 2000.

—— 30 November 2000: 'EZB lässt Leitzinsen in Euro-zone unverändert', Download: 15 December 2000.

Handelsblatt, 19 April 2001: 'Deutscher Beitrag zur Geldmenge wächst unterdurchschnittlich' (Patrick Welter), in: Auszüge no: 19/2001, p. 4.

NZZ, 4 February 2000: 'Zins-Karussell' (NZZ Online).

NZZ, 20 June 2000: 'Aus Euro-11 wird Euro-12', in: Auszüge no 29, pp. 5–6.

NZZ, 7 December 2000: 'Konjunkturoptimismus der Bundesbank', <http://www.nzz.ch/2000/12/08/wi/page-article717NV.html>. Download 8 December 2000

NZZ, 15 December 2000: 'Die Euro-zone noch ohne ëNew Economy'', <http://www.nzz.ch/2000/12/15/wi/page-article71V5P.html>.

NZZ, 3 January 2001: 'Schrittweise Stärkung der Euro-Gruppe—Griechenland als neues Mitglied', <http://www.nzz.ch/2001/01/04/wi/page-article7333SM.html>. Download 4 January 2001

Nürnberger Nachrichten, 18 December 2000: 'Fronten sind verhärtet' (Rolf Obertreis).

Reuters, 3 February 2000: 'n-tv: Welteke hält EZB-Zinsschritt für notwendig' (Yahoo Deutschland).

Spiegel-online, 3 February 2000: 'Zuspruch und Kritik', <http://www. spiegel.de/wirtschaft/konjunktur/0,1518,62812,00.html>. Download: 7 February 2000.

Stuttgarter Nachrichten, 6 March 2001: ''Flotte Sprüche helfen dem Euro nicht'' (Interview with Florian Schültke, head of Publicis Dialog, on the commercial campaign for the new currency), in: Auszüge no 12, 6–7.

SZ, 29/30 January 2000: 'Abwertung ist kein Grund zur Sorge' (Interview with Martin Hüfner), p. 25.

SZ, 2 January 2000: 'Der Euro wird nicht verteidigt', p. 25.

SZ, 1 March 2000: 'Zinsorakel' (Helmut Maier-Mannhart), 25.

SZ, 17 March 2000: 'Der Euro treibt die Zinsen', 4.

SZ, 22 March 2000: 'Bankenaufseher gegen Bundesbank', 26.

SZ, 30 March 2000: 'Das Kreditgewerbe halt sich vornehm zurück', p. 27.

SZ, 25 April 2000: 'Kursverfall des Euro löst heftigen Streit aus', 1.

SZ, 27 April 2000: 'Zentralbank in der Zwickmühle', 27.

SZ, 3 May 2000: 'Kandidat mit Schönheitsfehlern' (Andreas Oldag), 2.

SZ, 8 May 2000: 'Was dem Hund die Wurst ist' (Johannes Willms), 19.

SZ, 9 May 2000: 'Sanierung nach Wiener Art' (Wolfgang Simonitsch), 23.

SZ, 29 May 2000: 'Länder machen Front gegen Eichel' (Oliver Schumacher), 25.

SZ, 13 June 2000: 'Österreich sucht Weg aus der Schuldenfalle', 25.

SZ, 22/23 July 2000: 'Starke Muskeln, schwacher Euro' (Andreas Oldag), 25.

SZ, 29 August 2000: 'Länder halten an Bundesbank-Struktur fest', 21.

SZ, 8 September 2000: 'Massive Kritik an Schröders Euro-Politik' (Oliver Schumacher), 1.

SZ, 8 September 2000/a: 'Zu viel Optimismus schadet' (Interview with Joachim Goldberg), 2.

SZ, 8 September 2000/b: 'Viele Theorien, aber keine Erklärung' (Nikolaus Piper), 2.

SZ, 8 September 2000: 'Euro fällt erstmals unter 0,88 Dollar' (Andreas Oldag/ Martin Reim), 25.

SZ, 11 September 2000: 'Der einsame Euro' (Andreas Oldag), 5–6.

SZ, 15 September 2000: 'Notenbank-Käufe stützen Euro' (Thiemo Heeg), 25.

SZ, 25 September 2000: 'Banken: Spekulation verunsichert' (Felix Spies), 26.

SZ, 28 September 2000: 'Dänemark stimmt über den Euro ab' (Anne Rentzsch), 2.

SZ, 30 September/1 October 00: 'EU hält Tür für Dänemark offen' (Andreas Oldag/ Anne Rentzsch), 1.

SZ, 30 September/1 October 2000: 'Euro-Feinde auf dem falschen Pfad' (Andreas Oldag), 4.

SZ, 4 October 2000: 'Dänemark bleibt bei Vorbehalten gegen EU' (Anne Rentzsch), 7.

SZ, 17 October 2000: 'Freundliche Einladung', 25.

SZ, 18 October 2000: 'Todsünden eines Bankers' (Helga Einecke), 3.

SZ, 19 October 2000: 'Wim, bleibe stark!' (Helga Einecke), 27.

SZ, 27 October 2000: 'SZ-Interview mit dem Wirtschaftsprofessor und Währungskritiker Manfred J. Neumann: "Der Euro steht in einem Jahr pari" ', 27.

SZ, 28 November 2000: 'Gewerkschaften im Clinch mit der EZB' (Helga Einecke), 21.

SZ, 14 December 2000: 'Prominente sollen Stimmung für den Euro machen' (Ilona Wissenbach, Reuters), 32.

SZ, 15 December 2000: 'EZB sieht Wende beim Eurokurs' (Helga Einecke).

SZ, 27 December 2000: '2001 sieht Wende beim Eurokurs'SZ, 28 December 2000: 'Die Bundesbank zentral führen', 24.

SZ, 29 December 2000: 'Der Euro steigt, die Skepsis bleibt' (Andreas Oldag), 4.

SZ, 4 January 2001: 'Das Jahr des Euro' (Nikolaus Piper), 4.

SZ, 26 January 2001: 'Eichel fordert die Bundesländer heraus' (Oliver Schumacher), 23.

Tagesspiegel, 10 September 2000: 'Europa spricht nicht mit einer Stimme' (Martina Ohm), in Auszüge no 43, 4–5.

—— 3 December 2000: 'Ernüchterung bei der EZB/Dicke Luft im Euro-Tower' (Rolf Obertreis).

—— 15 December 2000: 'Europäische Zentralbank', <http:// 195.170.124.152/ archiv/2000/ 12/14/ak-wi-wi-4.html>.

——— 25 February 2001: 'Euro-Countdown' (Martina Ohm).

VWD, 24 November 2000: 'EuroTower: Strategie à la Buba?' (Hans Hutter), in: Auszüge no 57, 15.

VWD, 6 December 2000: 'Reale Konvergenz eine neue Euro-Hürde?' (Hans Hutter), in Auszüge no 58, 10.

VWD, 19 December 2000: 'Buba/ Remsperger: EZB-Projektionen ändern nicht strategische Position' (Markus-Alexander Frühauf).

VWD, 3 January 2001: 'Quo vadis Bundesbank?' (Hans Hutter), <http//www. vwd.de/print.prl?id =125695>. Download: 4 January 2001.

VWD, 14 February 2001: 'Eichel winkt ein hoher Bundesbank-Gewinn' (Hans Hutter), <http//www.vwd.de/print.prl?id=150117>. Download: 15 February 2001.

VWD, 4 April 2001: 'Dicker Bundesbank-Gewinn für Berlin mit Vermerk' (Hans Hutter), <http//www.vwd.de/print.prl?id=181139>. Download: 5 April 2001.

Welt am Sonntag, 23 April 2000: 'Euro hat guten Ruf verloren' (Interview with Juergen B. Donges), 53.

—— 31 December 2000: 'Feiert der Euro sein Comeback?' (Ulrich Porwollik), 49.

—— 4 March 2001: 'Die Politik hat beim Euro Fehler gemacht' (Interview with Ernst Welteke, president of the Deutsche Bundesbank), in: Auszüge no 12, 4–5.

Yahoo Deutschland, 1 February 2000/a: 'DGB gegen Zinserhöhung durch EZB' (Stephan Kosch, VWD), <http://de.biz.yahoo.com/000201/34/j2ti.html,>. Download: 2 February 2000.

Yahoo Deutschland, 1 February 2000/b: 'Euroschwäche nährt Zinsspekulationen' (AP), <http://de.news.yahoo.com/000201/11/j2wl.html>. Download: 2 February 2000.

—— 1 February 2000/c: 'Prof. Walter (Deutsche Bank): EZB bereitet Zinserhöhung vor' (Hans Hutter, VWD), <http://de.biz.yahoo.com/000201/34 /j26a.html>. Download: 2 February 2000.

—— 1 February 2000/d: 'Schwacher Euro macht EZB-Zinsschritt möglich' (Elke Pickartz, Reuters), <http://de.news.yahoo.com/ 000201/11/j2en.html>. Download: 2 February 2000.

—— 16 March 2000/a: 'DIHT und Volksbanken begrüflen Zinserhöhung' (dpa), <http://de.news.yahoo.com/000316/11/n2sm.html>. Download: 20 March 2000.

—— 16 March 2000/b: 'EZB-Reaktionen/ DGB übt scharfe Kritik an Zinserhöhung' (Stephan Kosch, VWD), <http://de.biz.yahoo.com/000316/34 /n32m.html>. Download: 16 March 2000.

——— 16 March 2000/c: 'EZB-Reaktionen/ Pro und Contra von BdB und DAG' (Hans Hutter, VWD), <http://de.biz.yahoo.com/000316/34/n2yb.html>. Download: 20 March 2000.

——— 16 March 2000/d: 'EZB zieht die Zinsschraube an von BdB und DAG' (Hans Hutter, VWD), <http://de.news.yahoo.com/000316/11/n2xe..html>. Download: 20 March 2000.

—— 16 March 2000/e: 'EZB-Zinserhöhung von Finanzwelt begrüßt' (dpa), <http://de.news.yahoo.com/000316/11/n39s.html>. Download: 20 March 2000.

—— 31 August 2000/a: 'DIHT und Gewerkschaften kritisieren Zinserhöhung' (dpa), <http://de.news.yahoo.com/000831/3/11kd6.html>. Download: 31 August 2000.

—— 31 August 2000/b: 'EZB zieht die Zinsschraube an' (AP), <http://de.news.yahoo.com/000821/12/11kem.html>. Download: 31 August 2000.

—— 29 November 2000: 'EMU-Monitor—EZB sollte Leitzinsen wieder erhöhen' (Reuters) <http://de.news.yahoo.com/001129/71/17d2d.html>.

—— 14 December 2000: 'DSGV und VÖB sehen EZB-Geldmengenbeschluss als Stabilitätssignal' (Andreas Kißler vwd), <http://de.biz.yahoo.com/ 001214/11/18 abs.html>. Download: 15.15.00.

—— 2 January 2001: 'EZB und EZB-Watcher begrüflen Griechenland im Euro-Gebiet' (Hans Hutter vwd), <http://de.biz.yahoo.com/010102/11/196y3.html>. Download: 3 January 2001.

—— 7 January 2001: 'Umfrage: Trotz Kurszuwächse kein allgemeines Vertrauen zum Euro' (dpa-AFX), <http://de.biz.yahoo.com/010107/36/19ha3.html> Download: 8 January 2001.

GREECE

*Anthony Papayannides**

1. Greece joins the Euro-zone: political parties, economic actors and public opinion

Greek public opinion and the Greek political system regarded Greece's accession to the Euro-zone to be as a major political achievement. Just after the general election of 9 April 2000—fought in part with EMU-participation as ammunition in the hands of the Simitis/PASOK Government, which renewed its mandate at the polls—the Prime Minister was crystal-clear when presenting his Government's programme in Parliament:

> Our first priority is to achieve our march towards the European Monetary Union. Our most important date is June 19th, 2000 when the European Council will decide on this issue.

He also stated:

> The vote of the Greek people has acknowledged the progress of our country those last four years. It has acknowledged the overhaul of our economy and our march towards EMU, which has crowned the new role of Greece in the European Union and on the international scene.

The same appreciation of the importance of the country's accession to the third and final stage of EMU (albeit one and a half years later than the original 11 members of the Euro-zone) can be found in most political and economic circles.

The 2001 Budget Report of the Ministry of Finance states:

> The 2001 budget signals the beginning of a new era for the country. Greece's entry into the Euro-zone gives new prospects for development, employment and social welfare [. . .] The accession of Greece is the result of a seven-year attempt to stabilize the economy targeted to lower inflation to EU levels and to promote growth. Having achieved these, economic policy will be focused on leveling up the living standards in the EU average and fighting unemployment.

The main opposition party is 'New Democracy'. Its spokesman for Economics, Professor George Alogoskoufis, acknowledges that:

> The accession of Greece to EMU is undoubtedly a major achievement in the economic history of our country.

* EKEME, 6 Kriezotou Street, GR-10671, Athens.

But the balancing statement is not far away:

> Although Greece's accession should have been self-evident within the frame of our country's European future, major costs were incurred by Greek society, due to the extensive economic imbalances of the eighties [. . .] Accession is not the miracle cure for the economy.[199]

The overall stance of New Democracy has been to praise accession to EMU, while at the same time deploring Greece's late entry (and the consequential costs to the Greek economy). The need for structural change was also emphasised, and the government's lack of resolve on that front was noted. Such reserved approval is the norm in the rest of the political spectrum. Only the anti-EU Communist Party (and the PASOK-splinter DIKKI) has been opposed to EMU accession.

In the 30 December 2000 issue of the largest-circulation Greek Sunday paper *TO VIMA* all contributors were positive about accession to the Euro-zone. The governor of the Bank of Greece, Lucas Papademos, summarised the general feeling when writing:

> The full accession of Greece to EMU on January 1st constitutes a watershed for the Greek economy [. . .] With the introduction of the euro a long and arduous period of anti-inflationary policy is completed, leaving behind a high degree of microeconomic stability.

However:

> Benefits from EMU accession are conditional [. . .] on national monetary policy, along with other macroeconomic policies, not being overturned.

For the Foundation for Economic and Industrial Research/IOBE (sponsored by the Federation for Greek Industry):

> Greece's entry into the Euro-zone is considered an important development that can greatly facilitate the economy's integration in the global market. Participation in the EMU is not an end in itself. It is a powerful means that can help the Greek economy to seize opportunities and avert risks posed by the growing international competition.

EMU is viewed as:

> a catalyst of change for Greece; the adoption of the single currency is expected to bring important changes in three central areas of economic life:
>
> - It will, first change the economic environment, as conditions will increasingly converge to a pattern common for all Euro-zone countries;
> - It will, secondly, affect economic behaviour, establishing in Greece a culture of stability and encouraging a competitive outlook;
> - Thirdly, it will create a new framework for economic policy dedicated to stability, competitiveness and growth.[200]

[199] *Economicos Tachydromos*, 7 Apr 2001.
[200] IOBE Bulletin No 25/July 2000.

EMU accession is certainly not easy. The tone becomes rather ominous in the very next issue of IOBE Bulletin (No 26/October 2000):

After entry to EMU there is a sense of fatigue in economic policy; a major goal of economic policy is now real convergence through the radical modernisation of the Greek economy. But such real convergence has no quantitative criteria nor a concrete time-schedule as was the case with nominal convergence.

Odysseus Kyriakopoulos, chairman of the Federation of Greek Industry, in a roundtable discussion including maverick left-wing politician Mimis Androulakis, echoed the same opinion:

ANDROULAKIS: The Greek economy could have avoided rushing into EMU, but only if we had a serious government, a serious state. I am favourable to EMU participation, exactly because in Greece we have no serious state: if this were not the case, I would have preferred for Greece to have kept an independent monetary policy for some more time.
KURIAKOPOULOS: Exactly because our country is such as it is, it was necessary for us to join EMU. It was good for Greece to join EMU; to reach this goal it was necessary to have concrete objectives [. . .] Now the question is where to go: last June we succeeded the EMU test; but right afterwards we should have set ten further goals! The first should have been competitiveness of the economy'.[201]

The president of the General Confederation of Greek Workers (Christos Polyzogopoulos) during the 20 March 2001 Roundtable on Social Security crystallised the labour movement's stance on EMU accession:

An achievement of historic proportions, built on the efforts of the man-of-the-street, of the Greek market. A promise of a more stable future for the Greek economy—but we should now witness the promise coming true and in no way be asked for a protracted period of ever-stricter incomes' policies.

The effort to introduce labour market flexibility was concluded in November 2000. At that point, legislation was passed that made the labour market only marginally more flexible; according to many commentators, it actually increased the regulatory burden on business. The other major front of post-EMU-accession structural reform was the area of social security. This was not opened until April 2001, one year after the elections and the run-up to EMU accession. It followed a report from the British government's actuaries, although the report's most radical conclusions/proposals were set-aside even before being formally presented.

Structural change has proved much more difficult—compared with nominal convergence—than was expected. Realisation of this is only slowly permeating public opinion. Public opinion remains strongly attached to Greek participation in EMU: 75 per cent of Greeks made accession-positive responses in a poll conducted for the daily

[201] *Economicos Tachydromos*, 7 Apr 2001.

Eleftherotypia on the eve of accession (31 December 2000). At the same time, according to *Eurobarometer*, 61 per cent of Greeks consider overall participation in the EU to be 'positive' (compared with 50 per cent of EU approval rate). EMU expectations are stated to be a major component of future benefits to be obtained from Greece's EU participation; for 72 per cent of Greeks EU accession is thought to be a 'source of benefits for the economy'.

It is interesting to note that the euro's tribulations on the international markets were met with much concern in Greece. The press commented abundantly, however no argument negative to accession was brought forward on that basis. 61 per cent of Greeks said that they are concerned by the euro's weakness, while 30 per cent feel unconcerned.

Greek society's growing resolve to accede to EMU can be illustrated by an episode at the end of April 2000, just after the elections in Greece and shortly before accession to the Euro-zone was finalised. Hans Reckers, a member of the board of the Bundesbank, told Reuters of his doubts as to the sustainability of the Greek inflation rate, and about the real compatibility of Greece's public debt (then 104 per cent of GDP) with the Maastricht criteria. He believed Greece's accession should have been postponed. For days afterwards, the press and the public rallied in opposition to Reckers' statement.

In conclusion, it could be said that the single-minded policy orientation of the modernising Simitis/social democrat government—in favour of EMU accession—has operated as an overall political aim that has kept Greece steadily on course at a time of economic strain and foreign-policy uncertainties. The Greek economy remains largely public while lip service is generally paid to market liberalisation; economic change comes slowly.

Overall, Greek public opinion experienced EMU as an opportunity to demonstrate that tangible goals could be attained and that 'real' equality was possible within Europe. After a first period of Euro-hesitant opinion (dating from before Greece's accession to the EEC until the mid-1980s) and a further period of Euro-discovery (from the era of the Mediterranean programmes and the Structural Funds until the final sprint to the EMU in the mid-1990s) Greece is now discovering Europe from a new perspective: not as a threat or a source of charity, but as an area of opportunity. There is also a sense of acceptance—of real and effective acceptance—by a core of first-speed group.

2. The end-run of the drachma to join the Euro-zone

The year 2000 was the threshold year in which the Greek economy was deemed to be compliant with the Maastricht criteria, and thus accepted as a member of the Euro-zone. Pursuant to the 19 June 2000 ECOFIN decision, the Bank of Greece harmonised its basic interest rates with those of the ECB (then at 4.75 per cent) on 27 December 2000, and the exercise of monetary policy was passed to the Euro-system's institutions.

The Greek drachma (GRD) had joined the ERM of the EMS in March 1998, at a central rate of 357 GRD/ECU (with the wide fluctuation margin of +/–15 per cent). The same fluctuation range was applicable until the drachma joined the Euro-zone under the ERM-II, with a central rate of 353.109 GRD/euro (the change was due to technical reasons). In order to counter inflationary risks that could have jeopardised Greece's road to the third stage of EMU, a 3.5 per cent revaluation of the central rate of the drachma was decided on 17 January 2000, bringing it to 340.750 GRD/euro. It was at that rate that the June 2000 ECOFIN decision provided for the drachma to be irrevocably locked in parity to the euro; it is at that rate that the currency was thus locked on 1 January 2001.

The ECB Convergence Report 2000 was straightforward:

> Over the reference period from April 1999 to March 2000, the average rate of HICP inflation in Greece was 2 per cent, ie 0.4 per cent lower than the level of the reference value of 2.4 per cent as defined in Article 121.1 of the Treaty and Article 1 of the Protocol on the convergence criteria [. . .]. Seen over the period since 1998, HICP inflation in Greece has been significantly reduced, and recently came closer to a level which can generally be considered to be consistent with price stability [. . .]. The Greek drachma has been participating to ERM of the EMS since 16 March 1998 and it joined ERM–II at the start of Stage Three of EMU. During the two-year reference period, the drachma normally traded significantly above its cental rates.

Throughout the crucial year 2000, the monetary authorities applied a restrictive monetary policy in order to avoid a resurgence of inflation (the Greek economy had just achieved the necessary convergence with the Maastricht criteria, but inflationary pressures remained latent while the oil price-sensitivity of the economy was high). The Bank of Greece proceeded to implement eight successive cuts to its basic interest rates, on 26 January, 7 March, 18 April, 28 June, 3 September, 14 November, 28 November, finishing with the final alignment with ECB rates on 27 December. The major cuts were brought about in the second half of the year, while 40 per cent of their importance was felt within the last two months. Overall, the Central Bank's rates were cut by six percentage points within the year: this convergence with ECB rates was made significantly easier by the ECB's successive rate hikes (totalling 1.75 per cent within the year 2000).

The passage of the drachma to the euro has been smooth enough, especially in the latest stages. This is particularly notable considering that:

(a) The Greek economy had to effect its end-run in a context of resurgent inflation.
(b) The year 2000 was an election year in Greece; a closely fought contest ended in re-election of the Simitis government. The Simitis team had

made EMU accession its main political objective, but only after a tough campaign, in which the temptation to shift to a less restrictive macroeconomic policy stance was great.

(c) The financial markets were suffering protracted turmoil: the Athens Stock Market—which had a buoyant 1999—crashed during 2000. This created widely felt tremors throughout the economy.

(d) Credit expansion rates, especially for house mortgages and consumer credit, had risen fast enough to create concern among the monetary authorities. To stem credit expansion, restrictive measures were uneasily applied to the commercial banks.

It was a difficult but smooth adjustment of the Greek economy to euro conditions.

3. Technical adaptations of the frame of monetary policies to the euro

During 2000, successive decisions by the Monetary Policy Committee of the Bank of Greece brought about the full harmonisation of Greek monetary policy with the Euro-system. The main decisions dealt with:

- the harmonisation of open-market operations,
- the system of financing facilities and mandatory deposits of the banking system in drachma and in foreign exchange,
- the regulation of contractual relations of the Bank of Greece with other monetary policy counterparts.

The main Monetary Policy Committee legislative act for the alignment of open-market operations with ECB practice is Bank-of-Greece Act 32/7.3.2000, by which the Bank of Greece's financing ceilings for Greek banks were lifted. In June 2000, the system of mandatory deposits to the Bank of Greece was harmonised with the Euro-system practice (Act 37/30.6.2000). A unified rate of 2 per cent was then applied in place of the previous 12 per cent, with a calculation basis identical to the ECB's. It was also made possible for banks operating in Greece to use all of their mandatory deposits on a given date (provided that they were within their requirements on a monthly average). Since 1 January 2001, Regulations (EC) 2818/98, 2819/98 and 1921/2000 of the ECB have been put in force, fully integrating the Greek currency into the Euro-system's minimum reserve requirements practices. In his March 2001 Monetary Policy Report to the Parliament and the government, the governor of the Bank of Greece wryly described the cat-and-mouse game that was played among the Central Bank, the commercial banks and credit institutions. This was especially the case in the second half of 2000 when the liberalised environment coincided with expectations of interest rate cuts, thus inciting the banks to play in the markets actively. The course was nevertheless maintained and the final sprint to the euro sustained no damage. However, market expectations that the drachma's final conversion rate would differ from the agreed 340.750 GRD/euro were quashed.

Special attention was paid to the system of acceptance of Government paper as security for the conduct of open-market operations (as provided by the Statutes of the Bank of Greece). The shift from the Greek nominal valuation to market valuation, as provided by ECB rules, required legal adaptation and the establishment of electronic systems. This allowed for the creation of a reliable database that linked the secondary market for government paper and the Hellas Real-time Money transfers Express System/HERMES in drachma. The system was put into operation in March 2000, and was linked to the trans-border payment system TARGET. (Euro-HERMES was in operation from 4 January 1999, along with the payment systems of the other EU countries). All of these systems have been adopted, in consultation and co-operation with commercial banks and other credit institutions since May 2000: virtual real-time functioning was successfully attempted with the participation of the ECB in October and November 2000. All systems bugs were ironed out and hesitations on the part of market participants were overcome. Credit institutions were smoothly integrated into the operations of the Euro-system on 2 January 2001.

4. Legal/institutional adaptations—The final alignment

The Statutes of the Bank of Greece were radically amended in December 1997 (Law 2548/19.12.97 'Rules applicable to the Bank of Greece'). This allowed for the Bank's independence and the independent conduct of monetary policy. Although the press and the financial community had voiced concerns about the Bank's policy options—mainly its schedule of interest rate cuts and its opposition to credit expansion, but also about the stance of the Central Bank's governor during the Stock Exchange tribulations—no challenge was presented to the effective conduct of monetary policy.

A further amendment to the Statute of the Bank of Greece was effected in April 2000: the Bank's General Council agreed to the amendments, the ECB was consulted (17.4.2000), the amendments were voted for at the general meeting of the Bank on 24 April 2000, and then ratified by Law 2832/13.6.2000.

This circuitous route illustrates the intricate legal equilibrium of a Central Bank operated as a Société Anonyme under the authority of the legislature and within the Euro-system. Suggestions about how to change the legal status of the Bank of Greece were finally put aside without real debate. The fact that the Bank's origin is to be found in an international Treaty (under the League of Nations) might have played a role in this. The year 2000 Statute amendments brought the Bank of Greece fully in line with EC Treaty requirements, so as to operate under EMU's third stage. The amendments also provided for sanctions to be applied in cases arising from the conduct of monetary policy, where the ECB does not have exclusive powers. In addition, the Bank of Greece's supervisory powers were determined with reference to payment systems, and with special concern for the avoidance of systemic risk and the regulation of competition.

All ECB Regulations and Directives that concern the conduct of monetary policy have also been implemented or transposed into the internal legal order. This occurred mainly through decisions of the Monetary Policy Committee following extensive consultation with the ECB and Euro-system committees (Monetary Policy Report 2000–1, March 2001, 79).

- The full adaptation of monetary policy instruments and procedures was concluded in the three days from 30 December 2000 to 1 January 2001. More specifically:
- The Bank of Greece transferred the balance of its participation to the registered capital of the ECB (2.0564 per cent), as well as the relevant share of its foreign exchange.
- The balances of the drachma elements of the financial institutions' accounts at the Bank of Greece concerning monetary policy operations were switched to euro.
- The Bank of Greece's accounting was changed to euro and its balance sheet was integrated into the Euro-system balance.
- In order that government paper would be acceptable within the Euro-system as a basis for the injection of liquidity, all Greek government paper was denominated in euro after 2 January 2001.

All problems resulting from the transformation of the financial system were absorbed through consultations: no legal challenges and no litigation have yet emerged. It is only the rapid scaling down of interest rates (against a background of falling inflation) that is creating conflicts, mainly in price escalation systems and in the fixing of interest rates in contracts. These have so far been addressed through the application of general civil law rules, with no specific reference to EMU-related legislation.

5. The remaining inflationary pressures of the Greek economy

Greece was accepted as a member of the Euro-zone with a harmonised CDI of exactly 2 per cent in March 2000; thereafter, the slide of the euro and the disruption of the oil market throughout the second half of 2000 (continuing in 2001) led to an increase in the mean inflation rate from 2.2 per cent in mid-summer to 2.9 per cent in December 2000. More dispiriting is the measurement of year-on-year CPI, which had reached 3.7 per cent in December: core inflation also showed resurgence, reaching 3.4 per cent by the end of 2000.

In addition to the euro-US dollar rate and oil price fluctuations, several factors played a role in this evolution. Monetary expansion in the Greek economy occurred at a rate of 10.4 per cent in 2000 (against 5.5 per cent for the whole of 1999), while the relevant target (for the M4N measure) was put at a 5–7 per cent range. Credit expansion—mainly through the growth of banking credit to the private sector (28.5 per cent)—grew by 20.2 per cent in 2000 (compared with 12.2 per cent in 1999). The Bank of Greece as a partial explanation for this evolution has invoked the relaxation of credit restrictions. However, the rapid cut of interest rates must have had a preponderant role. The operation of the Greek economy in the new era of low, ECB-fixed interest rates might establish a permanent 'new era inflation' bias in the country.

The Bank of Greece's official prediction is that inflation will be kept low—'the impact of main inflatory factors in Greece will be overall favourable for stability in 2001'—but there is also a warning in the Governor's Report on Monetary Policy (March 2001):

> Greece cannot rely only on the common monetary policy to establish stability, since common policy has as its objective low inflation in the whole of the Eurozone and not in each single country. Thus, national economic policy must assume a more active role.

The tightening of income policy (with salary increases of 3.5–4 per cent in 2001, against 4.2 per cent in 2000, and with lower increases in the public sector) combined with the overall fiscal policy, are assuming an increasingly stabilising role. When approving the revised stabilisation and growth programme for the Greek economy (on 12 February 2001), the ECOFIN Council had recorded a projected fiscal surplus of 0.5 per cent of GDP (compared with a deficit of 0.9 per cent for 2000), growing from a primary deficit of 7 per cent of GDP. Ominously, the Greek Government had accepted that:

> if growth ends lower than expected, for example, due to lower investment or higher oil prices, the same objectives as to the fiscal stance will be kept; to do so, special emphasis will be given to the use of public funds.

This rather opaque statement was clarified in practice at the end of March 2001. At that point, deep budget cuts and rearrangements—mainly of defence expenditure, but also in all public spending—were introduced amid exensive political and public opinion turmoil.

IRELAND

*Alan Stuart**

1. Political and economic aspects

1.1 Public opinion and awareness of the euro

It is unfortunate that there has been little research into general public attitudes towards the single currency since the euro was introduced into Ireland on 1 January 1999. The Euro Changeover Board of Ireland (ECBI) has used a distinguished market research firm to conduct its own opinion polls to analyse Irish public awareness of the euro and aspects of the latter.[202] Four surveys have been conducted by the ECBI so far: July 1998, April 1999, July 2000 and November 2000. However, it must be emphasised that, rather than investigating *attitudes* towards the euro *per se*, the opinion polls have simply measured *awareness* of the single currency among the Irish population. The results make for some interesting reading.

In the more substantive opinion poll of July 2000, 92 per cent responded correctly when asked to name the new currency. This compares with a figure of 59 per cent in July 1998 and 88 per cent in April 1999. The lowest level of awareness was among those aged over 65 years, housewives, and those in the lower socio-economic income categories. In July 2000, approximately 65 per cent correctly named 2002 as the year in which the euro will be introduced, and of these 72 per cent said that the introduction would happen in January. By November 2000, these figures were 77 per cent and 83 per cent respectively. Awareness is highest among younger people and those in the upper middle class (AB) social bracket. In the July survey, roughly 70 per cent claimed to have seen pictures of euro notes and coins (compared to 30 per cent in 1998), with incidence lowest among those aged over 50, women over 65, lower income categories, residents of the Munster region, and housewives.

Also in July 2000, a question asked whether respondents had seen anything priced in both euros and Irish pounds. Six in every seven Irish

* Institute of European Affairs, Europe House, 8 North Georges Street, Dublin 1. This paper covers Ireland for 1999 and 2000, since there was no Irish *Eurospectator* Report for 1999. The author is grateful to Professor Brigid Laffan, Director, and Dr Ben Tonra, Deputy Director, of the Dublin European Institute, University College Dublin, for helpful comments and suggestions with this paper.

[202] The Euro Changeover Board of Ireland (ECBI) was established by the Irish Department of Finance on 5 May 1998 to oversee the detailed implementation of the changeover to the euro, and to provide public and consumer information regarding the changeover.

adults (up from 65 per cent in 1999) had seen dual pricing, especially on supermarket receipts, statements, and utility bills. Two thirds of adults (down from 75 per cent in April 1999) said that they had seen, read or heard something about the euro. The proportion is highest among the top income category, residents in Connacht/Ulster and the under 35s, but lowest among over 65s, members of the farming community, and housewives. In the July 2000 survey, most information about the euro came from financial institutions (50 per cent) and shops/supermarkets (39 per cent). Information was 'gathered' from television (75 per cent), and newspapers and magazines (61 per cent).

When given a range of choices in the July survey, almost half (47 per cent) of the respondents put the Irish Pound value of the euro as between 78 and 80 pence, with only 12 per cent giving the exact figure. In contrast, 11 per cent said that the IR£1 was worth €1.27. Roughly 40 per cent were unable to even hazard a guess at the direct and indirect exchange rates. By November 2000, 38 per cent were able to name the correct exchange rate. Correct evaluation is highest among the under 35s, males, the upper middle classes (AB), and those who know the introduction date. Awareness is lowest among the over 65s, females, housewives, the unskilled working class group (DE), and Dubliners. In the July survey, around 42 per cent said that they had no idea how long the Irish currency would remain in circulation, with the figure being highest among over 65s and lower income categories. Just 13 per cent estimated the length of time as up to six weeks after the euro's introduction.

Overall, the survey results show disappointing results for a country that has always been such an enthusiastic supporter of European integration. A lack of simple awareness of basic 'Euro facts' has manifested itself in certain demographic cohorts of the Irish population. Without reliable opinion polls it is impossible to assess the overall popularity of the euro among the Irish public, who do have a general awareness of the euro's effective existence as the Irish currency since January 1999. Unlike in many other European countries, the debate over the *Treaty on European Union* (Maastricht Treaty) did not lead to a significant public discussion about the loss of monetary sovereignty. Instead, the 1992 Irish referendum on the Maastricht Treaty was confused with several other issues, including abortion rights for women in Europe.

Unfortunately, since 1 January 1999 there has only been one public opinion poll in Ireland specific to the euro and to the Irish people's *attitudes* towards EMU (rather than their simple awareness of it), but this poll was taken before the actual introduction of Stage Three.[203] Table 1 shows the results of the survey. A number of interesting results were obtained in

[203] This MRBI opinion poll was carried out on 12 and 13 May 1998 for *The Irish Times*.

Table 1: Opinion on Effects of EMU and a Single Currency upon Ireland's Economic Performance (per cent)

	Improve	Damage	No Difference
Total	41	24	25
Co. Dublin	42	24	26
Rest of Leinster	46	22	21
Munster	36	22	25
Connacht/Ulster	41	27	31
Urban	43	23	25
Rural	39	24	26
18–24 years	48	21	24
25–34 years	46	26	21
35–49 years	41	22	27
50–64 years	35	23	28
65+ years	33	25	25
Married/ Widowed/Separated	39	23	26
Single	44	24	24
ABC1	45	25	21
C2DE	38	22	28
FIF2	41	24	25
Male	46	20	25
Female	36	27	25
Fianna Fáil	45	19	26
Fine Gael	39	30	25
Labour	33	32	31
Progressive Democrats	36	18	27
Other	44	29	17

No opinion responses were 10 per cent approximately

response to a question about whether EMU and a single currency will improve, damage, or make no difference to Ireland's economic performance.

The first result to note is that, for all demographic cohorts, a consistent majority believes that the euro will improve Ireland's economic performance. Those who believe it will make no difference slightly outnumber those who believe it will damage the economy. When the results are analysed by region, Dublin and the rest of Leinster are the most Europhile areas, while urban dwellers are slightly more in favour of EMU than rural people. Support for the euro is greatest among younger people and opposition to it generally increases with age. No significant pattern can be discerned in the attitudes towards the euro of different social classes, though males are slightly more in favour of it than females are. Fianna Fáil supporters are the group most in favour of the new currency, while there is a lower-than-average figure of euro-support among supporters of the Progressive Democrats. In the absence of more recent polls, it is difficult to assess how public opinion has changed since this survey but, with the euro's weak value stimulating the economic boom, it is unlikely that 'anti-euro' opinion has increased significantly.

1.2 Irish financial institutions' attitudes towards EMU

For reasons of political neutrality, the Central Bank of Ireland[204] and the Irish Bankers Federation[205] do not profess official organisational opinions about the euro. However, their publications are referred to in an attempt to gain an impression of how financial sector commentators have viewed the introduction of the euro to Ireland. The Central Bank of Ireland publishes quarterly bulletins outlining the performance of the Irish economy and the Euro-zone as a whole, and general opinions can be elicited from the authors of these reports.

The general consensus among authors of the Central Bank of Ireland reports has been that EC interest rates and the weak value of the euro on foreign exchange markets have given the Irish economy an unwelcome stimulus to aggregate demand at a time when a sustained boom is being experienced and there is almost full employment. High inflation has begun to re-appear in Ireland since the introduction of the euro, and many feel that European monetary conditions are causing the Irish economy to grow unsustainably beyond its long-term trend, leading to an 'overheating' of domestic consumption. The major academic and professional banking debate about whether Ireland should proceed with EMU centred upon whether or not the United Kingdom would enter the Euro-zone. Opinion was divided on this matter. Some argued that, even without the UK, EMU entry would still lead to net output (0.4 per cent GNP) and employment (10,000 jobs) gains (ESRI, 1996). Others argued that the lack of correlation with the business cycles in Germany and other likely Euro-zone countries was seriously underestimated when compared with the correlation with the UK. On these grounds, they disputed Irish entry without the UK (Neary and Thom, 1998). Figure 1 from Neary and Thom (1996) shows the correlation of EU Member States' demand or nominal shocks (represented by inflation) and supply or real shocks (represented by output growth) with Germany.[206] The lack of correlation

[204] The Central Bank of Ireland is also known in the Irish language as *Banc Ceannais na hÉireann*.

[205] The Irish Bankers Federation is the professional body representing the banking industry in Ireland.

[206] The structural vector autoregression (VAR) technique used in Figure 1 is not without

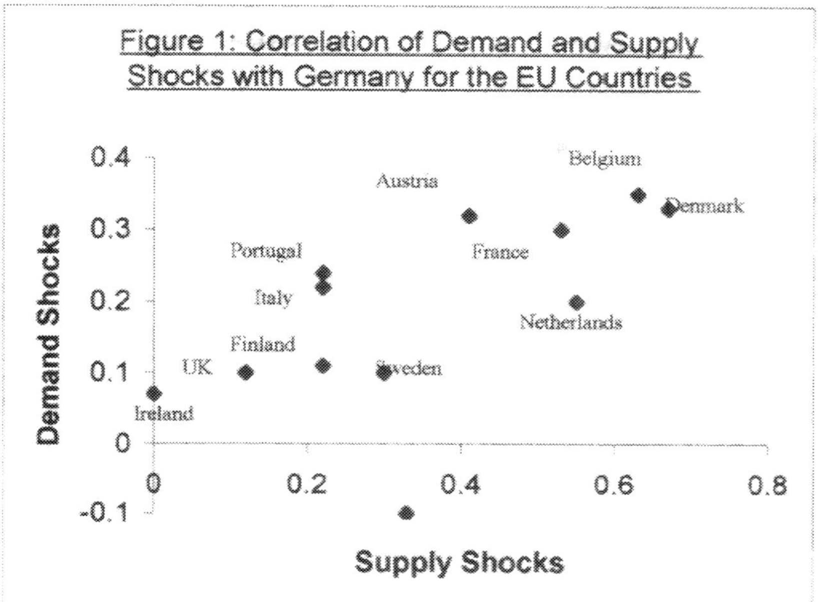

in the results tends to suggest that Ireland does not belong to the European 'core' in this group, and therefore might not be part of a European Optimal Currency Area.

A recent *Irish Banking Review*[207] article showed how the punt's[208] sterling dependency has fallen since the start of EMU Phase Three. The main concern has instead shifted to shocks to the US economy and the dollar/euro exchange rate, as well as the sterling/euro exchange rate. The inflationary consequences of both a strong pound sterling and high oil prices was not envisaged as a likely scenario in the years before EMU, yet this is exactly what has materialised in Ireland after its EMU entry. Sterling appreciated strongly in 1997, and it has remained strong on financial markets ever since. Many Irish bankers robustly believe that, due to the increases in the UK's services prices and labour costs relative to its major trading partners, sterling is overvalued and cannot maintain its present value. The high price of imports adds a cost-push stimulus to Irish inflation, while the low price of exports adds a demand-pull impetus to an already overheated economy. Due to such an overvaluation, many banks

its critics among econometricians. Yet Neary and Thom (1996) note that the results do tend to illustrate a clear lack of convergence of European business cycles.

207 The *Irish Banking Review* is the official journal of the Irish Bankers Federation.

208 The 'punt' is the Irish language word for 'pound'. It is used to refer to the Irish pound on foreign exchange and financial markets to distinguish it from the British pound sterling.

have downgraded their estimates of a sudden sterling depreciation on Irish output to a greater degree than they would have done in the years before the start of Stage Three.

Yet, from the long term perspective, Ireland's UK export and UK import share of total exports and imports has declined steadily (although the latter not quite as dramatically as the former). Figure 2 shows that UK exports declined from 73 per cent in 1960 to 21.7 per cent by 1999, while UK imports have declined from 50 per cent in 1960 to 32.6 per cent in 1999. It is too early to tell whether the punt's entry into the euro has altered such trends. Although there has been a decline in the exposure of the manufacturing sector to a sterling shock, exposure to a dollar shock has increased. Yet the dollar/euro exchange rate is also overvalued. The present day competitiveness of Irish manufacturers could suddenly reverse in the medium term in the presence of a US equity price shock that could have a 'knock-on' effect in the UK as well. Using the NiGEM macro econometric model, two prominent Irish economists have estimated an initial decline of 3 per cent GNP and 3.3 per cent employment if US equity prices fell by 25 per cent. According to their estimations, the decline in output and employment in later years would be lower (Duffy and Fitzgerald, 2000).

In addition to the important issue of sterling volatility, EMU has affected Irish monetary flows and financial markets in other significant ways. As is evident from Figure 3, less than 30 per cent of Ireland's payments are with the Euro-zone, and about 80 per cent of these simply

Figure 2: Share of UK Trade for Ireland 1960-1999

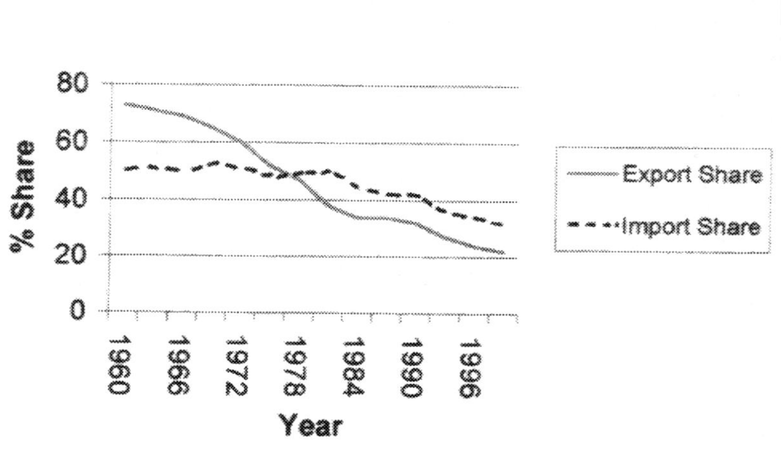

refer to the Irish Financial Services Centre in Dublin.[209] The elimination of the exchange rate risk premium as a component of systemic risk on real Irish short-term interest rates has led to lower real interest rates. Such a decline is evident when one considers the 17 per cent real interest rate required to keep the punt within the narrow ERM band at the end of 1992 during the currency crisis. Irish real interest rates also overshot the long-term real rate during the wide-band period, so depositors gained in real terms when the punt's depreciation into its euro rate was less than expected. After entry into EMU, real interest rates turned out to be negative due to the higher inflation level in Ireland, while short-term interest rates were being set by the ECB for the Euro-zone as a whole. The lack of a Fischer effect adjustment in real interest rates has further stimulated an asset price boom in Irish property markets that has manifested itself most severely in the greater Dublin area. Ironically, Ireland now needs higher real interest rates to prevent domestic aggregate demand from overheating the economy.

In addition to lower real interest rates, EMU was expected to deliver

Figure 3: Share of EMU-Area in Ireland's International Payments (%)

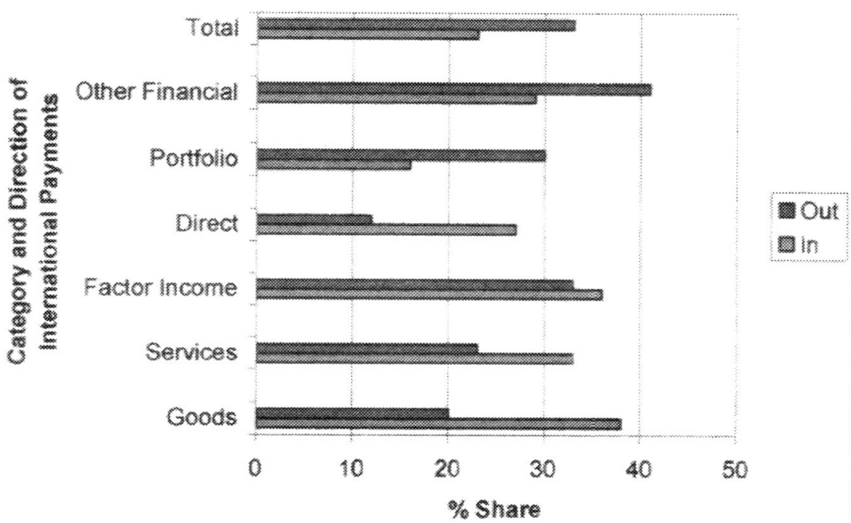

[209] The International Financial Services Centre (IFSC) is a tax-incentive area in Dublin designated for the promotion of the financial services sector in Ireland.

lower financial transaction costs. However, retail money transmissions charges remained high after EMU entry, a fact that Honahan (2000) attributes to the lack of common procedures for making retail financial payments across the Euro-zone. Curiously enough, the start of Stage Three seems to have had little influence over the Irish banking sector's international mergers and acquisitions. The entry of UK banks into Irish deposit and mortgage markets, and the acquisition by the four main Irish commercial banks of subsidiaries in Poland, the UK and elsewhere, show such activity having little regard for the creation of the Euro-zone in 1999.

One of the most important consequences of EMU for Ireland was expected to be the convergence in inflation rates to low European levels. Yet a lack of convergence has been evident from Ireland's increase from its trend inflation level since 1999. Despite being critical of expansionary fiscal budgets pursued by the ruling Fianna Fáil-Progressive Democrats coalition government, the Central Bank of Ireland generally feels optimistic about inflation converging to European levels. By December 2000 the inflation rate in Ireland had reached 6 per cent, while Euro-zone inflation was merely 2.75 per cent. The Central Bank of Ireland's Director General, Pádraig McGowan, attributes the 3.75 per cent inflation differential to a number of factors. In the context of the depreciating euro, about 0.50 per cent of the differential is due to the greater exposure of Ireland to non-euro currencies than the rest of the Euro-zone. About 1 per cent of the differential is attributed to higher productivity in the traded sector, pushing non-traded sector prices up in a Balassa–Samuelson effect. Another 0.75 per cent can be attributed to indirect tax increases, while only 1 per cent is seen as resulting from excess demand-pull factors in the Irish economy (McGowan, 2000).

Although the Central Bank of Ireland sees inflation as emanating mainly from external factors, it has criticised the government's failure to propose a contractionary fiscal policy to return Irish growth to its long-run steady state level. Asset price increases and infrastructure deficits are two areas where, after its rapid growth, the congestion of the Irish economy has been accentuated by lax fiscal policy, the weak euro, and the low real interest rates of the ECB mentioned earlier. The construction sector has been stretched to its fullest capacity and only an appreciating euro and higher real interest rates will ease the present infrastructure deficits.

Although there was not a spokesperson available at any of the four main commercial banks to discuss the loss to banks of foreign exchange revenue due to EMU, a prominent member of EMU planning at one bank highlighted some of the Irish commercial banks' concerns with EMU[210] at a conference by the Institute of European Affairs in Dublin in February

210 Pat McArdle, Head of the EMU Planning Unit in Ulster Bank, gave the address on behalf of commercial banks.

Table 2: Indebtedness to Irish Banks: Percentage of GNP

	Total	Personal	Building & Construction	Financial	Other
1994	71	33	5	8	24
1995	70	34	5	7	23
1996	73	35	5	7	24
1997	79	37	6	9	24
1998	85	39	8	11	25
1999	101	44	10	18	28

2000.[211] The number of participants in the Irish foreign exchange markets has fallen with the centralisation of euro dealing by banks and company treasurers, with turnovers declining by up to 30 per cent. The spokesperson commented that 'turnover in the foreign exchange, money, bond and indeed equity markets has diminished sharply as markets have either disappeared or liquidity has moved to larger trading centres'. However, the official response of the Irish banks has generally been one of support for the euro's introduction. With the lower interbank-offer rate there has been an explosion of credit expansion, with total indebtedness rising from 71 per cent of GNP in 1994 to 100 per cent in 1999 (see Table 2). The indebtedness of the property sector, as a proportion of GNP, doubled between 1994 and 1999. While overall levels of indebtedness are not currently high by international standards, continued growth at the current pace would raise concerns about the financial stability of the Irish banking system. The Central Bank of Ireland has continued to raise credit institutions' awareness to maintain prudent standards, especially in the mortgage market, and it is exploring ways in which counter-cyclical policies should be undertaken by lending bodies. Table 2 shows outstanding credit by Irish banks to various sectors of the economy.

1.3 Political aspects of the euro

Contrary to the situation in other Member States, the euro did not prove to be a major source of contention either within or between the four main political parties during the referenda debates on the Maastricht and Amsterdam Treaties. European integration has never been a major source of political cleavage—in the sense defined by mainstream political science—in Irish politics (Lipset & Rokkan, 1967). Public debate about the Maastricht Treaty was confused with domestic upheaval about abortion rights for

211 The Institute of European Affairs was founded in 1991 as a self-governing body devoted to the study of Irish policy on European integration.

women in Europe, and the Amsterdam Treaty referendum was never cohesively debated because it was held on the same day as the referendum about the highly significant Belfast Agreement on a peace plan for Northern Ireland. Three main political issues have arisen that might affect Ireland's commitment to the euro and further European integration:

(a) The combined effects of Ireland's rapidly increasing prosperity and eastern expansion of the EU will soon turn the country into a net financial contributor to the European Union. Although it is unlikely that any political party will object to EU membership, expansion, and integration on these grounds, Irish people may pressurise their politicians into a variety of 'pork barrel' budgetary measures. The splitting of the Republic of Ireland into two European regions to obtain more Structural Funds can be seen as a harbinger of what is to come in this regard.
(b) As Ireland's business cycle has become unsynchronised with larger Euro-zone countries, the increasing problem of a 'one size fits all' monetary policy is becoming an issue with Irish voters. If inflation increases beyond a certain threshold, anti-euro sentiment may prove significant.
(c) Concerns about Irish sovereignty and the accountability of European institutions are becoming more widespread in Irish politicians' speeches and the press. 'Spillover' integration in contentious areas might provoke a nationalist backlash among Irish voters. This would affect political parties and other interest groups.

1.4 Political parties

Since European integration has never been an inter- or intra-party political cleavage in Ireland, it is difficult to elicit any definite views about the euro from the Irish political parties. Yet, by interviewing public relations spokespeople and by examining press releases and speeches of their members, the following general descriptions can be drawn.

Centrist Fianna Fáil is the largest Irish political party and is currently in coalition government in Ireland. The party holds 76 of the 166 seats in the Dáil,[212] and 6 of Ireland's 15 European Parliament seats. The party has been in government for all of Ireland's referenda on European membership and integration, and has expressed continued support for Ireland's membership of the single currency. At a recent speech, party leader and current Taoiseach (Prime Minister) Bertie Ahern stated that 'many new jobs would not be created, were we not an integral part of a large single market with a single currency'.[213] Similar speeches by other party

212 The Dáil is the Lower House of the Irish Parliament.
213 The comments were made in a speech given to the European Movement Ireland Monday, 6 Nov 2000 in Dublin.

members who are also currently cabinet ministers echo such sentiments. The party also professes that the creation of the euro will enable Ireland to take a leading part in Europe's international affairs, and it does believe that 'pooled' monetary sovereignty will prove to be beneficial to all EU Member States. In an attempt to curtail diminishing support for European integration with the reduction of Structural Funds for Ireland, party spokespeople have also highlighted the cultural and social enrichment of Irish life due to European membership.

The centre-right Fine Gael party, currently in opposition with 53 of the 166 Dáil seats and 3 of the 15 Irish European Parliament seats, supported the European integration project from the time of Ireland's entry into the EEC in 1973. Party policy has wholeheartedly supported the EMU provisions in the Maastricht and Amsterdam Treaties. Despite the difficulties that Ireland has experienced in Stage Three since 1999, the party remains convinced that EMU's benefits for Ireland outweigh its costs, and it quotes the Economic and Social Research Institute (ESRI) Report (see Section 1.2) as support for this position.[214] In a policy pamphlet entitled 'Plan for the Nation', published in November 2000, the party confirms its belief that—even without the UK—Ireland's membership of EMU is beneficial. It also proposes that, in order to respond appropriately to the rigidity of the euro, a continued emphasis upon sound public finances, the development of a trained and educated workforce, active encouragement of market diversification, and more flexible systems of wage and salary compensation are needed.

The social democratic Labour Party, currently in opposition with 22 of the 166 Dáil seats and 1 of Ireland's 15 European Parliament seats, is also firmly committed to Ireland's membership of the euro, and to deeper European integration and enlargement. The secretary to the party's Irish MEP commented that the party was committed to the EP Party of European Socialists' policies on the completion of EMU and believes that it will bring net benefits to Europe's workforce. In a statement to the Dáil in June 1999, party leader Ruairí Quinn confirmed his party's commitment to deeper European integration and asked whether EU Member States wish 'to stop at the completion of the single market and single currency . . . or do they wish to see Europe's capacity to address issues like drug trafficking, the future of our environment, the elderly and unemployment increase?' The party also believes that EMU will benefit Ireland's workers, even without the UK.

The liberal Progressive Democrats party, with 4 Dáil seats but no MEPs, has also been a supporter of European integration and EMU since

[214] The Economic and Social Research Institute is a not-for-profit organisation that aims to bring the latest thinking in economics and the social sciences to bear on the actual and potential problems of Irish society.

its foundation in 1985. The party is currently in coalition government and its party leader, Mary Harney, holds the post of Tánaiste (Deputy Prime Minister). Party members have made speeches and press releases confirming their commitment to EMU, as well as further co-operation in other areas if such steps bring economic benefits to Ireland. However, the Progressive Democrats is probably the most 'Euro-cautious' of the main parties and Harney has expressed concern about entering EMU without the UK. Although no reference was made to the euro per se at the party's national conference in November 2000, both a party member of the Committee of the Regions and a party Irish Senator gave lectures strongly encouraging greater European co-operation and expansion. Although the party has signalled its intention to support the Treaty of Nice, it remains to be seen whether an integrationist—as opposed to expansionist—momentum can be maintained with its rank-and-file members.

The environmentalist Green Party has 2 Dáil seats and 2 Irish MEPs. While not Euro-sceptic per se, the party has objected to the perceived democratic unaccountability of many European institutions and it is opposed to EMU. The party campaigned hard against the Maastricht and Amsterdam Treaties, and recent party conventions reaffirm their disappointment with a lack of sustainable environmental and social mechanisms to regulate market forces in the European single market and single currency area. Such policies are surprising in light of the strong pro-integrationist stance of the green parties in the larger EU Member States. The Irish Green Party will experience difficulties with the other European green parties in this regard in the future.

The extreme nationalist Sinn Féin party, with 1 Dáil seat and no MEPs, has been generally anti-European and opposes the Republic of Ireland's membership of EMU. The primary impetus behind such an approach is that, with the UK not participating, EMU will lead to increased economic divergence between Northern Ireland and the Republic of Ireland. A recent speech by the Sinn Féin vice-president also espoused the 'freedom to pursue our own political and economic objectives' and opposed 'economic policy dictated from an undemocratic European Central Bank'. Their one Dáil Deputy, Caoimhghín Ó Caoláin has recently commented that 'successive governments have already surrendered too much powers and control of our economy to the EU', and he went on to advocate rejection of the Nice Treaty in the forthcoming referendum. Although the party has little support in the Republic of Ireland, its ultra-nationalist doctrine might yet prove attractive to some Irish voters.

At this juncture, it is also worth highlighting the results from a recent expert survey carried out by one of Ireland's leading political scientists regarding Irish party positions on several dominant saliences (policy dimensions) (Laver, 1998). The technique used is that of an 'expert survey' involving the subjective opinions of political experts in ranking political parties on various policy saliences to suggest coalition-forming possibilities. It is a technique widely applied in the political science rational choice literature. The survey involved the responses of 30 Irish political scientists ranking the various parties on certain policy dimensions according to the best of their opinions. One of these dimensions was European policy, and the results are shown for the six Irish parties discussed in this report. They are rated on a scale of zero to twenty, depending upon the perceptions of the political scientists concerned.[215] Although European policy does not have as high a policy salience in Ireland as economic policy or Northern Ireland policy, it is judged to be the next most important topic. The results are shown in Table 3 below.

As was expected from the policy descriptions above, Table 3 shows that European policy effectively pits the Green Party and Sinn Féin against all the others, with only insignificant changes in all parties' policy positions since 1992. However, it must be remembered that these two parties have only a tiny percentage of the Irish vote. As already mentioned, in practice European policy has not proved divisive in Ireland.

1.5 Anti-Europe interest groups

The most prominent anti-European policy and decisively anti-euro interest group in Ireland is The National Platform, a non-party pressure group that aims to unite Euro-critics of all political persuasions who are opposed to further European integration. An interview with its Secretary, Dr Anthony Coughlan, revealed some of the group's aims and ideals. The National Platform, in its own words, believes 'that stable and friendly co-operation between states and peoples can only be based upon respect for their national independence and sovereignty'. It believes that a single currency will prove disastrous for Ireland and states that the project 'is politically profoundly undemocratic and economically unsustainable'. The organisation has long

Table 3: European Policy Saliences of Irish Political parties

	SF	Green	Labour	FF	FG	PD
1997	6.61	5.97	14.53	14.60	16.97	15.17
percentage change 1992–7	+2.32	−1.23	+0.24	−1.76	−0.99	−2.72

215 The political scientists were asked to rate the Irish political parties upon the scale of: Oppose more integration with the European Union (low) versus Promote more integration with the European Union (high).

standing connections with Danish, Norwegian, and British opponents of the EU, and since 1992 it has developed links with similar movements in France, Spain, Poland and Slovenia (among others). The organisation is affiliated with The European Anti-Maastricht Alliance (TEAM), which links together some 40 organisations in 13 different European countries, only allowing member organisations that have non-racist constitutions. Coughlan has served as international co-ordinator of TEAM. The group has also been successful in winning three significant Irish Supreme Court cases about the government's conduct of Irish referenda, which will have an effect upon any further Irish referenda on European integration. It is also signalling its intention to campaign against the forthcoming Treaty of Nice in 2001.

1.6 Trade unions

The European Affairs spokesperson of the Irish Congress of Trade Unions, Frank Vaughan, spoke about the confederation and its affiliated members' attitudes to the euro. The ITUC and its members have all been generally pro-EMU and no significant inter- or intra-union differences have emerged to this effect. The ITUC opposed Irish entry into the EEC in 1973 on the grounds that tariff removal would harm Irish workers. However, they have since become firm supporters of European integration and supported the 'Yes' side in the referenda on the Maastricht and Amsterdam Treaties. Unlike many Irish academic and financial commentators, Vaughan claimed that the trade unions were 'more or less happy' with the rate at which the punt entered the euro (DM 2.48). He also believes that, if the Irish indicative planning Social Partnership agreements are flexible enough to adjust to external shocks, membership will bring net gains to the Irish economy and Irish workers. The ITUC is also committed to European expansion and further integration. On the issue of whether the euro will affect Ireland's competitiveness, the ITUC believes that Ireland should aim for a 'high-skill, high-wage' economy, and not try to compete in 'low-skill, low-wage' sectors with newly industrialising countries. Competing for foreign investment in appropriate sectors will be paramount to maintaining full employment in Ireland in the absence of independent exchange rate policy.

1.7 Employers' organisations

The Irish Business and Employers Confederation (IBEC) is the main organisation representing Irish employers. It has a membership of approximately 7,000 companies from all sectors of economic and commercial life in Ireland. Its EMU project co-ordinator, Gary Rynhart, was interviewed about the organisation's attitudes towards the implementation of the euro and EMU. According to Rynhart, the opinions of Irish employers are generally highly favourable towards EMU, and they believe that reductions in transaction costs and the need for foreign currency hedging will lead to significant gains for Irish firms in their trade with the Euro-zone. They also strongly believe that EMU is a necessary step to ensure completion of the Single Market. Fears of the loss of independent exchange rate policy, according to Rynhart, are exaggerated because competitive devaluations only delay necessary labour market reforms. He expresses concern about the lack of UK participation, but he nevertheless believes that, on balance, Ireland will be a net gainer since dependence on the sterling has decreased sharply and will continue to do so. Rynhart also claims that most members were happy with the competitive level at which the punt entered the euro, and he does not believe that a higher level of entry would have been more appropriate. Again, the loss of an independent ability to set interest rates is of concern, and he said that 'many sectors of the economy, particularly the housing market, need an interest rate about 4–5 per cent higher than Ireland currently has'. Yet the general belief of IBEC economists and senior officials is that the Irish business cycle will converge to that of the Euro-zone as time progresses, and that a single monetary policy will confound its critics and enhance intra-European trade and political co-operation. Rynhart strongly emphasised the paramount requirement for flexibility in the social partnership negotiations, if Ireland is to remain competitive within the constraints of the Euro-zone. IBEC also supports European expansion, believing that it will create new markets and provide fresh labour to fuel Irish economic growth.

2. Trends towards spillover

Trends towards spillover, as predicted by the neo-functionalist paradigm of European integration, have provoked a significant amount of debate in the wake of the Irish decision to enter EMU. For many Irish Euro-sceptics, EMU was seen as further striking proof that a nascent federal Europe is underway, and steadily declining support for the 'Yes' side in Ireland's European referenda has given rise to much public discussion as to whether further EU integration is desirable. In the 1971 referendum on EEC accession, 73 per cent voted 'Yes'. This figure dropped to 69.5 per cent in 1987 with the referendum on Single European Act, 68.7 per cent in 1992 when the Treaty on European Union (Maastricht) was being considered, and 60.4 per cent in 1998 when the Amsterdam Treaty was being voted upon. When the debate on the Nice Treaty comes to the fore, it is likely that the four main political parties will switch their ideological positions to one of 'widening' rather than 'deepening' Europe. As Ireland becomes a net budget contributor, the general public might simply object to any further form of integration or expansion on a purely financial basis. A number of different 'spillover' areas shall now be examined.

2.1 Tax harmonisation

Tax harmonisation in the wake of EMU has provoked by far the most heated discussion of any area of proposed further integration in Ireland. A strong general consensus that taxes harmonisation would be very harmful for the Irish economy has emerged among the political parties, trade unions, employers' organisations and state bodies. The primary focus for this debate has been corporation tax, as it has been argued that Ireland's recent economic success was based upon its corporation tax rates and structure acting as an incentive to multi-national enterprises to locate in the country. Any attempt to move to qualified majority voting in the Council of Ministers on taxation issues is seen as threatening Ireland's competitive edge over the country's peripheral location. Ireland's corporation tax structure is highly complex with differing rates; it basically consists of an incentive 10 per cent rate for manufacturing and International Financial Services Centre firms in Dublin and a standard rate of 24 per cent for other firms. A lower rate of 12.5 per cent applies to other companies whose profits do not exceed £50,000 per annum. A deal with the EU Commission will lead to a single standard rate of 12.5 per cent by 2005. Such a competitive rate is highly resented by other Member States, and pressure to alter it will intensify in the years to come. Ireland also resents indirect tax harmonisation due to a greater reliance on revenue from VAT and excise duties and the higher rates that apply. Pressure to move to the origin principle instead of the destination principle as a prerequisite to indirect tax approximation is also resisted.

2.2 Social policy

Although not as controversial an area of integration as tax policy, social policy—about whether or not further integration should proceed in the wake of EMU—also generates discussion in Ireland. It is difficult to elicit any clear policies on this area of spillover from Irish political parties, as it does not feature prominently in any of their published speeches or policy documents. Broadly, the Labour party expresses a desire to pursue a moderately corporatist approach to harmonising social legislation, while the Progressive Democrats argue that a neo-liberal flexible approach is necessary to deal with the rigidities of EMU and they oppose any development that elaborates upon the Social Charter and the Social Protocol. Fine Gael and Fianna Fáil lie somewhere in between these two viewpoints. As might be expected, the ICTU favours further employment and workplace directives and regulations, and it would surely support any such measures that will be introduced in the future. IBEC, in contrast, strongly opposes any developments that violate labour market flexibility under EMU, and it advocates supply-side measures to maintain full employment in Ireland. A general debate that has been underway in Ireland is the 'Boston versus Berlin' debate over social policy (that is, whether the country should aim for a low-tax liberal welfare state model or a high-tax social democratic welfare model). The present government has been trying to aim for the former. Some see the debate as the start of a possible ceiling on Ireland's participation in economic integration if it threatens the concerns of vital sectors of the economy. Yet the emphasis upon a neo-liberal rejection of social policy spillover is moderately surprising given Ireland's near-full employment at the end of 2000.

2.3 Macroeconomic policy co-ordination

With the advent of EMU, control over monetary and exchange rate policy has been removed from Member States. Yet the Growth and Stability Pact also aspires to constrain the use of *fiscal* policy to adjust one's economy to asymmetric output shocks. It can be argued, as the reliable Mundell-Fleming model so clearly highlights, that fiscal adjustment to real shocks offers only a temporary reprieve from output's inevitable adjustment to its long-run natural level. The gradualist monetarist consensus argues that inflation will result in the long term if a fiscal expansion is used to offset an adverse supply shock. The same belief about the long run neutrality of money applies to exchange rate devaluations. Co-ordination of fiscal policy should therefore not necessarily be seen as ceding too much sovereignty to organs of supranational co-operation. Yet since the introduction of EMU in Ireland, there has been dissatisfaction with the EU Commission's public commentary about the inflationary aspects of Irish fiscal policy. Rather than suffer from adverse shocks, the Fianna Fáil-Progressive Democrats coalition has fuelled an already booming economy by a mixture of tax cuts and expenditure increases in fulfilment of commitments to the trade unions within the context of social partnership. Such lax fiscal budgets have aroused concern, even though the government has run a primary surplus in its budgets since the introduction of EMU. As mentioned in Section 1.2, the Central Bank of Ireland has expressed concern at the government's renegade action, and opposition political parties have criticised the government for damaging Ireland's standing with the EU Commission. The massive fiscal stimulus of the most recent budget in December 2000 spurned strong condemnation from across Europe for its inflationary consequences. Yet the present government's opposition to any EU constraints remains steadfast on an area that it regards as national sovereignty. The deadlock looks set to continue unabated for the rest of the present coalition's term of office.

2.4 The neutrality debate

The press and other commentators have jokingly referred to Irish neutrality as 'between a rock and something hard'. Indeed, the inclusion of the Second Pillar (Common Foreign and Security Policy) into the Maastricht Treaty provoked intense debate concerning the position of Ireland's neutrality in a more integrated Europe of EMU (Cheating, 1996). The fears were primarily orientated towards whether or not the Western European Union (WEU) was to be formally incorporated in the European Union, and if so whether it would just be a puppet of NATO. Apart from Tadjikistan, Ireland was the only European country not to take part in NATO's Partnership for Peace (PFP) consultative forum before 2000. The four largest political parties—while wishing to preserve Irish neutrality from full membeship of NATO—have gradually faced up to the *realpolitik* of the post-Cold War world, where the necessity of taking part in international peace-keeping and peace-enforcement missions has to be a priority. However, the general consensus has been that Irish participation in such missions should only proceed when officially mandated by the United Nations. At present, the two small parties—Sinn Féin and the Green Party—are vehemently opposed to any steps that would include Ireland in a European military alliance. Indeed an attempt by the previous Fine Gael-Labour-Democratic Left coalition government to take Ireland into the PFP was rejected by the Democratic Left party.[216] The present Fianna Fáil-Progressive Democrats coalition succeeded in negotiating Ireland's entry into the PFP forum, but Irish people generally oppose any attempt to form a European military alliance. With the accession of Finland, Austria and Sweden to the EU, Ireland has other neutral countries with which to ally itself in preventing any such measures.

3. Legal framework

The start of Stage Three of EMU did not cause any major legal upheaval in Ireland, and domestic banking and commercial law have by and large accommodated the changeover with relative ease. Indeed, most of the euro changeover provisions appear to be of a mainly functional nature, and a central finding of this report has been that no civil law cases involving the use of the euro have emerged during the first two years of Stage Three. The general attitude of dealing with problems as they emerge reflects the Anglo-Saxon common law tradition in Ireland, as opposed to the code-based systems prevalent on the European continent. Most legal provisions necessary for the changeover were introduced in Economic and Monetary

[216] Democratic Left was a small socialist party that merged with the Labour Party in January 1999. It strongly opposed membership of NATO's PFP.

Union Act 1998, which is itself effectively the domestic enactment of Council Regulation (EC) no 974/98 of 3 May 1998 and Council Regulation (EC) no 1103/97 of 17 June 1997. The provisions governing institutional and regulatory changes to the Central Bank of Ireland in the wake of EMU are enshrined in the Central Bank Act 1988. It is to these two Acts that the focus of this paper's attention now turns.

3.1 Domestic provisions in the Economic and Monetary Union Act 1998

The primary purpose of this legislation is to remove incompatibilities between Irish monetary law and the EU legal framework for the use of the euro, which comprises Regulations 974/98 and 1103/97. For instance, section 7 of the Act confirms that contracts may be denominated in euro during the transition period, despite the fact that euro notes and coins will not be in circulation. What is unclear in the Act is whether a *pacta sunt servanda* obligation to pay or be paid in euro is binding upon the contracting parties during the transition period. Section 9 allows for the Minister for Finance to decide upon an 'earlier operative date' to shorten the maximum six month period after 31 December 2001 during which punts and euros shall operate beside each other as legal tender. A Department of Finance ministerial order, due to be signed in May 2001, suggests 9 February 2002 as the end of the dual currency operation period.

Section 10 provides that no person, other than the Central Bank of Ireland and 'such persons as the Minister may designate by order', will be obliged to accept more than 50 euro coins in any single transaction. This provision was made to ease cash handling requirements, especially in the retailing sector, but it could lead to difficulties during the specie changeover phase after 31 December 2001. An extension of a prohibition on counterfeiting is provided for in section 12.[217] Two provisions relate to the fact that the costs of issuing euro coins (and the proceeds from such issues) shall be paid from (and paid into) the General Fund of the Central Bank.

An amendment to the Copyright Act 1963 provides for the copyright of the European Central Bank in relation to euro notes, and the copyright of the Minister for Finance in relation to the national face of euro coins issued under section 11 of the Act.[218] The Act also allows for all measures and instruments pertaining to the Dublin Interbank Offer Rate (DIBOR) to apply to the Euro Interbank Offer Rate (EURIBOR) from 1 January 1999. The provision allowed for the smooth transition of inter-bank lending rates with the introduction of the new currency into Ireland.

Section 23 of the Act deals with transition period redenomination of

217 A separate bill to combat counterfeiting is due to be put before the Dáil in 2001.
218 The harp is the Irish national symbol on euro coins.

Irish government debt into euros by the National Treasury Management Agency (NTMA).[219] Subsection (2) allows the Minister for Finance to redenominate any Euro-zone currency debt into euros during the transition period, *provided* that the Member State of which the debt is denominated has redenominated all or part of its national currency general government debt into euros. It also obliges the Minister to issue notice to this effect in *Iris Oifigiúil*.[220] Subsection (3) also allows state bodies to redenominate their debt into euros providing the financial institutions concerned agree to do so.

The Act also provides for the redenomination of company share capital into euros. Section 25 allows companies that wish to redenominate their share capital into euros during the transition period to do so, provided that shareholders pass a resolution approving it. In cases where redenomination of share capital into euros would lead to a decrease in share capital due to inconvenient amounts, section 26 provides that—by a special shareholders' resolution—the amount of the decrease will be paid into a fund known as the Capital Conversion Reserve Fund. The Act also penalises a company that fails to lodge a copy of such resolutions with the Registrar of Companies within 15 days of it having been passed.

Another provision amended the Minister's power to suspend certain transactions in the national interest under existing legislation. From now on, this power shall not prejudice the Central Bank of Ireland's responsibilities under the Statute of the European System of Central Banks (or Euro-system). A few final provisions also allow for the issuing of commemorative coinage to celebrate the completion of Stage Three of EMU.

3.2 The Central Bank Act 1998 and its implications

The main piece of legislation dealing with regulatory and institutional changes to the Central Bank of Ireland is the Central Bank Act 1998. What follows are some of its more important provisions.[221]

Section 4 of the Act amends the central bank's duties to include 'any function or duty' required by or under provisions of the Treaty or the ESCB-ECB Statute. The section also outlines the duties of the governor to inform the board of the bank of ESCB decisions. In addition, allowance is made for the authority and responsibilities of the governor to be vested in the director general of the bank in the case of ill health or 'any other

[219] The National Treasury Management Agency (NTMA) is the Irish government body assigned with the liability management duties of managing Irish government debt.

[220] *Iris Oifigiúil* is the official journal in which the Irish government announces all official legal rulings and public appointments.

[221] The author is grateful to two anonymous representatives of the Central Bank of Ireland for assistance with this section of the Legal Framework.

cause'. Section 5 enshrines the policy goals of the ECB as those of the Central Bank of Ireland. It states the following:

> the primary goal of the Bank shall be to maintain price stability, and without prejudice to the generality of the aforesaid, the Bank may perform such functions and exercise such powers and carry out such duties as are conferred or imposed on it by the Treaty, the Statute or any Act of the Oireachtas or instrument made thereunder.[222]

Another provision allows for the Minister for Finance to request the governor (on behalf of the board of the bank) to consult with him regarding the execution of any duty imposed upon the bank, other than ESCB duties. The minister can request the governor to inform him of the pursuit of the primary policy objective of price stability under the Act. The section also states the following secondary policy goals:

> Without prejudice to the objective of maintaining price stability, the Bank shall support the general economic policies in the Community with a view to contributing to the achievement of the objectives of the Community as laid down in Article 2 of the Treaty.

The Act also allows the board of the bank, by unanimous vote of all the directors, to request the President of Ireland to remove the governor from office on the grounds of 'serious misconduct'. Yet any decision to remove the governor may be subject to a reference to the European Court of Justice. Section 8 of the Act requires investment trust companies, money brokers and financial intermediaries to furnish the Central Bank of Ireland or the ECB with information and returns concerning the business to which their licenses relate. Any other information required by the central bank and the ECB to fulfil their duties can be requested.

The Act also governs the accountability of the governor to the Oireachtas. Section 17 states the following:

> Subject to the requirements of the Treaty and of the Statute, the Governor of the Bank shall, if so requested, attend before a Joint Committee of the Oireachtas that is assigned the role of examining matters related to the Bank and shall furnish the Committee with such information as may be requested . . .

The Joint Committee on European Affairs was assigned the role of supervising the bank in this regard, and this author attended one of these sessions where the present governor, Maurice O'Connell, presented a statement to the committee outlining his views of the Irish economy's performance in the Euro-zone. The committee has been pleased thus far with the present governor's performance bringing Ireland into the Euro-zone, and it appears that this aspect of the Act has been working quite well since January 1999.

222 The Oireachtas is the collective name of the lower house (Dáil) and upper house (Seanad or Senate) of the Irish Parliament.

Although it was always implicit in the appointment of the bank's governor, the Act explicitly forbids the governor from standing for election as a director of any credit institution, financial institution, or insurance undertaking. If the governor holds such a directorship at the time of his/her appointment, the position must be divested within ten days. These measures guarantee the independence of the governor from commercial, as well as political, interference.

The Central Bank Act allows for the efficient transfer of monetary and regulatory structures during the transition phase. Most of the legal provisions are simple functional measures necessary to ensure the smooth transfer to the completion of Stage Three of EMU, and no legal problems have so far emerged as a result of the Act.

3.3 National law from the EU perspective

After speaking with, and formally interviewing, numerous legal experts in Ireland, I conclude that there are no conflicts between national legislation and EU legislation concerning the euro. This conclusion was reached after consultation with the Irish Parliamentary Legal Advisor, barristers from the Honourable Society of King's Inns and solicitors from the Law Society of Ireland (who are experts in banking and European law), representatives from the Central Bank of Ireland, and academic law lecturers. None of the aforementioned individuals perceive any such conflicts arising in the future.

3.4 The application of the law

The experts mentioned in Section 3.3 of this report commented that they have no information about any proceedings or judgments in Irish civil courts concerning the changeover to the euro or EMU. This includes legal areas such as the law of contracts and obligations. Also, to the best of their knowledge, no *obiter dictum* comments by an Irish judge have been made in any Irish civil case concerning the euro to date.

Bibliography

Duffy, David and Fitzgerald, John (2000): 'Has Ireland's Exposure to a Sterling Shock Changed?' in *Irish Banking Review* (Winter 2000).

Economic and Social Research Institute (1996): *Economic Implications for Ireland of EMU* (Dublin: ESRI).

Honahan, Patrick (2000): 'Ireland in EMU: Straitjacket or Skateboard?' in *Irish Banking Review* (Winter 2000).

Cheating, Patrick (1996): *European Security: Ireland's Choices* (Dublin: Institute of European Affairs).

Laver, Michael (1998): 'Party policy in Ireland: Results from an Expert Survey' in *Irish Political Studies* (1998: 13: 159–71).

Lipset, Seymour Martin and Rokkan, Stein (1967): *Party Systems and Voter Alignments: Cross-National Perspectives* (London: Collier-Macmillan).

McGowan, Pádraig (2000): 'Ireland: Experiences in EMU' in *Central Bank of Ireland Bulletin* (Winter 2000).

Neary, Peter & Thom, Rodney (1996): *Punts, Pounds and Euros: In Search of an Optimum Currency Area* (Dublin: University College Dublin).

ITALY

Marina Mancini and Silvia Nenci

1. Political and economic aspects

Silvia Nenci*

1.1 Public opinion and the euro

1.1.1 Surveys

Eurobarometer survey (Eurobarometer No 54) questioned more than 16,000 citizens of the European Union in November and December 2000. It shows that 55 per cent (–3 per cent in comparison with Spring 2000) of Europeans support the single currency, while 37 per cent do not. The Member States in which support is strongest are Italy (79 per cent), Luxembourg (75 per cent), Belgium (72 per cent), Greece (70 per cent), Ireland (69 per cent), Spain (68 per cent) and the Netherlands (64 per cent). The majority of public opinion is against the euro in Sweden (26 per cent), the United Kingdom (21 per cent), Denmark (41 per cent) and Finland (45 per cent). The results show that 79 per cent of Italian citizens are in favour of the euro (–2 per cent in comparison with previous six months), 17 per cent are against it (+3 per cent) and the remaining 4 per cent are indifferent.

With respect to public opinion towards the Union's institutions and bodies (Eurobarometer survey No 53): the European Central Bank is one of the three most widely trusted Community institutions and bodies (53 per cent of preferences), along with the European Parliament (67 per cent) and the European Commission (58 per cent).

The survey reveals that at least 8 in 10 Italians claim to have received information about the single currency, a significant improvement since autumn 1999. Television, newspapers and magazines and financial institutions are the principal vehicles for information about the euro in Italy.

The annual ISTAT (the National Statistics Institute) survey of Italian knowledge and opinions regarding the introduction of euro—carried out among 7,000 citizens—shows that 90 per cent of the Italians interviewed know that there will be a single currency in the European Union from 2002. The demographic analysis shows some significant differences: women seem to be less informed than men (86 per cent versus 92 per cent) and people over 65 years old seem less informed than young people (77

* Istituto Affari Internazionali—Rome, Via Angelo Brunetti 9, Palazzo Rondinini, I-00186, Rome; Supervisor: Prof. Natalino Ronzitti, LUISS University, special counsellor at the IAI—Rome.

per cent versus 95 per cent). The survey also highlights the trend that the level of knowledge about the euro tends to increase with higher levels of education and income.

Italians support for the euro is strong, but they know little about it.

A public opinion poll of 600 people from 17 to 74 years of age, conducted by Eurisko in autumn on behalf of the Treasury Minister, shows that almost all Italians know of single currency (98 per cent). But the poll also indicates that only 10 per cent of those interviewed know that the double currency period has been shortened from six to two months, and only a third know the exact value of euro in relation to the lira (Dalla lira all'euro, 2000).

The Eurisko opinion poll also indicates there is still considerable ignorance about the countries involved in the third stage of EMU. Only 1 per cent of the people interviewed know exactly which countries, other than Italy, have adopted the single currency, and at least half the Italian people cite the four larger countries (Italy, France, Germany and Spain). Answers to the opinion poll also showed a significant drop in Italian acceptance of the euro. It is the second shrinkage recorded since 1997 when a restrictive fiscal policy was implemented to meet Maastricht criteria.

Italian citizens consider the common single currency to be a 'weak' currency. Only 50 per cent of people interviewed are optimistic about the benefits linked to the introduction of the euro.

According to an opinion poll issued on the eve of a key EU summit, France, Germany and Italy are among the countries most committed to the European Union, although they do not always agree on the pace of integration. The poll, carried out by the IPSOS institute for France's European Affairs Minister, shows that most of those questioned believe that European institutions should have more political clout in order for citizens to feel that they belong to the EU.

IPSOS conducted the poll in France, Germany, Britain, Spain and Italy in Autumn 2000, with 1,000 people questioned in each country. 'Today 34 per cent of Europeans questioned believe that they will consider themselves European citizens the day a head of state is elected by all Europeans,' IPSOS said (6 December 2000). That feeling was most prevalent in France, Germany and Italy, where 34 pe rcent of those questioned shared that view (compared to 24 per cent in Britain and 22 per cent in Spain). However, the poll showed that Europeans remain attached to national sovereignty, especially in Britain (67 per cent), Germany (56 per cent) and France (53 per cent).

A troubling view is expressed in an Autumn 2000 Nielsen opinion poll conducted on behalf of the Indicod—Istituto di studio per i beni di consumo—among 5,000 citizens over eighteen years old. 73 per cent of the Italians interviewed believed that the euro would cause confusion and problems to consumers.

The annual opinion poll by the Louis-Harris Institute, conducted on behalf of some important European daily newspapers, shows a less positive situation. Only 41 per cent (53 per cent in the previous opinion poll) of the people interviewed in seven European countries (France, Spain, Germany, Italy, Netherlands Greece and Luxembourg) are happy about the substitution of the euro for the national currency. Looking at the individual country analysis, only 29 per cent of the German people will willingly renounce the Deutsche Mark. The Netherlands and Luxembourg have the most optimistic populations (61 per cent and 72 per cent respectively), while the British are the least positive (20 per cent). The Louis-Harris opinion poll shows an unusual result for Italy: only 48 per cent of the Italian people would be happy about the introduction of the common single currency.

1.1.2 Articles in the press

During 2000, public debate focused on the weakness of the euro vis-à-vis the US dollar and the reasons for this.

This debate can be synthesised in a few articles taken from two important Italian daily newspapers. *Corriere della Sera*, from Milan, observed that there are no truly valid explanations for the weakness of the euro:

> The European economy is picking up and ought to be pushing up the euro with it, while the dollar ought to have suffered from trade deficit figures. However, this was not the case.

With respect to explanations for the euro's continuing slide, in April the Milan daily quoted three different opinions: the lack of true political unity on the Old Continent, the monetary control exercised by the European Central Bank, and the various fiscal policies. The *Corriere della Sera* argued that 'the best answer to why the euro cannot keep up with the dollar is that "Europe is not America" ', reporting the opinion expressed in the fifth report from the Einaudi Centre written by economist Mario Deaglio (Corriere della Sera, 20 April 2000). There were many contingent factors (the Italian premier's resignation, a fall in investor confidence in Germany, the roller-coaster rush on the US bourses) which mixed to exacerbate an underlying weakness, and thus proved to be particularly difficult for the euro during the first months of the year.

In its editorial of 26 October, *La Stampa*, the Turin daily newspaper, observed that the markets were letting the euro slide because the European economy was not as strong as the American economy (which was not slowing at the pace that pundits had expected). The Turin daily went on to say that the European Central Bank was more concerned about economic recovery than inflation, which was the Fed's greatest enemy. It was thus keeping European interest rates well below those in America. This did nothing to convince people to sell dollars and buy euro.

Another reason for the euro's plight was the difference between European and US interest rates. Corriere della Sera quoted those who blamed the ECB for doing nothing to defend its currency. It also reported the attack against the ECB, which accused it of being non-existent on the markets and indirectly responsible for the strengthening of speculators.

Regarding the ECB's decision to increase interest rates by a quarter of a point in September, Corriere della Sera published a flanking editorial co-written by Franco Modigliani (Nobel Prize laureate, economist) and Giorgio La Malfa (secretary of the Republican Party), slamming the central bankers for raising rates. They wrote:

> The ECB announced that, which everyone more or less expected: a quarter percentage point hike of the discount rate, which is now 4.5 per cent. The decision saddens, but does not surprise us: we find it to be a serious error at a moment at which the Europe of the euro has just started a modest economic recovery and unemployment has begun to show signs of falling; if it is effective, the rate hike will determine a new period of slow growth.

In the same daily, economist Paolo Savona agreed with a proposal floated by the renowned American economist Fred Bergsten to allow the G7 nations to make a joint, concerted effort to boost the euro, saying 'calm' measures like raising the key lending rate would not halt the Euro's overall 'slide' (*Corriere della Sera*, 2 September 2000).

As a possible reason for the weak defence of the euro by ECB, La Stampa cited the lack of any statement in support of a stronger euro from the Group of Seven summit, and the fact that many European exporters and politicians wanted a weak euro to help exports and reinforce the recovery (*La Stampa*, 20 April 2000).

1.2 Financial institutions

1.2.1 The weakness of the euro

The weakness of the euro against the US dollar, which characterised the year 2000, did not particularly worry financial institutions.

Wim Duisenberg, the European Central Bank President, has often explained that the increases in interest rates were instituted to contrast the risk of inflation and not to support the euro, as the European fundamentals showed a positive trend.

During a parliamentary debate in March, the same view was expressed by Luigi Spaventa, President of the Commissione Nazionale per le Società e la Borsa (Consob). According to Spaventa, the euro-dollar exchange rate was not a real threat to the monetary stability of the Euro-area, because it was in line with the historical trend of the euro's synthetic index.

Economist Paolo Savona held the international monetary disorder—and not the European fundamentals—responsible for the euro-dollar exchange rate (Radiocor, 14 January 2000).

Italian Treasury Minister Vincenzo Visco did not show concern about euro either. Speaking after a European policy meeting in May, Visco played down the inflation outlook for the Euro-zone, affirming that the fall in the euro-dollar exchange rate was not consistent with fundamentals. He went on to say that, instead of relaxing their budgets following the launch of the euro, policy-makers must make clear Euro-zone economic strategies and reaffirm their commitments to fiscal consolidation. He stated that monetary policy decisions have become more delicate with such a strong depreciation of the currency, and it must be managed carefully to avoid future problems (Bridgenews Global Markets, 8 May 2000).

The Italian Finance Minister agreed with the above view. Speaking after an Ecofin meeting of European economy and finance ministers in Brussels in July, Ottaviano Del Turco said he was optimistic about the euro's potential appreciation (Bridgenews Global Markets, 17 July 2000).

On the subject of the single currency's state of health, the European Central Bank Executive Board member Tommaso Padoa-Schioppa restated the line dear to the ECB:

> It is the market that has got it wrong. I think the market trend will change before the factors at the root of the current trend (such as the growth differential between the EU and the United States, structural problems, and the lack of political union) have been reversed.

The ECB council member added that rates in Euroland were still low, and interest rate increases were dictated by the need to ward off the threat of inflation. This was because monetary policy's 'new deal' had one primary duty: to prevent inflation, and not to keep pace with it. In any case, 'there is a threat to price stability' but, as it was due to oil prices and exchange trends, 'it is decidedly more reversible than the threat held out by large pay raises'. The state of the 11s economy was good (indeed, 'exceptionally positive', better than it had ever been in the last 15 to 20 years) and could thus afford the current level of rates, which Padoa-Schioppa described as 'fairly low'. The central bank had paved the way for economic performance. Indeed, it was up to the monetary authority to prolong growth and to the governments—via structural and budgetary policies—to raise it. Padoa-Schioppa concluded that the European economy could afford to exceed the rate of 3 to 3.5 per cent forecast for 2000 and 2001, but only if it succeeded in launching the requisite structural reforms (Il Sole-24 Ore, 14 June 2000). He said the Euro-zone—especially Italy—should move ahead by taking steps to make structural changes in order to enhance competitiveness. The euro, like all important global currencies such as the dollar and the yen, will also see upswings and downswings in its value in the future, but he affirmed that the European single currency will recover value and consolidate its position against the dollar even before European political union occurs (Bridgenews Global Markets, 21 December 2000).

1.2.2 ECB policy measures

Financial operators expressed varying opinions about ECB policy measures.

At the Cernobbio meeting on the Italian economy, the economic and political leaders made many considerations in relation to the ECB's 31 August decision to increase the euro's interest rates. Some of them claimed the interest rate hike was insufficient, while others believed it to be just right. Still others bemoaned the increase entirely. Alessandro Profumo, chairman of the Unicredit savings group, believed the hike was not big enough. Economist and ex-industry minister Paolo Savona agreed with him, stating that 'small movements' were not enough, and that Europe needed stronger measures and a monetary policy that more closely resembled that of the US. But the chief of the banking association Abi, Maurizio Sella, said the rate hike was accurate. He called it 'equilibrated' and said that the decision balanced the protection of the economic interest with the need to contain inflation (*Ansa*, 1 September 2000).

Franco Modigliani held the European Central Bank President responsible for the euro's collapse in relation to the US dollar. He said ECB economic policy was too concerned with inflation targets, and not concerned enough with the economic development of Europe.

According to Confindustria, the main Italian confederation of enterprises, increases in the price of oil, the euro's weakness, and economic recovery drove ECB to increase interest rates. But this measure will have serious effects in Italy, which is characterised by high public debt, and slower economic growth than its European partners. Confindustria suggested the adoption of reforms specifically aimed at boosting Italy's competitiveness in foreign markets. There is no need to adjust wages to face the risk of imported inflation. This measure will result in a further increase in inflation and interest rates that could threaten economic growth and employment (16 March 2000).

The Italian Central Bank Governor, Antonio Fazio, highlighted the risk of a new inflation burst due to both current and structural factors. He believed in immediate action to avoid the use of restrictive monetary policies in the future, claiming that 'preventing is better than curing' (*La Repubblica*, 5 June 2000).

1.3 Institutional and procedural matters

The euro's weakness *vis-à-vis* foreign currencies were one of the main issues debated by Italian political, social and economic institutions last year.

In April, after a meeting between Euro-zone finance ministers and the European Central Bank President, Giuliano Amato (the then Italian Treasury Minister) said that the euro level did not reflect the strong growth in the Euro-zone's economy. Amato's statement was similar to those of almost all Euro-zone finance ministers, as was his statement that the euro had acquired stability despite the volatility of the financial markets. Looking at the Italian economy and the oil-fuelled inflation worries, Amato seemed optimistic about the reduction of inflation in the second half of the year (Bridgenews Global Markets, 7 April 2000). At the prestigious Ambrosetti conference held in Cernobbio in September, Amato (as Italian Prime Minister) confirmed his trust in the euro. Responding to the plunge of the euro to an all-time low against the US dollar, Amato blamed the strength of the US economy, and said that the euro's weakness was not a problem. He said the euro would 'certainly' appreciate (La Repubblica, 2 September 2000).

Romano Prodi, the former Italian Prime Minister and European Commission President expressed a similar view. He said that he has never been worried about the weakness of euro in relation to the Japanese yen and the US dollar. In the first months of the year, Prodi professed to be optimistic about the recovery of euro because the fundamentals of the European economy were sound. He said that the mistrust of the euro was short-lived, and people would become aware of its benefits later in the year when concrete preparations were under way for the currency's 'physical introduction' (AP Online, 1 May 2000).

Italian President Carlo Azeglio Ciampi shared this positive opinion about the euro and EMU. He said that the European single currency was a driving force for integration progress: 'In two years, 290 million citizens of the eleven states will use the same money, the same banknotes. We will all feel more European' (BBC International Reports, 1 January, 2000).

With regard to the euro's weakness, Ciampi said that it was 'unrealistic' to see the three major currencies—the EUR, USD and JPY—all stabilise. Therefore, he was not worried about the slump in the value of the European single currency since its launch in 1999. He stressed that European nations should promote structural reform to boost industrial competitiveness, and said the euro will inevitably move on an upward trend, if growth in the Euro-zone is sustained (Bridgenews Global Markets, 23 November 2000). Ciampi added that, in his opinion, there would be no postponement of the coming into force of the single currency after a two-month period of coexistence alongside the various national currencies (*Il Sole* 24 Ore, 19 October 2000).

Italian Foreign Minister Lamberto Dini was of the same opinion. In an interview with *La Repubblica* (1 September 2000), Dini said that he was confident about the outlook for the euro because the fundamentals were solid and the gap between European and US growth was diminishing. He added that he would have no concerns for the future, especially if governments across Europe took structural measures (such as labour flexibility, financial market rules, privatisations and the liberalisation of certain markets) to lessen the rigidities of their national economies. Dini also said inflation was in check and the only danger derived from the impact on domestic prices of global crude prices and the dollar. He expressed a positive opinion in September about the united intervention of leading central banks to support the faltering single European currency (*Ansa*, 25 September 2000).

Silvio Berlusconi, head of the centre-right Forza Italia party, and Giulio Tremonti, Senator of the same party, did not agree with the above views. Berlusconi described the euro as a 'disaster' that reflected the economic and political policies adopted by left-wing governments across Europe. 'In the old Europe, only Great Britain, Spain and Ireland are on the same footing as the US. I hope also Italy [will be soon]', Berlusconi told journalists on the sidelines of an October conference on EU enlargement (Bridgenews Global Markets, 27 October 2000). Speaking at the Cernobbio conference, Tremonti said Europe was governed by the 'Adams Family', likening the central bank to a dysfunctional family depicted on a popular television show. He called the ECB decision to raise the interest rate 'insignificant'. Tremonti added that Europe needed more economic liberty, fewer taxes and rules, and more enthusiasm.

Confindustria affirmed that ECB monetary policy measures are useless palliatives that could restrain economic recovery. The industrial association believed that structural reforms could assure strong economic growth without the risk of inflation, and could boost competitiveness (Press bulletin, 27 April 2000).

Pirelli's Managing Director Marco Tronchetti Provera, was not particularly worried about the weakness of the euro, if the European Union is able to establish an integrated political, financial and industrial framework within the next two years (*La Repubblica*, 4 May 2000).

Giovanni Agnelli, Honorary President of Fiat, said he was confident about the approaching parity between the euro and the US dollar, but was slightly worried about an overly rapid realignment. According to Agnelli, the weakness of the euro is primarily due to a different trend in the US and EU economies (*La Repubblica*, 2 September 2000).

Fiat Chairman Paolo Fresco told the Cernobbio conference that the central bank always has to balance two different needs: it must defend the currency's value and avoid introducing growth-reducing measures. He did not think rate hikes would slow economic growth. Meanwhile, the head of the Confcommercio retail association, Sergio Bille, expressed concerns that the interest rate hikes would be particularly hard on Italy, especially as the country has yet to realise all its badly needed economic reforms. He said that slow-moving reforms meant that rate hikes would cause 'extra disadvantages' for Italy, and:

> We have yet to complete the latest reform cycle and this renders us more exposed to external factors which could influence our policies . . . Rate hikes do not help consumption, and thereby the recovery of the internal market, and this could harm economic recovery (World News Connection, 1 September 2000).

Minister of Industry, Enrico Letta, expressed some concerns about the possibility of negative consequences for economic recovery as a result of the ECB decision to raise the interest rate. Trade unions were also critical of the interest rate measure. According to both the Confederazione Italiana Sindacati Lavoratori and the Confederazione Generale Italiana del Lavoro, the ECB intervention represented a risk for economic growth. The CGIL expressed a particularly severe opinion of the ECB monetary policy.

The banking association (Abi) had a different opinion. The Association fully agreed with ECB policy and did not voice concerns about the economic trend (Il Sole 24 Ore, 6 October 2000).

In February 2000, the European Union economy and finance ministers' meeting approved the Italian stability programme for 2000–2003. This detailed the country's plan to reach public finance targets agreed to in the Euro-zone's Stability and Growth Pact. The Ecofin Council noted 'with satisfaction' that, in spite of a slowdown in the national economy, Italy held the 1999 budget deficit at 2 per cent of GDP. The Council also gave the green light to the Rome government policy aimed at recovery and promoting the growth and equitable distribution of income. After affirming that Italy can expect to hold the current budget deficit at below 3 per cent of GDP with a safety margin, the Council said that Italy should be able to comply with the 'requirements of the Stability Pact' by 2003. However, the ministers insisted that Italy will have to continue to work on its public debt, and must reduce it below 100 per cent of GDP by the same date (*Ansa*, 28 February 2000).

The Ecofin Council also said the Italian government should show greater determination in tackling medium-term structural problems affecting public finances (concerning pension spending and spending linked to the ageing population). After applauding the Italian government's efforts to build supplementary pension funds as a step in the right direction, the ministers stated that this would not be enough by itself:

> A timely re-examination of the pension system parameters would allow the forecast increase in the ratio between pension spending and gross domestic product to be contained.

The Council went on to recommend continuing:

> the privatisation programme with vigour and increasing the impact of structural

reforms in the labour market, products and public administration, which is essential for heightening competitiveness and efficiency and revitalising the Italian economy.

The then Italian Prime Minister D'Alema expressed general satisfaction: 'Our objective, that of latching on to general economic recovery in Europe, has been reached', he affirmed.

1.4 Trends towards spill-over

By centralising governance of the currency in the European System of Central Banks, the euro has projected the integration process beyond the point of return. The Union will be ready to handle the greater and more incisive responsibilities, for which it is already gearing up: consolidating a common foreign policy, setting up a common military force, implementing the area of freedom, security and justice, and adopting the constitution of the European Union.

1.4.1 The debate on EU reforms

December's European Union summit resulted in various reforms of EU institutions to be promoted with the entry into force of the Nice Treaty or after the enlargement: re-weighting of votes among Member States, a quick move toward more majority voting, enhanced co-operation, as well as changes to the size of the Commission and the powers given to its president. Furthermore, leaders agreed on a new Article 7 that could act as a warning system and lead to the imposition of sanctions against Member States that do not respect the EU's fundamental rights of liberty, democracy and human rights.

At the EU summit in Nice, Italy was praised for its intermediate role, *ad adiuvandum* the French Presidency, and its supranational position. Furthermore, the Summit consented to the Italian and German positions on 'reinforced co-operation'.

On that occasion, Italy declared its two main objectives in reforming the EU structure: to reduce the intergovernmental haggling involved in EU decision-making, and to make institutions more accountable to public opinion in member nations.

Regarding the first objective, Prime Minister Amato noted during a parliamentary debate in December that, although the summit had seen too much defence of national interests, unanimous approval was no longer required in the most 'sensitive areas' of policy-making. He stressed that the final agreement ensured that no single country would be able to team up with another to block EU decisions. Amato admitted that there was no progress in the integration of tax policies (due mainly to British opposition), and said this was 'not encouraging'. Britain also resisted a common defence policy, but Amato said he believed that this was only a temporary delay and that this goal would be reached sooner or later (BBC International Reports, 14 December 2000).

The Italian Prime Minister stressed the need to promote structural reforms to support the European economy. These reforms have to take competitiveness, technology, and education into consideration (Parliamentary debate, 2 February 2000). He also underlined the importance of involving the United Kingdom in the process of strengthening EU institutions. He said:

> I simply cannot envisage any core of Europe existing without the UK. If there is to be a new heart of Europe, Britain must be in it. Otherwise, it will be a weak heart.

Amato's determination that the UK should form part of any European core was also part of a broader vision that such a core cannot be exclusive. According to Amato, the EU definitely needs to discuss creating a core of some kind so as to become more than just an economic space, especially after the arrival of new countries from Eastern Europe. The Prime Minister affirmed that the essence of Europe involves the integration—through co-operation and diversity—of major and minor countries with common interests. On defence policy, immigration and law and order, he believed there is scope for enhanced co-operation involving countries that can opt to join the core if they wish. Amato also believed Europe should create a common European political culture by means of a Bill of Rights (*Financial Times*, 6 July 2000).

There can be no further delay in reforming European Union institutions, said Italian Foreign Minister Lamberto Dini. Dini reviewed Italy's position in the reform debate among the 15 Member States. He said that the Union would have at least 27 members in the not too distant future. He said that, while Rome favours proposals to make the Union more federal, it opposed a number of other proposals. In particular, it opposed the development of a 'Franco-German axis', a sort of reinforced co-operation outside the guidelines of treaties. Dini also spoke about the European single currency and observed that 'a strong euro needs a strong economy and strong policies'. He meant that there should be greater co-ordination between national economic policies in support of a monetary union because 'it is wrong to believe that solitude reinforces the European Central Bank and thus ensures its freedom to perform' (*Ansa*, 2 October 2000).

With regard to the debate on EU reforms, Italian President Carlo Azeglio Ciampi said he sees the EU's proposed Charter of Fundamental Rights as 'the first part of a constitution, to be complemented with a second part devoted to defining the various institutions'. Ciampi said the Charter represented the EU's development from a primarily economic project to a common area of rights with values and rules that define the notion of European citizenship.

According to some analysts, Italian institutions demonstrated varying opinions and positions in the debate about EU reforms (Pasquino, 2000; Rossi, 2001). However President Ciampi denied that there were any divisions on this topic. Ciampi stated that Italy's desire to continue to be an active element within the EU was supported by 'a genuine popular sentiment'. He added that this sentiment had been seen in the Italian parliament on several occasions, 'with a broad agreement of voting on fundamental issues in EU policy' (BBC International Reports, 4 October 2000).

The European desire for reform will devise solutions allowing federal institutions, such as the European Central Bank to work in conjunction with others set up on intergovernmental lines.

> The deadlines facing us call for intense co-operation among all the institutions . . . The demanding work performed by the European Parliament, the Council and the Commission has to interact with the Member States' initiatives in the interests of the Union,

Ciampi said (*La Stampa*, 28 November 2000).

European Commission President Prodi affirmed the need to strengthen common policies. According to him, the lack of a common economic policy was the main reason for the euro's weakness. In addition, he expressed concerns about the lack of a political partner for the ECB, because a strong central bank is useless without a strong executive power (*Stern*, 12 September 2000).

Speaking at a conference on 'A Federal State and a Constitution for a New Europe' in November, Padoa-Schioppa said that, the lack of political union was not the primary cause of the euro's current weakness, but there was no doubt that greater political union would benefit the single currency. Looking back at the creation of the European single market, economic and monetary union and the euro, the Italian banker observed that Europe already had a *de facto* constitution through the series of agreements beginning with the Treaty of Rome. Nevertheless, he concluded that it would be best if Europe adopted a real constitution, even if it did face two basic obstacles: the fact that 'Europeans do not realise that the European Union is not complete and they do not realise how much has actually already been achieved' (*Ansa*, 13 November 2000).

Padoa-Schioppa favours the idea, often aired, of the 11 Euro-zone countries reaching economic policy decisions in concert:

> There is a lot to be done to enhance the strength of the European forum for economic policy consensus seeking and decision making.

Padoa-Schioppa added that the ECB would not be weakened as a result, since the two fields of action are quite distinct:

> There is room for a strengthening of the central government of the economy, and I believe it is in the ECB's interests that that room be taken up.

1.4.2 Fiscal policy and tax harmonisation

During a parliamentary debate, Minister of Treasury Vincenzo Visco warned against the risk of adopting the incorrect fiscal policy measures that had reduced economic growth in the past, and he underlined the need to check public expenses. He affirmed that the euro has produced impressive gains for Europe and for Italy, but that investors have sent the currency's value plunging because of the inability of the EU members to make coherent decisions (Parliamentary debate, 27 July 2000). During a September meeting of EU finance ministers in Versailles, Visco said Britain was the crux of the problem as it is not a member of the common currency but it is able to block progress on key matters such as the harmonisation of taxes within the Euro-zone. Visco said the euro had been a dramatic success in Italy because it had imposed constraints and limits that politicians could not be trusted to enforce. In Italy, he added, the problem is often that 'our politicians, trade unions and entrepreneurs are unable to understand what is going on, they don't care about the economy'. Visco went on to say that having economic policies dictated by the European Central Bank in Frankfurt 'is a nice constraint because it means you cannot spend too much or embark on extravagant programs'. He shares the view of the European Commission that 'you are not allowed to cut taxes if you do not cut spending'. He added that the introduction of cyclical rather than structural measures in several countries was another source of confusion for financial markets:

> When you talk about tax reform, in my opinion, you should talk about structural reform . . . [Italy has] completely changed the fiscal rules, and now our taxation system is one of the most modern in the world. But no one realises that because we did not reduce taxes.

Visco said that primary public spending in Italy is now among the lowest in the EU, on the same level as Britain. This would give him ample leeway for tax cuts, were it not for inherited economic problems. He had not been surprised by Italy's progress from economic rake to fiscal virtue: 'Our problem . . . is our political system, and you should start worrying if the present majority changes' (*International Herald Tribune*, 11 September 2000).

Finance Minister Del Turco expressed a different opinion. He said that the Italian government would be forced to develop a 'clear and visible' tax reduction and fiscal reform plan.

Bank of Italy Governor Antonio Fazio strongly urged the House and Senate budget committees to quickly implement the reforms outlined in the government's economic and financial planning document (the DPEF) and to consider adopting a bigger tax cut. Fazio said the 2001–4 financial blueprint was heading in the 'right direction', but stressed that realising essential reforms, such as tax cuts, and lowering public spending were imperative (ANSA, 18 July 2000). At the general meeting of the Italian central bank, the governor affirmed that euro depreciation only fostered European industrial competitiveness in the short term. Fazio stressed the need for both tax and social policy harmonisation to facilitate the movement of labour across Europe. Italy obtained monetary stability in 1994 thanks to the adoption of a deflationary monetary policy, the narrowing of the gap between public expense and income, and the adoption of the single currency. 'Nowadays structural factors emerge such as the industrial fragmentation and weak capacity of product innovation' said Fazio. He believes the positive international economic trend offers the opportunity to implement legislative, social and tax reforms. Italy needs to link the budget deficit reduction with an increase in public investments (Banca d'Italia, 2000).

During the parliamentary debate on 14 March, Consob President Luigi Spaventa also underlined that harmonisation efforts were still not sufficient in the EU.

1.4.3 Competitiveness

During the parliamentary debate on 11 July 2000, President of the Industrial Association Antonio D'Amato said Italy had lost competitiveness and he stressed the importance of adopting structural reforms to foster economic growth and to facilitate the liberalisation process.

The Confindustria report, in co-operation with Ernst & Young (Confindustria, Ernst & Young 2000), affirmed that the euro's weakness was related to neither economic nor institutional structural factors. The EU's failure to adopt specific policies to face structural problems (specifically, social and labour measures) and to strengthen its institutions was evident. The Report criticised the European competition policy as well. This policy allowed for the removal of protections and fostered the liberalisation process, but it interfered with the ability to pursue an effective regional policy. Expansive monetary policies have to be adopted along with structural reforms. According to Confindustria, it is necessary to focus on microeconomic issues more than on macroeconomic ones. The large European market—believed to be as competitive as the US market and characterised by economies of scale—has only partially been realised. The final aim is not total harmonisation, but an extensive adoption of the 'mutual recognition' criteria. The Confindustria Report suggested adopting a new Maastricht method characterised by deadlines, ranking, parameters and targets such as tax and social expenses reduction, labour liberalisation and single market completion.

Bank of Italy Governor Fazio issued a strong warning that Italy was increasingly losing competitiveness against its main trading partners and urgently needed wide-ranging reforms to improve productivity, growth, and job creation. During the annual address to the bank's general assembly, he said the country could achieve a growth of 2.7 per cent provided exports increased significantly after the dismal performance of recent years. Fazio's prescription to revitalise the Italian economy was a familiar one: he suggested innovation, flexibility, more investment, lower taxes and tighter public spending. He repeated that current spending growth should be contained and lowered as a percentage of GDP, while reductions in the tax burden should gradually be amplified in the medium term. The continued reduction of the deficit should go hand-in-hand with more public investment (Bridgenews Global Markets, 31 May 2000).

The International Monetary Fund's visit to Italy in March resulted in a favourable view of the country. The IMF team was positive about the prospects for Italian economic growth, although it did urge the government to speed up its reforms, starting with pensions, unemployment, public deficit and fiscal reform (*La Stampa*, 27 March 2000).

1.4.4 Pension reform

Regarding social policy, Wim Duisenberg has often affirmed that ageing populations threaten the balancing of public accounts. For this reason, he suggested clear efforts to reform national social systems.

Italian union and government officials say Italian pensions are safe in the future, though the new system may have to be phased in faster than current law permits. The Italian labour minister and trade unions, in particular, did not appreciate Duisemberg's reproach.

CGIL leader Sergio Cofferati denied being concerned with the matter: 'We reformed the pension treatment in 1995 and we revised it in 1997. Now we are getting the first results'.

Cesare Salvi, Labour Minister, expressed a more caustic opinion: 'It is the same old story! . . . but we will go on.' During a parliamentary debate in April 2000, Salvi confirmed that ECB's reproach did not concern Italy.

Trade union and government authorities defended the government's pension reform schedule in response to renewed criticism from the Organisation for Economic Co-operation and Development (OECD). The June OECD report gave optimistic figures for economic growth but reprimanded Italy's slowness in tackling its pension system, underscoring that the projected spending trend suggested the need for further reform. But Treasury Minister Visco defended the government's reform schedule, saying that 'we are perfectly on time—the [pension reform] review will begin in January 2001' (BBC International Reports, 7 June 2000).

1.4.5 The labour market

The ECB annual report urged EU Member States to make structural reforms in order to ensure more labour flexibility and increase employment. According to former Prime Minister Massimo D'Alema, the wages differential has already been introduced in Italy, while economist Luigi Paganetto affirmed that the wages differential is a short-term measure that is unable to both solve employment problems and create development conditions.

The Bank of Italy disagreed with them. According to its representatives, further efforts could be made to improve the relationship between wages and productivity.

Cipolletta, former Confindustria General Director, and Bolzoni, Confapi (Confederazione Italiana della Piccola e Media Industria) President, was also in favour of a further wages differential. Cipolletta asserted that the wages tool is crucial to boost economic recovery, and Bolzoni suggested the introduction of new forms of labour contracts (Il Sole 24 Ore, 13 April 2000).

Franco Modigliani said that mass unemployment existed within the European Union because European central bankers desired it. He stated that high levels of joblessness were due to the European Central Bank's tight monetary policy (Morning Star, 5 April 2000).

In a series of recommendations approved for Italy and for the other EU Member States in September, the European Commission said Italy had made some progress in 1999. But it noted that the structural problems of its labour market had yet to be tackled. Setting priorities for government action, the Commission said it was indispensable

> to continue the implementation of pension reforms and other systems of benefits in order to stem the outflow from the labour market.

It also said Italy must 'keep up its efforts to reduce the tax burden on nonqualified work'.

In its recommendations, the European Commission called on Italy to 'take effective action to prevent long-term unemployment', to 'adopt and implement a coherent strategy for continuous training, complete with national targets', to 'improve the employment opportunities of women' and to bring the national employment information system up to speed. It had positive comments about the adoption of tax breaks for new jobs and more flexible contracts. But it noted that a string of indicators showed Italy was still lagging behind most of the EU and had to close the gap (6 September 2000).

Padoa-Schioppa declared that unions represented a formidable obstacle to achieving flexibility in Italy; flexibility was the secret of America's economic success. 'Union activity is increasingly limited to older people, those who are higher up on the professional ladder. This results in a conservative unionism, which penalises the interests of the young' he said (La Repubblica, 21 February 2000).

2. Legal framework

Marina Mancini**

2.1 Changes in the legal framework

2.1.1 Law of treaties

On behalf of the European Community, Italy negotiated two important agreements with San Marino and Vatican City in 2000. These agreements establish the use of the euro by San Marino and Vatican City as a consequence of the adoption of the single currency by Italy. The Italian lira is used as the official currency in San Marino and Vatican City, as in Italy. Thus, the Italian substitution of the Italian lira with the euro was intended to be followed by the substitution of the Italian lira with the single currency in San Marino and Vatican City.

In Declaration no 6, attached to the Final Act of the Treaty on European Union, the European Community committed itself to facilitating the re-negotiation of the agreements between Italy and San Marino and the Vatican City on monetary relations, which seemed necessary as a consequence of the introduction of the euro. Monetary relations between Italy and San Marino and the Vatican City were regulated by the Agreements of 21 December 1991[223] and of 3 December 1991,[224] respectively. Both agreements reproduced the text of previous agreements concluded in 1939 and renewed every ten years.[225]

Council Decisions 1999/97/EC[226] and 1999/98/EC[227] of 31 December 1998 entrusted Italy with the negotiation of the agreements with San Marino and Vatican City, and established that the Commission and the European Central Bank (within its competencies) join the negotiations. These decisions were based on Article 111.3 (ex Article 109.3) EC. According to this article, the Council is competent to make arrangements for the negotiation and conclusion of agreements concerning monetary or foreign exchange regime matters that need to be stipulated between the Community and one or more countries or international organisations.

** Istituto Affari Internazionali—Rome, Via Angelo Brunetti 9, Palazzo Rondinini, I-00186, Rome.

223 Implemented in Italy by Law No 118 of 14 Feb 1994, which was published in the Italian Official Journal No 43 of 22 Feb 1994, Supplement.

224 Implemented in Italy by Law No 119 of 14 Feb 1994, which was published in the Italian Official Journal No 43 of 22 Feb 1994, Supplement.

225 With regard to this, see Cafaro (1999), 259, n 47.

226 OJ [1999] L 30/33, 4 Feb 1999.

227 OJ [1999] L 30/35, 4 Feb 1999.

Although it is not expressly stated, it is believed that the Council may also delegate the negotiation and the conclusion of such agreements to the Member States.[228]

The agreement between Italy and San Marino is very similar to the agreement between Italy and the Vatican City. San Marino and the Vatican City are to use the euro as their official currency from 1 January 1999 and to grant legal tender status to euro banknotes and coins from 1 January 2002. They are consequently obliged to apply the Community rules on euro banknotes and coins. Moreover, they are obliged to follow the calendar fixed by Italy for the introduction of euro banknotes and coins and the withdrawal of lira banknotes and coins (Article 1).

San Marino and the Vatican City may issue euro banknotes and coins for a maximum nominal value, of 1,944,000 and 670,000 euros, respectively, per year from 1 January 2002 (Article 3). However, at the year in which the Pope is substituted, the Jubilee takes place, or the Ecumenical Council is opened, the Vatican City is allowed to issue 210,000 Euros in addition to the maximum nominal value (Article 7).

The total volume of euro banknotes and coins allowed to Italy is to be approved by the European Central Bank and must be calculated by adding the annual nominal value of euro banknotes and coins issued by San Marino and by the Vatican City to the volume of euro banknotes and coins issued by Italy. Before 1 September every year, San Marino and the Vatican City must inform Italy of the nominal value of euro banknotes and coins they intend to issue in the next year (Article 4). Euro banknotes and coins of San Marino and of the Vatican City must be exclusively minted by the competent Italian institution (Zecca) (Article 6).

San Marino and the Vatican City may issue euro banknotes and coins from 1 January 2002; they may issue lira banknotes and coins until 31 December 2001. Lira banknotes and coins issued by San Marino and the Vatican City have the same legal tender status as those issued by Italy. The total volume of banknotes and coins allowed must be calculated by adding the annual nominal value of lira banknotes and coins issued by San Marino and the Vatican City to the volume of lira banknotes and coins issued by Italy (Article 7 of the Agreement between Italy and San Marino, Article 8 of the Agreement between Italy and the Vatican City).

San Marino and the Vatican City commit themselves to co-operating closely with the European Community in the fight against counterfeiting of euro banknotes and coins (Article 8 of the Agreement between Italy and San Marino, Article 9 of the Agreement between Italy and the Vatican City).

Financial institutions located in San Marino and the Vatican City may have access to payment systems within the Euro-area on the conditions

[228] See Cafaro, op cit, 250 et seq.

specifically fixed by the Bank of Italy with the consent of the European Central Bank (Article 9 of the Agreement between Italy and San Marino, Article 10 of the Agreement between Italy and the Vatican City).

Finally, the Agreement between Italy and San Marino of 21 October 1991 and the Agreement between Italy and the Vatican City of 3 December 1991 are abrogated (Article 10 of the Agreement between Italy and San Marino, Article 11 of the Agreement between Italy and the Vatican City). In any case, these agreements were close to expiry. They were concluded for ten years and, by virtue of a protocol providing for their provisional application before the exchange of ratifications, they were applied immediately after being signed. They would, thus, have expired in 2001.

The agreements between Italy and San Marino/Vatican City allow San Marino and the Vatican City to adopt the euro. Various Member States strongly opposed these agreements. In particular, France (traditionally a secular state) did not want banknotes and coins issued by the Vatican City to be legal tender on its territory. Moreover, it feared the above-mentioned agreements might create precedents and give rise to claims by the Principality of Monaco, whose banknotes and coins are not legal tender on French territory.[229] A parallel arrangement was indeed negotiated by France with Monaco.

2.1.2 National law

Article 155 of Law no 388 of 23 December 2000 concerning the state budget for 2001[230] contains provisions about the replacement of the lira by the euro. In particular, it provides that lira banknotes and coins will continue to be legal tender until 28 February 2002. As euro banknotes and coins will become legal tender on 1 January 2002, the lira and the euro will have both legal tender status on Italian territory from 1 January 2002 until 28 February 2002.

The Euro Committee document concerning the last phase of the transition to the euro, specifies the measures to be taken for the substitution of the Italian currency with the single currency before 1 January 2002, between 1 January 2002 and 28 February 2002, and after 28 February 2002. Euro banknotes and coins will be furnished to traders before 1 January 2002 in order to facilitate the use of the euro in retail trade from the first days of 2002. The competent provincial offices will distribute euro coins to banks and post offices from 1 September 2001. The local branches of the Bank of Italy will distribute euro banknotes to banks and post offices from 15 November 2001. Banks and post offices will furnish

[229] See Cafaro, op cit, 263 et seq.
[230] Published in the Italian Official Journal No 302 of 29 Dec 2000.

euro coins and, in the last days of 2001, euro banknotes to traders. The traders will be obliged to retain the euros until 1 January 2002; only from that date will the use of euros be permitted.

From 1 January 2002, banks will be changing lira banknotes and coins for those in euros without fees. They will change lira for euros to their customers to a maximum of 1,000,000 lira per day and, if requested in advance, without limits. For non-customers, they will change lira for euros to a maximum of 500,000 lira per day.

Once withdrawn from circulation, lira coins and banknotes will be lodged in the competent provincial offices (coins) and in the local branches of the Bank of Italy (notes) and will later be destroyed. In order to reduce the volume of lira coins to withdraw from circulation, the micro 50-lire and 100-lire pieces lost legal tender status in October 2000.

After 28 February 2002, the banks will continue to change lira for euros free of charge until a date that is yet to be fixed. Local branches of the Bank of Italy will change lira for euros free of charge until 1 March 2012.

2.2 National law from the EC perspective

Article 15 of Regulation (EC) no 974/98 of 3 May 1998[231] states that national banknotes and coins will continue to be legal tender for a maximum of six months after the transitional period. It adds that this period may be curtailed by national rules.

According to widespread opinion, the curtailment is necessary in order to reduce the risk of confusion that the co-existence of national banknotes and coins with euro banknotes and coins could arouse, and to meet the requests of the traders who could bear high costs because of such co-existence.

In accordance with this opinion, the Council Decision of 8 November 1999 established that national banknotes and coins must continue to be legal tender from a minimum of four weeks to a maximum of two months after the end of the transitional period.

Article 155 of Law no 388 of 23 December 2000 is in full conformity with Article 15 of Regulation 974/98 and with the Decision of 8 November 1999; it provides that lira banknotes and coins will continue to be legal tender for two months after the end of the transition period.

2.3 The application of the law

With regard to the application of the legislation concerning the introduction of the euro, only one case can be reported. On 20 February 1999, the local police station of Ovada issued a fine against Mr Giuseppino Repetto.

[231] OJ [1998] L 139/1, 11 May 1998.

The latter appealed to the Prefect of the Province of Alessandria against the fine. With Order of 28 June 1999, the Prefect found for Mr Repetto because the copy of the fine released to him did not mention the amount due in euros.

The legitimacy of the order is very doubtful. The Euro Committee document concerning the last phase of the transition to the euro points out that, from 1 January 1999, pecuniary sanctions can be paid in lira or in Euros. To this end, it is not necessary to mention the amount due in euros. It is sufficient to mention the amount due in lira, with the specific proviso that it can be paid also in euros.

2.4 Institutional aspects

2.4.1 Relationship between the Bank of Italy and the Italian government

The Bank of Italy is now totally independent from the government. In recent years it has been made consistent with the EC Treaty's model of an independent national central bank. To this end, Law no 82 of 7 February 1992,[232] Legislative Decree no 385 of 1 September 1993,[233] and Law no 483 of 26 November 1993[234] were enacted.

More recently, the Statute of the Bank of Italy was modified by Decree of the President of the Republic of 24 April 1998.[235] This decree was issued in conformity with Article 10 of Legislative Decree no 43 of 10 March 1998.[236]

2.4.2 Relationship between the Bank of Italy and the European Central Bank

The Bank of Italy is now an integral part of the European System of Central Banks; it acts according to the directions and instructions of the European Central Bank. Among them, the following guidelines need to be mentioned: the Guideline of 3 November 1998 on the implementation of Article 52 of the ESCB-ECB Statute; the Guideline of 22 December 1998 on the common rules and minimum standards to protect the confidentiality of the individual statistical information, collected by the European Central Bank assisted by the national central banks; and the Guideline of 22 April 1999 on the authorisation to issue national banknotes during the transitional period.

232 Published in the Italian Official Journal No 37 of 14 Feb 1992.
233 Ibid, No 230 of 30 Sept 1993, Supplement.
234 Ibid, No 282 of 1 December 1993
235 Ibid, No 99 of 30 Apr 1998.
236 Ibid, No 61 of 14 Mar 1998. With regard to this decree, see *Eurospectator 1999: Italian Report*, EUI Working Paper Law No 2000/7, 64 et seq.

Bibliography

Banca d'Italia (2000), *Bollettino Economico*, No 35, October.

—— *Relazione all'Assemblea Generale Ordinaria dei Partecipanti*, 31 May, Rome.

Bruni, Franco (2001), 'L'Italia e la politica internazionale', in *Annuario di Politica Internazionale*, ISPI-IAI 2000 (mimeo).

Cafaro, Susanna (1999), 'I primi accordi della Comunità in materia di politica monetaria e di cambio', in *Il Diritto dell'Unione Europea*, 243–68.

Capriglione, Francesco (1999), 'Moneta', in *Enciclopedia del diritto*, Milano, Giuffré, Vol III, aggiornamento, 747–72.

Ciampi, Carlo A (2000), 'Se non ora, quando?', in *Global*, no 6.

Confindustria (2000), *Benchmarking Competitivo: redditività delle imprese e carico fiscale*, <http://www.confindustria.it>.

Croci, Osvaldo, Bowles, Paul, MacLean, Brian K. (2001), 'Banca d'Italia, Banca centrale europea e questione dell'autonomia, in *Queste Istituzioni*, 33–48.

De Cecco, Marcello (2000), 'Monete e mercati in Europa', in *Il Mulino* No 3, 551–60.

European Commission (2000), Eurobarometer. *Public Opinion in the European Union*, no 53.

—— *Eurobarometer. Public Opinion in the European Union*, no 54.

Pasquino, Gianfranco (2000), 'La classe politica italiana e l'Europa', in *Il Mulino*, no 4, 922–923.

Ministero del Tesoro, *Bilancio e Programmazione Economica (2000), Dalla lira all'Euro*, October.

—— *Comitato Euro—Rapporto sull'utilizzo dell'euro in Italia*, 31 marzo 1999—31 marzo 2000, Roma.

Napoletano, Giuseppe (2000), 'La riforma della Banca d'Italia per l'accesso alla terza fase dell'Unione economica e monetaria', in *Banca, borsa, titoli di credito*, 71–92.

Padoa Schioppa, Tommaso (1999), 'L'Euro: una moneta di collegamento tra popoli e culture', in *Europa Europe*, 44–8.

—— (2000), 'Euro e politica', in *Il Mulino* No 5, 1107–13.

Perissich, Riccardo (2000), 'Come convincere gli europei ad essere europei', in *Global*, no 6.

Righi, Alessandra and Siciliani, Isabella (2000), *La conoscenza e le opinioni degli italiani sull'introduzione dell'Euro*, ISTAT.

Rossi, Lucia S (2001), 'La conferenza intergovernativa', in *Annuario di Politica Internazionale*, ISPI-IAI 2000 (mimeo).

Triulzi, Umberto (1999), *Dal Mercato comune alla Moneta unica: le politiche di integrazione dell'Unione europea*, Edizioni SEAM, Roma.

THE NETHERLANDS

Jeannette Mak and Frank Elderson

1. Political and economic aspects

Jeannette Mak*

1.1 Introduction

As there was no Dutch report in the 1999 *Eurospectator* series, this report will consider developments in the Netherlands that year concerning EMU and the euro.

Before turning to more recent developments, it seems useful to devote a few words to the discussion, or lack thereof, on EMU in the Netherlands before the introduction of the euro on 1 January 1999.

The Dutch attitude towards the euro can be characterised as one of permissive consensus. While both the general public and the élites regard EMU as being beneficial to the country, the former seems rather indifferent towards it. In May 1999, the President of the *De Nederlandsche Bank NV* (DNB) gave two explanations for the lack of debate in the Netherlands: the general pro-European attitude of the Dutch, and the considerable public confidence in institutions in the Netherlands.[237] The latter is a well-established concept in the traditional understanding of Dutch politics, and it has often been mentioned as explanation for the lethargic public attitude towards the EU.[238] As a result, limited debate has taken place on the EMU and the euro in the Netherlands, and only three incidents seem worth mentioning. In combination, they did create some uproar and might thereby explain the sharp drop in public support for the euro in spring 1997.[239]

The first case was an initiative by a group of 70 well-known Dutch economists who protested against the single currency by placing a public statement in a number of newspapers on 13 February 1997. The economists argued that EMU was based on dubious economic assumptions, and that it would lead more to unemployment and social tensions, than to a modern European social welfare state. The criticisms were mainly aimed at

* European University Institute, Department of Social and Political Sciences, Via dei Roccettini 9, I-50133, Firenze.

237 Speech of Dr Wellink, President of the Nederlandsche Bank, 15 May 1999, <http://www.dnb.nl>.

238 RB Andeweg, and GA Irwin, (1993), *Dutch Government and Politics*, Macmillan Press Ltd., London.

239 G Reuten, K Vendrik, and R Went (1998), *De prijs van de Euro*, Van Gennep BV, Amsterdam.

the convergence criteria, the Stability Pact and the mission of the ECB, which was only committed to price stability. According to the economists, the loss of macro-economic instruments would lead to downward (fiscal) policy competition amongst the Member States, which would have repercussions on the social quality of the EU. The first reaction to the statement from the political and financial élite was that the comments were too late as the country had made the decision to participate in EMU back in 1991. This strongly discouraged further debate. The economists were also countered by the traditional arguments concerning the benefits of European integration as a whole, and by stressing the importance of a 'strong euro'. The latter can be explained by the clear belief in the 'strong currency thesis' in the Netherlands.[240]

In reaction to the debate about the euro, the *Socialistische Partij* (SP), a small left-wing political party, profiled itself as the nation's anti-euro front and pleaded for a referendum on EMU in the Netherlands. However, this suggestion was not seriously discussed at the political level. Of more importance was the personal 'crusade' of Mr Bolkestein, former leader of the VVD (the Dutch liberal party), against a possibly weak euro. Prior to the ultimate decision about which counties would participate, he stressed that his party would not accept participation by any Member States that did not *fully* meet the convergence criteria. As a result, a public debate took place on the participation of Italy in EMU. In January 1998, only 20 per cent of the Dutch population were in favour of Italy's membership of EMU; 38 per cent was against it, fearing that it would undermine the 'strength' of the euro. As many as 42 per cent of the respondents had no opinion on this matter. Of those respondents who opposed Italy's participation, 56 per cent thought the Netherlands should withdraw its EMU candidacy if Italy were to participate.[241]

The DNB President attributed the drop in support for the euro in early 1997 to both the discussion raised by the 70 economists and an increasing concern for the 'strength' of the euro.[242] The latter was most likely stimulated by the critical position of Mr Bolkestein. Given the traditional élite consensus on EMU, the major actors in the Netherlands regarded the discussion initiated by Mr. Bolkestein as 'non issue'.[243]

[240] Lof, E. (1998), 'Economische taboes', in Reuten, Vendrik, and Went, (1998), op cit.

[241] NIPO (1998), *Toetreding Italië tot EMU belangrijk item voor Nederlandse kamerverkiezingen*, Amsterdam, The Netherlands, 20 Jan 1998, <http://www.nipo.nl>; fieldwork carried out 17–18 Jan1998.

[242] Speech of Dr Wellink, President of the Nederlandsche Bank, 15 May 1999, <http://www.dnb.nl>.

[243] Interview with senior official, Dutch Ministry of Finance, The Hague, Nov 2000.

1.2 Public opinion

Eurobarometer findings suggest that over the years, public opinion towards EMU and the euro has been stable and more positive in the Netherlands than in most Member Sates; other survey data draws a picture of a more critical, and increasingly, sceptical Dutch public. According to Eurobarometer, 71 per cent of Dutch respondents said they were in favour of the euro in spring 1999; this was a clear drop from the 79 per cent that supported the euro in autumn 1998.[244] In Autumn 1999, support had recovered slightly, with 75 per cent saying they agreed with the single currency.[245] In Spring 2000, public opinion had again become more sceptical, with 67 per cent of Dutch people being in favour of the euro.[246] Early opinion polls, carried out on request of the DNB, seem to confirm these Eurobarometer findings. According to their survey in Spring 1999, four out of five adults in the Netherlands supported the euro.[247]

However, other research suggests that the Dutch are much more negative towards the single currency. In May/June 1999, the Dutch consumer organization *de Consumentenbond* found that only 46 per cent of the population had a positive attitude towards the euro, while 42 per cent had a negative opinion.[248] A survey carried out by the NIPO[249] and published just before the Danish referendum on the euro on 28 September 2000, showed that as many as 53 per cent of Dutch adults would vote against the euro if they were asked for their opinion in a referendum. Only 31 per cent of the respondents said they were in favour of the single currency at that time. If the government had still had the choice, 46 per cent of the population thought it should have left EMU, while 37 per cent did not regard this to be necessary.[250] Meanwhile, a DNB survey argued that the Danish referendum, in which the population rejected their country's membership of EMU, had not severely influenced public opinion about the euro in the Netherlands. Half of the respondents were polled prior to the Danish referendum, and the rest were questioned later. The two groups did not show significant differences.[251]

[244] *Eurobarometer*, No 50 and 51.

[245] Ibid, No 52.

[246] Ibid, No 53.

[247] De Nederlandsche Bank (1999), *De Euro in Nederland*, uitkomsten van de achtste DNB-euro-enquête, Onderzoeksrapport WO&E, nr. 580/9913, Mei 1999, Amsterdam, The Netherlands; fieldwork carried out between 1 and 12 Mar 1999.

[248] 'Euro sluipt langzaam dagelijks leven binnen', in *Consumentengids*, Aug 1999: 47–8.

[249] An independent Dutch public opinion research bureau.

[250] NIPO (2000), *Komst van de euro wekt vooral negatieve verwachtingen*, 2Vandaag/Nipo Onderzoek, Amsterdam, The Netherlands, 26 Sept 2000, <http:// www.nipo.nl>; fieldwork carried out between 22 and 24 Sept 2000.

[251] De Nederlandsche Bank (2000a), *Voorbereiding Euroconversie stagneert*, uitkomsten van de tiende DNB-euro-enquête, Onderzoeksrapport WO&E, nr. 640/0035, Nov 2000, Amsterdam, The Netherlands; fieldwork carried out in Sept–Oct 2000.

The different surveys are not very clear about the number of people who changed their opinion about the euro after its introduction on 1 January 1999. According to the Spring 2000 DNB survey, 15 per cent of people had changed their opinion concerning the euro in the past year; of this group, two thirds had become more sceptical.[252] The NIPO research in Autumn 2000 showed that a larger number of people had changed their mind in the last year: only 61 per cent of the people had the same opinion, 22 per cent had become more positive, and 7 per cent had become more negative.[253] The latest DNB survey (Autumn 2000) draws a more negative picture and finds that 22 per cent of the Dutch population had become more negative concerning the euro since 1 January 1999.[254] Nevertheless, according to another NIPO survey, Dutch attitudes to the single currency in December 2000 were still among the most positive of EU Member State populations. 52 per cent of Dutch respondents said they were generally satisfied with the replacement of the guilder by the euro.[255]

The surveys deviate considerably in their findings, but two conclusions can nevertheless be reached. While the Dutch seem to be more positive towards the single currency than the population of the EU as a whole, their support is less stable and unconditional (as suggested by the Eurobarometer data). At the same time, general Eurobarometer findings have been confirmed by alternative research in the Netherlands. The surveys carried out by both the DNB and the NIPO found fluctuations in support for age and education. Younger and older people are, on average, more sceptical towards the single currency than those in the group ranging from 30 to 50 years of age. People with a lower level of education not only have a more negative attitude towards the euro, but also a more *unstable* opinion. Finally, these sources confirm that, in general, men are more supportive of the euro than are women. According to the Eurobarometer data, the Dutch generally have a more positive opinion about their country's EU membership than they have about the euro. This is a deviation from the European trend in which people are, on average, more supportive of the single currency than of their countries' EU membership.

The DNB surveys argue that the perceived benefits of the euro are more likely to be of a micro-economic nature, such as price transparency and easier payments. Objections are primarily politico-cultural; the loss of cultural identity is often mentioned as a major disadvantage.[256] There also

[252] De Nederlandsche Bank (2000), *Eurodynamiek verliest Momentum*, uitkomsten van de negende DNB-Euro-enquête, Onderzoeksrapport WO&E, nr. 617/0012, April 2000, Amsterdam, The Netherlands; fieldwork carried out between 21 Feb and 3 Mar 2000.

[253] NIPO (2000), op cit.

[254] DNB (2000a), op cit.

[255] Nipo (2001), 'Zorgen om Europa zijn de wereld nog niet uit', 15 Jan 2000; fieldwork Dec 2000.

[256] De Nederlandsche Bank (1999), *De Euro in Nederland*, uitkomsten van de achtste DNB-euro-enquéte, Onderzoeksrapport WO&E, nr. 580/9913, May 1999, Amsterdam, The Netherlands; fieldwork carried out between 1 and 12 Mar 1999.

seems to be a fear of 'a weak euro'. Two concerns have been identified in the DNB data over the years. The first was the rounding of prices in euro, and the second was the external value of the euro. The major public fear has recently shifted from the rounding of prices to price stability.[257] In its May/June 1999 survey, the *Consumentenbond* found major concern about the euro's value. This fear is expected to have grown as a result of the deterioration of the euro's exchange rate against the US dollar.[258] According to a September 2000 NIPO survey, as many as 63 per cent of respondents thought that life would be more expensive after the changeover.[259]

It is currently difficult to conclude from survey data the extent to which the external value of the euro has influenced general support for the currency and/or might do so in the future. In his reaction to the Autumn 2000 NIPO survey, the DNB's President Wellink commented that the outcomes were more negative than he had expected. He clearly attributed the sceptical public opinion to the deteriorating exchange rate of the euro against the dollar.[260] In September 2000, about half the population expected the exchange rate to improve over time;[261] by December 2000, the Dutch (and the Germans) were very worried about the deterioration of the value of the euro against the dollar. More than three quarters of the respondents voiced this concern.[262]

Whereas the Dutch feel, and indeed are, better informed than the average citizen of EU Member States, they do not receive significantly more information than the populations of the other states. In spring 1999, 79 per cent of Dutch people said they had received information about the euro, as compared with 60 per cent six months earlier.[263] In Autumn 1999, the number of people having received information dropped to 74 per cent.[264] In Spring 2000, the figure had risen again; but with 82 per cent of Dutch people stating they had received information, the Netherlands was just below the EU-11 average of 84 per cent.[265] This may be regarded as surprising as, in relative terms, the Dutch government spends far more money than the other participating Member States on information and communication activities concerning the EMU and the euro. According to the DNB, fewer people in Autumn 2000 (compared with the two previous surveys) felt they had sufficient knowledge about the euro and EMU: 69 per cent felt they had enough information in

257 Interview with senior official, Dutch Ministry of Finance, The Hague, Nov 2000.

258 Interview with a representative of *Consumentenbond* (Dutch Consumer's Organisation), The Hague, Nov 2000.

259 NIPO (2000), op cit.

260 NIPO (2000), op cit.

261 DNB (2000a), op cit.

262 Nipo (2001), *Zorgen om Europa zijn de wereld nog niet uit*, 15 Jan 2001; fieldwork Dec 2000.

263 *Eurobarometer*, No 51.

264 Ibid, No 52.

265 Ibid, No 53.

Autumn 2000, compared with 72 per cent six months earlier, and 79 per cent a year before. This seems to contradict the fact that there was more information available and that the objective knowledge of people had actually improved. The DNB gave the possible explanation that, as the introduction of the euro draws nearer, people felt they need more specific knowledge and they worried more about the consequences of the deteriorating exchange rate of the euro against the dollar. It is telling that fewer people than before could mention the correct conversion rate between the guilder and the euro, and it seems that people think that this is being affected by the external value of the euro.[266]

Finally, the existence of the ECB is relatively well known in the Netherlands, as compared to the other Member States.[267] This may be partly due to the fact that Wim Duisenberg is Dutch. Moreover, in spring 1998, 84 per cent of the Dutch population thought that there had to be a European Central Bank that is independent of the Member States, while 87 per cent thought the ECB had to be accountable to the EP. Both scores are the highest found in any Member State.[268]

1.3 Financial press and financial institutions

The Netherlands' financial sector is generally very positive about the EMU, but it simultaneously defends its particular interests quite fiercely concerning the switch to the euro. The Netherlands' Bankers Association (NVB) noted the successful introduction of the euro on 1 January 1999, but also emphasised the expenses involved. It stressed the actual costs for the banks and the loss of profit on currency exchange within the Eurozone. It also pointed out that the very short dual circulation phase in the Netherlands puts a large burden on the banking sector, and it explicitly justified bank charges on currency exchange and international payments.[269] Nevertheless, NVB expects the euro to raise benefits for the private sector by 3.5 bn euro a year; this means that the costs of the changeover will be recovered within one year. Direct benefits are primarily expected from lower transaction costs, limited risks of exchange rate fluctuations, and simpler bookkeeping. Moreover, Dutch enterprises are expected to profit indirectly from a larger market share, better transparency, and lower inflation and interest.[270]

The DNB president has been equally optimistic about EMU over the

[266] DNB (2000a), op cit.

[267] *Eurobarometer*, No 51.

[268] European Commission (1999a), *European Public Opinion on the Single Currency*, Special Edition, DGX, Brussels, Jan 1999.

[269] NVB, *Jaarverslag 1999*, Amsterdam, 31 Oct 1999.

[270] New Year's speech, President of the NVB, 8 Jan 2001, Amsterdam, <http://www.nvb.nl>.

last two years. Since February 1999 he has stressed the importance of the internal stability of the single currency, as opposed to 'external strength', and he has pressed for moderation of wage rate demands ever since.[271] In mid-2000, the bank's president was still quite satisfied with the favourable economic situation in the Netherlands, but he showed concern about the relatively high inflation rate and again emphasised the tight labour market in the Netherlands (which was expected to result in substantial demands for wage rises).[272] In November 2000, a spokesman confirmed that the DNB is mainly content with the positive effects of EMU so far, as it has contributed to an exceptionally long period of continued economic growth in Europe.[273]

1.3.1 Monetary decisions of the ECB and the euro-dollar exchange rate

Just after the introduction of the euro in January 1999, the financial press speculated that the euro would appreciate against the dollar and that this might be disadvantageous to the European economy. Moreover, it pointed out that the external exchange rate of a currency is primarily a *political* matter.[274] The first monetary decision of the ECB—the surprisingly large interest rate cut by 0.5 per cent on 8 April 1999—was generally regarded as positive and mainly intended to stimulate economic growth.[275] The following decision to raise the interest rate by the same 0.5 per cent in November 1999 was equally perceived to be the correct decision. It was regarded as a decisive action that left no doubts about the ECB's priority of price stability, and that would tranquillise speculation about further increases in interest rates. Moreover, the press assessed the decision as having been announced well beforehand. Finally, the ECB's initiative was believed to be particularly well suited to the Dutch economy's healthy economic growth and relatively high inflation rate.[276] However, the rather positive opinion about the ECB's performance was to change rather quickly.

In early 2000, the Dutch financial press did not consider that the dropping exchange rate of the euro against the dollar would itself be disadvantageous for the European economy.[277] Nevertheless, when it became clear in March 2000 that the combination of the deteriorating exchange rate

[271] Speech by Dr Wellink, President of the Nederlandsche Bank, 25 Feb 1999, Amsterdam, <http://www.dnb.nl>.

[272] Ibid, 27 June 2000 and 15 Sept 2000, <http://www.dnb.nl>.

[273] Interview with senior official, DNB, Amsterdam, Nov 2000.

[274] *NRC Handelsblad*, 'De sterke euro heeft ook weer bezwaren', 5 Jan 1999.

[275] *De Volkskrant*, 'Duisenberg brengt rente fors omlaag', 9 Apr 1999.

[276] *De Financiele Telegraaf*, 'renteverhoging voorkomt hardere ingreep later', 5 Nov 1999.

[277] Ibid, 'Zakke Euro stimulans economische groei EU', 8 Feb 2000 and 'Export Eurozone vaart wel bij lage Euro', 3 Mar 2000.

and increasing oil prices were putting pressure on the inflation rate, the ECB was judged to be powerless. While price stability remained its main objective, the ECB slowly came to be regarded as being under political pressure as a result of the euro's exchange rate fluctuations. It was suggested that the ECB should take bolder steps (than minor interest adjustments) to maintain confidence in both the institution and the currency.[278] After its third upward adjustment of the interest rate by 0.25 per cent in 2000, the ECB's lack of clear initiative was fiercely criticised. Its weakness was attributed to the inherent nature of compromise between the different national central banks, each of which pleads for the monetary policy that best suits its national interest. While the lower exchange rate of the euro against the dollar was still regarded as being beneficial to the European economy, the inflationary consequences were not. It was again stressed that exchange rate interference is not part of the ECB's official objective. The interest adjustments were also criticised for having no positive effect on the exchange rate.[279] In June 2000, after the ECB's unexpectedly large interest rate increase (half a percentage point to 4.25 per cent), the financial press was more positive and judged that the European good had prevailed over nationally defined priorities. While the ECB's initiative was regarded as a clear and positive sign, it nevertheless had a limited effect on the euro exchange rate. Furthermore, the ECB's decision to make the interest rate flexible was expected to place a slight upward pressure on the rate.[280] The main concern about the euro's lower exchange rate against the dollar again seemed to be the effect on inflation; by that time, the Netherlands' inflation rate was above the European average.[281] The single currency's deteriorating external value was mainly attributed to high economic growth in the US, which could not be matched by the EU.[282] This was enforced by the expectation of a slow-down in European economic growth as a result of high oil prices and the ECB's interest rate increases. In August 2000, concerns about the inflation rate, the even further deteriorating exchange rate of the euro against the dollar, and the idea that new interest rate adjustments would have a limited impact, led the financial press to speculate about the ECB's exchange rate interventions. In the Netherlands, ECB intervention was preferred over further

[278] *NRC Handelsblad*, 'Euro geeft centrale bankiers hoofdpijn', 1 Mar 2000 and *De Financiele Telegraaf*, 'rubriek finanscoop: kantjeboord', 3 Mar 2000.

[279] *NRC Handelsblad*, 'Euro volgt bank niet', 28 Apr 2000 and *De Financiele Telegraaf*, 'Euro zakt verder ondanks renteverhoging door ECB', 28 Apr 2000.

[280] *De Financiele Telegraaf*, 'ECB verhoogt rente 0.5 per cent', 8 June 2000 and *NRC*, 'Centrale bankiers zien het graag wat somber in', 9 June 2000.

[281] *Het Financieele Dagblad*, 'Eurodepreciatie heeft aanzienlijk inflatoir effect', 5 May 2000, 'Inflatie Eurozone schiet voorbij bovengrens ECB', 19 July 2000, 'Inflatie Eurozone blijft op hoog niveau', 19 Aug 2000.

[282] *Het Financieele Dagblad* 'ABN Amro ziet Euro dalen tot $ 0,80', 19 May 2000, 'Euro breekt $ 0,90-grens door kracht economie VS', 9 Aug 2000, 'Is bodem voor de Euro echt in zicht?', 12 Sept 2000.

interest rate increases, especially due to the clear anxiety that the relatively high inflation rate would lead to demands for wage increases and would thus affect economic growth.[283] The 0.25 per cent interest rate increase on 31 August 2000 was criticised: it had been anticipated and had hardly any influence on the exchange rate. The limited increase was attributed to the ECB's concern not to hamper economic growth.[284] Intervention was consequently, and increasingly, regarded to be the lesser of two evils. However, the financial press did not expect there would be sufficient support for this instrument, and the ECB was again criticised for its lack of initiative.[285]

As a result of its timing (just before a meeting of the G7 and the referendum on the euro in Denmark), the ECB's first intervention of 22 September 2000 was believed to have been a primarily political decision.[286] In reaction, some papers tried to put the euro/dollar exchange rate into perspective, and pointed to other macro-economic benefits of EMU. In this respect, it was explicitly mentioned that in 2000 the Dutch government presented its first budget surplus in decades. The lack of political agreement on the euro was again being criticised at this time.[287] The subsequent unexpected raise of the interest rate on 5 October 2000 was regarded as follow-up of the support purchases of the euro and mainly intended to fight inflation. The ECB was thought to be following the tradition of the Bundesbank by trying to surprise the financial markets with its initiatives. Although this strategy was believed to prevent speculation on the financial markets, it was equally argued it would make the euro a more risky investment, which in turn would result in a lower exchange rate. On the one hand, the interest rate increase was regarded as a justifiable step given the high price of oil and the fear of inflation.[288] On the other hand, the ECB was again advised not to change the interest rate based on considerations about the external exchange rate alone.[289] The already limited success of both initiatives was regarded as being neutralised when it became clear that the 'American Fed' was reluctant to support the ECB in further interventions, and that the ECB was unlikely to act on its own.[290]

283 *NRC Handelsblad*, 'Déjà vu dreigt voor de euro-economie', 25 Aug 2000.

284 *De Financiele Telegraaf*, 'ECB verhoogt rente met 25 basispunten', 31 Aug 2000.

285 *Het Financieele Dagblad*, 'Euro hoeft niet op spoedige redding te hopen', 11 Sept 2000, 'Euro bereikt dieptepunt tegenover dollar en yen', 12 Sept 2000, 'Nieuwe diepten euro na uitblijven steunaankopen', 12 Sept 2000.

286 *Het Financieele Dagblad*, 'Euro veert op na massale steunactie', 23 Sept 2000.

287 *NRC Handelsblad*, 'De hoogste tijd voor drie hoeraatjes voor de Euro', 28 Sept 2000.

288 *NRC Handelsblad*, 'Sint Duisenberg steeds guller met surprises', 6 Oct 2000 and *Het Financieele Dagblad*, 'Duisenberg verrast markt met rentestap', 6 Dec 2000.

289 *De Financiele Telegraaf*, 'Rentestap van Duisenberg zinloos', 9 Dec 2000.

290 *Het Financieele Dagblad*, 'Euro zakt verder in moeras door uitblijven ingreep', 26 Oct 2000.

In October 2000, Duisenberg was heavily criticised for telling *The Times* that he regarded new interventions in the euro exchange rate as unlikely. It was judged that he was loosing strength and importance.[291] While some newspapers criticised the media circus around the ECB, it was simultaneously argued that neither EMU nor the EU as a whole, seem to have the political strength to breed confidence.[292] The two interventions of 3 November 2000 were regarded as pointless. Not only did the exchange rate remain unchanged, but it also was argued that some fatal mistakes were made. The intervention took place without the co-operation of the Federal Reserve and just before key American financial figures were to be presented.[293] The limited effect of the intervention of 5 November 2000 was equally attributed to the fact that it was a forced solitary action of the European central banks without the help of the US.[294] Finally, the improving exchange rate of the euro against the dollar in late 2000 was almost completely attributed to reports about the slow-down in US economic growth.[295]

To summarise, a slight difference in emphasis can be detected between the two most prominent financial newspapers in the Netherlands. *NRC Handelsblad* has paid more attention to the absence of political unity about monetary affairs in the EU, whereas the more technical *Financieele Dagblad* has emphasised the purely financial aspects and criticised the ECB for lack of vision and initiative. They also differed in their judgments about the President of the ECB. *NRC Handelsblad* put the criticism of Duisenberg into perspective by arguing that the institution is new and requires compromise between 11 central banks. Nevertheless, Duisenberg's typically open and communicative style was judged to be working against him. While it was previously thought to have given citizens confidence in the single currency by actively explaining ECB policy to them, this has instead led to instability and a loss of confidence.[296] *Het Financieele Dagblad* seemed slightly more sceptical towards Duisenberg, and it blamed him for not being able to 'sell' the euro very well.[297] The newspaper was particularly critical after Duisenberg's interview with *The Times*.[298] It stated that, while his public image as a casual and down-to-earth bank director might be well appreciated in both the Netherlands and the ECB

291 *NRC Handelsblad*, 'Van gebeten hond tot zielenpiet', 20 Oct 2000.

292 *NRC Handelsblad*, 'Greate Pier in Frankfurt', 20 Oct 2000.

293 *NRC Handelsblad*, 'ECB krijgt het tij niet eem', 4 Nov 2000.

294 *NRC Handelsblad*, 'Weer interventie van Europese Bank', 6 Nov 2000.

295 *Het Financieele Dagblad*, 'Groeivertraging in VS zet euro hoger', 5 Dec 2000 and 'Euro stijgt naar hoogste niveau in vijf maanden', 23 Dec 2000.

296 *NRC Handelsblad*, 'De katvanger van Frankurt', 10 Nov 2000.

297 *Het Financieele Dagblad*, 'Wanneer komt Trichet toch eigenlijk?', 25 Sept 2000.

298 *Het Financieele Dagblad*, 'President Duisenberg maakt het leven van ECB moeilijk', 17 Oct 2000, 'Duisenberg stuurt euro bijna naar nieuw dieptepunt', 17 Oct 2000 and 'Mister euro verspeelt krediet', 18 Oct 2000.

internally, the international financial scene clearly expected a more professional attitude (and, in particular, a smoother media presence).[299]

Just before the introduction of the euro, newspapers in the Netherlands had expressed their concern about the independence of the ECB. It was specifically stated that the Euro-11 might attempt to exert indirect influence on the ECB with regard to the euro's exchange rate. The division of competencies with regard to the exchange rate was perceived to be blurred. The press thereby showed great vision concerning later developments.[300] Following the actual deterioration of the exchange rate of the euro *vis-à-vis* the dollar, the discussion in the EU on the political influence of the Euro-11 gained importance. In this framework, in late 2000 the NVB (The Netherlands' Bankers Association) admitted to be worried about undermining the independence of the ECB. It argued that the deteriorating exchange rate of the euro against the dollar was, in itself, of limited economic significance. Given the Euro-euphoria at its introduction, the rate could only have slid afterwards. Furthermore, the EU's economic situation is good, while the inflation rate in the Netherlands—although above the target set by the ECB—is at a historically low level. Therefore, the NVB regarded the ECB's interventions to be of political, rather than of economic, importance. Finally, the reversed euro-dollar expression was granted psychological explanatory value for the weakening confidence in the euro.[301] In this respect, it is telling that the National Platform for the Introduction of the Euro (NFE) addressed the issue in terms of the *improving* exchange rate of the dollar —as opposed to the *deteriorating* exchange rate of the euro—in December 2000 for the first time.[302]

Nevertheless, according to the DNB survey of Autumn 2000, the euro's exchange rate fluctuations had a big impact on the attitude of enterprises (especially the larger ones with a strong international focus) to the euro. 84 per cent of these enterprises were said to have become more negative towards the single currency since its introduction, and were said to have done so as a result of the falling exchange rate against the dollar. The private sector's more sceptical attitude concerning the euro was translated into enterprises increasingly assuming that there would be greater costs and fewer benefits as a result of the actual introduction of the euro (DNB 2000a). The opinion about the euro held by both the general public and the private sector was widely believed to have become more negative in Autumn 2000. However, the Dutch (financial) élite did not appear to be

299 *Het Financieele Dagblad*, 'Duisenberg is meer dan een stand-up comediaan', 26 Sept 2000 and 'Duisenberg biedt te weinig beschutting bij tegenwind', 18 Oct 2000.

300 *NRC Handelsblad*, 'De Gideonsbende van Frankfurt: Europese Centrale Bank: de machtigste instelling van Euroland', 17 Dec 1998.

301 Interview with a NVB (Netherlands Banker's Association) representative, Amsterdam, Nov 2000.

302 Nationaal Forum voor de Introductie van de Euro (2000), *Conclusies NFE Bijeenkomst*, 12 Dec 2000, The Hague, <http://www.Euro.nl>.

seriously worried about it. Effects on public support for the euro were deemed to be of limited importance as the decision on EMU had already been taken. Moreover, one expected that—given the good economic situation in the Netherlands—public opinion would support the euro in the long run.[303] It was nevertheless speculated that the Netherlands might worry more about public acceptability of the euro than it pretended to do.[304] The media was also criticised for its role in discussion about the euro. While there are few outspoken anti-European or anti-euro media organisations in the Netherlands, they were nevertheless blamed for stressing the deteriorating exchange rate of the euro against the dollar, and for reporting on it in a negative way. A senior official of the Ministry of Finance explicitly reproached the popular press for playing on public concerns.[305] Both this official and a representative of the DNB admitted that it might have been a mistake on the part of the authorities to argue in their information and communication activities that the euro would become a 'strong' currency. People were found to have understood this slogan in terms of the external exchange rate only.[306] In reaction, the NFE stated in the conclusions of its December 2000 meeting that the members of the forum should make a bigger effort to emphasise the positive results EMU had already achieved. These benefits were formulated as the contribution to economic growth, decreased public debt, relatively low inflation, and a good investment climate.[307]

1.3.2 Referendum on the euro in Denmark on 28 September 2000

Following the Danish 'no', it was doubted whether the relatively indifferent reaction of European leaders was justified. The Danes were believed to have rejected EMU for political and emotional reasons, rather than for economic or rational ones.[308] The main importance of the Danish rejection was assumed to be its effect on public opinion in both the UK and Sweden (countries that would consequently be less likely to join the single currency). The European élite was advised to take the result of the referendum seriously and to pay more attention to the attitude of the general public towards the euro. Moreover, there was some concern about the future of both the euro and the EU as a whole. While the Danish 'no' was believed to lead to a stronger plea for flexibility within the EU, it would

[303] Interview with a NVB representative and interview a DNB senior official, Amsterdam, Nov 2000.
[304] Interview with senior EC officials, The Hague, Nov 2000.
[305] Interview with a senior official, Dutch Ministry of Finance, The Hague, Nov 2000.
[306] Interview with a senior official, Dutch Ministry of Finance, The Hague, Nov 2000 and interview a DNB senior official, Amsterdam, Nov 2000.
[307] NFE (2000), op cit.
[308] *De Volkskrant*, 'Euro krijgt psychologische tik door Deens 'NEJ', 29 Sept 2000; *Het Financieele Dagblad*, 'Denen leggen hun vinger op zere plek', 30 Sept 2000.

also mean that the new Euro-Member States were more likely to be the EU's accession states with their relatively weak economies. This was regarded to be negative for EMU's future.[309]

1.3.3 Accession of Greece and further enlargement of EMU

Given the discussion in the Netherlands surrounding the accession of Italy to EMU, the lack of discussion concerning the accession of Greece can be regarded as rather surprising. While some critics expected a downward pressure on the euro exchange rate as a result of Greece's EMU membership, relatively little attention was paid to it in the financial press. It was nevertheless hoped that inclusion of Greece in EMU would stimulate the accession of Denmark, Sweden and the UK.[310] At the same time, the Greek government's ability to qualify for participation in the single currency in such limited time—by cutting both the budget deficit and the national debt—was regarded to be a beneficial result of EMU. The same budgetary discipline could arguably be expected from future prospective Euro-members.[311] The fact that Finance Minister Zalm is in favour of a strict application of the convergence criteria to accessing countries from Central and Eastern Europe did not trigger any fierce reactions—favourable or otherwise—in the financial press.[312]

1.4 Institutional and procedural matters

In line with the consensus amongst the political élite on EMU and the euro, no big disagreements can be detected on the subject among the three coalition partners of the current government: PvdA (the socialist party), VVD (the liberal party) and D66 (the liberal-democratic party). The two biggest opposition parties, CDA (the Christian-democratic party) and *Groen Links* (the Greens), both stress the importance of further political integration in order to support a successful EMU.

In 1999, *after* the introduction of the euro, a book entitled '*Eurodebat*' was published in the Netherlands. The contributors to the book are all from 'Clingendael', the semi-governmental Netherlands Institute of International Relations, and the Minister of Finance wrote the foreword. According to the latter, the book gives a good overview of all the arguments for and against EMU and the euro, and it underlines that there has not been any debate on the subject in the Netherlands. Rood states that—given the consensus on European integration among the political élites—it

309 *NRC Handelsblad*, 'Denemarken feest, Europa treurt' and 'Hamlet en de euro', 29 Sept 2000, and *De Volkskrant*, 'een veelzeggend neen', 29 Sept 2000.

310 *De Financiele Telegraaf*, 'Grieken volgend jaar in euro', 5 June 2000.

311 *Het Financieele Dagblad*, 'Griekenland en de euro-doemdenkers', 19 Jan 2001.

312 *NRC Handelsblad*, 'EU handhaaft strenge criteria voor de euro', 11 Sept 2000.

is actually rather surprising that there was some debate on the euro in the Netherlands.[313]

This consensual attitude towards EMU in the Netherlands is reflected in the approach of the Dutch government towards the switch to the euro. The Ministry of Finance is responsible for the changeover to the euro in the Netherlands. As early as February 1996, the Ministry set up the 'National Platform for the introduction of the Euro' (*Nationaal Forum voor de introductie van de euro*—NFE). This platform was meant to prepare Dutch society for the single currency and to ensure that the change from the guilder to the euro would be as smooth as possible; it meets four times a year and is presided over by the Minister of Finance. The primary aim of the Platform is the exchange of information, expertise, and ideas, and the identification of problems. Finally, the Platform should disseminate information on the euro throughout the introduction procedure. In addition to the Ministry of Finance and the Ministry of Economic Affairs, representatives of the following organisations take part in the NFE: three different trade unions (*CNV*, *FNV*, *MHP*), the Dutch employers' organisation (*VNO–NCW*), the Dutch consumers' organisation (Consumentenbond), the Dutch organisation for the agricultural sector (*LTO-Nederland*), the Dutch organisation for SMEs (*MKB-Nederland*), the Dutch Central Bank (*DNB*), the Netherlands Bankers' Association (*NVB*), the pension funds, the Dutch organisation for retailers (*Raad Nederlandse Detailhandel*), the Dutch organisation for the insurance sector (*Verbond van Verzekeraars*), and the organisation of Dutch municipalities (*VNG*). These organisations are all represented at the top level.

The Dutch government has specifically stated that it does not want to monopolise the introduction of the euro, and it regards the changeover to be the common responsibility of the authorities and society as a whole.[314] At first glance, this co-operative picture seems to be confirmed by the partners involved. Four participating organisations and institutions of the NFE,[315] representing different interests, were asked for their opinions about collaboration within the platform. They all agreed that the atmosphere was very good. However, the representatives became more sceptical when asked for more details about the co-operation.

The MKB representative said that the NFE was slightly biased towards financial institutions as the Ministry of Finance is 'after all their traditional partner'. However, she acknowledged the benefits of the NFE and admitted that the dialogue and exchange of ideas had contributed to an earlier

313 HHJ Labohm, JQTh Rood, and A Van Staden (1999), *Eurodebat*, Lemma BV, Utrecht, The Netherlands.

314 <http://www.euro.nl>.

315 DNB, Consumentenbond, MKB-Nederland and NVB.

identification of problems.[316] While the MKB blamed the NFE for being rather elitist, the representative of the NVB criticised the co-operation from the opposite angle. On the one hand he acknowledged that the Netherlands authorities as a result of the NFE imposed few things, and that the Dutch approach (as compared with that of other Member States) is probably the friendliest one for the society as a whole. On the other hand, he described the co-operation as rather problematic and even wondered whether more efficient small group decision-making (by the élite) would have resulted in significantly different solutions.[317] The *Consumentenbond* had a very pragmatic approach towards the NFE: its main aim is to make the switch to the euro as smooth as possible for the consumer. Since its members are divided on the issue, as a result the organisation does not have a pro- or contra-position towards EMU and the euro. It sees its main role to be the communication of concerns and problems from the public to the politicians and the NFE. According to the *Consumentenbond*, the Ministry of Finance was rather successful in paying attention to diverse interests.[318] According to the representative of the Dutch central bank in the NFE, the latter was 'clearly working for the common good'.[319]

Nevertheless, there has been fierce disagreement about a number of practical aspects within the NFE. The main topics of dispute concerned the duration of the dual circulation phase, double pricing and some practical aspects of the changeover to the euro.[320] Finally, disagreement has arisen about whether the notes and coins could be distributed before 1 January 2002 in order to avoid confusion during the first days of 2002. Minister of Finance Zalm has strongly opposed this.[321] Nevertheless, the government has made some concessions on the front-loading of euro coins; notes will not be made available before the official introduction date. According to the Ministry of Finance, the main disagreements in the NFE—which have been relatively easily solved by financial concessions by the government—have been about costs. SMEs are allowed to deduct the costs from their taxes, while the banks have been granted 125 million guilders to avoid passing costs to retailers when they exchange additional notes and coins.[322]

316 Interview with a MKB–Nederland (Dutch Organisation for SMEs) representative, Delft, Nov 2000.

317 Interview with a NVB (Netherlands Banker's Association) representative, Amsterdam, Nov 2000.

318 Interview with a *Consumentenbond* (Dutch Consumers' Organisation) representative, The Hague, Nov 2000.

319 Interview with a senior official of the Dutch central bank, Amsterdam, Nov 2000.

320 Interview with a senior official of the Dutch central bank, Amsterdam, Nov 2000 and interview with a senior official of the Dutch Ministry of Finance, The Hague, Nov 2000.

321 *De Volkskrant*, 'EU zal euro niet eerder verspreiden', 11 Sept 2000.

322 Interview with a senior official of Dutch Ministry of Finance, The Hague, Nov 2000.

The Dutch government is thought to be strongly opposed to any political pressure regarding the ECB, and Finance Minister Zalm has often given his clear personal opinion concerning this matter. As long as the ECB keeps inflation under control, no serious attention is being paid to criticism of the institution. In its yearly overview of EU developments ('*de staat van de Europese Unie*') in September 2000, the Dutch government explicitly stated that the Euro-11 was nothing more than just an informal forum in which one exchanges ideas and perspectives about economic developments in the Euro-zone.[323] After the ECB exchange rate intervention in September 2000, Prime Minister Kok hastened to say that the intervention had occurred without any political pressure.[324] In November 2000, the Dutch government repeated that it was hesitant towards strengthening the Euro-11/12, and added that this would undermine unity on economic matters within the EU as a whole.[325]

The traditional political objectives concerning European integration appear to be of major importance in the Dutch government's general approach towards the single currency. EMU is expected to have a major impact on European reality. While the Netherlands was the only Member State during the negotiations on the Maastricht Treaty to favour further political integration, EMU seems to be expected to slowly create that political union.[326]

1.5 Trends towards spillover

All major actors in the Netherlands expect spillover to occur, and they are generally rather positive about such a development. However, they have a more pragmatic attitude when it concerns a concrete policy area such as tax harmonisation. On the one hand, they favour a Europe-wide playing field in order to maximally profit from the euro; this would mean harmonised taxes. On the other hand, the opponents of tax harmonisation clearly differ according to the kind of tax that would need to be harmonised, and whether this would mean winning or loosing. Nevertheless, opposition to tax harmonisation is mainly attributed to politicians as it touches upon the core of sovereignty.[327]

[323] Ministerie van Buitenlandse Zaken, (2000a) *De Staat van de Europese Unie 2000-2001*, De Europese Agenda 2000–1 vanuit Nederlands perspectief, 19 Sept 2000, The Hague.

[324] *Het Financieele Dagblad*, 'Euro veert op na massale steunactie', 23 Sept 2000.

[325] *NRC Handelsblad*, 'Eurogroep zoekt invloed op beleid ECB', 4 Nov 2000.

[326] Interview Senior Civil Servant, Dutch Ministry of Finance, The Hague, Nov 2000.

[327] Interviews Representative NVB (Netherlands Banker's Association), Amsterdam, Representative *Consumentenbond* (Dutch Consumers' Organisation), The Hague, Representative MKB-Nederland (Dutch organisation for MSEs), Delft, all Nov 2000.

2. Legal framework

Frank Elderson**

2.1 Changes in the legal framework

2.1.1 Introduction

Unlike most other EU Member States, the Netherlands was not covered by last year's *Eurospectator* national reports. This overview thus pays some attention to previous developments, instead of being strictly limited to the changes in the legal framework in the course of the year 2000. In a variation on Shakespeare's 'what is done, cannot be undone', this survey will not attempt 'completely to compensate now [for] what was not done before'. Instead, Section 2.1.1 will contain a very broad overview of the most important features of the law as it stood at the end of 1999; this will serve as a basis for Section's 2.1.2 description of the main changes in the legal framework in 2000.

2.1.1 Brief overview of the main features of the law as it stood at the end of 1999[328]

2.1.1.a Bank Act 1998

The Netherlands' main legislative innovation in the context of EMU has been the adoption of the Bank Act 1998.[329] It replaced the Bank Act 1948 and provides for the independence[330] of *De Nederlandsche Bank NV* ('DNB') and its integration into the ESCB.[331] This summary will not attempt to give a comprehensive overview of the structure and of the

** Senior Lawyer, Legal Department, De Nederlandsche Bank NV, PO Box 98, NL-1000 AB, Amsterdam. The author wishes to thank A Arda, RMG Bax, G Bom, J Pöhland, JWM. Schoots, R Smits, and C Wensing, all with the DNB Legal Department, for their useful comments and assistance. The views expressed herein are those of the author only and cannot be attributed to DNB.

328 This overview is partly based on: René Smits (rapporteur for the Netherlands), Frank Elderson (editor), 'National report for the Netherlands on Legal Consequences of the Single Currency', *Report for FIDE 2000, XIX Congress*, Helsinki 1–3 June 2000, in: SEW 4 (2000) Apr 124.

329 *Bankwet 1998* of 9 Apr 1998, Official Journal ('*Staatsblad*') 1998, 200, as amended most recently by *Wet van 11 november 1999, Staatsblad* 1999, 507.

330 Section 3(3) Bank Act 1998, provides as follows: '[i]n implementation of the Treaty, the Bank may, in carrying out its tasks and duties under subsections (1) and (2) [DNB's ESCB-tasks], seek and take instructions exclusively from the ECB'. Personal independence is guaranteed by the provisions of section 12 Bank Act 1998. The members of the Governing Board shall be appointed for terms of seven years and can only be relieved from office on the grounds mentioned in Art 14.2 ESCB–ECB Statute. Section 23(5) Bank Act 1948, which made non-compliance with instructions of the Minister of Finance a ground for dismissal and which obviously would have been incompatible with Article 108 EC, has been abrogated.

331 Section 1(2) Bank Act 1998, provides that '[t]he Bank is an integral part of the ESCB in respect of the tasks and duties which the Treaty confers upon that System'.

provisions of the Bank Act 1998;[332] instead, it highlights some aspects that seem to be of specific interest. In line with the 1996 EMI Convergence Report,[333] and effective from the date of the establishment of the ESCB/ECB, the Minister of Finance's power to give instructions to DNB in the monetary field has been abrogated.[334] In addition, the supervisory powers of the government representative on the supervisory board, and his/her ancillary competence to obtain information, have been restricted to non-ESCB related activities of DNB.[335] In its March 1998 Convergence Report,[336] the EMI—which had been consulted about the draft Bank Act 1998—reported on incompatibilities with the EC Treaty and the ESCB-ECB Statute. However, the EMI found one 'imperfection'. The provision in section 3(1)(a) of the draft Bank Act 1998 states that 'the Bank shall . . . co-define and implement monetary policy'. The EMI pointed out that it is not the DNB, but its governor, 'who will do so in his/her capacity as a member of the Governing Council of the ECB'.[337] Although the Bank Act 1998 initially entered into force[338] without this imperfection having been addressed, the situation was remedied by a November 1999 amendment of the Bank Act 1998.[339] Section 3(1) subsequently reads as follows: 'the Bank shall make a contribution, within the framework of the ESCB, towards the fulfillment of the following tasks: a) to define and implement monetary policy . . .'. In order to further accommodate the EMI's concerns, the November 1999 amendment added a new subsection 4 to

332 An informative introduction is H. Weenink's 'Nieuwe Bankwet: bevoegdheden DNB herzien' [New Bank Act: revision of DNB's competences], in: *Bank- en Effectenbedrijf*, Dec 1997, 38–41.

333 See EMI, *Progress towards convergence 1996*, November 1996, 132.

334 This power was laid down in section 26 Bank Act 1948, *Staatsblad* 1948, I 166. It had always been considered as *ultimum remedium* and had never been exercised. However, even the mere existence thereof was, of course, incompatible with the independence requirement of Art 108 EC.

335 Section 13(2) Bank Act 1998 states that '[o]ne member of the Supervisory Board shall be appointed by the Government, each time for a term of four years'. Pursuant to s 14(1) Bank Act 1998, this government-appointed Supervisory Board member may at the request of the Minister of Finance or at his own initiative and 'with due observance of Article 107 [now: 108] of the Treaty' obtain from DNB's Governing Board data and information about the manner in which DNB performs its tasks. On the basis of s. 14(2) Bank Act 1998, the Governing Board shall provide the government-appointed Supervisory board member the requested data and information 'with the exception of the data and information which, pursuant to the Treaty . . . are secret'.

336 Report required by Art 121 (ex Art 109j) EC, March 1998 (further: *EMI Convergence Report* 1998).

337 *EMI Convergence Report 1998*, 302, 333 and 335. See also the *European Commission Convergence Report 1998* (prepared in accordance with Art 121 EC), 25 Mar 1998, 52.

338 On the date of the establishment of the ECB and the ESCB (i.e., 1 June 1998), see *Besluit van 20 april 1998 houdende vaststelling tijdstip inwerkingtreding Bankwet 1998* [Decision of 20 Apr 1998 regarding the date of entry into force of the Bank Act 1998], *Staatsblad* 1998, 244.

339 *Wet van 11 november 1999, Staatsblad* 1999, 507.

Section 12 of the Bank Act 1998, providing that with regard to the tasks and activities performed by DNB to achieve the maintenance of price stability 'the Governing Board shall acknowledge the President's capacity as member of both the Governing Council and the General Council'. As a result of these two amended provisions, the Bank Act 1998 now clearly acknowledges that the competence for ESCB monetary policy rests exclusively with the ECB's Governing Council.[340] In order to facilitate the exchange of views between DNB and the Netherlands parliament in the monetary field, section 19 Bank Act 1998 provides that 'the President of the Bank may, with due observance of Article 107 [now 108] of the Treaty and Articles 10.4 and 38 of the Statute of the ESCB-ECB, be heard by the First and Second Chamber of Parliament at their request'.[341] Also in the framework of preparations for the start of the third phase of EMU, DNB has adopted new articles of association[342] and new rules of procedure. In addition to the ESCB-related competencies, the Bank Act 1998 provides for objectives, tasks and activities of DNB at the national level (such as the supervision of financial institutions).[343] Finally, Section 4(4) Bank Act 1998 contains a catch-all[344] provision that allows DNB to perform tasks 'other than those referred to in this Act'. Such other tasks must be 'in the public interest' and permission must have been granted by Royal Decree. Section 9(c) Bank Act 1998 contains an equivalent provision for 'activities'. An example of a Royal Decree granting approval for non-ESCB activities (although based at the time on Section 21 Bank Act 1948) is the Royal Decree regarding the approval of DNB activities in the field of the exchange of guilder into euro coins.[345]

340 See the ECB Opinion of 2 Aug 1998 (CON/98/38), which has been deposited for inspection at the Office of Parliamentary Documentation, as mentioned in Second Chamber of Parliament, session 1998–9, 26, 233, No 3, 1, n 1.

341 Cited is the wording as in force after the Nov 1999 amendment of s 19 Bank Act 1998. At the time of the establishment of the ESCB, s 19 provided that the DNB president could be heard only by the 'competent committees of the Second Chamber of Parliament'. On the other hand, the Nov 1999 amendment deleted the possibility of the DNB president being heard 'on his own initiative'.

342 See the website of *De Nederlandsche Bank* at <http://www.dnb.nl/english/e_publicaties/index.htm>.

343 Section 4(1) Bank Act 1998 provides that the Bank 'shall have the task of supervising financial institutions in pursuance of the relevant statutory regulations'. These 'relevant statutory regulations' are the following: *Wet toezicht kredietwezen* 1992, 23 Apr 1992, *Staatsblad* 1992, 722, as most recently amended by *Wet van 28 October 1999, Staatsblad* 1999, 509 [Act on the Supervision of the Credit System 1992]; *Wet toezicht beleggingsinstellingen*, 27 June 1990, *Staatsblad* 1990, 380, as most recently amended by *Wet van 28 October 1999, Staatsblad* 1999, 509 [Act on the Supervision of Investment Institutions] and *Wet inzake wisselkantoren van 15 December 1994, Staatsblad* 1994, 903, as most recently amended by *Wet van 28 October 1999, Staatsblad* 1999, 509 [Exchange Offices Act].

344 Albeit, of course, within the limits of Art 14.4 ESCB-ECB Statute.

345 *Koninklijk Besluit houdende goedkeuring van de werkzaamheden van DNB op het gebied van verwisseling van guldensmunten door euromunten*, 23 Jan 1998, *Staatsblad* 1998, 62, as most recently amended by Royal Decree, 30 Aug 1999, *Staatsblad* 1999, 389.

2.1.1.b Further legislation which required adaptation in view of Article 109 EC

In its 1998 Convergence Report (pp. 334, 335) the EMI mentioned the following Acts that needed to be amended in order to ensure compliance with Article 109 EC Treaty (the legislative action taken in pursuance of the EMI's observations is indicated between brackets):

- *Coinage Act*[346] (the 'pre-third phase' provision on the Minister of Finance's competence to issue coins[347] has been amended[348] to take into account the ECB's power to approve the volume of the issuance of coins and the EU Council's competencies with regard to the denomination and technical specifications of coins.[349] Furthermore, section 1 Coinage Act has been amended[350] to provide for the duration of the transitional period between 1 January 2000 and 31 December 2001 by allowing both the euro and the guilder to function as units of account in the Netherlands monetary system);
- *Act on the Exchange Rate of the Guilder*[351] (has been repealed by the *Act on the Common Exchange Arrangements of the Euro*)[352];
- *Act on External Financial Relations 1994*[353] (has been amended by making the exercise of certain powers of the Minister of Finance vis-à-vis DNB conditional upon such exercise not being in breach of provisions of the EC Treaty);
- *Act on the Supervision of Securities Trade 1995*[354] (the ECB has been added to the list of institutions exempted from the Minister of Finance's supervision of securities institutions);
- *Archives Act 1995*[355] (this Act has not been amended within the framework of ensuring compliance of Netherlands legislation with Article 109 EC (see below Section 2.2));

[346] *Muntwet 1987, Staatsblad* 1987, 451, as amended by Act of 27 April 1994, *Staatsblad* 1994, 336, Act of 26 Mar 1998, *Staatsblad* 1998, 200 and Act of 7 Dec 1998, *Staatsblad* 1998, 713 [Coinage Act 1987].

[347] Old s 6 Coinage Act 1987.

[348] By means of s 23 Bank Act 1998; see the present s 6 (3) Coinage Act 1987.

[349] See Art 106(2) EC.

[350] *Wijziging van de Muntwet 1987*, 7 Dec 1998, *Staatsblad* 1998, 713 [Amendment of the Coinage Act 1987].

[351] *Wet inzake de wisselkoers van de gulden*, 25 May 1978, *Staatsblad* 1978, 332, last amended by Act of 6 Feb 1997, *Staatsblad* 1997, 63.

[352] See section 4 of the *Wet inzake gemeenschappelijke wisselkoersarrangementen van de euro*, 26 Mar 1998, *Staatsblad* 1998, 201.

[353] *Wet inzake financiële betrekkingen buitenland*, 25 Mar 1998, *Staatsblad* 1994, 258, amended by Act of 26 Mar 1998, *Staatsblad* 1998, 201 and by Act of 28 Oct 1999, *Staatsblad* 1999, 509.

[354] *Wet toezicht effectenverkeer 1995*, 16 Nov 1995, *Staatsblad* 1995, 574, as amended most recently by Act of 28 Oct 1999, *Staatsblad* 1999, 509.

[355] *Archiefwet*, 28 Apr 1995, *Staatsblad* 1995, 277, as amended most recently by Act of 4 Dec 1997, *Staatsblad* 1997, 580.

- *Act on the Public Access to Government Documents*[356] and the *Ombudsman Act*[357] (under sections 1a(1)(d) and 1(2) of the Act on the public access to government documents and sections 1a(1)(e) and 1(2) of the Ombudsman Act, and in as far as its ESCB-tasks are concerned, on the basis of a Decision[358] DNB has been exempted from the regimes of these two Acts).

In addition to the Acts mentioned in the EMI Convergence Report 1998, a number of other existing Acts and Regulations have been amended, and new Acts and Regulations have been adopted. The most important of these are the following:

- *Act on the Supervision of the Credit System 1992*[359] (the references to the *Bank Act 1948* have been replaced by references to the relevant sections of the *Bank Act 1998* (see section 21(1) *Bank Act 1998*), and the relevant changes brought about by the EC Treaty have been taken into account (*e.g.*, by repealing section 19 *Act on the Supervision of the Credit System 1992* on the ground that monetary instruments previously regulated therein are henceforth regulated by the ECB instead of the DNB, and by repealing section 89 *Act on the Supervision of the Credit System 1992* as a consequence of the abolishment of the Minister of Finance's power to give instructions to DNB on the basis of section 26 *Bank Act 1948*) (see section 21(2) *Bank Act* 1998));
- *Financial Transactions Emergency Act*[360] (the references to the *Bank Act 1948* have been replaced by references to the relevant sections of the *Bank Act 1998*; in addition, inter alia, section 15 *Financial Transactions Emergency Act*—providing for the possibility of DNB to accept, jointly with the Minister of Finance, under certain emergency situations, other forms of collateral than those specified in the *Bank Act 1948*, has been repealed, since the monetary competence has been transferred to the ECB) (see section 22 *Bank Act 1998*);
- *Act on the Common Exchange Arrangements of the Euro*[361] (in the absence of procedural arrangements regarding common exchange arrangements between the euro and the currencies of the 'outs' in the EC Treaty, this Act authorises the Netherlands Minister of Finance to

356 *Wet openbaarheid van bestuur*, 13 Oct 1991, *Staatsblad* 1991, 703, as amended most recently by Act of 18 June 1998, *Staatsblad* 1998, 356.

357 *Wet Nationale Ombudsman*, 4 Feb 1981, *Staatsblad* 1981, 35 as amended most recently by Act of 18 June 1998, *Staatsblad* 1998, 356.

358 *Besluit van 11 september 1998, Staatsblad* 1998, 580.

359 See n 340.

360 *Noodwet financiëel verkeer*, 25 May 1978, *Staatsblad* 1978, 348, as last amended by Act of 16 Mar 1998, *Staatsblad* 1998, 200.

361 *Wet inzake gemeenschappelijke wisselkoersarrangementen van de euro*, 26 Mar 1998, *Staatsblad* 1998, 201. The entry into force of the various provisions of this Act is regulated by the Royal Decree of 26 May 1998, *Staatsblad* 1998, 311.

enter into such arrangements (on behalf of the Netherlands and after consultation with DNB) collectively with the other Euro-zone Member States);

- *Act on the Redenomination of Debt*[362] (states and implements the modalities of the redenomination of (public and private) debt securities governed by Netherlands law. The method used is the rounding of debt to one of the nearest whole euro units. In case of rounding down, a sum in cash for the difference (which will remain interest-bearing) is payable to the holder);
- *Act on the Replacement of Reference Rates of Interest*[363] and the *Regulation on the Replacement of Reference Rates of Interest*[364] (provide for the replacement by EURIBOR and EONIA of previously maintained national reference rates);
- *Act on the Transition to Taxation in Euro*[365] (provides for a transitional regime according to which citizens and companies have the option to file their tax returns regarding the years 1999, 2000 and 2001 either in guilders or in euro; the tax due will be calculated in the currency of choice of the person or entity filing the tax return; tax returns filed after 1 January 2002, but having regard to periods prior to that date, may still be calculated in guilders);
- *Act of 17 December 1998*[366] (implements the *Settlement Finality Directive*[367] by amending the *Bankruptcy Act and the Act on the Supervision of the Credit System 1992* in order to abolish the retro-active effect of insolvency procedures ('zero hour rule'), in so far as payment orders and orders for the delivery of securities are concerned. These are processed in systems that have been designated as such by the relevant authorities and of which the European Commission has been notified to).

2.1.2 Developments during the year 2000

2.1.2.a Protection of the euro: Act of 11 November 1999 and Euro-counterfeiting Bill

Section 2.1.2 covers events in 2000. Nevertheless, the Act of 11 November 1999[368] is dealt with here because its subject matter is closely related to

[362] *Wet Schuldredenominatie*, 23 Nov 1998, *Staatsblad* 1998, 659.
[363] *Wet vervanging referentierentes*, 17 Dec 1998, *Staatsblad* 1998, 716.
[364] *Regeling vervanging referentierentes*, 4 Jan 1999, Government Gazette 1999, 2.
[365] *Wet overgang belastingheffing in euro's*, 17 Dec 1998, *Staatsblad* 1998, 723.
[366] *Staatsblad* 1998, 714.
[367] Directive of 19 May 1998 on settlement finality in payment and security settlement systems, OJ [1998] L 166/25, 11 June 98.
[368] Act providing for the introduction of a prohibition against making, having and distributing printed matter or other objects which, in connection with the introduction of the euro, could wrongly be taken to be legal tender, as well as for adjustment of the Criminal Code, *Staatsblad* 1999, 494.

the Euro-counterfeiting Bill that was introduced in November 2000. In the Act of 11 November 1999 the Netherlands legislature laid down a number of criminal law provisions in order to implement the European Commission's Recommendation[369] that Member States take measures to avoid, *inter alia*, the production, issue and distribution of collector coins, tokens and medals that are similar in design to euro coins. These implementing measures were deemed necessary by the Netherlands legislature because—in the absence of case-law on this point—it was uncertain whether the existing prohibition of section 440 Criminal Code[370] also covered objects resembling coins and banknotes that do not (yet) have legal tender status (that is, euro coins and banknotes prior to 1 January 2002). Section 1 of the Act of 11 November 1999 contains a prohibition effective until 1 January 2002, which, broadly summarised, prevents the production, distribution and storage of printed material and other objects that might give the impression that they can be used as euro coins and/or euro banknotes. Section 1 will not be effective as of 1 January 2002. The Act of 11 November also covers the reverse situation. Guilder coins and banknotes will no longer be legal tender, after the double circulation period ends (in the Netherlands: 28 January 2002). Nevertheless, it will still be possible to exchange the 'old' guilder coins and banknotes at commercial banks and DNB for some time (for the applicable periods, see below). It was felt that during this period, the production, distribution and storage of objects that might give the impression that they can be used as former guilder coins and banknotes, should be prohibited in order to avoid confusion among the public. Such a prohibition has been laid down in section 2 of the Act of 11 November, which will enter into force on 1 January 2002; it will be effective, together with the entire Act of 11 November, until 1 January 2010. Finally, by adding a new section 84*ter* to the Criminal Code, section 3 of the Act of 11 November 1999 ensures that the counterfeiting of both former and future legal tender coins is covered by the prohibition of counterfeiting laid down in section 208 Criminal Code. Section 84*ter* will also be effective until 1 January 2010. Although the Act of 11 November 1999 addressed the problem of euro-counterfeiting to a certain extent, the provisions of the May 2000 Council Framework Decision[371] required further legislative action. To this end, a Euro-counterfeiting Bill[372] was

[369] Commission Recommendation of 13 Jan 1999 concerning collector coins, medals and tokens, OJ [1999] L 20/61, 27.1.1999.

[370] Which prohibits 'the making, distributing or having for the purpose of distributing of printed matter or other objects in a form which makes them resemble currency notes or banknotes or specie'.

[371] Council Framework Decision of 29 May 2000 on increasing protection by criminal penalties and other sanctions against counterfeiting in connection with the introduction of the euro, OJ [2000] L 140/1, 14 June 2000.

[372] *Wetsvoorstel houdende wijziging van het Wetboek van Strafrecht met betrekking tot valsheid in muntspeciën en munt- en bankbiljetten* [Bill providing for amendment of the

introduced on 14 November 2000. A number of elements of the Council Framework Decision are covered by the existing provisions on counterfeiting in the Criminal Code. However, the following acts will also be prohibited when the Bill becomes law: (i) receiving, obtaining, transporting, exporting and re-exporting forged or counterfeit money, as well as receiving and obtaining substances and objects intended for counterfeiting, and (ii) illegally circulating, receiving, obtaining, having, importing, exporting and re-exporting notes and coins that are legal tender and have not yet been, but are intended to be, brought into circulation. In addition, the definition of materials that can be used for counterfeiting will be extended to include computer programmes. These proposed changes will lead to the amendment of sections 209, 210, 213, 214, 214bis and 215 Criminal Code.

2.1.2.b Adaptation of legislation in relation to the introduction of the euro

Although the directly effective Euro-regulations[373] render such an operation unnecessary from a strictly legal point of view, it has been decided on grounds of 'clarity, efficiency and practicality' to convert all amounts in Netherlands legislation hitherto denominated in guilders (or other Community currencies) into new round euro amounts. Outlines for this vast legislative operation were set out in a February 2000 memorandum to parliament.[374] According to this memorandum, five legislative 'products' will be needed: (i) a *verzamelwet* [Collective Act], (ii) a *verzamelrijkswet* [Collective Act of the Kingdom of the Netherlands], (iii) a *verzamel-algemene maatregel van bestuur* [Collective General Administrative Order], (iv) a *verzamel-algemene maatregel van rijksbestuur* [Collective General Administrative Order of the Kingdom of the Netherlands] and (v) a '*bezemwet*' [literally: 'sweeping Act', that is, an Act amending earlier legislation].

In the course of 2000, proposals for the *verzamelwet* and the *verzamelrijkswet* were presented to the Second Chamber of Parliament. These concern, first the Bill providing for adjustment to the euro,[375] which deals with the adaptation of all 'ordinary' Acts of Parliament, and secondly, the Bill for an Act of the Kingdom of the Netherlands providing for adjust-

Criminal Code regarding counterfeiting in respect of specie and currency notes and banknotes (Euro-counterfeiting Bill)], Second Chamber of Parliament, session 2000–1, 27 494, 1 and 2.

[373] Notably Art 4 of Regulation 1103/97 and Art 14 of Regulation 974/98.

[374] Second Chamber of Parliament, session 1999–2000, 27 042, 1, 1: ***Beleidsbrief inzake aanpassing van wetgeving in verband met de invoering van de euro*** [Policy statement on the adoption of legislation in connection with the introduction of the euro], 7 Feb 2000 (thereafter: Feb 2000 Policy Statement).

[375] *Aanpassingswet euro*, Second Chamber of Parliament, session 2000–1, 27 472.

ment to the euro,[376] which has regard to the adaptation of legislation of the Kingdom of the Netherlands. Of the some 10,000 changes needed, about 90 per cent can be dealt with relatively simply by 'technical conversion'. This means that the present guilder amount will be divided by 2.20371 (the irrevocably fixed conversion rate of the euro in terms of the Dutch guilder), after which the result will be rounded off in accordance with the rounding rules of Regulation 1103/97. The remaining 10 per cent (still some thousand legislative provisions) will require a policy decision of some sort.

In an Annex to the above-mentioned February 2000 Policy Statement, a number of 'rules of thumb regarding the introduction of the euro' have been formulated. We mention some by way of illustration: provisions that have become obsolete will not be converted (rule 3); technical conversion will be applied if possible (rule 5); if technical conversion is not an option, the amount will be rounded off to a round euro number, taking into account the overall objective to implement the entire legislative euro conversion operation in a budgetary neutral way[377] (rule 6); the denominations of euro coins or banknotes will be taken into account if possible (for example, a €0.20 coin instead of the NLG 0.25 'quarter') (rule 8); these 15 rules are intended to give guidance and deviations could occur in specific instances. In such cases, the relevant Explanatory Memorandum will specify the grounds for departing from this set of rules (rule 15). The proposed Act providing for adjustment to the euro contains a proposal to repeal section 113, Book 6 of the Netherlands Civil Code.[378] This section provides that '[f]or payment in Netherlands legal currency, if the sum of money owed is not five cents or a multiple thereof, it is rounded off to the closest amount divisible by five, with a minimum of five cents'. This provision was made necessary by the abolition of the guilder cent in 1983. With the introduction of the euro, the cent (eurocent) will re-appear, thus rendering this provision superfluous.

2.1.2.c Euro Temporary Act on regulation procedures

On 12 April 2000, the Euro Temporary Act on regulation procedures entered into force.[379] This Temporary Act is closely linked to the legislative efforts described in the previous paragraph. The amendment of the

[376] *Rijkswet aanpassing rijkswetten euro*, Second Chamber of Parliament, session 2000–1, 27 473 (R 1668).

[377] In the field of criminal law, it has been decided that the present maximum penalties will simply be divided by two (instead of by 2.20371) in order to avoid impractical, broken numbers. Although this will result in an increase of the maximum penalties, no major budgetary consequences are to be expected, as maximum penalties are hardly ever imposed.

[378] *Aanpassingswet euro*, Second Chamber of Parliament, session 2000–1, 27 472, 3, 25.

[379] *Tijdelijke wet regelgeving euro*, 16 Mar 2000, *Staatsblad* 2000, 149.

many different pieces of subordinate legislation that will be covered by the various collective orders mentioned above will be subject to a relatively large number of different procedural requirements. The Acts on which these pieces of lower legislation are based often require some form of parliamentary involvement, if the subordinate legislation is to be amended, but the way in which this occurs may vary from one category of order, decree, etc., to another.[380] In order to enhance the efficiency of what is already a very complex legislative undertaking, the Temporary Act does away—albeit, exclusively in the context of the 'euro conversion legislative operation'—with all these different procedures. For the same reason, all otherwise obligatory consultation procedures (with the exception of the requirement to consult the *Raad van State* (Council of State)) have been suspended.

2.1.2.d Amendment of certain provisions of Book 2 of the Civil Code

On 1 September 2000, an Act entered into force to amend Book 2 of the Netherlands Civil Code (NCC) in connection with the introduction of the euro.[381] A rather extensive academic debate has evolved around the various issues raised by the introduction of the euro in the field of company law. Rather than summarising these discussions here, a reference is made to the literature mentioned in the Explanatory Memorandum[382] to the Act. In summary, Regulations 1103/97 and 974/98 and the new provisions in Book 2 NCC, created a system that offers each *naamloze vennootschap* [public limited company] and *besloten vennootschap* [private limited company] the option to choose one of three possibilities regarding whether or not to amend its articles of association. A company may either (a) refrain from making any amendment to its articles of association on the basis of Article 4 Regulation 974/98, or (b) amend its articles of association pursuant to the ordinary regime of Book 2 NCC, or (c) amend its articles of association pursuant to the extra-ordinary (somewhat simplified) regime introduced by the Act amending Book 2 NCC.

Some other changes to company law during 2000 merit notice. In addition to the ordinary regimes applicable to the above-mentioned *naamloze vennootschap* and *besloten vennootschap*, Book 2 NCC contains provisions on the '*structuur-naamloze vennootschap*' [large public limited

[380] These procedures may, for example, consist of the requirement that a certain amount of time elapses between the official publication of an intended amendment and its entry into force in order to enable the parliament to oppose this, if it so wishes.

[381] *Wet tot wijziging van boek 2 BW in verband met de invoering van de euro*, 8 June 2000, *Staatsblad* 2000, 267 and *Besluit houdende vaststelling van inwerkingtreding van de Wet tot wijziging van boek 2 BW in verband met de invoering van de euro*, 4 July 2000, *Staatsblad* 2000, 289 [Decision on the entry into force of the Act amending Book 2 of the Civil Code in connection with the introduction of the euro].

[382] Second Chamber of Parliament, session 1999–2000, 26 823, 3, 2.

company] and '*structuur-besloten vennootschap*' [large private limited company]. These special regimes are applicable to public and private limited companies that surpass certain thresholds in terms of number of employees and issued capital.[383] By means of a Royal Decree dated 4 July 2000 (and in force as of 1 September 2000),[384] this issued capital threshold has been converted into an amount in euro and slightly raised, thus resulting in a threshold of €13 million. The minimum capital of a private limited company (NLG 40,000) also needed to be converted into euro. Technical conversion would have resulted in an amount of €18,151, which would have been impractical because this number cannot easily be divided into shares with an equal nominal value. Therefore, the minimum capital of a private limited company was set at €18,000 by Royal Decree dated 22 July 2000 (and in force as of 1 September 2000).[385]

2.1.2.e Cash changeover

In line with the 8 November 1999 Ecofin Council declaration that it would be 'helpful if financial institutions and certain other groups, notably cash-in-transit companies and retailers, were provided with notes and coins some time before 1 January 2002',[386] DNB can frontload credit institutions with euro coins and banknotes as of 1 September 2001. DNB will enter into contracts with the subject credit institutions in order to cover the risks associated with frontloading, and in order to prevent the frontloaded euros from being put into circulation prior to 1 January 2002. Third parties—such as retailers, but not the general public—can then be sub-frontloaded by their own credit institutions. On the basis of a covenant between the Ministry of Finance and DNB, the latter will play a coordinating role in a number of areas in which the cash-changeover will occur:

(i) in the storage and distribution of euro coins;
(ii) in the production, storage and distribution of euro banknotes; and
(iii) in the intake of guilder coins and banknotes.[387]

Although euro banknotes will not be provided to the general public prior

383 In very general terms, the gist of the structure-regime is to give more power within the company to the board of supervisory directors (and, thus, safeguard the influence of the company's employees, which have a representative on the board of supervisory directors) and less power to the general meeting of shareholders than is the case under the ordinary regime.

384 *Besluit financiële benedengrens structuurregeling*, 4 July 2000, *Staatsblad* 2000, 290 [Decision on the financial lower threshold of the structure regime].

385 *Besluit minimumkapitaal in euro besloten vennootschap*, 22 July 2000, *Staatsblad* 2000, 322 [Decision on minimum capital in euro of the private limited company].

386 Deposited for inspection at the Office of Parliamentary Documentation, Second Chamber of Parliament, session 1999–2000, 25 107, 37, Annex 3, sub 3.

387 See Second Chamber of Parliament, session 2000–1, 25 107, 47, 3.

to 1 January 2002,[388] small amounts of euro coins will be made available in two modalities:

(i) as of 17 December 2001, all inhabitants aged six and older will receive a free coupon entitling them to a starter kit containing eight euro coins, one of each denomination (that is, a total value of €3.88); and
(ii) from the same date, larger packages of euro coins with a value of NLG 25 can be purchased.

The coupon can also be used to purchase the larger package with a €3.88 discount. Some of the main further features of the cash changeover scenario are the following:[389]

- the guilder will loose its legal tender status as of 28 January 2002;
- as of 1 January 2002, retailers are to give change only in euro;
- as of 1 January 2002, automatic teller machines will dispense euro banknotes exclusively (including the smaller denominations of €5 and €10);
- until 1 April 2002, the public may turn in their guilder coins and banknotes at their credit institution free of charge; from that date until 31 December 2002, credit institutions may charge a fee for this service;
- DNB will, free of charge, convert guilder coins (until 1 January 2007) and banknotes (until 1 January 2032) into euro.

2.1.2.f Act on the financing of decentralised public authorities

The *Wet financiering decentrale overheden*[390] [Act on the financing of decentralised public authorities] deserves to be mentioned briefly. It makes part of a framework of new measures to co-ordinate different levels of government in the field of public finance. This Act—which has been adopted, but has not yet entered into force—regulates the conditions under which decentralised public bodies (such as provinces, municipalities and *waterschappen* [district water boards]) may borrow, lend, grant guaranties and manage financial derivatives (section 2). It requires a minimum cash amount to be held by a decentralised public body (section 3), and more detailed rules may be laid down by ministerial decree. The average quarterly floating debt may not exceed the minimum cash amount. If it nevertheless does so for two consecutive quarters, the relevant supervisor (depending on the decentralised public body concerned) may give an *aanwijzing* [instruction]. If no improvement takes place, the supervisor may—under certain conditions—require that new loans may only be

[388] See Second Chamber of Parliament, session 2000–1, 37, 6.
[389] Ibid, 4.
[390] Act of 14 Dec 2000, *Staatsblad* 2000, 587. The date on which this Act will enter into force will be determined by Royal Decree.

contracted after its prior approval. In addition, the supervisor may set a maximum for the debt in current account of the public body concerned (section 4). Rules regarding the maximum permitted interest rate risks may be set by ministerial decree (section 5). If the 3 per cent EMU government deficit norm is in danger of being exceeded as a consequence of the deficit of the decentralised public bodies, rules may be laid down by general administrative order with the object of controlling the latter's deficit. Such rules will not take effect until four weeks after their publication in the *Staatsblad*. Both Chambers of Parliament will be immediately informed of such publication (section 7). Rules concerning the reporting obligations of decentralised public bodies *vis-à-vis* their respective supervisors may be laid down by ministerial decree (section 8).

2.2 National law from the EC perspective

No conflicts or redundancies have been identified vis-à-vis Community law, and the Netherlands legislation and regulations adopted during 2000. At most, two Commission communications could be identified as not being followed in full. One of these is the Commission Communication on the use of the euro symbol (€).[391] In this communication, the Commission 'invites all currency users to use the symbol . . . whenever a distinctive symbol is needed for the description of monetary amounts in euro, *e.g.*, in price lists and invoices, on cheques and in any other legal instruments'. The communication contains no language that would indicate that the Commission intended to exempt statutory law from the (very broad) description of 'any other legal instruments'. Nevertheless, in proposing the use of the abbreviation 'EUR' to forthwith indicate Euro amounts (instead of the wide variety of ways to indicate guilder amounts currently used in Netherlands legislation),[392] the Netherlands government failed to give any explanation for the apparent discrepancy with the Commission's recommendation. Instead of prescribing the use of the recommended euro symbol, the Netherlands government intends to incorporate a requirement to use the 'EUR' abbreviation in the '*Aanwijzingen voor de regelgeving*' [Directions for Lawmaking].[393]

391 Commission Communication COM(97) 418 of 23 July 1997 on the use of the euro symbol (€).

392 Sometimes numbers are used (eg f 1000), sometimes words (thousand guilders) and sometimes a combination of the two (as in *f* 10 million guilders). The letter f or *f* (meaning 'florin') is used to indicate an amount in Dutch guilders, in the same way as the $ symbol is used to indicate an amount in US dollar.

393 See Second Chamber of Parliament, session 2000–1, 27 472, 3, 6. The Directions for lawmaking have been laid down by Decision of the Prime Minister of 18 Nov 1992, been published in the Governement Gazette 1992, 230, entered into force on 1 January 1993 and have been amended various times since. They are meant as a set of guidelines for cabinet members and their ministries in the field of rulemaking. They have no formal statutory status, but are occasionally eluded to in case law.

A second Commission document concerns the Commission's recommendation on measures to facilitate the preparation of economic operators for the changeover to the euro and has not been complied with fully.[394] In the Second Chamber of Parliament, Minister of Finance Zalm, stated that some of the recommendations will not be followed. Among these are the recommendation to 'as early as possible in 2001 pay . . . employees' wages and salaries in euro' (Article 2(2)), and the recommendation that '[p]ublic administrations, insurance companies and utility companies . . . should set their tariffs in euro during the third quarter of 2001' (Article 2(4)).

Another issue that might deserve being raised under this heading—as an imperfection, rather than as an example of a 'conflict or redundancy vis-à-vis Community law'—is the fact that the above-mentioned 'Directions for Lawmaking' fail to explicitly take into account the obligation that national authorities consult the ECB 'regarding any draft legislative provision in its field of competence' (see Article 105(4) EC). Directions 263, 268, 345 and 346 mention the European Commission and regulate how the European Commission's advisory role in certain fields should be incorporated in the Netherlands legislative process. However, the ECB is not mentioned. Although it could be argued that ECB opinions fall under the 'other opinions' referred to in Direction 268(c) and (d), it seems that the consultation obligation laid down in Article 105(4) EC is of sufficient importance to merit being dealt with explicitly in the Directions. In the same vein, the *aanhef* [salutation] of legislative acts makes a standard reference to the fact that the *Raad van State* (the Council of State, which among its other competencies, it is also the government's highest advisory body on legislative issues) has been consulted. There is no analogous practice *vis-à-vis* ECB consultation: no mention is made of the ECB having been consulted in Acts within the ECB's fields of competence. Altering the standard text of the salutation would require amending the Constitution,[395] which would seem too onerous a procedure to follow. However, some mention in the parliamentary documents that the ECB has been consulted would seem to enhance the transparency and the quality of the legislative process. A rare example of this suggested practice is the mentioning of the ECB opinion in the Explanatory Memorandum to the Act on the redenomination of debt.[396]

Finally, the Archives Act 1995[397] should be mentioned as a remnant of

[394] OJ [2000] C 303/6, 24 Dec 2000.

[395] Supplementary Art XIX Netherlands Constitution explicitly provides how the standard text of the salutation should read. See also Directions 109 and 110, Governement Gazette 1998, 45.

[396] See Second Chamber of Parliament, session 1998–9, 26 233, No 3, 1, n 1 which mentions that the ECB Opinion dated August 2, 1998 (CON/98/38) has been deposited for inspection at the Office of Parliamentary Documentation.

[397] *Archiefwet*, 28 Apr 1995, *Staatsblad* 1995, 277, as amended most recently by Act of 4 Dec 1997, *Staatsblad* 1997, 580.

the legal convergence exercise in the preparation for the third phase of EMU. As we have seen, the Archives Act 1995 was already mentioned in the EMI Convergence Report 1998. The EMI observed that the Act is applicable to DNB and that it was 'being reviewed in the light of the confidentiality regime within the ESCB under Article 38 of the Statute'.[398] The Act is indeed applicable to DNB, but no amendments have been made so far. This means that there is presently a discrepancy between the period after which documents are available to the public on the basis of the Archives Act 1995 (in principle 20 years)[399] on the one hand, and the period applicable on the basis of the Rules of Procedure of the ECB, on the other (in principle 30 years).[400]

2.3 The application of the law

To our knowledge, during the year 2000 there were no proceedings or judgments regarding private or public law issues in the field covered by this contribution.

2.4 Institutional aspects

To our knowledge there are no developments of interest to be reported under this heading.

398 *EMI Convergence Report 1998*, 335.

399 See ss 12 and 14 Archives Act 1995.

400 Art 23.3 of the Rules of Procedure of the ECB, which have most recently been amended on 7 Oct 1999, OJ [1999] L 314/32, 8 Dec 1999.

SPAIN

Juan Carlos Monedero Fernández-Gala and Manuel López Escudero

1. Political aspects and trends towards spillover Juan Carlos Monedero Fernández-Gala*

1.1 La continuidad del *relativo* optimismo europeísta

Si en el informe *Eurospectator* 2000 manifestábamos la vinculación entre el pasado autoritario de España y el alto grado de europtimismo (una visión de Europa que la equiparaba con modernización, prosperidad y democracia), doce meses después las variaciones respecto de esta afirmación se mostraban mínimas valorando el conjunto del periodo. El año transcurrido ha traído una mayor presencia del euro en la vida cotidiana de los españoles, aunque sólo fuera por el tortuoso camino recorrido respecto del dólar y la cobertura mediática otorgada al mismo, y, sin embargo, las encuestas correspondientes a este año no recogen prácticamente variaciones. Sólo a finales de año empieza a verificarse un cambio que quiebra esa tendencia, hasta el punto que allí donde el *efecto 2000* ocupó los más oscuros presagios económicos, el 2001 iba a iniciarse con un euro que protagonizaba el papel del malvado de la película. De cualquier forma, esa tendencia pertenece más bien al informe del 2001, por lo que sólo aparecerá tangencialmente en este *Eurospectator 2000.*

Hace dos años uno de los elementos clave para presentar a la opinión pública española la virtud del euro era entenderlo como 'el mejor aliado para las hipotecas'[401]. Se vinculaba el euro a una baja inflación y a tipos de interés moderados, aspectos de interés para muchas personas debido al elevado número de créditos bancarios vinculados a la vivienda existentes en España. Sin embargo, la mala marcha de esos indicadores no ha sido cargado en el debe de la moneda única.

La Asociación Hipotecaria Española realizó un estudio en el año 2000 donde mostraba que, con la salvedad de Bélgica, Francia e Irlanda (que quedaban fuera del estudio, si bien Irlanda había mantenido tasas más bajas), las hipotecas españolas seguían siendo en marzo de 2000 las más bajas de la Unión Europea. Mientras la media europea estaría en el 6'6 por ciento, la española estaba en el 4'95 por ciento, lo que permite explicar el mantenimiento del optimismo español al margen de las variaciones de la

* Facultad de Ciencias Politicas, Universidad Complutense de Madrid, Campus de Somosaguas, E-28223, Madrid.

401 Titular aparecido en el diario económico *Expansión* el 23 de junio de 1998.

primera etapa del euro. Es un dato de gran relevancia, pues la subida de los tipos de interés por el Banco Central Europeo suponía un aumento mensual, en la revisión de la hipotecas de junio de 2000, de 6 euros (mil pesetas) por cada 6000 euros (aproximadamente 1 millón de pesetas) prestados, lo que suponía un incremento sustancial del gasto mensual de los españoles en hipotecas. Hasta esa fecha, por tanto, no se percibe el euro como responsable de las variaciones hipotecarias. El Gobierno español tomaría cartas en el asunto y en la ley de acompañamiento de los Presupuestos Generales del Estado de 2000 estableció la exención fiscal de los costes de cancelación de hipotecas y de la renovación de préstamos, con el fin de que los usuarios pudieran renegociar de manera más ventajosa sus préstamos con otras entidades bancarias, aumentando así la competencia y, presumiblemente, reduciéndose los precios. No hay que olvidar que de los 460 billones de pesetas de préstamos hipotecarios en Europa, 25 billones corresponden a España, de manera que la marcha del euro, el precio del dinero, las hipotecas y la actitud de los españoles respecto de la moneda única van a ir de la mano.

Sigue funcionando, como ya se ha señalado, una imagen mítica de Europa que genera una mayor identificación en lo abstracto que en lo concreto y que sigue haciendo cohabitar una gran confianza en Europa con un gran desconocimiento de la realidad institucional europea. Ya apuntamos que, el hecho de que en España no haya existido nunca un debate en profundidad sobre Europa que haya llegado a la opinión pública, hace que la aceptación sin mayores cautelas de todo lo que venga de las instituciones comunitarias sea una constante (la argumentación *europea* tiene un gran peso propio cuando es esgrimida por las autoridades nacionales). Aún más si consideramos que las élites políticas son sin excepciones europeístas. En España no hay fuerzas políticas contrarias a la construcción de Europa. (Incluso el nacionalismo ve posibilidades de rebajar dentro de Europa su vinculación con España). Ese sentir pasivo de los españoles respecto de la Unión Europea lo ha recogido la publicidad institucional escogida por las autoridades españolas para dar a conocer el euro: una escalera mecánica que lleva al ciudadano, sin esfuerzo, hacia el final del trayecto. La Unión Económica y Monetaria es un proceso que lleva a los ciudadanos al margen de su esfuerzo[402].

Tampoco en el periodo electoral desarrollado en España en 2000, que dio la mayoría absoluta al Partido Popular de José María Aznar, fue 'Europa' un lugar de confrontación, pese a ser las elecciones un momento propicio para debatir asuntos como la política monetaria. Todo lo más

402 La no participación de la ciudadanía española en el proceso de introducción del euro permite explicar por qué desde determinados sectores se exige al Estado que cubra todo el esfuerzo del paso a la moneda única. En otros términos, quienes no han tenido participación en la decisión de introducir el euro, no ven tampoco la razón de aportar un esfuerzo o un coste personal en algo que sienten como impuesto.

que ha generado el euro en la ciudadanía es cierta inquietud vinculado a las dificultades de una nueva mecánica de cambio o a los problemas del redondeo. No es de extrañar que una de las campañas publicitarias para familiarizar a los españoles con el euro sea en forma de humor, mostrando a una familia (hecha con plastilina) confrontada a situaciones cotidianas atravesadas de ironía que acercan el euro a los ciudadanos desde su imagen afable.

1.2 La opinión pública española respecto del euro

En el Eurobarómetro número 51, publicado en julio de 1999, el 70 por ciento de los españoles apoyaba el euro, frente al 15 por ciento que se situaba en contra. España ocupaba el quinto lugar en el resultado neto (55 por ciento). El informe de abril de 2000, los apoyos habían subido al 72 por ciento y la oposición también había subido tres puntos hasta el 18 por ciento. España seguía ocupando la quinta posición (54 por ciento). El siguiente barómetro, número 53 de octubre de 2000, mantenía la tendencia, subiendo el apoyo hasta el 75 por ciento, manteniéndose la oposición en el 18 por ciento. España ascendía un puesto en la escala de resultados netos (57 por ciento). Respecto de la media europea, los ciudadanos españoles muestran una confianza superlativa en el euro: 75 por ciento a favor del euro, frente al 65 por ciento de media en el Euro11 (y del 58 por ciento en el Euro15), y 18 por ciento en contra del euro, frente al 27 por ciento en contra en el Euro11 (el 33 por ciento en el euro15).

Aunque el Eurobarómetro 54, elaborado a finales de 2000, vendrá a romper esta tendencia optimista, los resultados durante el año 2000 muestran ese entusiasmo generalizado (en el eurobarómetro 54 el apoyo desciende al 68 por ciento, perdiéndose siete puntos, y la oposición se sitúa en el 24 por ciento, seis puntos por encima).

Sin embargo, si comparamos el eurobarómetro construido por la Dirección General para la Educación y la Cultura de la Comisión Europea con la encuesta elaborada por España a través del Centro de Investigaciones Sociológicas (nº 2392, de mayo de 2000), vemos fuertes divergencias, siendo más cautos los resultados del estudio español respecto de ese entusiasmo por la moneda única. Nos inclinamos a dar más credibilidad a la información que brinda el estudio del CIS por dos razones: (1) la mayor representatividad de la muestra, registrándose en el caso del CIS dos veces y media más de preguntas (1000 encuestas en el caso del Eurobarómetro frente a 2500 entrevistas en el caso del CIS); (2) la formulación de la pregunta. Esto es importante, pues mientras que el Eurobarómetro pregunta por el posicionamiento respecto del euro (quedando la pregunta en el ámbito abstracto en donde hemos dicho que los españoles siguen comportándose en términos de una Europa idealizada), el CIS opta por una pregunta más concreta y más dura: 'Ahora

	A favor	En contra	Resultado neto	Media Euro 11	Media Euro15
Eurobar.51 (julio 1999)	70 por ciento	15 por ciento	55 (quinta posición)	46	33
Eurobar.52 (abril 2000)	72 por ciento	18 por ciento	54 (quinta posición)	42	28
Eurobar.53 (octubre 2000)	75 por ciento	18 por ciento	57 (cuarta posición)	38	25
Eurobar.54 (2001)	68 por ciento	24 por ciento	44	—	18

quisiera que me dijera si está Usted muy de acuerdo, bastante de acuerdo, poco de acuerdo o nada de acuerdo con el hecho de que nuestra moneda nacional, la peseta, desaparezca para ser sustituida por el euro'. Si bien la pregunta en la encuesta española acerca más a la cuestión concretándola, no deja de ser cierto que también condiciona la respuesta. Por un lado hay una apelación sentimental a la moneda ('nuestra moneda nacional') y, por otro, hay un posicionamiento no neutral respecto del futuro de algo con lo que se ha convivido diariamente, ya que se menciona en la pregunta que la peseta va a 'desaparecer'.[403] Igualmente, la proporción de personas que 'no saben' es superior en la encuesta española. En definitiva, ambas encuestas, pese a interrogar sobre una misma realidad, no son homogéneas.

El estudio del CIS reproduce las que ya señalamos en el informe *Eurospectator 1999* como constantes de la opinión de la ciudadanía española respecto de los aspectos europeos y, por tanto, respecto del euro: (1) optimismo abstracto; (2) mayor inclinación por posturas nacionales ante cuestiones concretas; (3) gran desconocimiento de lo que significa la Unión Europea, que se manifiesta en la falta de consistencia entre las diferentes respuestas y en la falta de conocimiento del funcionamiento de la UE.

El 41'8 por ciento de los españoles, según el estudio del CIS, aprueba la desaparición de la peseta. Desagregando ese porcentaje, 'muy de acuerdo' está sólo el 8'2 por ciento, mientras que el 33'6 por ciento está 'bastante de acuerdo'. Por el contrario, el 50'4 por ciento desaprueba la desaparición de

403 El problema de la falta de homogeneización de los diferentes estudios europeos aparece una vez más en toda su crudeza. Como ya apuntamos en el informe anterior, sólo estudios cualitativos podrìan permitirnos avanzar en esa dirección su perando los problemas que los estudios cuantitativos crean.

Percepción del beneficio/perjuicio de la pertenencia de España a la UE en relación a los precios

	mayo 1998	mayo 1999	mayo 2000
más bien beneficiosa (1)	26 por ciento	25 por ciento	20 por ciento
ni beneficiosa ni perjudicial	20 por ciento	21 por ciento	18 por ciento
más bien perjudicial (2)	32 por ciento	34 por ciento	45 por ciento
(1)–(2)	–6	–9	–25
no sabe	22 por ciento	20 por ciento	17 por ciento
no contesta	0 por ciento	0 por ciento	0 por ciento

Fuente: CIS, estudio 2.392

Grado de acuerdo con la desaparición de la peseta para ser sustituida por el euro

	mayo 1998	mayo 1999	mayo 2000
muy de acuerdo	10 por ciento	7 por ciento	8 por ciento
Bastante de acuerdo	30 por ciento	34 por ciento	34 por ciento
muy+bastante de acuerdo (1)	40 por ciento	41 por ciento	42 por ciento
poco de acuerdo	24 por ciento	28 por ciento	25 por ciento
nada de acuerdo	22 por ciento	22 por ciento	25 por ciento
poco+nada de acuerdo (2)	46 por ciento	50 por ciento	50 por ciento
(1)–(2)	–6 por ciento	–9 por ciento	–8 por ciento
no sabe	12 por ciento	8 por ciento	7 por ciento
no contesta	2 por ciento	1 por ciento	1 por ciento

Fuente: CIS, estudio 2.392

Beneficio/Perjuicio del establecimiento de la moneda única para los intereses españoles

	mayo 1998	mayo 1999	mayo 2000
más bien beneficiosa (1)	42 por ciento	45 por ciento	41 por ciento
ni beneficiosa ni perjudicial	14 por ciento	13 por ciento	13 por ciento
más bien perjudicial (2)	22 por ciento	20 por ciento	26 por ciento
(1)–(2)	20 por ciento	25 por ciento	15 por ciento
no sabe	22 por ciento	22 por ciento	20 por ciento
no contesta	0 por ciento	0 por ciento	0 por ciento

Fuente: CIS, estudio 2.392

la peseta y su sustitución por el euro ('poco de acuerdo' el 25 por ciento y 'nada de acuerdo' el 25'4 por ciento). Llama la atención que el porcentaje de los que *no saben* se limita al 6'7 por ciento. Estos datos son poco consistentes con el 75 por ciento que se muestra a favor del euro en el Eurobarómetro número 53. Entre el estudio del CIS y el eurobarómetro hay una diferencia de 33 puntos para una, supuestamente, misma realidad.

Esta inconsistencia con los valores del Eurobarómetro se reproduce dentro del propio estudio del CIS cuando se cruzan respuestas que debieran manifestar coherencia entre ellas. Tenemos que el 77'4 por ciento muestra una actitud favorable ante la UE y un escaso 11'2 por ciento manifiesta una actitud desfavorable (el optimismo abstracto al que nos hemos referido). Sin embargo, al 45'1 por ciento le sería indiferente 'si mañana le dijeran que la Unión Europea se ha disuelto, que ya no existe', porcentaje al que habría que sumar el 4'3 por ciento que señala que 'le alegraría algo', y el 2'3 por ciento al que le 'alegraría mucho'. Por tanto, tenemos un 51'7 por ciento que no muestra el mínimo aprecio por la existencia concreta de la UE. ¿Cómo compatibilizar esto con ese 77'4 por ciento que muestra una actitud favorable a la UE?

Mayor coherencia interna muestran las respuestas respecto del euro. En lo que respecta a si la moneda única traerá más beneficios o más costes a los países miembros, el 27'3 por ciento se inclina por sus consecuencias positivas, el 15'8 por ciento cree que todo permanecerá igual y el 31'6 entiende que supondrá más costes que beneficios. Cuando se pregunta para el caso de España, el 40'6 por ciento entiende que será más bien beneficiosa, el 13'2 por ciento ni beneficiosa ni perjudicial, y el 26'1 por ciento más bien perjudicial. (En esta pregunta, el porcentaje de las personas que 'no saben' asciende al 20 por ciento). Esta última respuesta coincide con los porcentajes de aquellos que están de acuerdo con la sustitución de la peseta por el euro (41'8 por ciento), si bien se verifica un *efecto prudencia* que hace que los que creen que no va a ser ni beneficiosa ni perjudicial (13'2 por ciento) y una parte de los que no saben (20 por ciento) se sumen a los que entienden que va a ser perjudicial (26'1 por ciento) para mostrarse en desacuerdo con la desaparición de la peseta (50'4 por ciento). E igualmente coincide con los porcentajes de aquellos que entienden que la pertenencia de España a la UE le ha beneficiado (55 por ciento), le ha perjudicado (14 por ciento) o ni le ha beneficiado ni perjudicado (18 por ciento). Similar consistencia muestra la encuesta cuando se consideran las respuestas a la pregunta de si con la pertenencia de España a la UE se han acortado las diferencias con la media europea, pues el 55 por ciento creen que esas diferencias se han reducido, el 13 por ciento creen que han aumentado y el 14 por ciento creen que no ha habido variación.

Las encuestas públicas no recogen la actitud de los ciudadanos respecto de los efectos de la Unión Económica y Monetaria en el crecimiento económico, desempleo y políticas sociales (las preguntas vinculan de manera abstracta estos aspectos a la Unión Europea), por lo que no es sencillo aventurar un análisis al respecto. Tampoco se interroga acerca de la trasparencia e independencia del Banco Central Europeo ni de la relación del euro respecto del dólar o el yen (aunque la presencia en la opinión pública de la evolución del euro respecto de la moneda americana permite prever una creciente inquietud). Sólo una de las preguntas del estudio del CIS interroga acerca de la percepción de la ciudadanía respecto de la relación ingresos/precios futura en relación con el euro. En términos similares a otras respuestas, el 14'2 por ciento espera que los ingresos suban más que los precios (optmismo); el 26'8 espera que los precios suban más que los ingresos (pesimismo); el 39'6 por ciento cree que permanecerán igual (indiferencia), y el 19'2 por ciento no tienen respuesta (ignorancia). Sin embargo, podemos colegir que las respuestas, de existir las preguntas, reproducirían los elementos señalados (aunque esto no es más que una hipótesis).

Insistimos en que, de cualquier forma, el hecho de que a uno de cada dos españoles no le preocupe la desaparición de la UE pone en cuestión las apreciaciones concretas respecto del euro. Recordemos que el 62'2 por ciento de los españoles se consideraban sobre todo 'ciudadanos españoles'; el 23'1 por ciento 'europeo y español al mismo tiempo'; y sobre todo 'ciudadano europeo' el 6 por ciento. Aún un 8 por ciento no se encontraría ubicado dentro de esas categorías (recuérdese el pluralismo nacional de España). Europa no pertenece a la reflexión política cotidiana de los españoles. Un ejemplo claro lo encontramos en la aportación española al presupuesto comunitario. El proyecto de Presupuestos Generales del Estado para el 2001 señala que los pagos comunitarios a España ascienden a 16.747,44 millones de euros. El total de la aportación española es de 7.414,35 millones de euros. Por tanto, el saldo financiero es de 9.333,09 millones de euros favorable a España. Pese a la magnitud de esta diferencia, sólo el 23'8 por ciento de los españoles sabe que España aporta menos a la UE de lo que recibe. El 31'3 por ciento cree que los españoles entregan al presupuesto comunitario más de lo que recogen y el 12'3 por ciento entiende que España recibe más o menos lo mismo que aporta. El 32'4 por ciento ignora los términos de esa relación. En conclusión, poco más de dos de cada diez españoles sabe cuál es la vinculación de España con el presupuesto comunitario. El 33'3 por ciento cree que Suiza pertenece a la UE y un 34'1 por ciento cree lo mismo respecto de Noruega; el 31'5 por ciento no sabe que Finlandia pertenece a la Unión y el 23 por ciento ignora lo mismo de Irlanda. No en vano, al 56'1 por ciento de los españoles, las noticias relacionadas con la Unión Europea le interesan poco o nada. Lo que no impide que, como hemos apuntado, el 77'4 por ciento manifieste un actitud favorable hacia la Unión Europea. Una vez más señalamos que la opinión de los españoles respecto de Europa no está consistentemente formada.

La Sociedad Estatal de Transición al Euro (SETE) ha realizado varias encuestas con motivo de sus campañas de introducción del euro (consistentes principalmente en simulaciones en sitios públicos)[404]. El resultado de estas encuestas (poco fiables estadísticamente) es que 'la sociedad española da muestras de tener prácticamente asumido este cambio, y estar mentalizada para afrontarlo'. La SETE encargó también un estudio cualitativo a la empresa ASP titulado 'La sociedad española ante el proceso de introducción del euro'. El estudio se hizo entre el 28 de abril y el 27 de julio y reunió a diez grupos de discusión con personas de distintos sectores profesionales y estratos socioeconómicos. Las preguntas formuladas hacían referencia al euro, con el fin de evaluar el nivel de información del público, su preparación y su preocupación sobre el cambio de moneda. Las conclusiones y recomendaciones finales son: (1) los niveles generales de información, preparación y preocupación permiten anticipar que, de planificarse bien las necesidades de cada colectivo, la introducción se realizará de manera satisfactoria. Algunos grupos no alcanzarán por sí mismos una preparación óptima, por lo que necesitarán estímulos y ayuda externa; (2) las necesidades de información no son homogéneas. Existen colectivos más necesitados (amas de casa, personas mayores, comerciantes de poblaciones pequeñas y medianas) Será preciso, por tanto, intensificar las campañas de información en estos colectivos. Son precisamente estos colectivos los más preocupados por el uso de las dos monedas durante el periodo de convivencia; (3) en la gran mayoría de la gente existe el temor a posibles alzas de precios en los primeros días de 2002.

Para solucionar estos problemas, se propone la conveniencia de que se disponga de euros antes de enero de 2002 (algo que, por otro lado, ya está recogido en el II Plan Nacional de Transición al Euro) y la recuperación del valor del uso de los céntimos, evitando igualmente el redondeo al alza. Esto último parece que será algo de gran utilidad en España, pues especialmente las personas mayores operaron con monedas de fracción de peseta, lo que facilitará su manipulación con los euros. Para los comercios y pequeñas y medianas empresas se recomienda en el estudio de ASP la conversión anticipada a euros de los catálogos de precio, la aplicación del doble etiquetado y la adaptación contable e informática previa.

1.3 El punto de vista empresarial

En el año 2000 el Banco Bilbao Vizcaya[405] expresaba las ventajas e inconvenientes de la Unión Económica y Monetaria, resumiendo un punto de vista generalizado entre los empresarios españoles:

[404] La SETE, organismo público para apoyar la introducción al euro, ha centrado sus esfuerzos en campañas corporativas de imagen de inciertos resultados. No consta que este organismo haya puesto en marcha una evaluación de su trabajo.
[405] <http://www1.el pais.es/bbv>.

(1) Ventajas económicas: mayor dimensión económica el área euro; disminución de los costes de las transacciones intercomunitarias; disminución del grado de incertidumbre respecto de los movimientos de los tipos de cambio; fomento de la integración económica, con mercados financieros más amplios y profundos; refuerzo de la estabilidad y mayor transparencia de precios; euro como moneda internacional de reserva, con la consiguiente mayor influencia internacional de la UE; reducción de los tipos de interés en los países periféricos de la UE (España, Grecia, Italia, Irlanda, etc.).

(2) Inconvenientes: cesión de soberanía monetaria nacional (imposibilidad de variar los tipos de interés); cesión de la política cambiaria como mecanismo de ajuste (imposibilidad de modificar los tipos de cambio); reducción de la soberanía presupuestaria (limitaciones del déficit público); costes derivados de la sustitución de las monedas nacionales por el euro; ausencia de una política presupuestaria europea; potenciales problemas de desempleo imposibles de combatir al faltar instrumentos de política económica (combatibles con transferencias de riqueza de las regiones más ricas a las pobres que llevara a una convergencia real).

Los resultados de la encuesta *La empresa española ante el euro* de abril de 2000, realizada por la Cámara de Comercio muestra las siguientes conclusiones. En primer lugar, el 65 por ciento de las empresas consideran que la implantación del euro traerá ventajas, frente al 27 por ciento que considera que traerá inconvenientes (para el comercio los inconvenientes suben hasta el 35 por ciento, reduciéndose las ventajas al 57 por ciento). En cuanto al grado de información, el 74 por ciento se considera informado y el 25 por ciento insuficientemente informado. En lo que se refiere a los precios, el 81 por ciento cree que los mismos se mantendrán, el 13 por ciento que aumentarán y el 3 por ciento que tendrán una reducción. Atendiendo a los principales problemas que las empresas tienen respecto del euro, el más referido es el redondeo (37 por ciento), seguido de la contabilidad (32 por ciento), de la informática (30 por ciento), la conversián de precios (25 por ciento) y la fiscalidad (24 por ciento).

Una reflexión diferenciada la ha desarrollado el sector agrícola (no olvidemos que el 45 por ciento del presupuesto comunitario está destinado a este capítulo). Este sector ve disminuir crecientemente su papel económico, pese a que en España trabaja aún en él el 7'4 por ciento de la población. España ocupa el primer lugar en la producción mundial de aceite de oliva, es el primer productor comunitario de cítricos y es el cuarto productor mundial de vinos. En total, España produce el 14 por ciento de la producción agrícola comunitaria. Desde este sector se entiende que la puesta en marcha del euro significará una mayor transparencia en los precios (mejorando el sistema anterior sobre la base del llamado *ecu*

Ventajas e inconvenientes de la implantación del euro en la empresa

	1998	1999	2000
ventajas	56 por ciento	63 por ciento	65 por ciento
inconveniente	30 por ciento	29 por ciento	27 por ciento
no sabe/no contesta	14 por ciento	8 por ciento	8 por ciento

Fuente: La empresa española ante el euro, Cámara de Comercio, abril de 2000

verde), que a se vez se traducirá en una mayor competencia que favorecerá a España en los productos en los que es más fuerte: aceite de oliva, frutas, hortalizas y vino. A su vez perjudicará a la producción de aquellos bienes en los que se es menos competitivo: lácteos, vacuno, cereales y arroz.[406] Según el propio sector, la introducción del euro servirá para lograr una mayor estabilidad monetaria en lo que se refiere a pagos de la PAC, ayudas y precios de intervención, como en los intercambios interiores. La imposibilidad de devaluar también es visto por el sector como algo positivo al ser un ámbito de precios muy rígidos y muy ligado a las variaciones en la moneda. En los aspectos negativos de la incorporación del euro, además de los comunes del coste de adaptación o la doble contabilidad, se señala la afloración de dinero negro, que encarece el coste de la tierra de manera especulativa. Este aspecto, siendo importante no ha recibido una gran atención ni en la opinión pública ni por parte de las autoridades.

Señalemos también la importancia que se está dando desde las instituciones financieras a la introducción del euro como factor de estimulación de la competencia. Como señala la consultora Analistas Financieros Internacionales, 'la introducción del euro ampliará y profundizará el mercado hipotecario en el área euro, facilitando la consecución de un mercado único para los préstamos hipotecarios, que hoy en día todavía dista mucho de esa situación'. De esta forma, el euro servirá como elemento impulsor de una mayor comunitarización de un ámbito tan sensible a los ciudadanos españoles como es el mercado hipotecario.[407]

1.4 El Banco de España

En el *Informe Anual 1999 del Banco de España* (BE), que se publica a mediados de 2000, la máxima autoridad monetaria española desgrana lo que ha sido la primera etapa del euro desde la perspectiva española. Para el BE, en el primer año de pertenencia de España a la UEM, este país ha

[406] 'El euro y el sector agrícola', en *Noticias euro*, núm. 24, Ministerio de Economía y Hacienda, 2000.
[407] <http://www.afi.es>.

mantenido los niveles de estabilidad macroeconómica que le permitieron entrar en la Unión Monetaria, alcanzando incluso algunas 'correcciones adicionales de algunos de los desequilibrios que aún permanecen, como el déficit público, y manteniendo acotado el incremento de su tasa de inflación, inducido por el encarecimiento de la energía'. Siguiendo el análisis, el BE señala que España 'ha experimentado altas tasas de crecimiento de la actividad y del empleo, que le han permitido avanzar en el proceso de convergencia real con la zona del euro'. Pero no deja de destacar igualmente los problemas más evidentes de la economía española: 'Sin embargo, el deterioro del déficit comercial y la persistencia del diferencial de inflación ponen de manifiesto la necesidad de vigilar la expansión de la demanda global y de imprimir una mayor flexibilidad a la oferta de la economía, eliminando los obstáculos de carácter estructural que impiden la ampliación de su potencial crecimiento'.

Pese a la puesta en marcha de la UEM, el Banco de España recuerda que ésta no garantiza sin más la homogeneidad de las condiciones monetarias y financieras en los distintos países del área euro, ya que éstas dependen, entre otros factores, de los mecanismos a través de los cuales se propagan los impulsos monetarios, mecanismos que reposan en la 'estructura y funcionamiento de los diferentes sistemas financieros nacionales'. Para el BE, 1999 fue testigo de tres hechos de gran relevancia para la evolución de los mercados y de los flujos financieros: el inicio de la tercera etapa de la Unión Económica y Monetaria; la entrada en vigor de la reforma de la Ley del Mercado de Valores; y los cambios en la fiscalidad de un buen número de activos financieros. Estos cambios tendría a su vez efectos sobre la competencia entre los mercados, que fue mayor, e impulsaron los procesos de 'desintermediación financiera y de internacionalización de las carteras de los inversores y de las fuentes de financiación de los prestatarios finales'.

En una entrevista realizada al Gobernador del Banco de España, Jaime Caruana, quien sustituyó a Luis Angel Rojo por finalización de su mandato en 2000, apunta algunas ideas en la misma dirección.[408] Para el actual Gobernador del BE, los procesos de liberalización y apertura al exterior habrían proporcionado a España 'impulsos de disciplina y transformación extraordinariamente beneficiosos para la economía española', siendo la entrada en la UEM 'un paso decisivo en el proceso de apertura y modernización de nuestro país'. Consecuencia directa de la pertenencia de España a la moneda única, serían la 'estabilidad macroeconómica, bajos tipos de interés, cambios en las expectativas de precios y en las pautas de negociación salarial, impulso a las reformas estructurales, consolidación fiscal, e intensa creación de empleo', además de que tendría ventajas adicionales al 'incrementar nuestro peso en el contexto internacional'.

[408] Entrevista a Jaime Caruana, en *Noticias Euro*, Ministerio de Economía y Hacienda, septiembre de 2000.

En lo que respecta al problema más evidenciado de la economía española, es decir, la inflación, Jaime Caruana cree que España debe 'aumentar su potencial de crecimiento no inflacionista y para ello precisa mejorar sus estructuras productivas, elevar el nivel de competencia en los mercados de bienes y servicios y lograr que el mercado de trabajo funcione con eficacia'. Y concluye: 'se trata, en suma, de aumentar nuestra competitividad. Y ha de procurar también gestionar adecuadamente la política fiscal y de mantener en todo momento el control del gasto público y su adecuada composición que favorezca el crecimiento'.

En lo que atañe a los procesos de comunitarización que impulsa la existencia de una moneda única, el Gobernador entiende que 'el número de fusiones transnacionales en el ámbito de la Unión Europea ha sido, hasta ahora, relativamente pequeño, especialmente en banca al por menor. Sin embargo, es previsible que el propio avance de la UEM potencie este proceso. En este sentido, la supervisión financiera va a tener que hacer frente al reto de la supranacionalidad y, en mi opinión, la mejor forma de enfrentarse a él es potenciar la cooperación entre los supervisores nacionales de los distintos países involucrados. Ello supone, por una parte, un mayor y mejor intercambio de información, y por otra parte una cierta convergencia a las mejores prácticas supervisoras.

El papel futuro de las entidades bancarias españolas también es analizado, estando estas empresas sometidas a dos tipos de retos. Por un lado, de carácter estratégico ligado a la creación de un mercado bancario paneuropeo. Por otro, retos de carácter operativo vinculados a la sustitución de la peseta por el euro. Para Caruana, los bancos españoles afrontan con gran eficacia ambos desafíos. Las fusiones y alianzas y las mejoras en la gestión de riesgos son elementos de gran relevancia al respecto.

En cuanto al momento concreto en que los ciudadanos operen con euros, el Gobernador señala la conveniencia de evitar retrasos y de acelerar el uso regular del mismo. La predistribución de monedas y billetes debiera facilitar la reducción de la convivencia de la peseta y del euro. De cualquier modo, su punto de vista al respecto es optimista, de manera que cree que en la primera quincena de enero de 2002 el proceso de puesta en circulación de las nuevas monedas y billetes esté completado. La aprobación del II Plan Nacional de Transición al Euro (ver parte legal de este estudio) tendría como principal objetivo que este proceso se realice de la manera menos traumática posible, si bien el periodo de dos meses de convivencia de la monedas (reducido desde los seis meses marcados inicialmente) sigue siendo superior al de otros países.

1.5 Los sindicatos: la apuesta por el *spillover*

Los principales sindicatos españoles mantienen el mismo grado de apoyo a la moneda única manifestado desde la primera fase. Como ha señalado el

Secretario General de la Unión General de Trabajadores (UGT), Cándido Méndez, 'la implantación del euro ha sido un éxito', si bien no por ello no dejan de lado determinadas inquietudes, principalmente la depreciación del euro respecto del dólar (que si bien favorecería las exportaciones, terminaría debilitando la confianza en la moneda). En esa dirección, los sindicatos insisten en la necesidad de alcanzar una *armonización fiscal*, incrementar la tasa de crecimiento y reducir las tasas de paro. Para Cándido Méndez, 'es imprescindible un énfasis mayor en las políticas coordinadas hacia el crecimiento económico sostenible y el empleo. Y pensamos que la unidad política de Europa es el marco necesario para la fortaleza de su moneda'[409]. En esa exigencia de ampliar los aspectos comunitarios en consonancia con la moneda única, la UGT reclamó, con motivo de la Cumbre de Niza en diciembre de 2000, garantías para los derechos de negociación colectiva, acción sindical y huelga en el ámbito europeo. Para ello no dudan en reclamar una reforma del proceso de toma de decisiones: 'Las decisiones por mayoría deberían convertirse en la norma general de la política social europea'[410].

El análisis que se realiza desde Comisiones Obreras (CC.OO.) va en la misma dirección. Por una lado, se entiende la política monetaria desarrollada por el Banco Central Europeo, caracterizada por su apuesta restrictiva aumentando ligeramente los tipos de interés en siete ocasiones desde el 2'5 por ciento (abril 1999) al 4'75 por ciento (octubre 2000). La superior fortaleza del dólar respecto del euro se achaca a la mayor fortaleza económica de los Estados Unidos, con un ciclo de crecimiento que dura ya una década. De ahí que recomienden 'hablar más de apreciación del dólar que de depreciación del euro'[411]. Se repite la idea de que un euro depreciado favorece las exportaciones—mejorando la capacidad de esos sectores-, pero también abarata las importaciones, colaborando en la creación de inflación, además de disminuir la confianza en la moneda. De ahí que establezcan una dura crítica a lo que entienden que es 'la ausencia de una unión política para adoptar decisiones creíbles con capacidad de generar la suficiente confianza interna y externa', recordando que 'la experiencia del último año muestra que las elevaciones del tipo de interés del dinero no es un mecanismo eficaz para revalorizar la moneda comunitaria. Más al contrario, una decisión de estas características ha venido siempre acompañada de una nueva depreciación del tipo de cambio de la moneda europea'.

409 Cándido Méndez, 'Un gran proyecto europeo', en *Noticias euro*, núm.19, Ministerio de Economía y Hacienda, 2000.

410 Boletín de Información Sindical, núm.7, 5 de diciembre de 2000.

411 'Situación de la economía española y Presupuestos Generales del Estado 2001. Posibles repercusiones de su aplicación', Confederación Sindical de Comisiones Obreras, 2000, 13–15.

La confianza en la moneda única sirve incluso para criticar a los empresarios españoles, a quienes se acusa de tener una actitud poco emprendedora y una escasa voluntad a la hora de asumir riesgos:

> los resultados negativos (. . .) entorpecen las posibilidades futuras de la sociedad española para generar riqueza, aunque la integración en el euro ha limitado sus efectos nocivos. De no haber pertenecido a la moneda única, los desequilibrios mencionados [paro, tasa de actividad, inflación y endeudamiento con el exterior] hubieran generado una depreciación muy superior de la peseta, acompañada de un severo crecimiento de los tipos de interés nominales, muy por encima de los marcados actualmente por el Banco Central Europeo.[412]

El otro gran reto del sindicalismo español está en alcanzar una mayor eficacia en la negociación colectiva en el ámbito europeo, complemento, entienden, necesario de la existencia de una moneda única: 'Mayor coordinación en el ámbito europeo, de forma que desde las diversas federaciones sectoriales de los distintos Estados pueda responderse adecuadamente a decisiones transnacionales'[413]. Esa negociación colectiva va ligada a la construcción de un Estado social europeo con gran presencia de un sector público en el centro del modelo europeo de bienestar. Para CC.OO., la UE produce un desplazamiento de los núcleos de decisión empresariales, legislativos y judiciales, así como de las relaciones laborales. Las transformaciones en las posibilidades nacionales de ajustes monetarios llevaría a que los empresarios intentaran transferir los ajustes imponiendo límites a la negociación colectiva, abaratando costes laborales. La inexistencia de una política fiscal comunitaria centralizada impediría encontrar soluciones menos lesivas para los intereses de los trabajadores. El riesgo sería 'encontrarnos así frente a la paradoja de que la Unión Monetaria produce una fragmentación y atomización empresarial y sindical, entrando en competencia unos países con otros a través de la negociación colectiva o a través del dumping social (. . .) Para las organizaciones sindicales en toda Europa supone todo un reto'. La conclusión final a la que llega el principal sindicato español es que 'Habrá que convenir en la necesidad de reforzar el sindicalismo europeo a través de la CES para que su capacidad de intervención permita alcanzar acuerdos con las patronales europeas, así como incidir de manera efectiva en las decisiones adoptadas en los distintos foros europeos'. En definitiva, los sindicatos apuestan claramente por la comunitarización del resto de políticas públicas que deben garantizar un Estado social.

1.6 Los partidos políticos

Como hemos señalado, en marzo de 2000 hubo elecciones generales en

[412] Ibid*em*. 163
[413] Documentos aprobados en el VII Congreso, Comisiones Obreras, 2000.

España, que fueron ganadas por mayoría absoluta por el Partido Popular. Las principales fuerzas políticas hicieron referencia durante la campaña electoral a cuestiones europeas, pero en ningún caso se abrió ninguna disputa al respecto. Europa no es un motivo de fricción entre los partidos políticos españoles y el euro es el actual símbolo de esa Europa sobre la cual no hay discusión (como ya se señaló en el anterior informe, la recurrente petición de Izquierda Unida de celebrar en el Parlamento un debate anual específico sobre la Unión Europea no ha sido considerado necesario por el Partido Popular, bastando, se ha argumentado, con la discusión después de cada cumbre europea).

En el programa electoral del Partido Popular, *Elecciones generales 2000: El compromiso del centro*, uno de los principales elementos que se señalan es que, frente al anterior Gobierno socialista, ellos habrían 'participado en la constitución de la Unión Monetaria Europea y en la implantación del euro', presentando este hecho no como un esfuerzo colectivo sino como obra exclusiva de los últimos cuatro años. Como se ha venido exponiendo en este informe, sólo el desconocimiento ciudadano respecto de Europa permite este tipo de planteamientos. El conjunto de ideas recogidas al respecto en este programa insiste en la necesidad de avanzar en la convergencia con Europa, respetándose en todo caso las exigencias de estabilidad presupuestaria (no se hacen referencias a las obligaciones europeas recogidas en el Pacto de Estabilidad) y manteniendo estables las variables macroeconómicas marcadas por el Banco Central Europeo, haciéndose especial referencia a la contención de la inflación en el entorno del 2 por ciento, a la reducción del déficit público y del gasto público, y a una mayor liberalización de mercados y de factores productivos.

En el capítulo dedicado estrictamente a Europa no hay apenas referencias concretas ni al euro ni a la política monetaria, poniendo el centro de la atención en los procesos de liberalización. El compromiso del Partido Popular se dirige a una política macroeconómica que proporcione estabilidad en toda la Unión; reformas fiscales que generen menor distorsión y mayores posibilidades de luchar contra el fraude; alcanzar los objetivos de liberación y de cambio normativo en todos los sectores de la economía para que todos los Estados tengan similares condiciones de competencia y acceso a los mercados; mejora de la regulación nacional y comunitaria que garantice niveles efectivos de competencia; fomentar el conocimiento y la investigación. Respecto del euro se manifiesta que: 'El euro ha venido a incrementar este papel importante que desempeña la Unión Europea en el contexto económico mundial. La moneda única es en estos momentos una de las grandes monedas mundiales y su voz ha de escucharse en defensa de los intereses y valores europeos'. En esa dirección se destaca la labor de armonización: 'En los foros económicos internacionales, como el Fondo Monetario Internacional, el Banco Mundial o el G-7, el euro está presente con una sola voz'. Como se ve, no existen referencias más comprometidas acerca de futuras comunitarizaciones de otros ámbitos ni se hace mención alguna al Banco Central Europeo como instrumento monetario. Europa, en consonancia con la percepción que de la misma tienen los ciudadanos, permanece en ese lugar abstracto positivo que, de alguna manera, hace de la UE un lugar ajeno a lo político.

El Partido Socialista Obrero Español, quien después de 14 años de gobierno había pasado su primera legislatura en la oposición, presenta en su *Programa Electoral para las Elecciones Generales 2000* una imagen mucho más política de Europa. Para el PSOE, Europa sigue siendo la mejor garantía para la paz, la estabilidad, el progreso y el bienestar social. Para ello entienden como necesaria la reforma institucional de la UE, que incorpore a nuevos pueblos al modelo europeo; el impulso para la incorporación de todos los miembros de la Unión a los Acuerdos de Schengen; el incremento de la cooperación jurídica y judicial en el ámbito de la Unión, aproximando las legislaciones civiles, penales y procesales; el refuerzo de la paz, apoyando las políticas de estabilidad en todo el continente; el impulso de la adopción de políticas comunes que contribuyan a la convergencia progresiva de las condiciones laborales y sociales de todos los trabajadores y pensionistas europeos. Para ello proponen levantar el veto del PP a la Directiva Europea sobre participación de los trabajadores en los Consejos de Administración, impulsando igualmente el acuerdo en torno a la armonización fiscal, la eliminación de paraísos fiscales, el tratamiento de los movimientos internacionales de capitales y la coordinación de las políticas presupuestarias y de empleo.

En el ánimo electoral, se critica al PP por lo que se define 'política miope, errática, sin objetivos definidos, que ha conducido a tener una posición secundaria en Europa'. En referencia concreta a la moneda única se afirma que 'La orientación de una política económica socialista en esta situación tiene que partir de un reconocimiento: la realidad del euro cambia algunos parámetros esenciales de la política económica, que ya no puede seguir haciéndose como antes'. Esto les lleva a asumir dos compromisos: 'La convergencia real con Europa es la prioridad que orienta toda nuestra oferta política' y 'El respeto a la convergencia nominal y, en concreto, a los compromisos presupuestarios asumidos en el Pacto de Estabilidad es el condicionante esencial que graduará los ritmos de aplicación de nuestras políticas a lo largo de la legislatura'. En esta dirección establecen que para ellos la convergencia real no es sólo una aproximación en los niveles de renta per cápita, sino una aproximación al nivel medio de bienestar. Sin embargo, sí recogen las limitaciones que implica la moneda única. De ahí que, la existencia del euro, continúan, implica que 'una política de demanda no puede basarse en subidas salariales y aumento del déficit público'.

Para Izquierda Unida (que perdería en las elecciones la mitad de los votos obtenidos en 1996), la visión de Europa es la más política (es decir, la más referida a intereses colectivos en transformación). Esta formación 'opta por una verdadera Unión Europea, alejada del modelo mercantilista y financiero actual, una integración política con mecanismos auténticamente democráticos', destacándose la crítica al 'déficit democrático' de la UE. En el ámbito propositivo, IU plante lo siguiente: establecimiento de un control y fiscalización de los movimientos de capital para limitar la especulación financiera y relanzar la inversión productiva generadora de empleo; desaparición de los paraísos fiscales; creación de un impuesto que grave las transacciones de capital a corto plazo sobre los mercados de divisas (tasa Tobin), dedicándose la recaudación a programas de ayuda al desarrollo; aumento del presupuesto de la UE y de las acciones estructurales dirigidas a la cohesión; aprobación de una Carta Social Europea con categoría de Tratado que establezca los mínimos laborales, sociales y fiscales 'para compensar las consecuencias de la implantación del mercado y la moneda únicos'.

El programa de IU es el único que hace referencia concreta a las cuestiones relacionadas con la moneda única que configuran el eje del estudio *Eurospectator*. En las *Prioridades económicas de IU* se establece: 'Una oposición al llamado 'Pacto de Estabilidad', porque supone medidas de ajuste para acabar con el déficit público de los Estados sin tener en cuenta el contexto económico de cada país'. De ahí que propongan 'Flexibilizar el 'Pacto de Estabilidad' con la formación de fondos de garantía y préstamos supraestatales'. En esa línea también se propone la creación de una 'Hacienda europea cuyos recursos provengan de las aportaciones directas' de la ciudadanía, con independencia del Estado en el que residan y según las capacidades individuales. En lo que respecta a las autoridades monetarias, se recoge en este programa que 'El Banco Central Europeo y los diferentes Bancos centrales de los Estados deben estar bajo la dirección y vigilancia de las instituciones políticas elegidas democráticamente. Este mismo criterio tendría que seguirse para el nombramiento de sus máximos responsables. Su objetivo prioritario debe ser la creación de empleo'. Concluyen con una propuesta de financiación de su programa. Para logra los objetivos señalados de debiera 'Elevar la cuantía del Presupuesto Comunitario para reforzar la cohesión, más necesaria ahora ante la puesta en marcha de la Unión Monetaria y la ampliación de la Unión Europea a los países del Este'.

En definitiva, se repite la aceptación generalizada en los principales partidos políticos españoles del proceso europeo, no habiendo surgido ninguna oposición ni siquiera con motivo de las dificultades en que está sumida la moneda única en su relación con el dólar. Europa sigue sin ser un motivo de disputa política. Ahora bien, los planteamientos de los principales partidos (PP y PSOE) siguen la línea de presentar a Europa con una mezcla de exigencia externa/inevitabilidad y de positiva abstracción. No tenemos todavía elementos empíricos que permitan verificar ninguna línea de futuro al respecto, pero los escasos instrumentos conceptuales que poseen los ciudadanos españoles en su relación con la Unión Europea deben dejar abierta la hipótesis de un fuerte alejamiento del compromiso europeísta de los españoles en caso de dificultades económicas. Los resultados de las encuestas de finales de año, influidos por la marcha del euro, marcan esa tendencia, sólo solventable en tanto en cuanto Europa sea incorporada como una reflexión participada por todos los ciudadanos y ciudadanas y no como un *factum* al que se enfrentan acríticamente.

1.7 El euro en los medios de comunicación

El año se iniciaba con grandes dosis de optimismo respecto del euro, valorándose de manera generalizada sus primeros doce meses como 'inequívocamente favorable', 'un éxito' o, en sus vertientes más críticas, con un amable 'discreto encanto del euro'. Doce meses después todo parecía haber cambiado y al entusiasmo inicial le ha seguido una suerte de pesimismo colectivo sobre el futuro del euro. El diario *El país*, el de más tirada y prestigio de España, titulaba en el último día del año su información sobre el euro con un contundente 'Riesgo de colapso'. A comienzos de 2001, las críticas han arreciado y todo un año de vaivenes han terminado haciendo mella tanto en el ánimo de la información en la prensa como en los ciudadanos (Ya hemos señalado que este informe cubre el año 2000. Sin embargo, es necesario señalar el fuerte cambio de tendencia que se recoge en los primeros meses de 2001, pues, de lo contrario, la valoración de 2000 parecerá un paréntesis inconexo).

Las primeras informaciones del año, más allá del apuntado optimismo, referían cuestiones prácticas, tales como la adaptación de las empresas, especialmente las pequeñas y medianas, los problemas de convivencia de la moneda nacional y el euro o las dificultades de la población para manejar la nueva unidad de cambio. Los rasgos entusiastas estaban vinculados a las 'presunciones de los más pesimistas', que a menudo habían planteado la práctica imposibilidad de que España se vinculara desde su inicio a la moneda única o de que el proyecto colectivo de unificación monetaria cuajase (Recordemos que el año se iniciaba con la amenaza catastrofista del *efecto 2000*). Sin embargo, ya desde enero de 2000 se empezó a apuntar lo que sería, junto a la depreciación del euro respecto del dólar, el asunto central de la información en España sobre la moneda única: el aumento de la inflación y la incapacidad de las autoridades españolas para gestionar la subida de precios, en manos exclusivas del Banco Central Europeo.

Pronto en España empezarían a relacionarse la debilidad del euro frente al dólar, la carestía del petróleo y el repunte de la inflación, uno de los principales problemas, junto al desempleo, de la economía española.

Mientras que en otros países de Europa la depreciación del euro ayudaba al relanzamiento de la economía, favoreciendo las exportaciones y mejorando las posiciones del sector manufacturero (que vende sus productos principalmente fuera del área del euro), en España ponía en peligro los equilibrios macroeconómicos, pues el grueso de las exportaciones españolas tiene lugar dentro del área del euro, de manera que la subida de precios que provoca un euro depreciado y una política de tipos de interés bajos deteriora directamente su competitividad, además de que encarece las importaciones (España comenzaba el año con un mayor déficit comercial, el 52'4 por ciento más alto, debido a que mientras las exportaciones habían ascendido el 5'6 por ciento, las importaciones lo habían hecho el 14 por ciento).

El Índice de Precios al Consumo de abril de 2000, del 0'4 por ciento situaba la tasa anual de inflación en España al 3 por ciento, mientras que en Alemania era del 1'5 por ciento, en Francia el 1'3 por ciento y el Italiano, que había logrado reducirlo, del 2'3 por ciento (El objetivo que se había marcado el Gobierno español para todo el año era del 2 por ciento). Sin embargo, algunos medios de comunicación dejaban claro que no podían buscarse exclusivamente fuera de España las responsabilidades, haciendo del euro el 'chivo expiatorio' de unos problemas con origen nacional (el creciente precio de los servicios y el alto precio del suelo). Por su parte, las autoridades españolas insistían en achacar las culpas al euro y al precio de petróleo. José Folgado, Secretario de Estado de Economía o Rodrigo Rato, Ministro de Economía, apuntarían a la debilidad del euro como factor clave, señalando igualmente la dualidad implícita en la situación de la moneda única, que favorecía el crecimiento económico pero con el consiguiente problema del encarecimiento de los precios. Las liberalizaciones propuestas por el Ministro Rato para el Consejo Europeo de junio en Feira, Portugal (gas, electricidad y transportes) irían dirigidas a reducir los efectos de la inflación en la economía española.

El clima publicístico catastrofsta produjo una serie de respuestas. En mayo de 2000, José Manuel Fernández Norniella, Presidente del Consejo Superior de Cámaras de Comercio, publicaba un artículo llamando a la calma: 'Euro, ¿oportunidad fallida?[414]. Tras reconocer que el euro había registrado un mínimo histórico, limitaba la relación entre el precio de la moneda única y la salud de la economía europea, recordando que la economía norteamericana tenía una mayor capacidad para atraer capitales. Para este autor, la tarea del euro no es competir con el dólar, sino asegurar la estabilidad y la eficiencia de los mercados europeos, tarea que estaría cumpliendo con gran rigor y éxito al facilitar la diversificación de fuentes de financiación, las concentraciones y la flexibilidad.

Las subidas de los tipos de interés realizadas por el BCE fueron muy

[414] José Manuel Fernández, 'Euro, ¿oportunidad fallida?', en *El país*, 22 de mayo.

bien recibidas por el Gobierno, los partidos políticos y los medios de comunicación españoles. En junio la inflación interanual española estaba ya en el 3'6 por ciento de manera que la subida de tipos al 4'5 por ciento anunciada ese mes fue recibida con alivio. También el verano fue utilizado para lanzar un recordatorio sobre la introducción de la moneda el 1 de enero de 2002, al constatarse desde la administración cierta confusión sobre las fechas y el retraso en algunos sectores, incluidas las corporaciones locales, en la adaptación de sus equipos informáticos a la moneda única.

En septiembre de 2000 tenía lugar la sexta subida de tipos de interés desde 1999. Era la primera vez que todos los países de la UE alcanzaban o sobrepasaban el 2 por ciento de inflación. España ya había alcanzado el 3'7 por ciento, sólo superada por Irlanda y 1'3 por ciento por encima de la media europea. El cambio oficial orientativo de la peseta respecto del dólar (aunque la peseta ya no cotice en los mercados) era de 191'70 pesetas por dólar, un récord que no se recordaba desde hacía más de quince años. El cambio oficial el 1 de enero de 1999, cuando la peseta se incorporó al euro, era de 143,35 pesetas por dólar. La depreciación desde entonces había sido del 33'7 por ciento. Unos días después la divisa europea volvía a caer y arrastraba de nuevo a la peseta, costando un dólar 195'15 pesetas (un mes más tarde ya estaría en 197. En octubre alcanzaría la *barrera psicológica* de 200 pesetas por dólar). En Madrid, la revista The Economist realizaba unas jornadas con el título: 'La identidad europea, ¿realidad o utopía? Medidas internas como aumentar el número de suministradores de carburante, aumentar el suelo disponible, reducir el gasto público, flexibilizar el mercado laboral o reducir los beneficios de las empresas (reduciendo los precios de venta) eran propuestas desde diferentes sectores. Desde el Gobierno español se apuntaba a la necesidad de una mayor 'modernización' del mercado laboral, si bien se mostraba el desacuerdo con la armonización de la fiscalidad sobre carburantes tomada según el principio de la mayoría (frente al de la unanimidad) en la Unión Europea.

Las intervenciones en solitario del BCE para apoyar al euro ocuparon un lugar principal en los medios de comunicación en noviembre, mientras que las críticas al Presidente Duisenberg no tuvieron en España la importancia y virulencia que tuvieron en otros países. Muy al contrario, las autoridades españolas mostraban su satisfacción por las medidas tomadas (recordemos que el año anterior el Ministro Rato llegó a manifestar su descontento con la política monetaria del BCE que, fomentando tipos bajos de interés, perjudicaba a la economía española). Diciembre se cerraba con una recuperación del euro respecto del dólar, que era celebrada con declaraciones optimistas de todos los actores sociales. Un dólar costaba 180 pesetas a finales de año, coincidiendo con los primeros síntomas de debilidad de la economía norteamericana. Eso no evitaría que el año se cerrase con una llamada de atención acerca del escaso tiempo restante para la entrada física en vigor de la moneda única y una constatación de que la euforia inicial respecto del euro había dejado paso al 'desaliento', especialmente en las encuestas realizadas previamente a la recuperación a finales de año de la moneda europea.

En lo que respecta a las noticias recogidas en los diarios de información económica sobre la moneda única, el tema que más páginas ocupó, además de la depreciación del euro respecto del dólar, fueron el IVA y la armonización fiscal. En términos generales, los asuntos principales tratados en los diarios fueron: las denuncias y sanciones de la Comisión y el Tribunal europeos a las rebajas españolas del IVA (dentro de los intentos del Gobierno español de atajar la inflación); los intentos de los quince por articular la armonización fiscal del ahorro; los intentos de Bruselas de acelerar la armonización del IVA; la celebración en Madrid del Consejo de Gobierno del BCE (homenaje al Gobernador del Banco de España, Luis Angel Rojo, que dejaba el cargo); el enfrentamiento entre España y Francia acerca de la política monetaria, al estar las economías de estos países en situaciones diferentes y necesitar políticas de precio del dinero incompatibles entre sí; la aprobación del II Plan Nacional de Transición al Euro; la emisión de los últimos billetes en pesetas.

La Conferencia de Niza entre el 7 y el 10 de diciembre insistió, como recogería el grueso de la prensa española, más en los aspectos nacionales que en los comunitarios, presentándose en España como una victoria del Gobierno y un aumento del peso específico español dentro de la Unión Europea. El optimismo de los resultados de esa cumbre no se trasladarían a la opinión pública. El decisivo año 2001 empezaba su andadura con el crecimiento del euroescepticismo. Los últimos meses para la entrada en vigor definitiva de la moneda única no dejan ya hueco para manifestaciones entusiastas que no vayan acompañadas de hechos constatables por la ciudadanía española.

2. Legal framework

Manuel López Escudero**

Durante el año 2000 las novedades en el ámbito jurídico más relevantes que se han producido en España en relación con la Unión Económica y Monetaria han sido tres, a saber: la elaboración de un proyecto de Ley General de Estabilidad Presupuestaria, la adopción de un segundo Plan Nacional de Transición al Euro y la aprobación del Reglamento de Régimen Interno del Banco de España.

Además, el Banco de España ha desarrollado diversas Orientaciones del Banco Central Europeo referentes al sistema TARGET en la medida en que

** Universidad de Granada, Facultad de Derecho, Departamento de Derecho Internacional Público, Plaza de la Universidad s.n., E-18001, Granada.

afectaban al componente español de dicho sistema,[415] que es el Servicio de Liquidación del Banco de España, y relativas a cláusulas utilizables en las operaciones de política monetaria.[416] No se ha producido, en nuestra opinión, ninguna cuestión jurídica relevante a efectos del presente informe. El Banco de España ha adoptado otras resoluciones, como la que contiene las normas de funcionamiento del Servicio Español de Pagos Interbancarios, gestionado por la Cámara de Compensación de Madrid, o las referentes a los índices de referencia de los préstamos hipotecarios, cuyo análisis excede los objetivos de este informe.

En lo que respecta a la aplicación judicial de la normativa referente a la introducción del euro o al Banco de España, aún no tenemos conocimiento de litigios que se hayan planteado ante órganos jurisdiccionales de instancias superiores.[417]

2.1 El proyecto de ley general de estabilidad presupuestaria

La vertiente económica de la UEM quedó articulada de forma insuficiente en el Tratado de Maastricht, ya que no se transferían competencias a las instituciones comunitarias, limitándose los artículos 98 a 104 TCE a establecer un procedimiento de coordinación de las políticas económicas nacionales y a imponer a los Estados varias normas de disciplina financiera y presupuestaria, en especial, la prohibición de déficit públicos excesivos. El deseo de algunos Estados como Alemania de asegurar el respeto de la disciplina presupuestaria en la fase final de la UEM se tradujo en la adopción por el Consejo Europeo de Amsterdam de junio de 1997 del llamado Pacto de Estabilidad y Crecimiento (en lo sucesivo, 'PEC'). El PEC está formado por una Resolución del Consejo Europeo de 17 de junio de

[415] Circular 8/2000 del Banco de España, de 22 de diciembre de 2000, sobre entidades participantes en el TARGET-SLBE, sistema de reembolso y otras modificaciones de la normativa del Servicio de Liquidación del Banco de España (*BOE* n° 312, de 29 Dec 2000, 46596).

[416] Resolución del Banco de España de 10 de octubre de 2000 (*BOE* n° 304, de 20 Dec 2000, 44783).

[417] Sólo hemos localizado una Resolución de la Dirección General de los Registros y del Notariado de 22 de junio de 2000 (*Repertorio Aranzadi de Jurisprudencia, RJ 2000/7342*) referente a la aplicación de los artículos 21 y 31 de la Ley 46/1998 de introducción del euro, que regulan la redenominación en euros de la cifra del capital social y de las acciones y participaciones sociales en empresas, así como las obligaciones de las profesiones oficiales (notarios, registradores dela propiedad, etc.) al respecto. Se trataba de la escritura de constitución de una sociedad de responsabilidad limitada, cuyo capital social era de 500.00 ptas., y en la que se aplicó correctamente el tipo de conversión para fijar en euros dicho capital, pero se cometió un error en la aplicación del tipo de conversión de pesetas a euros al fijar el valor de las participaciones sociales. La Dirección General entiende que la escritura es válida pese a este error, porque la expresión en euros del capital social es obligatoria durante el período transitorio, según el artículo 21 de la Ley 46/1998, y constituye motivo de suspensión de la inscripción de dicha escritura (apartado 2 del artículo 31 de la Ley 46/1998), pero no es motivo de suspensión la expresión en euros de del valor de las acciones o participaciones sociales, según el apartado 3 del este ultimo precepto.

1997,[418] por el Reglamento nº 1466/97,[419] basado en el apartado 5 del artículo 99, y por el Reglamento nº 1467/97,[420] fundado en el segundo párrafo del apartado 14 del artículo 104. Su objetivo básico es conseguir que los Estados miembros en la fase definitiva de la UEM estén obligados a mantener situaciones presupuestarias saneadas, próximas al equilibrio o con superávit, para alcanzar la estabilidad de precios y un crecimiento fuerte y sostenible que favorezca la creación de empleo.

Durante el año 2000, el Gobierno español ha elaborado un proyecto normativo de gran interés jurídico y que pretende asegurar el respeto del PEC por parte del Estado español. Se trata de dos proyectos de ley complementarios, el de la Ley General de Estabilidad Presupuestaria[421] y el de la Ley Orgánica complementaria a la Ley General de Estabilidad Presupuestaria,[422] que se encuentran en fase de tramitación parlamentaria. Con estos proyectos se pretende dar rango de ley interna al cumplimiento de las obligaciones presupuestarias resultantes para España de los artículos 98 a 104 TCE y del PEC, así como profundizar en el contenido de estas normas reforzando el deber de las administraciones públicas internas de gestionar sus presupuestos de forma equilibrada o con superávit.

Estas leyes de Estabilidad Presupuestaria, que se aplicarán a todas las administraciones públicas, revisten particular importancia en un Estado bastante descentralizado, como es el caso de España, porque corresponsabiliza a todas las administraciones con el objetivo de la estabilidad presupuestaria. Además, se trata de una propuesta legal que pretende romper con la tradicional cultura de condescendencia con los déficit públicos que ha imperado en la economía española hasta el proceso de convergencia seguido para la incorporación a la moneda única.

El Gobierno fundamenta la competencia del Estado para adoptar estas leyes de Estabilidad Presupuestaria en el artículo 149.1.13ª de la Constitución española, que confiere competencia exclusiva al Estado en materia de '*Bases y coordinación de la planificación general de la actividad*

418 Resolución del Consejo Europeo de 17 de junio de 1997, sobre el Pacto de Estabilidad y Crecimiento (*DO C* 236, de 2 Aug 97, 1).

419 Reglamento (CE) nº 1466/97 del Consejo, de 7 de julio de 1997, relativo al refuerzo de la su pervisión de las situaciones presupuestarias y la supervisión y coordinación de las políticas económicas (*DO L* 209, de 2 Aug 97, p. 1).

420 Reglamento (CE) nº 1467/97 del Consejo, de 7 de julio de 1997, relativo a la aceleración y clarificación del procedimiento de déficit excesivo (*DO L* 209, de 2 Aug 97, 6).

421 Su texto se presentó ante el Congreso de los Diputados el 2 de febrero de 2001 y se encuentra publicado en el *Boletín Oficial de las Cortes Generales. Congreso de los Diputados*, Serie A, nº 29–1, de 9 de febrero de 2001, 1. También está disponible en <http://www/cpmgresp/es/cgo-bom/iniciativas/publicaciones>.

422 Su texto se presentó ante el Congreso de los Diputados el 2 de febrero de 2001y se encuentra publicado en el *Boletín Oficial de las Cortes Generales. Congreso de los Diputados*, Serie A, nº 30–1, de 9 de febrero de 2001, 1. También està disponible en <http://www.congreso.es/cgi-bin/iniciativas/publicaciones>.

económica'.[423] El objetivo de estabilidad presupuestaria constituye un elemento básico de la política económica del Estado y su consecución debe imponerse a todas las administraciones para garantizar su cumplimiento. No obstante, las Comunidades Autónomas tienen reconocida autonomía financiera por el artículo 156 de la Constitución española[424] y puede plantear dudas de constitucionalidad la imposición del criterio de estabilidad presupuestaria a dichas entidades territoriales, porque se limitaría con ello su autonomía financiera. Esta circunstancia explica la presentación por parte del Gobierno de dos proyectos de ley diferentes, aunque complementarios, la ley ordinaria sobre estabilidad presupuestaria que se aplicará a la administración central, a la de la Seguridad Social y a la administración local, así como a los entes de ellas dependientes, y la ley orgánica, que se aplicará a las administraciones de las Comunidades Autónomas y organismos dependientes de ellas.

El artículo 2 del Proyecto de Ley General de Estabilidad Presupuestaria delimita las entidades públicas a las que se aplica, que son:

- La Administración General del Estado y organismos dependientes de ella.
- Las Entidades que integran el Sistema de la Seguridad Social
- La Administración de las Comunidades Autónomas y organismos de ellas dependientes.
- Las Entidades Locales y los entes públicos vinculados con ellas.
- Las entidades públicas empresariales, sociedades mercantiles y demás entes de Derecho Público dependientes de dichas administraciones que se financian con ingresos comerciales. En este caso, la estabilidad presupuestaria conlleva la necesidad de equilibrio financiero mediante la adopción de estrategias comerciales de saneamiento que eviten pérdidas y generen beneficios. Se trata, en definitiva, de que las empresas del sector público no generen pérdidas que obliguen a las administraciones a inyectarles fondos, con el consiguiente riesgo de endeudamiento para éstas.

En el caso de las administraciones estatal, autonómica y local el principio de estabilidad presupuestaria conlleva la situación de equilibrio o superávit computada en términos de capacidad de financiación, completándose dicho principio con los de plurianualidad, transparencia y eficiencia en la asignación y utilización de recursos públicos.

[423] Como fundamento constitucional adicional, se esgrimen los títulos competenciales exclusivos del Estado referentes a '*Sistema monetario: divisas, cambio y convertibilidad; bases de la ordenación del crédito, banco y seguros*' (Art 149.1.11ª de la Constitución) y a '*Hacienda general y Deuda del Estado*' (Art 149.1.14ª de la Constitución).

[424] En concreto, el apartado 1 del artículo 156 establece que '*Las Comunidades Autónomas gozarán de autonomía financiera para el desarrollo y ejecución de sus competencias con arreglo a los principios de coordinación con la Hacienda estatal y de solidaridad entre todos los españoles*'.

El Título II del Proyecto de Ley General de Estabilidad Presupuestaria establece las disposiciones comunes, que se aplicarán a todas las administraciones, con objeto de conseguir la mencionada estabilidad. En primer lugar, las administraciones deben adecuar su normativa presupuestaria para el logro de la estabilidad y deberán elaborar un plan económico-financiero de saneamiento a medio plazo en caso de incurrir en situaciones excepcionales de déficit presupuestario. En segundo lugar, las Cortes Generales aprobarán el objetivo de estabilidad presupuestaria referido a los tres ejercicios siguientes para el conjunto del sector público y para cada una de las administraciones, a propuesta del Consejo de Ministros, en la que se adjuntará el cuadro macroeconómico de horizonte plurianual contenido en el Programa de Estabilidad. Por último, se fija la corresponsabilidad de todas las administraciones por los incumplimientos de las normas de disciplina financiera y presupuestaria de obligado cumplimiento para España en el marco de la UEM, señalándose que cada administración asumirá en la parte que le sea imputable las responsabilidades derivadas de tales incumplimientos. Con ello, el Estado puede repercutir sobre las administraciones autonómica y local las consecuencias del incumplimiento de normas de derecho comunitario de los que él es el único responsable ante las instituciones comunitarias.

Establecidas estas disposiciones comunes, el Proyecto de Ley contiene normas específicas para cada uno de los tres niveles de la Administración Pública española, estatal, autonómico y local.

En lo que respecta al sector público estatal o administración central, los Presupuestos Generales del Estado deben respetar el límite máximo de gasto no financiero aprobado por las Cortes Generales y, si se incurre en déficit, el Gobierno debe remitir a las Cortes un plan económico-financiero de corrección del desequilibrio, con indicación de las medidas para volver al equilibrio presupuestario en un plazo máximo de tres años. Se contempla, también, la creación de un 'Fondo de contingencia de ejecución presupuestaria' en los Presupuestos Generales del Estado por importe del 2 por ciento del límite máximo de gasto no financiero, que servirá para hacer frente a las situaciones que requieran financiación no contemplada en el Presupuesto. Cuando la liquidación presupuestaria arroje un saldo deficitario, el Gobierno someterá a las Cortes un plan económico-financiero de corrección y, si el saldo es excedentario, el superávit de la Administración General del Estado se destinará a reducir su endeudamiento neto, es decir a saldar Deuda Pública, y el superávit del Sistema de Seguridad Social se destinará al 'Fondo de Reserva de la Seguridad Social', que se ha creado para atender las necesidades futuras del sistema.

En relación con la administración local, el Proyecto de Ley prevé la determinación del objetivo de estabilidad presupuestaria por parte de las Cortes a propuesta del Gobierno y previo informe de la Comisión Nacional de la Administración Local. Las Entidades Locales que incurran en déficit deben presentar un plan económico-financiero de saneamiento ante el Ministerio de Hacienda, que se encargará del seguimiento de su aplicación. Para obligar a las Entidades Locales a cumplir estos planes y asegurar su estabilidad presupuestaria, su capacidad de realizar operaciones de crédito y emisiones de deuda se supedita al respeto de este objetivo.

En lo que respecta a las Comunidades Autónomas, el Proyecto de Ley Orgánica complementaria a la Ley General de Estabilidad contiene las disposiciones específicas para asegurar el respeto del equilibrio presupuestario. El Proyecto pretende imponer sólo a las Comunidades Autónomas el objetivo de estabilidad presupuestaria, dejándoles libertad total para, dentro de este límite, determinar las vías de ingresos y gastos, con objeto de no atentar contra su autonomía financiera, consagrada por el artículo 156 de la Constitución. El Proyecto de Ley confiere un importante papel al Consejo de Política Fiscal y Financiera de las Comunidades Autónomas, que emitirá un informe previo sobre el acuerdo del Gobierno en el que se somete a las Cortes Generales el objetivo de estabilidad presupuestaria para el conjunto del Estado y que, una vez fijado dicho objetivo, determinará para cada Comunidad Autónoma un objetivo específico de estabilidad presupuestaria. Las Comunidades Autónomas que incurran en déficit o que liquiden su presupuesto con déficit, deben presentar a este mismo Consejo un plan de saneamiento económico-financiero a medio plazo para que verifique su conveniencia y, en su caso, lo apruebe. El mecanismo definitivo para que una Comunidad Autónoma se vea obligada a respetar el objetivo de estabilidad presupuestaria es la posibilidad del Estado de supeditar a su cumplimiento la concesión de autorización a las administraciones autonómicas para realizar operaciones de crédito y emisiones de deuda. Este régimen debe aplicarse a todas las Comunidades Autónomas, excepto a las que disponen de regímenes forales especiales de financiación, esto es, Navarra y el País Vasco, para las que se establecerá un procedimiento específico.

2.2 El canje de pesetas por euros

Mediante la Declaración común de 8 de noviembre de 1999 sobre la introducción de los billetes y monedas en euros, el Consejo ECOFIN propuso a los Estados la reducción del período máximo de seis meses de doble circulación de billetes y monedas denominados en unidades monetarias nacionales y en euros a un tiempo máximo de entre cuatro semanas y dos meses. Para tener en cuenta esta recomendación y establecer algunas precisiones adicionales sobre la logística de la introducción del euro, España ha adoptado en julio de 2000 el II Plan Nacional de Transición al Euro[425] y

[425] II Plan Nacional de Transición al Euro: el Canje de Pesetas por Euros, disponible en <http://www.euro.mineco.es/plan2/plan2.htm>.

ha introducido las modificaciones pertinentes en su Ley 46/1998, de 17 de diciembre, sobre la introducción del euro con objeto de plasmar jurídicamente los contenidos de dicho Plan. Esta modificación legislativa se ha realizado mediante la reforma de varios preceptos de la Ley 46/1998, previstos en el artículo 67 de la Ley 14/2000.[426]

En lo que respecta al II Plan Nacional de Transición al Euro, elaborado como el I Plan, por la Comisión Interministerial para la coordinación de las actividades dirigidas a la introducción del euro, sus objetivos principales son: garantizar la producción y distribución de los 7.800 millones de monedas y 1.924 millones de billetes denominados en euros, correspondientes a España; organizar de forma eficiente la retirada de billetes y monedas denominadas en pesetas; asegurar una rápida introducción de los billetes y monedas en euros para que la mayoría de las transacciones se desarrollen en euros desde el 15 de enero de 2002; y mejorar la información del público respecto a este proceso de sustitución. Para conseguir estos objetivos, el II Plan organiza las actividades a desarrollar en tres etapas:

(1) Etapa de predistribución: Esta etapa, que se extenderá desde el 1 de septiembre hasta el 31 de diciembre de 2001, comprende un conjunto de actuaciones orientadas a facilitar la existencia de una masa crítica de billetes y monedas en euros en la primera quincena del mes de enero del año 2002.

Los billetes y monedas en euros correspondientes a España, que están siendo fabricados por la Fábrica Nacional de Moneda y Timbre, comenzarán a ser predistribuidos de forma escalonada en los meses finales del año 2001, realizando un proceso de prealimentación fiduciaria en euros. Así, las empresas de seguridad y de transporte de fondos comenzarán, a partir del 1 de septiembre de 2001, el proceso de predistribución capilar de monedas y billetes en euros entre las entidades de crédito y de gran distribución comercial. A su vez, las entidades de crédito comenzarán a distribuir los billetes y monedas en euros a los pequeños comercios y al sector de hostelería a partir del 1 de diciembre de 2001. El gran público, por su parte, podrá adquirir durante la segunda quincena del mes de diciembre de 2001 paquetes de monedas, denominados *starter kits*, con 43 unidades monetarias en euros, por un valor unitario equivalente a 2.000 pesetas. Así, los ciudadanos podrán ir familiarizándose con las monedas en euros y se acelerará la sustitución de las pesetas por euros.

La adaptación del parque de máquinas expendedoras automáticas se va realizando ya, con objeto de permitir a sus fabricantes que dichas

[426] Ley 14/2000, de 28 de diciembre, de Medidas Fiscales, Administrativas y del Orden Social (*BOE* n° 313, de 30 Dec 2000, 46631. Esta es la ley de acompañamiento a la Ley de presupuestos para el año 2001.

máquinas puedan operar con monedas en euros desde el 1 de enero de 2002. También se han organizado medidas para facilitar el uso de monedas y billetes en euros entre poblaciones sensibles, como los invidentes.

El II Plan Nacional prevé, por último, en esta etapa la constitución de un Comité de seguimiento para reaccionar de forma rápida ante los posibles problemas que puedan plantearse con la predistribución de billetes y monedas en euros.

La Ley 14/2000 ha aportado cobertura jurídica a las decisiones del Estado en relación con esta etapa de predistribución, introduciendo un nuevo párrafo en el apartado 1 de la disposición final segunda de la Ley 46/19998, que permite al Gobierno 'dictar las normas que puedan ser necesarias para la distribución de cantidades limitadas de billetes y monedas en euros antes de 1 de enero de 2002, con el fin de facilitar la transición a la nueva moneda'. La predistribución de billetes y monedas denominados en euros antes de que se inicie su introducción fiduciaria el 1 de enero de 2002 genera diversos problemas jurídicos, que el Banco Central Europeo trata de resolver mediante la adopción de la Orientación BCE/2000/1,[427] cuya aplicación por parte de los bancos centrales nacionales es supletoria respecto de las disposiciones adoptadas por los Estados miembros. La principal dificultad jurídica de la predistribución anticipada es la cobertura de los riesgos crediticios y de daño, hurto y robo de las monedas y billetes predistribuidos. A este respecto, el artículo 68 de la Ley 14/2000 ha previsto que se aplicará el artículo 14 de la Ley 41/1999, de 12 de noviembre, sobre sistemas de pagos y de liquidación de valores a las garantías constituidas a favor del Banco de España para asegurar el cumplimiento de las obligaciones derivadas del proceso de distribución de billetes y monedas en euros con anterioridad al 1 de enero de 2002 o del ejercicio del resto de funciones. La constitución de estas garantías deberá constar por escrito y ser inscrita en el registro correspondiente, aunque no requerirá la intervención de fedatario público ni ningún otro requisito formal. Además, el artículo 68 de la Ley 14/2000 permite que se utilicen como garantías de la distribución anticipada de monedas y billetes en euros frente al Banco de España las que se vienen aplicando para asegurar el cumplimiento de obligaciones derivadas de la ejecución de las operaciones de política monetaria y crédito intradía.

(2) Etapa de doble circulación: Esta etapa se extenderá desde el 1 de enero hasta el 28 de febrero de 2002. La Ley 14/2000 ha modificado el apartado 2 del artículo 4 de la Ley 46/1998 en los términos siguientes:

[427] Orientación BCE/2000/1 del Banco Central Europeo, de 10 de enero de 2001, por la que se adoptan determinadas disposiciones sobre el cambio de moneda en el año 2002 (*DO L* 55, de 24 Feb 2001, 80).

los billetes y monedas denominados en pesetas continuarán siendo válidos como medio de pago de curso legal con pleno poder liberatorio, en cuanto subdivisión del euro al tipo de conversión, hasta el 28 de febrero de 2002. A partir de dicho momento, tales billetes y monedas perderán su curso legal y *sólo* conservarán un mero valor de canje en los términos previstos en esta Ley y sus disposiciones de desarrollo.

De esta forma, España se aviene a la recomendación del Consejo y reduce de los seis meses inicialmente previstos a dos meses el período de doble circulación de monedas y billetes en pesetas y euros.

Esta reducción del período de doble circulación va a ser posible por el esfuerzo de predistribución antes descrito y porque el artículo 24 de la Ley 46/1998 obliga a las entidades de crédito a realizar operaciones de cambio de pesetas por euros e impide el canje inverso, cambiar euros por pesetas. Además, el II Plan prevé que los cajeros automáticos de las entidades financieras distribuyan en su mayoría exclusivamente billetes en euros desde el 1 de enero de 2002 y que todos los hagan desde el 15 de enero. Por otra parte, se potenciará la devolución del cambio por parte de los comercios minoristas a sus clientes exclusivamente en euros desde el 1 de enero de 2002, mediante la difusión entre éstos de euroetiquetas y su adhesión a un Código de Buenas Prácticas, elaborado en la Comisión Especial Observatorio Consumo-Empresas, que aparece como anexo al II Plan. Se pretende, así, acelerar el proceso de cambio fiduciario de pesetas por euros y reducir las posibles molestias que para los operadores económicos puede suponer la convivencia física de dos tipos de unidades monetarias de curso legal.

(3) Etapa de retirada y canje: La retirada de los billetes y monedas denominados en pesetas y su canje por los correspondientes valores en euros se iniciará desde el 1 de enero de 2002, que es cuando estos últimos comienzan a circular. Los billetes y monedas en pesetas retornarán al Banco de España y a la Fábrica Nacional de Moneda y Timbre para su destrucción.

El plazo de canje de los billetes y monedas en pesetas en las entidades financieras se mantiene inalterado y concluye el 30 de junio de 2002, pese a que éstos pierden su poder liberatorio desde el 28 de febrero de ese año. A partir de esa fecha, estos billetes y monedas denominados en pesetas se podrán canjear por tiempo ilimitado en el Banco de España. En todo caso, el canje siempre será gratuito, tal como impone el artículo 24 de la Ley 46/1998.

2.3 Disposiciones Referentes al Banco de España

En lo que respecta al estatuto jurídico del Banco de España, su Consejo de Gobierno aprobó el 28 de marzo de 2000 el Reglamento Interno del Banco de España,[428] que viene a completar a la Ley 13/1994, de 1 de junio, de Autonomía del Banco de España.[429] El Reglamento Interno contiene algunas normas de desarrollo de la Ley de Autonomía cuyo contenido es relevante a los efectos de nuestro informe.

Los artículos 4 a 6 del Reglamento Interno contienen disposiciones referentes a la aplicación por parte del Banco de España de los actos jurídicos del Banco Central Europeo (BCE), que no se incluyeron en la Ley de autonomía. El artículo 4 establece la obligatoriedad para el Banco de España de los actos jurídicos vinculantes del Banco Central Europeo y encomienda al Secretario General la custodia y archivo de las notificaciones certificadas de dichos actos, pudiéndose fijar, además, mediante circular interna un sistema de tratamiento documental de estos actos vinculantes del BCE. El artículo 5 establece que las Orientaciones e Instrucciones del BCE son puestas en conocimiento del Gobernador, Subgobernador y demás órganos competentes del Banco de España por razón de la materia para que adopten o propongan las medidas necesarias para su debido cumplimiento.[430] Las Recomendaciones y Dictámenes del BCE se comunican sólo al Gobernador para que decida sobre la conveniencia de su aplicación por el Banco de España, según estipula el artículo 6 del Reglamento interno.

El Reglamento Interno aclara, también, el régimen de impugnación y de control jurisdiccional de los actos del Banco de España, que el artículo 2 de la Ley de Autonomía regulaba de forma concisa y sin precisar adecuadamente la actuación del Tribunal de Justicia de las Comunidades Europeas. En efecto, el artículo 15 del Reglamento Interno establece que los actos administrativos del Banco de España en el ámbito monetario, que éste adopta como miembro del Sistema Europeo de Bancos Centrales, sólo son susceptibles de recurso ante la Sala de lo Contencioso-Administrativo de la Audiencia Nacional. Por el contrario, los actos administrativos del Banco de España en ejercicio de competencias distintas de las monetarias que le atribuye el derecho interno español son impugnables en recurso de alzada ante el Ministro de Economía y las decisiones de éste ante la Sala de lo Contencioso-Administrativo de la Audiencia Nacional. Esta Sala es competente, también, para conocer de los recursos contra las decisiones de naturaleza normativa (circulares y circulares monetarias) del Banco de España.

[428] Resolución del Banco de España de 28 de marzo de 2001, por la que se aprueba el Reglamento de Régimen Interno del Banco de España (*BOE* n° 83, de 6 Apr 2001, 14323).

[429] El texto consolidado de esta Ley, con las reformas introducidas en ella por la Ley 66/1997 y por la Ley 12/1998, que está en vigor desde el 1 de enero de 1999, puede consultarse en <http://www.bde.es/infogene/be/legisla/leyauton.htm>. Sobre su contenido, nos remitimos al informe español presentado en el marco del proyecto Euro Spectator en 1999, publicado en *EUI Working Papers Law n° 2000/8*, 31–42.

[430] Sobre la ejecución indirecta de los actos del BCE, véase el reciente trabajo de Zilioli and Selmayr, 407–24.

El artículo 16 del Reglamento Interno alude a la competencia del Tribunal de Justicia, pero con una técnica jurídica bastante deficiente. En efecto, el apartado 1 de este precepto no hace más que reiterar la competencia del Tribunal de Justicia, en virtud del artículo 229 TCE, para conocer los recursos de anulación contra las decisiones del Banco Central Europeo que impongan sanciones, de conformidad con los procedimientos previstos en los Reglamentos (CE) nº 2532/98 y nº 2157/99. Es una reiteración completamente inútil y cuya inclusión en el Reglamento Interno del Banco de España no se justifica. El apartado 2 del artículo 16 contiene otra reiteración similar, cuando señala que 'los actos o las omisiones del BCE estarán sujetos a la revisión y a la interpretación del Tribunal de Justicia en los casos previstos en el Tratado y con arreglo a las condiciones establecidas en el mismo'. Sí resulta pertinente la inclusión en el artículo 16.2 del Reglamento Interno de la referencia a la competencia del Tribunal de Justicia para conocer de los recursos por incumplimiento por parte del Banco de España de las obligaciones resultantes de los Estatutos del SEBC y del BCE. Hubiera sido conveniente mencionar expresamente que la fase precontenciosa en la instrucción de estos recursos de incumplimiento la lleva a cabo el BCE, de conformidad con el apartado 6 del artículo 35 de dichos Estatutos, así como prever la actuación concreta del Banco de España y de sus órganos rectores en el marco de estos recursos de incumplimiento (órgano competente para responder al escrito de requerimiento y al dictamen motivado del BCE, defensa ante el Tribunal de Justicia, etc.).

Por último, el apartado 3 del artículo 16 del Reglamento Interno recoge la competencia del Tribunal de Justicia para conocer de los recursos contra la decisión de relevar de su mandato al Gobernador del Banco de España, en caso de violación del Tratado CE o de una norma relativa a su aplicación. La disposición, que retoma el recurso previsto en el apartado 2 del artículo 14 de los Estatutos del SEBC y del BCE, es también muy escueta y no se regulan las consecuencias de la interposición de estos recursos.

Bibliography

López Escudero, M and Monedero Fernández-Gala, JC (2000), 'Spanish Report', *EUI Working Papers Law nº 2000/8*, 31.

Linde Paniagua, E and Mellado Prado, P (ed), *La unión económica y monetaria: balance y perspectivas*, Madrid, Colex, 2000.

Liñán Nogueras, DJ (1999), 'El Banco Central Europeo', in A. Mangas Martín and D. J. Liñán Nogueras, *Instituciones y Derecho de la Unión Europea*, Madrid, McGraw-Hill, 121–35.

López Escudero M (2000), 'La UEM (II): coordinación de las políticas económicas nacionales. Proyección exterior de la UEM', in M López Escudero and J Martín y Pérez de Nanclares (ed), *Derecho Comunitario Material*, Madrid, McGraw-Hill, 2000, 399–408.

Zilioli, C. and Selmayr, M. (2000), 'The European Central Bank, its System and its Law', *Yearbook of European Law* 1999/2000, 347.

SWEDEN

*Eric Clapham**

1. Political and economic aspects

1.1 Public opinion

During the year 2000, both the Social Democratic Party and the blue-collar workers' trade union confederation—LO—decided to officially support Sweden joining the third stage of the EMU. As a result of those decisions, most important institutions in Swedish society are in favour of membership. This includes political parties representing almost 80 per cent of the electorate, most trade unions and all employers' confederations.

At the same time, the long-term trend towards increasing public support for EMU membership was broken during the year 2000. *Statistics Sweden* conducts biannual surveys of Swedes' attitudes towards EMU, and they showed a steady increase in support from 1997. However, the trend was broken with the May 2000 poll, and support continued to decrease throughout the year. Towards the end of the year there was some measure of stabilisation in the opinion polls, at a fairly low level of support for the EMU (see Table 1 and Graph 1; during early 2001 support has begun to increase somewhat again). At any rate, Swedish participation in the third stage of EMU now appears more distant than it did at the end of 1999.

Sweden ranks among the more EU-sceptic countries in Europe, and it is currently perhaps the most sceptical after the United Kingdom. According to Eurobarometer no 54 (Autumn 2000), only 34 per cent of Swedes think EU membership is a good thing, and a mere 25 per cent feel Sweden has benefited from EU membership on average. This is the lowest figure in the union. A majority of the population is against the euro in Sweden, Finland, Denmark and the United Kingdom. Only the United Kingdom's population is more critical than Sweden's.

However, Sweden—together with Greece, Italy, Spain and Denmark—belongs to the group of countries with most positive attitudes to enlargement. The majority of the Swedish population, thus, appears to sympathise with a loose but large union, rather than a small and well-integrated union. It has been claimed that Swedes feel that 'we want to leave the Union, and we want everybody else to join' (Economist, 2001). Nevertheless, Swedes do sympathise with the European spirit on some issues. A large majority of the population feels that Sweden should adopt

* Stockholm School of Economics, Handelschögskolans adress, PO Box 6501, S-11183, Stockholm.

the same quotas as the rest of the EU regarding private import of alcoholic beverages, rather than keeping its current restrictive regulation (see Table 6).

As regards a breakdown based on demographic variables: urban dwellers, the well educated, the young, and men, tend to be more positive towards the single currency, just as in other EU countries (Tables 2 and 3). However, the Swedish difference in the approval ratio between men and women is comparatively large, and has been above twenty percentage points in polls. Danish Aktuelt published an article on 13 March 2000 entitled 'The women decide on the euro', commenting on the fact that women in both Sweden and Denmark are especially sceptical towards the single currency (UD, 2001).

The development towards a more negative stance on the EMU in Sweden during the year 2000 could potentially be explained by several factors. First the development in Sweden broadly mirrored the development in the EU as a whole, as captured by Eurobarometer surveys. In early 1999 the euro received considerable attention and the public's impression of the new currency typically improved. The effect of the introduction then decreased; instead, the impression of the euro as a weak currency—due to the depreciation *vis-à-vis* the US dollar—became more important (see Graphs 3 and 4). Klas Eklund, the chief economist at the SEB bank, argues that the euro exchange drives Swedish EMU opinion, and that this is unfortunate because the changes in the rate do not affect the basic arguments for or against Swedish membership (Dagens Industri, 2 February 2001).

Secondly, the outcome of the Danish referendum is likely to have played some role in Sweden. On 28 September 2000, a majority of 53.1 per cent rejected Danish membership in the third stage. The participation rate of 87.4 per cent was quite high, revealing keen public interest in the issue. Those opposed to membership in Sweden typically pointed out that the outcome of the Danish election improved Sweden's possibilities of remaining outside; those in favour stressed the need for each country to follow its own course.

A third aspect is that the Swedish economy has performed comparatively well since the mid-1990s, after having gone through a severe recession during the early 1990s (see Graph 2). Swedish EU and EMU membership has often been promoted as a necessity. As an outsider, Sweden risks being left behind and encountering increasing economic difficulties. The development during the last few years has given the impression that Sweden is perfectly capable of surviving outside the Euro-zone. A comparatively strong Swedish economic performance need not always reduce support for the EMU, but it appears to have that effect at present. Mats Hallgren, argues 'Good economy strengthens No to EMU' (Svenska Dagbladet, 16 June 2000):

The Swedish economy performs wonderfully, even though the country is outside the EMU and the single currency, the euro. The Swedish economy grows faster than that of the Euro-zone, unemployment is lower, prices are more stable and the Swedish currency has strengthened against the euro. Sweden seems to do well without the euro. Then why join the EMU when we can remain outside? We might as well say no, then everything will remain the same. We can calmly remain seated where we are.

Thoughts such as these probably explain why EMU resistance has strengthened since spring.

Fourthly, there has been fairly limited public debate about EMU since the Social Democratic congress in March 2000, when that party decided on a positive stance towards the EMU. The Financial Times argued that the Commission's simultaneous decision not to allow the merger between Swedish lorry manufacturers Volvo and Saab might have undermined the momentum in Swedish opinion (UD, 2001, 22). Whether or not this is true, there are few incentives to engage in debate for the time being as a decision on Swedish participation on the third stage of the EMU has been postponed. In the above-mentioned article, Mats Hallgren continues:

During an extra congress in March party leader Göran Persson explained in a lively fashion why the Swedish welfare society was safer within the EMU than outside. But the public opinion is not controlled by one-off measures. If Social Democracy is serious about its yes to EMU (and one presumes that is so) it will require a long-term sustained economic and political pedagogic effort.

In an article in Svenska Dagbladet (2 October 2000), the opposition and party leader of the Moderate Party, Bo Lundgren, was not surprisingly critical:

When Göran Persson and the Social Democrats now have taken a position in favour of Swedish EMU membership and for a Swedish referendum on the issue, he must also realise that he has a great personal responsibility for public opinion. The Prime Minister should long ago have made clear how he views the process that would lead to Swedish membership. The government he leads must take initiative to establish an agenda. Citizens have the right to know in what direction the country is headed. The argument Göran Person uses to rid himself of the issue—to say that Sweden cannot join before we know that Swedish wage formation works—is an artefact of his own government.

It should be noted that arguing in favour of EMU has no political cost for Mr Lundgren, whose voters typically approve of EMU. Mr Persson, on the other hand, risks scaring EMU-sceptic voters away from his party by engaging in debate on the issue.

Aftonbladet, a newspaper politically affiliated with LO, had an editorial entitled 'Stop mumbling about the EMU' (30 September 2000):

Those in favour of EMU have been scared by Danish opinion and do not dare to take up the debate with those who claim the EMU leads to misery and eternal market liberalism. Apart from a few weeks during the spring when the Social Democratic congress decided to say yes to EMU, it has been noticeably silent among those on the yes side.

In an interview in *Dagens Nyheter* (22 November 2000), the chief economist at LO also expressed a wish for a more active government EMU policy. According to that newspaper,

> [t]he government's EMU-policy is much too passive. That is stressed by LO's new chief economist Dan Andersson . . . Dan Andersson thinks the government would gain greater respect if it pursued a more active policy: 'I believe the wait-and-see policy is fundamentally wrong.'

The government had earlier set up a committee to promote knowledge among the public about the EMU, which was lead by Georg Andersson, a former Social Democratic Minister of Immigration. The committee distributed 20 million krona among various organisations in 1999. However, according to one survey, the interest in participating in courses about the EMU at reduced cost was limited; groups with special needs—such as the physically or mentally challenged and those with little knowledge of Swedish—were particularly difficult to reach (Dagens Nyheter, 20 January 2000). During 2000, the committee was disbanded, but, after the Danish referendum, Prime Minister Göran Persson indicated that more money would be made available once a date has been set for the Swedish EMU referendum (Dagens Nyheter, 30 October 2000).

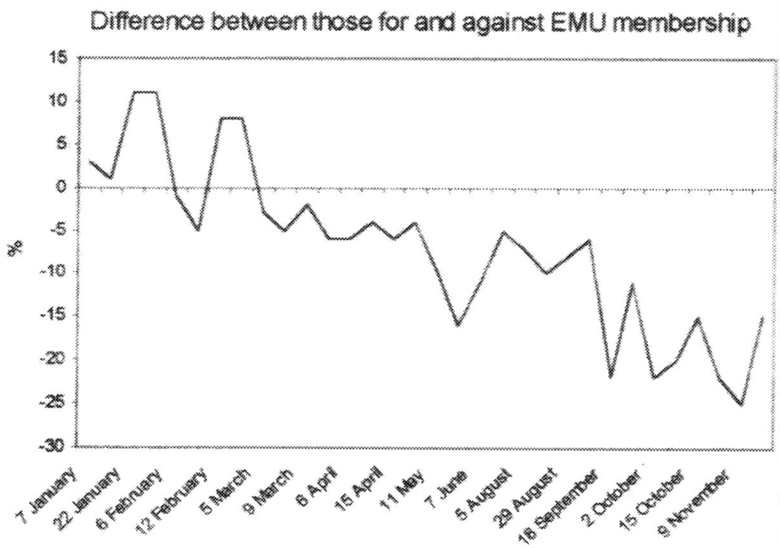

The above graph is based on Table 1.
Graph 1. Development of public opinion during the year 2000

Table 1. Swedish public opinion during the year 2000

Publicised polls by private organisations on Swedish EMU membership during the year 2000. Four private firms regularly conduct and publicise polls, namely Demoskop, Gallup, Sifo and Temo, and they are based on samples of about 1000 individuals. Questions asked are variants of 'Would you vote in favour or against Swedish EMYU membership in a referendum?'

Institute	Yes	No	Don't know	Publicised
Gallup	39	36	25	7 January
Demoskop	43	42	16	12 January
Gallup	44	33	23	22 January
Temo	42	31	27	25 January
Sifo	40	41	18	6 February
Demoskop	39	44	17	9 February
Gallup	42	34	23	12 February
Temo	40	32	28	26 February
Sifo	39	42	19	5 March
Demoskop	39	44	17	9 March
Gallup	35	37	28	9 March
Temo	35	41	24	28 March
Sifo	38	44	18	6 April
Gallup	36	40	24	10 April
Demoskop	40	46	14	15 April
Gallup	36	40	24	6 May
Demoskop	37	47	16	11 May
Sifo	33	49	18	4 June
Demoskop	39	50	11	7 June
Gallup	34	39	27	10 June
Demoskop	40	47	13	5 August
Sifo	36	46	18	20 August
Temo	37	45	18	29 August
Demoskop	42	48	10	8 September
Skop	37	59	4	18 September
Gallup	31	42	27	1 October
Demoskop	32	54	14	2 October
Sifo	32	52	16	7 October
Gallup	28	43	29	15 October
Temo	30	52	18	23 October
Demoskop	31	56	13	9 November
Demoskop	36	51	13	8 December

Source: The Temo website <www.temo.se/dok/proj/EMU/EMUsamtliga.htm>

Table 2. Long-term development of public opinion

The Statistics Sweden biannual poll is the most comprehensive in Sweden, comprising a sample of approximately 6500 individuals.

Would you vote in favour or against Swedish EMU membership in a referendum?

	Yes	No	Don't know	Gender gap
Nov 1997	22.9	48.5	28.6	12.8
May 1998	28.9	44.6	26.5	13.2
Nov 1998	34.4	36.6	29.0	15.3
May 1999	36.9	38.7	24.4	19.6
Nov 1999	38.5	34.8	26.7	17.1
May 2000	32.6	42.0	25.4	14.5
Nov 2000	27.8	47.2	25.0	13.4

Gender gap gives the difference between the fraction of men in favour of EMU membership and the same figure for women.

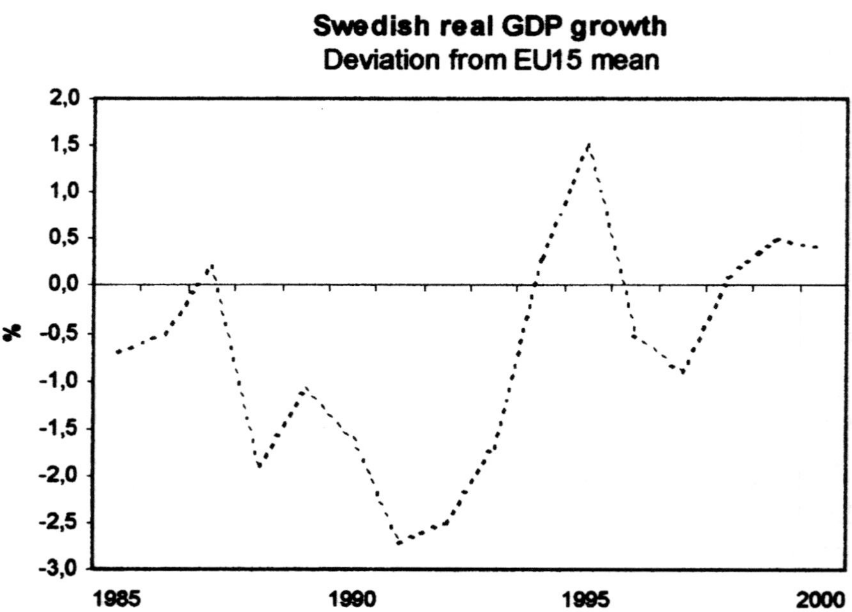

Graph 2. Economic development

Table 3. Statistics Sweden November 2000 poll

This is a breakdown of the same type of survey as in Table 2.

Would you vote in favour or against Swedish EMU membership in a referendum?

	Yes	No	Don't know
Age			
18–20 years	34.4	44.1	21.6
21–29 years	29.0	47.6	23.4
30–39 years	29.0	47.0	24.0
40–49 years	29.2	50.0	20.8
50–59 years	30.7	46.9	22.4
60 years	22.4	46.4	31.3
Region			
Rural	20.7	60.9	18.4
Urban	35.2	34.7	30.1
Political sympathies			
Centre Party	19.4	54.5	26.1
Christian Democrats	24.9	49.2	25.8
Greens	15.7	70.5	13.8
Left Party	10.9	74.2	14.9
Liberal Party	50.0	27.6	22.4
Moderates	51.8	26.4	21.8
Other Parties	17.1	60.0	22.9
Social Democrats	24.5	48.7	26.8
Don't know	22.9	47.4	29.7
Employer			
Public sector	25.4	50.0	24.6
Private sector	32.2	46.1	21.7
Private sector breakdown:			
Blue collar	25.3	53.4	21.3
White collar	39.7	38.2	22.2

Table 4. Public opinion about the Social Democratic congress

The Social Democratic party will hold a conference in March 2000 to decide on the EMU issue. Do you think the Social Democratic Congress will say that Sweden should join the EMU now or that Sweden should join later or do you think they will say no to Swedish membership?

	%
Yes	36
Yes later	52
No	3

Source: Poll conducted by Temo and publicised 23 November 1999.

Table 5. Public opinion about an EMU referendum

Do you think Swedish EMU membership should be determined by a referendum or do you not think so?

	%
Referendum	73
No referendum	23
Don't know	4

Source: Poll conducted by Demoskop during 28 February to 6 March 2000.

Table 6. Import of alcoholic beverages

Do you think Sweden should have the same rules for private import of alcoholic beverages as other EU countries (10 litres of spirits, 90 litres of wine and 110 litres of beer) or should we maintain the present Swedish regulation (1 litre of spirits, 5 litres of wine and 15 litres of beer)?

	All	Men	Women
European rules	64	73	55
Swedish rules	33	24	42
Don't know	3	3	3

Source: Poll conducted by Sifo on 14–17 February 2000.

Table 7. Election results

The most recent elections for the National parliament were held in 1998, and for the European Parliament in 1999.

	National 1998	European 1999
Centre party	5.1	6.0
Christian Democrats	11.8	7.6
Greens	4.5	9.5
Left Party	12.0	15.8
Liberal party	4.7	13.9
Moderates	22.9	20.7
Social Democrats	36.4	26.0
Other	2.6	0.5
Participation rate	81.4	38.8

1.2 Financial markets

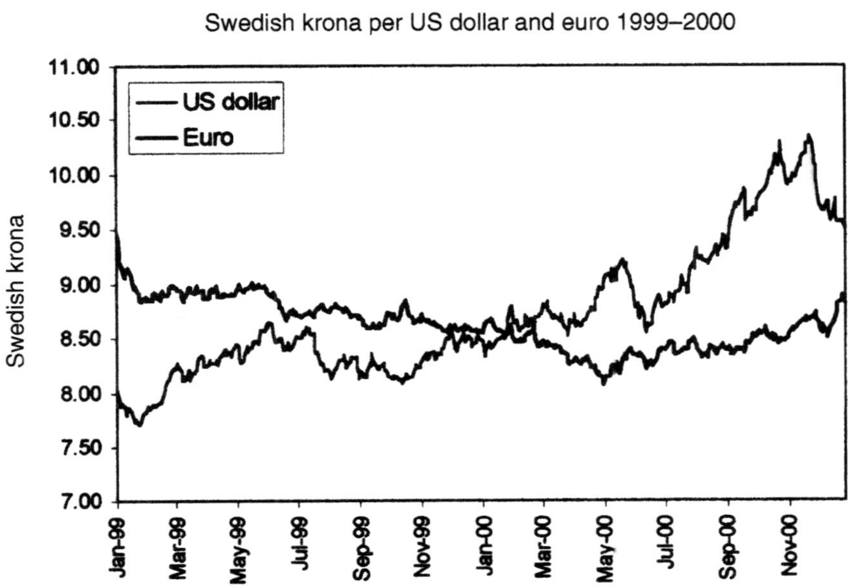

Graph 3. Exchange rates

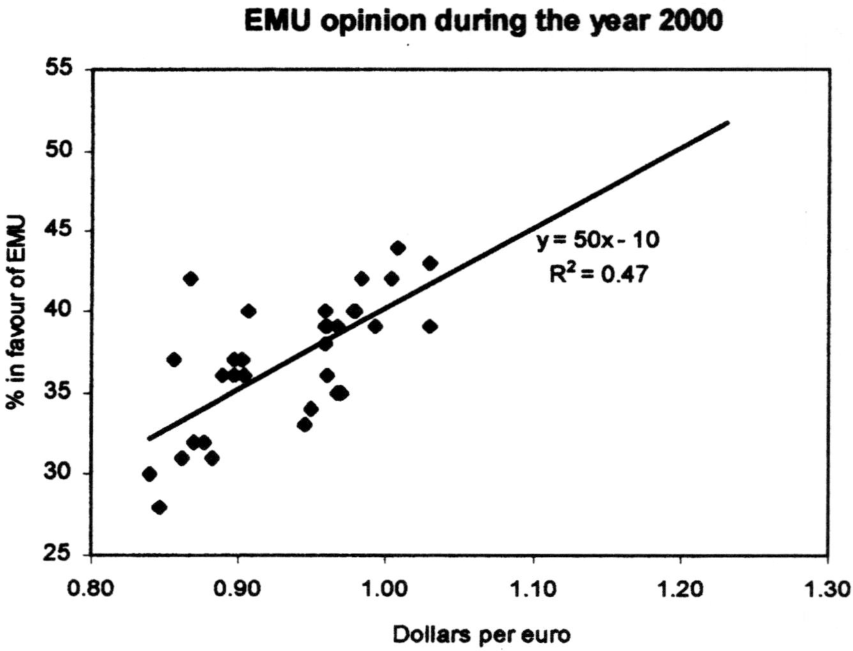

This scatter diagram relates the support for EMU membership in the polls listed in Table 1 to the exchange rate between the euro and the US dollar at the same time. Obviously the simple graph should be interpreted with extreme caution; nevertheless, it predicts that a majority of Swedes will support the euro if its exchange rate goes above 1.20 dollar per euro. Over the same time period there is no relationship between EMU support and the euro exchange rate *vis-à-vis* Swedish krona.

Graph 4. Opinion and exchange rate

1.2.1 Opinion about EMU membership

On the whole, Swedish economists have become more favourable to Swedish EMU membership over time. The daily financial newspaper *Finanstidningen* (4 January 2000) conducted a poll comprising all economics professors, and all chief economists at financial institutions in Sweden. Respondents were asked 'if it is in Sweden's economic interest to join the EMU'; 63 per cent answered 'yes', while 29 per cent answered 'no'. The newspaper concluded 'it is time to revise the commonly held view that economists strongly disagree on the EMU'. Those in favour argued that EMU would reduce transaction costs and improve access to the common market. Many also argued that EMU was primarily a political decision. In the words of one economist, 'EMU is questionable from the viewpoint of economics, but is nevertheless a part of the EU membership. It is ultimately in the economic interest of Sweden to strengthen its position within the EU.' One anti-membership economist said, 'Flexibility in the Swedish economy is still uncertain. Further, the viability of the EMU remains unproven.'

1.2.2 Openness and transparency of the ECB

Sweden adopted a floating exchange rate as a result of financial turmoil during the autumn of 1992. Thereafter, the Swedish Central Bank—the Swedish Riksbank—has developed a new strategy for monetary policy based on an explicit inflation target, regular official inflation reports and continuous dialogue with financial markets. Several economists participated in this process, not least Lars E.O. Svensson (Professor of Economics at the Institute for International Economic Studies at Stockholm University and, among others, a scientific adviser to the Swedish and New Zealand central banks). In an interview he says (Dagens Industri, 16 December 2000):[431]

> The Swedish Riksbank has since 1992 gradually developed into one of the world's most professional central banks, in the same division as the Federal Reserve and Bank of England. Had Sweden been a member of the EMU we would have been forced to have unnecessarily high interest rates.

He was also asked to give advice to Wim Duisenberg:

> First, express a more precise inflation target. Today it is at most 2 per cent. It would be better to say 1.5 per cent plus/minus a tolerance interval of 1 percentage unit. Secondly, tear down the 'First pillar', the money stock indicator. The two so-called pillars only cause confusion. Both theory and practice show that the money stock is no good indicator of future inflation. The only reasonable approach is to combine all information in the 'second pillar' and make a lucid inflation prognosis that is published and acted upon.

Johan Schück, commented on the need for openness in monetary policy (Dagens Nyheter, 19 August 2000):

> Some disagreement does not hurt. In the Riksbank leadership, the 'interest rate hawk' Eva Srejber makes a valuable contribution by stubbornly persisting with her own opinion, which is contrary to that of the other members of the executive board. She shows that there is more than one approach to monetary policy and that no interest rate decision is beyond questioning. [. . .] Things are different in the European Central Bank where a council of seventeen people makes interest rate decisions. [. . .] At their meetings there is no open vote and no discussion protocols are published. Hence the EMU countries lack the transparency that currently exists in Sweden and the UK.

Members of the politically appointed General Council of the Riksbank

431 Some of Professor Svensson's work can be found at his personal home page <http//www.iies.su.se/leosven>. A recent paper is Svensson (2000).

agree that improved openness is required in the EMU (debate article, Dagens Nyheter, 12 December 1999):

> The first thing that seems important is that accuracy and openness is improved. The underlying principals for how the central bank reasons and what the central bank considers important should be made available to the public. An openness of this type would be achieved (1) by publicising inflation reports and protocols from meetings with the ECB council and the ECB executive board and (2) by letting members of the executive board hold speeches for the EU parliament and the various national parliaments and (3) by letting the members take part in the debate on monetary policy also in other respects.

The former Social Democratic Minister of Finance Kjell-Olof Feldt wrote a column titled 'Swedish model should be brought to the EMU' (*Dagens Nyheter*, 21 January 2000):

> The Swedish Riksbank has shown that it is possible to combine political independence with a high degree of openness and continuous dialogue with the outside world. In fact the interested part of the Swedish people seem to know more about the Riksbank and have greater trust in its work than it had in the good old days when politicians ruled. That would be something to bring into the EMU once we are there.

1.2.3 ECB and monetary policy

In an analysis of the ECB interest raise, Mats Hallgren wrote in an article with the title 'The ECB fooled the market again' (*Svenska Dagbladet*, 10 June 2000):

> The European Central Bank has once again done what it says it wishes to avoid, namely take financial markets by surprise. That occurred at the meeting last Thursday with Wim Duisenberg as chairman. The market was fully convinced there would be a raise [. . .] of 0.25 percentage units. The raise was double that.

Minister of Trade, Leif Pagrotsky, is against Swedish EMU membership and has repeatedly been voted the most popular member of the government in polls. In an interview (*Dagens Nyheter*, 15 February 2000), he says that he believes in the new economy and comments on monetary policy in general, while admitting that he is primarily thinking about the ECB:

> A cowardly central bank does not dare take risks and raises interest rates too early in the business cycle. It pushes its one goal, to keep inflation down, too hard. That delays a necessary modernisation, where the new parts of the economy, for instance in the IT-area, must be given room to grow.

However, not everything about EMU is bad. In an analysis entitled 'Euro-problems are exaggerated', Johan Schück writes (*Dagens Nyheter*, 20 October 2000):

The euro is not the disaster that it is often claimed to be. Certainly the single currency is weak compared to the US dollar. But the EMU countries still have a low rate of inflation, apart from the effects of the high oil price . . . The weakness of the euro has put pressure also on Wim Duisenberg and no mistakes are tolerated. His statements in The Times this Monday were careless, since he talked about the sensitive issue of supportive currency purchases. However, what he actually said was perfectly reasonable.

Interventions in the currency markets received relatively limited attention in the Swedish media. The attitude was generally not negative, but the effectiveness of the approach was questioned. For instance, Lars E.O. Svensson felt that other measures would be more effective (Dagens Nyheter, 4 November 2000). According to him, 'it would matter more if the ECB decided, as the Swedish Riksbank, to regularly publish an inflation report. The exchange rate should not be a big issue'. Robert Bergqvist, chief analyst at the SEB bank, also commented on currency interventions (Finanstidningen, 16 November 2000):

Currency intervention is a weapon that becomes increasingly blunt the more often it is used. The market looses confidence in the central bank and the supportive purchases ultimately have the opposite effect . . . Fundamental factors like growth and economic policy must be in focus if the euro is to strengthen.

1.2.4 Convergence programme

EU member states that are not participating in the third stage of EMU present an annual convergence programme, while members present stability programmes. Sweden presented its first convergence programme in December 1998, a first update in November 1999, and the second update in November 2000. The year 2000 update is based on forecasts, estimates and proposals in the Budget Bill for 2001. The 10 November 2000 press release goes on as follows:

The convergence programme shows that Sweden's economy is on a very positive track. Employment is rising and unemployment is falling. At the same time inflationary pressure is moderate. GDP is expected to increase by 3,9 per cent in 2000 and 3.5 per cent in 2001. Net lending in the public sector is estimated at 3.4 per cent of GDP in 2000 and 3.5 per cent in 2001. Consolidated gross debt in the public sector, the so-called Maastricht debt, is expected to decline to 53.2 per cent of GDP in 2001.

1.3 Institutions

1.3.1 Political parties

Sweden has a parliamentary system with proportional elections every fourth September. Seven parties are currently represented in the parliament

(Riksdag), and the outcome of the last election (in 1998) is given in Table 7. The Social Democrats are in government with the support of the Green Party and the Left Party. The other four parties (Moderates, Liberal Party, Christian Democrats and Centre Party) make up an opposition whose degree of co-ordination varies.

Left-of-centre parties tend to be against EMU membership, and those right-of-centre in favour. While conservative Eurosceptics and pro-EMU people do exist on the left, they are uncommon. At the beginning of the year 2000, five of the seven parties had an official opinion: the Moderates and the Liberal Party are in favour of EMU membership, while the Centre Party, the Left Party and the Greens are against. The remaining two parties—the Social Democrats and the Christian Democrats—had party congresses during the 2000, where a favourable stance towards the EMU was agreed.

1.3.2 Social Democratic Party

The Social Democratic Party's executive committee (verkställande utskottet) decided on 7 January 2000 to favour Swedish EMU membership. Two main preconditions for membership were given, namely a Swedish business cycle reasonably aligned to that of the Euro-zone, and wage formation consistent with Swedish competitiveness. As discussed in last year's *Eurospectator* report, this was also accepted by the extraordinary party congress during 10–12 March, with 234 votes in favour and 113 votes against. However, party leadership was forced to accept the formulation that EMU membership is to be decided in a referendum rather than to be put to the people. The latter could mean that, in a general election, EMU would simply be one issue among others.

The 'yes later' approach of the Social Democratic congress was consistent with the expectations of most Swedes, according to a poll made by Temo during November 1999 (see Table 4). After the congress, Mats Hallgren made the following analysis (Svenska Dagbladet, 13 March 2000):

> Now the goal has been reached, Göran Persson said after the Social Democratic Party had said yes to EMU during the weekend. Now there is a clear majority in parliament for EMU membership . . . On paper the change may have been radical but reality has not changed much. Party leadership was forced to accept a promise about a referendum in order to get the congress to accept its proposal. Hence the EMU issue has changed from an if to a when, but uncertainty persists . . . When will there be a referendum? The Social Democrats have set up two preconditions . . . There really is a third precondition that should be fulfilled. Public opinion must be positive to the EMU and stable so that one can feel certain that the referendum will produce a 'yes'. A 'no' to EMU would have untold consequences for Sweden as EU-member. Göran Persson has said himself that a 'no' really is impos-

sible . . . In one way the weekend's decision means a change. The EMU issue can now be dismissed from the political agenda and Göran Persson can concentrate on winning the next election. Perhaps that was what Göran Persson really meant when he said, 'the goal has been reached.'

At the Unibank Seminar on 'Perspectives on European Integration' in Copenhagen, Lars Calmfors, a Labour economist who is professor at the Institute of International Economic Studies at Stockholm University, gave a speech with the title 'Sweden and the EMU' (Calmfors, 2000b). He said:

In the liturgy of the Swedish EMU debate, the Social Democrats have moved from the earlier position of 'No, not now' to 'Yes, but not now' or perhaps even 'Yes, but later' . . . The economic considerations will probably not play so large a role for a Swedish decision to join the EMU. It will mainly be a political decision. It seems as if the Social Democratic leadership has decided that Sweden should in a few years time join the EMU. I think they will go for it as soon as they believe that they can win the referendum that has been promised, and do this without splitting the party and losing votes to the Left Party [the former communists] and the Greens, who are both opposed to EMU membership.

The next Social Democratic Party congress is scheduled for November 2001 in the city of Västerås. During that congress a new party programme will be adopted, and the committee is currently preparing a draft (Social Democratic Party, 2000). The draft takes a clear stance in favour of EMU and it is generally tilted more towards what could be described as 'social liberalism' than 'traditional socialism'. The document is already the subject of considerable internal debate and has attracted criticism from traditionalists within the party. Regarding EMU, the draft says (p. 28):

Sweden should join the European Monetary Union. The issue of Swedish membership should be put to the Swedish voters.

The party's stance on the EU begins with the following statement in the draft:

Sweden should be an active member of EU and work to strengthen and develop co-operation within the union. We want to work to ensure that issues about ecological sustainability, employment and employees' rights, consumer protection, gender equality and the struggle against racism and xenophobia receive a central position in European co-operation.

At a meeting on 29 October 2000, the board of the Social Democratic youth organisation—SSU—also decided to favour EMU membership. The majority was the smallest possible—7–6 votes—and the decision is formally a recommendation to the organisation's August 2001 congress to support EMU membership. Mikael Damberg, chairperson of the youth organisation, explained why he would like Sweden to join EMU (Borås Tidning, 30 October 2000):

The most important reason is that we wish to create a democratic counterweight to the market, a greater European co-operation where we can resist currency speculation and thus secure welfare and jobs in Sweden.

1.3.3 Other parties

On 2 December 1999, the board of the Christian Democratic Party decided to recommend to its upcoming congress (riksting) to favour Swedish membership of EMU. The congress decided on 29 January 2000 to say 'yes' to EMU, with a majority of 209 votes in favour and 68 against. The meeting also decided to work for an EMU referendum during the year 2001. The party leader Alf Svensson said afterwards that 'No-one can deny that we have had a long careful debate'. The party spokesman on economic policy, Mats Odell, noted that 'There has been a positive debate and that is a result of the open debate climate we have had all along.' (KD, 2000)

The Centre party is the only party outside the left-of-centre part of the political spectrum that opposes EMU membership. One of its better-known anti-EMU members is Hans Lindkvist, and in a debate article he encourages the party to promote EMU resistance more actively (Östersundsposten, 13 November 2000):

The Centre Party must now build on the increasing EMU-resistance after Denmark's 'no' to the euro and actively work to stop all plans for Swedish EMU membership . . . It is time to start the debate now when the government and the Social Democrats do everything they can to cause confusion using new phoney investigations about buffer funds and renewed talk about even more educational measures to tell a stubborn public what it ought to think . . . My question is the following: Where are all those opposing EMU to go? Not everyone wishes to go for the Left Party and the Greens. The Centre Party must seek to prevent that. Here the Centre Party has its great opportunity if we actively pursue a campaign and inform about our arguments for a 'no'.

The Left Party is the third largest party and a strong opponent of EMU membership. The report 'EMU, welfare and gender equality' explains the basic facts of EMU in the section 'What is the EMU' (Left Party, January 2001, p. 7):

The economic and monetary union EMU is primarily an important part of the development towards a federal Unites States of Europe. The economic policy underpinning the EMU has a clear right wing profile. EMU's construction is based on the idea that elected politicians should not control the economy, but only set up simple rules. The market will do the rest . . . The overriding economic policy objective of the EMU is to fight inflation. [Why did low inflation become an important objective?] Essentially it is about changing the balance of power to the detriment of wage takers and democratic institutions and to the advantage of capitalists and employers.

1.3.4 Politics and the EMU referendum

The political system has effectively committed itself to a referendum on participation in the third stage of the EMU, although such a referendum can formally only be advisory under the Constitution. There is also great support among the Swedish public for settling the issue through a referendum. In a published poll, 73 per cent said they would like an EMU referendum (see Table 5). However, Olof Petersson, a professor of political science at Uppsala University, says that many political scientists oppose a referendum due to the experience of the 1994 referendum about EU membership and the tension it created between those in favour and those against (Finanstidningen, 22 January 2000).

Of course, Sweden is not a Member State with special status as regards the Maastricht Treaty. The government must therefore persuade an international audience that Sweden will eventually honour its obligation to join the Euro-zone. On the other hand, it must persuade the Swedish public that it will hold a referendum and honour its outcome. A few years ago, Ulf Bernitz, professor of European integration law at Stockholm University, wrote (debate article, Svenska Dagbladet, 20 June 1997):

> Especially worrying in my mind is that responsible politicians do not dare make it clear that Sweden is legally bound to enter the EMU. In Sweden a pseudo-debate is pursued, and it sets off from the faulty premise that Sweden is free to choose whether to be an EMU member or not in the long run.

Romano Prodi commented on the situation in an interview (Dagens Nyheter, 12 April 2000):

> In practice, Sweden has the same freedom of choice as Denmark and the United Kingdom to say 'no' to the EMU, although Sweden lacks this right formally. It is not a legal matter but a simply a matter of what the people decides.

At an earlier stage it was often said that the government had wanted to make a formal commitment to join the Euro-zone before Sweden assumed presidency of the EU on 1 January 2001. During late 1999 and early 2000, some believed a decision was soon to come. For instance, Olle Djerf, the chief economist at Merita Nordbanken, collaborated with three other economists to write (Djerf, 2000, 135):

> The most probable development is that the issue will be settled by a referendum well in advance of the next parliamentary election in 2002 . . . Given that the [Social Democratic] party leadership and the congress approves, a referendum already during the year 2000, say in September, is likely. If the referendum results in a 'yes' to EMU, Sweden can apply for EMU-membership and enter ERM2 during the autumn of 2000.

In an article with the title 'Better to wait with EMU' (Dagens Nyheter, 27 May 2000) Johan Schück wrote:

The public opinion is such that the 'yes'-side has every reason to delay a referendum since the risk of defeat is overwhelming. As things are now a referendum can be expected at the earliest in 2003 and membership around the year 2005. Further delays are possible.

In February 2001, Prime Minister Göran Persson confirmed that there would be no referendum before the next election. British Prime Minister Tony Blair has similarly declared that his country will hold a referendum no more than two years after the upcoming British election, expected to be held in May 2001. An article entitled 'Persson is waiting for a yes' contained the following analysis (Dagens Industri, 26 February 2001):

> The logic is as follows: Swedish voters do not want to join the EMU. But nor do they wish to see Sweden alone outside the currency union. If the British vote 'yes' to EMU the Swedish opinion can quickly turn in favour of a 'yes' . . . The main scenario is therefore that both the British and the Swedes will have a referendum sometime during early spring 2003. The British first and then the Swedes a few weeks later.

1.3.5 Ecofin Council and Euro-group

The Euro-group is becoming an increasingly influential forum, possibly at the expense of the Ecofin Council. Being outside the Euro-zone, Sweden is not a member of the Euro-group, and there has been some debate about whether this undermines Sweden's influence in the EU. Regarding the increasing importance of the Euro-group, the Minister of Finance Bosse Ringholm said (Finanstidningen, 18 July 2000):

> We have no problems with this. It is in everybody's interest that we are better organised.

Sweden was not represented in Euro-group during its EU presidency in the first half of 2001. Mr Ringholm felt this should not pose any problems (Finanstidningen, 2 March 2000):

> I had a conversation with German Minister of Finance Hans Eichel last week. We discussed the issue and agreed that there are no obstacles for Sweden to remain informed about what happens in the Euro-group . . . I think it is very exaggerated that Sweden cannot chair the Euro-group. It is of no importance under the circumstances.

1.3.6 Trade unions: LO

Sweden is the world's most unionised country. There are three major trade union confederations: SACO, for university graduates; TCO, for white-collar workers; and LO, for blue-collar workers. Both SACO and TCO have been in favour of EMU membership since before the year 2000.

The Social Democratic Party is the political arm of the workers' movement, while LO is the trade union arm. During 2000, LO also decided to favour EMU membership during its September congress labelled 'The Democracy Congress 2000'. The Metal Workers' Union presented a motion to the congress demanding an affirmative stance concerning the EMU. Another motion was made by the Transport Workers' Union, which demanded a referendum.

The LO executive council had to decide whether or not it recommended to the Congress to accept these motions. Its meeting of 4 April approved Swedish EMU membership, with 16 votes to 2. Each vote represents an affiliated trade union, and it was the Commercial Employees' Union and the Transport Workers' Union that opposed membership. According to the council, the preconditions for Swedish membership were a stable wage system and the implementation of 'buffer funds' to reduce the risks of cost and structural crises associated with a fixed exchange rate. Further, a referendum is to be held on EMU membership, but not before the general elections in September 2002. This implies that LO established more far-reaching preconditions for accepting the EMU than did the Social Democratic Party.

During March 2000, the LO team of economists presented their independent report 'A difficult choice—a booklet about the EMU' (LO Economists, 2000). This functioned as background material for the LO September 2000 congress, where an EMU decision would formally be made. Overall the economists felt that the advantages of membership dominate, primarily in terms of reduced transaction costs and increased Swedish influence in the EU. A main disadvantage is the assessment that the Euro-zone is not an optimal currency area, and the decision to join should therefore not be rushed. In the summary, the economists say (p. 7):

> Sweden should wait with the single currency until we are better able to judge the stability of our new wage formation and have made necessary improvements in our stabilisation policy [i.e. buffer funds]. When these conditions have been fulfilled it is natural that the Swedish people have an opportunity to speak their minds. If they say 'yes', we should abandon the krona and adopt the euro.

Many voices were raised against EMU membership during the September congress. After twenty delegates had presented critical speeches, the LO leadership had at the end (on 4 September) to withdraw the following formulation: 'LO shall at a referendum recommend its members to vote in favour of adopting the single currency, if wage formation has been proven to be sufficiently stable and buffer funds have been established'. Two days later a new formulation was presented: 'Given that wage formation has been proven to be sufficiently stable and buffer funds have been established, LO is positive to co-operation in the third stage of the single currency'. This was eventually accepted by 269 votes to 143.

1.4 Trends towards spillover

1.4.1 Stabilisation policy

On 30 October 2000, the government appointed a commission to consider the consequences of EMU membership for Swedish stabilisation policy. The commission, in particular, is to analyse fiscal policy, and the need for new instruments and institutional reform to promote the implementation of efficient stabilisation policies. The experiences of current EMU members are to be studied and discussed.

Bengt KÅ Johansson heads the commission (among others, he was Social Democratic minister responsible for wage policy during much of the 1980s). Another member is Lars Calmfors, who headed an earlier and more extensive commission on Swedish EMU membership in 1995 and 1996 (SOU, 1996). A preliminary report is to be presented no later than 30 June 2001, and a final report is due before 31 December 2001.

One of the commission's main tasks is to consider the concept of 'buffer funds' and other means of improving real wage flexibility. Buffer funds were invented by the Finnish trade union movement, and the idea is to create a mechanism that can substitute for a depreciating currency during recessions. Corporations pay excess taxes or fees during good years. These are accumulated in funds that are then used to finance primarily reduced wage costs in some form, thus improving competitiveness even though the exchange rate is fixed. This will be useful during asymmetric shocks (that is, shocks to economic activity that affect only some parts of the Euro-zone and that cannot, therefore, be combated with one common monetary policy). Buffer funds are now being implemented on a modest scale in Finland and will eventually amount to 2–3 per cent of annual labour costs. They have been agreed upon by trade unions and employers' confederations, which administer them jointly. The funds will be used to finance a portion of unemployment insurance and pensions during recessions. LO has argued that the scheme is also suitable for Sweden. During the LO congress in 2000, the implementation of buffer funds was specified as a necessary condition for Swedish EMU membership (as mentioned above). However, the Swedish employers' confederation has shown limited interest in the idea. Thus, buffer funds will probably have to be implemented by legislative means in Sweden, rather than through a voluntary agreement between trade unions and employers as in Finland.

The new commission had a mixed reception. Östersundsposten, a newspaper opposing Swedish EMU membership, ran an editorial on 31 October entitled 'Bluff with buffer funds', where it was argued that 'the buffer bonds are primarily a way of making EMU more acceptable to trade union people'. Stefan Carlén, a trade union economist at the Commercial Employees' Union, claims the buffer funds were used to trick the Finnish trade unionists to accept EMU. The Metalworkers' trade union has been one of the major proponents of buffer funds. Göran Johansson, its leader, indicated that the buffer funds are necessary, if Swedes are to accept EMU: 'They must know that during a crisis companies can lower their wage costs without threatening job security' (Dagens Nyheter, 3 March 2000). Employers' confederation SAF claimed that it is LO—and not wage formation—that is the problem that needs to be fixed (SAF, 2000).

Lars Calmfors published an article in Ekonomisk *Debatt*, the journal of the Swedish Economics Society, entitled 'EMU and unemployment' (Calmfors, 2000a), where he also discusses buffer funds. He differentiates between the effects of EMU on equilibrium unemployment and fluctuations over the business cycle. As regards the equilibrium level, he finds no clear pattern (p. 130):

> A number of mechanisms can be identified through which an EMU membership may affect equilibrium unemployment. The effects however tend in different directions and based on current research it is not possible to draw any conclusions about the net effect. Definite statements about the EMU creating or destroying jobs do not have any place in a serious discussion.

He is less uncertain when it comes to variation over the business cycle (p. 131):

> In my mind an EMU membership does imply worsening conditions for stabilisation policy, even if you take plausible adjustment mechanisms in the labour market into account.

Professor Calmfors discusses three possible institutional arrangements to limit the impact of EMU: buffer funds, profit sharing schemes, and wage indexing. He finds that buffer funds and wage indexing could potentially be helpful. Profit sharing schemes are found to increase equilibrium employment, but not employment variability. He also discusses the option of the government reducing employers' fees during a recession, which could be financed by running down net assets or by raising other taxes. He refers to the measure as an internal devaluation in the latter case. The conclusion is:

> Although it may be difficult in practice to carry out large reductions in government employers' fees, it is difficult to see any alternatives if a big cost adjustment must be achieved during a structural crisis. My opinion is that it is then the best instrument at hands.

1.4.2 Prices level and EMU membership

In late November 2000, the Swedish Board of Trade, the Swedish Competition Authority and the Swedish National Board for Industrial and

Technical Development jointly published the report 'Sweden—a part of the single market. Why do differences in prices remain' (NUTEK, 2000).[432] It points out that (1):

> As to Swedish consumers, membership of the Single Market should result in lower prices. For every percentage point that prices are forced down, household budgets stand to gain considerably.

In 1998, prices for important consumer items such as pasta and rice, non-alcoholic beverages, chemo-technical household products and toiletries were, on average, 30–40 per cent higher in Sweden than in the EU. Detergents were 90 per cent more expensive in Sweden. Nevertheless, the gap between Sweden and the EU average has consistently narrowed since Sweden became a member in 1995. The report concludes, 'participation in the EMU and the introduction of a single currency would hasten this development' (6).

Johan Schück wrote an article (Dagens Nyheter, 10 June 2000) with a similar message:

> Sweden is capable of keeping lower interest rates, in spite of higher growth, than the EMU Member States . . . On the other hand there may be long term gains from membership associated with increased competition on previously fairly protected national markets. In the end that could lead to lower prices, for instance for services from banks and insurance companies.

1.4.3 Practical preparations

In August 1999, the government assigned twelve public authorities to undertake an analysis of the consequences of possible introduction of the euro. In this connection, the Swedish Agency for Administrative Development (Statskontoret) was assigned to head a co-operation group for the twelve authorities covered by the government's assignment. The group was to support individual authorities in conducting their analyses. The emphasis and focus were to be on common issues for the authorities concerned, and on the interfaces between the authorities.

The analysis was completed in March 2000 and presented in a report (Statskontoret, 2000). It considers four different time scenarios:

- Advanced preparation period: 12–15 months, transitional period: 1 year.
- Advanced preparation period: 12–15 months, transitional period: 2 years.
- Advanced preparation period: 3–5 months, transitional period: 2 years.

[432] The Swedish National Board for Industrial and Technical Development (NUTEK) has been split into three different agencies and this particular investigation now falls under the domain of the Institute for Growth Studies.

- Advanced preparation period: 24–27 months, transitional period: 0 years ('Big bang').

'Advanced preparation period' refers to the period from the date of the decision to join until the date Sweden actually joins and fixes the exchange rate. The transitional period then begins and continues until only the single currency is in circulation. The first scenario is the most plausible.

The report concludes that there is a need for continued monitoring of the development in the Euro-zone, and also a need to increase knowledge about the EMU in the central government administration. The report also suggests a range of standards concerning the level of public service, information, rounding, historical data and computer interfaces.

1.4.4 Taxes

Sweden has been the OECD country with the highest overall tax level since the 1960s. The Swedish tax level currently stands at just over 52 per cent of GDP, while the OECD average is 37 per cent. There is an on-going debate as to whether globalisation, as well as EU and EMU membership, will force Sweden to make adjustments.

The Left Party (2001, p.12) says that the European Commission feels that the Swedish tax pressure 'is too high and that further measures should be taken to limit public sector expenditure. That is a very clear indication of what awaits us as EMU members'. The Chamber of Commerce newspaper had an article with the title 'Sweden will adjust to European tax rates irrespective of EMU membership' in which Claes Nordmark, a tax expert at KPMG, was interviewed (6 October 2000). The current adjustment of corporate and capital taxes will eventually be followed by other examples, and Claes Nordmark thinks that Swedish taxes will be adjusted downwards. This is still to happen on a large scale.

2. Legal framework

2.1 Background

Prime Minister Ingvar Carlsson presented Sweden's application for EU membership on 1 July 1991. At the opening of the negotiations between Sweden and the EU on 1 February 1993, the then EU minister, Ulf Dinkelspiel, made the following statement:

> A final Swedish position relating to the transition from the second stage to the third stage will be taken in the light of further developments and in accordance with the provisions in the Treaty.

The statement was repeated on 9 November 1993 and recorded in the minutes of the meeting. In the Government Bill 1997/98:25 on Sweden and the Economic and Monetary Union it is noted that (pp. 4–5):

Sweden's negotiating position on EMU was the subject of consultations between the then Government and Opposition. It was judged to be more appropriate to make a unilateral declaration than to try to get the same formal opt-out that Denmark and the United Kingdom have . . . The question of Sweden's membership in the EU was the subject of a referendum on November 13, 1994. One of the preconditions for the referendum was that membership in the EU would not automatically lead to participation in the monetary union, and that a separate decision on EMU would be taken by the Riksdag.

Sweden joined the Union on 1 January 1995, following a referendum on 13 November 1994 in which 53 per cent voted in favour of membership. On 19 October 1995, the government appointed a commission to consider the consequences of Swedish participation in the third stage of EMU. The commission, led by Professor Lars Calmfors, presented its conclusions in October 1996 (SOU, 1996): the Swedish economy should not join the third stage in 1999, but should wait until its economy had improved. Flexibility-enhancing reform was deemed necessary, especially with regard to the labour market.

In the Government Bill 1997/98:25, accepted by parliament on 4 December 1997, the government proposed that Sweden should not join the third stage in 1999, but should remain prepared to do so at a later date. The main argument for this policy was the lack of public support for the euro, as documented by public polls and other indicators.

Sweden currently participates in the second stage of EMU. After Greece joined on 1 January 2001, Sweden is one of three EU member states that are not participating in the third stage (the others being Denmark and the UK). Unlike Denmark, neither Sweden nor the UK is a member of ERM2. The Swedish currency has had a floating exchange rate since the financial turmoil of autumn 1992. The Swedish currency had been unilaterally tied to the ECU until 1991 when it replaced a currency basket arrangement that had been in operation in various forms since 1977.

2.2 Swedish legal convergence

According to the Maastricht Treaty, a convergence report is to be prepared biannually. The 1998 report from the EMI (European Monetary Institute) considered all 15 EU Member States. The 2000 report from the ECB covers only Greece and Sweden, which were the two remaining states without a special status still outside the Euro-zone.

In the ECB's convergence report 2000, Sweden is deemed to meet the Maastricht convergence criteria in terms of budget deficit, government debt, long-term interest rates and price stability. Further, the report note that Swedish legislation has 'been adapted to meet the requirements of the Treaty and the ESCB-ECB Statute for the independence of Sveriges Riksbank' (71, s 5.2.1). These changes are a result of Government Bill

1997/98:40 and were already pending at the time of the previous convergence report in 1998. They have been in force since 1 January 1999 (see also the previous *Eurospectator* report).

However, as Sweden remains outside ERM2 it does not meet the requirement of a stable exchange rate. Further, legal convergence remains to be completed, especially concerning the status of the central bank and the ECB. The convergence report notes (section 5.2.4, p.73):

> Swedish legislation, and in particular the Statute of Sveriges Riksbank, does not anticipate the Bank's legal integration into the ESCB, although Sweden is not a Member State with a special status and must, therefore, comply with all adaptation requirements under Article 109 of the Treaty.

Robert Sparve, who is the department head of the secretariat of the central bank board, in an article of his comments on the convergence report (Dagens Nyheter, 4 May 2000):

> The demands from the ECB have been presented before and Sweden will surely fulfil them, if it decides to enter the EMU. The EMU countries would like Sweden to join and are hardly prepared to go beyond making statements . . . Nobody wants to push this to its limits by setting up time limits or—as a final measure—by taking Sweden to court.

The failure of legal convergence is due to the current form of the Riksbank Act and of the Constitution Act (Regeringsformen). The Constitution Act (Chapter 9, paragraphs 11 to 13) states that the government has overall responsibility for issues concerning the national currency, that the Swedish Riksbank is responsible for monetary policy, and that only the Riksbank may issue notes and coins. Legislation concerning access to public documents needs to be further considered in relation to the confidentiality requirements under Article 38 of the ESCB–ECB Statute.

Lack of legal convergence is particularly serious with respect to the provisions of the Constitution Act, which can only be amended by two majority decisions in parliament, with a general election in between. Sweden and Finland are the only EU countries in which the central bank is an authority directly under the control of parliament, and that is why the division of power between the central bank and parliament is stipulated directly into the Constitution. Finland can alter its Constitution directly by a qualified majority in parliament, but that is not possible in Sweden. The next Swedish general elections take place in September 2002 and 2006. So, if the first decision to alter the Constitution is not made before the September 2002 election, legal convergence cannot be completed until 2007.

Robert Sparve has argued (Dagens Nyheter, 22 July 2000) that the political system should make the first decision to adjust the Constitution as soon as possible after the upcoming election, in order to retain the possibility of completing legal convergence in 2003. This has been criticised as being democratically unacceptable, as it would make a mockery out of a future referendum on EMU membership. Sparve argues that the first decision is not final and it only preserves the opportunity to complete legal convergence by 2003. If the result in the referendum were to be negative, the second decision to alter the Constitution could simply be cancelled or postponed. Sparve also pointed out that the 1997 decision by parliament not to join the third stage in 1999 included a clause that Sweden should remain prepared to join at a later stage. That, according to Sparve, calls for the passing of the necessary constitutional changes as soon as possible, so as to keep alive the possibility of joining in 2003.

A counter-argument has been that EU legislation always takes precedence over national legislation. That is correct, but the Maastricht Treaty specifically says that national legislation must be changed. A further counter-argument is that Sweden would probably be accepted as an EMU member even if the constitutional change was only pending (that is, if it had passed through parliament once and was likely to do so again later). Sparve argues this need not occur:

> I am not so sure other Member States will accept this. The EU has a gigantic task of integrating almost as many new Member States as currently make up the Union. Many new Member States will encounter convergence difficulties not least in the legal area. It is close at hands for the EMU countries to say that if Sweden does not fully apply the legal convergence requirement, how can we uphold a strict policy towards other future Member States, which also wish to become members of the EMU? And what happens if Sweden for some reason does not complete the constitutional change? Only one decision does not have any legal consequence beyond having reached halfway. If parliament does not consider the question a second time—for instance, after the government has repealed the bill, or parliament rejects it—then what? Should Sweden leave the EMU and reintroduce the krona? I think the government will find it difficult to persuade its EU colleagues to accept 'half decisions'.

Finally, Sparve calls on politicians to take action:

> Grab the bull by its horns and explain to voters why constitutional issues come up even before the people have had a chance to make their voices heard in a referendum!

2.3 Accounting in euro

As a result of the passing through parliament of Government Bill 1999/2000:23, it is now possible for limited liability companies to register shareholders' capital and to keep accounts in euro. The law entered into force on 1 March 2000, as discussed in last year's *Eurospectator* report. The government is currently considering extending the right to keep accounts in euro to any foreign currency.

Bibliography

1. Articles and Books

Calmfors, Lars (2000a), 'EMU och arbetslösheten [EMU and unemployment, article in Swedish with English summary]', Ekonomisk debatt, 28.2, 117–32.

Calmfors, Lars (2000b), Sweden and the EMU—Perspectives and Policy Challenges, speech to the Unibank Seminar on 'Perspectives on European Integration', Copenhagen, May 11, 2000, available at <http://www.iies.su.se/~lcalmfor/Kopenhamn.pdf>.

Djerf, Olle et al (2000), 'EMU medlemskapets betydelse för svensk lönebildning [The consequences of the EMU membership for Swedish wage formation, article in Swedish with English summary]', Ekonomisk debatt, 28.2, 117–32.

ECB (2000), Convergence report 2000, May 2000.

Economist (2001), Goran Persson, a Swede leading Europe, 10 February 2001.

European Commission (2000), Eurobarometer, no 53–4.

KD (2000), Rikstinget sa ja till EMU [The congress said yes to EMU], press release from the Christian Democratic Party, 29 January 2000

Left Party (2001), välfärd och jämställdhet [EMU, welfare and gender equality], January 2001.

LO Economists (2000), Ett svårt val—en skrift om EMU [A difficult choice—a booklet about the EMU], available in Swedish only at <http://www.lo.se/pdf/EMU.pdf>.

NUTEK (2000), Sweden—a part of the single market: Why does [sic] the differences in prices remain?, publication classification NUTEK Info 051–2000, available at <http://www.itps.nu/pdf/inrem.pdf>.

SAF (2000), LO är ett större hinder mot EMU än lönebildningen [LO is a greater obstacle to EMU than wage formation], press release from the Swedish Employers' confederation, 5 May 2000.

Social Democratic Party (2000), Draft party programme, available in Swedish only at <http://www.sap.se>.

SOU (1996), Report by the EMU investigation (The Calmfors report), Government public investigations SOU 1996:158.

Statskontoret (2000), Swedish public authorities and the euro—common issues, report by the Swedish agency for administrative development, available in English at <http://www.statskontoret.se/pdf/200008A.pdf>.

Svensson, Lars E.O (2000), What is Wrong with the Eurosystem's Money-Growth Indicator, and What Should the Eurosystem Do about It?, Briefing Paper for the Committee on Economic and Monetary Affairs (ECON) of the European Parliament for the Dialogue with ECB, available at <http://www.iies.su.se/leosven/papers/ep011.pdf>.

UD (2001), Sverigebilden—Sverige i utländsk press år 2000 [Sweden in foreign media during the year 2000], 3 January 2001.

2. Government bills

Government Bill 1997/98:25, Sweden and Economic and Monetary Union (available in English at <http//www.regeringen.se/euro/english>).

Government Bill 1997/98:40, Riksbankens ställning [The position of the Riksbank].

Government Bill 1999/2000:23, Redovisning och aktiekapital i Euro [Accounting and shareholders' capital in Euro].

3. Daily newspapers

Various editions of the following daily newspapers have been referred to in the text: *Aftonbladet, Borås Tidningar, Dagens Industri, Dagens Nyheter, Finanstidnigen, Svenska Dagbladet and Östersundsposten.*

4. Opinion polls

Data from opinion polls conducted by Demoskop, Gallup, Sifo and Temo.

5. Web sites

<http://www.regeringen.se/euro/english>: Government site with information about the euro. Contains relevant government press releases, government bills and more. The Swedish version is somewhat more extensive (at <http://www.regeringen.se/euro>).

<http://www.riksdagen.se/english/eu>: The parliament web site on the EU. Some general information but of less interest than the government site above. Swedish version at <http//www.riksdagen.se/eu>.

<http://www.rsv.se/english>: The National Tax Board has investigated the consequences of EMU membership for Swedish tax administration. Swedish version at <http://www.rsv.se/skatter/euro>.

<www.statskontoret.se/euro>: Swedish agency for administrative development (Statskontoret) is responsible for administrative development related to the euro in the public sector. Their website contains a few reports in English, but is otherwise in Swedish.

UNITED KINGDOM

Alexis Krachai, Hosein Jahanshahi, Lazaros Panourgias, and Mads Andenas

1. Political and economic aspects

Alexis Krachai* and Hosein Jahansashi**

1.1 Public opinion

1.1.1 Summary

Opposition to the euro has risen since 1999 and now fluctuates at around 60–65 per cent. This is a consequence of a significant increase in opposition recorded between September and December that reversed the 6 per cent rise in support recorded between January and August. The effect that a governmental campaign would have on the balance of voting continues to be seen as an important issue. But, as a result of the government failing to begin such a campaign, any influence it might have in a future debate could be declining. The public increasingly feels that membership of the single currency is not as inevitable as it was in 1999, and more people now (up to 6 per cent) feel that Britain will never join the single currency.

1.1.2 General attitude towards the euro

Britain's proposed membership of the single currency continues to be the underlying theme in the majority of political and economic debate and, as in 1999, public opinion remains heavily opposed to membership. Monthly opinion polls conducted by ICM Research asked respondents:

> If there was a referendum, would you vote to join the single European currency or vote not to join?[433]

When averaged for the year, results showed that 24.5 per cent of the public was in favour of joining, 62.4 per cent was opposed, and 12.9 per cent was undecided. When compared to the results obtained in 1999, this represents a 4.6 per cent decline in support for joining, an increase in opposition of 5.7 per cent and a 1.2 per cent increase in undecided opinions.

* Research Officer, Federal Trust for Education and Research, Dean Bradley House, 52 Horseferry Road, London: SW1P 2AF.

** Research Assistant, Federal Trust for Education and Research, Dean Bradley House, 52 Horseferry Road, London: SW1P 2AF.

433 <http://www.icmresearch.co.uk>.

Although indicative of the continued opposition towards the euro, this increase from 1999 was a product of the marked increase in opposition recorded in the last four months of the year when support declined by 13 per cent and opposition grew by 14 per cent. Prior to this—in the period from January to August—ICM opinion polls saw support for the euro rise from 25 per cent to 31 per cent, while opposition fell from 63 per cent to 57 per cent. It was thus polls in the last third of 2000 that produced an increase in annual averages of opposition levels towards the euro from 1999. These annual averages mask the significant 6 per cent rise in support for the euro that was recorded between January and August. This raises an important question: what caused the negative shift in public opinion between September and December? Although results indicate that public opinion remains hostile to the euro, pro-Europeans claim that this is because the government has yet to begin campaigning in favour of EMU. They argue that public opposition towards the euro will decline, and support for joining will increase, once this campaign is underway. This claim is supported in part by MORI[434] polls that asked:

> If the government were to strongly urge that Britain should be part of a single currency, how would you vote?

The averaged results of this poll show that—faced with government support—the percentage difference (balance) between those in favour of membership and those against would be 22.5 per cent against joining. This figure is significantly smaller than the 30.5 per cent margin recorded for the 'basic' euro question on voting intentions. According to polls, if the government were to actively promote membership of the single currency, the gap between those in favour and those against membership would fall by 8 per cent. This is commonly described as the 'halo effect' and has enthused pro-Europeans that believe that the high levels of opposition exist because the government is yet to actively promote membership. It is claimed, public opinion will swing once a campaign begins, and a referendum could be won in favour of membership. Further practical evidence in support of this claim was recently broadcast on the television programme *Panorama*. The purpose of this broadcast was to follow the course of a 'sample' referendum campaign in a single street. At the start, the majority of opinion was against the euro. Following a week of campaigning, residents voted in favour of joining the single currency. This programme concluded that the public could have their opinion and views changed, if faced with simple economic arguments that set out the case in favour of membership.

434 Market and Opinion Research International, web site address at <http://www.mori.co.uk>.

Eurosceptics disagree. They argue that public opposition towards the euro will not simply be swayed by a government campaign. Political commentators, including Peter Riddell of the Times newspaper, have also argued that government procrastination has ensured that:

government campaigning would now carry less weight.[435]

Comparing MORI opinion poll results from 1999 and 2000 reinforces this view. As mentioned, polls in 2000 showed that the 'balance' in voting intentions would decrease by 8 per cent in response to strong government support for membership. However, corresponding results obtained in 1999 suggested this gap could have been 10 per cent.

Although the majority of the British public currently opposes British membership of the single currency, questions posed by MORI and ICM show that many expect EMU membership will take place. This suggests that the public distinguishes between what they would like to happen and what they expect to happen. In a MORI poll conducted in October, 68 per cent of respondents said it was 'likely' that they will use euro notes/coins by 2010, while 80 per cent expected they would be in use by 2015. ICM also asked:

Leaving aside how you would vote, in 10 years time, which of the following do you think is most likely?

40 per cent of respondents replied:

'The euro will be the currency of most of Europe, Britain included', 25 per cent said Britain would have 'retained the pound', 24 per cent believed the 'Euro would fail' and 11 per cent 'did not know'.

Enthusiastic pro-Europeans argue that these results suggest that opposition to the euro is widespread but 'shallow'. However, when comparing results from polls in January and November, it is clear that this perception of inevitability declined over the course of 2000. Polls conducted in each of these months asked:

Irrespective of what you think about the single currency, do you think that Britain will replace the pound within . . . 5 years, 10 years, 15 years, longer than that, never, don't know?

In January, 32 per cent of people felt that membership would occur by 2005. By November, this figure had fallen to 22 per cent. This trend was also represented in the figures expressed for membership by 2010, with expectations falling from 34 per cent to 30 per cent. Most significantly, however, in the same period there was a 6 per cent increase in the proportion that felt that Great Britain would never become a member.

435 P Riddel (2000), 'Britain still firmly against joining the single currency', *The Times*, 30 June 2000.

1.1.3 Analysis

These results and trends highlight a number of issues that warrant further examination and analysis. The first and arguably most important is the way in which the euro and the European Union are reported and perceived in the media, and the impact this has on public opinion. This relates not only to the economic and political arguments surrounding the single currency but also to the wider perception of the European Union. Other factors have been the lack of a coherent campaign in favour of the euro, the failure of the government to lead this campaign, and the perceived success of the British economy while it remains outside the Euro-zone.

> Britain's European debate is often feverish and one-sided.[436]

This is due to the domination of an organised, well funded and politically backed Eurosceptic press and lobby that is only opposed by a small contingent of largely passive pro-European journalists and disjointed lobby groups hampered by a lack of clear political support. In the media, this Eurosceptic lobby is led by a number of widely read newspapers that not only shape public opinion and opposition towards the euro but also, in the effort to maintain circulation levels, cater for a public that increasingly expects, and positively responds, to anti-European coverage. They argue that membership of the euro would damage British economic interests and that the introduction of a single currency will lead to a closer political union and the arrival of a European super-state. It is also argued that replacing the 'pound' will undermine British sovereignty. It repeatedly warned against this loss of sovereignty, even though the pound has been operating in a globalised economy dominated by international financial markets and global business transactions. It is this fear of political union and the predicted loss of sovereignty that drives the Eurosceptic press, and that is arguably the key factor behind the high levels of opposition.

Opposition towards the euro is also a product of opposition towards all things European. Surveys of British press coverage reveal that nearly all reporting about the European Union is, at best, neutral. In a speech given in October, Keith Vaz, Minister for Europe rightly argued that:

> The Eurosceptic media exaggerates the negative and plays down the positive in its coverage of Europe. You have to look hard for the good European news in the . . . media.[437]

As a result of this biased reporting and the nature of the arguments offered by Eurosceptics, the promised referendum will currently be a vote as much

[436] *The Economist* (2000), 'The good European—Why Britain's Prime Minister needs to change tack on Europe', *The Economist*, vol 354, no 8158, 19.

[437] K Vaz, (2000), 'Manchester: The EU is Good for You', Speech given by UK Minister for Europe, 6 Oct 2000.

about the merits of the euro as on the European Union as a whole. Public opinion about the euro cannot currently be separated from the general perception of the European Union; that is, pro-Europeans say, until the government begins to make the economic case for membership.

The government maintains that a referendum will only be held once it has decided that the British economy is aligned with the economy of the Euro-zone. This decision will be based on the five economic tests that were announced by the Chancellor Gordon Brown in 1997. Until the government decides to return and look at the status of these 'tests', the government's position is that it is:

> in favour of a successful single currency; in practice, the economic decisions must be fulfilled.[438]

During a recent parliamentary question time, Tony Blair said that a review of the economic situation would occur within two years. This was the first indication that the government was preparing for a decision to be made on economic convergence and also the timing of a referendum. But the counterpart of this declaration is that before that time, the government will be unable to embark on a campaign for fear of undermining its own position.

The government is also unwilling to embark on a pro-euro campaign in the run up to an anticipated general election in May 2001. With fewer than one in five voters in favour of joining the single currency, the government believes that urging membership would jeopardise its chances in the forthcoming election. This reasoning has seen the Labour government continually try to anaesthetise the issue of the euro and remove it from frontline political debate. Meanwhile, the Conservative Party is striving to make the euro a central issue with the slogan 'Keep the Pound". The Labour government's stated policy has given rise to a difficult situation where the government is reluctant to give a strong pro-euro lead and the public is against membership. However, as noted above, opinion polls suggest that support for the euro will not increase until the government takes a positive lead on the issue.

The high levels of opposition towards the euro can also be seen as a consequence of the government's failure to accept that the decision to join the euro will ultimately be an economic, rather than a political, choice. This stands in stark opposition to the majority of the public who are opposed to the euro on political grounds. Hence the Eurosceptic lobby and the Conservative Party base their arguments on political issues: protecting British sovereignty. Until the Labour government accepts that the majority of the public see this decision as having a political dimension, it will be very difficult for it to combat the Eurosceptic arguments that currently acknowledge, respond to and reinforce peoples' worries.

[438] Answer by Rt Hon Tony Blair MP, Prime Minister's Questions, 14 June 2000.

Ironically, the government's position and long-term strategy has not been helped by the recent success of the British economy and the failure of the euro on the currency markets. At the beginning of 2001, the fall of the euro to below parity with the dollar, and the strength of the pound received more than normal media exposure for a financial story. Although not immediate, this had the effect of raising questions in the public perception as to the long-term stability of the euro. In such circumstances, why should Britain replace the successful pound with what is perceived to be a failing euro?

1.2 Financial institutions

1.2.1 Aim of ECB monetary policy

The ECB's monetary policy strategy is aimed at achieving price stability over the medium term. Price stability has been defined as:

> A year-on-year increase in the Harmonised Index of Consumer Prices (HICP) for the Euro-area of below 2 per cent.[439]

The definition is intended to securely anchor inflation expectations. In addition, it provides a clear yardstick against which the ECB's monetary policy can be held accountable for the achievement of its primary objective.

The ECB's monetary strategy consists of two so-called 'pillars'. The first pillar monitors money supply: M3 growth. The second pillar analyses economic variables. Based on these criteria, the ECB alters interest rates to maintain price stability over the medium term.

1.2.2 ECB monetary policy decisions in 2000

1.2.2.a M3 growth

During 2000, the 'loose target', or the reference value for M3 growth, has remained at 4.5 per cent per annum. This has been based on certain assumptions that point to a goal of steady growth in the Euro-zone over the medium term.

1.2.2.b Interest rates

On 5 January 2000, at its first meeting of the year, the Governing Council of the ECB held rates on the main refinancing operations (MROs) unchanged at 3.0 per cent. Rates were raised six times during the course of the year, by 25 basis points each time. On 5 October the ECB made its last rate rise of 2000. The main rate was increased to 4.75 per cent.

[439] European Central Bank, <http://www.ecb.int>.

1.2.2.c Straight from the president's mouth

Speeches by ECB President Dr Duisenberg in October and November outlined the reasons for the rate rises. In October, at the European Business School in London, he said:

These decisions were taken to counteract the emergence of risks to price stability in the Euro-area. The analyses conducted under both pillars of our strategy corroborated our decisions. The analysis under the second pillar indicated that external shocks, namely the strong increase in oil prices and the depreciation of the euro, were increasingly putting pressure on prices. A passing through to consumer prices was facilitated by the faster pace of economic growth that was progressively materialising in the Euro-area. At the same time, the analysis of monetary and credit aggregates under the first pillar of the strategy was also signalling the existence of very generous liquidity conditions in the Euro-area. This also pointed to potential upside risks to price stability.[440]

In November, at the Amsterdam Institute of Finance, he said:

As for the developments in consumer prices in the Euro-area, annual HICP inflation rose to 2.8 per cent in September, compared with 2.3 per cent in August. This increase mainly resulted from the acceleration in energy prices. A contribution was also provided by the higher year-on-year change in prices of non-energy industrial goods in the HICP to 0.8 per cent, from 0.6 per cent in August 2000. This, in combination with the slight increase in the annual rate of change in processed food prices, led the rate of annual HICP inflation, excluding energy goods, to increase to 1.6 per cent in September 2000, from 1.5 per cent in August.

Owing to developments in energy prices and the decline thus far in the euro, consumer price inflation may remain above 2 per cent for longer than was expected some months ago. It is important to recognise that these are temporary price increases resulting from external factors which monetary policy cannot counteract. The ECB, like all other central banks, is not able to influence consumer price inflation in the short term owing to the time lags of monetary policy. Moreover, such first-round effects do not infringe upon the ECB's objective of price stability, since the latter is to be fulfilled in the medium term. In order to ensure the maintenance of price stability precisely over the medium term, it is, however, crucial that longer-term inflation expectations of economic agents do not increase. In this respect, the past decisions to increase ECB rates should have contributed to maintaining confidence in price stability over the medium term.[441]

1.2.3 Reactions in the United Kingdom

Broadly speaking, financial institutions and associations have been

[440] Speech by Dr Willem F. Duisenberg at the European Business School London, 12 Oct 2000.
[441] Speech by Dr Willem F. Duisenberg at the Amsterdam Institute of Finance, 10 Nov 2000.

indifferent to ECB decisions. A brief outline of the reactions of the various players follows.

1.2.3.a The Bank of England

The Governor of the Bank of England has made the Bank's position clear. Although the ECB has performed well in its operationally independent role, Sir Eddie George remains sceptical of a single pan-European monetary policy:

> The 'one-size-fits-all' short term interest rate within the Euro-zone—which is the inevitable consequence of a single currency—will not in the event prove to be appropriate to the domestic monetary policy needs of all the participating countries.
>
> Countries may have divergent cyclical positions. They may face divergent fiscal positions, which would affect their appropriate fiscal/monetary policy mix in different directions—though this should be contained by the Growth and Stability Pact. Or their domestic policy needs may diverge as a result of economic shocks of some sort—a classic, but unique, example was German re-unification, but the more recent global economic disturbance was perhaps another example.
>
> The risks of divergent monetary policy needs within a monetary union are certainly real. If they materialised to any very significant extent, the resulting tensions could be serious, because alternative mechanisms—such as labour migration or fiscal redistribution through a central budget—which help to mitigate sectoral or regional disparities in the national context—are less developed at the Euro-zone level. Some commentators point to the present inflationary pressures in Ireland as an example of the problems that could arise where the single monetary policy is easier than the national situation might require—though I am not sure how far one can sensibly generalise from the Irish experience. It is equally possible to envisage circumstances in which the single monetary policy is too restrictive for some countries.[442]

1.2.3.b Systemic issues arising from ECB monetary policy decisions

Meanwhile, with respect to the practical implications of a centralised monetary policy in the Euro-zone, the Bank concluded in June that:

> The Euro-system operational framework to implement monetary policy is widely considered to have functioned well.[443]

In November, the Bank expressed its confidence in the way in which the ECB dealt with overbidding for fixed-rate tenders by market counterparties, one of the main technical issues that had developed.[444] The ECB's

[442] Speech by Rt Hon Eddie George, Governor of Bank of England, at British Swiss Chamber of Commerce, 12 Sept 2000.

[443] Bank of England, *Practical Issues Arising from the Euro*, June 2000.

[444] Ibid.

solution was to switch to variable-rate tenders. This effectively eased pressure (though we will not indulge in technical detail here).

1.2.3.c The Treasury

The Treasury is maintaining its 'wait and see' approach and is adhering to the five economic tests that Gordon Brown outlined in 1998.

1.2.3.d The London Investment Banking Association (LIBA)

LIBA is the principal trade association in the UK for firms that are active in the investment banking and wholesale securities industry. It did not issue any press releases regarding the ECB and its actions,[445] and it does not consider the single currency to be a main issue of concern.

1.2.3.e The National Association of Pension Funds (NAPF)

The members of NAPF own approximately 25 per cent of the shares traded on the London Stock Exchange (LSE). In January 2000, a NAPF survey revealed that:

> 95 per cent of private sector and 94 per cent of public sector pension schemes were not planning to adjust their investment portfolios following the introduction of the euro.[446]

A second telephone survey of 100 pension administrators recorded 93 per cent of respondents non-plussed by the euro and—through association—by the actions of the ECB. When questioned for reasons, the answers fell into three areas:

> 'It is just another currency'; 'it is not important because it is not yet a reality'; and 'because our investment is entirely UK based.'

NAPF Director General at the time, Ann Robinson, said:

> The impact of the euro, and the UK's position within it, is still shrouded in uncertainty. Unless trustees are certain of the future performance of the Euro-zone, and the UK's position either inside or outside EMU, the new currency alone will not justify expensive portfolio re-adjustment.

1.2.3.f The Association of British Insurers (ABI)

The members of this organisation own approximately another 25 per cent of the shares traded on the LSE. The ABI believes that: '*The costs and*

[445] <http://www.liba.org.uk>.
[446] <http://www.napf.co.uk/05_jan_2000.htm>.

benefits to UK insurers of UK entry to EMU are finely balanced. Therefore, the Association is neither in favour of, nor opposed to, UK entry.'[447]

The ABI is neutral regarding the ECB's monetary policy decisions.

1.2.3.g Mortgage associations

ECB interest rate decisions directly affect those with mortgages. The UK is a nation of homeowners. At the start of 2000, the ECB rate was 300 basis points lower than the UK main rate, and ended the year 125 basis points lower. For the whole period in question, it would have been in the home-buyers' interest to adopt the single currency. According to one consumer group, had the UK been in the Euro-zone:

> UK interest rates would be likely to be significantly lower and less variable than they have been in the past.[448]

1.2.4 Reactions from the financial press

In the Financial Times, the consistent headline regarding the ECB policies for much of the year was the weakness of the currency. Rate decisions were mainly analysed in this context. In October, the Financial Times and The Economist lambasted Duisenberg for making revealing comments regarding intervention—or, rather, the lack of—by the main central banks in support of the euro. The Economist labelled him a liability.

In addition, the UK financial press has often expressed a view that the ECB's actions are being strongly influenced by Germany. On the eve of the first rate rise (in February), the Financial Times ran an article implying that the ECB would first need to gain approval from the Bundesbank. Additionally, subsequent comments by the German Finance Minister Hans Eichel, were quickly seised as evidence that politicians can still influence ECB policy.

On the whole, the specialised UK press have been sceptical of the ECB's ability, and have not hidden their disapproval of Duisenberg.

1.2.5 Reactions regarding the weakness of the euro *vis-à-vis* other currencies

For much of the year the euro lost ground against all the major currencies, particularly the dollar and the pound.

Much of this was due to positive sentiment towards the US. Private and institutional investors were drawn by the technology boom, higher produc-

447 <http://www.abi.org.uk/theEuroArea>.

448 Consumers in Europe Group, *Introducing the Euro*, Feb 2000, 8.

tivity rates, and hopes of higher returns. During 2000, Europe recorded a substantial net outflow of direct investment. This weakened the currency, and two interventions in the currency markets by central banks (in September and November) could do little to reverse negative sentiment towards the euro. It was only after signs of a US recession grew, and the presidential election debacle, that the euro regained some ground against the dollar.

In the UK, there was much ado about the strength of sterling relative to the euro and the harm this was doing to British exports. The year ended with announcements of closures in the car and steel industries. The sterling's strength and the euro's weakness were making UK exports non-competitive in the global market.

The odd couple was the euro–yen relationship. Japan's economy has been sickly for a decade; the banking sector is in need of urgent reform and there is a deflationary problem. Yet, the euro continued to weaken vis-à-vis the yen for much of the year. Markets and the financial press regarded this as an extremely worrying development for the new currency.

1.3 Institutional and procedural matters

The positions of the three main political parties towards the euro are largely associated with shaping and responding to public opinion. The Labour Party is theoretically in favour of British membership, but only if the economic case is proven and the euro is seen as a success. It repeatedly claims that the decision to join the euro should be based on economic rationales rather than political and constitutional factoring. In the run up to a general election they have made efforts to remove the euro from mainstream political and public debate. The Liberal Democrats also hold this position but are more open to debate. They 'see UK entry as perfectly feasible but that early government steps are needed.'[449] They call for a positive decision on a referendum and strong governmental support for a 'yes' vote. In contrast to these positions, the Conservative Party has tried to make the euro a central issue of the political debate. They are at the forefront of the 'Save the Pound' campaign and are attempting to use the high levels of public opposition towards the euro as a basis upon which to gain more parliamentary seats at the next general election.

Business community views continue to be split and a number of lobby groups have been launched to actively promote each side of the argument. The Confederation of British Industry (corporate membership) is currently polling its members on their views on EMU. This follows a similar poll conducted in 1999, which returned a 'clear 'yes', but not an unconditional

[449] Liberal Democrats (1999), 'Britain Adoption of the Euro: Report of the Expert Commission', Established by the Rt Hon Charles Kennedy MP, London, Liberal Democrats.

one'.[450] The Confederation of British Industry recently said that it would not continue to actively campaign for British membership until the government begins to take a firm lead on the issue. In contrast, the Institute of Directors (individual membership) has taken the firm position that it is against Britain joining the single currency. It has been at the forefront of a new organisation 'Business for Sterling', a lobby group that enjoys strong support from a number of high profile business benefactors. The Trade Union Congress—the co-ordinating body for a large number of individual Trade Unions—is largely in favour of membership and has urged 'the government to be frank and open about Europe and run a consistent pro-European campaign'.[451] The dominant opinion in the City of London continues to be that its long-term competitiveness and central position in the world financial markets depends on euro membership, despite some opposition from interests benefiting from UK's exclusion from EMU.

Other aspects of EMU and the euro's performance and management were examined in a high profile House of Lords European Union Committee Report. It was published in November and provides a detailed account of the various views of the cross-party committee, parliament and business representatives who were called to give evidence. There is common agreement that:

> It continues to be difficult to disentangle the economic elements which are a direct consequence of EMU and the economic elements which are, for example, a consequence of cyclical upswing at the macro-economic level.[452]

Macro-economic trends in the Euro-zone were interpreted as showing strong signs of revival after the launch of the euro in January 1999. Gross Domestic Product was recorded as having risen by 2.3 per cent in 1999 and, at the time, 3 per cent growth was predicted for 2000.[453] The recorded fall in unemployment across the Euro-zone (from 9.5 to 9.2 per cent) in the first half of 2000 was also welcomed, but it was recognised that these figures masked national variations. Witnesses from business and financial institutions concluded that the euro had performed 'very well indeed',[454] and that the economies of the Euro-zone were 'working pretty well.'[455]

[450] The Confederation of British Industry (1999), 'Policy Statement', London, released 20 July 1999.

[451] Trade Union Congress (2000), 'Monks urges government to be "frank and open" over Europe', Press Release, 14 Nov 2000.

[452] House of Lords Select Committee on the European Union (2000), *How is the Euro Working*, 21 Nov 2000, London.

[453] Gross Domestic Product per capita at constant market prices (percentage change year on year). Source: Eurostat.

[454] Evidence given to the House of Lords Committee by Dr Norbert Walter, Chief Economist, Deutsche Bank.

[455] Evidence given to House of Lords Committee by Sir Edward George, Governor of the Bank of England.

The ECB was complimented on the interest rate rises that were decided upon between February and October. It was concluded that the bank's 'analysis and reasoning was well considered'.[456] However, questions were raised as to how the bank came to its decisions and whether it was monetary growth or non-monetary factors that influenced decisions. The effect was that it was difficult for financial markets and institutions to predict decisions because they were unable to determine which of the 'two pillars' had more weight in the decision-making process.

The increased transparency of the ECB was welcomed, as was the publishing of more data. It was recognised, that by not publishing minutes or voting records of the governing council the ECB might arouse suspicions or attract criticism. However, it was felt to be inappropriate to publish these records because doing so would place undue pressure on national representatives sitting on the board. A number of institutional and business representatives felt that publication 'would run the risk of exposing individual members of the Governing Council to criticisms or pressures from their own countries'.[457] The ECB announcement that they would publish all future internal economic forecasts was welcomed as promoting a greater understanding of its monetary policy.

It is largely felt that the ECB should be subject to scrutiny from some democratically elected body. The institutional witnesses that gave evidence during the committee's deliberations supported this view. The European Parliament's role in this matter was recognised, and efforts to strengthen this link were welcomed. It is seen as impracticable and unreasonable to expect the ECB to be accountable to national parliaments. There may also be:

> a case for strengthening the arrangements for the ECB's reporting to the Council of Ministers (ECOFIN) and to the Euro-group of Finance Ministers of participating Members States.[458]

However the independence of the ECB has to be rigorously observed and maintained.

The euro's performance on the foreign exchange markets has been a point of concern, but it was felt that the press has exaggerated fears. Suggestions have been made that this poor performance was largely caused by over-inflated initial expectations, as was the initial exchange rate against the dollar. The combined consequence of these factors is that, in November, the 'current level of the dollar-euro rate [did] not correctly reflect economic fundamentals.'[459] A persuasive argument offered by Bank of England, Governor Sir Eddie George, suggested that this weakness

[456] House of Lords Committee, 2000, London.
[457] Evidence given to House of Lords Committee.
[458] House of Lords Committee, 2000, London.
[459] Evidence given to House of Lords Committee by Sir Edward George.

essentially reflected a net outflow of long-term capital from Europe to the United States. If this flow ceases, or perhaps reverses, market fundamentals would be reasserted.

Questions were also raised as to the suitability of a 'one-size-fits-all' monetary policy. Pressure on this policy has not been slight, due to improving economic performance since the launch of the euro. But worries exist as to the policy's long-term stability, if faced with a pan-European or global economic downturn.

1.4 Trends towards spillover

1.4.1 Tax harmonisation

The main political parties agree that the threat of tax harmonisation is real. There is a feeling in the UK that a single monetary policy will eventually lead to a single fiscal policy; this would result in higher taxes in the UK and would damage its competitive position in the world. In December, the Labour Party portrayed the Nice Summit as a battle to keep Britain's veto on taxes; the British Prime Minister Tony Blair, succeeded in doing this.

The Conservative Party's Eurosceptics have voiced their fears regarding EMU. The Conservative leader, William Hague, stated that, after monetary union:

> the UK's tax to GDP ratio would have to rise by at least one sixth to bring it in line with the rest of the European Union.[460]

However, other voices in the UK do not foresee any real drive towards tax harmonisation.[461] Their belief is that Member States will not compete on fiscal policy—whether corporate or income tax—as feared. If corporate tax is the issue, the reasoning goes that low tax and high tax Member States attract different types of business. If a business needs good infrastructure, a well-educated workforce and sound public services, it will be prepared to pay for these investments. Therefore, the types of business that locate in high tax Member States are not likely to relocate on the basis of low taxes.

If income tax is the issue, low rates of labour mobility among Member States negate any necessity for governments to harmonise taxes, otherwise they face losing revenue.

[460] Speech by the Rt Hon William Hague to CBI conference.

[461] Dick Taverne, (2000), 'The Euro and Taxes', in S Haseler and J Reland (eds), *Britain & Euroland*, by the Federal Trust, London, Kogan Page, 15–23; Ussher, Kitty (2000), *The Spectre of Tax Harmonisation*, Centre for European Reform.

1.4.2 Social policy

According to a TUC press release in January, the Government could afford to raise public spending by an extra £31 bn over the next three years and remain in line with EMU restrictions.

The effects of EMU on pension provision have been recognised.[462] A pan-European market provides wider opportunities for pension funds to diversify their investments; this might lead to higher returns for pensions. The European Commission's proposed EU Directive on the Supervision of Institutions for Occupational Retirement Provision was adopted in October. It was intended to establish a common prudential framework for the regulation of occupational pension funds in the EU, and to prepare the ground for the eventual realisation of cross-border schemes. The Confederation of British Industry (CBI) was quick to realise the implications of this and has been working through UNICE to ensure that the Directive fully accommodates the features of the UK pension system. The CBI's comments were incorporated into the UNICE response to the draft Directive.

However, there is a general fear among British businesses that Community law is burdening business with excessive red tape. The Institute of Directors—representative of small business—never ceases to repeat this criticism or reflect this fear.

1.4.3 Co-ordination of macroeconomic and monetary policy

There is a fear that a 'one-size-fits-all' monetary policy might eventually cause problems for the macroeconomic stability of Member States. If fiscal policy measures were also restricted, the feeling in the UK would be that effective sovereignty was all but surrendered. This is not a problem at present. The UK economy is currently in convergence with Euroland. But what if this was to change in the next economic downturn? If labour mobility is low and there are not sufficient funds in the central budget, where will the stabilisers come from? Could the current budget perhaps be reformed?

1.4.4 External projection of the euro

There is feeling that the euro has lost credibility externally. The UK press has rarely missed an opportunity to criticise the ECB, its monetary policy strategy and its president.

The Bank of England has focused on the forthcoming parallel use of the

[462] Federal Trust, *Can Europe Pay for its Pensions* (London, Kogan Page, 2000).

euro. Preparing small and medium enterprises (SMEs) has been of particular concern. Sir Eddie George has voiced that concern:

> A higher external profile is needed for the euro. Especially, for Member States such as the UK that should be expecting increased trade with the Euro-zone.

A second Outline National Changeover Plan (NCP) was published in March. A key focus of the NCP is planning in the public sector. The Inland Revenue, Customs and Excise and the Department of Social Security are planning to invest around £20 million in total during 2000/2001.[463]

Finally, with regard to the global projection of the euro, the leader of the Pro-Euro Conservative Party John Stevens, has made the following comments:

> The euro is a neutral instrument, an instrument of immense power, but a neutral one nonetheless. It can allow Europe to drive much more effectively towards a European bloc economy, protected if that is what is desired, or it can assist tremendously the stability of a global free trade order, if that is desired in preference. The people who are going to decide this are ultimately the electors of Europe. At the present moment they have sent us off on one course and the significance, from the point of view of the UK, is that this course is going to be extremely uncomfortable for outsiders the longer that they stay out.[464]

2. The euro, EMU and UK law

Lazaros E. Panourgias* and Mads Andenas**

2.1 Overview

The legal preparations for the introduction of the euro in the UK reflect the general discussion about EMU. Both the government and the opposition, and most of the press, have had an interest in focusing on the obstacles facing EMU and the euro. This is reflected in parliamentary debates and in otherwise informed comment. The *Economist* and the *Financial Times* have, at regular intervals since Maastricht, given prominence to some development that was supposed to block or slow down the introduc-

[463] Bank of England, *Practical Issues Arising from the Euro*, June 2000, 92.

[464] Stevens, 'The Foreign Policy of the Euro', in S Haseler and J Reland (eds), *Britain & Euroland*, by the Federal Trust, London (Kogan Page, 2000), 101.

* LL.B. (Athens Law School); LL.M. (Georgetown University Law Center); MA (Fletcher School of Law and Diplomacy); Greek States Scholarships Foundation Scholar in Banking Law; Member of the Athens (Greece) and New York Bar. Legal Adviser, EBRD, and Research Fellow, British Institute of International and Comparative Law, Charles Clore House, 17 Russell Square, London WC1B 5JP,

** MA (Oxon); Ph.D. (Cantab). Senior Teaching Fellow, Institute of European and Comparative Law, and Fellow, Harris Manchester College, Oxford University. Director, British Institute of International and Comparative Law, Charles Clore House, 17 Russell Square, London, WC1B 5JP.

tion of the euro. There has also been very good coverage of the various technical problems, and this far exceeds the press coverage in other Member States. The general expectations have reflected this, and they have also reflected the perception that the euro was not going to become a reality and that, in any case, the UK's entry into the euro would be far in the future. The government has also faced another problem; any preparations it has undertaken have been seen as a promotion of the euro. This particularly applied to any kind of technical preparations for a UK entry to the euro, and such preparations were basically abandoned in 1999. The fear of being seen to promote the UK's entry into the euro seems to have resulted in general preparations being based on an assumption that the UK will remain outside.

The discussion about the euro takes place on several levels, and it is not all rational. The lack of rationality has had an impact on the legal preparations, mainly by slowing them down. The climate has not been conducive to practical legal preparations—either as an 'in' or as an 'out'—for the euro. Some positions and arguments in the discussion are predictable. Export-oriented industry points to the costs of staying out, particularly at a time when a weak euro and a strong pound would reduce its competitiveness. Other arguments surprise. In political discussion, the Conservative Party claims that abolishing the pound would lead to the British government losing regulatory power over the level of unemployment. Of course, this asserts a Keynesian theory of macro-policy to which it does not otherwise subscribe. It has been described as one of the ironies of the British euro-debate that economists and politicians who repudiate Keynesian policy at home become fervent Keynesians when they contemplate the horrors of British membership of the single currency. The Bank of England is showing an increasing sympathy for Keynesian theory and the fine-tuning of the national economy when it argues against the euro in a similar vein.[465] Governor George has launched a thinly veiled anti-euro campaign that seems to offer no more principled resistance than preserving the Bank of England. The Bank is a great institution whereas Europe is here today, gone tomorrow.

There have been developments on a contractual level by which companies have sought to insulate themselves from the consequences of the UK staying outside. A number of companies, principally in the car manufacturing industry, are making arrangements to pay their subcontractors in euros. This has aroused some interest, but the fact that

465 The main line of argument is that Britain should not give up national control over instruments of economic policy, and it is very much framed as an issue of national sovereignty. This goes beyond possible concerns about the effectiveness of a single monetary policy without co-ordination of fiscal policies, to political integration and concern with effectiveness of monetary policy arrangements.

other companies (such as Rolls Royce) have followed a parallel practice with complete invoicing from subcontractors in US dollars has made this less interesting.

UK legislation has not yet dealt with many issues that will eventually arise from the replacement of the pound by the euro in the financial markets. It is expected[466] that the treatment of these issues by UK legislators will be similar to the arrangements adopted by the participating countries. However, it is a long way from reaching a political consensus, or even a workable majority for the continuing and enhanced participation of the UK in the EU. Many developments currently indicate that popular opinion is moving in the opposite direction. A Bill—*European Union (Implications of Withdrawal)*[467]—was introduced in the House of Lords on 14 December 2000 to discuss implications for the economy, national security, the Constitution, and the costs faced by the United Kingdom, if it were to withdraw from the EU. There is no prospect of the Bill being adopted, but it will serve as a focal point for opposition to the EU.

Community legislation is the basis for the euro's legal effects in the UK, as it is in other Member States. Council Regulations 1103/97 of 17 June 1997 on *Certain Provisions Relating to the Introduction of the Euro*,[468] enacted on the basis of Article 308 (ex 235) EC, is binding and directly applicable[469] in the UK. However, it will not apply to conversions between sterling and the euro.

Council Regulation 974 /98 *on the Introduction of the Euro*[470] will, in practice, apply to debts or other legal obligations expressed in currencies of participating countries,[471] although it is not directly applicable in the UK as it is enacted on the basis of Article 123.4 EC. In addition, even if the euro does not become legal tender in the UK until the UK joins the euro, it could be used in contracts or for other purposes (such as accounting, pricing, etc). UK legislation has already provided for accounting, tax, invoice, conversion and securities issues in relation to the euro.

466 Bank of England, *Questions Relating to Possible UK Entry Into EMU*, <http://www.bankofengland.co.uk/Euro/qanda.htm>.

467 *European Union (Implications of Withdrawal) Bill* [H.L.], as introduced in the House of Lords on 14 Dec 2000, <http://www.parliament.the-stationery-office.co.uk/pa/ ld200001/ Idbills/009/2001009.htm>.

468 *Council Regulation 1103/97 on certain provisions relating to the introduction of the Euro*, OJ [1997] L 162/1 (thereafter Council Regulation 1103/97).

469 The reference to Art 308 (ex 235) EC, contrasted to Art 123.4 EC, in Council Regulation 974/98, confirms that the Council Regulation 1103/97 is applicable in all Member States. See also European Commission, Directorate General II/Economic and Financial Affairs, *The Legal Framework for the Use of the Euro*, Brussels, Nov 1997.

470 *Council Regulation 974/98 on the introduction of the Euro*, OJ [1998] L 139/1 (thereafter Council Regulation 974 /98).

471 '"[P]articipating Member States" shall mean those Member States which adopt the single currency in accordance with the Treaty' (Art 1 of Council Regulation 1103/97).

2.2 Private law issues

2.2.1 Continuity of contracts

Under English law, the governing law of the contract[472] will apply to the issue of continuity.[473] Thus, Council Regulation 1103/97—applicable in all Member States—will apply to contracts governed by English law. There will be no application to relations involving the sterling, but it will be applicable when debts are denominated in currencies of the participating Member States. This means that substitution of the euro for the currencies of the participating Member States will not result in 'altering any term' or 'discharging or excusing performance' under contracts governed by English law.[474]

The applicability of English law to the continuity question beyond the reach of the Council Regulations remains an issue. It is argued that relevant English law doctrines can still apply, especially if considering the legislative history of political compromise in the drafting of Article 3 of Council Regulation 1103/1997. They also complement the EU Regulations.[475] Although Regulations should prevail in a case of conflict, it is worth examining domestic law because it remains uncertain how the UK courts will dispose of related arguments.

Exceptions to the principle of continuity can be founded in the doctrine of frustration in contracts governed by English law: impossibility or illegality of performance (or similar situations) due to circumstances arising after the formation of a contract can lead to discharge of the contract.[476] The development of strict requirements for its application[477] limits or excludes its use in establishing revocability of contracts on the basis of the introduction of the euro. The currencies of the participating Member States, in which debts are denominated, will be replaced—not abolished—by the euro.[478] And

[472] See AV Dicey and JHC Morris, *Dicey & Morris, The Conflict of Laws* (13th edn 2000), p. 1261 for the law applicable to a contract in the UK.

[473] The *Contracts (Applicable Law) Act 1990* has incorporated in the UK legal order the Rome Convention (*EEC Convention on the Law Applicable to Contractual Obligations*).

[474] 'The introduction of the euro shall not have the effect of altering any term of a legal instrument or of discharging or excusing performance under any legal instrument, nor give a party the right unilaterally to alter or terminate such an instrument. This provision is subject to anything which parties may have agreed' (Art 3 of Council Regulation 1103/97).

[475] See J Mance, 'Possible Legal Problems Affecting Financial Transactions at the Time of European Monetary Union', 8(11/12) EBLR 266 (1997), 269 for the sustainability of arguments based on principles such as the 'impossibility' or 'intolerable harshness', in spite of the application of Art 3 of Council Regulation 1103/97. On potential conflicts in jurisdictions of other Member States see also RJ Botter *et al.*, *Introduction of the Euro in the Various Members, An Inventory of the National Rules*, <http://amue.lf.net/efiles/Euroframe/national/index.html>, 7.

[476] On the doctrine of frustration under English law see G Treitel, *The Law of Contract* (10th edn 1999).

[477] See Mance, above n 475, at 270.

[478] Arts 2, 3 of Council Regulation 974 /98.

mere substitution of performance does not establish frustration.[479] It is interesting to note that the replacement of the Minimum Lending Rate[480] by a new reference rate (the base rate of the main clearing banks), was effected in the UK financial markets without legal problems. More specifically, the replacement of one currency by another does not establish frustration under English law.[481] There is no substantial change other than a change in the abstract 'unit of account'.[482] It is unlikely that such change will sustain the strict frustration test as illustrated by Lord Bingham in *J Lauritzen AS v Wijsmuller BV*:

> Since the effect of frustration is to kill the contract and discharge the parties from further liability under it, the doctrine is not to be lightly invoked, must be kept within very narrow limits and ought not to be extended.[483]

It is expected to be equally difficult—if not more so in the UK context—to establish frustration of contract[484] on the basis of financial hardship.[485]

2.2.2 Conversion and rounding

Council Regulation 1103/97 also provides for rules of conversion and rounding. It clearly does not apply, when debts and other legal obligations are expressed in sterling. However, Regulation 1103/97 will have effect in the United Kingdom with reference to debts expressed in currencies of participating Member States. Conversion and rounding issues will be regulated by the *lex monetae*[486] for contracts governed by English

479 See Mance, above n 475, p. 270 on the non-application of the frustration doctrine to contracts, affected by the Suez Canal crisis, whose performance was significantly altered (performance was possible only through the Cape of Good Hope instead of the Suez Canal).

480 Reference rate for interest obligations published by the Bank of England until 1981.

481 See W Blair, 'Contracts and Monetary Union', 8 (10) EBLR 228 (1997), 230. See also Dicey & Morris, above n 472, 1578 on the continuity of contracts in case of currency change as a fundamental principle in general.

482 See R Goode, *Payment of Obligations in Commercial and Financial Transactions* (1993), 131: '[the replacement of one currency by another] does not frustrate the payment obligation, for the unit of account is an abstraction, a measure of value, not a tangible object of delivery obligation. All that happens when the unit of account is changed is that the debtor's obligation to pay a given number of old units becomes converted into an obligation to pay the equivalent in new units at the conversion rate prescribed by the law creating the new currency.' This is consistent with Knapp's definition of the 'unit of account' itself as an abstraction determined by its relation to its predecessor currency, its 'recurrent linking', on the basis of a specific conversion rate (G F Knapp, *The State Theory of Money* (1924), 21).

483 *J Lauritzen AS v Wijsmuller BV* [1990] 1 Lloyd's Rep 1.

484 Mance, above n 475, at 270.

485 Id, 270, 271 for the possibility of a more successful invoking of the doctrine of frustration in case of interest rate differentials or long-term foreign currency swaps. See Blair, above n 481, at 230 for the non-application of the frustration doctrine also in cases of currencies or interest rates differentials.

486 *Lex monetae* is the law of the country of the currency, in which the debt is denominated. The *lex monetae* is 'that law as it exists from time to time' and as such it encompasses the promulgated rate of conversion that links an 'old' and a 'new' currency in case of a

law.[487] Thus, the country of issue of the currency that the debt is denominated will apply. This will be Council Regulation 1103/97 as complemented by more detailed legislation of the Member State in question.[488]

Council Regulation 1103/97 will not apply to sterling. While the UK remains outside the EMU, conversions between the sterling and a participating currency (or the euro after 2002) will occur in the same way as conversion and rounding of existing foreign exchange transactions or conversions. For contracts governed by English law, the applicable foreign exchange rate will be the one at which the participating currency or the euro can 'be bought in London in a recognised and accessible market, irrespective of any official rate of exchange' on the day of payment.[489] Still, the parties to a transaction can agree that the conversion and rounding rules provided by Council Regulation 1103/97 also apply to conversions between the sterling and the participating currencies, or the sterling and the euro. Unlike other countries, the UK has not enacted any detailed regulations for conversion and rounding.

2.2.3 Substitution of euro for the currencies of the participating Member States

It has been argued that Council Regulation 974/98, covering the substitution of euro for the currencies of participating Member States,[490] is not directly applicable in the UK.[491] The argument suggests that the Regulation should only apply to participating countries because it is based on Article 123.4 of the EC. Nevertheless, Council Regulation 974/98 will have legal effect in the UK to the extent that debts or other legal obligations are denominated in currencies of the participating Member States. For such contracts governed by English law, it is the *lex monetae* (the law of the currencies of the participating Member States, including Council Regulation 974/98) that will determine the qualities of the currency of debt denomination at the time of payment, and this will also cover replacement of the currency.[492]

currency change (*Dicey & Morris*, above n 472, at 1576 et seq.). See also id, for the application of the rate of conversion as promulgated by the *lex monetae* in the case of replacement of the old German Mark by the Reichsmark in 1924 and in the case of the introduction of the euro.

[487] Even if not governed by English law, the proceeding in an English court will have the same result: either the law of a Member State will be directly applicable or the third-country law will most likely also respect the *lex monetae* and give effect to the law of the Member State in question.

[488] See Botter R.J., above n 475, for information with reference to relevant provisions in the Member States.

[489] *Dicey & Morris*, above n 472, 1600, 1601.

[490] Arts 2, 3 of Council Regulation 974/98.

[491] See Mance, above n 475, 266 finding certain pointers in support of this view without committing himself.

[492] *Dicey & Morris*, above n 472, p. 1576 .

It is difficult to follow the view that the Regulation should apply directly only in participating countries (the Euro-countries), and to the UK through *lex monetae*. Even outside the Euro-area, a regulation based on Article 123.4 EC cannot be treated as foreign law. The Regulation is part of Community law and courts (British or continental) will have to treat it as such. It is the *Community* that has entered the third stage of EMU. The special regime for Britain and Denmark (and the derogations) are just exceptions to the material application ('champ d'application matérielle') of the Regulation. The territorial application of the Regulation is clearly irrelevant.[493]

The final formula at the end of the Regulation is that 'the present regulation is directly applicable in all the Member States'. This is a confusing and erroneous translation of 'le présent règlement est directement applicable dans tout État membre'. It means that the Regulation does not need any kind of transformation, approbation or publication in the Member States, and that it is applicable *in*, rather than *to*, the Member States.

A number of UK-incorporated companies have share capital denominated in currencies of participating states. Do companies need to take any steps to alter their share capital as a result of the conversion into euros?

The best view is that such capital has automatically, by operation of law, been redenominated into euros (although companies may wish to take action to deal with issues of inconvenient par values of shares which result from conversion). Due to the rounding provisions, there could be a small increase or decrease in the aggregate nominal value of the share capital. As a matter of best practice, it may be advisable to follow the procedures for increasing or reducing share capital in section 121 and Chapter IV of the Companies Act 1985. Furthermore, conversion is likely to have produced shares with nominal values that are not whole numbers. Accordingly, a company could issue bonus shares, consolidate the shares and subdivide them into whole number values. The view of Companies House is that shares denominated in currencies of participating states have not automatically converted into euros. Companies House suggests that a company must either (a) repurchase the shares or (b) cancel them in accordance with a court order, file a resolution converting the authorised share capital into euros, and reissue the shares in euros. Companies House has given no basis for its view, which seems plainly wrong

2.2.4 Accounting

The existing framework adequately addresses accounting issues that could

[493] This better view also have authoritative support in *Dicey & Morris*, above n 472, 1577, n 27. There are convincing reasons of consistency and certainty of Community law in favour of this view.

arise from the use of the euro regardless of the UK's entry into the EMU. The Statement of Standard Accounting Practice 20 on 'foreign currency translation' (SSAP 20)[494] and the Abstract 21 on 'accounting issues arising from the proposed introduction of the euro' (UITF Abstract 21),[495] as complemented by Information Sheet 30[496] of the Urgent Issues Task Force (UITF), cover issues of financial reporting in relation to the introduction of the euro.

Companies can already prepare financial reports in foreign currencies, including euro, and there is no obligation for exclusive or additional reporting in euro. Exchange gains or losses from dealings in currencies of the participating Member States before the exchange rates became irrevocably fixed will be reported in the profit and loss accounts.[497] Expenditures[498] arising during the years that are related to euro preparations must be reported separately in the financial statement from those incurred at the end of the year. General preparation for the euro can be disclosed in the company's operating and financial review.[499] If the company already has an accounting policy of capitalising this type of assets, euro-related costs incurred on existing assets that 'give rise to an asset'[500] (that is, that enhance the asset's potential for future economic benefits), must be capitalised and depreciated in the method provided. If the costs maintain the assets, they must be written off as they are incurred.[501] Provision for costs will be recognised in the accounting period during which they are sustained.[502] The euro will have no impact on the accounting policy with regard to the deferment of gains or losses from anticipatory hedges.[503]

It must be noted that smaller companies subject to the Financial Reporting Standard for Smaller Entities are not required to comply with UITF Abstract 21. However, they must consider it when the euro's impact on their operations is strong.[504]

494 Statement of Standard Accounting Practice 20, 'Foreign currency translation' (SSAP 20), Apr 1983 (as amended in Nov 1997 and in Dec 1998).

495 UITF Abstract 21, 'Accounting issues arising from the proposed introduction of the Euro' (1998), <http://www.asb.org.uk/publications/publication115.html> (UITF Abstract 21).

496 UITF Information Sheet 30, 'Further accounting issues arising from the introduction of the Euro' (1998), <http://www.asb.org.uk/publications/publication152.html> (UITF Information Sheet 30). It addresses euro implications for compliance with SSAP 20.

497 UITF Abstract 21, ss 11-13. See also Accounting—business preparations for the euro factsheets No 12, <http://www.Euro.gov.uk/facts.html> (Accounting).

498 Such costs could be 'administrative planning, staff training, the provision of information to customers, modification of software and the adaptation of hardware, such as vending machines, retail outlets' cash registers or banks' automatic teller machines'. See UITF Abstract 21, s 2.

499 See Accounting, above n 497.

500 Assets are 'rights or other access to future economic benefits controlled by an entity as a result of past transactions or events'. FRS 5 'Reporting the Substance of Transactions'.

501 UITF Abstract 21, ss 6, 7, 17.

502 Ibid, s 8.

503 Ibid, ss 14, 15.

504 Ibid, 21.

2.2.5 Invoices

There is no requirement to invoice in euro or to accept invoices in euro.[505] When an invoice is in sterling and the debtor offers to pay in euro, there is the option—but no requirement—to accept it.[506] As mentioned above, a number of companies are beginning to contract in euro with their domestic UK providers.

2.2.6 Tax issues

2.2.6.a 'Euroconversion'

The European Single Currency (Taxes) Regulations[507] provide mainly for the tax implications of 'Euroconversion' in relation to a currency, asset, liability, contract or other instrument.

'Euroconversion' is defined:[508]

(a) in relation to a currency as: 'the conversion or restating of that currency or that amount into euro and any rounding of the resulting amount within a euro'.
(b) in relation to an asset, liability, contract or instrument as:

'(i) the simple redenomination of that asset, liability, contract or instrument, or (ii) in the case of a relevant asset, the simple redenomination of that asset accompanied by either or both renominalisation and reconventioning, or (iii) the substitution (whether by way of exchange, conversion replacement or otherwise) for the asset, liability, contract or instrument of an equivalent replacement asset, liability, contract or instrument'.

Pursuant to the Regulations, a currency amount, asset, liability, contract or instrument that results from 'Euroconversion' of the original currency, asset, liability, or contract respectively will, for tax purposes, be treated as if it were the same as the original.

When the euro results in a change in the variable interest rate that, in turn, causes a change in the variable payment rate (specified by the original contract) and the contract is rescinded, the new contract will be treated as if it were the same as the original and it were concluded on the same date. The same will apply in case of similar changes in the interest rate of currency contracts, including options.[509]

[505] See Accounting, above n 497.

[506] Banking—business preparations for the Euro factsheets No 12, <http://www.Euro.gov.uk/facts.html> (thereafter Banking).

[507] Statutory Instruments 1998, No 3177, The European Single Currency (Taxes) Regulations 1998, <http://www.hmso.gov.uk/si/si1998/1998317703.htm> (thereafter European Single Currency (Taxes) Regulations 1998).

[508] Art 3 European Single Currency (Taxes) Regulations 1998.

[509] Arts 8, 9 European Single Currency (Taxes) Regulations 1998.

Part II (Articles 4–6) provides for the tax deductibility of costs from redenomination of shares and securities in euro in the case of investment companies or companies engaged in trade or life assurance business.

2.2.6.b Tax payments in euro

Customs & Excise and the Inland Revenue have respectively accepted payment in euro of VAT, customs duties, excise duties, Insurance Premium Tax, Landfill Tax and Air Passenger Duty, and all taxes and National Insurance since 1 January 1999.[510] All records and accounts, except for VAT and duty accounts, can be kept in euro.[511]

Tax invoices cannot be in euro only. If the invoices consist of several items and are drawn in euro, a report in sterling is not necessary for each item if the total net value at each VAT rate, and the VAT amount at each rate, appear in sterling.[512] Tax returns must be completed mainly in sterling. Only Box 22—Single Administration Document (SAD) for the invoice value on Customs declarations can show amounts in euro. Intrastat declarations must be prepared in the currency of the Member State of submission.[513]

2.2.7 Listing securities in euro

The London Stock Exchange (LSE) allows issuers to list euro-denominated securities. Its existing trading platforms allow for the trading of securities denominated in euro or more than 32 other currencies.[514] The listing fees for euro-denominated securities are much lower than the fees payable by international issuers in most markets.[515] In addition, euro-denominated depository receipts (EDR) are traded on LSE's SEAQ International.[516] EDR is also quoted in euro and its dividends are payable in euro.[517] Eurobonds (EEB) and bonds (ECB) denominated in euro are also available.[518] Along with EDRs, they are subject to the listing rules of the UK Listing Authority (UKLA).[519]

510 Tax and the Euro—business preparations for the Euro factsheets No 17, <http://www.Euro.gov.uk/facts.html> (thereafter Tax and the Euro).

511 Ibid. at 2, 3.

512 Ibid.

513 Ibid.

514 *Listing in London, the first choice: Listing euro products*: http://www.londonstockexchange.com/about/pdfs/europroducts.pdf.

515 Ibid.

516 The Stock Exchange Automated Quotation system for international equity market securities.

517 Ibid.

518 Ibid.

519 The UKLA will be integrated into the Financial Services Authority (FSA) on 31 March, 31 as under the Official Listing of Securities (Change of Competent Authority) Regulations 2000 the FSA is now responsible for the admission of securities to the Official List, <http://www.fsa.gov.uk/ukla>).

2.3 Institutional issues

2.3.1 Monetary policy

Since 1998, the Bank of England has enjoyed operational independence in the exercise of monetary policy. The Monetary Policy Committee (MPC) is solely responsible for the formulation of monetary policy, and it meets monthly to set interest rates. Its goal independence is limited as it must pursue the government-defined inflation target (currently 2.5 per cent).

The Bank of England Act 1998 regulates the Bank's accountability and transparency. The MPC's decisions must be announced immediately after its meetings. Unlike the ECB, minutes of MPC meetings must be published. An annual report must be submitted to Parliament, MPC Members must appear before Parliament's Treasury Select Committee, and quarterly reports must be published. In case of a deviation of more than 1 per cent from the inflation target of 2.5 per cent, the Bank's Governor must write an open letter to the Chancellor.

Besides accountability and transparency requirements, the 1998 Act also ensures a role for the Treasury. In cases of 'extreme economic circumstances', Treasury can issue monetary policy directives for the public interest, but only for a limited period. Treasury can also participate through an observer at the Monetary Policy Committee.

2.3.2 Government debt management

The Debt Management Office (DMO) under the HM Treasury was established in 1998. Its task is to direct the Bank of England's role[520] in sterling debt management, the sale of gilts, oversight of the gilts market and cash management for the government. The DMO Chief Executive has operational independence in debt and cash management and day-to-day operations. The power to formulate the policy and financial framework of DMO's operations is entrusted to the Chancellor of the Exchequer.[521] The reform of government debt management was part of the process of establishing operational independence for the Bank of England.

2.3.3 Supervision

The euro can be expected to have important consequences for the regulation of European financial markets. German and French initiatives in this

[520] For the Bank's activity in the gilts market and its importance for financial stability see *UK Financial Services following the Launch of the Euro*, Speech by David Clementi, Deputy Governor of the Bank of England, Economist Conferences, 23 Apr 1999, <http://www.bankofengland.co.uk/speeches/subject.htm>.

[521] United Kingdom Debt Management Office, <http://www.dmo.gov.uk/>.

field have created certain expectations of a new system at the EU level, or at least within the Euro-area.

Prudential supervision is continuously redefined at the EU level. The existing supervisory framework is decentralised because it operates on the basis of the home country control principle, combined with essential harmonisation of supervision requirements and mutual recognition. The prevailing view[522] has been that there is no need for a supervisory body at the EU level,[523] and the European Central Bank[524] enjoys only a limited advisory and co-ordinating role.[525] The main supervision powers continue to rest with the national supervision authorities, based on the home country control principle. However, this has functioned only in relation to the licensing of financial institutions, and even there with many exceptions; otherwise, there is double regulation. This is difficult to accept in an internal financial market. Meanwhile, to the extent markets now interact and the internal financial market has progressed, national regulators do not have effective means of maintaining financial stability.

Until recently, the expectation in the UK was that little would come from possible attempts to develop the European dimension of financial market regulation. Results would be based on the arrangements surrounding the European Central Bank. The UK supervision structure is not formally affected by the evolution of the EU supervision arrangements in the Euro-zone because the relevant Treaty provisions will not apply in the UK. However, it remains interdependent with the systemic stability developments in the Europeanised banking system.

The recent German and French initiatives have been played down, as have expectations about a new European settlement within the Euro-area. Even the financial press does not seem to report developments in this field. There is general support for maintaining UK institutions, and no willingness

522 For an interpretation of the Treaty to allow for 'extensive' supervision powers of the ECB on the basis of the 'applied monetary policy' effect see Panourgias L.E. and Andenas M., *PS+SS+R→; Supervision and Lender of Last Resort adaptations in European Monetary Union: Maximising the sum of price stability-PS (monetary policy), systemic stability-SS (supervision and lender of last resort) and representation-R (independence and accountability)*, draft paper on hold with the authors.

523 At the EU level, the Banking Supervisory Committee, the Banking Advisory Committee, and the Contact Group, have only an advisory/co-ordinating role and no formal prudential rule-making or supervisory power.

524 The ESCB is composed of the ECB and fifteen national central banks (Art 107.1 EC, Art 1.1 ESCB-ECB Statute, annexed to the Maastricht Treaty on European Union). The ESCB lacks legal personality and it is merely 'the common roof for the joint existence of the ECB and the national central banks in a system with common principles and common rules', Zilioli and Selmayr, 'The European Central Bank, its System and its Law', 1 EUREDIA 187, (1999), 203.

525 Arts 105.5, 105.4 EC, Arts 3.3, 25.1 ESCB-ECB Statute. On the co-ordinating role of the ECB see also Smits, 'The Community and International Contexts', in *Banking Supervision in the European Community, Institutional Aspects*, Report of a Working Group of the ECU Institute under the chairmanship of Jean-Victor Louis (1995), 33, 45.

to transfer authority, so that a new European system can emerge. This leads to very little incentive for discussion of the pending institutional developments in the Euro-area.

Nonetheless, the UK system appears to be an interesting model in the discussion for reform of financial market regulation in the EMU.

The Bank of England no longer has statutory responsibility for prudential supervision of the UK banking system[526] as the Bank of England Act 1998 transferred banking supervision to the Financial Services Authority (FSA). The 1998 Act did not provide for detailed rules but instead envisaged the enactment of new legislation. The Financial Services and Markets Act (FSMA) was adopted in June 2000 and provides for the legislative framework for the FSA as a single financial regulator with regulation and supervision responsibility for the entire financial services industry. This builds on the Scandinavian model of universal regulators and has been followed by governmental proposals for reform in Ireland and Germany. It is expected that all the legislation and preparations necessary for the implementation of the FSMA will be completed in 2001.[527] The FSA has assumed the powers of the following supervisory bodies: the Securities and Investments Board (SIB), the Supervision and Surveillance Department of the Bank of England, the Investment Management Regulatory Organisation (IMRO), the Personal Investment Authority (PIA), the Securities and Futures Authority (SFA), the Insurance Directorate of the Department of Trade and Industry (subsequently transferred to HM Treasury), the Building Societies Commission (BSC), the Friendly Societies Commission (FSC), and the Chief Registrar and Registry of Friendly Societies (RFS).

The FSA is accountable to the Treasury Minister. It has to submit an annual report to the Treasury regarding the fulfilment of its objectives, and it must regularly submit evidence to the Treasury Select Committee. The annual report must also be forwarded to Parliament.[528]

Although supervision is transferred to the FSA, the Memorandum of Understanding between Treasury, the Bank of England and the Financial Services Authority, provides that the Bank of England has the power to act as a Lender of Last Resort (LOLR) in individual and systemic liquidity

[526] The Bank of England's statutory responsibility for prudential supervision was provided for the first time in 1979 by the Banking Act 1979. Before this, supervision was exercised on an informal basis through 'moral suasion'. It is interesting for the discussion of centralising supervision at the ECB level that the Bank of England was independent in the conduct of supervision, while it lacked independence with regard to monetary policy.

[527] *Implementing the Financial Services and Markets Act*, FSA/PN/095/2000, 18 July 2000 <http://www.fsa.gov.uk/pubs/press/2000/095.html>. See also The Year Ahead, Speech by Howard Davies, Chairman of the Financial Services Authority, BBA Banking Supervision Conference, London, 19 June 2000, <http://www.fsa.gov.uk/pubs/ speeches/sp51.html>.

[528] See *Accountability*, Financial Services Authority, <http://www.fsa.gov.uk/accountability>.

crises.[529] The Memorandum also provides for information gathering and sharing arrangements between the Bank of England and the Financial Services Authority, as well as for cross-representation in their decision-making bodies.[530] Finally, in the case of LOLR it provides for consultations in the context of the Standing Committee (representatives of the Bank of England, the FSA and the Treasury), and timely solicitation of Treasury approval.

The evolution of the EMU supervision arrangements can be constructively informed by the UK supervision structure. The operation of FSA as a single financial regulator can offer valuable lessons in the discussion about the development of consolidated supervision of the entire financial services industry, rather than a merely European SEC or banking regulator.[531] In addition, the combination of the Bank of England's LOLR power and the sophisticated information-sharing agreements with the FSA can further support the argument for centralisation of the LOLR, regarding both individual and systemic liquidity crises, and supervision powers at the ECB level.

The Bank of England has retained broad responsibility for financial stability. This is defined in much the same way as the Bank used to define its responsibility for banking supervision (before that responsibility was taken away from the Bank). Other central banks have used similar terminology, to some extent. One interpretation is that the Bank of England retains the level of responsibility for the banking and the broader financial sector that it had before the First Banking Directive forced a continental European model of banking supervision (with licensing and actual formal continuous supervision) on it.

2.3.3.a Capital adequacy

The FSA has welcomed the EU Commission's Consultation paper for the revised Basle Accord, and especially the Commission's emphasis on protecting consumers and investment firms. It also agrees with the Commission's commitment to implement the new rules at the same time as the new Basle Accord; that is, by the end of 2004. The FSA considers that the Basle Accord—although targeted at large international banks—will

[529] See s 2 of the *Memorandum of Understanding between HM Treasury, the Bank of England and the Financial Services Authority*, Bank of England, <http://www.bankofengland.co.uk/financialstability/mou.htm> (thereafter *Memorandum*).

[530] Apart from continuous contacts and a secondment programme, the Memorandum provides that the Deputy Governor of the Bank of England, in charge of financial stability, will be a member of the Financial Services Authority Board, and the Chairman of the Financial Services Authority will represent the FSA in the Court of the Bank of England. Ibid.

[531] On FSA lessons for the EU securities markets regulations see C Briault, *FSA Revisited and Some Issues for European Securities Markets Regulation* (Dec 2000), <http://www.fsa.gov.uk/pubs/other/FSArevisited.pdf>.

have a considerable impact on all banks and building societies, as well as on investment firms.[532]

The FSA has also decided that derivatives involving more than one currency of the participating Member States will continue to be regulated as derivatives up to maturity, for capital adequacy purposes. It will continue to apply a 50 per cent limit on counter-party risk weighting, and it will allow netting between long and short positions for such derivatives.

2.3.3.b *Three Rivers*

Although the UK is outside the institutional reach of EMU supervision arrangements, it remains subject to the EU prudential requirements formulated in the context of the development of the internal, EU banking market. While EMU does not develop further institutional structures, the effectiveness of such prudential requirements is important for a stable and effective system of EMU supervision.

In light of the institutional implications of the prudential requirements, the *Three Rivers*[533] case is of particular interest for the debate on further centralisation of supervision at the ECB level.[534] In the *Three Rivers* case, the House of Lords has given a first judgment[535] on the issue of Bank of England's liability for its supervision of the Bank of Credit and Commercial International (BCCI). It has rejected liability for the Bank of England on the basis of Community law. After an unsatisfactory interpretation of tort liability of the supervisors and direct effect, the House of Lords has refused to recognise enforceable rights for depositors on the basis of the First Banking Directive. It has also failed to refer the issue to the European Court of Justice under Art 234 EC.[536]

The effect of the *Three Rivers* judgment is compounded if we consider that the French courts held that the Bank of England's negligence broke

[532] *FSA welcomes European Commission capital adequacy proposals*, FSA/PN/019/2001, 5 Feb 2001, <http://www.fsa.gov.uk/pubs/press/2001>.

[533] *Three Rivers District Council and Others v Governor and Company of the Bank of England*, [2000] 2 WLR 1220.

[534] For an extensive and critical analysis of the comparative and community law aspects of the *Three Rivers* case see Andenas, 'Liability for Supervisors and Depositors' Rights—the BCCI and the Bank of England in the House of Lords', 2 EUREDIA 388 (2000).

[535] The issue of liability for misfeasance in public office under English law was expected to be discussed some time in 2001.

[536] For the duty to refer see Andenas, above note 534, pp. 408-409, citing the Opinion of AG Jacobs in the *Stockholm Lindöpark* case (C-150/99, *Swedish State v Stockholm Lindöpark Aktiebolag* and *Stockholm Lindöpark Aktiebolag*): 'According to the case-law, it is in principle for the national courts to determine whether the conditions for State liability for breach of Community law are met. In some case cases, the Court has none the less considered that it possessed the necessary information to make an assessment, whilst in others it has indicated circumstances which the national courts might take into account. I consider, in any event, that the question of the grant of rights to individuals is more properly a matter for this Court' (para 52 of the Opinion).

the causation between the damage to French depositors and the non-feasance of the French authorities.

Adding to concerns about the effectiveness of the current supervisory system, the House of Lords failed to take supervision developments in other jurisdictions sufficiently into account. It only referred to the case of Denmark, and it inaccurately stated that there was no formal banking supervision before the first Banking Directive.[537]

The First Banking Directive presents one of the first regulatory initiatives to liberalise the European banking system. To address systemic risk implications as well as to promote equal conditions of competition, it also provided for minimum prudential standards. Among these were the protection of depositors and the duties of banking supervisors. *The Three Rivers* case raises questions about the adequacy of the decentralised framework based on minimum harmonised prudential standards.

The *Three Rivers* case has shown the degree of potential divergence in the incorporation of the Directives' minimum standards in the Member States. The problems are demonstrated by the ways the UK and French courts treated the issue in the BCCI case. UK courts have ensured the wider application of the law by limiting the role of depositors' protection, while French courts based a wider application of the French law on a broader recognition of the depositors' protection objective. In both jurisdictions, the cases turned on an interpretation of the First Banking Directive, and both extended the reach of their national jurisdictions in relation to Community law. However, this outcome required conflicting interpretations of the Directive.

In addition to the issue of the accountability of the banking supervisors and the effectiveness of banking supervision in UK, the *Three Rivers* case suggests a review of the effectiveness of the current EU supervision arrangements. It definitely provides support to efficiency arguments for further centralisation of the EU banking supervision system. The case is about exactly what the First Banking Directive was intended to prevent: that regulators can claim non-responsibility because of the involvement of regulators of other Member States.

2.3.3.c Payments systems

The Bank of England's responsibility for financial stability includes the power to oversee the payments systems.[538] This responsibility covers the CHAPS Euro (Clearing House Automated Payment System for Euro),[539] a

537 Andenas, above n 534 pp. 389–90. It must be noted that a formal banking supervision system has existed in Denmark since the nineteenth century (ibid).

538 *UK Financial Services following the Launch of the Euro*, op. cit.

539 Bank of England, *The Bank of England and Payment and Settlement Systems*: <http://www.bankofengland.co.uk/markets/payments/index.htm>; *What is CHAPS* <http://

Real-Time-Gross-Settlement-System (RTGS) payments system for euro payments. CHAPS is also the link[540] to TARGET (Trans-European Automated Real-Time Gross Settlement System), the ECB-operated and supervised payments system that links the Member States' payments systems.[541] The large volume[542] of euro payments effected through CHAPS makes its safe and efficient operation particularly important for effective use of the euro. It should also be noted that the CHAPS Clearing Company and the Bank of England have agreed to the development of the 'New Chaps' system, which is planned to replace the CHAPS Euro and the CHAPS Sterling from August 2001. Part of the rationale is to facilitate the future introduction of the euro in the UK.[543]

ECB Regulations under Article 22 ECCB-ECB Statute will not apply to the UK, as they do not apply to Member States with derogation or an opt-out. Still, the ECB Regulations will affect CHAPS's operation to the extent that it is linked to TARGET, and the ECB Regulations refer to it. The ECB and 'in' Member States are also expected to co-operate with the 'outs' for monetary and financial stability purposes. In that context, it was agreed that the Bank of England would be primarily responsible for the supervision of ECHO (Exchange Clearing House), which operates an inter-bank multilateral netting scheme for the clearing of foreign exchange transactions.[544]

www.apacs.org.uk/about_apacs/htm_files/chaps.htm>. See ibid. for the separate operation of a CHAPS Euro and CHAPS Sterling since Jan 1999.

540 CHAPS provides access to TARGET for banks of all Member States regardless of their location (ibid.).

541 TARGET *the Trans-European Automated Real-Time Gross settlement Express Transfer system—update 2000*, Sept 2000, <http://www.ecb.int/target/gi/tagi01.htm>.

542 'To date, CHAPS Euro has a 10 per cent of market share of the volume of payments sent via TARGET, and some 17 per cent of the value, with volumes and values growing daily. A new daily peak volume of 21,767 euro payments was recorded on 30 May 2000. This is an increase of 13 per cent on the previous peak. The all time daily peak value for euro and TARGET payments was euro 232 bn on 29 September 2000' (*What is CHAPS*, above n 539).

543 *What is CHAPS*, above n 539.

544 See R Smits, *The European Central Bank, Institutional Aspects* (1997), 307.

THE EURO-GROUP AND ECONOMIC POLICY CO-ORDINATION

*Jean-Victor Louis**

1. Introduction

The Maastricht Treaty introduced a new Title on Economic and Monetary Policy in the Rome Treaty that provides for a well-known asymmetric regime between Economic Union and Monetary Union. This situation is very clearly expressed in the wording of Article 4 (ex Article 3a) of the EC Treaty. The economic policy is based on 'the close co-ordination of Member States' economic policies', while the Monetary Union comprises 'the introduction of a single currency . . . and the introduction and conduct of a single monetary policy and exchange rate policy'.

There is some paradox in the requirement of closer economic policy co-ordination. On the one hand, Member States have been deprived by the realisation of the EMU of their (limited) freedom to make use of the exchange rate as an instrument to counter asymmetric shocks. They want to preserve the possibility of using other macro-economic instruments, like price and fiscal policies, to fight against possible imbalances. On the other hand, a closer co-ordination of a broad range of economic policies is considered to be a requirement for the smooth functioning of the monetary union. This has become an exclusive competence of the Community, the ECB and the political institutions.

This asymmetry is reflected in the institutional arrangements. The Monetary Union includes an important institutional creation: the European System of Central Banks (ESCB) and the European Central Bank (ECB) at the centre. As provided in the Delors Report, the existing institutional framework for economic policy co-ordination was considered to be sufficient for the needs of the Economic Union. The Ecofin Council would be the main instrument in this perspective, in association with the Commission and with the assistance of the Economic and Financial Committee (succeeding the former Monetary Committee). The Economic Policy Committee would remain in charge of assisting the Council and the Commission in the macroeconomic field. More remarkable is the intervention of the European Council in the process of elaborating the broad

* Professor, European University Institute, Florence, and Université Libre de Bruxelles.

guidelines of the economic policies of the Member States and the Community (Article 99.2, ex Article 103.2 EC).

At its meeting in Luxembourg in December 1997, the European Council created a new informal organ, first called the Euro-11 or Euro-council, and now designated as the Euro-group, in order to enable the (now 12) ministers of the Euro-area Member States to discuss questions related to their specific responsibilities in the single currency field.

The Euro-group plays a role in the co-ordination process established under the Treaty, as it is described in the report (the Helsinki Report) presented by the Ecofin to the European Council at its meeting in Helsinki in December 1999.[545] This draws on the experience acquired since the beginning of the third stage of EMU. Although this document notes broad satisfaction with this experience, it also expresses some criticisms and makes prudent suggestions for the future.

After analysing the concept of economic policy co-ordination and reviewing the existing procedures, we will look for some perspectives on the development of the 'economic leg' (Lamfalussy, 1999, p. 148) of the EMU.

2. The co-ordination, its nature and its limits.

The co-ordination of economic policies is not a novelty introduced by the EC Treaty and the EMU, as planned under the Maastricht Treaty. Already the EEC Treaty provided, as an important mission of the Council, for the co-ordination of general economic policies (ex Article 145 EC). 'Strengthening the co-ordination of economic policies' was a leitmotif of many decisions taken in the 1970s, after the adoption of the Werner Plan on the staged realisation of an EMU. It was generally intended, although this is questionable, that Article 145 (now Article 202) EC could only provide for obligations concerning the examination procedure of the general economic policies by the Council. No transfer of power concerning the content of these policies was intended.

The legal picture has not fundamentally changed with the Maastricht Treaty, but a procedure for co-ordinating national policies has been provided in the Treaty itself. The budgetary discipline, plus the Stability and Growth Pact, complete the picture. This situation was 'rationalised' in the above-mentioned Helsinki Report. The economic policies have to be conducted with 'full respect' for four principles: subsidiarity, independence (of the ECB) and respect for the competencies of the diverse actors, market economy and close co-ordination.

For the first time, this objective of '*close* co-ordination' ('*closer* co-ordination', under Article 99.3, ex Article 103.3 EC—emphasis added) has

[545] See Report of the Ecofin Council to the European Council on the coordination of economic policies, 29 Nov 1999, 13123/1/99, REV 1.

been enshrined in the Treaty itself (Article 4.1, ex Article 3a.1 EC). For the Ecofin, this principle concerning the conduct of economic policies by the Member States, includes the Treaty obligation that the Member States consider their economic policies 'as a question of common interest' (point 2.4 iv of the Helsinki Report). This requirement is mentioned in Article 99.1 (ex Article 103.1) EC. The expression—used in the former Article 107.1 of the EEC Treaty for par values of the currencies, when national authorities had full competencies in the field of monetary policy—has to be understood as the recognition that the 'ultimate responsibility' for economic policies resides in the hands of the Member States.[546] The Member States must conduct these policies 'with a view to contributing to the achievement of the objectives of the Community' (Article 98, ex Article 102a EC). Co-ordination is not just about avoiding frictions between competing policies. It can be regarded as 'the way to respond jointly to changes in the economic environment' (Viñals, 1999, 82). Article 4.1 (ex Article 3a.1) EC evokes 'an economic policy, which is based on the close co-ordination of Member States' economic policies' (Smits, 1997, 66), and it has been rightly mentioned that the Treaty can be interpreted as requiring:

> the definition of an integrated policy, which differs radically from the method of convergence used for the entry to the Monetary union. It is no more a question of fixing the same objectives to national economies, but to determine the contribution that each of them must bear to the realisation of a common objective.[547]

This corresponds to the definition given by a classical Dictionary of the verb 'co-ordinate': it means 'to make (various different things) work effectively as a whole'.[548]

The originality of a genuine co-ordination process has been underlined (von Hagen, 1999, 79), although the term 'has long been part of the Community vocabulary'. The same author observes that 'it is hardly in the habits of organising reciprocal adjustments to national decisions' (ibid.). The more so, if co-ordination is used in order 'to elaborate in common a set of policies based on the differentiated use of economic policy instruments which remain at the disposition of the participants to the co-ordination process' (Jacquet, 1998, 37). This kind of 'strategic' co-ordination is based on the capacity of the authorities to exercise their discretionary policy in a jointly organised way' (ibid.).

Article 99.3 (ex Article 103.3) EC mentions 'closer co-ordination' next to 'sustained convergence' as an objective of the procedure of multilateral

546 See J Cloos, G Reinesch, D Vignes, and J Weyland, *Le Traité de Maastricht*, Brussels, Bruylant, 1994, 239–40.

547 A Gauron, in *Co-ordination Européenne des politiques économiques*, Conseil d'analyse économique, Paris, La Documentation Française, 1998, 107.

548 See *Cambridge International Dictionary of English*, Cambridge: Cambridge University Press, 1995, 3403.

surveillance. There is an evident link between these objectives and participation in EMU; these requirements are essential for both the adoption of the single currency, and for the smooth functioning of the Monetary Union. The Declaration of 1 May 1998 (of the Ecofin Council and the ministers meeting within the Council, attached to the recommendation concerning the Member States participating in EMU) mentions closer co-ordination as one of the measures necessary for obtaining all the advantages of EMU and the Single Market.[549] This is further emphasised in the Helsinki Report, which underlines that the completion of the single market and the single currency accelerates the economic integration in the Community. Hence the increasing interest in the economies of the partners, the imperatives of avoiding free-rider attitudes, of creating equitable conditions of competition, and of contributing to the global realisations of the EU in terms of growth and employment (point 2.5 thereof).

The report nevertheless underlines the '*specific* interdependence' created by participation in the Monetary Union. This makes the pertinence of co-ordination within the Euro-area 'particularly strong', as is demonstrated by the Treaty itself (in the context of budgetary discipline), by the Stability and Growth Pact, and by the creation of the Euro-group.

Co-ordination of economic policies is thus a vital requirement. But, as a result of the process of co-ordination, the Member States subscribe to commitments that are closer to soft law than to hard Community law. As underlined by the Ecofin, 'the present political framework allows for different forms of co-ordination 'from "dialogue" to "binding commitments" ', without specifying if these commitments are legal obligations or political undertakings. In its 2001 Communication on 'Strengthening Economic Policy Co-ordination', the Commission observes that this co-ordination 'within the Euro-area is based on consensus. It does not aim to impose a decision on a particular Member State but to convince it to apply the policy deemed to be desirable'.[550] This co-ordination comprises three elements, for the Commission:

- a common assessment of the economic situation;
- agreement on appropriate economic policy responses and
- acceptance of peer pressure and, where necessary, adjustment of the policies being pursued.

Nevertheless, nothing in the Treaty would impede the Council in its adoption of a legally binding decision, on the basis of Article 202 EC. The procedure of Article 99 EC is, indeed, about common examination and 'peer pressure', and its instruments are not binding 'recommendations'. It is a kind of 'negative' co-ordination—as it has been described by some

549 OJ [1998] L 139/28.
550 COM (2001) 82 final, 7.2.2001.

economists—that is intended to avoid errors. Article 100.1 (ex Article 103a) EC provides another legal basis for the Council. It has replaced Article 103 of the EEC Treaty (related to very short-term measures), and it allows the Council to decide upon measures appropriate to an economic situation. It is obviously a provision for a period of crisis, as the example given of a possible case of intervention demonstrates. The Article refers to 'severe difficulties' arising 'in the supply of certain products'. The need for a unanimous Council decision indicated that this Article was not intended to be an instrument that could easily be relied upon. If ratified, the Nice Treaty will substitute the unanimity in this provision with qualified majority vote, but the mechanism under paragraph 2 may still only be used if difficulties arise independently of the will of the State concerned.

Having stated the importance the Treaty attaches to the co-ordination of economic policies and the potential for enhanced co-ordination—but also the limits imposed upon it—it is necessary to briefly describe the procedures applicable under the Treaty and secondary law.

3. The co-ordination procedures

The three pillars of Economic Union are the co-ordination provisions (Articles 98 and 99 EC), a code of conduct in budgetary affairs (Articles 101 to 103 EC), and the rules about excessive deficits (Article 104 EC). The Stability and Growth Pact (SGP)[551] constitutes a sort of link between economic policy co-ordination and budgetary discipline. In particular, Regulation 1466/97 (based on Article 99.5 EC and adopted in the framework of the SGP), complements the mutual surveillance procedure.

The 'broad economic policies guidelines (B.E.P.G.)' provided in Article 99.2 EC lie at the centre of the co-ordination process. This is evident from a reading of the Treaty itself, although if one reads the already mentioned Helsinki Report, it remains a programme for the future. Point 21 of the Helsinki Report states that 'the B.E.P.G. will be placed at the centre of the process of co-ordination', and the President's conclusions of the December 1999 Helsinki European Council confirm that the 'Broad Economic Policy Guidelines provide the framework for the definition of overall policy objectives and orientations' (point 32). At its Luxembourg meeting, the European Council had already insisted on the opportunity to use the 'broad guidelines' as 'an efficient instrument for a sustained convergence among the Member States' (Resolution of the European Council of 13 December 1997, point 4). The repetition of this objective in successive

551 The Pact consists in the Resolution of the European Council of 17 June 1997, Regulation 1466/97 of 7 July 1997 on the strengthening of the surveillance of budgetary positions and the surveillance and coordination of economic policies, OJ [1997] L 209/1 and Regulation 1467/97 of the same date on speeding up and clarifying the implementation of the excessive deficit procedure, OJ [1997] L 209/6.

resolutions of the European Council seems to demonstrate that this ideal has not yet been achieved.

There is a sharp contrast between the expectations placed in the B.E.P.G. and the opaque, complex procedure provided for their adoption. The Helsinki Report observes that the recourse to multiple, possibly overlapping procedures has not allowed the public and the markets to obtain a clear idea of the process of co-ordination (point 18). This particularly applies to the cumbersome process of adoption of the B.E.P.G. Article 99.2 EC is clearly a provision resulting from a compromise between different positions between and within national administrations (Balleix-Barnejee, 1999, 166, 314–15, 325). The desire to involve the European Council in the process—without conceding decision-making power to it—is responsible for the complexity of Article 99.2 EC. The Commission, the Ecofin Council, the European Council and, eventually, the Ecofin Council again, are involved in the procedure. The Parliament is officially consulted beforehand by the Commission on a facultative basis: 'It participates in the annual orientation debate between the Commission and the Council, that precedes the formulation of the B.E.P.G.; it gives an opinion on the recommendations of the Commission on the B.E.P.G.' (see Helsinki Report, point 39), and it is also informed of the Council's recommendation concerning the Guidelines (Article 99.2 EC).

More remarkable is the soft law nature of the B.E.P.G. In its Resolution of 11 February 1999,[552] the European Parliament considers the 'non-binding nature of the broad economic guidelines and the results of multilateral surveillance which can only be implemented by means of recommendations' as a 'weakness' (Preamble, under D a). The co-ordination of a broad spectrum of economic policies (for a list of the policies concerned, see the report to the European Council of Vienna, of 11–12 December 1998, on the co-ordination of economic policies, Annex to Annex II of the Presidency conclusions; compare Fini, 1999, 57) is indeed considered to be a requirement for the smooth functioning of a Monetary Union. The European Council has itself repeatedly insisted on the necessity to include a number of policies in the B.E.P.G. and to give them a more precise content. But the continuous reference to the principle of subsidiarity marks the limit of the political will of the Member States to receive 'instructions' as a result of the co-ordination process.[553] In this context, the fine-tuning of the B.E.P.G. adoption timetable and increased vigilance in the surveillance of their implementation (recommended by the Ecofin Council) is due to have only limited effectiveness. The sanction for economic policies incompatible with the

[552] Adopted on a report of Mr José Barros Moura, on the constitutional consequences of the EMU in the context of the enlargement, A4-0030/99, 25 Jan 1999.

[553] See, eg, the last paragraph of point 4 of the Resolution of the European Council of 13 Dec 1997 or the Declaration of the Ecofin Council and the Finance ministers, quoted above, of 1 May 1998, point 9.

B.E.P.G. allows the Commission to make recommendations for the adoption of recommendations by the Council. It is also possible for this recommendation to be made public on a proposal by the Commission (Article 99.4 EC). In the Helsinki Report, the Council affirms that it is prepared to make use of this instrument, but it observes that it is wise to make a moderate use of it in order to make it maximally effective (point 32).

In the 1999 resolution quoted above, the European Parliament considers this kind of 'peer review' system of multilateral surveillance to be a 'weakness'. It is noteworthy that the Parliament does not repeat its concern on this point in its Resolution of 4 October 2001.[554] There is no doubt that the governments judge this feature positively. It underlines the 'club' concept of co-ordination and seems to work quite well if there is a broad consensus about what has to be achieved. But this kind of consensus can be based on the unwillingness to take objectively necessary measures. The result of this process can be viewed as a kind of negative consensus.[555]

There is a sharp contrast between the powers given to the Community in order to fight excessive deficits under Article 104 and the soft law features of economic co-ordination.

It nevertheless has to be mentioned that two significant elements have been added to the co-ordination framework laid down by the Maastricht Treaty: the Stability and Growth Pact and the Euro-group.

Regulation 1466/97, included in the Stability and Growth Pact, is important for the co-ordination process. It was approved on the basis of Article 99.5 EC, which provides for the Council's adoption of 'detailed rules for the multilateral surveillance procedure'. This Regulation obliges the Member States to present either a pluri-annual (four years) stability programme (for the Member States participating in the euro) or convergence programs (for the 'outs'). The difference is based on the remaining competencies of the Outs in the field of monetary policy, and the necessity to avoid 'real exchange rate misalignments and excessive nominal exchange rate fluctuations' (Article 10.1). These programmes include information particularly related to the commitment of the Member States to achieve the medium-term objective of a close to balance, or in surplus, budget (as provided by the Stability and Growth Pact). This Regulation also creates an early warning mechanism in order to prevent the occurrence of an excessive deficit (Article 6.3). This 'warning' takes the form of a recommendation under Article 99.4 EC. In the Helsinki Report, the Ecofin Council has made an explicit reference to this mechanism (point

554 Resolution on the Commission communication on strengthening economic policy coordination within the Euro-area, A5-0307/2001 (Rapporteur Pervenche Berès).

555 As Philippe Lemaître observes, concerning the role of budgetary policy debates, they do not necessarily result in a consensus, their role is 'de s'éclairer sur les intentions des uns et des autres, de se comprendre, de faire jouer la fameuse pression des pairs', *Le Monde*, 8 July 1998.

33) that has apparently not been used thus far (Dec 2001). Perhaps it was felt—as often happens in official reports—that quoting applicable legal texts acts as a warning has a kind of independent effectiveness.

In parallel with the adoption of the Stability and Growth Pact, the Intergovernmental Conference (Amsterdam, 1997) has adopted a new Title on Employment (Title VIII, ex Title VIA) to be inserted in the EC Treaty, and the European Council agreed to the 16 June 1997 Resolution on Growth and Employment. There are clear relations between these texts and the process of co-ordinating economic policies. On the basis of the conclusions of the European Council, Title VIII provides for the adoption of an employment strategy (Article 125 EC), the elaboration by the Council and the Commission of an annual report on employment (Article 128 EC), and the adoption of employment guidelines. Under Article 128.2 EC, these guidelines must conform to the B.E.P.G. of Article 99.2 EC. Under the terms of the Resolution, the Council is called upon to take the pluri-annual employment programme into account when formulating the B.E.P.G. (point 5).

With reference to the conclusions of the Luxembourg and Vienna European Council meetings, the Helsinki Report asks for a strengthening of the synergies between the employment guidelines and the B.E.P.G. (point 28). It also underlines the necessity to ensure a greater coherence between the work of the Ecofin Council and the one of other Councils: in particular, the 'Internal Market', 'Industry' and 'Labour and Social Affairs' Councils (point 34). It points to the usefulness of these Councils' contributions and those of the committees that prepare their work. These contributions could be used for the preparation of the B.E.P.G., especially concerning structural measures (the 'Cardiff process'). An interesting co-ordination process timetable is attached to the Helsinki Report. In this context, mention should also be made of the 'macroeconomic dialogue', agreed upon at the Cologne European Council in June 1999, that links all the actors (including the ECB) in order to ensure a better mutual understanding (see point 29 of the Helsinki report).

The other novelty, in comparison with the situation resulting from Maastricht in the field of economic co-ordination, is the creation of the 'Euro-11 Group or Council'; this has more recently been known as the 'Euro-group'. After dramatic discussions with the British Government at the Luxembourg European Council of 13 December 1997, it was decided to establish this informal grouping. This Resolution allows Ministers from the States participating in the Euro-area to 'meet informally among themselves to discuss issues connected with their shared specific responsibilities for the single currency. The Commission and the ECB when appropriate, will be invited to take part in the meetings.' The Euro-group generally met for two hours before the formal Ecofin meeting, but it is now convened the previous day. It has organised a procedure of 'cross examinations' of economic policies and situations. The Group will follow, on a permanent basis, the budgetary situation of participating Member States (Helsinki Report, point 33). This surveillance could result in the Ecofin Council's activation of the early warning system provided by Regulation 1466/97. Thus, a link exists between the informal and the formal procedures.

At every opportunity, the European Council and the Ecofin Council stress the precarious institutional position of the Group, which can only be changed by modifying the Treaties. Nevertheless, as it is necessary to have specific co-ordination within the Euro-area, the same European Council has placed specific responsibilities on the Group. This is especially the case for the external projection of the Monetary union.

Article 111.4 EC provides that 'the Council shall, on a proposal from the Commission and after consulting the ECB, acting by a qualified majority decide on the position of the Community at international level as regards issues of particular relevance to EMU'. Nevertheless, the European Council has decided that the informal preparation of the questions concerning the EMU, to be discussed within the G7, will take place within the Euro-11 Group (see the Resolution of European Council of Vienna of 11 and 12 December 1998, point 1). This understandable decision risks substituting a formal one (where both the Council and the Commission play their usual institutional roles) with an informal procedure (where a non-binding conclusion is adopted by consensus). This constitutes an example of a situation where differentiation among the Member States could disrupt the institutional balance of powers and—if the discussion within the Euro-group is not followed by a formal procedure at the level of the Ecofin Council—replace a compulsory decision with a commitment that is not legally binding.

The goals of achieving a single institutional framework and equality of the Member States impede the creation of an organ with decisive powers, if this organ does not include all the Member States. Such a structure would not have a clear basis on primary Community law. It would have little meaning to institutionalise an organ without formal powers. The provisions on closer co-operation of the Amsterdam Treaty (as they have now been modified by the Nice Treaty) have not changed this situation, since they do not allow for exceptions to the unity of the institutional framework (see Article 43.1,b of the TEU). Member States are allowed to make use of the institutions (see Article 43.1 TEU, 40.1 TEU and 11.1 EC) but are not allowed to create new ones, when only some Member States take part in the deliberations.[556] On the other hand, Article 11 EC (before and after Nice) provides that no new competence may be created by the bias of closer co-operation. This process aims only to avoid delay or paralysis in the

[556] See also D Servais, Ph Vigneron and R Ruggeri, 'Le Traité de Nice: Son impact sur l'union économique et monétaire', *EUREDIA*, 2000–4, p. 477 et seq, 496–7.

implementation of existing competencies. As the Ecofin Council has the power to adopt only non-binding B.E.P.G. and recommendations, if the latter are not respected, the Euro-group cannot receive the power to take more compelling action through the procedure of closer co-operation.[557]

It is difficult to judge whether the Euro-group has emerged as an important instrument of economic co-ordination, or if it has to be considered as a talk shop. Many observers and participants contrast the interest of the debates within the Group (where there are only two persons per Member State) with the rather boring and formal discussions in the (overcrowded) Ecofin Council. As an informal grouping, it lacks the power to make decisions in the absence of a consensus, and it knows that it cannot interfere with the exercise of internal governmental responsibilities. It is completely unarmed if there is a conflict among (important) Member States, but it is also true that the Ecofin Council also lacks compulsory powers other than under the excessive deficit procedure of Article 104 (ex Article 104c) EC.

Using his position as chairman of the Euro-group during the French Presidency in the first semester of 2000, Laurent Fabius has tried to strengthen the Group. The French Finance Ministry has contemplated ideas such as the creation of a troika, the increase of the duration of the presidency from six months to one year, the designation of a Mr Euro (a perspective opposed by the president of the ECB), the creation of a permanent secretariat, and so on. These ideas have been met with either scepticism or open hostility from the partners of France and the ECB; this opposition was augmented because the suggestions were accompanied by declarations about interest and exchange rate policies, as well as an idea about a possible role for Euro-area Ministers in the adoption of an inflation objective.[558] Apart from the new official denomination, the Group has decided to meet the day before the Ecofin meetings and to extend the list of subjects to be debated: 'Il n'y a pas de sujet tabou entre nous', if we believe the opinion of Mr. Fabius.[559] And indeed, the Group is not only interested in fiscal policy, but also in structural questions, employment, financing pensions, the cost of health care, and other such matters. This increases the concern of those who question the legitimacy of the Finance ministers to interfere with important social problems,[560] and who advo-

557 In its Communication of 7 February 2001 (COM(2001) 82 final) the Commission mentions the possibility 'if the case arises' to introduce 'other co-ordination instruments' 'in particular on the basis of Article 99.5 of the Treaty' by way of the reinforced co-operation procedures (ibid, para 18).

558 *Le Monde*, 3 Aug 2000: 'L'Europe monétaire, cauchemar politique'.

559 Ibid, 24 July 2000: 'Une présidence pour les Européens'.

560 See 'Vergrijzing is geen financieel problem', *De Financieel-Economische Tijd*, 23 May 2001. This article includes an interview of Belgian social affairs Minister Frank Vandenbroucke who claims that the question of ageing is a social challenge with financial aspects and not the reverse.

cate the creation of a Council of 'super-ministers' with the government authority required to co-ordinate the national positions and defend them within the Council. However, the creation of a Committee for social protection under the new Article 144 EC, introduced by the Nice Treaty, could challenge the role of the Group and of the Economic and Financial Committee by examining some of the questions the Euro-group has already started to work on (such as the consequences of an ageing population). That would contribute to the fragmentation of the co-ordination process.

In its conclusions, the European Council of Nice endorsed the increased role of the Euro-group. It

> welcomes the improvements made to the workings of the Euro-group and its visibility. It also welcomes the intention to extend the range of matters dealt with in this forum, with due regard for the conclusions of the European Council meeting. These improvements intended to enhance the co-ordination of economic policies will help to boost the growth potential of the Euro-area.

With this conclusion, the European Council officially recognised the role of the Euro-group as a forum for economic policy co-ordination. Indeed, the preparation of the Ecofin Council discussion on, for example, the B.E.P.G., has become one of the important tasks of the Group. But, if the extension of the subjects treated by the Euro-group has been approved by the European Council, the reference to the Luxembourg conclusions clearly indicate that the Group has to remain informal and that the 'decisions' are to be taken by the Ecofin Council.

Due to the inevitable abstention of the Swedish Presidency during the first semester of 2001, the Belgian Presidency of the Euro-group has been in charge for a full year. It very much accords with the French concept of the Group. For the Belgian Finance minister it is much more than just an informal club of Finance Ministers.[561] He is in favour of a 'permanent dialogue' with the ECB that could contribute to the efficiency of the *policy mix*. Notwithstanding this, Reynders has expressed his preference for the strengthening of the informal system (as he told a Belgian economic newspaper).[562] The 'strengthening' can result in the provision of a system of conference calls in order to allow for quicker reactions. He is not personally in favour of the creation of 'something more formal like a specific council for the Euro-area'[563] (because the monetary union should remain an open house) or a high representative (like a Mr Solana) for the euro.

[561] *InfEuro*, n°18, 2001–2, p. 5.

[562] *L'Echo*, 11 Mar 2001.

[563] A proposal made by P Jacquet and J Pisani-Ferry, 'La coordination des politiques économiques dans la zone Euro : bilan et propositions', in Conseil d'analyse économique (ed.), *Report 27. European Issues*, <http://www.premier-ministre.gouv.fr/GB/PM/CAE/REPORT27.HTM>.

The Belgian chairman of the Euro-group, and also of the Ecofin Council in the second semester, will more regularly (once every two months) participate in the meetings of the ECB Governing Council, as allowed by the Treaty. On the vexed question of who is Mr Euro, Reynders answers that he and Duisenberg share the responsibility, considering the allocation of competencies for exchange matters. Like the Commission,[564] he is not in favour of a centralised economic government of the Euro-area.

After this rapid description of the process of co-ordination of economic policies, it is not surprising to observe that the Helsinki Report mentions a strengthening of the transparency and legitimacy of the process as one of the objectives to be achieved (section 5). Paragraph 35 of the conclusions of the Lisbon European Council of 23 and 24 March 2000 calls for the simplification and better co-ordination of the B.E.P.G. and the Luxembourg, Cardiff and Cologne processes, 'in particular through other Council formations contributing to the preparation by the Ecofin Council of the Broad Economic Policy Guidelines'. As we have already observed, it is clear that the European Council does not contemplate a possible institutionalisation of the Euro-group or an in-depth reform of the Council's composition. For the European Council, 'No new process is needed'; this can be interpreted in different, but not contradictory, ways. No further process has to be added to the Treaty provisions (on the B.E.P.G.) and the Luxembourg, Cardiff and Cologne processes, but there is similarly no need for a substantial revision of the institutional set-up.

In the next section, we will look at an important but discrete actor of policy co-ordination. The Economic and Financial Committee (EFC) plays an important role in the preparation of the work at ministerial level, and it is also an interface between the ECB, the political institutions and the Member States. We will also say a word about the Economic Policy Committee (EPC).

4. The Economic and Financial Committee (EFC) and the Economic Policy Committee (EPC)

Article 114.2 (ex Article 109c.2) EC provides for the creation of the Economic and Financial Committee; this is as a successor of the Monetary Committee, created by Article 105 of the EEC Treaty. The Economic and Financial Committee plays an important role in the elaboration of all the decisions taken by the Ecofin in economic and financial matters. It is defined by the Treaty as a consultative and preparatory organ for both the Council and the Commission (on the EFC, see *Díez* Parra, 1999, 49 et seq., especially 56–7), but it is *de facto* more than that. It is very infre-

[564] See Pedro Solbès, 'Euro: coordonnons nos politiques économiques', *Les Echos*, 19 Mar 2001.

quently that a document that has reached a consensus in the framework of the EFC is seriously challenged at ministerial level. Although its preparatory works are 'without prejudice' to the COREPER's role (see Article 114.1 EC, 3rd indent), it is only on very rare occasions—to speak diplomatically—eg when very important institutional questions are at stake, that a substantive discussion occurs there when a EFC document reaches the Council level. Realignments within the Exchange Rate Mechanism 2 (ERM 2) are, *de facto*, an EFC job (for example, see the revaluation of the drachma on 15 January 2000). The Helsinki Report, so often quoted in the present paper, reached the European Council without a substantial input at ministerial level. The EFC is an essential piece in the process of economic policy co-ordination as it is now practised. Ministers have sometimes complained individually about the way in which the EFC had streamlined the Commission's draft Broad Economic Policy Guidelines (see on the B.E.P.G. of the Summer 1998, the comments of the Belgian Press, *De Standaard*, 6–7 June and the *Financieel-Economische Tijd*, 6 June 1998 on the attitude of the Monetary Committee, at the time).

Its impressive authority is due to the tradition of quality work and to its composition Member States, the Commission and the ECB each designate two members of the Committee. Member States appoint one high official from their Central Bank and one from their Finance ministry. These persons are selected among 'experts with *outstanding competencies* in the economic and financial field' (Council Decision of 21 December, OJ [1998] L 358/109, Article 2—emphasis added). It might be interesting to compare this with the requirement that the members of the ECB Executive Board should be 'persons of recognised standing and professional experience in monetary and banking matters' (Article 112, ex Article 109c EC). The Decision's text was obviously drafted by the Monetary Committee (before its disappearance). One should notice that the ECB is represented by its Vice-Chairman and another member of the Executive Board, and that the NCBs are also 'represented' at a very high level. All these experts exercise their functions in the general interest of the Community (Statutes of the EFC, Decision of the Council of 31 December 1998, OJ [1999] L 5/72, Article 3), but the members appointed by the Finance ministers have a privileged position. The president of the Committee is elected from among these members. Those designated by the central banks and the Commission do not vote, when advice or an opinion is given on questions on which the Council may subsequently take a decision (ibid., Article 4).

The Committee has rapidly become—perhaps more than its predecessor, the Monetary Committee (if that is possible to say)—a very influential organ. Its work certainly enhances the technical level of the documents officially produced by the Ecofin, but it is a very secretive organ (on the compatibility of this pervasive practice of confidentiality with the requirement of transparency, laid down by the Amsterdam Treaty, in Article 255, see the question asked by Diez-Parra, 1999, p. 56, who speaks of 'confidencialidad indiscriminada'). It is very remarkable that—perhaps paradoxically, due to its discretion—the EFC has succeeded in escaping criticisms from the European Parliament about its lack of transparency. The EFC has also derived a culture of consensus from its predecessor, and this explains the cautious tone of many of its documents. In this context, it is difficult for new ideas to prevail or clear-cut positions to be taken.

The EFC has a specific role to play in the dialogue between the ECB and the political authorities. In its Resolution of 13 December 1997, the European Council of Luxembourg decided that the EFC would be the framework where the dialogue could be 'prepared and continued' between Treasury high officials and those from the National Central Banks and the ECB. The EFC Statute makes reference to this function in Article 2, third indent (Diez Parra, 1999, 55). The fact that the NCB members of the EFC are not necessarily involved in the working of the main organs of the ECB could limit the potentialities of this dialogue. But most of them are participating in the committees (provided in Article 9 of the Rules of Procedure of the ECB, OJ [1999] L 125/34), including NCB officials, who assist the decision-making organs of the ESCB.

The status of an EFC that plays a consultative role for both the Council and the Commission has been contested. It now has its seat within the Commission, where its secretariat is also located, although it benefits from a large measure of autonomy. Some believe it should become a committee of the Council. It clearly cannot be assimilated with Council committees such as the COREPER, the 133 committee for trade policy or the special agriculture committee (CSA), nor the committees created in the framework of the CFSP. Its transformation into a Council committee would not only contradict some aspects of its mission, but would also present a problem for the continued presence of officials from independent central banks (NCBs and ECB).

The EFC prepares the meetings of the Euro-group. The Commission has proposed that either a Euro-group working party or the Euro-group meeting itself should be responsible for dealing with ex-ante co-ordination, whether it is done physically or via video conference.[565]

If the role of the EFC is not very well known to the external world, this is perhaps all the more true of the *Economic Policy Committee*, a consultative organ created by a decision of the Council of 18 February 1974 (OJ [1974] L 63/21). The Council's decision provided for the regrouping of various existing committees, and it held that the committees should be composed of officials in charge of the preparation of short and medium term economic policies in their own countries, as well as of others such as

[565] See its Communication quoted earlier.

the delegates of the Planning Authorities (where they exist) and officials of the Research Departments of Central Banks. The Committee is especially responsible for macroeconomic studies. Like the EFC, it helps the Council, the Commission or the Euro-group. A new EPC statute was adopted by the Ecofin Council at its session of 29 September 2000, in accordance with Article 209 of the Treaty.[566] The Committee will be composed of four members from each Member State, the Commission and the ECB. They will be selected from among senior officials possessing outstanding competence in the field of economic and structural policy. The Secretariat will be supplied by the Commission. If a vote is requested, opinions and reports will be adopted by a majority of members. The purpose of the Committee is to contribute to the preparation of the work of the Council by co-ordinating the economic policies of the Member States and the Community, and to advise the Commission and Council by providing economic analyses, opinions on methodologies and draft formulations for policy recommendations (particularly on structural policies for improving the growth potential and employment in the Community). The Committee's tasks include the support of the work of the Council in the formulation of the B.E.P.G. in the specific areas listed in the Decision, with a special focus in structural reforms. The EPC will provide the technical framework for the macro-economic dialogue involving representatives of the Committee (including the ECB), the EFC, the Employment Committee, the Commission and social partners. In addition, it delivers annual reports on structural reform.[567]

5. Possible orientations

The present situation of the economic pillar within the Union is less than satisfactory.

The Stability and Growth Pact is not a substitute for more adequate economic co-ordination. It has been said that it is a minimal, rules-based form of budgetary co-ordination, but that it does not provide for the kind of collective response to external challenges that the EMU requires (Fitoussi, 1999, 54).

The ECB has an interest in having an interlocutor in economic affairs. It has been rightly affirmed that it is a fallacy to believe that the weakness of the economic pillar provides a better guarantee of the independence of the Central Bank. Unilateral interventions by governments are to be feared more outside a structured dialogue in a clearly organised framework (von Hagen, 1999, 71–72). This is apparently completely ignored by those who claim that the 'asymmetry' between the limited powers of the Council and

566 See OJ [2000] L 257/28.
567 See its third report for 2001, ECOFIN/EPC/171/01-EN, 6 Mar 2001.

the constitution of the ECB as a European 'Geldsregierung' (the Executive Board) reflects the necessary 'depolitisation' of the monetary policy (Selmayr, 1999, 373, 378).

In an interesting contribution, Miriam Campanella has presented the relations between what she calls the ECOFIN-11 and the ECB in military terms.[568] She is evidently right when she evokes the political pressures and the resistance of the ECB. But perhaps this vision has been too heavily influenced by the attitude taken by Lafontaine, as Finance and Economic Minister at the beginning of the Schröder Government, and the policy of the French socialist government in its first year of existence. It seems exaggerated to describe the policy of the Euro-11 as a whole in autumn 1998 as a strategy aimed at regaining decisional power over monetary issues.[569] However, as she observes (quoting Thomas Eliott), the 'confrontation' between the ECB and the Euro-11 ended 'not with a bang but with a whimper'.[570] In his report on workshops of the CEDECE Grenoble conference of 1998, Jacques Bourrinet notes that 'Il convient surtout de prendre conscience que l'antagonisme de principe entre politiques et banquiers centraux concernant la cohésion économique et sociale est en train de s'estomper dans l'union économique et monétaire'. (Colloque de Grenoble 1998, La Documentation française, 2001, 343). In this respect, he quotes a speech by Daniel Strauss-Kahn made in London on 9 November 1998. Strauss-Kahn declared: 'Personne n'a jamais démontré que la redistribution des richesses par le biais de l'inflation ou de l'augmentation de la dette publique fasse progresser la justice sociale'.

In an eloquent illustration of the need to strengthen the EMU's economic leg, Alexandre Lamfalussy has insisted on the necessity that the ECB have some counter-part, to which to address itself (Lamfalussy, 1999, 149). The EMU needs a governmental organ with teeth, able to impose on Member States indispensable policy measures that complement the monetary action taken by the ECB. Dialogue with the ECB that respects both the independence of the monetary authority and effective co-ordination of economic policies is necessary. It is true that prior co-ordination may not be imposed on the ECB (Duisenberg, 1999); it would be contrary to its independence if the ECB were obliged to consult the Ecofin, the Eurogroup or the EFC before adopting monetary policy decisions (EMI, 1997, 3). But the ECB knows very well that it must avoid irreconcilable orientations of the monetary and the political authorities. To refuse to have a policy mix imposed upon it is perfectly legitimate and in conformity with the Treaty. To deny that bad relations between the political and the mone-

568 'The Battle between the ECOFIN-11 and the European Central Bank: A Strategic Interaction Perspective', in *The State of the EU*, op cit., 110 et seq.

569 Ibid, 117.

570 Ibid, 126.

tary authority can constitute a kind of policy mix *'par défaut'* is another matter (see Fitoussi, 1999, 130–1).

The EMU was born before the existence of a fully-fledged political union. Political and monetary powers were dissociated for the first time (Padoa-Schioppa, 1999a, 579). There is no doubt that this is an element of weakness in the European construction. There is no European Treasury Minister as there is not yet a European Foreign Minister; perhaps there will never be such a concentrated power in the Union. In any case, it is clear that the present institutional framework is not satisfactory. If it is true that various forms of co-ordination can be relied on, it is not acceptable that a decision cannot be imposed upon a Member State when necessary. One author has asked for the imposition of financial sanctions, as a measure of last resort, on persistently free riding Member States that refuse to implement the orientations resulting from the co-ordination process (Fini, 1999, 60).

The Ecofin Council is in charge of the co-ordination process. That gives extraordinary responsibility to the Economic and Finance or Treasury Departments, which has mostly been exercised at higher civil servant level. In this context, it is remarkable to see the Helsinki Report insisting on transparency and legitimacy. The present co-ordination process is neither transparent nor democratic. Considering the importance of this process, it should be asked whether Ecofin is the right place for the necessary strategic co-ordination (Herzog, 1998, 99). The required collaboration with other Councils is underlined by the Helsinki Report, which considers the importance of the responsibilities and the diversity of policies involved. One has perhaps to look further. Some believe the role of the European Council should be increased (Herzog, ibid.). We do not believe that one can expect too much from the action of this entity that is overburdened with a lot of items that impede it from giving its own views about issues that are—at least in part—very technical. The European Council is not a suitable place for effective action in the field of economic policy. We have advocated the institution of superministers in charge of European affairs. These Ministers would be responsible for the co-ordination of European policies at home, and would be able to participate in a Mega-Council. Such a Mega-Council's decisions would integrate all the aspects of macroeconomic policies that need to be co-ordinated at the European level at a given moment in time (Louis, 1999, 3–4). The generalisation of coalition governments in the EU means this suggestion will not easily be adopted. But, in our opinion, neither Prime Ministers nor Ministers for Foreign Affairs could do the job.

More coherence inside the Union would facilitate the external projection of EMU. The contemporary repetition of the imperative that the Union speak with one voice is a mere exhortation without practical effect.

Member States seem to believe that there is some advantage to be had if they act as free riders, and they tend to have restrictive views about the list of matters that require a common Union position.

Nor does the current Euro-group offer a solution. Regardless of the efforts made by ministers in Brussels to increase transparency, how can one expect national parliaments to implement measures that are not legally binding, that are perhaps not popular, and that have been decided behind close doors? If members of the Euro-area legitimately want to have the option to deliberate and decide among themselves about interests specific to the area, the Group's institutionalisation requires a revision of the Treaty.

The fight against asymmetric or generalised shocks does not only suppose the ability to take decisions but also the opportunity to use funds. The Treaty offers rather limited possibilities. When the Treaty of Nice will enter into force, the activation of the crisis mechanism will no longer be based on unanimity (new Article 100 EC), but the 'no-bailing-out' provision of Article 103 EC, which is not exactly inspired by ideas of solidarity, has also a certain constitutional value in this respect. However, the Community budget is limited (1.27 per cent of the GNP of the Member States). So, the idea of a substantial federal budget does not seem to be a realistic notion (Fitoussi, 1999, 215), although some authors (Fini, 1999, 60) contemplate the creation of a kind of insurance fund.

6. Concluding remarks

We have underlined the singularity of a central bank and a currency without a State (see Padoa-Schioppa, 1999b, point 27: '*banchieri centrali di una "moneta senza Stato"* '). We share the view that 'in the long run, the single currency has to become the expression of a united political entity more complete than the present one' (my translation of Padoa-Schioppa, 1999b, ibid.).

The ECB is strong in a weak institutional context. It has no Treasury Minister or Minister for the Economy and Finance. It has many opportunities to talk with assemblies of national authorities, but these ministers have no power to make binding decisions about the economic policies that would be necessary in order to achieve a coherent Community position. They usually make consensual decisions about non-binding recommendations. Far from being an advantage for the ECB, this can make a scapegoat of the institution (Boyer, 1999, 93). More effective co-ordination of economic policies—especially budgetary policies—should reassure the Central Bank (Jacquet, 1998, 41).

This lack of persons able to speak for Europe in the fields covered by EMU is one of the European Union's great current weaknesses. We deliberately point to EMU, and not only to monetary policy. That position could surprise those who believe that, as economic policies remain largely in the hands of national governments, these governments should also be able to exercise that discretion in the international sphere (see point 10 of the Resolution of the European Council of December, 13, 1997, already quoted). The Treaty itself makes a distinction as to the representation of the Community at the international level. Under Article 111.4 (ex Article 109.4) EC, the Council shall decide upon the representation of the Community in compliance with the allocation of powers laid down in Articles 99 and 105 EC. The first provision (Art 99) relates to the co-ordination of economic policies, the second (Art 105) relates to monetary policy. We take the view that this distinction does not allow Member States to participate independently—without the participation of the Community—in the co-ordination of economic policy outside the Community framework (see Louis, 2000). This particularly applies to representation in groups such as the Economic and Finance G7, G8. But it is well known that Europe's struggle to speak with one voice is not only due to the lack of an economic governmental body. It also results from the EU Member States' different positions regarding the monetary union.

Differentiation has been the price to be paid in order to realise EMU despite the refusal of the United Kingdom and Denmark to participate (at least from the beginning). Closer co-operation could be the remedy to the institutional imbalance created by the Maastricht Treaty. Indeed, it is not realistic to think that there will be unanimous agreement about the kind of political union involved in the strengthening of economic policy co-ordination in a union of more than 25 members. Considering all the limits imposed on the recourse to the provisions concerning closer co-operation (despite their reform by the Nice Treaty), their wording is not currently adequate for bringing about the kind of reform that would be needed.

In our view, if one wants to give more force to economic policy co-ordination—including the Community's competence to take compulsory measures—one cannot avoid revising the Treaty.

We would object to a kind of economic Schengen that would duplicate the institutional framework and organise the co-ordination process in an intergovernmental context, outside the Community legal order. Such a solution would be legally objectionable because the responsibility of managing the EMU has been conferred on specific institutions within the Community pillar of the Union, and it would also be politically unacceptable to the non-participating Member States.

One could choose to either confer more power on the Union's institutions (with the possibility of functionally differentiating between the status of the Member State concerned *vis-à-vis* the single currency) or to institutionalise closer co-operation through the Euro-group (but, considering the political impact of such an orientation, that would only be possible in the framework of an avant-garde scheme). Another perspective is the preservation of the present institutional arrangement, but as we have explained, this can only be a second-best solution.

Bibliography

Balleix-Barnejee, Corinne, *La France et la banque centrale Européenne*, Paris, PUF, 1999.

Bourrinet, Jacques, Rapport de synthèse sur les ateliers concernant 'les moyens et les politiques de la cohésion économique et sociale', in Colloque de Grenoble, quoted above, 333–44.

Boyer, Robert, *Le gouvernement économique de la zone Euro*, rapport du groupe présidé par Robert Boyer, Commissariat général du Plan, *La Documentation française*, Paris, mai 1999.

Chemain, Régis, *L'Union économique et monétaire, Aspects juridiques et institutionnels*, Paris, Pédone, 1996.

Cowles, Maria Green, and Smith, Michael (ed.), *The State of the Union*, vol. 5, OUP, 2000.

Díez Parra, Ignacio, 'El Comité económico y financiero', *Noticias de la Unión Europea*, N° 175/176, Agosto/Septiembre de 1999, 49 et seq. A French translation has been published under the title: 'Le comité économique et financier' in *EUREDIA*, 2000–1, 97–114.

Duisenberg, Wim, *Presentation of the ECB's Annual Report 1998 to the European Parliament.* Introductory Statement, 26 October 1999, <http//www.ecb.int>.

EMI, *Legal convergence in the Member States of the European Union as at August 1997*, October 1997.

Fini, Francesco, *Réussir l'Union économique et monétaire*, Groupement d'Études et de Recherches 'Notre Europe', Paris, 1999.

Fitoussi, Jean-Paul (sous la direction de), *Rapport sur l'état de l'Union européenne 1999*, Paris, Fayard, Presses de Sciences Po, 1999.

——— *Rapport sur l'état de l'Union européenne 2000*, Paris, Fayard, Presses de Sciences Po, 2000.

Hagen, Jürgen von, 'Co-ordination of Economic Policies and Employment', in A Lamfalussy et al (ed), *The Euro-Zone: A New Economic Entity*, Brussels, Bruylant, 1999, 61 et seq.

Herzog, Philippe, 'Contrôle démocratique et gouvernance de la coordination des politiques économiques', *Co-ordination européenne des politiques économiques*, Conseil d'analyse économique, Paris, La Documentation Française, 1998, 87 et seq.

Jacquet, Pierre, 'L'Union monétaire et la Co-ordination des politiques économiques', *Co-ordination européenne des politiques économiques*, op cit, 35 et seq.

Lamfalussy, Alexandre, 'Introduction', in A Lamfalussy et al (ed), *The Euro-Zone: A New Economic Entity*, Brussels, Bruylant, 1999.

Louis, Jean-Victor, 'La future réforme institutionnelle', *Bulletin d'information*, GEPE, Bruxelles, 1999, N° 32 (1999).

——— 'Les relations internationales de l'Union économique et monétaire', in *Droit international et Droit communautaire. Perspectives actuelles*, Paris, Pédone, 2000, 387–413 (2000).

——— 'L'UEM et la gouvernance économique', in *L'Union européenne et l'Euro: aspects économiques, institutionnels et internationaux*, Commission Européenne, Bruxelles, 2000, 155–64.

Padoa-Schioppa, Tommasso, 'Les enseignements de l'aventure européenne', *Commentaire*, N° 87, automne 1999 (1999a).

——— *Moneta, Commercio, Istituzioni: Esperienze e Prospettive della Costruzione Europea*, Trieste, 19 Novembre 1999, <http//www.ecb.int> (1999b).

Selmayr, Martin, 'Die Wirtschafts- und Währungsunion als Rechtsgemeinschaft', *Archiv des öffentlichen Rechts*, 1999, 357 et seq.

Servais, Dominique, Vigneron, Philippe and Ruggeri, Rodolphe, 'Le Traité de Nice: son impact sur l'union économique et monétaire', *EUREDIA*, 2000–4, p. 477 et seq.

Smits, René, *The European Central Bank. Institutional Aspects*, The Hague, Kluwer, 1997.

Viñals, José, 'Comments', in A Lamfalussy *et al* (ed.), op. cit., p.82 et seq.

Wellink, AHEM, 'De implicaties van de EMU: de economische-beleidscoordinatie nader beschouwd', *De Nederlandsche Bank Kwartaalbericht*, December 1997, 1 et seq.

'Le Gouvernement économique européen: quels instruments d'interférence dans la politique monétaire Européenne au service de la cohésion économique et sociale?' in *La cohésion économique et sociale: une finalité de l'Union européenne*, Vol. II, *Les outils et les politiques*, Actes du colloque de Grenoble, 19–21 octobre 1998, La Documentation française, 2001, 251–63.